The Life and Times of

William Shakespeare

1564–1616

Hildegard Hammerschmidt-Hummel

The Life and Times of

William Shakespeare

1564–1616

Hildegard Hammerschmidt-Hummel

Translated from the German by Alan Bance

CHAUCER PRESS

Published in 2007 by Chaucer Press
20 Bloomsbury Street
London WC1B 3JH

Designed and produced for Chaucer Press
by Open Door Limited, Rutland

Translation main text: Professor Alan Bance; Chronology: Graham Nattress,
Editors: Victoria Huxley, Tom Templeton
Indexer: Ingrid Lock
Author's website: www.hammerschmidt-hummel.de

Title: The Life and Times of William Shakespeare 1564–1616
ISBN: 1904449557

CONTENTS

INTRODUCTION

Since at least the mid-eighteenth century, an aura of genius, mystery, even divinity has surrounded William Shakespeare. The German writer, theologian and philosopher Johann Gottfried Herder imagined him seated 'high upon a crag', his 'head in the rays of Heaven'. It has been difficult to reconcile this elevated poet, who seemed to be remote from common humanity, with the somewhat prosaic facts of his real existence. The traditional account of the son of a humble craftsman in a small provincial town appeared incompatible with the image of a quasi-mythical Bard creating immortal plays.

The relative scarcity of documentary evidence from Shakespeare's life has resulted in elaborate theorizing to fill in the gaps, and important unanswered questions.

What did Shakespeare do in the so-called 'lost years': the period from 1585-1592 for which no documentary evidence of his presence in England exists?

How did a man who – as it seemed – never left his native country evoke renaissance Italy so vividly?

Why did he (with the exception of *Romeo and Juliet*) abruptly switch from writing comedies and histories to writing tragedies?

Why has so much secrecy surrounded the life of the bard that even great intellects thought that someone other than the man from Stratford – as, for instance, Sir Francis Bacon, the Earl of Oxford or Christopher Marlowe – must have written the plays?

There has always been a danger that further searches into the Bard's life and identity to answer these questions would lead to less clarity, not more. Shakespeare scholars at the end of the twentieth century assumed that nothing really new was to be found.

But, to my surprise, during a decade of research in England and on the Continent, I came across exciting new documentary evidence in the form of written historical sources and images, all hitherto neglected by Shakespearean scholars – or not recognized by them as relevant new source material for Shakespeare's life and work. From this novel documentary and circumstantial evidence it was possible to outline a completely new image of Shakespeare, an image which takes us far beyond previously charted territory.

RELIGION

In this book, I conclude that Shakespeare must have been a Catholic who received a Catholic education on the Continent and travelled to Rome three times during the 'lost years'.

In our overwhelmingly secular society, it is useful to be reminded of the fact that in Shakespeare's day, religion was central to the life of every individual. Deeply concerned about the plight of his Catholic countrymen, whose lives were blighted by Queen Elizabeth I's extremely harsh anti-Catholic penal laws, Shakespeare also appears to have been a life-long member of the Catholic underground network of the day.

Until recently little attention has been paid to the fact that Shakespeare was born into a Catholic environment and that he, his parents, relations, teachers and friends steadfastly adhered to the old faith, despite the banning and brutal suppression of Catholicism and the determination of Elizabeth I to stamp it out during her lifetime. This accounts for the failure to recognise that the times in which Shakespeare worked were extremely difficult and turbulent and imposed the most severe constraints upon him, constantly forcing him both as a man and a writer to avoid the attentions of the secular and religious authorities, and, as a Catholic, to lead a secret life.

A mass of circumstantial evidence, but also some documentary evidence shows that Shakespeare's parents were recusant Catholics. Thus the 14-year-old Shakespeare would have been sent to the Catholic college in Douai (or Rheims where it was located between 1578 and 1593). The young poet would have attended this college from 1578 to 1580. Partially erased names from the college records of this time, and the wealth of Catholic knowledge that permeates his plays solidify this thesis. The young Shakespeare then went to work as a tutor for the ardently Catholic Alexander de Hoghton in Lancashire, where, as further research reveals, he was initiated into the Catholic underground network, and remained a member, paid from stipends in Alexander de Hoghton's will, for the rest of his life.

Recorded conversations between the Elizabethan writer Robert Greene and a hitherto unidentified Shakespeare, published in Greene's *Groatsworth of Wit* in 1592, have the young Stratfordian explaining that he spent the last seven years, i.e. from 1585-1592, as an 'interpreter of the puppets'. This expression is almost certainly a code for 'mediator between the priests'.

In the year 2000 I discovered entries in the Pilgrim Book of the English College in Rome suggesting that Shakespeare stayed there on at least three occasions between 1585 and 1592, under pseudonyms always referring to his hometown Stratford-upon-Avon, including the suggestive 'Gulielmus Clerkue Stratfordus' ('William, Clerk of Stratford'). The lack of information on Shakespeare's whereabouts at this period of his life accord with the secrecy necessary to spare members of the Catholic underground from being discovered, tortured and executed.

Close reading of Shakespeare's plays in the 1590s reveal his familiarity with Italy – and with Catholic thought and rites. In this decade Shakespeare became a more or less covert supporter of the Earl of Essex who was then a most influential figure in Elizabethan politics and intended, among other things, to halt the persecution of Catholics in England. Shakespeare's play *Henry V* can be read as a thinly-veiled paean of praise to the charismatic Essex. His Roman tragedy *Julius Caesar*, with its sympathetic and graphic portrayal of a tyrannical ruler murdered by conspirators, would have been an especially inflammatory and risky subject matter at the end of the Elizabethan era. Indeed, Shakespeare's English history play *Richard II* was performed at the behest of Essex supporters the day before his ill-fated rebellion, complete with the banned scene in which the monarch is deposed. After Essex's execution for high treason the play was performed many times in the open streets of London as well as in private houses to keep the memory of the hero of the English people – and of the English Catholics – alive. Six months after the execution of Essex, Queen Elizabeth I remarked to the legal historian and antiquarian William Lambarde: 'I am Richard the Second, know ye not that?'

Shakespeare was careful enough to avoid punishment for his support of the Earl of Essex, but he refused to write lines of lament over the death of Queen Elizabeth. After the failure of the Essex Rebellion his work took a deeply pessimistic turn. He never again wrote a comedy, but turned his pen instead to world weary tragedies, cynical problem plays and and finally to reconcialiatory romances and one late history.

In 1613, now retired to Stratford, Shakespeare purchased the eastern gatehouse at Blackfriars, in London, which had long been a secret hiding place for priests and other fugitive members of the Catholic underground. It seems that Shakespeare made provision in his will that the gatehouse be secured for this purpose permanently.

As a supremely successful author, already revered in his own lifetime, Shakespeare was a particular object of Puritan loathing, especially after his death. Implacably hostile towards art, the theatre, and images in general, the English Puritans repeatedly tried to have the hated playhouses prohibited throughout Elizabethan and Jacobean times. In 1642 they shut down all the theatres, including Shakespeare's famous Globe Theatre in Southwark, built in 1599 and rebuilt after the fire in 1613. But in contrast to all other theatres, which were not pulled down until the 1650s, the Globe was razed to the ground as early as 1644. Discussions of Shakespeare's still missing manuscripts generally overlook the great loss of the actors' costumes, props and scripts that this event must have involved. Another incident that deserves more attention is the moment in 1637 when a Puritan Stratford councillor, together with an undersheriff, stormed into New Place, Shakespeare's imposing mansion in Stratford, at that time the home of Susanna Hall, his widowed daughter. Despite Mrs Hall's vehement protests, the intruders confiscated 'various books' and 'objects of great value' from 'the poet's „Study of books".' Incidentally, the victorious Puritans made sure to tell the imprisoned monarch, King Charles I, executed in 1649, that he would have done better to read the Bible than Shakespeare's plays.

THE DARK LADY

Another matter of great controversy in Shakespearean biography has been the identity of the 'dark lady', subject of the greatest sonnet cycle in the English language, in which a turbulent three-way relationship between the poet, his noble young friend and his mistress is described.

Shakespeare makes up one point of the love triangle, and scholarship has often picked on the third Earl of Southampton as the 'fair youth', but the identity of the 'dark lady' has been a yet more controversial question.

Research I carried out on the famous Elizabethan painting, *The Persian Lady* in the Royal Collection at Hampton Court, dating from the last decade of the sixteenth century, has played a crucial role in answering this question.

From a detailed comparison between *The Persian Lady* and an authenticated portrait of the third Countess of Southampton, Elizabeth Wriothesley, née Vernon, it became clear that they are one and the same. A gynaecologist has closely examined *The Persian Lady*, stating that the lady in the painting was eight to twelve weeks away from childbirth.

According to close linguistic and literary analysis, the sonnet inscribed in the bottom right corner of *The Persian Lady* proved to be written by William Shakespeare. This sonnet also proved to be the missing final sonnet of the Dark Lady sequence. The author of the new sonnet complains that the fruit of his love now belongs to 'others'.

From the great mass of historical, biographical and pictorial sources, facts, proofs and circumstantial evidence, I have established not only that the lady referred to in the sonnets was Elizabeth Vernon, who married Southampton when she was about ten weeks away from childbirth (in late August 1598), but also that Vernon's first child, Penelope, born on 8 November 1598, ostensibly fathered by Southampton, was in fact Shakespeare's daughter.

Since Penelope later married the Hon. William Spencer, who succeeded to the title of second Baron Spencer of Wormleighton in 1627, one byproduct of this conclusion is that the ninth Earl Spencer, his sisters, among them Princess Diana, and the current heir to the throne Prince William (as well as his brother Prince Harry) must be descendants of William Shakespeare.

OUTER APPEARANCE, ILLNESSES AND DEATH

'Your face, my thane, is as a book where men May read strange matters,' Lady Macbeth tells her husband. And now we may try to read Shakespeare's. He was a 'handsome, well-shaped man', as John Aubrey remarked in the seventeenth century. But Aubrey's testimony has received little or no attention until now.

Using ultra-modern facial recognition techniques developed by the German FBI (BKA) and other scientific methods, I have established that four representations of Shakespeare are highly accurate depictions of the man from different periods of his life. These are the Chandos portrait (on display in the National Portrait Gallery in London), the Flower portrait (in the Royal Shakespeare Theatre Gallery, Stratford-upon-Avon), the Davenant bust (in the London Garrick Club), and the Darmstadt Shakespeare death mask (on permanent display in the Castle of Darmstadt, Hesse Land and University Library). All prove that Aubrey's statement was correct.

Renaissance artists depicted their sitters faithfully and accurately, even showing any visible symptoms of illness. One intriguing conclusion reached by doctors who studied the authenticated representations, is that Shakespeare suffered from Mikulicz Syndrome, as well as a Caruncular Tumour and Skin Sarcoidosis, the symptoms of which can be seen progressively worsening in depictions from later in his life. It is quite likely that the Sarcoidosis – an immune system disorder which, after a protracted course, usually proves to be fatal – would have caused Shakespeare's early death at 52. Looking back now, I still find it striking how well the new findings about Shakespeare's life fit in with what was already known about him, but also how much they are in agreement with the lives of most of the English Catholics in the Elizabethan and Jacobean periods. As to Shakespeare's unique literary career, it is remarkable how often the poet referred to, commented on, or even tried to influence the great issues and events of his time – and yet he succeeded, despite this topicality, in creating universal and unsurpassed masterpieces; the greatest literary work the world ever has ever seen.

I sincerely hope that this new, richly illustrated and well documented Shakespeare biography will find many readers in the United Kingdom and other English-speaking countries; readers who are not only deeply interested in the true story of the life and times of William Shakespeare but will, at the same time, examine the new results in a critical but fair way and finally form their own opinions. With what is, in many ways, a new kind of attempt to move closer to the historical truth, I hope to launch a discussion that may lead to further research and insights into Shakespeare's life, work, and times.

Wiesbaden, April 2007
Hildegard Hammerschmidt-Hummel

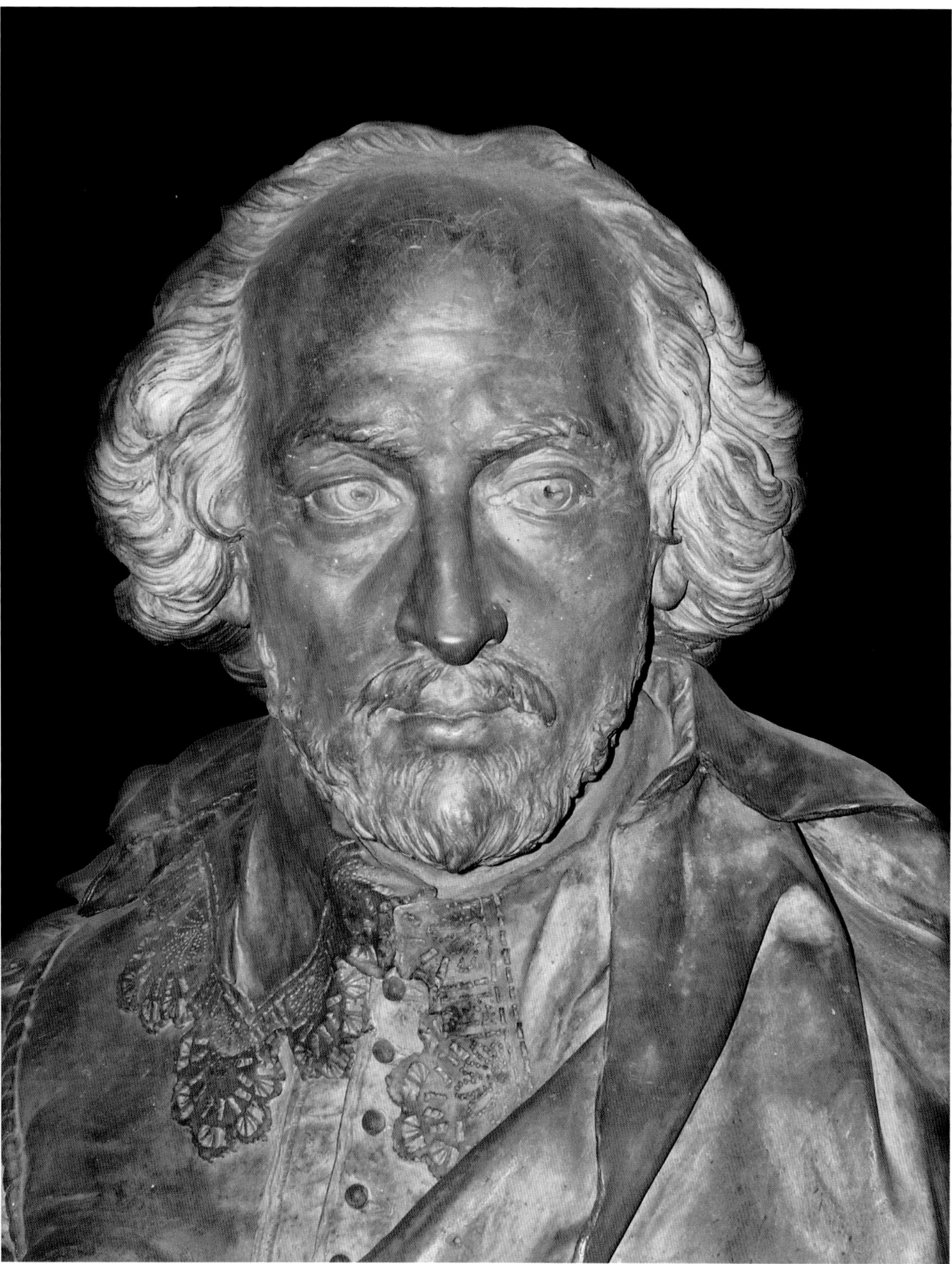

Fig. 1 – The Davenant bust of Shakespeare, terracotta, c. 1613, Garrick Club, London – scientifically authenticated, dated and ascribed to Nicholas Stone by H. Hammerschmidt-Hummel in her book *The True Face of William Shakespeare. The Poet's Death Mask and Likenesses from Three Periods of His Life* (London: Chaucer Press, 2006).

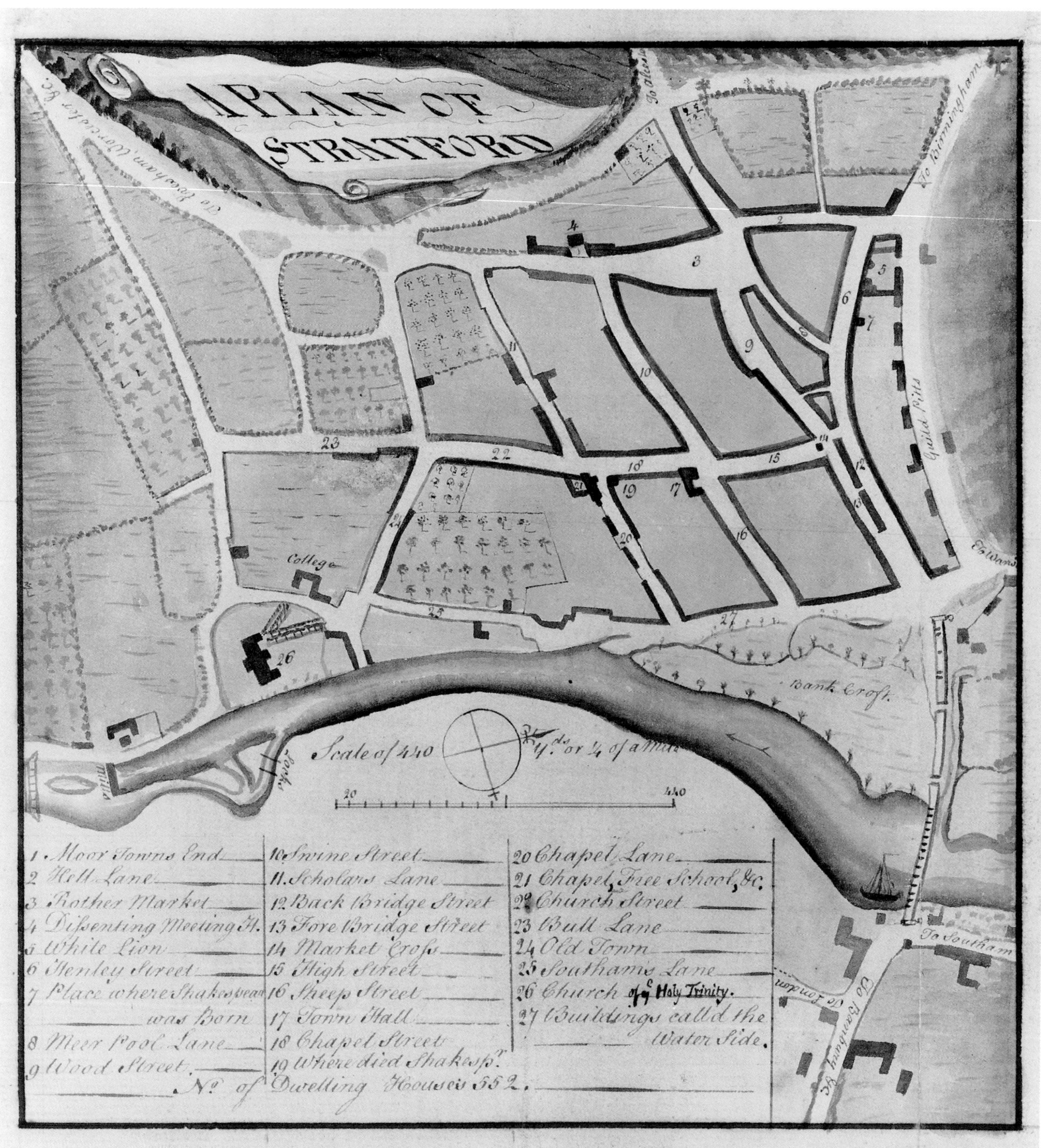

Fig. 2 – Above: 'A Plan of Stratford'. Town plan of Stratford-upon-Avon, Warwickshire, dating from the year 1759. The most important public buildings, squares and monuments are listed, including Holy Trinity Church (26), Chapel Free School [the Grammar School] (21) – Rother Market (3) and the Market Cross (14). The houses in which William Shakespeare was born, lived and died are also marked: 'Place where Shakespeare was Born' (7), Henley Street (6), and 'Where died Shakespr. (19). This refers to New Place on the corner of Chapel Street (18) and Chapel Lane (20), the mansion in which Shakespeare spent the final years of his life.

I. CHILDHOOD AND YOUTH

BIRTH AND BAPTISM IN STRATFORD

William Shakespeare's birthday is celebrated on the 23rd of April, the day dedicated to St George, patron saint of England. The English playwright and poet was born in Stratford-upon-Avon in 1564 and died there on the same auspicious day in 1616.

William was christened on Wednesday, 26 April 1564 by John Bretchgirdle, the Anglican vicar of Holy Trinity, Shakespeare's local parish church in Stratford upon Avon. *(Figs. 5a-b)*. The Latin entry in the baptismal register[1], now in the possession of the Shakespeare Birthplace Trust in Stratford, reads: 'Gulielmus filius Johannes Shakspere' ('William, son of John Shakespeare') *(Fig. 6)*. Since it was customary at the time for the baptism to be performed three days after birth, this document strongly suggests that he had been born three days earlier, on 23 April 1564. Moreover, the Book of Common Prayer, introduced in 1559, instructed that christenings should not be performed later than the Sunday after birth. Queen Elizabeth I, for instance, was born on a Sunday, 7 September 1533, and was baptised on the following Wednesday. Shakespeare's parents probably observed both the three-day period and the instruction that no Sunday should fall between birth and baptism.

Fig. 3a – William Shakespeare's birthplace, Henley Street, Stratford-upon-Avon.

Fig. 3b – The room in which Shakespeare was probably born. The furniture dates from the Elizabethan-Jacobean period.

When William was born, England was in the grip of great religious turmoil. In April 1564, Queen Elizabeth I was thirty years old and in the seventh year of her reign, which had been dominated by religious issues from the outset. At the very beginning of her government she had settled the religious question by re-enforcing Protestantism by law, and creating a lasting foundation for the Church of England as the established state religion. Yet large parts of the population, namely those who clung to the old (Catholic) faith, either completely refused to accept the new religion, accepted it half-heartedly or merely pretended to convert. This situation was a constant irritant for the government in London.

William's home-town Stratford-upon-Avon, was then a small market town on the banks of the broad, meandering River Avon *(Fig. 2)* located in Warwickshire and possessing some of the finest woodlands of England: the Forest of Arden. In the sixteenth century Stratford was surrounded by fertile fields and extensive sheep pasture. Its prosperity came from its commercial position and the wool trade.

William was the eldest son of a family who lived in a house in Henley Street which they owned *(Figs. 3 a-b)*. The Shakespeares could thus count themselves very fortunate, for at that time, England was experiencing a period of economic and social upheaval from which Stratford and the surrounding area were not spared.

After the Catholic Queen Mary died in 1558 and the new queen, Elizabeth I, re-introduced the Protestant faith, Stratford-upon-Avon's townspeople – later to change sides several times during the seventeenth-century Civil War – kept a low profile. At first, the lives of practising Catholics were not profoundly affected; it was only later that they were exposed to massive pressure and oppression.

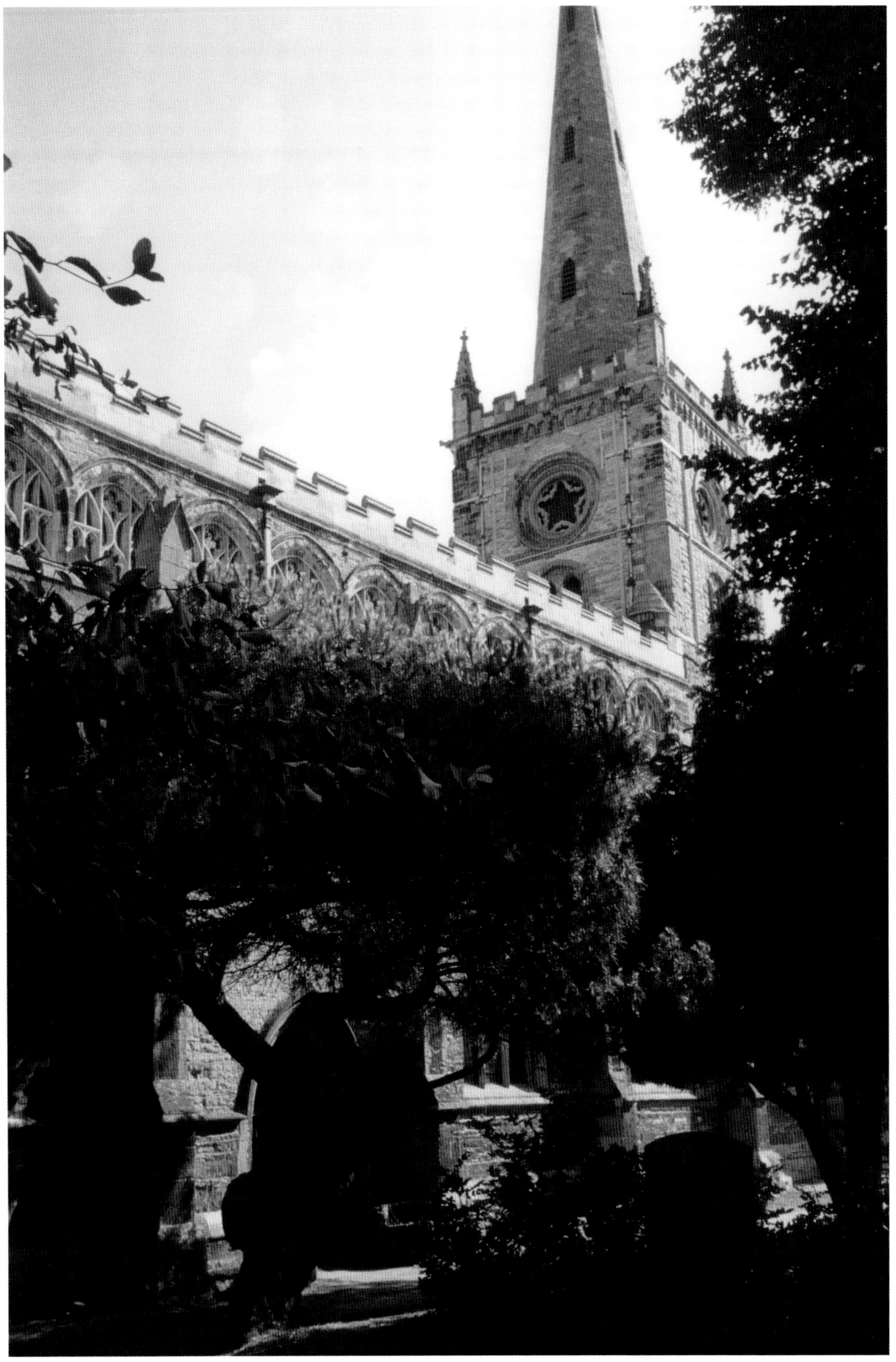

Fig. 4 – Side view of Holy Trinity Church, Stratford-upon-Avon.

Fig. 5a – Old baptismal font in Holy Trinity Church, Stratford-upon-Avon. William Shakespeare was probably christened in this very font.

Fig. 5b – The baptismal font, now restored.

Stratford was well situated as a trading centre, having a large stone bridge, Clopton Bridge, important for the access it gave to the north-west of the kingdom. The great strategic importance of Clopton Bridge was later demonstrated during the Civil War, when it was demolished by the parliamentary troops in order to prevent the Royalist army from moving north-west. The bridge was built in 1492 by Sir Hugh Clopton as a gift to his home town, as was the Guildhall he had rebuilt that same year. Sir Hugh had also built for himself an impressive house by the north side of the Guild Chapel, called New Place. It was to be purchased by William Shakespeare in 1597 and eventually become his home. In 1491, Clopton had served as Lord Mayor of London. This prestigious office also brought him much material wealth.

Stratford also boasted a church in the Gothic or Perpendicular style *(Fig. 4)*. Before the dissolution of the monasteries by Henry VIII between 1536 and 1539, it had formed a unity with the adjoining college. This college or seminary had been supported and run by the Stratford Guild of the Holy Cross, and it too was abolished and destroyed by Henry VIII in the same year.

Due to the great demand for wool and cloth for both domestic and overseas trade, many landowners enclosed their fields and began to breed sheep. This enabled them to make large profits, with very little investment. Their tenant farmers were no longer needed and thus they were summarily evicted. Enclosures were a notorious social phenomenon that impoverished much of the rural population. The results were also seen in Stratford, where the poor were dependent on charity allocated from Town Council funds.

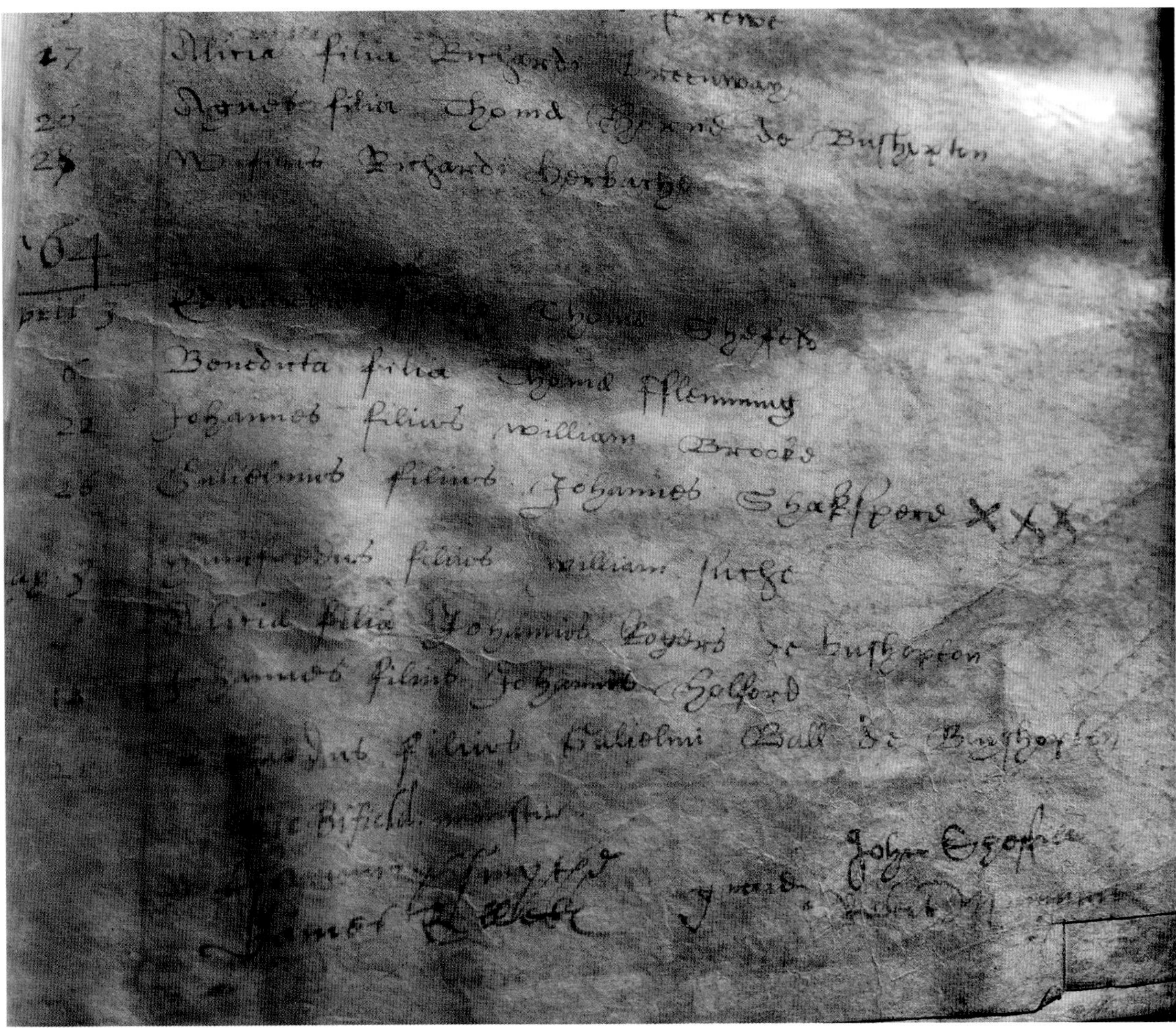

Fig. 6 – Entry for William Shakespeare's baptism in the Stratford parish register, 26 April 1564.

PARENTS AND SIBLINGS

William's parents, Mary Arden and John Shakespeare, must have known each other as children or teenagers, although they came from different social backgrounds. Mary Arden was the youngest of the eight daughters of the wealthy landowner and gentleman, Robert Arden, whose large estate was in Wilmcote, north-west of Stratford-upon-Avon. Arden also owned several hundred acres of land and two farmhouses in Snitterfield, north-east of Stratford. The family lived on the estate in Wilmcote. Their manor house was impressive, its eleven rooms decorated with fashionable painted tapestries *(Figs. 7-8a)*.

John Shakespeare was the elder son of Richard Shakespeare, an Arden tenant. Richard Shakespeare enjoyed great respect and standing, and leased a large tract of Arden's estate in Snitterfield. So, as a child, John Shakespeare lived with his family in a house belonging to his future father-in-law, Robert Arden. Contemporary records referring to John Shakespeare's position before he moved to Stratford call him an 'Agricola' or 'Husbandman', and occasionally also a 'Yeoman'. His status, therefore, was not far below that of a 'gentleman'.

John must have had basic skills in reading, writing and arithmetic, and was good at keeping accounts. Both John Shakespeare and his

Fig. 7 – Palmer's Farm in Wilmcote near Stratford-upon-Avon, an elegant mansion dating from Shakespeare's time, known since the eighteenth century as Mary Arden's house. This is most probably the childhood home of Shakespeare's mother. Palmer's Farm, located next to Glebe's Farm (see Fig. 8a), is the only authentic Elizabethan manor house in the area.

Fig. 8a – Glebe's Farm, Wilmcote. Recent British research claims that Glebe's Farm was Mary Arden's birthplace (see Roger Pringle, 'Mary Arden's House: the discovery, the excitement and the consequences', *Shakespeare*, No. 1, Spring, 2001) This identification is based on a document dating from 1587 which states that Agnes Arden, Robert Arden's widow and Mary Arden's stepmother, had 'recently moved into' Glebe's Farm (see *The Shakespeare Houses*, described by Roger Pringle, Norwich, 1999, rev. 2001, p. 30). However, the fact that Robert Arden's widow moved into Glebe's Farm, a relatively modest dwelling, about thirty years after her husband's death in 1556, does not allow us to conclude that Glebe's Farm was the birthplace of Shakespeare's mother. It is much more plausible that the family lived in the manor house now known as Palmer's Farm (Fig. 7). For Robert Arden was a 'gentleman', who had eight daughters, and left his youngest daughter, Shakespeare's mother, a substantial property when he died (see p. 7f).

brother Henry were responsible for the bookkeeping and administration work for his father's leasehold property[2]. John would not have been able to perform these tasks or his later duties in Stratford if he had been illiterate. Although there is no documentary evidence that Shakespeare's father ever received any schooling, the range of his responsibilities make his education self-evident.

The Ardens of Wilmcote were a branch of the Ardens of Parkhall, an esteemed and long-established aristocratic Catholic family whose seat was at Castle Bromwich in the parish of Aston Cantlow, near Birmingham. Sidney Lee[3], a British Shakespeare scholar and genealogy expert, claims that the two families were definitely related. In his Shakespeare biography, published in 1898, he writes that Mary Arden, Shakespeare's mother, belonged to the lesser Wilmcote branch of the family.

Like many other members of the landed gentry in Warwickshire, the Ardens of Parkhall, and also their distant relatives, the Ardens of Wilmcote, adhered firmly to the old faith, despite the fact that the compulsory adoption of the Book of Common Prayer had been

Fig. 8b – The church in Snitterfield (left), John Shakespeare's home village, a few miles north of Stratford.

Fig. 8c – The church in Aston Cantlow (above). It was in this church that Shakespeare's parents were married in 1557.

repeatedly ordained by the government, in 1549, 1552, 1559 and 1571. Nor were they deterred by the harsh punishments reserved for Catholics who did not attend Anglican church services or refused to take communion, and participated in Catholic Mass and/or protected Catholic priests. In 1583, Edward Arden, the head of the Ardens of Parkhall, was executed for his alleged involvement in a Catholic conspiracy against the queen, the Arden-Somerville plot, initiated by his son-in-law John Somerville. Arden proclaimed his innocence to the very last, and stated that his only 'crime' had been to practise the Catholic faith.

In the same year, ten more Warwickshire citizens were arrested and thrown into the Tower of London, among them one John Arden, probably also a relative of Mary Shakespeare. John Arden was most cruelly tortured for his Catholic faith. In 1597, after fourteen years of imprisonment, Arden – together with John Gerard, a Jesuit priest – managed a spectacular escape from the Tower. Using a rope, the two men broke out of the most notorious and best-guarded prison in the whole of England.

Mary was her father's favourite daughter, and it was to her that Robert Arden left the core of his estate, in a will in which he once more clearly confessed his Catholic faith. In this will, dated

Fig. 9 – Oxford University: Clarendon Building (side view) and sculptures in front of the Sheldonian Theatre (on the right).

24 November 1556, Arden wrote: 'I bequeath my soul to Almighty God and to our blessed Lady, St. Mary, and to all the holy company of heaven and my body to be buried in the churchyard of St. John the Baptist' (Aston Cantlow). Mary inherited her father's property in Wilmcote, known as 'Asbies'. Consisting of 100 acres of land together with a house, it generated a large income. Mary also inherited £6-13s-4d in cash. She already owned a share of two estates in Snitterfield, where Richard Shakespeare and his two sons, Henry and John, lived as tenants of the Ardens. However, John Shakespeare must have left Snitterfield in order to learn a trade.

Mary and her sister Alice were executrices of their father's will[4], and consequently – like Mary's future husband, John Shakespeare – must have been able to read, write and count.

Mary was brought up in a very traditional Catholic household, and her favourable treatment in Robert Arden's will implies that she shared her father's strong Catholic beliefs. Mary seems to have remained a Catholic throughout her life, and, it is natural to assume, raised her children in the old faith. There are no such clues to the religion of the young John Shakespeare, though documents survive from later in his life that clearly indicate that he was a practising Catholic.

In 1557, a year after Robert Arden's death, John Shakespeare married Mary Arden, who was now a relatively wealthy heiress. The wedding took place in the final year of Mary Tudor's reign, so it would have been performed according to Catholic rites. Although no documentary evidence survives to prove that the couple were married in the church of St John the Baptist in Aston Cantlow (*Fig. 8b*), in whose grounds Robert Arden had been laid to rest, this may well be assumed. For it was customary for the marriage to take place in the bride's parish church.

John Shakespeare, probably already in his late twenties, was considerably older than his bride and must have possessed qualities that gave him an advantage over other suitors in competing for the hand of the young heiress. He was an ambitious young man and would have decided early in his life that he was not content simply to manage the leasehold property in Snitterfield. He would also have been aware that just one generation earlier, a Snitterfield villager had quite quickly risen to become one of the wealthiest men in England. This man was John Spencer, the founder of the Spencer dynasty, whose seat is in Althorp in Northamptonshire[5].

Spencer had purchased large areas of arable farmland in Warwickshire and Northamptonshire and enclosed it for sheep rearing, enabling him to produce wool on a large scale. He eventually received a knighthood. Shakespeare's grandfather, Richard Shakespeare, could have been personally acquainted with John Spencer, and this local entrepreneur may well have been a kind of model for John Shakespeare, who himself later became wealthy through wool-trading.

John realised that the best opportunity to gain social standing and to amass money and property lay in moving to Stratford-upon-Avon, just four miles from Snitterfield. He made the most of this opportunity, as demonstrated by his successful career. His shrewdness, efficiency, reliability and hard work soon earned him enough money to buy properties in Stratford and start a family. As a citizen of Stratford and the holder of important public offices, John Shakespeare was able to provide an excellent education for his children, in particular for his eldest son, William.

A Royal Charter issued during the reign of Edward VI (1547-1553) granted Stratford borough status. The charter was issued just a fortnight before the death of the young king, and it was not confirmed by Elizabeth I until 1560. From then on, the town was governed by a bailiff, who led a Town Council of fourteen aldermen and a further fourteen capital burgesses.

In this thriving town, John Shakespeare worked as a successful and highly respected glove-maker. There is evidence that he lived in Stratford from 1552 onwards, so it is most likely that in this town he completed his seven-year apprenticeship. He lived in a house in Henley Street. It is not clear whether, at that time, this house was rented or whether John Shakespeare had already managed to earn enough money to buy the property. At any rate, in 1556, roughly a year before his marriage, he purchased two houses in Stratford, one in Henley Street and one in Greenhill Street. This demonstrates that he was determined not only to become financially successful, but that he was also preparing to start a family.

In 1575, John Shakespeare bought two further properties in Stratford; their exact location is unknown. In 1590, he owned two adjoining properties on Henley Street, of which the more westerly is famous today as the 'Birthplace', the property to the east being known as the 'Woolshop'.

John Shakespeare must have become a young man of great standing in Stratford, with an impeccable reputation, for by 1556 he was holding his (as far as we know) first important public office, that of the 'Taster of Bread and Ale'. An English source from the year 1450 shows that ale from the public brewery was tested weekly for quality by two inspectors. Similar strict quality controls were imposed on bread. Before the introduction of potatoes[6], tea and coffee, these were the most important staples in the English diet. This office would have been a great honour for John Shakespeare, but it was just the start of his remarkable career in public life.

John and Mary Shakespeare had a total of eight children, all of whom were probably born and raised in Henley Street. Their first child, a daughter, was born in 1558 and named Joan, but she died in infancy. Joan was born towards the end of the reign of Mary Tudor and would have been baptised by Roger Dyos, the Catholic priest in Stratford. When Elizabeth ascended the throne and re-introduced Protestantism as the established religion, Dyos refused to give up his office. The Town Council members withheld his stipend in order to be able to replace him. John Shakespeare voted with the Protestant majority, but his motives for doing so are not known. It is likely that he did not wish to draw attention to himself as a follower of the old faith and he was probably also reluctant to risk his career at such an early stage. Years later, Dyos successfully sued Stratford Town Council and received ample compensation.

For three years, Stratford was served by travelling preachers, and it was not until 1561 that John Bretchgirdle took up a permanent position as the town's Anglican vicar. Unlike many other members of the Anglican clergy, Bretchgirdle was unmarried. He had a large library and the reputation of an obsessive bibliophile. In 1562, Bretchgirdle baptised Margaret, the second daughter of John and Mary Shakespeare. Margaret, too, died in infancy. In 1564, William, the first son, was born and was baptised by John Bretchgirdle. Bretchgirdle died in 1565 and bequeathed his Latin-English dictionary to the local grammar school. It is very likely that Shakespeare later used this dictionary when he attended the school.

In July 1564, Stratford was afflicted by the plague. The Shakespeares and their three-month-old son William narrowly escaped the ravages of the Black Death. The doors of those Stratford inhabitants who contracted the disease were marked with a red cross and the words: 'Lord have mercy on us'. The number of crosses increased at an alarming rate; the disease appeared to be unstoppable. About 200 people died in the epidemic, roughly one in seven of the citizens of Stratford. The old, the very young and the infirm were most at risk. The threat to William Shakespeare's life at such a young age can be demonstrated by the fact that the plague struck the family of Roger Green, one of the Shakespeares' neighbours in Henley Street, who lost four children. The plague finally stopped just short of the Shakespeares' house, and they were spared. The fact that William's mother came from a genteel household in which great attention was paid to hygiene and cleanliness, and that John Shakespeare, as a former taster of bread and ale, probably knew more about hygiene than the majority of his fellow citizens, were almost certainly contributing factors.

In August 1564, the Town Council held a crisis meeting to organise aid for the poor. For fear of contamination, the meeting was held outdoors in the garden of the Guild Chapel. William's father, now one of the fourteen capital burgesses, was also present. He must have felt very fortunate that he, his wife and child had all escaped the plague, and that year he made a generous donation to the needy citizens of Stratford.

Once the threat of the epidemic had passed, William, the longed-for first son of John and Mary Shakespeare, could grow up well cared for and in safety. When he was three, his brother Gilbert was born. In 1569, Mary Shakespeare gave birth to a girl, who was named Joan, in memory of their first-born child who did not survive infancy. Another sister, Anne, was born in 1572, but died at the age of six. Ten years after William's birth, Richard was born, and in 1580, the Shakespeares had their last child, a son, called Edmund. Many biographers believe they named him after Edmund Lambert, Mary Shakespeare's brother-in-law, who had married her sister Joan.

At that time, however, the Shakespeares and the Lamberts seem to have been locked in a family feud, which would become very bitter in later years. The feud concerned the manor of Asbies, which Shakespeare's mother had inherited from her father. In 1578, the Shakespeares were in urgent need of ready cash and mortgaged the property to the Lamberts for a period of two years and in the sum of £40. During this period, the Lamberts were to receive the income from the property in lieu of interest. This method of quickly raising cash was often

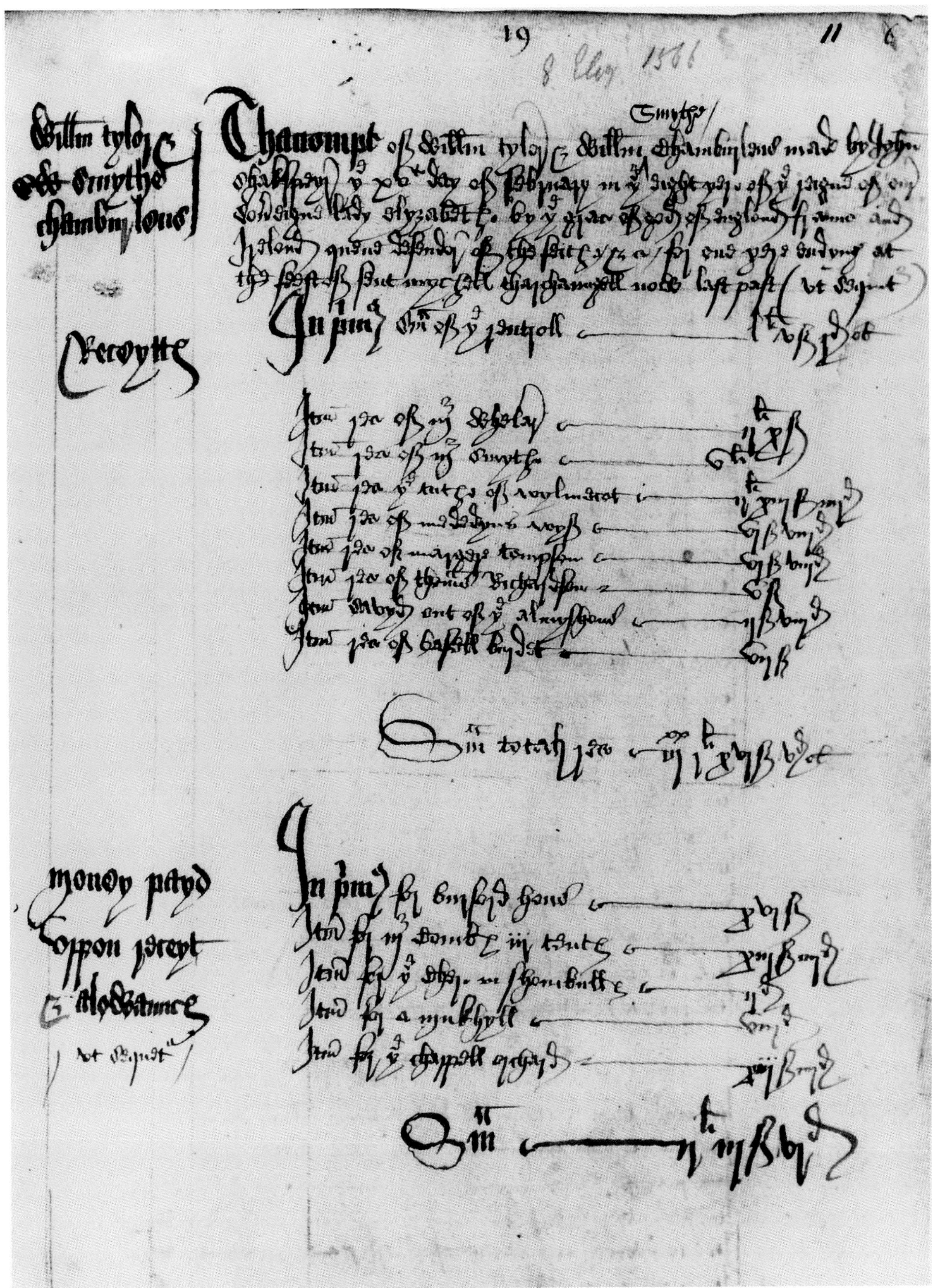

Fig. 10 – An extract from an Account Book of the Stratford Town Council kept by John Shakespeare for the year 1566.

recommended to English Catholics by their priests, as they found themselves in increasing financial difficulties.

In 1580, Asbies was supposed to be returned to the Shakespeares upon repayment of the £40, but this did not happen and, in fact, the Lamberts never returned the land. A protracted lawsuit ensued, which resulted many years later in the Shakespeares losing the case.

It is questionable whether Edmund Lambert acted as godfather to Edmund Shakespeare when he was baptised on 3 May 1580, as this was the year in which the dispute began. It is just as likely that, at this time, the child was named after Edmund Campion, the English Jesuit who left Rome in the spring of 1580 in the company of Robert Parsons, another Jesuit priest, and other priests and laymen, and arrived in England in June of the same year. Edmund Campion was one of the two leaders of a large Jesuit movement to re-Catholicise England, and many English Catholics, including the Shakespeares, may well have heard of him, even before he arrived in England. Campion had been an outstanding figure at Oxford University *(Fig. 9)* and had been celebrated as 'the English Cicero'. He had renounced Protestantism very early on in 1571, and had moved to Douai, then in Flanders but today in France, in order to become a Catholic priest, and later a Jesuit.

All of William Shakespeare's brothers died before him. He was outlived – by many years – only by his sister Joan, whose descendants can be traced down to the twentieth century. As far as is known, none of John Shakespeare's other children achieved anything remarkable or noteworthy. Only William possessed extraordinary talents. Favoured by his mother's inheritance and his father's rise in society, coupled with the particular circumstances of his upbringing and education, he created literary works of unique cultural and historical importance and influence.

Between 1557 and 1561, the versatile, capable, and well-regarded John Shakespeare held important public offices in Stratford. He was a juror, a constable and an assessor, legally appointed to impose the appropriate punishments for minor crimes and misdemeanours.

In 1561, three years before William's birth, John Shakespeare held a further important office, that of chamberlain, or treasurer. He and a colleague were now entirely responsible for managing the funds and income of the borough. John Shakespeare must have excelled as chamberlain, as he was re-elected in 1562. Even when his second term of office had ended, the Stratford Council did not cease to consult him on certain issues. John Shakespeare continued to audit and balance the accounts, as the still extant historical documents demonstrate *(Fig. 10)*. This alone makes it very clear that William Shakespeare's father not only excelled with regard to bookkeeping and the exemplary presentation of accounts, but must also have been highly literate.

On 4 July 1565, John Shakespeare was elected to the office of alderman of Stratford. From this time onwards he was known as Master Shakespeare. The title of master was reserved for educated people and those with a high social standing. John Shakespeare was sworn into office at a solemn and colourful ceremony on 12 September of the same year. He reached the height of his public career in 1568, when he became bailiff (the equivalent of a mayor) of Stratford, an impressive achievement for a glove-maker, wool-merchant and town councillor. Mary Arden would probably have regarded her husband's increase in social standing as a way of compensating for the loss of her own higher social status before marriage. It is also possible that John's determination and drive were rooted in a desire to provide a good standard of living and high social status for his wife, similar to that to which she had been accustomed. Mary herself must also have encouraged her husband in his ambitions.

The ceremonies associated with his public duties on special occasions, such as the solemn processions of town councillors wearing their formal robes of office, would have made a deep and lasting impression on the young William Shakespeare, who was just four years old when his father became a bailiff. Even day-to-day life in office was conducted ceremonially: the town bailiff and his deputies were escorted from their homes to meetings at the Guildhall, to church, to market days and to annual fairs by serjeants bearing the insignia of the bailiff. Over the years, William would also have noticed – surely not without pride – that his parents occupied a place of honour in the Guild Chapel and at Holy Trinity Church.

During his term as bailiff, John Shakespeare officially welcomed the queen's acting troupe and that of the Earl of Worcester, and allowed them to perform. The council at this time was already inclined to puritanism, and inviting actors to the town to perform was a noteworthy event that could by no means be taken for granted. As was customary, in Stratford as elsewhere, the actors gave a free performance for the bailiff, his family, the council members, their families and other special guests. It is certain, therefore, that, as a child, William Shakespeare attended theatrical performances by the country's finest troupes of actors. John Shakespeare may have welcomed them with an enthusiasm equal to that demonstrated by Hamlet in Act II, scene 2, as the hero greets a company of actors:

> You are welcome, masters; welcome all. – I am glad to see thee well. – Welcome, good friends. – O, my old friend! Why thy face is valanc'd since I saw thee last; com'st thou to beard me in Denmark? – What, my young lady and mistress! By'r lady, your ladyship is nearer to heaven than when I saw you last by the altitude of a chopine. Pray God, your voice, like a piece of uncurrent gold, be not crack'd within the ring. – Masters, you are all welcome. We'll e'en to't like French falconers, fly at anything we see. We'll have a speech straight. Come, give us a taste of your quality; come, a passionate speech.

Fig. 11 – The White Swan, an historic Elizabethan inn in Stratford-upon-Avon, not far from the house where Shakespeare was born.

Fig. 12a – Detail from wall painting in the White Swan: Tobias, Tobit's son, shown against a background of impressive medieval architecture.

When William Shakespeare returned to Stratford in later life as a celebrated playwright, well-respected citizen, gentleman and landowner, he would have witnessed the Stratford Council, whose meeting-place was directly opposite his residence, New Place, decree on 7 February 1612 that acting was outlawed. Furthermore, he would have witnessed the dramatic increase of fines for actors: from ten shillings to ten pounds.

Elsewhere in *Hamlet*, Shakespeare gives a hint of how he may have regarded the increasingly anti-theatre stance of the government of the time. Hamlet is particularly concerned about the way

Fig. 12b – Detail of a coloured fresco in the White Swan, depicting the story of Tobias, from the Apocrypha of the Old Testament, performed by amateur actors. The blind Tobit, wearing a fur-trimmed gown, is asking his son to cash a bill of debt from distant relatives. Behind the son stands the (still unrecognised) Archangel Raphael who will accompany him on the journey. The role of Tobit and his wife Hannah might have been played by John and Mary Shakespeare, William Shakespeare's parents. If this is so, the fresco, previously dated *c.* 1560, could have been painted in 1568 when John Shakespeare served as bailiff of Stratford and was allowed to wear a fur-trimmed gown.

in which the actors are to be treated and asks Polonius, the king's chief advisor, to treat the actors well:

> HAMLET.
> Good my lord, will you see the players well bestowed? Do you hear: let them be well used; for they are the abstract and brief chronicles of the time; after your death you were better have a bad epitaph than their ill report while you live.
>
> POLONIUS.
> My lord, I will use them according to their desert.
>
> HAMLET.
> God's bodykins, man, much better. Use every man after his desert, and who shall scape whipping? Use them after your own honour and dignity: the less they deserve, the more merit is in your bounty. Take them in.
>
> (Act II, scene 2)

In 1622, six years after the dramatist's death, Shakespeare's famous acting troupe the King's Men arrived in Stratford but were turned away by the puritanical Town Council. They were even paid for not performing, although they had a traditional right to do so.

Unlike his successors on the Town Council, John Shakespeare loved the theatre, and proved it while he served as bailiff of Stratford. He may even have performed the main role in an amateur production of a biblical play. A colourful fresco, dating from the 1560s, in the lounge of the White Swan Hotel in Stratford *(Fig. 11)*, depicts a theatrical scene from the Apocrypha, in which the blinded Tobit asks his son to go away to collect some money he is owed *(Figs. 12 a-b)*. At this time, amateur plays on biblical subjects were often performed, with burghers generally playing the main roles. The role of Tobit will therefore probably have been taken by a Stratford citizen. None of the figures have previously been identified. The painting

Fig. 13 – John Shakespeare's mark for the gloves he made.

Fig. 14 – 'Mary Shakespeare, née Arden'. This was initially thought to be a portrait of Judith Shakespeare, William Shakespeare's daughter, due to family resemblance. The style of clothing, however, indicates that this could be Shakespeare's mother. A swelling that can be seen on the upper lid of the left eye resembles the swelling seen on the authenticated Shakespeare portraits (Figs. 63 and 106). This portrait was discovered among the private possessions of Edward Fox*[1] and was later included in the collection at Nash House in Stratford-upon-Avon, where it remained until recently. According to the Birthplace Trust, the portrait is no longer extant and there is no record of it.

depicts Tobit in a very confident pose, wearing stunningly elegant clothing and even gloves, which he displays prominently. A slanting cross can be clearly seen on the inside of the left glove[7]. John Shakespeare often signed official documents with a very similar cross *(Fig. 13)* – it was his glover's mark, reminiscent of the cross of St Andrew and/or the base of his most important tool, the glover's donkey[8].

Tobit is also wearing a long, fur-trimmed overcoat or gown, another pointer that the man playing the role could be John Shakespeare, since as bailiff of Stratford in 1568 he would have been entitled to wear furs.

Strict Elizabethan dress regulations ('sumptuary laws') dictated that only members of the upper classes and holders of high public office were allowed to wear fur. The last sumptuary act from the time of Henry VIII, which came into effect in 1532, stated that sable was reserved for the royal family, and that lynx and black civet fur were to be worn exclusively by dukes, earls and barons.

The glover's mark on the left glove, the fur coat and the dating of this fresco are all strong indications that the role of Tobit was performed by the Stratford glove-maker, wool-merchant and bailiff, John Shakespeare. If this is true, then Tobit's wife – who is also elegantly dressed – must be Mary Arden, Shakespeare's mother. The round head of the female figure and what can be seen of her facial features are very similar to a portrait published as a black-and-white reproduction in *Shakespeare's Town and Times* by H. Snowden Ward and Catharine Weed Ward[9] around 1896. This portrait *(Fig. 14)* could be one of the family portraits found in New Place in the mid-eighteenth century, together with a likeness of Shakespeare. Henry Talbot, son-in-law of Sir Hugh Clopton and owner of New Place, had sold the property to a Protestant clergyman, the Revd. Francis Gastrell, in 1756. On 26 September 1758, an inventory of the items still at New Place was made. Among the papers of the Stratford historian and Shakespeare enthusiast, Robert Bell Wheler (d. 1857), was a record of these items,

Fig. 15a – 'Mary Shakespeare, née Arden' (?). A drawing by Sir Nathaniel Curzon of Kedlestone, copied from a painting and dating from 1708*[2]. Pictorial comparisons of the hairstyle, headdress and ruff, all typical of the 1550s and 60s*[3], show that this cannot be Shakespeare's wife Anne Hathaway (born 1556) as had initially been thought. By the time Anne and William married in 1582, this look was no longer fashionable. The drawing may well depict Mary Arden, Shakespeare's mother, who married John Shakespeare in 1557. The upper and lower lips, the corners of the mouth, and certain signs of illness, such as the thickening of the eyelids and especially the changes in the area of the left eye, remind us of the symptoms of illness in the portraits of Shakespeare (see *Figs. 1, 15c, 63,* and *106*), although the changes here are comparatively slight. Curzon must have made this drawing from a lifelike portrait of Shakespeare's mother which was still hanging in New Place in 1708 (see pp. 16–17).

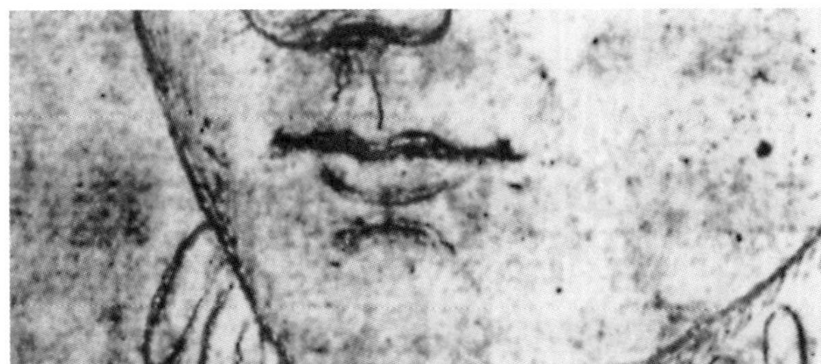

Fig. 15b – Detail of the mouth of the drawing in Fig. 15a.

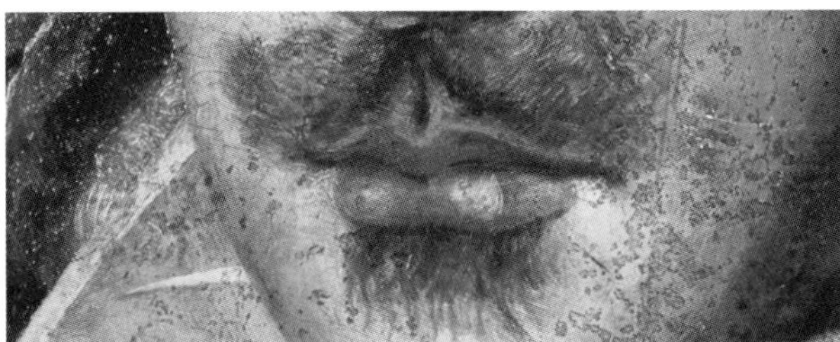

Fig. 15c – Detail of Shakespeare's mouth in the 'Flower' portrait showing how strongly his mouth resembles that of Fig. 15a, depicting – to all appearances – Mary Arden, his mother.

including a portrait of Shakespeare in the hall ('In ye Hall, Shakespeare's Head') and 'in the other rooms 6 Family Pictures'[10]. In the portrait included in the book *Shakespeare's Town and Times*, a distinct swelling can be seen on the left upper eyelid, which is very similar to the swelling seen in the authenticated 'Chandos' *(Fig. 63)* and 'Flower' *(Fig. 106)* portraits of Shakespeare. Until now, it had been thought that this was a portrait of Judith Quiney, Shakespeare's daughter, but the long, relatively narrow dress and the pattern of the material make this rather unlikely. Judith was born in 1585, and by the time she was about the age of the young woman portrayed in the painting, the fashion would have been quite different. The style appears to be more that of the late period of the reign of Mary Tudor, which would have been worn in the provinces in the 1560s. It still occurs in the early 1580s[11]. This indicates that the portrait is not that of Shakespeare's daughter, but of his mother.

If the fresco in the lounge of the White Swan Hotel[12] depicts John and Mary Shakespeare, it could date from 1568, the year in which John Shakespeare was bailiff. This would more or less be in agreement with previous attempts at dating the work: *c.* 1560. It is fortunate that this fresco survived the destructive attacks by the puritanical iconoclasts of the seventeenth century, and can still be enjoyed by twenty-first century visitors. A sketch made in 1708 *(Figs. 15 a-c)* also appears to depict Shakespeare's mother, and seems to be based on an accurate likeness.

The White Swan, which in the sixteenth century was an inn known as the King's Hall, is situated very near to Shakespeare's birthplace in Henley Street, where John and Mary Shakespeare lived, worked and raised their children. It can reasonably be assumed that John Shakespeare had close contact with the owner of this imposing inn, and that he probably met his friends here as William Shakespeare also could have done. There is a story that Michael Drayton and Ben Jonson visited their colleague and friend Shakespeare in Stratford in April 1616, just a couple of weeks before his death, had 'a merry meeting' and seem to have drunk too much, for Shakespeare fell ill with a fever from which he is supposed to have died. However, no written evidence exists to prove whether or not Shakespeare and his friends met in the King's Hall. The fact that the poet's health was already very poor at this point makes it unlikely that he left New Place. According to new research, Shakespeare had been suffering from a debilitating internal disease for many years, which most probably contributed to his early death (see pp. 317–318).

As bailiff of Stratford, John Shakespeare also held the important office of Justice of the Peace[13]. This meant a further enhancement of his already very high social standing. Although this was, and still is, an unsalaried position, it was much sought-after for the powers it bestowed. The most important task of the Justice of the Peace was to dispense justice. In addition to the usual court sessions at which minor breaches of the law were dealt with, there were four assize sittings a year. These fell in January, in the week after

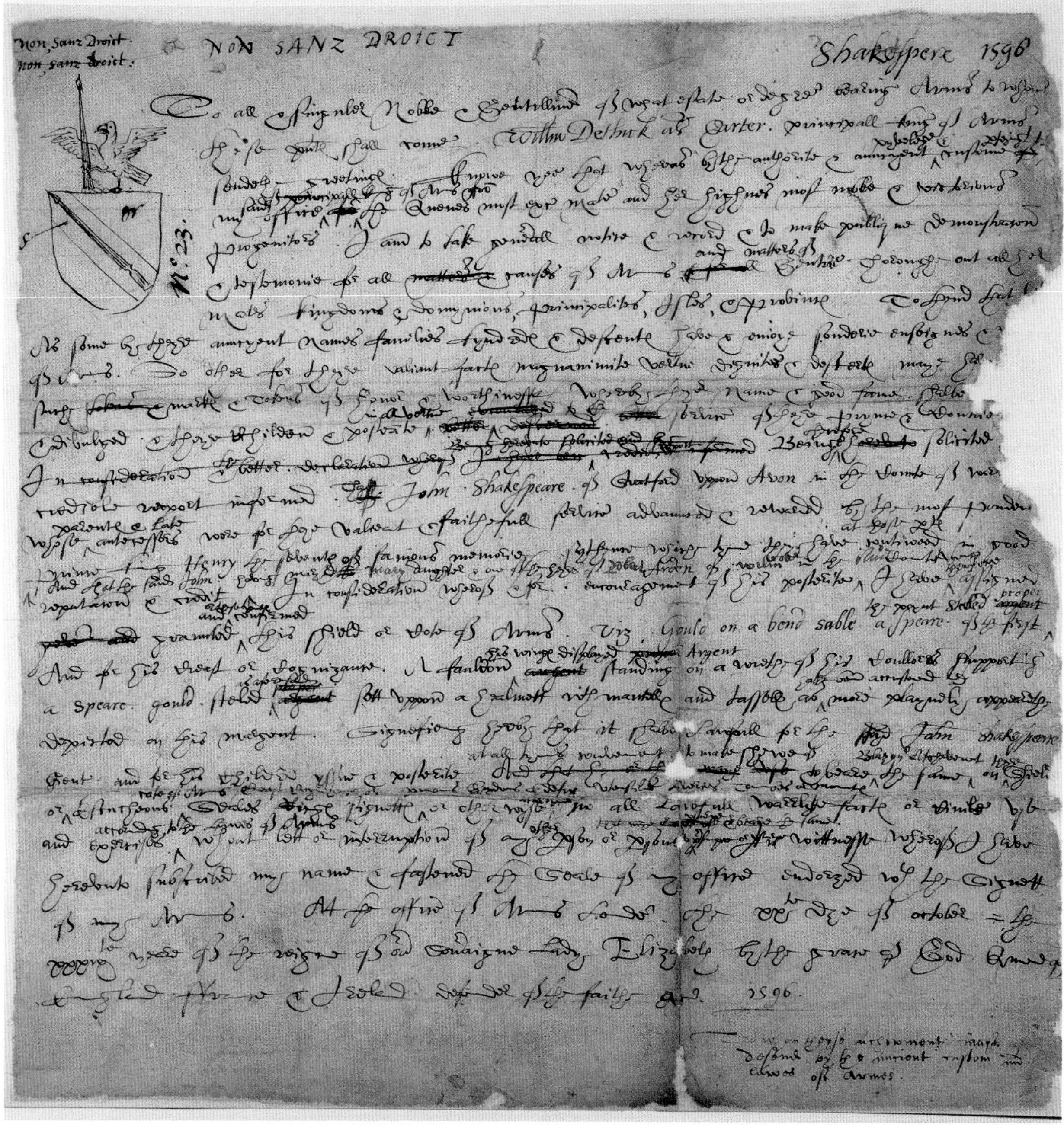

Non, Sanz Droict.

NON SANZ DROICT

Shakespere 1596

Fig. 16 – Draft of a response from the College of Heraldry to John Shakespeare's application for a family coat of arms in 1596, outlining the reasons why Shakespeare's father is entitled to a coat of arms: (1) John Shakespeare's grandfather had rendered outstanding service under Henry VII, (2) John himself had been a magistrate, a Justice of the Peace, a Bailiff and a Queen's Officer, and owned 'landes and tenements of good wealth & substance', and (3) had married 'the daughter of a gentleman'.

Easter, in July and in September. The Justice of the Peace presided over the assizes and was assisted by a scribe. Since many Justices of the Peace were laymen, they were usually supported by a group of legal experts, one of whom was required to be present at each session. In addition, the Justice of the Peace fixed prices, inspected and controlled weights and measures, licensed taverns, oversaw the maintenance of roads and bridges, and punished poaching, witchcraft, the practice of magic, and similar crimes or misdemeanours.

Fig. 17 – Shakespeare family coat of arms. Motto: NON SANZ DROICT (Not Without Right).

Among his new duties, John Shakespeare was responsible for ensuring that the Poor Law and Statute of Apprenticeship were observed, but he was also responsible for the implementation of the recusant laws. Recusants were those who rejected the Anglican divine service, and especially the sacrament of Holy Communion. As instructed in the Book of Common Prayer, parishioners had to receive communion at Easter and on two other Sundays during the year[14]. Most recusants were Catholics, but a few were non-conforming puritans. This will be discussed in greater detail in connection with John Shakespeare's religious beliefs.

Adrian Quiney, a rich Stratford silk and textile merchant, became Stratford's first bailiff in 1553. Quiney was also bailiff in 1559 and 1571, and John Shakespeare was elected as his deputy for his third term in office. The poet's father simultaneously held the office of Chief or High Alderman, and travelled to London with Quiney in 1572 in order to attend to matters of concern to the town. John Shakespeare was greatly respected by his fellow citizens, and his advice was keenly sought after. Even in old age, he was asked for advice in emergencies. When Sir Edward Greville attempted to take legal action against the town of Stratford in early 1601, John Shakespeare was one of the panel of five citizens chosen to advise the municipality in this difficult situation. He died at the beginning of September 1601, just a few months later[15].

As a child, William would have been very conscious of his father's high standing in the local community. It must be assumed that he admired his father greatly, and that the years during which John Shakespeare held public office had a lasting effect on William. This can be seen from the fact that Stratford remained at the centre of Shakespeare's life, and that he used the name of his home town as a pseudonym at the pilgrim's hospice of the English College (Collegium Anglicum) in Rome during his 'lost years' (1585-1592). Stratford was the place where William's own family lived and he returned to the town regularly, even after he had become very famous as a poet and playwright in London. Apart from one intriguing purchase of a house in Blackfriars in London towards the end of his life, Stratford was the town in which Shakespeare chose to invest all his money by buying extensive lands and property. There he eventually purchased a grand house, New Place, just opposite the Guild Chapel.

In 1576, at the age of twelve, William would have observed his father's efforts to acquire a family coat of arms, in recognition of his long and successful service to the town of Stratford. At last he seemed close to achieving the most coveted of his self-imposed goals; entering the ranks of the gentry, with the right to armorial bearings and the title of gentleman. Young William would also have seen his father's frustration at being deprived of this distinction. Years later, John Shakespeare applied once more for a family crest, successfully this time *(Figs. 16–17)*. On 20 October 1596, a document granting his petition was drafted under the guidance of William Dethick of the Heralds'

College. This time his son William, who by then had become famous and wealthy, may have taken a hand in the matter; no doubt his motives included self-interest. The Privy Council member Robert Devereux, Earl of Essex, and William Camden, the leading Elizabethan historian and antiquary, may also have exerted a positive influence. They were both extremely well-disposed to the, by now, renowned author Shakespeare. In 1597, Essex served as Earl Marshal of England and Head of the College of Heralds, of which Camden became a member in the same year[16].

In the 1570s, Alderman John Shakespeare presided conscientiously over the affairs of his town, and ministered to the concerns and needs of its population – to the great satisfaction of his fellow burghers. Yet in 1577, when he was in his fifth decade, and William was about thirteen, a change occurred in John Shakespeare's behaviour which has puzzled commentators ever since. John Shakespeare suddenly stopped attending council meetings, and gave no explanation for his absence. There must have been sound and cogent reasons for this complete change. John Shakespeare would never have disregarded his important public duties for a petty quarrel. The explanation for this fundamental turn in the life of Alderman Shakespeare must have been the massive internal and external conflicts brought about by the rigid religious policy of the government. Did John Shakespeare decide on this form of passive resistance and reject his public duties as a 'Queen's officer' (see caption to Fig. 16) because they were no longer compatible with his conscience and religious beliefs?

To answer this question, the increasingly severe anti-Catholic legislation imposed in the reign of Elizabeth I, and its devastating effects on the Catholic population of England, must be examined in greater detail than has hitherto been supplied in Shakespeare biographies and research.

ELIZABETH I'S ANTI-CATHOLIC PENAL LAWS AND THEIR CONSEQUENCES

In his book *Tudor England* (1950), the English historian T.S. Bindoff writes that Elizabeth I was the first English monarch to waive the right to punish her subjects for dissenting religious beliefs. Her concern, according to Bindoff, was not to save the souls of her subjects in the afterlife, but to save her country in this one. The truth is, however, that under Elizabeth I and James I those who remained true to Roman Catholicism and rejected the New Religion were subject to unbearable persecution and punishment. Mary Tudor, a strict Catholic, who became queen of England in 1553 had used fire and the sword to win back the land for the Catholic Church. In 1555, Hugh Latimer, a Protestant preacher and reformer, who had been Bishop of Worcester, and Nicholas Ridley, who as Bishop of Rochester and then of London, had promoted the religious reforms of King Edward VI, were tried and burned at the stake for heresy. On 6 November 1558 Mary acknowledged her half-sister Elizabeth as her successor – and died eleven days later. The last Catholic archbishop of Canterbury, Cardinal Reginald Pole, died the same day. When Elizabeth came to the throne on 17 November 1558, ten of the twenty-seven dioceses of England and Wales lacked a bishop. The late English historian Michael Davies wrote that of the seventeen Catholic bishops still officiating Bishop Kitchen of Llandaff was the only one who became an apostate. With regard to the fate of the other sixteen bishops, Davies states that two had died and two had gone into exile, that nothing was known about another of them, and that the remaining eleven Catholic bishops had died in prison. The bishops who perished in prison became martyrs in the eyes of the English Catholics[17].

Elizabeth I was crowned in St Paul's cathedral in London by a Catholic bishop *(Fig. 18)*. For the ceremony, the queen wore the dress (and an ermine-edged robe) her half-sister Mary had worn at her coronation. This served to dupe the

Fig. 18 – Coronation portrait of Elizabeth I. The new queen wore the same dress as her late half-sister, Mary I. Elizabeth was crowned in Westminster Abbey by a Catholic bishop in a Catholic ceremony, but she did not stay to take part in the Catholic Coronation Mass.

Fig. 19 – Sir Nicholas Throckmorton, conspirator and diplomat. Throckmorton devised cunning strategies to win the throne of England for Elizabeth. The new queen followed Throckmorton's counsel to keep her religious policies a secret at the beginning of her reign.

Fig. 20 – Portrait of Elizabeth I painted in 1585, the year of crisis. The unknown painter has depicted a stoat (ermine) with a crown around its neck close to the queen's heart. He thus seems to echo the ermine lining on the robe worn in her coronation portrait. This may also be an allusion to the disappointed hopes of the English Catholics.

Catholic population *(Fig. 19)*, for the queen did not take part in the Catholic Mass that formed part of the coronation service. In a famous portrait of the queen, painted in 1585, the year of crisis which was also the year in which Shakespeare disappeared from our view for seven years, a stoat (ermine) is painted near the queen's heart, in the same curved shape as the ermine lining on the robe in her coronation portrait. This pictorial reference echoes the Catholics' sense of betrayal by Elizabeth, for between 1558 and 1585 they had discovered through bitter experience that the queen's primary aim was not merely to suppress Roman Catholicism in England, but to eradicate it completely[18].

Thus, even at the outset of the Elizabethan age, the 'settlement' of the religious question was a central issue. The term 'religious settlement' gave the impression of reconciliation and appeasement, but in reality the population had once more to accept a change of religion, decreed by the government, which forced many to enter a period of active or passive resistance.

In 1559, a second Act of Supremacy and the Act of Uniformity were passed, a new Book of Common Prayer was introduced, and once more all ties with Rome were severed. Unlike the Act of Supremacy of 1534, passed by her father Henry VIII, who had thus become 'Supreme Head of the Church of England' and had sharply criticized Rome *(Fig. 21)*, the new Act of 1559 drafted by Elizabeth and her counsellors avoided the title of 'Head' and replaced it with 'Governor'. The queen's official title became 'the only supreme governor of this realm ...

Fig. 21 – 'The Allegory of the Reformation'. A satirical painting by an unknown artist, dating from *c.* 1568-1571. The dying Henry VIII is pointing to his son and successor, Edward VI, who triumphs over Rome.

as well in all spiritual or ecclesiastical things or causes, as temporal'. The 'Thirty-Nine Articles' came into force in 1563, being the historical doctrinal standard of the Church of England.

Whereas in 1555, one year after her marriage to Philip of Spain in Winchester cathedral, Queen Mary I had the leading Protestant clergymen burned at the stake as heretics, Elizabeth I – as mentioned above – arrested most of the Catholic bishops, but left her Catholic subjects unmolested, at least at the beginning of her reign. Outwardly, the government even strove for consensus, retaining elements of the Catholic liturgy and acting out of consideration for Catholic sensibilities in the choice of language for the new Book of Common Prayer. The queen's closest advisor was William Cecil, later granted the title of Lord Burghley *(Fig. 22)*; her favourite was Robert Dudley, Earl of Leicester.

The first setback to this conciliatory religious policy occurred when Mary Queen of Scots, a Stuart, whose claim to the English throne was supported by Catholics both in England and abroad, sought asylum in England in 1568. Her troops in Scotland had suffered defeat in a battle against the supporters of her murdered first husband, Lord Darnley. In 1569, Mary's presence incited a Catholic uprising in the north of England, which was brutally suppressed by the government.

When Pope Pius V excommunicated the English queen in 1570, new, more stringent anti-Catholic laws were introduced. Practising Catholics faced a conflict of loyalties. Many went into exile, mostly to the Spanish province of Flanders. The sons of Catholic middle-class and, in particular, upper-class families who remained in England were sent in large

THE
JOURNALS
OF ALL THE
PARLIAMENTS
During the REIGN of
Queen ELIZABETH,
BOTH OF THE
HOUSE of LORDS
AND
HOUSE of COMMONS.

Collected By
Sir *SIMONDS D'EWES* of *Stow-Hall* in the County of SUFFOLK, Knight and Baronet.

Revifed and Publifhed
By *PAUL BOWES*, of the MIDDLE-TEMPLE *LONDON*, Efq;

LONDON,
Printed for *John Starkey* at the *Mitre* in *Fleetftreet* near *Temple-Bar*. 1682.

Fig. **22** – Above, left: Elizabeth I presiding over Parliament. Frontispiece of *The Journals of All the Parliaments during the Reign of Queen Elizabeth*. To the right of the queen sits William Cecil, Lord Burghley, her First Minister and closest advisor. Above right: Title page of the *Journals of All the Parliaments*.

numbers to Douai in Flanders (today France). There William Allen *(Fig. 24)*, a former fellow of the University of Oxford, a Catholic-in-exile who later became a Roman Cardinal, had founded the first English College on the Continent, the Collegium Anglicum in 1568 *(Fig. 25)*. This college provided a Catholic education for English students, and also trained English priests. Between 1578 and 1593, because William of Orange's Protestant troops had conquered Douai, it was forced to move to Rheims to ensure the safety of the students and their teachers.

In Douai and Rheims, students could obtain an excellent basic academic education that was sufficient to qualify them as private tutors or teachers in England. The ambitious curriculum was based on that of the contemporary Jesuit colleges. Many students went on to advanced studies and became priests, working in the English Mission and thus playing an active role in restoring Catholicism into England.

These priests appealed to the conscience of their fellow-citizens, roused them from their inactivity, invoked the religion of their forefathers, and tried to win them back to Catholicism.

All this took place in great secrecy, in rural areas mainly in the houses of the Catholic landed gentry, where hiding places, 'priest chambers' or 'priest holes', had been constructed in order to protect the priests *(Fig. 26)*. To evade recognition, Catholic priests had to change their appearance and their names frequently. They often disguised themselves as servants.

The government and parliament reacted to the Jesuit movement[19] in the spring of 1581 by passing a new, draconian penal law, whereby all persons active in the English mission and all their followers were guilty of high treason. Priests who said Mass were threatened with a huge fine of 200 marks (roughly £133, the equivalent of about £20,000 today), and those who attended Mass not only had to pay a fine of over £60 but were also sentenced to a year's imprisonment. Anyone over the age of sixteen who did not attend Anglican divine services was fined £20 a month. Anyone employing a schoolmaster who refused to subscribe to the new religion had to pay a monthly fine of £10 and was sentenced to a year's imprisonment. Such

Fig. 23 – William Cecil, Lord Burghley, the most important member of Queen Elizabeth's Privy Council. For forty years – from 1558 to 1598 – he determined English policy. He was also the initiator of the harsh anti-Catholic legislation. Robert Parsons, the Jesuit priest who led the missionary movement to reintroduce Catholicism to England, regarded William Cecil as his greatest adversary. It has long been assumed that Shakespeare might have based the character of Polonius in *Hamlet* on Cecil. The new evidence presented in this book strongly supports this assumption.

Fig. 24 – Portrait of William Allen. The former Principal of St Mary's Hall, Oxford, Proctor of Oxford University and a Catholic living in exile, was the founder of the Collegium Anglicum in Douai, which opened in 1568. This was the first English college on the Continent where young English Catholics could receive a Catholic academic education.

Fig. 25 – The Collegium Anglicum in Douai as it was in Shakespeare's time.

illegal schoolmasters were deprived of their right to teach and sentenced to a year in custody.

The law also prescribed particularly severe punishment for citizens who incited their fellow citizens to treason, gave shelter to traitors and did not report these crimes within twenty days. If caught, they were deprived of their income and property and sentenced to life imprisonment. One third of the confiscated possessions went to the queen, another third to the poor in the respective district and the final third went to the informer. In view of such rich pickings there were plenty of informers, and the government had no difficulty in recruiting suitable spies.

Catholic priests who had abandoned their faith were the most feared on the Catholic side. For these renegades knew the hidden locations used by Catholics, and were familiar with the details of their teaching institutions. In 1584, Anthony Tyrrell, who had been educated at the English College in Rome and had been ordained priest there, spent twenty-four days at the hospice attached to the College. He collected information about the Pope and the plans of the English Catholics, which he afterwards passed on to Lord Burghley, Elizabeth's First Minister *(Fig. 23)*.

In 1580, a spy called Sledd betrayed Thomas Cottom, a young priest, who was the brother of the Stratford schoolmaster John Cottom. Sledd wormed his way into the young man's confidence while they were travelling from Lyon to Rheims. Thomas Cottom was tried and condemned as a traitor. His execution took place in 1582. In the

Fig. 26 – Concealed entrance to a secret 'priest's hole' in an English stately home, dating from the time of Shakespeare.

writings of the English Jesuits, Sledd was referred to as an 'Englishman and infamous Judas'[20].

In 1585 a further anti-Catholic law was introduced, banning all Jesuits and priests from England. Breach of this law was punishable by death. Anyone helping a priest or Jesuit was deemed to be guilty of high treason, and, if convicted, was sentenced to death. His property was confiscated. Subjects of the queen of England attending colleges and seminaries on the Continent had to return within six months to take the Oath of Supremacy. If they refused to do so, they too were considered guilty of high treason.

Anyone providing financial support for the Jesuits and priests, their colleges and students, was thrown into jail. Those who sent their children to be educated on the Continent without the permission of the government were forced to pay a fine of £100. Those who knew the whereabouts of a Jesuit or a priest and did not report it within twelve days were forced to pay a fine and were imprisoned. If a Justice of the Peace were found guilty of such an offence, he would be forced to pay a fine of 200 marks (*c.* £133).

A further anti-Catholic law passed in 1593 declared that recusants over the age of sixteen had to return to their homes (or the homes of their parents), and were only permitted to travel within a five-mile radius. If they broke this law, their property could be confiscated. A copyholder could be stripped of his income for life. All recusants had to register with the authorities. Anyone earning an income of less than £40 annually from their property, assets and livestock was forced to conform to the new religion, or had to swear to leave the country. Those who refused to swear the oath, or who swore the oath but broke it, were regarded as traitors and sentenced to death. Anyone suspected of being a Jesuit or a priest and refusing to answer questions about it, was immediately thrown into jail.

These laws had a devastating effect on English Catholics. They were not only deprived of their rights, excluded, criminalised, and persecuted, they also had to suffer draconian punishments. This was not to change officially until the Catholic Emancipation Act of 1829. Hitherto, this situation has been paid only marginal attention, if any, by leading English historians.

There are many signs that William Shakespeare – even before the great turning point in his works, after which he wrote only tragedies, problem plays and finally romances (with the exception of *Henry VIII*) – was disgusted by the renunciation of the old religion and the anti-Catholic laws, and appalled by the immorality and tyranny of those in power, and the resulting social and political injustice. This is particularly clearly demonstrated in Sonnet 66, written in the late 1590s (see pp. 205–206).

In Sonnet 29, Shakespeare makes an obvious reference to his own situation. He mentions his isolation ('I all alone') and his exclusion ('my outcast state'):

> When, in disgrace with Fortune and men's eyes,
> I all alone beweep my outcast state,
> And trouble deaf heaven with my bootless cries,
> And look upon myself, and curse my fate.

Until now, it has been thought that the poet may have been referring to his lowly social status, of which he would have been made very conscious by consorting with his friend and patron, the Earl of Southampton. This theory is supported by later lines in the sonnet:

> Wishing me like to one more rich in hope,
> Featur'd like him, like him with friends possess'd,
> Desiring this man's art, and that man's scope.

Against the background of my new findings presented in this book, showing that Shakespeare was a secret Catholic and was active in the Catholic underground, these verses can now be interpreted quite differently, and more accurately. When Shakespeare refers to his 'outcast state'[21], he seems to be pointing to his deprived, outsider existence to which he and other Catholics were condemned by their religion.

The English Catholics or recusants who did not conform to the Anglican Church and its institutions were outcasts and pariahs. Thus they often led a double existence: an official life in which they appeared to adhere to the religious laws, and a hidden life in which they practised the Catholic faith.

Shakespeare must have been one such recusant. As will be shown later, it was not only at the end of his life that he courageously risked almost everything to ensure that Catholicism would survive in England (see p. 303).

It is true that Shakespeare's lament in the first and second quatrains of Sonnet 29 is only a build-up to his final assertion that, thanks to the wealth gained from his love for his friend, he would not exchange his fate with any king. But the fact that the poet in the end uses his initial description for another purpose does not diminish its value as an historical statement, or its autobiographical relevance.

JOHN SHAKESPEARE – A SECRET CATHOLIC

While Lancashire was well-known in Elizabethan times as by far the most Catholic of English counties, Warwickshire also had a high proportion of Catholics. The large numbers of recusants in the diocese of Worcester, to which Stratford-upon-Avon belonged, made it a thorn in the side of the official church.

In 1596, the Bishop of Worcester, referring to the many recusants living in his diocese, wrote to William Cecil, Elizabeth's First Minister, claiming that his diocese was a particularly dangerous area. The bishop's observations were entirely correct. Many old-established aristocratic families lived there – above all in and around Stratford-upon-Avon – and they continued to practise the Catholic faith, in spite of the fact that they were breaking the law. These families included the Middlemores of Edgbaston, the

Sheldons of Beoley, the Throckmortons of Coughton, the Underhills of Idlecote, the Cloptons of Stratford, the Catesbys of Lapworth and – last but not least – the Ardens of Parkhall[22].

These and other Catholic families gave shelter to the Jesuit priests of the English Mission established in 1580 by Edmund Campion and Robert Parsons. The Jesuits distributed the 'spiritual testaments' devised by the Cardinal of Milan, Charles Borromeo[23]. By filling in and signing the Jesuit testaments, English Catholics would confess and confirm their faith anew. The Catholic conspirators of the 1605 Gunpowder Plot were the sons of the Catholic gentry of the English Midlands. Sir William Catesby, father of Robert Catesby, one of the leaders of the Gunpowder Plot, harboured Edmund Campion and his companions in Lapworth in 1580. Lapworth is just a few miles north of Stratford. In August 1581, Sir William Catesby was arrested for this and thrown into jail. His family were forced to pay draconian fines for having practised Catholicism. This forced them to sell many of their estates, much of their wealth accruing to the Crown. Sir William's son Robert was just a child when he witnessed the downfall of his family, and began at an early age to brood on revenge.

The Ardens of Parkhall, relatives of Shakespeare's mother, experienced a much worse fate in the 1580s, when Edward Arden, head of the family, was drawn into an amateurish Catholic conspiracy by his hot-headed son-in-law, John Somerville. This conspiracy was later called the Arden-Somerville Plot. Somerville planned to shoot the queen with a pistol. On his way to London he talked openly about his intention. He was soon arrested, along with Edward Arden and his wife Mary. Mary Arden of Parkhall, the namesake of the playwright's mother, was released, but her husband was convicted of high treason in 1583 and hanged. His head was displayed on a spike on London Bridge as a deterrent to others. The Protestant authorities raided the district in which his family lived, and the Shakespeares and their Catholic neighbours must have feared for their safety.

The Bishop of Worcester's concerns, expressed sixteen years after the beginning of the Jesuit missionary movement, were proved to be well-founded. Without doubt, his diocese was a centre of Catholic resistance, some of it organised. This is also proved by a written source which originated outside England, the so-called Rheims Report, an internal document for the use of those attending the Collegium Anglicum in Rheims, dating from 1580. The report states indirectly – for security reasons – that the diocese of Worcester was teeming with crypto-Catholics and that the Jesuit mission, led by Edmund Campion and Robert Parsons, was particularly strong in the north of England, i.e. Lancashire, but that it was also incredibly strong in another 'province', which appears to be the diocese of Worcester. According to the author of this report, between one and two hundred people regularly attended Mass and heard sermons in this 'province'. The Masses would not have been conducted in churches, but in secret venues offering ample capacity, such as the halls and reception rooms in the homes of the landed gentry[24].

Stratford was located in the geographical centre of this 'dangerous' region and was home to many Catholic recusants. In 1592, the government commissioned a register of all recusants, who were then – according to the letter of the law – subject to prosecution. The carefully compiled list of recusants in Stratford was sent to London, complete with annotations. It contained the name of Shakespeare's father.

Towards the end of the nineteenth century, the Protestant Reverend Thomas Carter claimed that John Shakespeare appeared on the list of recusants because he had rejected the official Church as a *puritanical* non-conformist. In his book *Shakespeare: Puritan and Recusant* (1897), he claimed that as a member of the Town Council, Shakespeare's father had backed the decision to destroy the paintings in Holy Trinity Church and the Guild Chapel (1562/3), and to sell the liturgical objects (1571). Sidney Lee, the eminent Shakespeare researcher, conclusively refuted Carter's argument. According to Lee, the Stratford Town Council had merely been following government orders. Lee's most striking counter-argument was that during his term in office as bailiff (1568/9) John Shakespeare allowed the Queen's Men and the acting troupe of the Earl of Worcester to perform in the town, and publicly welcomed them. Furthermore, he argued that John Shakespeare, with the help of his son William, had also consistently worked hard to acquire the title of gentleman and achieve a coat of arms. He had eventually been successful, not because he had been loyal to the government, but because of his services as a magistrate and the fact that he had married the daughter of a gentleman. Coats of arms, titles and, above all, the theatre, Lee called to mind, were all greatly despised by the Puritans[25]. So John Shakespeare must have been, not a Puritan, but a Catholic recusant.

There is further evidence of John Shakespeare's Catholicism. In 1577, his behaviour changed significantly. He stopped attending council meetings, neglecting his duties as an alderman. In the context of the political and religious atmosphere of the time, the reason for this behaviour could only have been that John Shakespeare no longer wished to act as the executor of a government that carried out deplorable acts of violence against property (such as the destruction of church paintings and the sale of Catholic liturgical objects) and that also took violent action against English Catholic priests who had been educated on the Continent and had returned to England as Catholic missionaries.

In 1577, the first Catholic priest was executed under the anti-Catholic law that had been passed in 1571. His name was Cuthbert Mayne, and he had been ordained at Douai. It appears to be no coincidence that this was the same year in which John Shakespeare chose to neglect his duties. The execution of Cuthbert Mayne could have been a decisive factor, causing him to withdraw from office and turn to passive resistance.

It has to be emphasized that such behaviour was totally untypical of Alderman Shakespeare. In all his public offices he had shown reliability, scrupulousness, a strong sense of duty and responsibility, i.e. those public virtues his Stratford fellow citizens appreciated in him, just as they appreciated his prudence and expertise. So one must bear in mind that it is hard to see any other obvious reason for John Shakespeare's conduct, apart from the inner conflict caused by the rigidity of the anti-Cantholic penal laws.

In 1571, Simon Hunt started work as a schoolmaster at Stratford Grammar School. Although officially the role of appointing the schoolmasters and vicars of Stratford would have been the task of the Earl of Warwick in his capacity as Lord of the Manor, a Town Council member as important as John Shakespeare would surely have had some say in the matter. After all, it was the council who paid the schoolmaster's salary.

William Shakespeare was seven-years-old in 1571, the usual age for starting grammar school. For John Shakespeare, the new schoolmaster's religion would have been as important as his qualifications. Hunt was another secret Catholic, who covertly educated the children in his care according to Catholic beliefs. After teaching for four years in Stratford, he openly declared his Catholic faith and travelled to Douai, where he became a priest. In 1578, he was accepted into the Society of Jesus in Rome, and in 1580 became Robert Parsons' successor as English Confessor at the Holy See.

Consequently, in his first four years at grammar school, William Shakespeare was under the care of a secret and particularly diligent and fervent believer in the old faith, and this must have had a great and lasting impact on him.

A Simon Hunt is recorded as living in Stratford at the end of the sixteenth century, but this cannot have been the schoolmaster. For the latter had left for Douai – together with Robert

Debdale of Shottery, one of his pupils from Stratford who also later became a priest.

John Shakespeare must have known that Hunt was a Catholic before 1571, i.e. before his son William entered the local Grammar School. Given John Shakespeare's obvious intelligence and the sources of information that would have been available to him as the former bailiff of Stratford, it is impossible to believe that he would have left to chance the religion of the schoolmaster to whom he would entrust his eldest son. Every piece of evidence about Shakespeare's father proves him to be a decision-maker and man of action, who was not only aware of everything going on in and around Stratford, but who probably had a say in everything that happened.

Hunt's successor, Thomas Jenkins, was a Protestant and later became an Anglican clergyman. In his case, the Protestant members of the Council had obviously managed to exert their influence. Shakespeare ridicules Jenkins in his comedy *The Merry Wives of Windsor* (see p. 43).

As mentioned above, from 1577 onwards John Shakespeare no longer attended council meetings and, as far as is known, made no official comment about this decision. He was not replaced in office until September 1586. During all this time, the poet's father only attended one council meeting, on 5 September 1582, when he voted for the new bailiff, his friend, the Catholic John Sadler. The fact that he broke his resolution to refrain from public life on this occasion meant that he must have been very keen to see Sadler elected. It is indeed of great significance that this was the very time, 1582, that William Shakespeare returned to his home town, having been involved – as will be shown later – in the Catholic underground movement in Lancashire, and being now in particular need of protection. So John Shakespeare's presence at the 1582 meeting must have been more than a coincidence, since a bailiff who was a friend of his father could secretly have shielded William.

When John Shakespeare began his period of 'boycott', William was thirteen-years-old and had therefore reached the age at which the sons of the English middle and upper classes were sent away for academic education to the two universities. As Catholics, this would have presented a problem for the Shakespeares, because it was impossible to graduate from Oxford or Cambridge without taking the Oath of Supremacy. Catholics refused to take this Oath, because they only acknowledged the Pope as the head of the Church and obeyed him in all spiritual matters.

So for the Catholic Shakespeare family – as for other English Catholic families – there was only one alternative: the Collegium Anglicum in Flanders, at that time the only place at which young English Catholics could study without taking the Oath of Supremacy. Studying at this college by no means meant that the young men were required to aim for holy orders. Instead, it offered them the chance to obtain a basic academic education in the humanities (Lower Studies). Students at the Collegium Anglicum were aged between fourteen and twenty-five, but thirteen-year-olds were also accepted, as demonstrated by the example of John Gerard, who later became a Jesuit priest[26]. In the early 1580s, even students as young as ten were allowed to enter the college, but they were sent on to other newly founded schools in the area or thereabouts, where they could receive an education more suitable for their age.

There are several significant indications that John Shakespeare was personally acquainted with William Allen, who founded the Collegium Anglicum. During the school years 1562/3 and 1563/4, a teacher named William Allen taught Latin at the Grammar School in Stratford. This William Allen seems to be the very same man who in 1568 founded the college in Douai and who later – just like Robert Parsons – became an eminent leader of the English Catholics in exile on the Continent. In 1561 he had fled from Oxford University on religious grounds and travelled to Louvain in Flanders[27]. In 1562, he secretly returned to England, remaining for some time in the Lancashire area, mainly staying with the Catholic landed gentry. There is also evidence that he lived in the Oxford area, where many families of the Catholic landed gentry had their seats. The city of Oxford itself was almost entirely Catholic. In 1561, the bailiff of Oxford informed the government that there were not three houses in Oxford not inhabited by Papists[28]. Allen's exact whereabouts was never disclosed. In 1565, after staying in England for four years, he was forced to flee again.

Stratford is less than thirty miles from Oxford, and had close connections with the university town. The masters of Stratford Grammar School were usually Oxford graduates. The dates of Allen's stay in England and the Oxford area coincide perfectly with those of the schoolmaster's employment in Stratford; from Michaelmas (29 September) 1562 until St Peter's Day (29 June) 1564 *(Fig. 30)*. When Allen left the school, William Shakespeare was just eight-weeks-old.

From what is known about the teacher William Allen, it is clear that he was a very significant person. The charter of the Stratford Grammar School stated that the teacher of Latin was to be paid by the schoolmaster out of his own wages, but William Allen was paid directly from the town funds. His name, however, was not entered in the records. This implies that he was being employed illegally, but that the Town Council welcomed his presence and supported him. In his second year, Allen quite suddenly abandoned his teaching post, obviously for compelling reasons. Instead of the normal wage of £4, he received just £3, showing that he had only taught for nine months.

Allen's salary was paid by John Shakespeare, one of the two officiating Stratford chamberlains, as proved by a pay receipt from the year 1564/5. Viewed against the religious background of the time, this can only mean that William Allen was a secret Catholic, who had been appointed as a teacher as part of an effort to protect him. As chamberlain, John Shakespeare must have known about the illegal employment of this obviously Catholic teacher at the Stratford Grammar School, and there is reason to believe that the poet's father was actively involved in the concealment.

William Gilbert, the assistant Latin teacher whom Allen seems to have supplanted, must also have been a Catholic. His name too was concealed, and an alias entered in the records (Gilbert *alias* Higges). He even received a payment from the Town Council, for an undisclosed purpose. This was highly unusual and in contrast to the detailed bookkeeping of the time, in which every sum was accounted for. When Allen was employed, Gilbert was not sent away, but was kept behind the scenes in reserve. When Allen left, or was forced to leave, Gilbert took up his position once again.

John Shakespeare could not have performed such transactions individually and without the approval of the Town Council. It can, therefore, reasonably be assumed that the Council members gave their consent to the Catholic education of the sons of the citizens.

If this William Allen was indeed the same man who later founded the Collegium Anglicum, then the Shakespeares would have had a direct link to Douai. They could have used this contact, or their indirect contact via Simon Hunt, William's former schoolmaster. If, following the example of many English Catholics, in 1577 the Shakespeares decided to send their son William to Douai/Rheims, either with or without using their contacts William Allen and Simon Hunt, then this decision would have coincided with John Shakespeare's resolution to withdraw from council meetings and not to perform his duties as an alderman, i.e. as 'an officer of the Queen', any longer. John Shakespeare thus began a new chapter in his life, closing the door on his successful career in public office. As the aldermen and bailiffs of the English boroughs had to enforce the anti-Catholic penal laws, this caused great inner conflicts for the many

Catholics among them; John Shakespeare would have shared this crisis of conscience.

The most significant impetus for John Shakespeare to withdraw from his office as alderman must have been the execution of the Catholic priest Cuthbert Mayne in 1577. It offended against a taboo, in a way that was not easy for Catholics to come to terms with. In addition, this event may well have persuaded the Shakespeares to send William to the Continent to receive a Catholic college education. Cuthbert Mayne was the Collegium Anglicum's first martyr and the spilling of his blood caused an upsurge in religious zeal among Catholics both in England and on the Continent. Even those Catholics who had acquiesced and followed the new religion – at least outwardly – were newly incensed. They began to turn in increasing numbers to the Catholic missionary priests who had secretly entered the country, acted secretly as pastors, and offered support to the Catholic population, hard pressed both materially and spiritually.

The question of whether John and Mary Shakespeare were committed Catholics who appeared to conform, or conformists who were encouraged to return to the Catholic faith by the priests from Douai or by Jesuits, can be answered confidently on the basis of thorough analysis of contemporary documents and reports. The Shakespeares were devout Catholics and remained so throughout their lives. It is most unlikely that they would not have sent their son, William, to Allen's College in Douai or Rheims, at that time the only place where he could have received a Catholic college education.

The basic course (Lower Studies) at the Collegium Anglicum lasted for two years, and the Shakespeares would have needed a considerable sum in cash to support their son during his stay on the Continent. A similar education at the universities of Oxford and Cambridge also lasted two years, and normally began at the age of fourteen, as long as the student displayed sufficient knowledge of Latin. Students completing their education would be awarded the degree of Bachelor of Arts (BA).

It is revealing that, on 14 November 1578, John Shakespeare mortgaged a large part of his wife's estate in Wilmcote, consisting of a house and fifty-six acres of land, for the sum of £40 and for a period of two years to his brother-in-law, Edmund Lambert. Also in November 1578, John Shakespeare mortgaged more land from the same property in Wilmcote (eighty-six acres) to a relative of his Snitterfield tenant, Alexander Webbe. Only one year later, John Shakespeare sold one-ninth of his property in Snitterfield (100 acres and two houses) to Robert Webbe, son of his tenant, for the sum of £40. Samuel Schoenbaum, the American Shakespeare scholar, writes that the selling price of this third piece of land was only £4. It seems, however, that he is merely repeating an error made by Sidney Lee, who later acknowledged it as a mistake and corrected it[29]. According to Schoenbaum, the reason behind these hasty transactions was 'a need for cash – immediate cash', but he does not offer any explanation as to why the poet's father was in such urgent need of this amount of ready money.

Earlier researchers have suggested that the funds were needed to pay the hefty fines imposed on those who failed to attend Anglican divine services. This cannot be the case, however, because the law whereby recusants over the age of sixteen had to pay a monthly fine of £20 if they failed to attend Anglican Church services was not passed until 1581. It is true that in 1580, John Shakespeare was heavily fined for failing to appear before the Queen's Bench in London, but this does not explain why he needed so much money in 1578. There is also no evidence that John Shakespeare acquired a large property or land in 1578 or 1579, which could also have accounted for these unusually large sums.

The only plausible explanation for John Shakespeare's pressing need for huge amounts in cash appears to be William's expensive two-year course of education on the Continent. If this is so, the money would have been spent on travel, lodgings, food, clothing, lessons, books and pocket money. It may also have been used to purchase souvenirs, such as crucifixes, statuettes of the Virgin Mary and rosaries. Many students at Allen's College acquired such items on the Continent to take home to their parents, as they were no longer on sale in England. William's schoolmate Robert Debdale, who was ordained priest in Douai, bought items such as these for his relatives in Shottery near Stratford. He asked a friend, the above-mentioned priest Thomas Cottom, to deliver them for him when visiting his brother, the Stratford Schoolmaster John Cottom, in 1580. The exchange, however, never took place because Cottom – as mentioned above – was spied upon in France by an English government informer and handed over to the authorities on arrival in England.

Other parts of the money could well have been donated to the college. The newly founded institution was in permanent need of funds, and was dependent upon contributions from English Catholics, particularly those whose sons attended the College. William Allen himself appealed to the parents to send their sons with generous amounts of money.

The cash raised by John Shakespeare must have totalled over £100. Considering the average yearly income of an Elizabethan craftsman[30], this amount would have covered the tuition fees very comfortably (even in expensive Rheims, where the Collegium Anglicum had moved in 1578) and would also have allowed a generous donation to the College funds.

In 1578, John Shakespeare obviously thought that by 1580 he would be able to raise the £40 needed in order to have the ownership of the property mortgaged to the Lamberts restored to him. In 1580, however, he was fined two sums of £20 by the Queen's Bench court in London[31]. He would thus have found it impossible to raise a further £40 in that year. The first fine was due for failing to appear before the court, whence he had been summoned to affirm the 'keeping the peace towards the Queen and her subjects' and be vouched for by a third party.

The second fine was imposed by the court in connection with a debt John Shakespeare had incurred towards John Awdley, a hatter from Nottingham. The details of this transaction are unclear, though it is known that Awdley was also required to appear before the same court and, like John Shakespeare, he was required to swear to keep the peace and be vouched for by a third party. Like John Shakespeare, he also failed to appear.

As long ago as 1930, in *A Life of William Shakespeare*, Joseph Quincy Adams, an American Shakespeare biographer, pointed out that John Shakespeare's summons to appear before the Queen's Bench is a significant event, which had so far received little attention.

Records show that more than 140 fines similar to that meted out to John Shakespeare were imposed in 1580. Given the fact that the movement to reintroduce Catholicism to England, led by the Jesuits Campion and Parsons, began in 1580 and that its preparations had been discovered by government spies on the Continent (especially in Rome, Paris and Rheims), there may well be a connection between the fines received by these 140 citizens and the escalating religious tensions.

Significantly, John Shakespeare received his fine during 'Trinity term' of the year 1580, in other words just after the arrival of the Jesuit priests led by Campion and Parsons. The fact that he was summoned at this time to swear that he would 'keep the peace towards the Queen and her subjects' can only mean that the government was uncertain of his loyalty. Again, there can only be one explanation – John Shakespeare's Catholic faith and his resulting actions.

Although he knew that he would face substantial fines, William Shakespeare's father obviously felt himself unable to recognise the queen as governor in all spiritual and ecclesiastical matters – for reasons of conscience. He would have been forced to make such a declaration, had he appeared before the court. John Shakespeare evidently saw no other possible course of action than to risk and/or pay a crippling fine. In 1580, the Queen's Bench and the English government were still satisfied with the payment of fines as punishment for failing to answer the summons. Only a year later, in reaction to the success of the Jesuit missionary movement, the government introduced a further anti-Catholic law, making the punishments meted out to recusants much more severe. Had John Shakespeare been summoned then, the consequences for him would also have been much more extreme.

In 1581, Edmund Campion was captured and personally questioned by Queen Elizabeth I. When she asked him if he recognised her as his queen, he answered in the affirmative. She then asked him if he recognised her supreme religious authority. If he had answered 'yes' to this, he would have been a free man and rewarded with a title and wealth by the queen. As Campion, however, could and would not recognise the spiritual authority of Elizabeth I, he was thrown into the Tower of London and viciously tortured. He was then accused of high treason, found guilty, and executed in a most brutal manner[32].

In the light of the religious and political context of the time, John Shakespeare and the 140 others must have been summoned to appear before the Queen's Bench because they were religiously 'unreliable' and therefore politically 'disloyal'.

The question remains, however, why it was that only around 140 people from all over the country were punished, given the large number of English recusants or Catholic non-conformists. How did the government discover their names, and by what criteria were they chosen? The indications are that these were not merely chance denunciations. They have, on the contrary, all the earmarks of a targeted attack, prepared by spies, on a particular group of people who were linked in some way. Circumstantial evidence suggests that they were the heads of families whose sons were then attending William Allen's College in Douai or Rheims. This educational institution was greatly hated by the government, but was very popular among Catholics. The college was founded in 1568, and by 1576 it already had eighty students. A year later, the number had increased by fifty per cent to about 120, and in 1583 by 150 per cent to roughly 200 students. If a select group of 140 people were summoned to appear before the Queen's Bench in 1580 for the aforementioned reason, this would roughly coincide with the number of English families whose sons were then being educated at Douai or Rheims. The fact that these men were not prepared to avow their loyalty to the crown, and did not even appear in court, preferring instead to receive a substantial fine, indicates that their views were in agreement with those who sent their sons to the Catholic college(s) on the Continent.

In Elizabethan times, the Collegium Anglicum in Douai was intensively targeted by spies, and it would not have been hard to discover the names of pupils and teachers at the college. It would have been harder, however, to discover their true identities, for almost everyone, for fear of discovery, used a pseudonym. The students usually used their mother's maiden name or that of their grandparents.

The English colleges on the European mainland – and in particular the Collegium Anglicum in Douai – were a permanent thorn in the side of Queen Elizabeth I and her Privy Council, for the government had to face the extremely irksome fact that the very flower of upper- and middle-class English youths migrated to the Continent in order to attend these colleges and receive a Catholic academic education. This must have been regarded as a form of 'voting with the feet'. The English government was also fully aware that on completion of their studies, the graduates became involved in the English Catholic

XIV.

"*Item*, laſtly I John Shakſpear doe proteſt, that I will willingly accept of death in what manner ſoever it may befall me, conforming my will unto the will of god; accepting of the ſame in ſatisfaction for my ſinnes, and giveing thanks unto his divine majeſty for the life he hath beſtowed upon me. And if it pleaſe him to prolong or ſhorten the ſame, bleſſed be he alſo a thouſand thouſand times; into whoſe moſt holy hands I commend my ſoul and body, my life and death: and I beſeech him above all things, that he never permit any change to be made by me John Shakſpear of this my aforeſaid will and teſtament. Amen.

"I John Shakſpear have made this preſent writing of proteſtation, confeſſion, and charter, in preſence of the bleſſed virgin mary, my Angell guardian, and all the Celeſtiall Court, as witneſſes hereunto: the which my meaning is, that it be of full value now preſently and for ever, with the force and vertue of teſtament, codicill, and donation in cauſe of death; confirming it anew, being in perfect health of ſoul and body, and ſigned with mine own hand; carrying alſo the ſame about me; and for the better declaration hereof, my will and intention is that it be finally buried with me after my death.

"Pater noſter, Ave maria, Credo.
"jeſu, ſon of David, have mercy on me.
Amen."

Fig. 27 – The Borromeo (Jesuit) Testament of John Shakespeare. William Shakespeare's father wrote a spiritual will copying the text written by Carlo Borromeo (1538-1584), Cardinal and Archbishop of Milan, and distributed by the Jesuit priests Robert Parsons and Edmund Campion. It is a declaration of his Catholic faith and thus a dangerous document that would have made him guilty of high treason had it been found, so he concealed it in the rafters of his house in Henley Street. It was discovered there by chance in 1757 by a builder named Joseph Moseley, and was handed to Mr Payton, a member of the Stratford Town Council. When the antiquary, John Jordan, was permitted to make a copy of the document in 1784, he found the first of the six pages to be missing. Jordan gave the document to the *Gentleman's Magazine* to print, but the magazine declined to do so. The original (without the first page) eventually came into the possession of the Shakespeare scholar, Edmond Malone, who was convinced of its authenticity and published it in Volume 1 (Part 2) of his 1790 book *The Plays and Poems of William Shakespeare*. Shortly before publication, the Reverend James Davenport, the vicar of Stratford, sent Malone Jordan's notebook, which contained the complete text of the testament. Malone published the missing page in his 'Additions and Appendices' at the end of the volume. Malone's literary executor, James Boswell, searched for the original in vain. It was probably removed and/or destroyed by someone who did not like the fact that John Shakespeare had made a Jesuit testament.

underground, either as priests or as laymen, and spread the word of the Catholic faith.

The extent of this insult to government can be gauged from the fact that William Cecil, when he fixed the day for Campion's execution, set a further warning example. He decreed that the priests Sherwin and Briant were to die along with Campion; the former vicariously for the Collegium Anglicum in Rheims, and the latter vicariously for the English College in Rome.

In the context of the religious, social and political events of the time, which have been overlooked or only cursorily examined in previous Shakespeare biographies, the combination of and events in John Shakespeare's life all point overwhelmingly to one conclusion – he and his family must have been adherents of the old faith.

Two further pieces of reliable historical evidence confirm that the Shakespeare family was devoutly Catholic. Not only did John Shakespeare fail to attend Council meetings and thereby neglect his duties as an alderman, he also avoided attendance at Anglican worship in Holy Trinity, his local parish church. In March 1592, the name of Shakespeare's father was placed upon the recusant list, along with the names of several others from Stratford-upon-Avon. This list is an authentic and unambiguous historical source, and it provides solid proof that John Shakespeare was a known Catholic. The list was compiled on the basis of a thorough investigation ordered by the Privy Council, and ensured that almost every Catholic recusant in the country was listed and subsequently punished. Schoenbaum has called such investigations 'inquisitions into the spiritual health of the realm'[33]. On behalf of the Privy Council commissioners were employed in every county to trace these men and report all those who offered protection and gave shelter to Catholic priests, Jesuits and (Catholic) refugees, as well as those who obstinately refused to attend Anglican services[34].

John Whitgift, Archbishop of Canterbury and Bishop of Worcester from 1577 to 1583, in whose former diocese Stratford-upon-Avon fell, had risen particularly swiftly in the hierarchy of the Anglican Church, and was a staunch supporter of this nationwide inquisition. John Shakespeare and another eight Stratford citizens were to be punished because they stubbornly refused to attend Sunday services at Holy Trinity Church, Stratford. Shakespeare and his co-accused countered this charge with a cunning argument with which they attempted to justify their actions. They stated that they did not attend church because they were afraid that they would be caught and consigned to prison by their creditors. Their claim was sent to London as part of the official report, and the excuse was accepted. This suggests that the Stratford councillors officially confirmed this story, in order to make it sound credible to outsiders.

The true reason for John Shakespeare's refusal to attend church can only have been his secret Catholicism. If his plausible excuse had not been accepted in London, John Shakespeare would have felt the full force of the recusant laws and would probably have lost all of his possessions, his freedom, and possibly his life, as did so many of his fellow English Catholics[35].

The fact that John Shakespeare still possessed substantial assets when he died in September 1601, despite hefty financial losses, indicates that this defence was a white lie. In fact, Sunday was the only day when John Shakespeare remained at home, when he ought to have been attending Anglican divine service. It calls to mind the method in Hamlet's madness; he used it selectively.

A further excellent contemporary source demonstrating John Shakespeare's Catholic beliefs is his Jesuit testament *(Fig. 27)*. The authenticity and importance of this source is no longer in doubt. Paragraph XIV reads:

> *Item*, I John Shakespeare do protest, that I am willing, yea, I doe infinitely desire and humbly crave, that of this my last will and testament the glorious and ever Virgin Mary, mother of god, refuge and advocate of sinners, (whom I honour specially above all other saints,) may be the chiefe Executresse, together with these other saints, my patrons, (saint Winefride) all whom I invoke and beseech to be present at the hour of my death, that she and they may comfort me with their desired presence, and crave of sweet Jesus that He will receive my soul into peace[36].

At the end, he writes:

> Pater noster, Ave Maria, Credo.
> Jesu, son of David, have mercy on me.
> Amen.

This was the spiritual testament, a written affirmation of the Catholic faith, composed by the Archbishop of Milan, Carlo Borromeo. The Jesuit priests Campion and Parsons received this text personally from Borromeo in Milan in April 1580. The Jesuits distributed large numbers of copies throughout England from June 1580 onwards. John Shakespeare probably obtained his from the Ardens of Parkhall, his wife's relatives, who are known to have harboured Jesuits and priests of the English Mission. He then must have copied out all fourteen paragraphs, inserting his name in each, and finally have signed the document. He must also have concealed it in the rafters of his house in Henley Street, where William was born, and where it was discovered by chance in 1757 when the roof truss was renovated. None other than John Shakespeare himself would have hidden it there. It is probable that this happened after the Arden-Somerville Plot of 1583, when there were raids carried out by aldermen on behalf of the government.

E.K. Chambers, a famous English Shakespeare expert, has stated that he believed the original document belonged to John Shakespeare. He thought, however, that it had no real significance with regard to his confession of faith, because in his opinion it dated from an earlier period. But as shown above, the Jesuit testaments did not appear in England until 1580, when the Jesuit movement to re-introduce Catholicism to England began.

In 1790, the Irish-born Shakespeare scholar Edward Malone studied five of the six pages of this Testament. He confirmed that it was the original document, and published it in Volume 1 (Part 2) of his edition *The Plays and Poems of William Shakspeare* (1790). Shortly before publication, he was able to obtain the text of the missing first page of the testament from a notebook belonging to the antiquary John Jordan. This was then printed in the 'additions and appendices'[37] of Malone's Shakespeare edition. After the Shakespeare scholar died, James Boswell, his literary executor, searched in vain for the original. The document went missing under unexplained circumstances. Since it has never been found, it may have been taken away or deliberately destroyed. It seems that there may have been a special interest in withholding this documentary proof of John Shakespeare's Catholicism from the public. By publishing the document, however, Malone had ensured that the content of this most valuable piece of evidence proving John Shakespeare's religion did not remain unknown.

Considering John Shakespeare's faith, his actions and his passive resistance to authority appear both logical and consistent. As a devout Catholic, he would have suffered a serious crisis of conscience while performing his duties as alderman in Stratford. It was the duty of every alderman, in London and throughout England, to act on behalf of the government and enforce the anti-Catholic penal laws. He would have had to report all fellow Catholics, who – like himself – rejected the Anglican Church; and he knew that those he reported would be treated as traitors and tried for high treason. He hoped to escape the dilemma by not attending council meetings.

His colleagues seem to have been aware of this crisis of conscience and respected his actions. In fact, he appears to have been treated by them with great clemency. For the council waited almost ten years before replacing John Shakespeare as alderman in 1586, after England had joined the Protestant forces in the Netherlands fighting Catholic Spain, and the internal Catholic threat, personified by Mary, Queen of Scots, had become more intense. The council did not impose any sanctions upon John Shakespeare, and even waived payments that were due from him. His colleagues also appeared to have been at pains to conceal his passive resistance, at no small risk to themselves. This may well be interpreted as a sign of the great respect they paid to him.

At a time when Catholic recusants in England were being ruthlessly stripped of their possessions, money and liberty under the new anti-Catholic legislation and many also lost their lives, John Shakespeare, a practising Catholic, rejected the New Religion, no longer carried out his duties as 'an officer of the Queen', and still managed to stay alive – financially relatively unscathed. Undoubtedly, his superior intelligence, his knowledge of the authorities and the law, his high standing as well as his compassion, all must have played a significant role in his survival.

One question remains, however: why is it that – with the exception of his first daughter, born while Mary Tudor was still on the throne – all of John Shakespeare's children, William included, were christened according to Anglican rites? A.L. Rowse and other scholars have used this argument, as well as the fact that William Shakespeare had his own children baptised at Holy Trinity Church, as proof that the poet himself was an Anglican. They were, however, overlooking the fact that Protestant baptisms (so-called 'heretical christenings') were recognised by the Catholic Church. English Catholics were naturally aware of this and so John and Mary Shakespeare, and later William and Anne Shakespeare, did not hesitate to have their children christened by the vicar of Holy Trinity Church. Thus they appeared to be conforming to the Anglican Church and obeying the laws of the Crown. But we may well assume that the Shakespeares – like most other English Catholic families at that time – would also have had their children secretly baptised by a Catholic priest.

SHAKESPEARE'S SCHOOLDAYS IN STRATFORD

By the time William Shakespeare began his schooling, the grammar school system had already been in place for generations. Most grammar school pupils completed their education at the universities of Oxford and Cambridge, the only universities in England at the time. After graduation, they entered the church and the law, or became doctors of medicine or schoolmasters.

By the early sixteenth century, literacy had increased substantially among the population, and attendance at grammar schools was surprisingly widespread. As early as 1516, the humanist Richard Pace felt obliged to warn the English nobility not to 'confine themselves to sport and leave the study of literature,' as he phrased it, to 'the sons of peasants.' Pace may seem to be over-reacting, but the fact was that education was no longer the privilege of the upper classes. By the end of the sixteenth century, approximately forty per cent of the male population could read and write and were numerate. This percentage was, of course, much smaller in rural areas than in the towns. The landed gentry and the merchant class shared an interest in keeping existing schools open and founding new ones. It is estimated that by 1600 there were 360 grammar schools in England, so that, statistically, there was one school to 13,000 citizens[38].

The most important of these institutions included Shrewsbury Grammar School (founded in 1552), Westminster School (re-

Fig. 28a – The interior of the main classroom in the grammar school. Preparatory school pupils used a smaller side-room.

Fig. 28b – King Edward VI Grammar School, Stratford-upon-Avon, re-founded in 1553. The structure of the building remained unchanged. As the son of the bailiff or mayor and Justice of the Peace, William must have attended this school. It is here that Shakespeare would have acquired the basic knowledge necessary for his further education.

founded in 1560), the Merchant Taylors' School in London (1561) and the grammar schools of Rugby (1567), Harrow (1571), St Bees (1583) and Uppingham (1584). The Stratford-upon-Avon Grammar School, re-founded by Edward VI in 1553 *(Fig. 28b)* was also one of the top schools in the country. The king signed the school's charter just fourteen days before his death, and seven years later it was approved by Elizabeth I. This information comes from the Stratford historian, schoolmaster and antiquary, the Reverend Joseph Greene (1712-1790), who dubbed Edward VI the 'good prince'[39] for the benefit he thereby bestowed upon the town of Stratford. There had formerly been a Guild School of Stratford, founded by a Mr Joleipe, a member of the Guild of the Holy Cross, during Henry VI's reign in the fourteenth century, but – just like the Guild itself – it had fallen victim to Henry VIII's greed.

Education at the Grammar School in Stratford, also known as the Free School, was free for the sons of the citizens of Stratford, just as the old Guild School had been free for boys living in the town. The schoolmaster received free accommodation and was paid the handsome sum of £20 a year by the Town Council. Of this sum, £4 had to be paid to an assistant teacher, whose responsibility it was to teach Latin to the students. The pay of the schoolmaster in Stratford was even higher than the salary of an academic at Oxford or Cambridge universities. The post was therefore in great demand – especially among Oxford graduates. For this reason, the school had excellent masters who provided a high level of education and learning.

As with most of England's grammar schools, a preparatory or elementary school, with (at least) one teacher, was attached to the Stratford school. The preparatory school teacher introduced the children to the ABC and was called the 'Abecedarius'. He taught reading and writing to children from the age of four or five onwards. In other words, he relieved the schoolmaster of the 'inconvenient duty' – as the Town Council once referred to it – of teaching the beginners.

The Reverend Joseph Greene wrote that there were smaller rooms in addition to the main classroom of the Grammar School *(Fig. 28b)*. It was in these rooms that the preparatory-school children were introduced to English, reading, writing and arithmetic[40]. The essential learning aid for the first-year pupils was the so-called 'hornbook'. This was a small, square piece of paper or parchment, set inside a wooden frame and covered with a thin, transparent layer of animal horn for protection. It had a handle on the lower edge, enabling it to be held upright. The alphabet was written on it from left to right, displaying all the lower case and upper case letters, then the vowels and finally combinations of vowels and consonants and vice versa. Hornbooks were used for teaching for at least the next 150 years.

William must have learnt the alphabet from a hornbook in about 1569 at the latest. The first continuous text that he would have been taught at preparatory school was the Lord's Prayer. This prayer would have been written directly beneath the combinations of consonants and vowels, and covered more than one half of the hornbook. Other preparatory school textbooks included *The ABC with the Catechism* and texts from the Book of Common Prayer. There was also a spelling book (*The Primer and Catechism*), which contained a calendar, an almanac, psalms and devotional texts.

Fig. 29 – A schoolmaster and two pupils stand beneath a bookshelf containing works by Cato, Cicero and other classical authors. Frontispiece of the comedy *Pedantius*, written anonymously in 1631.

Special emphasis was placed on pronunciation and spelling. Preparatory schools often taught the basics of mathematics and bookkeeping as well. Even at a young age, John Shakespeare kept the books for his father's leasehold property in Snitterfield, and he later administered the finances of the Stratford Town Council. The basic knowledge he needed for this he could have acquired in preparatory school.

Shakespeare makes several allusions in his plays to lessons in preparatory school, and even mentions the hornbook. In *Love's Labour Lost*, Moth says of the schoolmaster Holofernes: 'He teaches boys the hornbook' (V, 1). In *As You Like It*, Shakespeare writes: 'Then the whining school-boy, with his satchel / And shining morning face, creeping like snail / Unwillingly to school' (II, 7).

Shakespeare's description of a schoolboy reluctantly making his way to school is presumably an allusion to the strict discipline at Elizabethan grammar schools, in which there was extensive use of corporal punishment[41] *(Fig. 29)*.

Between 1569 and 1571 the Lancastrian Walter Roche, an Oxford graduate, taught the Latin pupils in Stratford. William must then have been attending the preparatory school attached to the Grammar School.

Between 1571 and 1575, the Oxford graduate Simon Hunt served as schoolmaster in Stratford *(Fig. 30)*. According to the standard educational practice at that time, the young Shakespeare would have entered the Grammar School at the age of seven and first been introduced to the Latin language by an assistant teacher and not by the schoolmaster himself.

All the lessons were usually held in a single schoolroom, so that Shakespeare might already have absorbed some of Hunt's lessons for the older pupils. From 1573 to 1575, William would have been taught by Hunt directly. For the subsequent three years, from 1575 to 1578, the Welshman Thomas Jenkins must have been his teacher. Like Hunt, Jenkins was also an Oxford graduate; he was a devout Protestant, later becoming an Anglican clergyman.

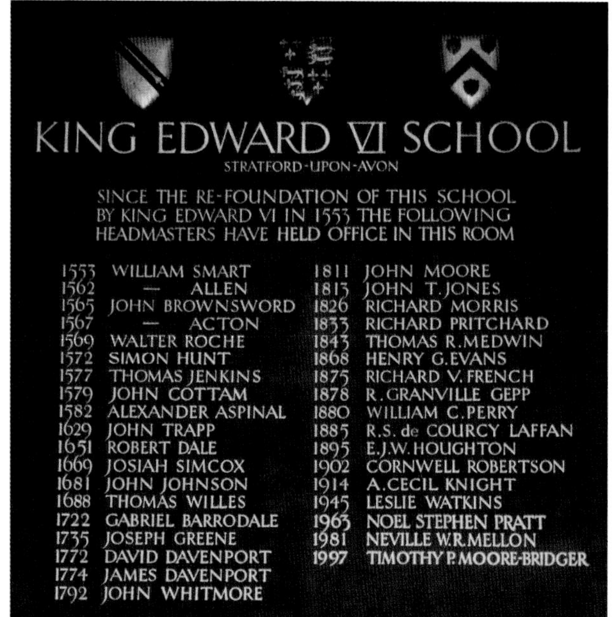

Fig. 30 – Plaque in the classroom of the Stratford Grammar School listing the names of previous schoolmasters. The name of Shakespeare's teacher, the crypto-Catholic Simon Hunt, can also be seen. Hunt revealed his religion in 1575 when he fled to Douai (in what was then Flanders), became a Catholic priest and moved to Rome. It is striking that the Christian names of two of the early masters are missing. The entry for 1562 only gives the surname 'Allen'. This, in fact, refers to William Allen, who is probably the same William Allen who later founded the College in Douai.

What was daily life like for an English grammar school pupil in the second half of the sixteenth century? What were the educational aims of the grammar school? What were the main subjects of instruction?

Historical sources show that the day always began at home with morning prayers, and then followed a rigid set pattern. After prayers, the children would wash and dress and comb their hair. They would then greet their parents, and the boys would leave the house with their satchels early enough to ensure that they were sitting in their places in the classroom before the school bell had finished ringing.

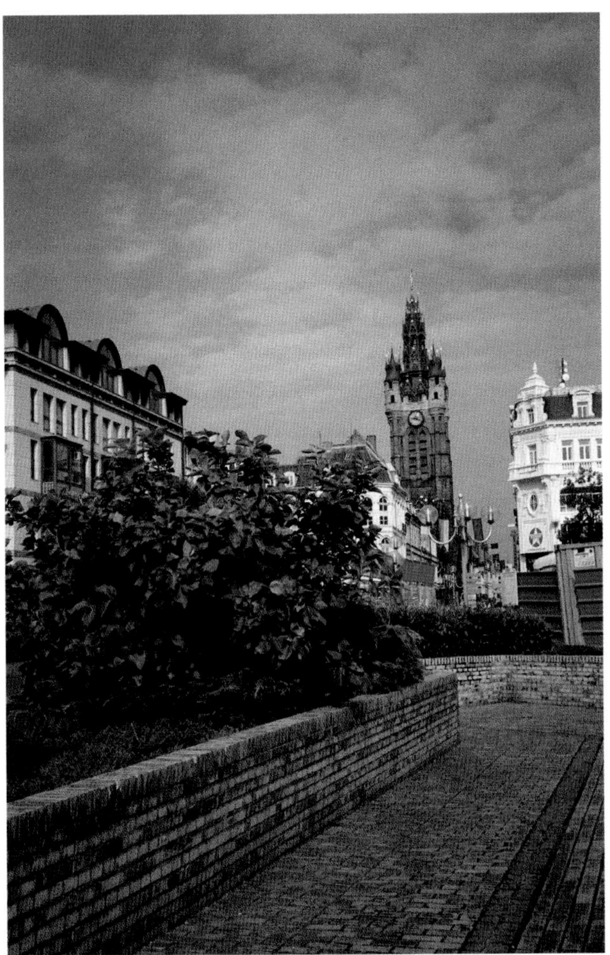

Fig. 31 – A view of Douai and its belfry. This is where William Allen founded the famous Collegium Anglicum in 1568. At that time it was part of Flanders, but today it is in France.

In summer, school began as early as 6 a.m.; in winter classes began at 7 a.m. School ended in the late afternoon, often at dusk, and in winter in full darkness. Since breakfast in England at that time was generally eaten at 6.30 a.m., many grammar school boys were only able to share the meal – consisting of bread, butter, beer, wine and various cooked meats – with their families in winter.

The school day began with prayers, psalms or Bible readings, and these would also bring the day to a close. Latin lessons formed the heart of the grammar school education, with particular emphasis on Latin grammar. The compulsory primer in all of England's grammar schools from the early sixteenth century was the book of grammar entitled *Rudimenta Grammatices*, written by William Lily or Lilye. Lily lived from approximately 1468 to 1522, and he was the first High Master of St Paul's School in London. His book (often referred to merely as *Lily's Grammar*) was well-known to every Grammar School pupil – Shakespeare included. In *The Merry Wives of Windsor* (IV, 1), he makes fun of one of the lessons from this book. The teacher, Sir Hugh Evans, is Welsh, like the Stratford schoolmaster Thomas Jenkins. Shakespeare mocks him and his Welsh-accented pronunciation. For example, Evans pronounces 'b' as a 'p', and the Latin words *hanc* and *hoc* become *hang-hog*. It is significant that the given name of the student in the play, who is questioned by his teacher in schoolmasterly fashion, is William. The playwright was probably recording actual memories of the class taught by his Welsh schoolmaster between 1575 and 1578.

A grammar school education fulfilled the humanistic educational ideal of the time. The primary aim was complete mastery of Latin, in order to be able to read and understand the Classical authors – Aesop, Plautus, Terence, Virgil, Horace, Sallust, Caesar, Cicero, Juvenal, Ovid and others.

The young Shakespeare was greatly fascinated and inspired by Ovid. In *Palladis Tamia*, or, *Wit's Treasury* (1598), a book in which English, Greek, Latin and Italian poets are compared, Francis Meres, a Cambridge graduate, describes the thirty-four-year-old poet and dramatist William Shakespeare as being on a par with Ovid, claiming: 'The sweet witty soul of Ovid lives in mellifluous and honey-tongued Shakespeare'. Meres added:

> As *Plautus* and *Seneca* are accounted the best for Comedy and Tragedy among the Latines: so *Shakespeare* among the English is the most excellent in both kinds for the stage; ... the Muses would speake with *Plautus* tongue, if they would speak Latin: so I say that the Muses would speak with *Shakespeares* fine filed phrase, if they would speake English.

HONI SOIT QVI MAL Y PENSE

THE MARINERS MIRROVR
Wherin may playnly be ſeen the courſes, heights, diſtances, depths, ſoundings, flouds and ebs, riſings of lands, rocks, ſands and ſhoalds, with the marks for th'entrings of the Harbouroughs, Havens and Ports of the greateſt part of Europe: their ſeueral traficks and commodities: Together w.th the Rules and inſtrumēts of NAVIGATION.

First made & ſet fourth in diuers exact Sea-Charts, by that famous Nauigator LVKE WAGENAR *of Enchuiſen And now fitted with neceſſarie additions for the uſe of Engliſhmen by*
ANTHONY ASHLEY.

Heerin alſo may be underſtood the exploits lately atchiued by the right Honorable the L. Admiral of Englād with her Ma.ties Nauie and ſome former ſeruices don by that worthy Knight
S.r FRA. DRAKE.

Fig. 32 – The title page of *The Mariners Mirrour* (1597). This lavish and comprehensive work contained all of the information necessary for seamen bound for European ports. Ships and sea voyages are prominent in Shakespeare's work, and they also played a significant part in his life. When travelling to Rome, Shakespeare and other English Catholics crossed through France and sailed from Marseilles to Genoa.

William's teachers in Stratford could scarcely have anticipated that their protégé, only two decades later, would stand at the pinnacle of English literature, and that his literary achievement would receive such public acclaim. But they could hardly have failed to notice his brilliance.

Although the main subject at grammar school was Latin, Greek and some Hebrew were also included in the curriculum. Additionally, the older boys were taught rhetoric, poetry and basic history, as well as mathematics, music and geography. The students also performed plays in Latin which were often written by the teachers, but which were occasionally also written or co-written by the pupils.

By the criteria of the time, high standards prevailed at Stratford Grammar School. It provided the future dramatist with an excellent basis for his further education. The oft-quoted dictum of Ben Jonson[42], that Shakespeare knew only 'little Latin and less Greek' must have been a considerable exaggeration. John Aubrey (1626-1697), the eminent English biographer and antiquary, a usually reliable source rightly countered Jonson in his *Brief Lives* (begun in 1667), claiming that Shakespeare 'understood Latine pretty well' because 'he had been in his younger yeares a Schoolmaster in the Countrey'. This schoolmaster theory has attracted a great deal of attention in recent research. It will be discussed and further developed later in this book.

The Tudor monarchs, especially Elizabeth I, realised the great importance of the teacher's role in religious education. In 1559, the queen decreed that all teachers should persuade their students 'to love God's true religion'. The Stratford schoolmaster Simon Hunt clearly took this duty very seriously, but as far as he was concerned, 'the true religion' was not Anglicanism, but Catholicism.

As mentioned above, Hunt relinquished his post as schoolmaster in 1575 and moved to Douai, to become a Catholic priest and later, in Rome, a Jesuit. He took one of his students from Stratford with him. His name was Robert Debdale, and he was one of William's schoolmates. Debdale came from Shottery and was a neighbour of Anne Hathaway, whom Shakespeare later married. In 1580, William's former teacher became the English Confessor at the College of Vatican Penitentiaries which was under the special protection of the Holy See in St Peter's in Rome. Hunt was the immediate successor of the Jesuit Robert Parsons, who – together with Campion – had led the Catholic movement to re-introduce the old faith in England. In the eyes of the English government Parsons was the most wanted traitor in the country.

Hunt died in 1585, while still in office. The circumstances of his death are a mystery. His Stratford student, Robert Debdale, died in the same year. Debdale had also become a priest in Douai. On 21 December 1585, he was martyred in England for his faith[43]. On 13 May 1582, Debdale's friend, the Catholic priest, Thomas Cottom, had also been executed in London for his beliefs. Cottom's brother John, who at the time was Thomas Jenkins' successor as schoolmaster at the Stratford Grammar School, was duly forced to resign his post.

As has already been shown, William's family and many others in the Stratford area were devout Catholics. This is particularly evident from the life of his father, who possessed a Jesuit testament. According to Joseph Gillow's *Bibliographical Dictionary of the English Catholics* (1885-1902, repr. 1968), the young Shakespeare was educated by a Benedictine monk named Dom Thomas Combe (or Coombes) from 1572 onwards.

COLLEGE EDUCATION ON THE CONTINENT

From the early 1570s, it was typical for young English Catholics from the middle and upper classes to attend the Collegium Anglicum on the Continent *(Fig. 31)*. The college had been founded by William Allen in Douai in 1568 and for reasons of security was relocated to Rheims between 1578 and 1593. It was so popular

Fig. 33 – 'Salle Jardine de France' in Douai. This large hall was built in 1609-10 in the Flemish baroque style. It replaced the former buildings of the Collegium Anglicum, which were no longer large enough to house all of the students. The building testifies to the great numbers of young English Catholics who secretly left their country to study at William Allen's College.

among English Catholics that, quite soon after its foundation, it was unable to admit the flood of new applicants who came by ship to Calais and other ports[44] *(Fig. 32)*. The Collegium Anglicum was in such great demand not only for religious reasons and for its high standards and excellent facilities, but also for its teaching concept modelled on the Jesuit pattern of education. The atmosphere was of 'magnificent liberality,' as Gregory Martin phrased it in a letter to his friend Edmund Campion in Prague. Martin added that the teachers did not have to 'keep order by stamping, raving, and flogging'. And a former student wrote that there was 'no need of any written law to keep the members in discipline'.

From the mass of circumstantial evidence we have, it is reasonable to conclude that the Shakespeares, too, must have sent their son William to Allen's College, as soon as he had reached the required entrance age of fourteen, which was in 1578.

Education at the Collegium Anglicum in Douai or Rheims followed Jesuit principles and was at a high level in Lower as well as Higher Studies. Lower Studies (called 'Humanities') provided students with a thorough grounding in the humanities. The curriculum was sub-divided into five courses, based on age and ability. The students read classical Latin authors, interpreted the subject matter and wrote essays. Particular emphasis was placed on verbal communication, in accordance with the Jesuit motto '*lege, scribe, loquere*' [read, write, speak]. In Douai, the most important class was Rhetoric, followed by Poetry, Syntax, Grammar and Rudiments. The standard course usually lasted three years. But it was possible to qualify in a shorter time, depending on the entrant's level of education and talent.[45]

The accommodation at the Collegium Anglicum in Douai was initially rather spartan, but the college was soon able to move to more commodious premises. After a few decades, it owned a large building, still impressive to this day *(Fig. 33)*. The layout of this type of college is demonstrated by the English College in St Omer near Calais, well documented in surviving pictorial material. It was built by Robert Parsons in 1593 and rebuilt in 1689 *(Figs. 34a and 34b)*. The sign over the grand entrance reads: 'FONDÉ PAR DES JÉSUITES ANGLAIS EN 1592' [FOUNDED BY ENGLISH JESUITS IN 1592] *(Fig. 34c)*. Since the college in St Omer was based on the Douai college, it is possible to gain a clear impression of the buildings and facilities in Douai.

The collegiate church was situated to the right of the grand entrance and alongside the printing press. Behind this were the kitchen, storerooms and kitchen garden, as well as the refectory, which was connected to a large spacious garden for the students to use. This was enclosed by a high wall on the left, by a low fence on the right, and by a complex of buildings on the far side. These buildings housed the various schools (departments) of the college, including, the particularly large school of rhetoric, the sick bay, the pharmacy and the physick garden, as well as the mill, bakery, butchery, brewery, carpentry workshop, the servants' quarters, and the stables.

The heart of the college in St Omer was a rectangular monastery-style building with a large courtyard. The main entrance was flanked by spacious reception rooms. The first floor contained an extensive gallery, and the second floor contained the huge college library, with its extensive collection of mainly Catholic texts.

The Catholic books at Oxford University had been ruthlessly destroyed. The Oxford University School of Divinity, which was situated over the lecture rooms, had been founded by Humphrey of Gloucester (1391-1447) to house his book collection, although it was not opened until 1480. This had been England's first university library, but it was destroyed in the Protestant raids of 1550. The facilities were abandoned and were used as a pig market until Sir Thomas Bodley (1545-1613) founded another library on the same site in 1598. The Bodleian Library opened in 1602. When the Swiss doctor Thomas Platter travelled through England in 1599, he was shown this very hall in Oxford, which he described as follows:

> Upon the loft in this hall, a new library was being constructed, and large books could already be seen chained to the shelves. The loft is divided into sections, and the university insignia, an open book with two crowns above and a single crown below, is painted above it. The book is inscribed 'sapientiae et felicitatis', meaning 'wisdom and happiness'[46].

Whether library books were chained to the shelves in the library at St Omer or Douai / Rheims is not documented, but the liberal atmosphere at these institutions makes it unlikely.

The dormitories occupied the right and left wings of the St Omer College. On the other side of the courtyard, which was planted with flowers, was the main wing. The principal had his quarters on the third floor, directly beneath the large bell-tower. Below them was the so-called 'small theatre'; the college's main theatre was on the first floor. The prominent sites of the two theatres in the main part of the college indicate the great educational importance attached to them. The theatres had a generous dressing room and shared a store room in a separate building, adjoining the right-hand side of the bell-tower building and probably connected to it via an inner door.

The colleges of Douai or Rheims (where Allen's institution was housed for fifteen years, from 1578 to 1593) were probably designed on similar lines.

If the young Shakespeare studied at Douai or Rheims he would have enjoyed conditions very conducive to his later career as a playwright. The theatrical performances at this college were modelled on the great Jesuit theatre of the time.

Fig. 34a – A perspective view of the English College in St Omer, built in 1592 and restored in 1689. It was one of the many colleges founded by the Jesuit priest Robert Parsons. This college and the Collegium Anglicum both expanded rapidly. The building contained a printing press, a small and a large theatre, a spacious theatre store room, a school of rhetoric and a large enclosed garden.

Jesuit drama developed in the last third of the sixteenth century, and theatre became a positive obsession during the seventeenth century. The latest theatrical techniques were used in the performance of exciting historical dramas and plays about the lives of the martyrs, in which the individual found himself caught up in a conflict between the material and the spiritual world. Despite its primarily religious (anti-Reformation) aims, Jesuit drama used theatrical means that appealed first and foremost to the senses. Religious messages were thus conveyed vividly and memorably. The approach of Jesuit theatre was essentially pluralistic, meaning that it featured a great variety of established theatrical devices, and was astonishingly indifferent to the Aristotelian

Fig. 34b –The former English College in St Omer today: the façade and entrance.

Fig. 34c – The inscription above the entrance gate, probably added when the building was restored in 1845. It mentions the founding of the college by English Jesuits in 1592, but without naming the founder, Robert Parsons.

theory of poetry that had been revived in the Renaissance. Aristotle's concept, especially his Three Unities of Action, Place, and Time, was not consistent with that of the Jesuit theatre.

The Jesuits were not averse to theoretical discussion, but often took an anti-Aristotelian line. By focusing on theatrical practice and performances, essentially they had broken free from all theoretical constraints, preferring hybrid forms of drama, and tragicomedy in particular. Ruprecht Wimmer's *Jesuitentheater, Didaktik und Fest* [Jesuit Drama: Didactics and Enjoyment] shows that the way the Jesuits loosely and indiscriminately described their plays as tragedy, comedy and tragicomedy indicates that they paid little heed to the classical definitions of these terms. According to Wimmer, the Jesuits' interest lay in justifying their hybrid forms, especially that of the tragicomedy.

Jesuit drama regarded the human race and the world in a positive light, despite their constant awareness of the threat of the power of Evil. The world was portrayed as a preparatory stage and/or an imperfect precursor for the afterlife. Thus the basic concept of Jesuit drama was the '*Tragoedia Christiana*' (Wimmer), to which all the theoretical principles of classical antiquity were subordinated.

A surviving illustration of the stage set for a performance of *Laurentius* in the Jesuit theatre in Cologne in 1581 *(Fig. 35)* tells us how a Jesuit set design must have looked. The aim was not to create artistic perspective and depth of space, as seen in the secular baroque theatre, but rather to create a simple (painted) structure following the lines of the rectangular stage.

To the right of the archway on the rear wall is a statue of the Virgin Mary standing on a pedestal. A crenellated fortification, apparently used as a platform for making speeches, is prominently positioned on the stage.

Centre stage is flanked by two large and naturalistic trees, complete with canopies of leaves. An obelisk leans against the vertical tree trunk, stage left, in front of which there is a small, free-standing monument.

Next to the bending tree trunk, stage right, there is another monument, upon which a board is hung. The supporting structure of the stage is clearly visible, above the heads of the audience, consisting of five broad barrels supporting the beams upon which the boards of the stage are laid. This illustration is of particular importance, because it dates from the year after Shakespeare must have finished his studies at the college in Rheims, and so he may well have seen this type of stage when he was there.

It was during his time at Allen's college that Shakespeare might also first have encountered the hybrid forms used in Jesuit drama, since he

Fig. 35 – An illustration by Broelman of the stage-set at the Jesuit theatre in Cologne for a performance of *Laurentius* in 1581. Jesuit drama ignored the Aristotelian principle of the unities of time, place, and action, and instead preferred hybrid genres. Stage design in Jesuit drama also neglected the symmetry and perspective of baroque architecture, and instead introduced elements from nature, such as trees.

came to make liberal use of them in his plays. In *Hamlet*, the playwright appears to allude, albeit ironically, to the pluralism of dramatic forms used in Jesuit drama. In a dialogue with Hamlet, Polonius is ridiculed. Bringing the 'news' that the actors have arrived (which Hamlet already knows), he takes the opportunity to show off his theatrical knowledge, boring the prince with his absurd classifications: 'The best actors in the world, either for tragedy, comedy, history, pastoral, pastoral-comical, historical-pastoral, tragical-historical, tragical-comical-historical-pastoral, scene individable, or poem unlimited.' (II, 2)

The fact that Shakespeare ostentatiously ignores the Aristotelian unities in his dramas (which was very much resented by the French critics of the eighteenth century, especially by Voltaire), may well be taken as a clue suggesting that, as a student at Allen's College, he became familiar with the theatrical concepts of the Jesuits. Hitherto no convincing explanation has been provided for when and where the young Shakespeare could have obtained his extensive general knowledge, academic education and his training as a playwright; nor where he could have developed his predeliction for hybrid dramas, especially the tragicomedy; and where he could have observed such complete disregard for Aristotle's theories. Now the scenario outlined above makes it quite clear that Shakespeare could have learnt all this during his education at the Collegium Anglicum – and to all appearances did so. If this assumption is true, then it was this training that launched and determined Shakespeare's subsequent career as a writer for the theatre. Neither Oxford nor Cambridge could have offered him a more favourable launching pad.

Previous Shakespeare biographers have overlooked the fact that comparisons between scenes from Shakespeare's plays and those in Jesuit drama had already been made in the early seventeenth century. We only need to look at an illuminating article, written by the English government spy John Gee in 1624, and entitled *New Shreds of the Old Snare, Containing The Apparitions of two new Female Ghosts, &c.*

Gee makes an ironic and satirical comment alluding to the exceptional skill of the Jesuit actors: 'The Jesuits being or having Actors of such dexterity, I see no reason but that they should set up a company for themselves, which surely will put down The Fortune, Red-Bull, Cock-pit, and Globe'. In other words they were good enough to have put the great London theatres out of business, including the Globe Theatre on the south bank of the Thames, which performed most of Shakespeare's plays. However, according to Gee in a jibe at the Jesuit Order, the Jesuits charged their audiences far too much, or came at too high a price, so to speak, and ghost scenes (such as in *Hamlet*), or the use of light, (as in what he calls *Pyramus and Thisbe*, referring to *A Midsummer Night's Dream*), in which moonlight is produced by means of a lantern, were Jesuitical effects more cheaply available in London theatres. The government spy is thus hinting that the ghost scenes in Shakespeare's plays are elements borrowed from Jesuit drama. (See p. 49 f.)

The assumption that the young Shakespeare was educated in Douai/Rheims can be further substantiated by allusions in the plays and also by external evidence.

A close reading of the plays reveals that the dramatist knew almost all of the terms of the five 'classes' (of the Humanities or Lower Studies) taught at the Collegium Anglicum: Rhetoric, Poetry, Syntax, Grammar and Rudiments. These classes were known almost exclusively to Catholic circles, apart from the English government spies and their paymasters. They indicate that the poet must have been a student at Allen's College in Douai or Rheims.

Shakespeare's dramas contain many classroom scenes and others in which Catholic terminology is used. For instance, in *The Taming of The Shrew*, the music tutor Hortensio, disguised as Licio, says that he would like first of all to teach his pupil Bianca the 'rudiments of the art' (of lute-playing) (III, 1).

Shakespeare's specific use of the word 'divinity' in *Twelfth Night* is another significant (linguistic) clue. In Act I, scene 5, Viola, disguised as Cesario, wishes to speak in private to Olivia, whom she adoringly calls a 'divinity'. Olivia then uses the same word, but with a different meaning: 'Give us the place alone; we will hear this divinity. [...] Now Sir, what is your text?' (I, 5).

The meaning of the word 'divinity' at that time, namely 'Doctor of Theology' or 'scholar', is no longer used in modern English. Even a 'Doctor of Divinity' is not referred to as a 'Divinity'. The word dates from a time when England was still a Roman Catholic country. Shakespeare uses this term towards the end of the Elizabethan era, at a time when Catholicism had been outlawed for several decades and when the use of Catholic terminology was distinctly dangerous. His use of the expression, therefore, is an indication of his Catholic background and seems to throw light on his own personal faith. It is an interesting fact that this passage from Shakespeare's *Twelfth Night* is not quoted in the great dictionary of the English language on historical principles, the *Oxford English Dictionary*. The entries in the *OED* principally list the various meanings of the same word, including those which are now obsolete. Obsolete definitions are generally illustrated with quotations from historical texts. If such terms occur in Shakespeare, he is usually cited.

In the English Catholic Colleges on the Continent, 'divinity' was the term used to describe a teacher of Theology in Higher Studies and so was part of the specific nomenclature used in these institutions. In Douai, the 'Divinities' were also the highest-ranking and most revered professors. They sat in the most exalted places in the refectory. If Shakespeare studied at Allen's College, he would have been aware of this usage of the word. His wordplay with the (Catholic) meaning of 'Divinity' in *Twelfth Night* proves that he was very familiar with this specific meaning of the word as well as with the environment in which it was used.

External evidence of Shakespeare's presence in Douai, other than clues from his plays, can be found in the so-called diaries of the Collegium Anglicum, in which many of the names were erased after they had reached England in the nineteenth century. It is significant that names were removed from the records in precisely those years when Shakespeare would have arrived at and left the college, namely 1578 and 1580. In one partially erased entry from 1578, the first name 'Guilielmus' (=William) is still visible; only the surname has been deleted. The obliterated name could have been that of Shakespeare. The editor of the diaries has marked this section with the word 'erased'. Another name under an entry for 1580 has been entirely erased, and is marked as '[26 erased]'[47].

It cannot be ruled out, of course, that the names erased are those of renegade students who were expelled, or those of English government spies who were unmasked. But in such instances, the whole name would presumably have been deleted. These deletions should be investigated using modern scientific techniques[48]. But even if the results showed that the name erased was not that of Shakespeare, this would still not be conclusive proof that Shakespeare did not attend the college. For obviously almost every student who studied at Allen's College used a pseudonym, for fear of betrayal or denunciation, and very often adopted this name for the rest of his life. The students often chose their mother's maiden name or the surname of a grandparent. When Shakespeare stayed in the household of the wealthy Alexander de Hoghton in Lancashire, apparently between 1580 and 1582, he used the name 'Shakeshafte', a name previously used by his paternal grandfather.

The envious Robert Greene's satirical use of the name 'Shakescene' to allude in 1592 to Shakespeare, his highly successful rival, represents another contemporary variation on his name.

Hitherto, the so-called 'lost years' have been a *tabula rasa* in Shakespeare's life, but later we will see that several times during this period Shakespeare used the name of his home town (or alterations of it) as a pseudonym (see pp. 77–82). This happened again at the end of his literary career in London in 1613 (see p. 310).

Students and teachers at Allen's College were in constant fear of discovery, and justifiably so. In 1587, a year before the Spanish Armada, none other than Shakespeare's fellow dramatist Christopher Marlowe (1564-1593) was sent to Rheims as a spy for the English government, apparently with instructions to discover the identities of those who taught and studied there and collect information about their activities[49].

It is also significant that Shakespeare spoke French, as demonstrated by passages from *King Henry the Fifth* (V, 2). Shakespeare could have learnt the language in Rheims, between 1578 and 1580.

In the courting scene between King Henry and Katherine, daughter of the French king, Shakespeare writes: 'KING: An angel is like you, Kate, and you are like an angel. / KATHERINE: *Que dit-il? Que je suis semblable à les anges?* / … / KING: I said so, dear Katherine, and I must not blush to affirm it. / KATH: *O bon Dieu! Les langues des hommes sont pleines de tromperies.* / KING: What says she, fair one? That the tongues of men are full of deceits?' (V, 2)[50].

In *The Taming of The Shrew* (II, 1), Shakespeare even alludes directly to Rheims as a place of study. It is significant that the character of Lucentio is introduced under a false name: 'this young scholar that hath been long studying at Rheims; as cunning in Greek, Latin, and other languages, as the other in music and mathematics. His name is Cambio.'

Since there was no university in Rheims, Shakespeare must have been alluding to the Collegium Anglicum. If so, then this comedy may well have been written before the college moved back to Douai in 1593. This is in agreement with a tradition that *The Taming of the Shrew* was written and performed in around 1592. The play was not published during Shakespeare's lifetime and appeared for the first time in the First Folio edition in 1623, i.e. seven years after Shakespeare's death. This suggests that the dramatist was trying to avoid the risk of censorship. But even in 1623 *The Taming of the Shrew* (and also *King John*) was not entered in the Stationers' Register. On 8 November 1623 only sixteen of the previously eighteen unprinted plays are to be found in this register, although all the poet's unpublished eighteen dramas did appear in the First Folio – as well as the eighteen ones that had already been published during his lifetime.

Marlowe, too, alludes to the Collegium Anglican in Rheims in a play written and performed around 1592. In Marlowe's *The Massacre at Paris* (V, 2), the French King (Henry III) stands over the corpse of the Duke of Guise, murdered on his orders, and speaks the following words, alluding to events of the time: 'Ah, this sweet sight is physic to my soul! / ... / Did he not draw a sort of English priests / From Douai to the seminary at Rheims, / To hatch forth treason 'gainst their naturall queen? / Did he not cause the king of Spain's huge fleet, / To threaten England, and to menace me?'

This was the 'official line', so Marlowe therefore had no cause to fear the censor.

Marlowe himself was spied upon in 1593 by the government informer Richard Baines, an apostate Catholic priest. It was Baines who proposed to Sir Francis Walsingham, chief of the English spy network, the wicked plan of poisoning the well at Allen's College, in order to wipe out the teachers and the students in one fell swoop. When William Allen learned of the vile plot, he is said to have turned as white as a sheet. In Marlowe's play *The Jew of Malta*, the character Barabas kills the nuns of a cloister with poisoned bread. It is most likely that this scene was based on Baines, whom Marlowe knew as a government informant.

The plot to poison the well of the Collegium Anglicum and the bloody story of St Bartholomew's Massacre in Paris 1572, when Catharine de Medici used the occasion of her daughter's marriage (the original 'blood wedding') to the Huguenot King of Navarre to slaughter the French Huguenots, show how closely fiction mirrored reality during Shakespeare's lifetime.

When Baines spied upon Marlowe, the dramatist revealed what he really thought about the English Catholics-in-exile. Thanks to the peaceful and harmonious picture he witnessed among the exiled community of priests and students at the English College in Rheims, Marlowe reached the conclusion that 'if there be any God or any good religion, then it is in the Papists'. The Protestants by contrast, Marlowe is reported to have remarked, were 'hypocritical asses'.

Marlowe's comments were surely reported to the government, thus sealing the young playwright's fate. In 1593, at the age of only twenty-nine, the young dramatic genius was stabbed to death by Ingram Frizer at the Bull Inn in Deptford, during a dispute in the presence of Nicholas Skeres and the spy Robert Poley. Frizer claimed it had been an act of self-defence, but the circumstances of Marlowe's death have never been fully clarified.

The various items of evidence presented here regarding the Catholicism of the Shakespeare family, suggest that their eldest son – like many Catholic adolescents of the English bourgeoisie and aristocracy – attended Allen's College, so that he enjoyed a Roman Catholic education and was not forced to take the Oath of Supremacy required to study at both English Universities. This is how Shakespeare would have gained his extensive and thorough education, as well as his basic knowledge of playwriting and acting. If no convincing counter-evidence is brought to light, it is reasonable to assume that William Shakespeare was given a large sum of money from the estate of his parents and enrolled at the Collegium Anglicum in Douai or Rheims in 1578. He would have left the college in 1580 after completing two years studying the humanities.

This story fits seamlessly with the facts of Shakespeare's later life, as can be seen in the next chapter.

EARLY EMPLOYMENT IN LANCASHIRE AND SHAKESPEARE'S INITIAL INVOLVEMENT IN THE CATHOLIC UNDERGROUND

The first clues to Shakespeare's early employment can be found in John Aubrey's *Brief Lives*. Aubrey came from a wealthy Herefordshire family and was an Oxford-educated antiquary, who made copious notes about his contemporaries over a long period of time, including details of their private lives. Aubrey met quite a number of the celebrities of the day and knew many of the elite. He would stay up far into the night, questioning them about their lives and the lives of others, even those of preceding generations, without informing his 'victims' of how he planned to use the details they disclosed. Today, we owe a debt of gratitude to Aubrey and his insatiable curiosity. He has left a large legacy of very valuable biographical material, spiced complete with anecdotes and trivial gossip, furnishing us with a personal portrayal of an era.

In the entry concerning 'Mr William Shakespeare', Aubrey mentions Shakespeare's early activities before he started his brilliant career as a poet and dramatist. In so doing, he also aimed at contradicting Ben Jonson's dictum which had already firmly established itself in the minds of the people. Jonson's famous verses 'To the Memory of my beloved, the Author Mr. William Shakespeare: and what he hath left us' were published in the First Folio edition of Shakespeare's plays in 1623. The editors of the first folio, John Heminge and Henry Condell, had clearly not expected Jonson's critical lines that Shakespeare had known little Latin and less Greek:

> And though thou hadst small *Latine*, and lesse *Greeke*,
> From thence to honour thee, I would not seeke.

Fig. 36 – A map of Lancashire produced in 1577. About three years after this map was published, Shakespeare was employed as an unlicensed private teacher in the household of Alexander de Hoghton, Lancashire. He may well have been familiar with this map.

SEPTENTRIO
LANCASTRIÆ
Comitatus palatin vera
et absoluta descriptio
Anno Dñi 1577
West Moreland diæ pars
EBORACENSIS PARS
DARBIÆ PARS
TRIÆ PARS
ORIENS
MERIDIES
KENDALL
KIRKBY LUNESDALE
LANCASTER
GARSTANG
PRESTON
KIRKHAM
BLACKBORN
COLNE
ROCHEDALE
BURY
BOLTON
WIGAN
MANCHESTER
STOPFORD
WARRINGTON
LIVERPOOLE
GISBORN

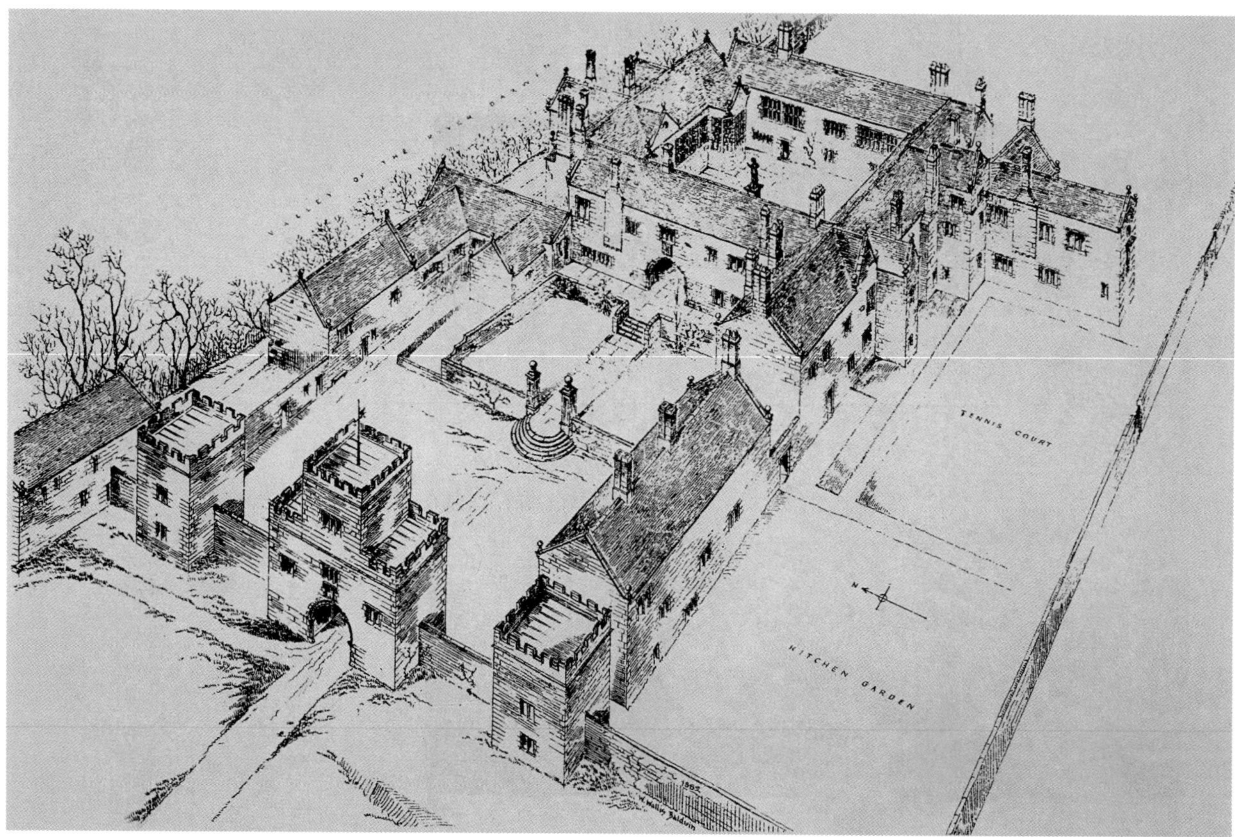

Fig. 37a – An old perspective view of Hoghton Tower in Lancashire. The house was restored and rebuilt in the 1560s on the orders of Sir Thomas de Hoghton the Elder, a friend of William Allen, the founder of the Collegium Anglicum. Sir Thomas later emigrated to Flanders because of his Catholic beliefs.

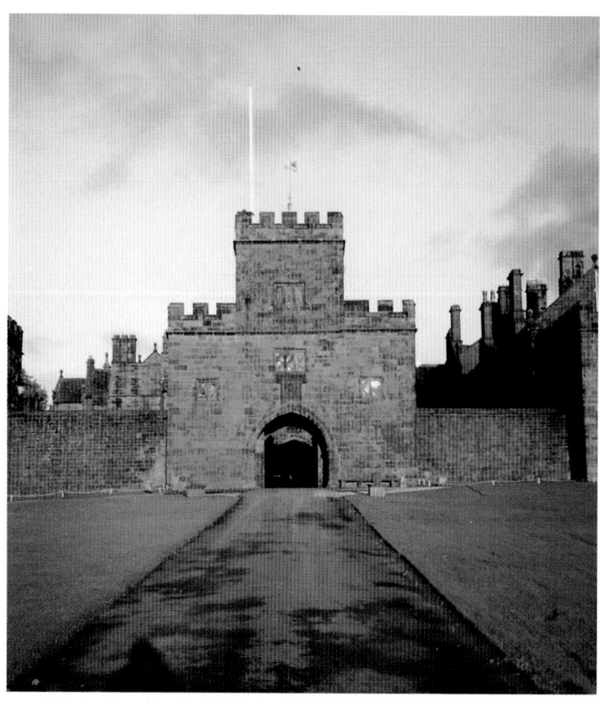

Fig. 37b – Hoghton Tower today.

Aubrey, born ten years after Shakespeare's death, corrected this impression of the playwright. He knew some of the Bard's contemporaries personally, including the actor William Beeston (*c.* 1606-1682), son of Shakespeare's fellow-thespian, Christopher Beeston (died 1638). Aubrey thus had reliable sources of information at his disposal. In 1598, Christopher Beeston and William Shakespeare played together in the main roles of Ben Jonson's cutting social satire *Every Man in His Humour*, in a production by the Chamberlain's Men at the Curtain Theatre. Aubrey knew better than Jonson, and firmly corrected him, using his sources to state that Shakespeare 'understood Latine pretty well', because 'he had been in his younger yeares a schoolmaster in the countrey'. Jonson's remark is today frequently quoted by those, who try (in vain) to question Shakespeare's authorship of the Works.

Fig. 38 – Portrait of Alexander de Hoghton. After the emigration of his brother, Sir Thomas de Hoghton, Alexander de Hoghton and his brothers Thomas and Richard inherited the family wealth. In 1580, Alexander became Shakespeare's first employer. He also seems to have had close connections with William Allen's College in Douai or Rheims.

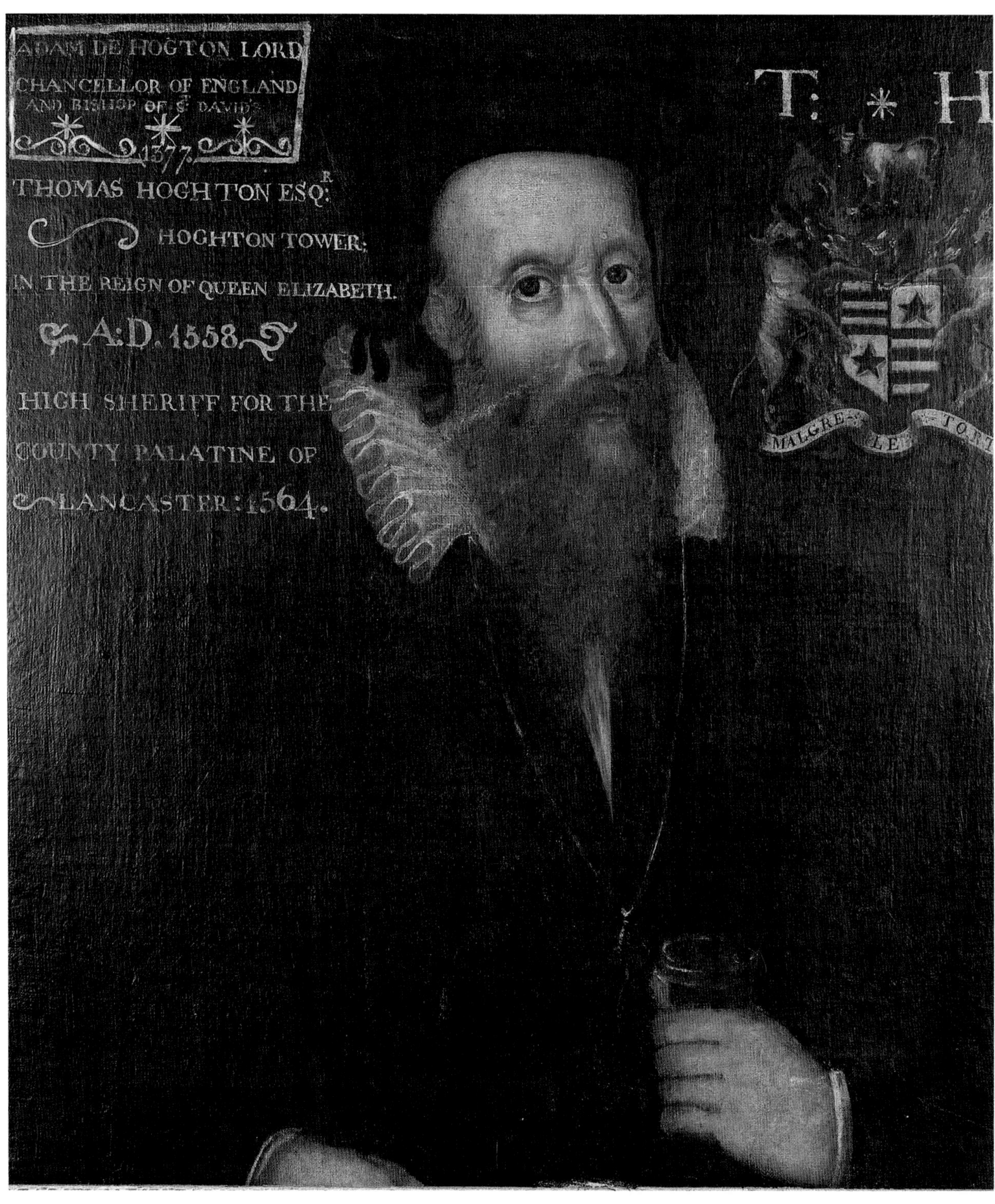

Fig. 39a – Portrait of Sir Thomas de Hoghton the Elder. Sir Thomas was an eminent English Catholic-in-exile who helped Allen found the English College at Douai. It seems very likely that Shakespeare knew him (see p. 61 and p. 157).

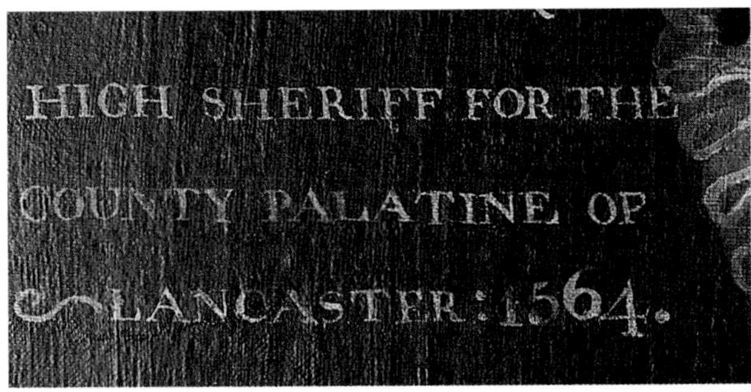

Fig. 39b – Detail of the inscription of Sir Thomas de Hoghton's portrait: 'High Sheriff for the County Palatine of Lancaster: 1564'.

Fig. 39c – Detail: The eyes of Sir Thomas de Hoghton.

Aubrey's schoolmaster tradition accords with a reliable Elizabethan source, which provides key evidence of Shakespeare's temporary stay with a noble Catholic family in the north of England *(Fig. 36)*. Oliver Baker (1937) and E. K. Chambers (1944) provided the earliest information about Shakespeare's employment as a young man, and it was then further investigated by the Shakespeare scholar E. A. J. Honigmann in his book *Shakespeare: The 'Lost Years'* (1985, 2nd ed. 1998), which aroused great interest. The book claims that the young man named in the will of the wealthy Catholic recusant Alexander de Hoghton, dated 3 August, 1581, as 'William Shakeshafte' is actually none other than William Shakespeare of Stratford-upon-Avon. According to Honigmann a family story, passed down orally, also claims that Shakespeare spent two years in the service of the de Hoghtons, an old-established Lancastrian family *(Figs. 37 a–b)*[51].

In his last will and testament *(Fig. 38)* Alexander de Hoghton was clearly very concerned for the welfare of William Shakeshafte and Fulke Gillom. He begs his friend, Sir Thomas Hesketh of Rufford Hall, head of a well-known recusant family in the area, to be good to the two young men currently living with him and urges him to take them into his service or help them 'find a good master'.

Since Shakeshafte and Gillom are mentioned by de Hoghton in connection with his 'players', about whose well-being he also appears to be very concerned, scholars believed that they could have been members of a company of players supported by de Hoghton. Honigmann thought otherwise, and proffered the suggestion that Shakespeare might have been a private teacher in de Hoghton's household. This would fit in with Aubrey's schoolmaster theory extremely well.

There is thus much convincing evidence to support the theory in every respect, especially however, since the time period (between 1580 and 1582) also matches perfectly with Shakespeare's biography. The fact that Shakespeare's name appears slightly altered in de Hoghton's will in no way rules out a reference to Shakespeare.

'Shakeshafte' was a family name, which, as mentioned above, Richard Shakespeare from Snitterfield, the dramatist's grandfather on his father's side, had already used. Between 1580-82 and 1585-92 and again in 1613, Shakespeare used several pseudonyms. These either point to the one his Snitterfield grandfather had adopted or to his own hometown, Stratford-upon-Avon (see pp. 80–82). In 1592, a then prominent London dramatist, who had led a dissolute life and was about to die, alluded full of envy, to his younger aspiring colleague Shakespeare, using the telling name 'Shake-scene' (see p. 98).

According to Honigmann, the link with Lancashire and the de Hoghtons could have been forged by the former Stratford schoolmaster John Cottom, who was also from Lancashire and had managed a small estate near the de Hoghton's country seat. Closer examination of the historical context shows a further, even more striking connection.

Sir Thomas de Hoghton the Elder *(Fig. 39a)* had rejected the English State Church in spectacular fashion in the late 1560s. Like many other Recusants, he emigrated to the Continent as a result of Elizabeth I's increasingly anti-Catholic policies, and was never to return to England. He died in 1580, in exile in Liège. His brothers inherited the family wealth.

Sir Thomas, one of the most important Catholics-in-exile, was homesick and tried to compensate for it through poetry. The queen herself had a great interest in his return, and sent his brother Richard to the Continent to plead with him to come back. The queen, however, required Richard to leave behind a large sum as a surety, to be returned to him only if he came back to England within two months. The queen's efforts were in vain, and Richard de Hoghton returned without his brother.

Several years before he emigrated, Sir Thomas took various measures to enable the Catholic faith to be practised in his home district, and to protect Catholic priests. Between 1562 and 1568, he had rebuilt Hoghton Tower in a grander style, and what seem to have been fortifications were added. Possibly, Sir Thomas – like many other Elizabethan landed gentry – used the reconstruction work to build secret hideaways for priests and to create hidden rooms, in which the Mass could be held in secret. Honigmann mentions the existence of one such feature in Hoghton Tower.

It is significant that when the official opening of the reconstructed house was celebrated in 1568, William Allen, another Lancastrian Recusant and a friend of Sir Thomas de Hoghton, was also present. This was the very year in which Allen founded the Collegium Anglicum in Douai. Sir Thomas the Elder supported the foundation of the institution and had a policy of ensuring the employment of its former students at Hoghton Tower, Lea Hall and/or Park Hall. In 1587, one year before the Spanish Armada, Allen was made a cardinal by Pope Sixtus V. If Spain had won the battle, Allen would have been made archbishop of Canterbury and so would have headed the re-established Roman Catholic Church in England. De Hoghton and Allen could have had no presentiment of this in 1568. But the link between Douai/Rheims the de Hoghtons had been firmly established, and this must have been a deciding factor for William Shakespeare's employment in Lancashire.

When Sir Thomas de Hoghton died in Liège in 1580, the Jesuit mission to England, under Campion and Parsons, had just begun. In the summer of 1580, Campion stayed with the de Hoghtons, where he was on relatively safe ground. In fact, Lancashire was solidly Catholic; recusant-hunters in the area had little hope of success, and were at risk of physical assault. The missionary priest's books were apparently stored in a hiding-place in Richard de Hoghton's house at Park Hall. Campion's hosts must have been Alexander de Hoghton (at Lea Hall) and/or his half-brother Thomas (at Hoghton Tower).

If Shakespeare taught the de Hoghton children, he did so unofficially. The employment of tutors without the necessary permission of the local Anglican bishop was illegal, but it was common practice, as it was the only way to ensure that the children of the Catholic gentry received a Catholic education[52]. After 1568, candidates produced by Allen's Collegium Anglicum had an advantage in obtaining such posts. These candidates were dependent upon employment in Catholic households because, legally speaking, they lacked proper educational qualifications. The Collegium Anglicum could not even grant them a degree, because such a degree would have had no official standing. If discovered, unlicensed teachers could be banned from teaching for life, but they and their employers were also in danger of being financially ruined and/or thrown into prison. As a result, the position of these teachers was very similar to that of English Roman Catholic priests.

It has been proved that the de Hoghtons were among those families who employed Catholic tutors. In 1592, Richard de Hoghton was reported to William Cecil by an apostate for having employed Catholic schoolmasters in his household for about twenty years. A recusant by the name of Richard Blundell, who taught singing and the virginal to children of the household, was also illegally employed as a teacher at Anne de Hoghton's estate in Lea, Lancashire. Shakespeare's early comedies, especially *The Taming of the Shrew*, show that the playwright knew a lot about private teachers and their lessons. Was the highly talented William Shakeshafte (Shakespeare) – specifically mentioned by Alexander de Hoghton in his will – one such unlicensed teacher in the de Hoghton household, and was he educated by William Allen, a friend of Sir Thomas de Hoghton the Elder? Was he sent directly from Rheims to the de Hoghtons, perhaps even by Allen himself? All the signs and evidence, in particular the similarity between the names Shakeshafte and Shakespeare and the evidence that the playwright must have been a student at Allen's college, strongly suggest that Shakespeare used the links forged by Allen and Sir Thomas de Hoghton, and that the answer to the question is a resounding yes.

If so, then Shakespeare would have been directly affected by the Schoolmaster Statutes of 1581, which threatened unlicensed private teachers (and their employers) with harsh punishments if exposed. Shakespeare would have been in danger of a heavy fine, and a permanent ban from teaching. He might also have been thrown into prison, with the customary opportunity to buy his way out withheld.

But William Shakespeare alias Shakeshafte, may have had yet another function in the de Hoghton household, which sheds further light on this section of his biography. Honigmann wrote that, having combed through hundreds of Elizabethan wills, after examining Alexander de Hoghton's will from 1581, he threw in the towel. He came to the conclusion that the very complicated settlements of the testator were eccentric and unclear[53]. In fact, the will is partially encoded, and when the codes are deciphered, they reveal the actual bequests of the testator, which for security reasons he was unable to state openly and clearly. He did, indeed, use an immensely complicated system of trustees, and allocated money to a very large circle of people. The will also indicates the existence of a secret organisation, with a hierarchical structure, whose members were paid for life (*Fig. 41*).

The main section of this last will and testament represents almost a quarter of the entire text, and is a detailed description of a highly unusual system of trustees. Two such trustees, Thomas Fleetwood and Robert Talbot and their heirs, were to receive a yearly income of £16/3s/4d during their lifetime and the lifetime of their lawful heirs (and astonishingly, until the death of the last of the thirty, individually named, servants of Alexander de Hoghton). This money was to be paid out twice yearly (at Whitsun and Martinmas) and was then to be distributed to a list of eleven further trustees, each named individually in the will, until the end of their lives. If a member of the group died, his share was to be divided among the remaining members. The will ensured the survival of this strictly hierarchical organisation, which was to be financially administered by the trustees after de Hoghton's death. Its hierarchical structure can be deduced from the different amounts of money bequeathed to each member. The organisation clearly had a leading member, who was entitled to the largest sum. Below him were four members, of equal standing, who received much less. Members on the next level, also consisting of four people, received only half of the amount that went to those above them. There were a further two people on the lowest level of the group, and their share was in turn only half of that received by the men above them[54].

The testator ensured that his intentions were executed according to his instructions far into the future by using trustees, who, he explicitly states, were to be solely accountable to God.

The key to unlocking the riddle behind Alexander de Hoghton's will is to be found in the terms 'players', 'play clothes' and 'instruments belonging to musics' [sic], which on initial reading seem completely innocuous. In the past, Shakespeare scholars took these terms at face value and concluded that Alexander de Hoghton was responsible for a theatre company for which he made provision in his will. He left the company to his brother, or – if his brother was unable to maintain it – to his friend, Sir Thomas Hesketh.

The manner in which, and the insistence with which de Hoghton expressed his wish that his 'players' should be looked after, and the way he recommended them to close confidants (his brother and friend) should have given earlier biographers pause for thought. Actors had noble patrons so that they would not be treated as vagabonds, i.e. publicly whipped and clapped in irons, but they were always financially independent and could earn their own living. This can be proved from a number of examples, including Shakespeare's company, the Chamberlain's Men or the King's Men. What kind of riches an actor could amass, especially in London, at that time is shown by the example of Edward Alleyn. Alleyn was the leading figure in the Admiral's Men, playing the main parts in Christopher Marlowe's plays. His earnings enabled him to buy an estate in Dulwich, south London, which still exists, and is now the home of the Dulwich Picture Gallery. He also founded a college in the same area that eventually became Alleyn's School, still a well-known public school today.

Neither in Elizabethan times, nor subsequently, was it usual for a nobleman to provide in his will for the accommodation, costumes and musical instruments of actors, as Alexander de Hoghton appears to have done. There must be more to this section of the will than meets the eye.

In the religious and political context of the Elizabethan age, especially in the late 1570s and early 1580s when the religious conflict reached its height, but also given the particular historical background of the recusant de Hoghton family, the peculiar English of the phrase 'instruments belonging to musics' cannot literally mean musical instruments. In addition, actors did not just need musical instruments alone: they used all sorts of props.

It was vital to resort to code when referring to anything concerning the Catholic faith, as this was often a question of life and death. We can assume that the group of people referred to in the will as 'players' are, in fact, not actors but priests. The expression 'play clothes' can only mean the vestments worn when officiating at Mass, and the strange phrase 'instruments belonging to musics' refers to the liturgical objects used in the saying of Mass (= 'musics'): chalices, patens, monstrances, missals and hymn books[55].

It would have been clear to initiates, therefore, that the recusant testator Alexander de Hoghton, brother of the famous Catholic-in-exile Sir Thomas de Hoghton and host of Edmund Campion, one of the two brilliant heads of the Jesuit movement, was concerned not so much with the accommodation and funding of actors, as with the accommodation and support of the persecuted (missionary) priests and regular clergy of the Catholic Church hunted by the spies of the government.

After this coded message, Alexander de Hoghton asks his friend, Sir Thomas Hesketh, to be particularly good to Fulke Gillom and William Shakeshafte, who lived with him at that time, and to take them into his service or find a good master for them:

> And I most heartily require the said Sir Thomas to be friendly unto Fulk[e] Gillom & William Shakeshafte now dwelling with me & either to take them unto his service or else to help them to some good master, as my trust is he will[56].

Fig. 40 – Portrait of Pope Gregory XIII. In April 1580, this Pope granted the Papal seal of approval to the Catholic Association, started by George Gilbert. The members of the Association were given the task of protecting the priests of the English Mission, finding them accommodation in the homes of Catholic English landed gentry, and persuading the Protestant population to revert to Catholicism. In October 1582, Gregory XIII introduced the Gregorian Calendar. In England, the Julian Calendar remained in use until 1752, and a distinction was made between the Old Style (OS) and New Style (NS) methods of dating.

This clearly shows the operation of the network of Elizabethan crypto-Catholicism: valued Catholic employees were recommended to Catholic employers so that they could be safely taken on by them. It is evident that Gillom and Shakeshafte (Shakespeare) were no mere servants. That is why, as Honigmann also concludes, they can only have been tutors in the household of Alexander de Hoghton.

This assumption is also supported by the familiarity with private teaching situations displayed by the dramatist in his work and, furthermore, by the practice common among the English gentry of employing unlicensed private Catholic teachers. We know that this was also customary in other branches of the de Hoghton family. Needless to say, this assumption perfectly fits Aubrey's schoolmaster tradition, as has been pointed out before.

Shakeshafte and Gillom were high-ranking officials in the secret Catholic organisation and received life-long payment for their services, as I discovered when studying Alexander de Hoghton's will. The young men belonged to the first rank of the organisation and received the second-highest payment:

Head: Thomas Sharp – £3 - 6s - 8d

First rank: Fulke Gyllom, William Shakeshafte Thomas Gyllom, Roger Dugdale – each receive £2

Second rank: Thomas Coston, Thomas Barker, Robert Bolton, Thomas Ward – each receive £1

Third rank: Roger Dickinson, William Ormesheye (alias Ascroft) – each receive 13s - 4d [57]

This organisation was founded in July 1580, probably along similar lines to, or as a sub-organisation of, Gilbert's Catholic Association, formed in April 1580 with the personal blessing of Pope Gregory XIII *(Fig. 40)*. Gilbert's Catholic Association was a group of young English Catholics dedicated to the protection of the Catholic priests of the English Mission and those attempting to reintroduce Catholicism in England. These young men accompanied priests on their journeys and prepared their accommodation in the houses of the Catholic English gentry.

On 20 July 1580, Alexander de Hoghton and his brother Thomas (the Younger) made an agreement which established a trust with the aim of financing the organisation. The purpose of the movement was described, highly cryptically, as 'divers good & reasonable causes & considerations'.

It is very likely that Edmund Campion and the priests and helpers travelling with him were guests of the de Hoghton brothers when they established their trust. Campion himself could have advised them on how to word the document so as to conceal its true purpose. 'The true purpose of the trust' seems to have been 'to support the secret existence of Catholicism in the region, even for generations after the death of the founders'[58].

At this time, Shakespeare was just seventeen-years-old, and especially trusted by Alexander de Hoghton. It seems that it was at this point in his life that he first learnt about the legal means and verbal manoeuvering used by the Catholic underground in England to ensure the survival of Catholicism under the most difficult of conditions. When Shakespeare later bought a house in Blackfriars, he used a similar network of trustees to achieve the same goals.

The trust established in July, 1580 by Alexander and Thomas de Hoghton (the Younger) was the first step taken by the secret organisation mentioned in the will dated 3 August, the true aim of which is no longer in any doubt. The existence of this trust is a further sign that the codeword 'players' must have been used to denote the priests and clergy of the Catholic Church, who needed the help and protection of the English Catholic recusants.

After his education on the Continent, William Shakeshafte (Shakespeare) became not merely a private tutor in the de Hoghton household, but was also a paid official in de Hoghton's underground Catholic organisation, and had committed himself as a young man to providing protection for Catholic priests, and sustaining the 'good & reasonable causes' of the de Hoghton trust.

The young Shakespeare may have been the author of an elegy that was written about a year after Edmund Campion's execution. This poem clearly proclaims the missionary's martyrdom, and is written in impressive poetical language. Shakespeare's parents and teachers were Catholics, and so was his first employer. The poet must also have worked in the Catholic underground. Furthermore, the Borromeo Testament written by Shakespeare's father shows that John Shakespeare had contact with the leaders of the Jesuit movement: Campion and/or Parsons. Finally, in a statement made in 1611 by the English cartographer and historian John Speed (?1542-1629) there is the line, 'this Papist and his Poet' (see p. 140). The poet was William Shakespeare, the papist Robert Parsons, the most politically-minded Jesuit priest. All this suggests that the young William Shakespeare, then only eighteen, may well be the author of the following sensitive lines, written with great empathy:

The scowling skies did storm and puff apace,
They could not bear the wrongs that
  malice wrought;
The sun drew in his shining purple face;
The moistened clouds shed brinish
  tears for thought;
The river Thames awhile astonished stood
To count the drops of Campion's sacred blood.

Nature with teares bewailed her heavy loss;
Honesty feared herself should shortly die;
Religion saw her champion on the cross;
Angels and saints desired leave to cry;
E'en heresy, the eldest child of hell,
Began to blush, and thought she did not well[59].

In the nineteenth century, this text was attributed to the Jesuit, Thomas Pounde of Belmont, who was very pugnacious on religious issues, and attacked the English martyrologist John Foxe (1516-1587) with particular venom. Foxe was the author of *The Book of Martyrs* (1563), the famous Protestant work which was the target of much Jesuit anger[60]. Pounde was a writer of aggressive polemical verse, and only a mediocre poet. He could not conceivably have authored these elegant verses to mourn the passing of Campion.

The author of this elegy writes, among other

Fig. 52 – Various Elizabethan silver coins. The heads bear a likeness of Queen Elizabeth I.

things, that the Thames miraculously stood still when Campion died. This phenomenon was first mentioned in an essay published by Robert Parsons in 1582. Since the writer is obviously referring to this, the verse could date from 1582 or shortly thereafter.

The poem has excellent lyrical qualities, unique references to nature, and subtle Christian metaphor and symbolism. Detailed linguistic analysis and comparison of elements have shown that the language of 'The scowling skies'[61] is very much in keeping with Shakespeare's other texts.

A conspicuous and pivotal pun in the elegy, namely 'Campion' and 'champion', is reminiscent of the polished style of Parsons, whose work contains many well-wrought puns similar to the one used in this elegy on Campion's martyrdom. Parsons had succeeded in escaping from England. After Campion's death, he was the sole leader of the movement to reintroduce Catholicism into England. He attacked the leading Elizabethan statesmen with the pun 'Chancellors of the Universities' and 'cancellers of virtue'. Parsons blamed William Cecil and the Earl of Leicester for the loose morals and the lack of virtue at the universities of Oxford and Cambridge. He made the observation that these grand universities did not bear comparison with the exemplary English seminaries and colleges on the Continent, concluding that the main representatives of the State and government, among them Cecil and Leicester, who held the positions of 'Chancellors' of the universities, were in fact 'cancellers of virtue'.

If Shakespeare was actually the true author of the elegy, and if he had adapted one of Parson's ideas, then this also supports the theory that John Speed's 1611 reference to 'this papist and his poet', encompasses both Parsons and Shakespeare. When the elegy to Campion was written, Shakespeare might still have been living in Lancashire. He must have returned to Stratford in the late summer of 1582.

II. SHAKESPEARE'S MARRIAGE, FAMILY, FLIGHT AND 'LOST YEARS'

MARRIAGE AND CHILDREN

The years 1582-1585 are probably the best documented in the life of William Shakespeare. It was in 1582, presumably in the summer, that the young Shakespeare returned to Stratford after many years of absence. In that year, England enjoyed particularly clement weather resulting in an unusually abundant harvest. The sight of pasture land and fields of grain around Stratford, the River Avon and the church steeple would have filled William's heart with joy and memories of his childhood and youth as he approached his home. At some point during the perfect summer of 1582, Shakespeare met Anne Hathaway, who came from nearby Shottery (*Figs. 42 a-b*), and courted her. A more intimate relationship developed, and by the time Shakespeare married her, Anne was three months pregnant. In late November 1582, the eighteen-year-old William Shakespeare and his twenty-six-year-old bride Anne became man and wife, but the circumstances of the wedding were to create problems.

William and Anne applied to the Bishop of Worcester for a marriage licence. The episcopal register shows that a marriage licence was issued to the couple in slightly altered names 'Willelmum Shaxpere et Annam Whateley de Temple Grafton'. John Whitgift, Bishop of Worcester, was a close confidant of Elizabeth I and became the Archbishop of Canterbury in 1583. He was an authoritarian, eager to abolish irregularities and mismanagement within the established Church. With regard to licences, he always saw to it that no legal problems could arise for him, his chancellor, Richard Cosin, and his registrar, Robert Warmstry; he made sure that unforeseen contingencies were covered by sureties. In the case of William and Anne, two wealthy farmers from Stratford-upon-Avon, Fulk Sandells and John Rychardson, stood surety to the amount of £40. On 28 November 1582, one day after registration, the 'Marriage Licence Bond' was issued.

There were two reasons why William Shakespeare and Anne Hathaway had to request approval and special permission to marry: firstly, the groom was a minor, and secondly, they had the marriage banns read only once. The Church of England, however, required (just like the Roman Catholic Church) that they should be read out in church on three consecutive Sundays. The couple could not afford to wait any longer, because Anne was already in her fourth month of pregnancy, and weddings were not permitted during Advent and the Christmas period, i.e. between 2 December 1582 and 13 January 1583. Anne's pregnancy was not mentioned in the application, and she was entered in the register as a 'maiden'.

Many Shakespeare scholars have found it difficult to understand why the bride's name and place of residence were changed. But since on 27 November the case of William Whatley versus Arnold Leight was brought before the Consistorial Court in Worcester, it was thought that the scribe - erroneously - took down 'Whateley' (still having this name in mind) instead of 'Hathaway'. This explanation seems quite plausible.

More problematic is the fact that the episcopal register for 27 November gives the bride's place of residence as Temple Grafton. Anne Hathaway was the daughter of the wealthy farmer, Richard Hathaway of Shottery, in the parish of Stratford. Therefore the statement the couple had made was probably not correct - unless she lived with relatives or held a post there. But we have no indication that this was the case. Therefore other explanations must be sought.

42a – Anne Hathaway's cottage in Shottery near Stratford-upon-Avon. A drawing by C. E. Hughes (made before 1899) from a photograph by Valentine & Sons. Shakespeare's wife Anne came from a wealthy farming family, as indicated by the family home, still preserved today (*Fig. 42b*). Anne was eight years older than William. The two must have met in the summer of 1582, when Shakespeare returned to Stratford after many years' absence.

In Temple Grafton (*Fig. 43a*) an elderly priest officiated who had remained a secret Catholic despite the new religious and political developments in England. His name was John Frith. He was a thorn in the side of the Bishop of Worcester. In 1580, Whitgift had already ordered Frith to uphold the new religious laws and forbade him to perform marriage ceremonies without his approval.

Elizabethan weddings were usually conducted in the bride's home parish, a custom which continued down the centuries. In 1709 *The Clergyman's Vademecum* stated: 'Twas an ancient custum that a marriage should be performed in no other church but that to which the woman belonged as a parishioner'. As the name of the priest who performed the ceremony was not necessarily required to appear on the licence, it is possible that the couple had conceived a plan that allowed them to be married almost immediately, and by a Catholic priest. They would have a single bann read out,

42b – Anne Hathaway's family home in Shottery today.

43a – The church in Temple Grafton. Sketch by Captain James Saunders, dating from *c.* 1800. All the pieces of evidence we have strongly suggest that William Shakespeare and Anne Hathaway were married here. At that time, John Frith, an old clergyman who had secretly remained a Catholic priest, was officiating in Temple Grafton. According to official contemporary reports, Frith looked after 'hurt or diseased hawks' (i.e. the persecuted Catholics) and was greatly mistrusted by the Anglican Bishop of Worcester.

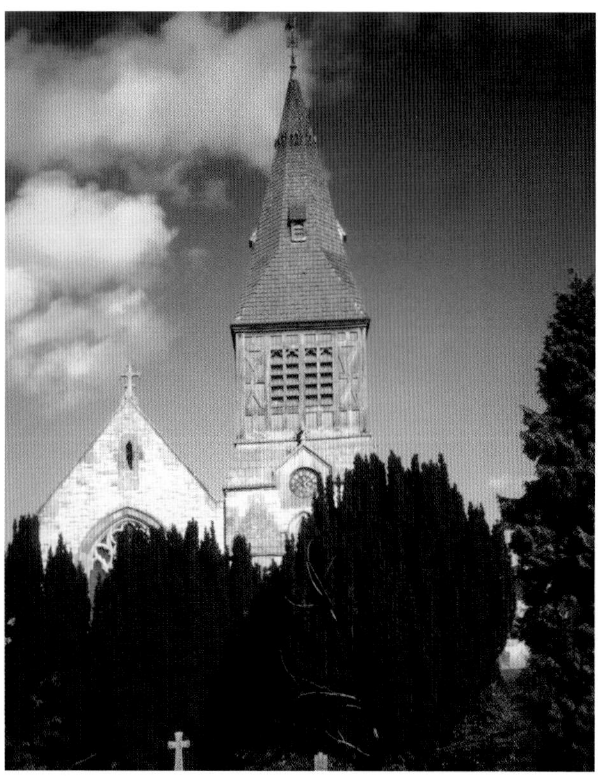

43b – The church in Temple Grafton. The old church (Fig. 43a) was replaced in the nineteenth century by this new building.

and give the bride's place of residence as Temple Grafton. They could then be married by its resident priest, the Catholic Sir John Frith (*Fig. 43b*), as has already been suggested by Heinrich Mutschmann and Karl Wentersdorf in *Shakespeare and Catholicism* (New York, 1952), pp. 93-95. According to Catholic doctrine, marriage is a sacrament and can only by performed by a priest. All this explains why William and Anne did not marry in the Protestant church of Stratford and why – despite detailed searches – no entry has been found for their marriage in neighbouring parishes. No documentation has survived to prove that the wedding took place in Temple Grafton, because the church register there is incomplete, the entries only beginning in 1612[62]. It is, however, very plausible that if William and Anne wanted to be married by the Catholic priest John Frith, they had indeed to think of a working strategy, because Frith would certainly never have obtained the bishop's consent to marry them.

In a contemporary Puritan account, *A survei of the state of the ministerie in Warwickshier (Dugdale Society, X, 5)*, Frith is characterised as 'an old priest & Unsound in religion; he can neither prech nor read well, his chiefest trade is to cure hawkes that are hurt or diseased, for which purpose manie doe usuallie repaire to him'. If Frith is said to heal wounded or sick falcons many of which 'repair' (return) to him, this is a coded reference to his suffering fellow Catholics to whom he gave help and succour. Special marriage licences such as that obtained by William and Anne had once been very rare, but they had now become almost commonplace, and there is evidence of ninety other licences of this kind having been issued around this period[63]. This can only mean that other couples were resorting to similar ways and means in order to be able to marry according to the Roman Catholic rite. The fact that the bishop and his employees protected themselves by sureties shows that they took into account the possible legal consequences of these acts.

About six months after the wedding, the Shakespeares' first child was born. She was christened Susanna at Holy Trinity Church in an Anglican ceremony on 26 May 1583. Since it was customary to christen a child on the third day after birth, she was probably born on 23 May 1583. A Protestant minister, Henry Heicroft, performed the baptism. But we have to bear in mind that Protestant christenings were recognised by the Catholic church. It is, however, very likely that the Shakespeares had the additional (Catholic) ceremonies supplied in the case of their daughter, as this was then a common practice among English Catholics.

The twins, Judith and Hamnet, were probably born on 31 January 1585. They were christened on 2 February, again in the church in Stratford, by Heicroft's successor, Richard Barton of Coventry. We can be certain that they also underwent a second, Catholic, baptism because their godparents, Judith and Hamnet Sadler, were Catholic recusants and rejected the new religion. Their names appear on the list of recusants in Stratford for the year 1606, as does the name of Susanna Shakespeare. The fact that the Shakespeares chose Hamnet and Judith Sadler as godparents for their twins is another indirect proof of their own Catholic faith. So by late January 1585, Shakespeare had fathered three children, for whom he appears to have felt great affection. In his later dramas, the playwright characterises his 'figures [...] by their individual characteristics and by how they behave towards children'[64]. For example, in *Julius Caesar*, on the eve of the battle of Philippi, Brutus shows fatherly concern for his pageboy Lucius, who has fallen asleep from exhaustion. He promises to be good to the boy if he (Brutus) survives. In *King John*, Hubert shows pity for the imprisoned young Prince Arthur. He was supposed to gouge his eyes out, but instead swears that he would not harm the child for all the treasures in the world. In *Macbeth*, Macduff is in exile in England when he learns that the tyrant has had his wife and all his children murdered. When a compatriot advises him to transform his grief into revenge, Macduff can only answer: 'He has no children'. He then asks, bewildered: 'All my pretty ones? Did you say all?' (Act IV, scene 3). The dramatist himself suffered terrible grief when his son Hamnet died at the age of eleven and was buried in Stratford on 11 August 1596 (see *Fig. 144*). Many scholars have assumed that the poet is alluding to this bitter blow when he describes the death of young Arthur in *King John*.

It is not known what William Shakespeare was doing during the three years he spent as a husband and father in Stratford. He could have worked in his father's wool and glove-making business. Another possibility is that he served as a town clerk in Stratford – one of the pseudonyms the poet used in Rome during the 'lost years' points in that direction (see p. 81). It is certain, however, that he received the yearly sum of two pounds bequeathed to him in the will of his Catholic employer Alexander de Hoghton. The sum was to be paid for his activities in helping to protect persecuted or fugitive priests, and the young Shakespeare may well have continued to engage in this work, although there is no documentary evidence to this effect.

There are, however, clear indications that Shakespeare's father tried to create favourable conditions for his son's life in Stratford. For this he was apparently even prepared to re-engage in public affairs, even if only briefly. In 1582, the year in which William returned to Stratford, his father once more attended a council meeting. During his long period of absence, from 1577 to 1586, when he was finally replaced as a councillor, John Shakespeare only attended that single meeting to vote for John Sadler, his friend and fellow Catholic, who was elected bailiff that year (see p. 31). It is not known how he was received, but the council must still have thought highly of him, since it had always tried to protect him from punishment.

Under the bailiff then in office, the Shakespeares and other Catholics of the town could live in relative safety. This included William Shakespeare, who – due to his Catholic education and his activities in the Catholic underground – was especially endangered. Life had become increasingly difficult for those who adhered to the old faith.

There is no genuine indication that the marriage between William Shakespeare and Anne Hathaway was an unhappy one. Fictional biographies, such as Robert Nye's *Mrs Shakespeare* (1993), imply that the marriage was stormy and claim that the poet and his wife engaged in sodomy, but the sole aim of such writings is to damage Shakespeare's character and reputation. Such 'biographies' distort history and blur the boundaries between fact and fiction for future generations. In fact, more is known about this aspect of Shakespeare's life than is generally believed. We know that Stratford remained central to Shakespeare's life. He acquired considerable property and land there, enabling his family to live almost as if they were part of the gentry.

The fact that, in 1585, after only three years of marriage, Shakespeare left his family behind was obviously not just for personal reasons. In our day, we are better placed than any other generation to understand that, in order to pursue his career as an actor and playwright, Shakespeare was later obliged to live in the capital, separated from his family. In his *Brief Lives* Aubrey tells us that the poet visited his family regularly when he worked as a playwright in London - even if the distance allowed him only a single annual visit during the summer. Anne, who survived William by seven years, even expressed the desire to be buried in her husband's grave. Her wish was not granted, possibly because the inscription on the stone slab covering Shakespeare's grave forbade anyone to disturb his mortal remains.

THE FLIGHT FROM STRATFORD AND SHAKESPEARE'S INVOLVEMENT WITH ENGLISH CATHOLICS-IN-EXILE

Shakespeare is known to have left Stratford after the christening of Judith and Hamnet. The true reasons for his sudden disappearance have never been clarified. It is still a riddle why the young father, still under twenty-one, abandoned his family and friends and vanished for so many years; but there are numerous clues. With his talents and the excellent education he had received, he may well have found it hard to settle down in this small provincial town. His feelings were probably those of Valentine of Verona in *The Two Gentlemen of Verona*, when he says to his friend Proteus at the beginning of the comedy:

> Cease to persuade, my loving Proteus:
> Home-keeping youth have ever homely wits.
> Were't not affection chains thy tender days
> To the sweet glances of thy honour'd love,
> I rather would entreat thy company
> To see the wonders of the world abroad,
> Than, living dully sluggardiz'd at home,
> Wear out thy youth with shapeless idleness.
>
> (Act I, scene 1)

It is, however, important to try to identify the reasons why Shakespeare left home at this particular moment in his life and why, for the next seven years, nothing is known of his whereabouts and activities.

One explanation that has been put forward is that Shakespeare had been caught poaching in the grounds of Sir Thomas Lucy (*Fig. 44*) who resided at Charlecote Park, near Stratford (*Fig. 45*). The story first emerged in the late seventeenth century, and has always caught the imagination of posterity. Two independent sources confirm it, and there is no reason to doubt its basic veracity; which does not, however, make it truly plausible as the main motive for Shakespeare's disappearance.

The Anglican minister Richard Davies, who died in 1708, was the first to report that William Shakespeare had been caught poaching 'venison & rabbits' on Sir Thomas's land. Davies stated that Lucy 'had him oft whipt & sometimes Imprisoned at last made Him fly his Native Country to his great Advancemt', and he continued 'His [Shakespeare's] revenge was so great that he is his Justice Clodpate and calls him

Fig. 44 – Funerary sculpture of the Protestant lord of the manor, Sir Thomas Lucy (1532-1600) in St Leonard's Church in Charlecote, Warwickshire. According to a local story, Shakespeare was caught poaching on Lucy's estate and was heavily punished by Sir Thomas, who was also a Justice of the Peace. Shakespeare may even have committed this crime on purpose – to create a pretext for his flight from Stratford in 1585.

ironically a great man & yt in allusion to his name bore three lowses rampant for his Arms'[65]. The reference to Justice Clodpate is generally believed by scholars to be an allusion to Shakespeare's comic character Justice Shallow in *Henry IV* (Pt. 2) and *The Merry Wives of Windsor*. The noun 'lowses' appears to be a direct link to Sir Thomas Lucy's coat of arms emblazoned with three 'luces' (pike fish). At the same time, 'luces' alludes to Lucy's name. The actual sting, however, is that, in the local dialect, the pronunciation of 'luces' was similar to that of 'lowses' (lice).

Soon after Shakespeare had invented Justice Shallow, this comic character was already being frequently referred to by the poet's contemporaries. Thus Charles Percy, the third son of the earl of Northumberland[66], who, through marriage, had become lord of the manor of Dumbleton in Gloucestershire, not far from Stratford-upon-Avon, wrote in a letter to his friend Carlington on 27 December (presumably) 1600 that he was so occupied with business matters that he could not come to London. He told Carlington that if he stayed any longer he would become so dull and silly that he could even be mistaken for Justice Shallow. These lines show that Shakespeare's Shallow must have been very well known at the time - not just by the London theatre audience, but also in the country; thus Shakespeare could count on the allusion to Sir Thomas Lucy being understood by both London and provincial audiences. The name Shallow had almost become a byword for a dull and ignorant man. Percy asks his friend to take pity on him and, above all, to send him news of events in the capital. As a postscript, he adds that he need not worry about sending him old news, because where he was, all news was still 'very new' whenever it reached him.

Sir Thomas Lucy was a puritanical political hardliner, who demanded draconian penalties for the adherents of the old faith. Therefore he was much feared by Catholic recusants, as, for instance, the minutes of the Parliament of 1583/84 are able to demonstrate (see *The Journals of all the Parliaments During the Reign of Queen Elizabeth*, published in 1682 – see *Fig. 22*). In his book, *William Shakespeare. A Documentary Life* (1975), Samuel Schoenbaum says of Lucy: 'As a Justice of the Queen's Peace, this puritanical squire exercised himself mainly over recusants, one of whom he literally uncovered, starving, in a haystack' (p. 86). At the same time, Lucy worked hard to strengthen property rights (no doubt in his own interest). Shakespeare's satirising of Sir Thomas in his most popular comedy (*The Merry Wives of Windsor*) will have found a ready audience among the

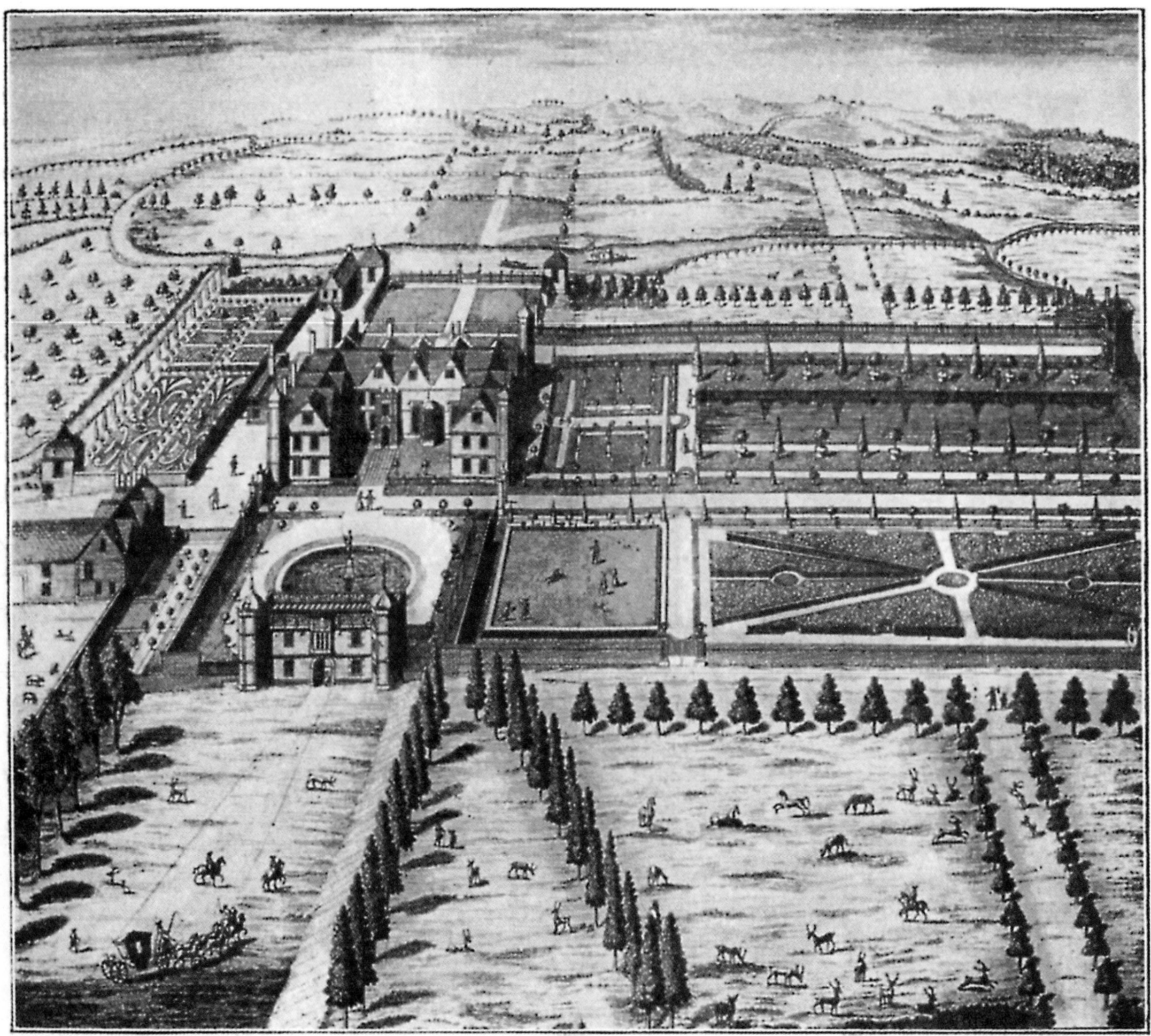

Fig. 45 – Perspective view of Charlecote, the country estate of the Lucy family near Stratford-upon-Avon. Copper engraving by Henry Beighton, based on a drawing by Elisha Kirkall (1685-1742).

nobility and gentry (in so far as they were not Puritans) of the upper and lower houses of Parliament, familiar with the London theatre and therefore well aware of the dramatist's target of ridicule.

A second account of the poaching story can be found in the first illustrated edition of *The Complete Works of Shakespeare*, printed in 1709. This edition was the first to provide an outline of the life of the great English poet. The account is attributed to the editor of the Works, dramatist and former lawyer Nicholas Rowe (1674-1718). Rowe's knowledge is based on information obtained from his friend, the famous Shakespearean actor Thomas Betterton (1635-1710) who travelled through Stratford and its environs about ninety years after Shakespeare's death, gathering information about Shakespeare. Betterton recorded that the writer had fallen into bad company as a young man, and had frequently joined in the sport of poaching in one of Lucy's parks. Shakespeare had been prosecuted by Sir Thomas with the full rigour of the law, and severely punished. The poet, however, had taken revenge on Lucy by writing a mocking ballad about him. According to Betterton, Sir Thomas responded by persecuting Shakespeare so intensely that he was forced to flee to London[67].

The opening scene of *The Merry Wives of Windsor* offers an indirect confirmation of the two anecdotal sources, and of the assumption that Shakespeare had Sir Thomas Lucy in his sights with the character of Justice Shallow[68]. The magistrate berates Falstaff for his poaching, and threatens to drag the delinquent before the most famous court in London, the Star Chamber. Immediately after his outburst of rage there is a reference to the 'dozen white luces' in his ancestor's coat of arms.

Two texts have been found that may be the satirical verses referred to, since both are claimed to be the ballad mentioned by Rowe:

TEXT I

Sir Thomas was too covetous,
To covet so much deer,
When horns enough upon his head
Most plainly did appear.

Had not his worship one deer left?
What then? He had a wife
Took pains enough to find him horns
Should last him during life[69].

TEXT II

A parliemente member, a justice of peace,
At home a poor scare-crowe, at London an asse,
If lowsie is Lucy, as some volke miscalle it,
Then Lucy is lowsie whatever befall it:
He thinks himself greate,
Yet an asse in his state,
We allowe by his ears but with asses to mate.
If Lucy is lowsie, as some volke miscalle it,
Sing lowsie Lucy, whatever befall it[70].

Text II contains much personal information about Sir Thomas Lucy, showing that these lines could only have been written by someone who knew him and the local vernacular. Being aware of the fact that Lucy was a member of parliament and a Justice of the Peace, the author ridicules him by referring to him 'as a poor scare-crowe' and an 'asse'. Compared to Text I these verses have much greater literary merit and are, therefore, more likely to have been authored by Shakespeare. The first text is too lame, its mockery based entirely on Lucy's greed, and on the word-play that bestows on him, a man who owns so many horned beasts and covets more, horns of his own (i.e. brands him a cuckold). The author of the second text also knows about the pun on 'Lucy'/'lowsie' that was in local currency. This author knew that Lucy thought greatly of himself but that, in reality, he had made an ass of himself. The 'someone' who knew all this could well have been Shakespeare. He was certainly very familiar with Lucy's circumstances at home, and moreover his father could have told him about events in London. At this time (1585), John Shakespeare was still officially a member of the Stratford Town Council. He knew the justice of the peace who was responsible for enforcing the laws and statutes of the government locally. Though he could make no public comment, no doubt he was well informed about Lucy and local politics.

The poet, however, had yet another motive for ridiculing Sir Thomas, a motive that was beyond mere personal revenge. As has already been mentioned, the owner of Charlecote was an infamous persecutor of recusants. In Parliament on 23 February 1585 he demanded an even crueller method of execution than usual for the 'Catholic traitor' Dr William Parry.

It is important to consider Shakespeare's own Catholicism and that of his family and friends, and the danger it entailed for them, in order fully to understand the reasons for his flight.

The execution of the Catholic priest Robert Debdale in 1585 may have provided William Shakespeare with good reason to disappear and thus escape the attention of the authorities. Naturally, when priests and

Catholics were executed, people close to them were also investigated by the local aldermen. In the case of Robert Debdale, this would have included the Debdale family in Shottery and their friends, including Anne Hathaway, Shakespeare's wife, as well as Simon Hunt, Robert Debdale's former schoolmaster in Stratford, who in Rome became the successor of the most wanted Jesuit Robert Parsons. The authorities' interest doubtless extended to Debdale's Stratford schoolfellows – tutored by the same teacher in the same (prohibited) faith – of whom William Shakespeare was one.

The family background of Shakespeare's mother probably provided another motive for him to leave Stratford and disappear. Mary Shakespeare was related to the Ardens of Parkhall, members of the nobility who were known to be steadfast Catholics. In 1583 Edward Arden, the head of this large family, had been executed in London after a spectacular trial for high treason.

In 1585, however, William Shakespeare himself would have been particularly endangered, so that he had to take preventive measures to protect himself. The most effective protection would have been to keep a low profile and remove himself from constant surveillance and the attentions of both established church and state.

Since he must have studied at the Catholic Collegium Anglicum in Douai or Rheims and was then employed as an unlicensed teacher in the household of the Catholic Alexander de Houghton in Lancashire, becoming at the same time a member of de Hoghton's secret Catholic organisation set up to protect Catholic priests of the English mission, the young Shakespeare had been offending against English religious laws for years. From 1585 onward, this would have been regarded as high treason, an act which was punishable by death. In 1585 Shakespeare must have consulted his family – in particular his father, who had signed a Borromeo testament and was himself in an extremely difficult position – and decided that he must leave home to escape his enemies, of whom the most formidable was the recusant-hunter Sir Thomas Lucy.

There are additional very important reasons why Shakespeare's flight from Stratford had to take place in the year 1585. In this year another severely anti-Catholic penal law was passed, which meant a terrible blow to the Catholic population. All Jesuits and priests were banned from the country and any breach of this law was punishable by death.

In 1585, recruitment began for troops to be sent to the Netherlands to support the Protestant Dutch in their battle for independence against Catholic Spain. As a Catholic and a member of a secret Catholic organisation, Shakespeare would have supported the Spanish side. In 1585 he would have run the risk of being press-ganged into the English army. This was another convincing reason to hide and/or disappear. In that same year, the fate of Mary, Queen of Scots was decided, and she was executed in 1587. The English Catholics had had great hopes of her, and her death appalled them, as it did Catholics-in-exile and other Catholic countries within Europe.

1585 was also the year in which opposition was hardening among the Catholics. There was a meeting in Rome where strategies were devised for an armed struggle against Protestant England to be waged by the leaders of the English Catholics-in-exile on the Continent (Robert Parsons and William Allen) with the help of the king of Spain and the Pope. Shakespeare, who since his employment as a private teacher in Lancashire was involved in the Catholic underground, could also have been called upon to take part.

All these constitute far more cogent reasons for Shakespeare to go into hiding than a few episodes of poaching. In Elizabethan England, poaching was common and was practically considered to be a 'gentleman's offence'. Escapades such as these were especially favoured by Oxford students. Many who later held high office in England had been involved in such pranks without damaging their careers.

This does not mean, however, that the story about Sir Thomas Lucy is not true. Shakespeare may even have deliberately poached on Sir Thomas's estate as part of a plan to provide a pretext for his escape. We may recall that, seven years later, John Shakespeare managed to avoid harsh penalties for himself and other Catholic recusants by using similarly convincing, but false, excuses.

Since nothing has hitherto been known about the seven years starting in 1585, scholars have often referred to this period in Shakespeare's life as the 'lost years'. There is, however, one important literary document that, if decoded, provides reliable clues to Shakespeare's activities at this time. The importance of this source has hitherto been overlooked. As will be shown later, there are three other documents that are able to prove that Shakespeare worked secretly in the Catholic underground between 1585 and 1592 and travelled at regular intervals to Rome, the centre of the Catholic faith and the centre for English Catholics-in-exile.

The largely ignored literary document was written by the London dramatist and pamphleteer Robert Greene, a Cambridge and Oxford graduate (1558-1592), who lived in London, had been very successful and enjoyed ridiculing his contemporaries (*Fig. 46*). He was renowned for his profligacy, which he bitterly regretted at the end of his relatively short life. In his *Groatsworth of Wit* (1592), a mainly autobiographical work written shortly before his death and intended as both a literary testament and a warning to others, there is a scene that, if decoded, proves to be very informative with regard to William Shakespeare. Greene describes a meeting between Roberto, a scholar, author and playwright – based on Greene himself – and a young man from the provinces. Their conversation includes a discussion about the relationship between actors and playwrights in England at the time. Roberto, clearly the elder of the two, seizes the opportunity to inquire as to the occupation of this elegantly dressed and very self-assured young man. He is amazed to discover that the young man is an actor, having assumed that he was 'a gentleman of great living', since his appearance and dress is indicative of rank and affluence. The stranger does everything he can to reinforce this impression, claiming that life had once treated him badly, but that times have changed: '*Tempora mutantur*'. The anonymous actor then mentions his possessions, and states that his collection of theatrical costumes must be worth at least £200. Roberto is astonished, and finds it hard to comprehend how a mere actor could prosper so greatly. In addition, he remarks that the actor's voice is rather unattractive. This is obviously a reference to the young man's regional accent. But this does nothing to shake the confidence of the stranger. Instead, he continues unabashed, though not entirely

Fig. 46 – The title page of the satirical pamphlet, *A Quip for An Upstart Courtier*, written by the Elizabethan playwright and pamphletist Robert Greene in 1592. Greene viciously attacked Shakespeare in *A Groatsworth of Wit* (1592). It is this document that contains the first proof of Shakespeare's presence in London. Henry Chettle, a printer and playwright, shortly afterwards vindicated Shakespeare in his *Kind-Harts Dreame*, referring to 'his honesty, and his facetious grace in writting, that aproues his Art'.

coherently, stating that as a writer who came from the provinces, he could supply 'beautiful speeches'; and that he once wrote 'morals' or 'morality plays'. His most significant remark, however, is that he spent seven years as an 'absolute interpreter of the puppets'. The stranger does not explain what he means by this, and Roberto does not ask.

At the end of the conversation, Roberto is hired by the dynamic young man as a playwright with the prospect of handsome pay. Being impoverished, he agrees to join the stranger and is accommodated by him in a house above shops near the city limits. The address, however, is not given.

There is no doubt that Robert Greene is describing an event from his own life, but who is this mysterious, charismatic actor? Since Greene, elsewhere in his book, sharply attacks a certain person as being an arrogant 'upstart crow', which – as scholars generally accept – is a clear reference to Shakespeare (see p. 98 f.), we may well assume that his boasting young actor is none other than William Shakespeare[71]. For in the scene just described, the anonymous young man's situation bears remarkable similarities to the life of Shakespeare as it would have been at the time: his occupation as an actor, his reference to having experienced hard times, his high level of education (evidenced by his knowledge of Latin) and his claim to be able to write speeches. Moreover, he claims to have been an 'author in the country' and to have written morality plays. This sounds very much like the period Shakespeare spent in Alexander de Hoghton's household in Lancashire where he was, according to Aubrey, a schoolmaster in the country and must also have written short texts and plays.

The depiction of the anonymous actor as being elegantly dressed, giving the impression of an affluent gentleman and owning £200 worth of theatrical costumes, is, however, very different from the usual image of Shakespeare as a playwright in London in the early 1590s. But we must bear in mind, after all, that Shakespeare's mother was a distant member of a family, belonging to the lower nobility, and that Shakespeare had been brought up in affluent circumstances, with an education to match. At the age of fourteen he received an income from his parents, and was later in receipt of a small lifelong pension for his work in de Hoghton's organisation. He also obtained a remarkable income from his work as an actor and successful playwright. Catholic priests and their helpers were frequently disguised as gentlemen and/or officers in order to command respect, especially when travelling. For example, Edmund Campion wore an officer's uniform when he returned to England in the year 1580. When staying in the homes of their aristocratic patrons, however, the same priests were often dressed as servants. Henry Chettle (*c.*1560-?1607), an English printer and dramatist, noted that Shakespeare had a confident appearance, great rhetorical skills, and a refined manner. These are all characteristics that he could have acquired from his teachers and sponsors, but also through his contacts with missionary priests, high-ranking English Catholics-in-exile and members of the English landed gentry.

According to the description and location of the house in which the stranger (obviously Shakespeare) lodged the writer and playwright (obviously Greene), it could have been a building in Blackfriars (perhaps even the eastern Gatehouse) that Shakespeare later purchased. For it is possible that the poet, who was active in the Catholic underground, was already using the house at this time.

By far the most convincing similarity between the anonymous player and Shakespeare is the fact that, according to the actor's own admission, he was engaged for seven years (from 1585 to 1592, the period identical with the 'lost years') in an activity which proves to be in perfect harmony with the poet's activities when he worked for the Catholic underground and Catholics-in-exile. Again a linguistic code is used (comparable to the reference to 'players' to mean

Fig. 47 – St Peter's Square with a view of St Peter's Church. Fresco from *c.* 1588, in the Vatican library in Rome.

priests in Alexander de Hoghton's will). When the unknown actor claims that he was an 'interpreter of the puppets' he is - as it appears - telling us that he was a mediator for the priests. If this interpretation is correct, Greene's document confirms that the poet played an important and dangerous role as middleman in the Catholic underground. Shakespeare's purchase of the house in Blackfriars in 1613 (see pp. 298 ff.) serves to confirm this.

New and important evidence proves that Shakespeare's most significant place of residence during his 'lost years' was, in fact, in Rome (*Fig. 47*)[72]. The evidence for this comes from an important historical document, namely the Pilgrim Book No. 282 of the English Pilgrim Hospice in Rome. The hospice was officially founded in 1362 but its origins date back to as far as 726. When the English College was founded in 1579, the old hospice was attached to it. The Pilgrim Book is a record of all the travellers who stayed at the hospice, recording their names, exact date of arrival and the precise length of their stay.

In October 2000, I travelled to Rome[73]. The object of my journey was the Venerable English College. Its first permanent rector, Father Alphonsus Agazzari, was appointed on 23 April 1579 when Pope Gregory XIII signed the Bull of Foundation. In early 1579, Father Robert Parsons had been given temporary charge. He served as rector of the college in 1588, the year of the Armada, and again from 1598 to his death in 1610.[74] This famous English College (Collegium Anglicum) produced many important English theologians and numerous martyrs. Its hospitality has been extended to popes (*Fig. 48*), kings and other royals, cardinals, members of the aristocracy and nobility, ambassadors, academics, poets, and writers. The Venerable English College still trains future priests for the Catholic Church in Britain.

Fig. 48 – A bust of Pope Gregory XIII, formerly in the Collegium Germanicum, Rome. In April 1580, Pope Gregory gave support to the missionary movement of the English Jesuits. He was one of the eminent visitors to the English College in Rome, which was rapidly gaining importance. Simon Hunt, Shakespeare's former Stratford schoolmaster, who died in Rome in 1585, was Robert Parsons' successor as English Confessor to the Holy See. He would have known Pope Gregory XIII personally.

Here I was to be allowed access to the ancient pilgrim-books. All the evidence I had collected showed that Shakespeare must have travelled in Italy between 1585 and 1589/90, and must have stayed in Rome in 1585. Would these authentic entries concerning English travellers to Rome who had lodged in the Hospice in the 1580s make any kind of reference to William Shakespeare from Stratford-upon-Avon?

There were three books: the bound catalogue of the College, together with two pilgrim-books, likewise bound (Liber No. 18 and Liber No. 282). Liber No. 18 dates from the late 15th century, while Liber No. 282 is from the late 16th century, containing entries from 1580 to 1656. It was Liber 282 that I was intensely interested in. Most Catholics who lived, studied or taught in English colleges on the Continent, used pseudonyms for security reasons. I picked up the book, cautiously undid the tape around it, and began to leaf through carefully. By chance, at first glance my eye very quickly fell upon three significant entries:

(1) 'P. Antonius Tirellus'. This concerned the Catholic priest Anthony Tyrrell, who was one of the first students at the English College in Rome. He later became a renegade, acting as a spy for the English crown. Tyrrell and his companions arrived on 7 September 1584, and stayed 24 days in the Hospice. On his return to England he passed on his insider information about the Pope and the plans of the English Catholics-in-exile to the government. It was Tyrrell who informed on the conspirator Babington, thus sealing the fate of Mary Queen of Scots. As Lord Burghley's spy, among other things he spent time in the Clink Prison in Southwark, where he held mass for Catholic prisoners and heard their confessions, which enabled him to pick up further information about them. However, Tyrrell changed sides several times. In January 1588 – before the launch of the Spanish Armada – he was supposed to preach in St. Paul's Cathedral in London, thereby publicly renouncing his Catholicism. But he stunned the congregation, and especially the Protestant authorities, with an impassioned confession of his Catholic faith. He was promptly arrested, but not before he had hastily managed to distribute his sermon in the form of a broadsheet. In October 1588 he succeeded in convincing Lord Burghley of his 'true repentance'. Remarkably, he was only overcome with remorse once the Spanish Armada had been defeated and Queen Elizabeth had solemnly given thanks for her victory in a divine service at St. Paul's. After Tyrrell really

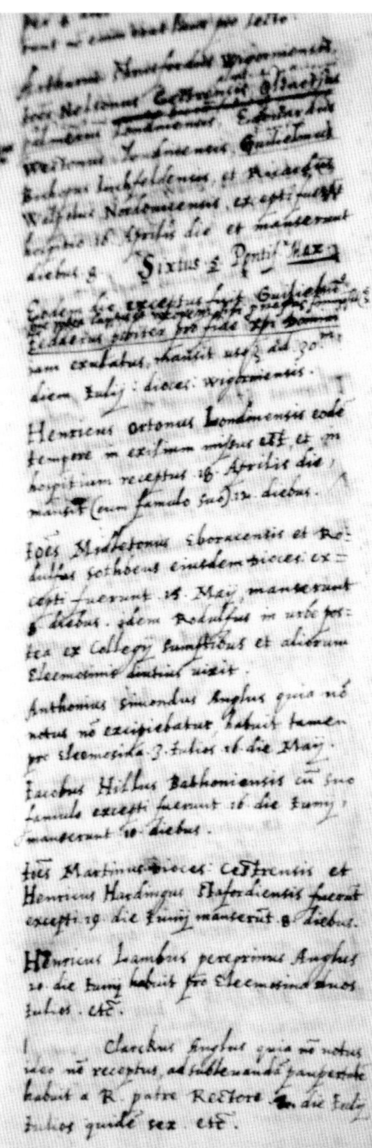

Fig. 49 – An extract from Pilgrim Book No. 282 of the Venerable English College, Rome. An entry from the year 1585 shows one of William Shakespeare's pseudonyms 'Arthurus Stratfordus Wigorniensis' (third line from the top). Shakespeare fled Stratford in February 1585 and arrived at the Pilgrim Hospice in Rome on 16 April 1585, using a pseudonym based on the name of his home town.

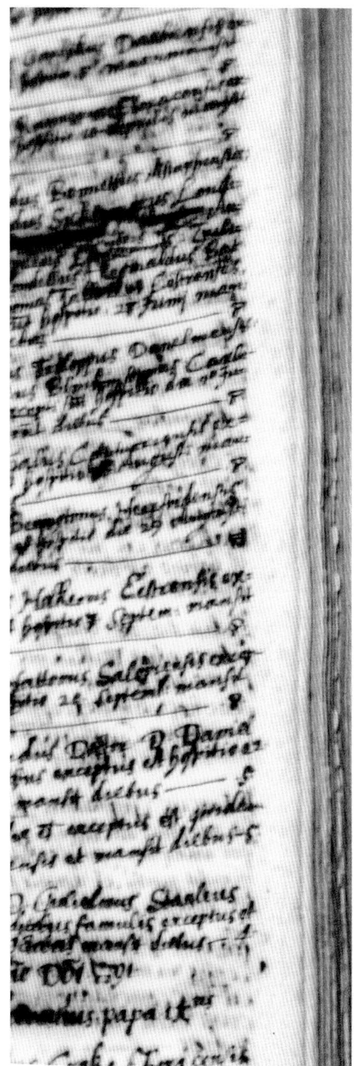

Fig. 50 – An extract from Pilgrim Book No. 282 of the Venerable English College, Rome. An entry for the year 1591 has been completely removed, presumably with the nib of a quill pen (eighth line from the top). Shakespeare visited Rome at two-year intervals during his 'lost years' (1585-1592), as three names entered in 1585, 1587 and 1589 are able to show that are all based on or referring to the town of Stratford. It is possible that he also stayed at the College in 1591.

had abjured the Catholic faith in a sermon delivered also in St. Paul's in December 1588, a text was published entitled 'The recantation and abjuration of Anthony Tyrrell (some time priest of the English College in Rome)'; the government employed it for propaganda purposes. The renegade Catholic priest now became an Anglican clergyman, marrying and living a secluded private life. Towards the end of his life, however, Tyrrell moved to what is now Belgium and died a natural death, once more reconciled with the Catholic Church.

The vicissitudes of Anthony Tyrrell's life can also serve to illustrate the pressures inflicted on Shakespeare and his contemporaries by the new, imposed religion. But William Shakespeare found ways and means to avoid these pressures and remain incognito.

(2) 'Reuerendus Dominus Alanus – Lancastriensis'. This entry refers to William Allen, founder of the Collegium Anglicum in Douai, who arrived in Rome on 4 November 1585 accompanied by the priest 'Gulielmus Mores' (William Morris), his nephew and confidant Thomas Hesket from Lancashire, and a student called Byars. Allen was appointed Cardinal by Pope Sixtus V in 1587 and was designated Archbishop of Canterbury, in case the invasion of the Spanish Armada in 1588 should prove successful. He was never to leave Rome again. When Allen died in 1594, he was buried in the crypt of the College church. His close friend, the Jesuit priest Robert Parsons, was interred next to him in 1610. Today the sepulchre in the former crypt of the church is empty, and practically inaccessible. I was able to establish this on 4 March 2000 during my first visit to the Venerable English College. Andrew Pinsent, a student at the College, spontaneously offered to show me the tomb. Napoleon had removed the monuments, sarcophagi and remains of Allen and Parsons, and had their lead coffins melted down.

(3) 'Arthurus Stratfordus Wigorniensus' (*Fig. 50a*). This name opens an entry recording the arrival of travellers in Rome on 16 April 1585, and their eight-day stay there. The Christian name is given as 'Arthur', and the family name is that of the town of Stratford, together with the diocese of Worcester, to which it belongs. Pseudonyms were commonly used for reasons of security among Catholics at that time. But who was hiding behind the pseudonym 'Arthurus Stratfordus Wigorniensis', in other words 'Arthur (from) Stratford (in the) Diocese of Worcester'? Today we know that Shakespeare had to apply to the Bishop of Worcester for his marriage licence (see p. 66); and today Stratford is, of course, associated above all with Shakespeare. Using the name of the town of Stratford, at the time in no way posed a risk of revealing his identity.

Long before I discovered this entry, I had assembled a body of evidence which led me to conclude that William Shakespeare stayed in Rome during the crucial year of 1585 (see pp. 74 ff.), as a member of a secret Catholic organisation (see pp. 61 ff.). Thus the 1585 entry 'Arthurus Stratfordus Wigorniensis' in the pilgrim-book of the Venerable English College (like two other coded entries in 1587 and 1589 respectively, referring to the same person, and discussed below) was no strange coincidence, but documentary evidence of Shakespeare's presence in Rome in April 1585, under a pseudonym that seems to demonstrate considerable pride. This evidence therefore fits well into the context of religious, social, and cultural history that this book has established on the basis of historical facts and contemporary sources.

Even when we look at the fine historical details, there is a clear correspondence. The group arrived in Rome on 16 April 1585, five days before Easter. However, according to the old Julian Calendar, in force in England until 1752, it was the 6th of April when they arrived. Shakespeare's twins, Judith and Hamnet, were christened on 2 February 1585 in the church in Stratford. Scholars unanimously accept that Shakespeare then left Stratford. It would therefore have taken him two months to reach Rome. This accords with the usual duration of the journey at that time. Travellers went by water and overland from England to Italy via France, stopping over in Rheims, Paris, Lyons, and Marseilles, sailing from there to Genoa, then proceeding – mostly on foot – via Florence and Siena to Rome.

Systematically and chronologically working through the pilgrim-book, from 1580 to 1592, I noticed other names, including two further obvious pseudonyms of Shakespeare's:

'D. Shfordus Cestrensis' [1587]: there is every reason to think that this is William Shakespeare. The strange family name 'Shfordus', without a Christian name, is probably a combination of 'Shakespeare' and 'Stratfordus' ('Sh[akespeare Strat]fordus'), as is strongly suggested, too, by the pseudonym 'Arthurus Stratfordus Wigorniensis' used in 1585. Citing 'Cestrensis' (meaning the diocese of Chester) instead of 'Wigorniensis' is obviously meant to divert attention from the correct diocese (Worcester). Between 1580 and 1582 the poet lived in Lancashire, a county that belonged to the diocese of Chester.

'Shfordus' stayed for quite some time in the Hospice of the English College in Rome, from 7 February (?) to 8 April 1587. This relatively long sojourn might indicate that he had important and time-consuming tasks to complete in Rome, perhaps on behalf of the secret Catholic organisation by which – as the will left by the recusant Alexander de Hoghton shows - he was also being paid. It may be assumed that this was the Catholic Association.

'Gulielmus Clerkue Stratfordiensis' [1589]: this pseudonym unmistakeably points to the person of William Shakespeare. The writer's real (Latinised) first name ('Gulielmus' = William) is combined with a Latinised form of the name of his home town ('Stratfordiensis'). 'Clerkue' ('clerk') may be a reference to the occupation the later playwright then practised. Originally reserved for clerics, after the Reformation the term was also applied to laymen. In those days of limited literacy, a 'clerk' would perform the duties of a secretary and/or bookkeeper, as well as conducting all written business transactions. 'Gulielmus Clerkue Stratfordiensis', which is to say 'William, secretary from Stratford', arrived in Rome on 22 September 1589 and stayed for eight days.

The three codenames ('Arthurus Stratfordus Wigorniensis', 'Shfordus Cestrensis' and 'Gulielmus Clerkue Stratfordiensis') found in the entries for 1585, 1587 and 1589 in pilgrim-book No. 282, lead – in conjunction with other findings reported in this book – to the firm conclusion that we are dealing here with none other than William Shakespeare himself, who visited Rome precisely in those years. These journeys to Rome at two-year intervals take place exactly in the 'lost years' period (1585-1592), about which nothing was previously known. They offer a convincing explanation of Shakespeare's whereabouts and the company he was keeping in this previously hidden phase of his life. By far the longest visit of the playwright to Rome occurred, significantly, in the year 1587, when intensive preparations were taking place on the Catholic side for armed conflict with Protestant England.

Shakespeare, who can be shown to have been in London from 1592 onwards, may also have gone to Rome in 1591, but this is not borne out by entries for that year in pilgrim-book No. 282. However, mention should be made of the fact that page 27 of the pilgrim-book I examined is badly damaged. Most of the damage consists of round holes that can hardly have occurred by accident. Page 27 contains some of the entries for the year 1591. It is particularly noticeable that one of the names in the fourth entry on this page has been completely erased. The rectangular hole created by this action (*Fig. 50b*) could have been caused by a sharp pen. An expert investigation of the damaged parts of this page using the latest scientific methods might perhaps yield more information, and possibly some indication of the name that has been so painstakingly eradicated from the table of the names of English travellers who visited Rome in the year 1591.

Back in Germany, I compared my transcripts from pilgrim-book No. 282 with the corresponding entries in volume VI of H. Foley's *Records of the English Province of the Society of Jesus* (1880). I found that the names of the persons and dioceses had not been reproduced in Latin, but transposed directly into English – not completely accurately, however. This was also clear from the examples of 'Arthurus Stratfordus Wigorniensis', 'D. Shfordus Cestrensis', and 'Gulielmus Clerkue Stratfordiensis', translated as

'Stratford, Arthur, Worcestershire', 'Sliford or Stiford, Dom., of Cheshire', and 'Clarke, William, Staffordshire'. In contrast to most persons mentioned in the pilgrim book, 'Arthurus Stratfordus' and 'Shfordus' have never previously been identified. The identification of 'Gulielmus Clerkue Stratfordiensis' as 'Clarke, William' is not tenable, given the confusion between the town of Stratford and the county of Staffordshire. The readings of the entries that I have put forward therefore prevail, especially as they have stood up to further investigations of their linguistic correctness and the plausibility of their content.

While I was looking at the published source, I once more scanned the list of names from 1580 to 1616. Alerted by my researches in the Venerable English College, I noticed among the 1613 entries the name 'Stratford, Richard'. The Latin version 'Ricardus Stratfordus' immediately recalled the entry 'Arthurus Stratfordus' from the year 1585. Since the name of his home town is here used once more as a pseudonym, we are clearly dealing with Shakespeare again. The playwright borrowed the Christian name either from his grandfather on his father's side, or from his brother Richard, buried on 4 February 1613. This corresponds to the custom of the persecuted English Catholics at the time, and can be seen as a covert reference to the poet's family allegiance. 'Ricardus Stratfordus' stayed at the Hospice for eight days. It is noticeable, however, that – probably to protect his cover – he did not supply any of the usual further information.

His last stay in this city, in October 1613, took place during the time when his professional career as a playwright was over, his contribution to the survival of the Old Faith complete, and his retirement to Stratford accomplished. It is surely not just by chance that 'Rome' occurs in his work about 290 times, but London is mentioned only about 60 times.

Looking back to Shakespeare's first trip to Rome in April 1585, it now seems most likely that the poaching incident in Charlecote was indeed just a pretext for leaving Stratford as quickly as possible. It seems his first acquaintance with the Eternal City occurred shortly before his 21st birthday, and that he had given himself the resounding name 'Arthurus Stratfordus Wigorniensis'. As far as is now known, Shakespeare proudly retained the name of his home town in all his later pseudonyms. His first visits to Rome had already fitted in well with the surroundings and the situation he found himself in at that time.

The fact that Shakespeare spent a considerable amount of time in Rome in 1587 also supports the theory that 'Guilielmus erased', the suspicious entry in the records at Douai or Rheims for the year 1587 (see p. 51), could originally have contained the name of the poet or one of his pseudonyms. We may well assume that the poet visited the Collegium Anglicum in Rheims during his travels on the Continent on the way to or from England. In the year 1587, when the Spanish king at the instigation of the leaders of the English Catholics abroad were preparing for an armed struggle to reintroduce the old faith into England, Shakespeare would have had a particular interest in staying in Rheims and sharing information. In that year, as has already been mentioned, Christopher Marlowe was sent there by the English government to gather information about students and teachers. It is not impossible that Shakespeare and Marlowe met in Rheims as secret envoys of the opposing sides. Just five years later, these cogs in the great machine of religious politics, Shakespeare and Marlowe, were the leading English dramatists vying for the favour of London theatre audiences.

These newly discovered historical sources are able to throw new light on the hitherto obscure 'lost years', generating a relatively clear picture of Shakespeare's activities during this most turbulent time. They provide a very plausible explanation as to why the poet needed to keep all of this so secret.

III. SHAKESPEARE'S RISE AS A PLAYWRIGHT IN LONDON

ARRIVAL, ACCOMMODATION AND CONTACTS

Until now, the date of Shakespeare's arrival in London (*Figs. 51–52*) is unknown, and the circumstances under which he came have been shrouded in mystery. There has been no lack of speculation, impossible to discuss in detail here. Shakespeare biographers represent a wide variety of opinions. In recent years, however, one of these assumptions has been presented again and again. In *Shakespeare: A Life*, the Shakespeare scholar Park Honan wrote that 'on a day of doubtful promise to himself, he [the young Shakespeare in his early twenties] would have bid farewell to his parents, three small children, and Anne, and set out on a road leading to the teeming, colourful, and oddly dangerous south'[75]. The journalist and biographer Anthony Holden proposes in *William Shakespeare, his Life and Work* that Shakespeare joined the Queen's Men after they appeared in Stratford in the summer of 1587: 'This was the occasion on which it may be surmised that twenty-three-year-old William, son of the glover who had seen better times, volunteered his services, bid a fond farewell to his parents, wife and three small children, and threw in his lot with the players, setting forth to seek his fortune in London'[76]. Although there are no sources to support Honan and Holden, they were not the first to make such a suggestion. Anthony Burgess's *Shakespeare*, a light-hearted, amusing and imaginative biography, takes many events from the playwright's life and turns them into an exciting story that reads like a novel or a melodrama. According to Burgess, the young Shakespeare could even have made an application to one of the clowns of the Queen's Men on their visit to Stratford in 1587 to be accepted as one of their number:

> In the summer of 1587, the Queen's Men paid a second visit to Stratford [...] The chief comic men of this company were Dick Tarleton and Will Kemp [...] In that last Stratford summer of his youth, Will would see a brilliant clown with sad eyes and a decaying body. It may have been to him that he made a stammering or confident application to be considered as a member of the company. [...] Something like that. Back from the inn where the players lodged to Henley Street, to bundle up his few clothes, beg a little money from his father, be sprayed by tearful farewells. And then cease to be Will of Stratford. The role of Sweet Master Shakespeare awaited him in a bigger town – filthy, gorgeous, mean, murderous, but the only place where a member of his new breed, without land, without craft, could hope to make money and a name. [77]

In *Will in the World. How Shakespeare became Shakespeare* Stephen Greenblatt imagines a somewhat similar scenario, suggesting that the theatre company Shakespeare may have joined in Stratford in 1587 did not head directly for London but toured the country, thus giving the future playwright the chance 'to hone his skills'. Greenblatt writes:

> If in June 1587 he was taken on by the Queen's Men, for example, the company would have continued to tour the towns and hospitable noblemen's houses of the Midlands. By August of that summer, the company, or part of it [...] had gone to the southeast, perhaps providing the young man his first glimpse of the chalk cliffs at Dover (which later figure so powerfully in *King Lear*). The company then worked its way through towns like Hythe and Canterbury toward the capital. Such a route would have given Shakespeare the chance in a comfortingly familiar provincial setting to hone his skills ... [78]

Fig. 51 – Hand-coloured map of London and Westminster, probably based on a drawing by George Hoefnagel and probably engraved by Frans Hogenberg. It was first published in *Civitates Orbis Terrarum* (1572).

However, the most that can be said with any certainty, on the strict basis of the factual evidence, is that the playwright must have been in London by early 1592 at the latest. This is supported by a scene in Greene's *Groatsworth of Wit* (1592) where the character Roberto (obviously Greene himself) meets a stranger who – as has been discussed above – was in all probability identical with Shakespeare. For this actor claims to have been an 'absolute interpreter of the puppets [=priests]' for seven years, i.e. precisely during the 'lost years' of 1585 to 1592. Shakespeare's presence in London by the latter date is also confirmed by Greene's *Groatsworth of Wit* because in this 1592 pamphlet the author alludes to a performance of Shakespeare's historical play *Henry VI*.

On the basis of the new information about Shakespeare's Catholic education in Rheims, his first job in a Catholic household in Lancashire, and his seven-year involvement with covert Catholicism and Catholics-in-exile on the Continent, it now appears very likely that the playwright took the same route back from the Continent as that taken by Catholic priests and laity who had worked in the service of Catholics-in-exile in Rome or elsewhere. There are many sources documenting these routes. Clergy and laity were all forced to avoid the English ports, which were closely watched. Those trying to return to the capital sailed up the Thames estuary to Gravesend, then took a small boat clandestinely upstream to London, in an attempt to evade surveillance (*Figs. 53 a–b*). In this context, William Harrison states in his *Elizabethan Journal*: 'if the ship is for London they take a boat between Gravesend and London and so escape examining'. This comment was made in

Fig. 52 – Thomas Wyck's *View of London from Southwark*, a seventeenth-century panorama of London in colour.

relation to the testimony of the recusant Edward Pemberton, who was interrogated on 29 November 1593, by order of the Archbishop of Canterbury[79]. The truth of Pemberton's testimony can be confirmed by the report about the arrest of Anthony Skinner and Richard Acliffe, who were caught at Gravesend while attempting to row upstream to London in a small boat, having set out from Calais. Skinner and Acliffe were interrogated by the Attorney-General and the Solicitor-General on 18 December 1591. The interrogation not only revealed that the pair were recusants; they were also found to have been out of the country for eight years, having spent most of this time in Rome. Skinner had been a servant to Cardinal William Allen, founder of the Collegium Anglicum in Douai and a friend of Robert Parsons, head of the movement to restore Roman Catholicism to England. Acliffe had worked in the service of Bishop Cassano[80]. The sources do not mention where the travellers landed, but it was probably at the landing-stage at Blackfriars, where sufficient cover was provided by the eastern gatehouse, whose tenant and family were on hand to offer help.

The grounds of the former monasteries at Blackfriars, Whitefriars, St Martin's le Grand, Holywell and others were known as 'Liberties', meaning that they were not under the jurisdiction of the aldermen of the City of London and still had the rights of sanctuary. This made them perfect locations for the activities of the secret Catholic movement. Anyone could seek sanctuary from the authorities there. They offered refuge, for example, for those escaping forced military service. These locations were also much sought after as sites for theatres, because the London aldermen, who strongly opposed the theatre, had no authority there.

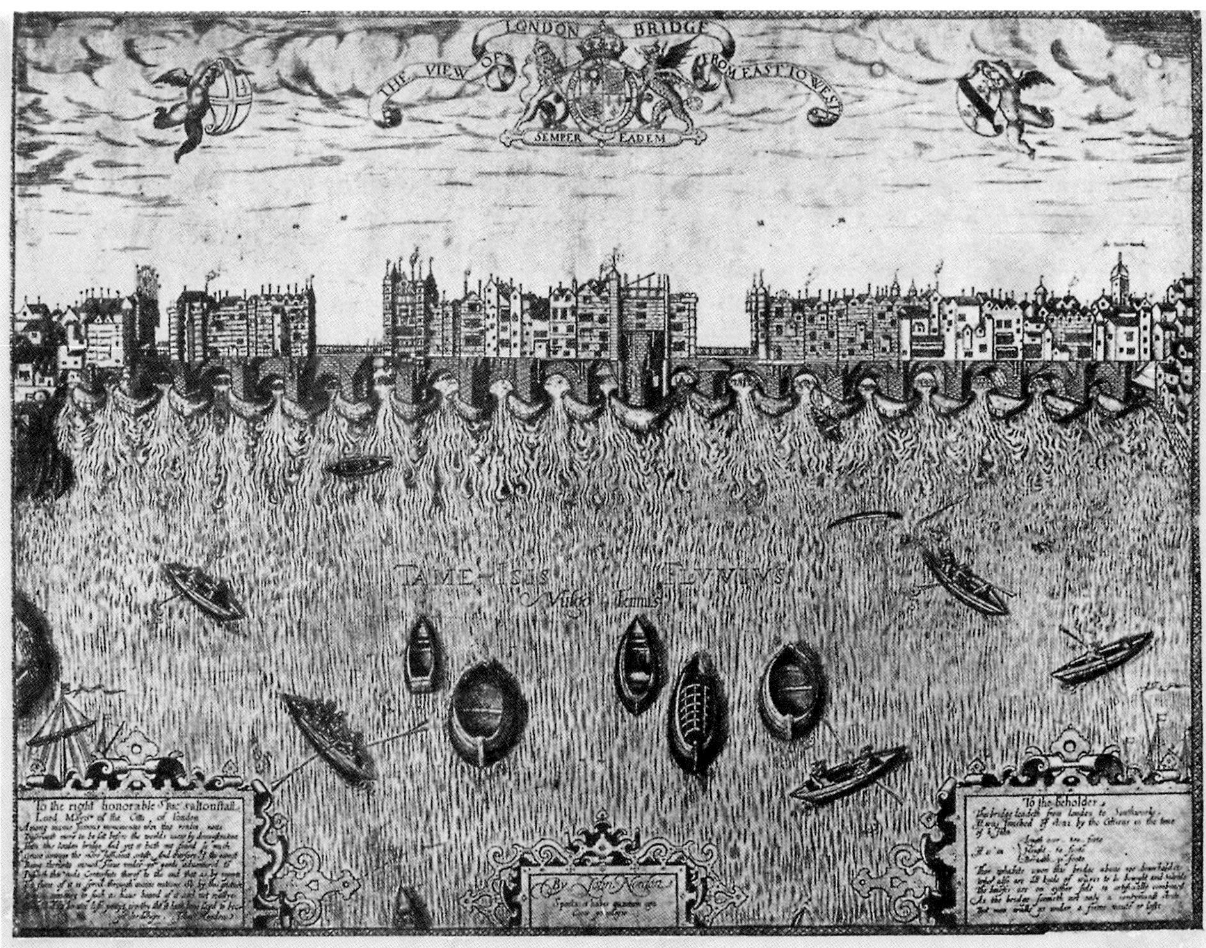

Fig. 53a – Illustration of the eastern side of London Bridge in the year 1597. In the foreground, the Thames and many small boats are visible. These crafts would have been used to transport people to and from Gravesend, where the larger ships docked. English Catholics and Catholic priests were secretly transported in and out of London in boats like this.

The route taken by English Catholics-in-exile up the Thames from Gravesend to London is thus well documented. Blackfriars was the most popular point of embarkation for Catholic priests and recusants attempting to flee England, and it was where they disembarked on their return journey. It is very probable that William Shakespeare also made this secret journey when he first came to London (*Fig. 54*) – evidently in early 1592. He would then have been able to live anonymously as one of the 200,000 citizens within the city walls (*Fig. 65*). Shakespeare's contacts with the Catholic underground meant that accommodation presented no problems for him. When he reached London, he did not need to justify his long absence to anyone. If he had returned to Stratford, however, he would have been accountable to the Anglican Church and the authorities for his whereabouts and his activities during the previous seven years.

Even so, while in London, Shakespeare had to keep a keen eye out for government informers, who were a force to be reckoned with. Spies were amply rewarded for their work and they succeeded in unmasking many priests, their flock, and those who offered them succour. Such people were then brought before courts, sentenced, and publicly executed.

On 1 November 1591, Richard Topcliffe, one of the government's chief spies, arrested the seminary priest Edmund Gennings (or Jennings), while he was saying Mass in full vestments at the

Fig. 53b – A picture of London as Shakespeare would have known it, with densely crowded houses and churches. This drawing was made by Oscar Mothes, based on an engraving by M. Merian in 1641. It shows the city as it looked twenty-five years before the devastating fire of 1666. Many large and small boats can be seen in the foreground, as well as the 'Steelyard' of the German Hanseatic League.

home of a certain Swithin Wells in Holborn. The ten people who were attending the Mass were also arrested. This led to scenes of violence, during which Topcliffe was thrown down the stairs by the servant of one of those present. Gennings, Swithin Wells and five other Catholics, including three Jesuits, were executed on 10 December 1591. Shortly before his execution, Gennings was challenged one last time to admit his treason. His reply was simple: 'If to say Mass be treason, I confess I have done it and glory in it'[81]. Topcliffe was so enraged by these words that he prevented the priest from saying anything further and saw to it that Genning's noose was cut down as soon as possible after the ladder had been removed. The hangman immediately cut off the priest's limbs while he was still alive, and pulled out his entrails. Harrison describes the gruesome scene: 'Gennings was thus thrown on his feet, but the hangman tripped up his

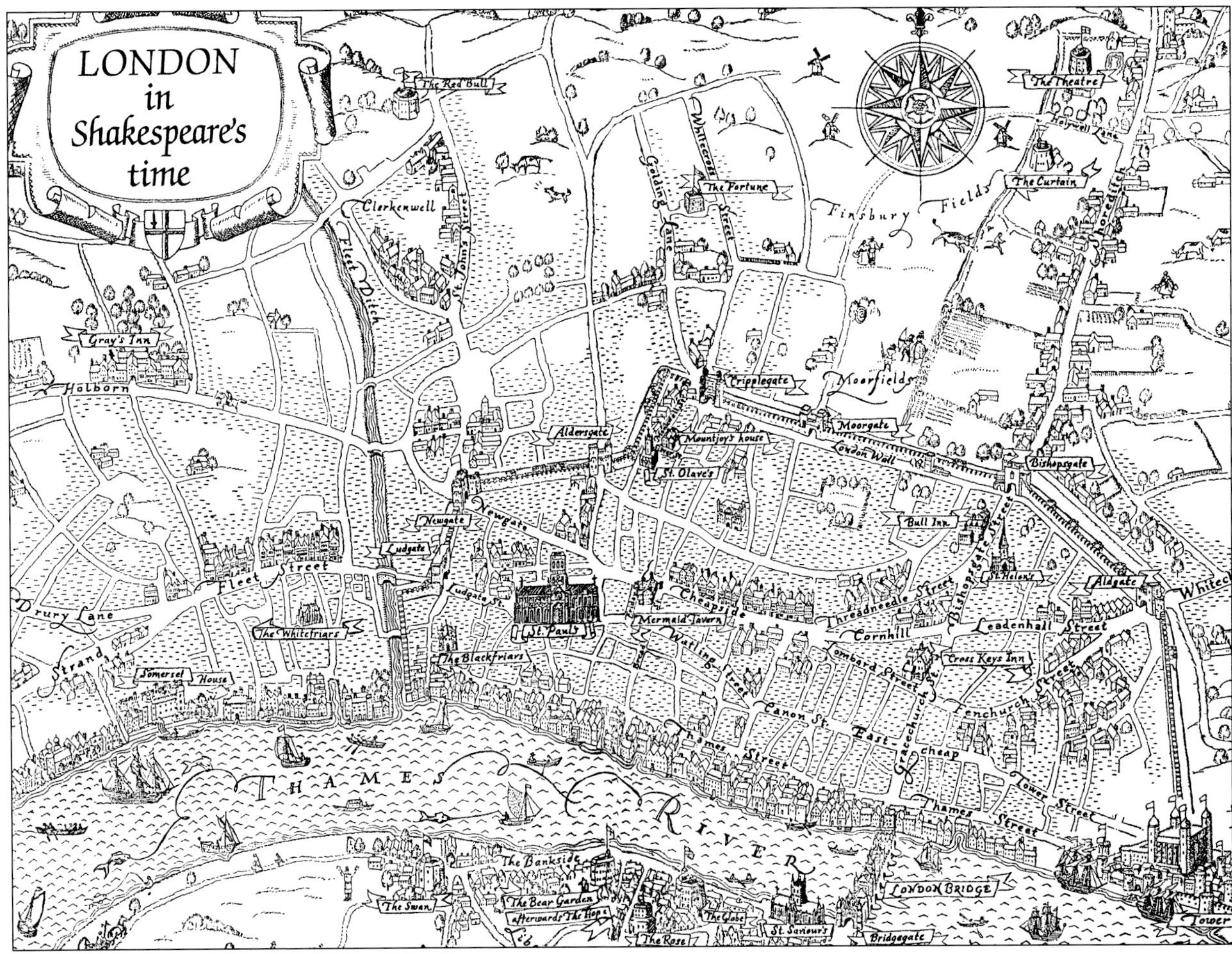

Fig. 54 – Street map of London in Shakespeare's time (reconstruction).

heels, cut off his members and disembowelled him. In this agony, Gennings began to call on St Gregory to the great astonishment of the hangman, who cried out with a loud voice, 'God's wounds! His heart is in my hand and yet Gregory is in his mouth'[82].

In *The Comedy of Errors*, an early comedy and possibly his first, the playwright describes the site where the merchant Aegeon is to be executed. He speaks of the 'melancholy vale', 'the place of death and sorry execution', which is located 'behind the ditches' of an abbey (Act V, scene 1). Scholars have long agreed that Shakespeare is referring to the execution of the Catholic priest William Hartley shortly after the victory over the Spanish Armada in 1588. This execution was not performed at Tyburn, the principal place of public execution in London from 1388 until 1783 (the approximate site of the gallows today being marked by a stone in the traffic island at the junction of Edgware Road and Bayswater Road), but instead upon the site of the former Holywell monastery in Shoreditch, where, in 1576, James Burbage had built his famous theatre. According to John Aubrey, Shakespeare, too, lived in Shoreditch, to be precise 'at Hoglane [Hog Lane]', today called Worship Street, 'within 6 dores [from] – Norton – folgate [Norton Folgate]'[83]. The dramatist may have been informed of Hartley's execution by Catholic sources in 1588, for the arrests and executions of priests were fully documented in the English colleges on the Continent, and the news spread fast among English Catholics at home and abroad. But it is also possible that Shakespeare first heard of the event later, when he lived and worked in Shoreditch as a playwright.

Fig. 55 – Noble lady with her lady-in-waiting. A sketch by the Swiss doctor Thomas Platter, made during his visit to London and England in 1599.

On his return to London, Shakespeare must have noticed that even stricter controls were now in place, especially since the 'Proclamation against Jesuits' of 21 November 1591, the purpose of which was to halt the considerable flow of young men attending the Jesuit seminaries and colleges on the Continent. In a speech made on 18 October 1591, the queen herself spoke of her 'good subjects', who were being thrown into moral conflict and lured into treason 'under a false colour and face of holiness'. The 'treacherous messengers in obscure places', she continued, were spreading the 'secret infection of treasons in the bowels of Our Realm'. Only constant and careful searching and the implementation of strict orders could stop this infection. The queen stated that it was known that the traitors entered the kingdom using 'secret creeks, and landing places', disguising their 'names and their persons', some of them 'in apparel as soldiers, mariners or merchants', pretending that they had been 'taken prisoners, and put into galleys, and delivered'. Others, the monarch went on, 'come in as gentlemen with contrary names, in comely apparel', claiming to have been travelling 'into foreign countries for knowledge'. Many behaved 'as ruffians', so that nobody could even begin to suspect that they were 'friars, priests, jesuits, or popish scholars'[84].

This description fits in with Robert Greene's reference to Shakespeare in the *Groatsworth of Wit*. The confident, nameless actor described by Greene is also dressed like a gentleman and claims to have spent seven years as an 'Interpreter of the puppets'.

All of this gives credence to the theory proposed at the start of this chapter that, at the end of his 'lost years', William Shakespeare also used the secret routes described by the queen in order to reach England, and disembarked unobserved at the landing-stage of the former monastery of Blackfriars.

Towards the end of 1591, the English government drastically tightened its controls on Catholic clergymen and recusants and other non-conformists. It also increased surveillance within its own ranks. On 19 December 1591, the members of a Special Commission set up to monitor and investigate the secret movements of Jesuits and lay priests on their return to England were ordered by the Privy Council to inform it in the strictest confidence whether any members of the Special Commission itself were suspected of being 'unsound in religion', whether they had family members who were recusants, or if any had harboured 'persons suspected to be backward in religion'. Their 'names and dwelling places' were to be handed to the Council, along with 'their opinions of the men'[85].

The government found these 'cleansing' strategies to be necessary because the unmasking of Jesuits and priests by aldermen and members of the Special Commission was often hindered by their own family members. The case of Sir Henry Bromley is a famous example. After the Gunpowder Plot of 1605, Bromley laid protracted siege to Hendlip House in Worcestershire because Henry Garnet, the Superior of the English Jesuits, was being hidden there. He eventually managed to capture Garnet

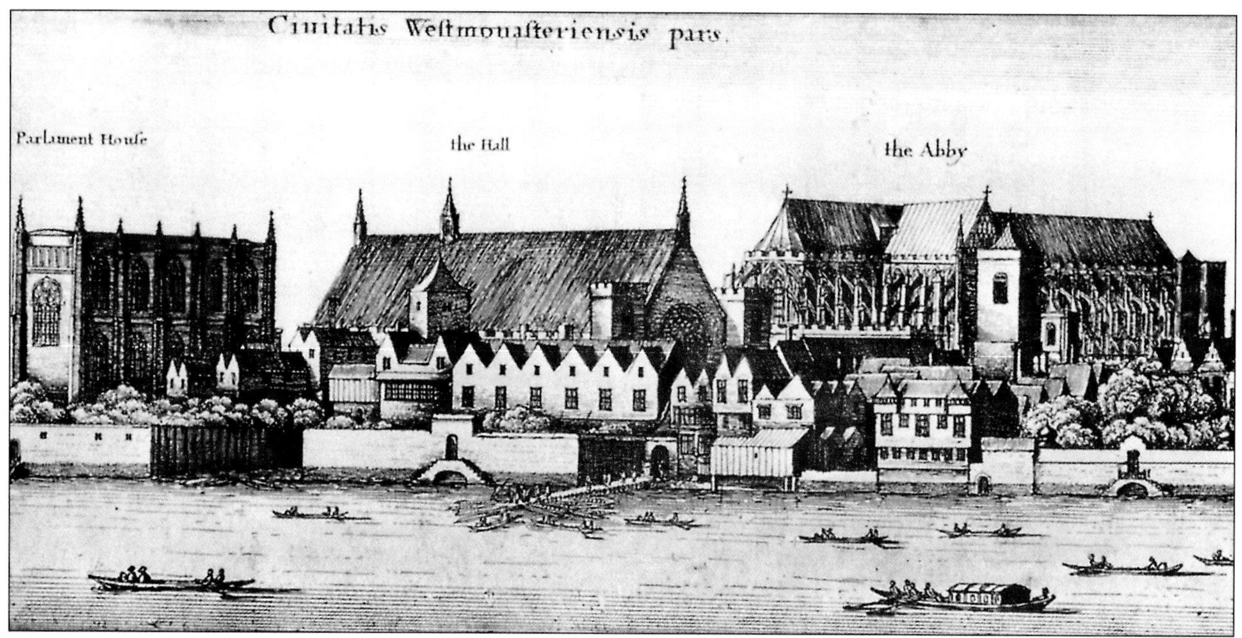

Fig. 56 – 'Civitatis Westmonasteriensis'. Westminster at the time of Shakespeare. From left to right: Parliament, Westminster Hall and Westminster Abbey.

and initially kept him prisoner in his own house, allowing him to dine at his table. During this time, Mrs Bromley was converted to Roman Catholicism (see p. 276).

Shakespeare lived in various parts of London, both within and without the city walls, and always as a lodger in other people's houses. Apart from acquiring one property in the capital in 1613, he invested his money only in Stratford, buying both property and land there. The fact that Shakespeare frequently changed his address in London and did not have a lavish and extravagant lifestyle, even when he became rich and famous, is highly significant. He opposed the government for religious reasons, and living as a tenant enabled him to move on quickly if necessary. It also had the additional effect of ensuring that his assets were seen to be as minimal as possible by the London revenue authorities. Thus he paid much less tax to a regime he did not support.

Initially, Shakespeare may have used accommodation provided by the Catholic underground. His first fixed address in London seems to have been in Westminster, the country's centre of power (*Fig. 56*). It is here that he may have purchased the *Archaionomia*, an anthology of English legal texts, edited by William Lambarde and published in 1568. A copy of this book in the Folger Shakespeare Library in Washington DC contains the signature 'W. Shaksp.[ere]'. Comparisons between this signature and the authentic signatures on the original manuscripts of the Blackfriars Gatehouse conveyance of 10 March 1613 (in the Guildhall of London), the Blackfriars Gatehouse mortgage of 11 March 1613 (in the British Library in London) as well as the playwright's will of 25 March 1616 (in the Public Record Office in London) all suggest that it could be genuine. This copy also contains an important annotation, probably added by a subsequent owner, stating: 'Mr Wm Shakespeare lived at No 1 Little Crown St Westminster NB near Dorset Steps, St James's Park'. If this information is correct, why did Shakespeare choose to live near the royal court (Whitehall), Parliament and the most important law courts of the country, rather than near the theatres? Anthony Holden argues that rents in Westminster were lower than inside

Fig. 57 – Portrait of the actor Richard Burbage, thought to be a self-portrait. He was the son of James Burbage who opened the first public theatre in Shoreditch in 1576. In 1594, Richard Burbage and William Shakespeare joined the Chamberlain's Men and quickly became their leading actors, making them by far the best acting troupe in England. The two worked very closely together, and were also great friends. Shakespeare left Richard Burbage money for a ring in his will. He also left money to John Heminge and Henry Condell for the same purpose.

The Workes of William Shakeſpeare, containing all his Comedies, Hiſtories, and Tragedies: Truely ſet forth, according to their firſt ORJGJNALL.

The Names of the Principall Actors in all theſe Playes.

William Shakeſpeare.	Samuel Gilburne.
Richard Burbadge.	Robert Armin.
John Hemmings.	William Oſtler.
Auguſtine Phillips.	Nathan Field.
William Kempt.	John Underwood.
Thomas Poope.	Nicholas Tooley.
George Bryan.	William Eccleſtone.
Henry Condell.	Joſeph Taylor.
William Slye.	Robert Benfield.
Richard Cowly.	Robert Goughe.
John Lowine.	Richard Robinſon.
Samuell Croſſe.	Iohn Shancke.
Alexander Cooke.	Iohn Rice.

Fig. 58 – Shakespeare and Burbage head the list of 'The Names of the Principall Actors in all these Playes', reproduced from the First Folio edition published in 1623 by Shakespeare's close friends and acting colleagues, John Heminge und Henry Condell.

or just outside the city, but this is not very likely. Holden also claims that the playwright had worked there as a clerk or scribe in a legal office since 1589, when his parents had a legal dispute with their relatives, the Lamberts, about the mortgaged Asbies estate which had never been returned to the Shakespeares. This theory is neither consistent with the new evidence concerning the 'lost years' nor with that of Greene's nameless actor (Shakespeare) who first appeared in London in 1592.

Shakespeare may have lived at No. 1 Little Crown Street for about two years. The boat trip from his home to the Rose Theatre, downstream in Southwark, would have been quick and easy. Shakespeare would merely have climbed into a boat at the landing-stage and given the boatman the direction 'Eastward Ho!'

As early as 1594, Shakespeare could have moved to Shoreditch, then a London suburb north-east of the city wall. For in that year, he joined the Chamberlain's Men, and along with the actor Richard Burbage (*Fig. 57*), son of the theatre owner James Burbage, became one of their two leading actors (*Fig. 58*). The move was necessary in order to avoid a long journey through the city. Shoreditch was located on the main northern access route to London. It had taverns, inns, brothels, bowling alleys and gaming-halls, generally offering cheap entertainment which meant that at that time it had a rather seedy reputation. It was home to actors, writers, bohemians, soldiers, prostitutes, illegal craftsmen, cut-purses, and beggars. The Burbages lived there, as did many other actors and members of the Chamberlain's Men. The playwright Christopher Marlowe (*Fig. 59*) is also known to have lived there. As has already been mentioned, the evidence that Shakespeare lived not far from The Theatre in Shoreditch comes from John Aubrey. The conscientious biographer noted that in a conversation with the actor William Beeston he learned that Shakespeare, 'was not a company-keeper' and 'wouldn't be debauched' and 'if invited to, writ he was in pain'. Aubrey commented that this made Shakespeare an even more admirable figure (cf. Bodleian Aubrey MS. 8, f. 45^{v}).

William Beeston, Aubrey's source, was the son of the actor Christopher Beeston, who used the alias Hutchinson, and was a prominent member of the Chamberlain's Men. Beeston performed on stage with Shakespeare several times in the 1590s, including performances of Ben Jonson's *Every Man in His Humour* in 1598. He knew the Bard well, but the young Beeston obtained most of his information about Shakespeare from the actor John Lacy (d. 1681), a skilled dancing-master who was a member of the King's Company during the Restoration and who excelled as a comic actor in the role of Falstaff. Lacy was also extremely well informed about Falstaff's creator.

Tax records show that before October 1596, Shakespeare lived for a while at St Helen's in the Bishopsgate district, not far from the playhouses known as The Theatre and the Curtain in Shoreditch. Shakespeare's personal wealth at that time was assessed at around £5. A document dated November 1596 indicates that he must have moved from there to the south bank of the Thames. Tax records prove that in 1599, he lived in the Liberty of Clink, in Southwark. This was close to the Globe Theatre, which opened in 1599. On 25 October 1598, Shakespeare's old friend from Stratford, Richard Quiney, who lodged at the Bell, in Carter Lane near Blackfriars, wrote an urgent letter to the dramatist in great haste, which was supposed to reach him in Southwark. However, Shakespeare obviously never received this letter because it was later discovered among Quiney's papers. Further correspondence between Adrian Quiney, Richard's father, and Abraham Sturley confirms that Shakespeare had offered them money.

Fig. 59 – Portrait of (?) Christopher Marlowe. When Shakespeare came to London in 1592, Marlowe was England's most famous poet and playwright. Being an atheist and a government spy, Marlowe, in 1587, spied upon the students and teachers at the Collegium Anglicum in Rheims. The still extant diaries of the college contain a partly erased entry, which could refer to William Shakespeare. This entry dates from the year 1587. It reads: 'Guilielmus [erased]'.*[4] It is possible that Marlowe and Shakespeare met in Rheims.

Richard Quiney travelled from Stratford to London several times between 1597 and 1601 to represent the town of Stratford on important matters. On 25 October 1598, he was summoned to appear in court and wrote to his friend Shakespeare, asking him to lend him £30.

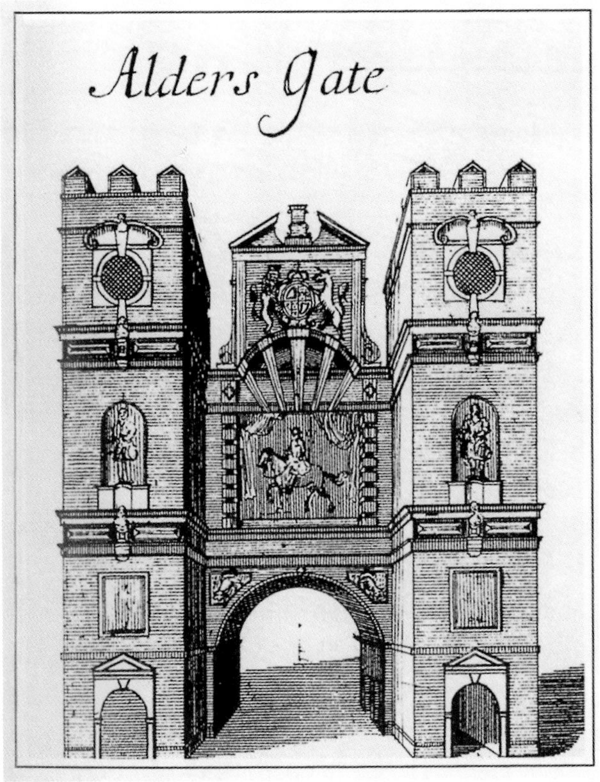

Fig. 60a – One of London's gates: Aldersgate.

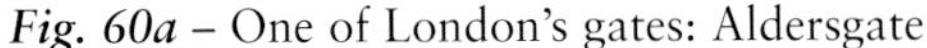

Fig. 60b – One of London's gates: Cripplegate.

It seems the matter was of crucial importance. Quiney feared that he would not be allowed to return from the court the following night, and he expressed the wish that the Lord be with Shakespeare and with them all. He closed the letter with an 'Amen'.

It is not known what debts Quiney is referring to in his letter to Shakespeare, but it may have been that he was being forced to pay a draconian fine of the type levied on recusants. The content and wording of the letter, especially its ending, suggest that the sum was not merely a business debt.

Further important information about where Shakespeare lived in London and his relationship with other people is provided by documents concerning a legal argument between a father and son-in-law about a dowry that was promised but never paid. From about 1601-02 until about 1606-7, the playwright lodged with the wealthy Huguenot refugee Christopher Mountjoy (d. 1620) who lived in Silver Street, opposite the Church of St Olave's and not far from the city gates of Aldersgate and Cripplegate (*Figs. 60 a–b*). Mountjoy and his family, his journeymen and apprentices produced valuable filigree headwear for the queen, the ladies of the Court and women in London society. When an apprentice of his named Stephen Belott fell in love with Mary, Mountjoy's daughter and wanted to marry her, Shakespeare was living with the Mountjoys and acted as a marriage-broker. The marriage took place on 19 November 1604. As a dowry, Belott was promised £60 and a £200 legacy in his father-in-law's will. Yet after eight years of marriage these promises had still not been kept, and in 1612 Belott sued his father-in-law. The witnesses who were asked to produce affidavits and to make a solemn declaration included a certain William Shakespeare, who is described as a gentleman and resident of Stratford; his age is given as (approximately) forty-eight. Shakespeare's detailed statement consists of five points. Among other things, he explains that he has known Mary and Stephen for approximately ten years and that he was involved in the arrangements for their marriage. He states that he is unable, however, to remember the details of the dowry.

Shakespeare's tenancy in Silver Street, where he seems to have rented rooms on the top floor, allowed him an insight into the art of 'hair-dressing' or 'tire-making', and also gave him a glimpse of the ladies of the Court and of London's High Society, who must have often come to Mountjoy's house. In *The Merchant of Venice*, there is a sample of what the playwright could have seen and marvelled at in the studio of his London landlord. In the play, Bassanio opens the leaden casket bearing Portia's portrait and exclaims with joy: 'Here in her hairs/ The painter plays the spider, and hath woven/ A golden mesh t'entrap the hearts of men/ Faster than gnats in cobwebs'. (Act III, scene 2). Shakespeare was obviously fascinated by the artful and impressive hair decoration and precious headwear produced by Mountjoy's workshop for fashionable Elizabethan ladies[86].

Shakespeare's relatively frequent changes of address in London, and the fact that he was only ever a lodger, should also be viewed against the backdrop of his secret Catholicism. If the playwright often dragged his feet over paying taxes to the revenue, this may have been because he did not wish to attract the attention of the church and/or the lay authorities.

The best method of identifying recusants was to keep a close eye on church attendance and participation in communion. Recusants were deemed to be guilty of high treason, because as far as the government was concerned, they owed allegiance to a foreign power, namely the Pope. This is demonstrated by a tragic case that occurred in Winchester.

On 25 March 1593, the young Catholic James Bird was sentenced to death and led to his execution in Winchester, according to the penal law of 1593. Bird had already been imprisoned for ten years for his beliefs. In order to obtain the desired verdict from the jury, the Lord Chief Justice Anderson explained:

> Here you have James Bird, a recusant. You know what a recusant means. A recusant is one that refuseth to go to church ; this no one refuseth unless he hath been reconciled to the Church of Rome. That man that hath been reconciled to the Church of Rome is a rebel and a traitor. Now know your evident duty.

As Bird stood on the ladder at the gallows, he made a final plea: 'Tell me,' he asked the Sheriff, 'what I die for?' The Sheriff answered that he did not know the reason, but that Bird himself best knew why he had been condemned. All Bird had to do was admit his crime and promise to go to church. Then 'the Queen's pardon' would be begged for him. But Bird replied: 'if by going to church I can save my life, surely all the world will see this, that I am executed solely for faith and religion, and nothing else. It was just this that I wished to elicit from you. Now I gladly die.'[87]

This shows the great danger Shakespeare was in – especially since he must have offended against the law several times: he had obviously been educated at the Collegium Anglicum in Rheims, had acted as an unlicensed private teacher in a Catholic household and had been a member of a secret Catholic organisation for protecting priests. He had also, as it appears, worked as an intermediary for priests during the 'lost years'. With the exception of the poet's employment in the Catholic household of the de Hoghtons, all this has remained undisclosed to Shakespeare biographers until now. This is why Samuel Schoenbaum, in his *William Shakespeare: A Documentary Life,* believed that Shakespeare had been 'tax evasive'. Schoenbaum, however, overlooked the point that the playwright may have withheld his taxes so as not to support the State and the established Church.

Shakespeare, it seems, took a keen interest in spiritual and temporal power structures, and was very much aware of which influential people in the capital were well-disposed towards Catholicism. On his arrival in London, the playwright would quickly have scanned the composition of the Privy Council, the body that devised and drafted new laws, supervised the implementation of the new religious policies and made the major political decisions. The Privy Council also controlled the widespread government spy network. The names of the Earl of Essex and his later patron, the Earl of Southampton, would have emerged straight away.

In 1592, the members of the Privy Council were Dr John Whitgift, Lord Archbishop of Canterbury; Sir Christopher Hatton, Lord Chancellor of England, Knight of the Garter; Sir William Cecil; Lord Burghley, Lord High Treasurer of England, Knight of the Garter; Charles Howard, Baron of Effingham, Lord Admiral of England, Knight of the Garter; Henry Carey; Lord Hunsdon, Lord Chamberlain, Knight of the Garter (and cousin of the queen); Thomas, Lord Buckhurst, Lord High Butler of England, Knight of the Garter; Sir Francis Knollys, Treasurer of the Queen's Household; Sir Thomas Heneage, Vice-Chamberlain to the Queen, Chancellor of the Duchy Lancaster; Mr John Wolley, Esquire, Secretary for the Latin Tongue, Chancellor of the most Honourable Order of the Garter; Mr John Fortescue, Esquire, Master of the Great Wardrobe and Under Treasurer of the Exchequer. In 1593 Robert Devereux, 19th Earl of Essex and a favourite of the queen, joined the council.

John Whitgift, the Archbishop of Canterbury, aged about sixty-two in 1592, was well known to Shakespeare. Between 1577 and 1583, he held the position of Bishop of Worcester and, during this period, had been responsible for Stratford. As bishop, he would have an eye on the most talented pupils from the grammar schools of his diocese to be educated at Cambridge or Oxford, so that they might occupy high positions in the Church or the State. The Stratford schoolmaster, Thomas Jenkins, would have given him a list of the most intelligent students, among them, no doubt, the name of William Shakespeare. Whitgift was the son of a rich merchant and had studied at Cambridge. He was a convinced and ambitious Anglican, and this ensured him a rapid rise in the hierarchy of the established church. In 1583, Elizabeth I named him Archbishop of Canterbury, making him the highest representative of the Church. He was a close friend and confidant of the queen, who playfully called him her 'little black husband'. In November 1582, when he was still Bishop of Worcester, William Shakespeare and his pregnant future wife, Anne Hathaway, managed to obtain permission to marry from Whitgift, with the help of two townsfolk, despite the fact that only one marriage bann had been read. It seems that the bishop was deceived as to the bride's place of residence, so that the wedding could take place in a location where an old Catholic priest still remained in office.

As the highest representative of the Church of England, Archbishop Whitgift was a martinet, and a harsh censor. He led a strong campaign against the Puritans, who published pamphlets in 1588 under the pseudonym Martin Marprelate, attacking the Church of England in general, and the Archbishop of Canterbury in particular. Satirical and erotic literature were the especial targets of Whitgift's censorship. The archbishop banned numerous books and pamphlets and had them burnt in a public ceremony on 4 June 1599. In popular parlance, this was known as 'the bishop's bonfire'.

Shakespeare must have come into contact with Thomas Heneage, the queen's vice-chamberlain, by 1594 at the latest. Heneage worked very closely with the queen and enjoyed her full confidence. On 2 May 1594, Heneage married Mary Wriothesley, Countess of Southampton, the widowed mother of Shakespeare's patron and friend. Through this marriage, the countess secured an influential protector for herself and her family in the highest government circles. This was most important, because the Southampton family had remained Catholic, and priests came and went from their London residence, Southampton House, said Mass there, and were given refuge and shelter. As the protégé and friend of Southampton, Shakespeare may also have enjoyed the protection of Privy Council member Heneage, especially since Heneage was also Chancellor of the Duchy of Lancaster. Some biographers justly believe that the playwright wrote *A Midsummer Night's Dream* – which culminates in the marriage of the royal couple Theseus and Hippolyta, and the couples Hermia and Lysander, and Helena and Demetrius – to celebrate the marriage between Sir Thomas Heneage and the Countess of Southampton.

Sir John Fortescue, who probably only conformed to the new religion for form's sake, was not unknown to Shakespeare either. This is revealed by events from his later life. The Fortescues were a Catholic family with many branches, belonging to the lower nobility. One branch of the family lived near Stratford, and its members were patients of Shakespeare's son-in-law, Dr John Hall, who was a physician. Sir John Fortescue, Master of the Queen's Wardrobe, was the uncle of the long-term (Catholic) tenant of the eastern gatehouse of Blackfriars – also called John Fortescue. The eastern gatehouse was situated directly opposite the Queen's Wardrobe, and had been used for decades as a most important institution of the Catholic underground. Raids on this house by the aldermen and sheriffs of the City of London were almost always unsuccessful. The most plausible explanation for this would seem to be that the tenant of this gatehouse, John Fortescue, always received timely warning when danger was imminent. These warnings must have come from his powerful uncle and neighbour, Sir John Fortescue, who would have been fully informed about planned government raids and who, as Master of the Queen's Wardrobe, could have given well-disguised signals.

Shakespeare even seems to have had connections from quite early on with the Earl of Essex, whose meteoric rise to power at the court in the 1590s was due to his relationship with Elizabeth I. One connection was through Southampton, his patron and friend, who in turn was a close friend and confidant of Essex. Southampton not only became his co-conspirator but also a co-leader of the Essex Rebellion. Another connection was through the queen's lady-in-waiting, Elizabeth Vernon, Essex's cousin and ward, who became Shakespeare's mistress – and his 'Dark Lady' of the sonnets (see pp. 170–179). There are many indications that, towards the end of the century, Shakespeare pinned all his political hopes on the Earl of Essex.

One of Shakespeare's most important early contacts in London, whom the playwright would have sought out straightaway, was his fellow Stratford pupil and friend, Richard Field. Richard was the son of the dyer Henry Field, who had lived with his family in Stratford near Shakespeare's family home and who had close business and personal relations with John Shakespeare. The level of trust between the two families is shown by the fact that William's father was asked to produce an inventory of Henry Field's property after his death. Incidentally, this is further proof that, despite some claims to the contrary, John Shakespeare cannot have been illiterate.

In 1579, at the age of fifteen, after he had left Stratford Grammar School, Richard moved from Stratford to London, where he completed a seven-year apprenticeship with the respected printer Thomas Vautrollier. When Vautrollier died in 1587, Richard married his widow and, by doing so, inherited the best printing business in England (*Fig. 61*). The successful London career of his Stratford schoolfriend was a stroke of luck for Shakespeare. Indeed, it was Field who printed the narrative poems *Venus and Adonis* and *The Rape of Lucrece* in 1593 and 1594. These poems made a stir, not only in literary circles in London, but even in educated circles beyond the capital. They made Shakespeare's name and won him the patronage and eventually the friendship of the third Earl of Southampton.

Fig. 61 – An Elizabethan printing press.

THE START OF SHAKESPEARE'S LITERARY CAREER

In comparison with most writers living in London in the early 1590s – with the exception of Thomas Lodge – Shakespeare had an exceptionally extensive and sophisticated knowledge of the world. He had received an excellent education and was well travelled, visiting France and Italy, and probably Spain and Navarre, through his contacts with Parsons. In terms of his knowledge and experience, he was very much the equal of his fellow playwrights such as Christopher Marlowe, Robert Greene, George Peele, Thomas Lodge and Thomas Nashe. In terms of rhetoric and stagecraft, his education was, if anything, superior to that of his fellow writers. Like William Shakespeare, Marlowe, Greene, Peele, Lodge and Nashe were also from artisan or middle-class families, but all had attended one of the two English universities. Only Thomas Kyd, son of a London scrivener, had no university education.

Shakespeare's life before 1592 had been exciting and dangerous, but he had remained discreetly out of the public eye, particularly during the 'lost years'. His career was about to take him straight into the limelight and bring him lasting fame.

When William Shakespeare entered the world of the London theatre, he excited both attention and envy. In April 1592, he was twenty-eight-years-old and somehow managed to put his finger on the pulse of the citizens of the nation's capital. His works appealed to practically all levels of society – noblemen, wealthy merchants, craftsmen, apprentices and servants. The trilogy of *Henry VI*, presumably his first work, won him exceptional popularity, much to the annoyance of his possible collaborators Greene and Peele. For seven years he had worked for English crypto-Catholics and Catholics-in-exile and had to lead a secret life. Now he was outshining all the established London dramatists – with the exception of Marlowe. These dramatists were smug about their academic education at Oxford or Cambridge but the middle-class young man from Stratford-upon-Avon had not only had more experience of the world, but was also privileged with regard to his specific theatrical training. Although a newcomer to the professional London stage, he confidently employed the theory and practice he had learnt during his excellent academic education on the Continent. These skills included the ability to adapt historical material for the stage, with a disregard for the classical Aristotelian unities of place, time and action. The latter found its expression in combining the elements of comedy and tragedy, and in preferring a quick succession of scenes and events that were often far removed from one another in terms of time and space.

Most of our knowledge of Shakespeare's presence and reception in London in 1592 is based on information provided by the above-mentioned writer and scholar, Robert Greene, who sharply attacked a new colleague (Shakespeare) as an 'upstart crow'. In contrast to the scene in which Greene deals with the young boastful actor whose encoded language with regard to his identity as well as his activities and whereabouts during the last seven years has been overlooked by previous Shakespeare commentators (with the exception of A.L. Rowse who had already suggested that the young actor was probably Shakespeare), the target of Greene's massive attack in *Groatsworth of Wit* on a most successful young colleague of his has long been known as Shakespeare. The Irish Shakespeare scholar Edmond Malone (1741-1812) was apparently the first to notice the allusion. Greene writes:

> Yes trust them not: for there is an up-start Crow, beautified with our feathers, that with his Tygers hart wrapt in a Players hyde, supposes he is as well able to bombast out a blanke verse as the best of you: and beeing an absolute *Johannes fac totum*, is in his owne conceit the onely Shake-scene in a countrey.

In the reference 'Tygers hart wrapt in a Players hyde', Greene is alluding to a line in Act I, scene 4 of Shakespeare's history *Henry VI (Part 3)*:

> O tiger's heart, wrapp'd in a woman's hide!

'Shake-scene' is clearly a reference to Shakespeare's name, and his ability to move and enthuse his public, a fact that Greene resented. Up until then, Greene had been the focus of attention in the London literary scene. His abuse was levelled at the man who challenged his dominance – William Shakespeare.

A glance at the programme of the Rose Theatre for 1592 proves that Greene had good cause to be envious of Shakespeare. The theatre had been closed in 1591 due to the Plague, but the theatre company known as Lord Strange's Men was given permission to resume the performance of public plays on 19 February 1592. The Privy Council sympathised with the Thames watermen who had had to suffer a severe loss of earnings when the theatre closed, since they relied on the large numbers of playgoers who needed to be ferried across to Southwark.

One of the plays performed by Strange's Men was Greene's sensationalist comedy *The Honorable History of Friar Bacon and Friar Bungay*[88]. The action takes place in the thirteenth century, and the main characters are the Franciscan monks of Oxford, Roger Bacon and Thomas Bungay, who make a brass head and claim that they can get it to speak with the help of the Devil. The head will speak its first words within a month, but both monks must constantly be present for the spell to work correctly. Friar Bacon assigns his servant Miles to stand watch day and night over the statue in his place. When the head speaks for the first time, uttering the words 'Time is', Miles considers the words not to be important enough to wake his master. Eventually, after also saying the phrases 'Time was' and 'Time is past', the head falls to the ground and breaks. Friar Bacon wakes up and is furious at his unreliable servant's behaviour. The play also has a romantic sub-plot involving the courtship of Margaret, the pretty daughter of a gamekeeper, by Lord Lacy and the Prince of Wales. Here were all the elements that would suit the public's taste, and the play promised to have a long run on the stage.

Yet the weekly review dated 26 February 1592 shows that Greene's *Friar Bacon* was not repeated. The plays performed included *Muly Mullocco*, *Orlando Furioso*, *The Spanish Comedy*, *Sir John Maundeville*, *Harry of Cornwall* and *The Jew of Malta*, Christopher Marlowe's popular drama of revenge. The weekly review dated 4 March 1592 reveals that Marlowe's play must have also been taken off. *Harry the Sixth* (clearly Shakespeare's history play *Henry VI*) was premiered on 3 March, as indicated by the diary entry 'Harey the vi'[89] written by the London theatre owner Philip Henslowe. *Harry the Sixth* was a great success at the Rose Theatre and featured regularly on the playbill – with the exception of the week 3-10 June 1592 – in the following weeks, until the theatre was compulsorily closed on 23 June: it did not re-open until Michaelmas (29 September). On this occasion, it was in response to an apprentices' riot that the authorities closed the theatres for several months. *Friar Bacon* played four times at the Rose Theatre between 19 February and 23 June, and the *Jew of Malta* played ten times, but *Harry the Sixth* was performed a total of fourteen times[90].

In early September 1592, Greene lay on his deathbed, and the theatre ban was still in effect. The once-celebrated dramatist would have had to come to terms with the fact that he had been put in the shade by the newcomer Shakespeare, whose genius he must surely have recognised and resented.

Groatsworth of Wit was entered in the Stationers' Register on 20 September 1592, three weeks after Greene's death. The Register – which also plays an important role in the collection and dating of Shakespeare's works – was the official listing of the printers' and booksellers' guilds, in which works to be published were entered. In the year 1586, the government had decreed that all books be licensed by the Archbishop of Canterbury and his assistants. This served not only to control the numerous English books being printed illegally at home and abroad – and in particular the Jesuit writings printed in England and distributed across the country – but also anything published by the members of the printers' guild, the Stationers' Company. The works were checked primarily for seditious material as well as for erotic content. The London printers, incorporated since 1557, were only allowed to produce books that had first been officially licensed in their register.

The archbishop's censors must have been generally displeased with what they found in Greene's *Groatsworth of Wit*, as it contained the author's declaration (though now repentant) that his life had been a wild, depraved mess, as well as a letter to his wife, whom he had completely neglected and deserted, and from whom he was now imploring forgiveness. The censors probably did not notice the oft-quoted attack on Shakespeare, which dealt a particularly heavy blow to the young author. When he wrote these words, Greene was already close to death, and the Elizabethans attached particular significance to the words of the dying. An important passage in the text of *Richard II* attests to this fact (Act II, scene 1), when the dying John of Gaunt lets those at his deathbed know:

> O, but they say the tongues of dying men
> Enforce attention like deep harmony.
> Where words are scarce, they are seldom spent in vain;
> For they breathe truth that breathe their words in pain.
> [...]
> More are men's ends mark'd than their lives before.

Greene not only attacked Shakespeare for his arrogance; he apparently also insinuated that he was guilty of plagiarism, that the 'upstart crow' had been 'beautified with our feathers'. The printer Henry Chettle (*c.* 1560-1607), whose press had issued Greene's pamphlet, restored Shakespeare's good name. Himself a successful playwright in later years, Chettle, who knew his way around the London theatre scene, defended himself against the charge that he had played a part in Greene's text. His pamphlet *Kind-Harts Dreame*[91], registered on 8 December 1592, contains an address to the reader in which he apologises for Greene's attacks on Shakespeare, as if they had been his own fault. Chettle also explains that it had been his observation that the quality of Shakespeare's conduct was in no way inferior to the excellent quality of his work. In addition, he explains that:

> The other [Shakespeare], whome at that time I did not so much spare, as since I wish I had, ... (especially in such a case) the Author [Greene] beeing dead, that I did not, I am as sory, as if the originall fault had beene my fault, because my selfe have seene his [Shakespeare's] demeanor no less civill than he exelent in the qualitie he professes: Besides, divers of worship have reported his uprightnes of dealing, which argues his honesty, and his facetious grace in writing, that aprooves his Art.[92]

Chettle's statements provide excellent documentary evidence that Shakespeare's extraordinary literary talent had already made a sensational impact on the elite at the very start of his career as a dramatist and poet. This brilliant beginning came to an abrupt halt after only a few weeks in early March 1592. As previously mentioned, the London apprentice riot caused a theatre ban, which remained in place until Michaelmas of the same year. Even before this period had expired, there was another outbreak of the Plague and the London theatres remained closed for a long time.

On 7 September 1592, the epidemic claimed its first victims. The depressing statistics produced on 31 December 1592 show that of 25,886 deaths in the capital, 11,503 were recorded as being due to the Black Death. When the number of Plague victims decreased slightly in the winter, the Lord Strange's Men were once more permitted to perform at the Rose Theatre, starting on 30 December. However, this was only to last until 2 February 1593, because the Plague returned with a vengeance from 21 January 1593, and a new theatre ban was issued on 28 January. Throughout 1593, London was afflicted by the epidemic, August being especially bad. In the week of 30 July to 5 August, there were 1,603 reported deaths, 1,130 of them from the Plague. A total of 1700 to 1800 victims were claimed by the Black Death in London and the surrounding district in the week of 7 August to 14 August 1593. On Boxing Day of that year, the Earl of Sussex's men resumed their performances at the Rose Theatre, but fearing a new outbreak of the epidemic, the authorities issued a renewed ban for London on 3 February 1594. This also included a five-mile radius around the capital. On 6 February 1594, the Rose Theatre was closed, where fourteen days previously, on 24 January 1594, Shakespeare's sensational tragedy *Titus Andronicus* had premiered. The drama took the form of the well known 'revenge plays' of the time. Another example of the genre is *The Spanish Tragedy*, by Thomas Kyd in which sheer madness – murder, suicide, a public execution, and even a seemingly well-bred lady biting out a gentleman's tongue – were brought to the stage for the sensation-hungry Elizabethan public. In similar vein, Shakespeare's play also presented heart-stopping acts of villainy – a rape, mutilation and even cannibalism.

During one of the first performances of *Titus Andronicus* in the year 1594, the young Cambridge graduate, Henry Peacham (*c.* 1573–*c.* 1643) made a sketch of the opening scene (*Fig. 62a*). This extremely valuable pen-and-ink drawing, which was only discovered in 1907, is the oldest preserved artist's representation of a performance of a Shakespearean drama. This drawing is kept in the library of the Marquess of Bath at Longleat in Wiltshire. It illustrates the costumes, props and stagecraft of the time, making it clear that the production complied with the rules of performance later described in D. Franciscus Lang's *Dissertatio de actione scenica* (1727) which were more or less

Fig. 62a – Pen and ink drawing by Henry Peacham of the first scene of Shakespeare's early revenge drama *Titus Andronicus*, made immediately after or during a performance of the play. It dates from the year 1594 and is the earliest known illustration of a Shakespeare play. Recent interdisciplinary research and a criminological image comparison*5 have revealed that the role of the kneeling Tamora, Queen of the Goths (right), was played by Richard Burbage, Shakespeare's friend. The role of the victorious Roman general, Titus Andronicus (opposite Tamora), must have been played by Shakespeare himself and Aaron (far right) most probably by the comic actor William Kempe*6. At Christmas 1594, Kempe, Shakespeare and Burbage performed before Queen Elizabeth I (see *Fig. 70* and p. 116).

compulsory for actors of the Baroque theatre. For example, the sketch illustrates the *crux scenica*, a standard method of placing the feet:

> When placing the feet [...] care must be taken to ensure that they never point in the same direction, but instead are ostensibly angled away from each other on the ground [...]. [93]

The most fascinating thing about Peacham's drawing, however, is that it presents for the first time the individual Elizabethan actors who are portrayed so realistically that they can be identified. What, among other things, proves that Peacham drew this scene at a contemporary production with live (male) actors is that he depicts Tamora, the play's female lead, with a clearly discernible Adam's apple. Tamora, Queen of the Goths, who is kneeling in the illustration, is played by Richard Burbage. This was the conclusion drawn from a forensic examination of the sketch, commissioned by the present author and performed by experts of the German Bundeskriminalamt (BKA=CID) in early 1995, comparing the magnified head of Tamora and an authentic portrait of Burbage (*Figs. 62 a-c*)[94].

There are several indications that the role of the victorious Roman commander, Titus Andronicus, was played by none other than Shakespeare himself. This is suggested by the similarity between the shape of Titus's head when magnified, as well as his facial features, and the likenesses of Shakespeare as authenticated by the present author: namely the Darmstadt Shakespeare death mask, the Chandos and Flower portraits but also the Droeshout engraving[95] the authenticity of which was confirmed by Ben Jonson and appeared in the First Folio edition of Shakespeare's plays, published in 1623. This claim is also supported by the fact that the drawing shows a scene from one of Shakespeare's own plays being

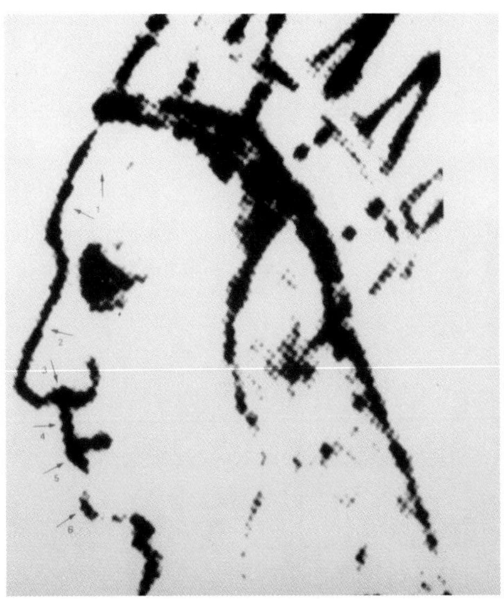

1. Forehead
2. Bridge of nose
3. Nostril
4. Upper lip
5. Lower lip
6. Chin

Fig. 62b – The head of Tamora. An image comparison made by the specialist Reinhardt Altman of the German Federal Bureau of Criminal Investigation (BKA=CID) in 1995 proves that six facial features in this illustration and in *Fig. 62c* (Richard Burbage) are a perfect match*[7]. The accuracy of Peacham's drawing is also demonstrated by the clearly recognisable Adam's apple.

1. Forehead
2. Bridge of nose
3. Nostril
4. Upper lip
5. Lower lip
6. Chin

Fig. 62c – The head of Richard Burbage showing the matching facial features*[8].

performed. Furthermore, it is a fact that Shakespeare and Richard Burbage were the leading players in the Chamberlain's Men, a theatre company that had been formed in the year 1594.

During the long periods when the London theatres remained closed, the playwrights and actors were more or less unemployed. Shakespeare evidently used these times to make his mark as a poet, poetry being a genre that enjoyed the highest esteem in Renaissance England. He wrote the narrative poems *Venus and Adonis* (1593) and *The Rape of Lucrece* (1594) and dedicated them to the young Earl of Southampton, thereby gaining his patronage and friendship.

During these unplanned breaks from the theatre, Shakespeare further devoted himself to the art of the sonnet, particularly highly esteemed by his contemporaries. It was a fashion in poetry that found special favour among the cultivated literary circles of the English capital.

On 1 June 1591, a hugely influential work had been published in London: the sonnet cycle *Astrophel and Stella* by Sir Philip Sidney, which contained a preface by the young Thomas Nashe. Here Nashe made the claim to other poets and poetasters that the author surpassed all others in his craft. This was no overstatement. Sidney's sonnet cycle inspired numerous imitations by English poets and generated a great wave of sonnet compositions. Shakespeare himself took to heart Sidney's exhortation at the end of the first sonnet in *Astrophel*: 'look in thy heart and write.' His own sonnets were not only deeply personal in nature; they also set new standards for this verse form.

Since Shakespeare belonged to the Catholic underground, his career as a dramatist would have opened up to him the opportunity to offer subliminal clues to his audience to the suffering of their oppressed and persecuted Catholic

Fig. 63 – Portrait of William Shakespeare (The Chandos Portrait) in the National Portrait Gallery, London. The authenticity of this painting was proved in 1995, 1998 and again in 2006 by interdisciplinary scientific research. Criminological forensic image comparisons with the authenticated portrait engraving of Shakespeare in the First Folio edition from 1623 (the Droeshout engraving, *Fig. 90b*) and the Flower Portrait (*Fig. 106*), carried out by BKA specialist Reinhardt Altmann, proved that seventeen facial features are in agreement and that there are no discrepencies. The montages of these images generated by so-called Trick Image Differentiation Technique also applied by Altmann in 1995 and again in 1998 (including the Davenant bust, *Fig. 1*), too show that they form a perfect match. Investigations by medical experts revealed that the symptoms of illness in the portraits were also consistent. The progression of these symptoms indicates that the sitter of the Chandos portrait must be much younger than the one in the Flower portrait, the timespan ranging from approximately ten to fifteen years. Hence it would be safe to say that this portrait depicts the playwright at the age of about thirty to thirty-five (cf. the author's book *The True Face of William Shakespeare*, London, 2006, p. 88).

countrymen. Yet, so far as is known, contemporary sources contain no references to Shakespeare's involvement in Catholic plots or acts of violence. Nor does he ever preach Catholicism in his writings. In his plays, however, there are numerous elements that point to his familiarity with Catholic views, customs, rites etc. Peter Milward's monograph *Shakespeare's Religious Background* (1973) supplies many examples of this.

The young Shakespeare had learned early on to escape the attentions of the State Church and government spies. He was well aware of the many hardships the Catholics had to suffer as a result of the new anti-Catholic penal laws. He knew that they were increasingly deprived of their rights and were often financially ruined. He also knew that shockingly high numbers of them were robbed of their liberties and their lives. Shakespeare had experienced the execution of clergymen and lay priests from his immediate environment (including Robert Debdale and Thomas Cottom), and as a young man of sixteen in Lancashire, despite great danger to his own life, had accepted the responsibility of a secret mission. On the other hand, Shakespeare seems to have been familiar with the tricks and ruses to which the recusants resorted when it came to outwitting even high representatives of the Church of England and the authorities of the State with regard to marriage ceremonies, baptisms and inventing plausible excuses for not taking part in Anglican divines services. In his earlier life, he had seen the world mostly from a more sheltered Catholic point of view. As an inhabitant of London, he was now exposed to the Protestant centres of power, having the opportunity to become closely acquainted with them and to see them in action: the Court, Parliament, the State Church, Puritanism, the law courts, and of course the aldermen of the City of London. Their puritanical views placed them on the extreme fringes of Protestantism, and they were hostile to the theatre.

NARRATIVE POEMS DEDICATED TO THE EARL OF SOUTHAMPTON

In 1593, William Shakespeare (*Fig. 63*) published his narrative poem *Venus and Adonis* (*Fig. 64*), based on Ovid's *Metamorphoses*, and became famous as a poet practically overnight. The printer and publisher – his schoolfriend from Stratford, Richard Field – had created what we might call a print masterpiece. This literary work was dedicated to Henry Wriothesley, the third Earl of Southampton (*Fig. 65*).

The young earl was intelligent and well educated. He had studied at Cambridge, excelling in the field of literature. He owned large estates (*Fig. 66*) and had already distinguished himself as a generous patron of poets and men of letters. The English dramatist Nicholas Rowe (1674-1718), a lawyer by profession, who first practised in the Middle Temple and later became poet laureate, recounted that Southampton had once given Shakespeare £1000 – probably to thank him for the narrative poems dedicated to him. Rowe, who records this in his biography *Life of Shakespeare* (1709), relied on the testimony of Sir William Davenant (1606-1668), a dramatist and poet laureate who admired Shakespeare. He was also Shakespeare's godson, possibly even his biological son (of which more later). There is no reason to doubt the accuracy of this tradition.

Like his family, Southampton adhered to the old faith. After the anti-Catholic penal law of January, 1581 came into effect, his father had been thrown into the Tower of London as a recusant. In August of the same year, Southampton's father ran into even greater difficulties when the Privy Council learned about his connections with Edmund Campion, who was executed for 'high treason' on 1 December 1581.

The earls of Southampton belonged to the majority of the English peers who had remained Catholic. A census dating from 1567, preserved in the Vatican archives, verifies that thirty-two members of the English high nobility stood firmly by their Catholic beliefs, twenty more sympathised very strongly with Catholicism, and only fifteen were active Protestants[96].

The Wriothesleys, however, were not members of the old aristocracy. Thomas Wriothesley, first Earl of Southampton and Baron Titchfield, was the grandfather of Shakespeare's patron and, as chancellor to Henry VIII, had personally participated, in the name of the king, in iconoclasm and the Dissolution of the Monasteries. He was rewarded for his efforts with the title of earl and extensive estates. Under Elizabeth I, his widow turned the family home, the former Titchfield Abbey (*Fig.* 66), into a secret bastion of Catholicism. The magnificent tombs of the Earl of Southampton's parents and grandparents, constructed in the 1590s, were made in Gheerart Janssen the Elder's sculptor's workshop in Southwark. Gheerart Janssen the Younger was later to create Shakespeare's tomb. The young earl, Shakespeare's patron, is depicted kneeling together with his sister Mary (*Fig.* 67). Many Catholic priests found refuge in Titchfield Abbey, before moving on to their next place of shelter, and priests also came and went at the earl's London residence in Holborn, Southampton House. In such an environment, Henry Wriothesley, second Earl of Southampton, became a firm believer and advocate of the old faith. Grappling with a moral conflict after the excommunication of Elizabeth I, he sought advice from the Catholic bishop John Leslie, Mary, Queen of Scots' representative in London, asking if he was obliged to obey his queen (in religious matters). He was arrested in 1571 and imprisoned in the Tower for eighteen months, although he did have a private apartment there, and was allowed to receive visitors. His petitions to Lord Burghley and the queen finally achieved the desired result. On 1 May 1573, the second Earl of Southampton was released from prison, but was immediately detained again at the house of William More. Since the earl's son, Henry, later to become Shakespeare's patron, was born

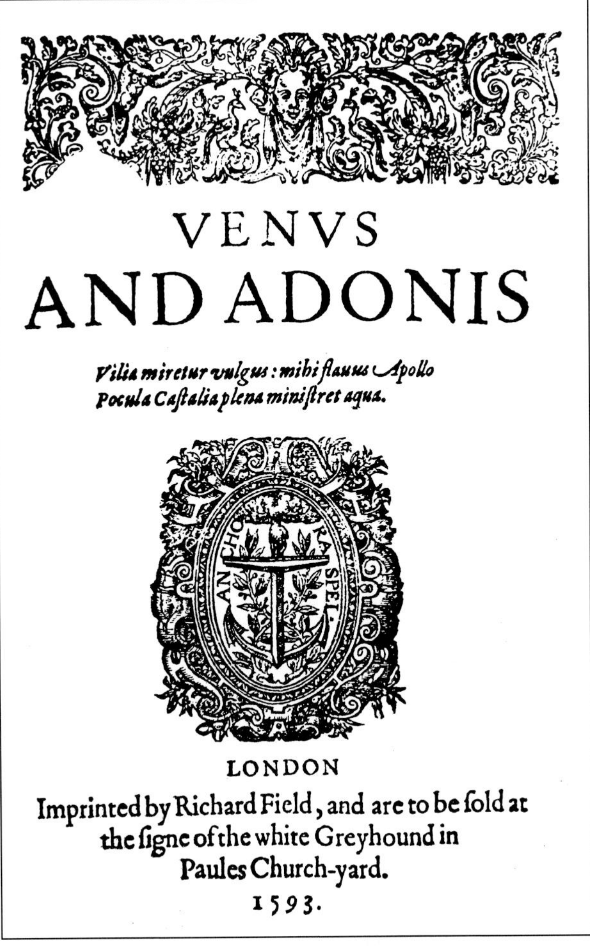

VENVS
AND ADONIS

Vilia miretur vulgus: mihi flauus Apollo
Pocula Caſtalia plena miniſtret aqua.

AN HOR KA SPEL

LONDON
Imprinted by Richard Field, and are to be ſold at
the ſigne of the white Greyhound in
Paules Church-yard.
1593.

Fig. 64 – William Shakespeare, *Venus and Adonis* (1593). The title page of the first edition of Shakespeare's narrative poem, printed by the playwright's Stratford schoolfriend Richard Field. This poem was particularly popular among students at the universities of Oxford and Cambridge, and frequently reprinted even during Shakespeare's lifetime. Shakespeare dedicated this poem to the young Catholic Earl of Southampton obviously in an attempt to win him over as a patron. Shakespeare refers to Southampton's physical appearance (*Fig. 65*) and compares him to Adonis.

approximately five months after the earl's release from prison, namely on 6 October 1573, he must have been conceived in the Tower. His life would take him back to the Tower in the February of 1601 since, after the Essex Rebellion, Southampton almost shared the fate of the Earl of Essex. His death sentence was commuted, however, to life imprisonment in the Tower through the intercession of his mother

Fig. 66 – Titchfield Abbey, near Portsmouth, residence of the Earl of Southampton and a former abbey, converted into a manor house. It is now in ruins, but its former splendour is still in evidence. Shakespeare probably visited Titchfield Abbey several times as a guest of his patron.

and his wife, the latter being the queen's former lady-in-waiting, Elizabeth Vernon, Essex's cousin. When James I ascended the throne in 1603, he immediately granted amnesty to the earl. The new king, whose succession Essex and Southampton had secretly supported at the end of the reign of Elizabeth I, restored all of the earl's former rights. Shakespeare's patron now played a prominent role at Court. He later abandoned the Catholic faith and became a Protestant, probably out of gratitude for the benefits he had received from the king. His Catholic compatriots – including, as it would seem, William Shakespeare – resented him for this, and his contemporaries nicknamed the Earl of Southampton 'The Malcontent'.

The emblem on the title page of *Venus and Adonis* shows an anchor dominated by the form of the cross. It is framed by the slogan: '*Anchora spei*' ('anchor of hope'). Field's mentor, the printer Thomas Vautrollier, had used this emblem once before in 1579 on the title page of the influential translation of Plutarch's *The Lives of the Noble Grecians and Romans*, which Thomas North had translated from the French edition published by Jacques Amyot. In the context of the life upon

Fig. 65 – Portrait of Henry Wriothesley, third Earl of Southampton. After the publication of Shakespeare's narrative poem *Venus and Adonis* in 1593, the young earl became Shakespeare's patron. It was certainly no later than 1594, after the publication of Shakespeare's second narrative poem *The Rape of Lucrece*, likewise dedicated to Southampton, that the two also became friends. Recent research has revealed that Southampton is the noble 'Friend' in Shakespeare's sonnets. He later became Shakespeare's rival in love (see pp. 168–185).

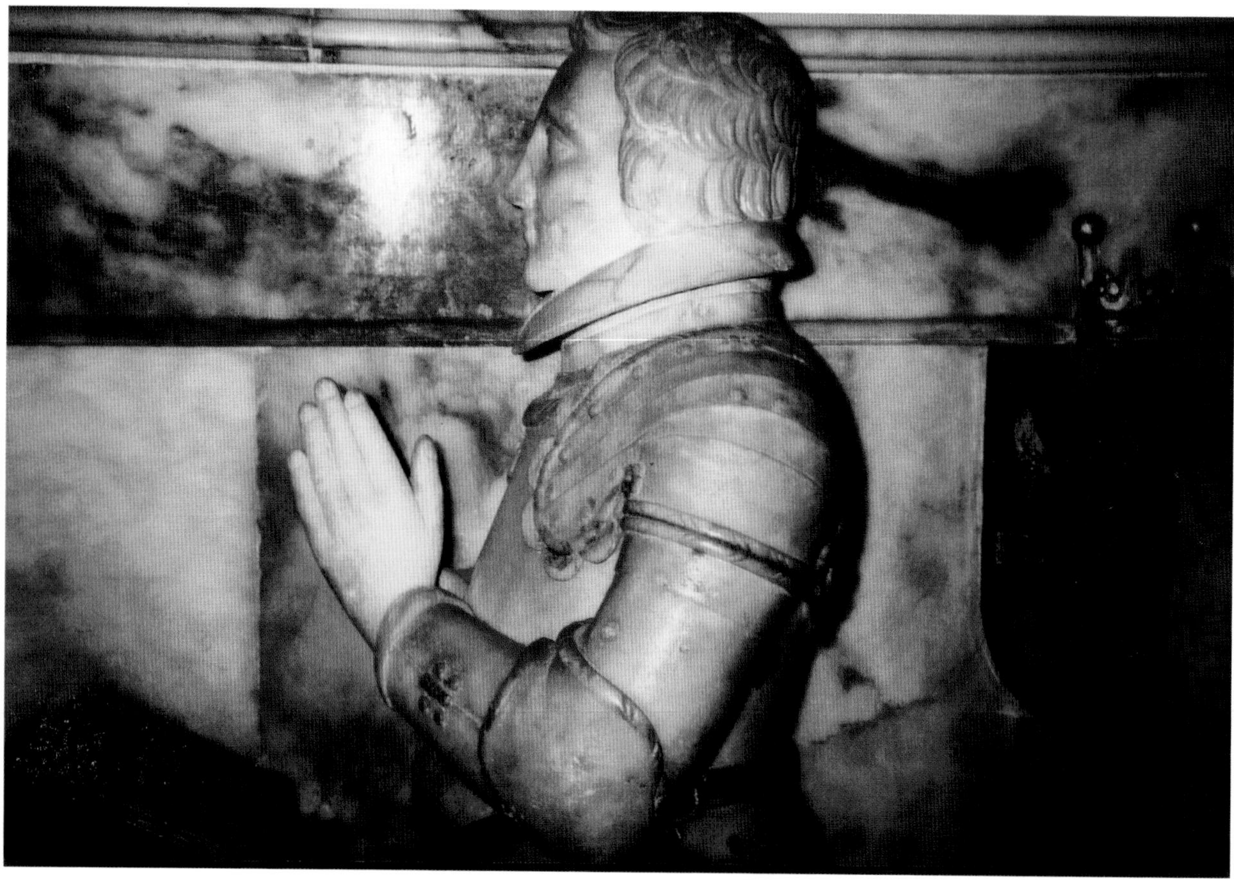

Fig. 67 – The third Earl of Southampton kneeling at the tomb of his parents and grandparents in St Peter's Church, Titchfield.

which William Shakespeare had just embarked, the images and text acquire a meaning that can be interpreted as relating to his new personal situation and his clandestine activity in the English Catholic underground. Did Shakespeare see Southampton as the 'Anchor of Hope' of English Catholicism? Initially, this would seem incompatible with the erotic content of *Venus and Adonis*. But as a newcomer to the English capital, Shakespeare was confronted with the need not only to make a name for himself with his poetic debut, but also to choose a topic that would sweep the young earl off his feet and enthral him, so as to be able to acquire him as a future patron.

Southampton was then only nineteen-years-old and a remarkably handsome young man with a narrow face, bright blue eyes and curls that hung down over his shoulders. This can be seen from his portraits, including the well-known miniature. In other words, the young earl was an Adonis and a heart throb, pursued by smitten females. His charms also attracted members of his own sex; this emerges from reports of alleged or actual events that took place in a field camp during the Earl of Essex's Ireland campaign of 1599. If women chased him, stalking him as it were, then this was not unusual in England at the time, particularly in the case of good-looking young men. On 10 January 1598, a Mrs Frances Pranell – on behalf of Katherine Howard – inquired 'whether Southampton will love her better or not' and what was going to happen with her. Some weeks later, Pranell, again on behalf of Katherine, asked whether she was to his liking and if she should hurry down to the country. The earl's reply was abrupt and dismissive. He made it plain that he wanted to know nothing of

Katherine and that he was annoyed by her importuning, in spite of the 'country pleasures' she had proposed[97]. At this time, he was already engaged to Elizabeth Vernon, a lady-in-waiting to the queen whom Shakespeare also loved. Southampton was irritated with his monarch and was about to leave for a trip to France.

Southampton, the beautiful, initially shy young man, had over the years persistently refused to commit himself, even to the match his foster-father, Lord Burghley, had intended for him, a stance that caused him to lose a great deal of property which went to Burghley's coffers. When Shakespeare wrote his first narrative poem and dedicated it to Southampton, he fashioned its main character in subtle ways ensuring, however, that the young earl would recognise himself, and that the reader would also see the parallels and be able to identify Adonis as Southampton.

Southampton could provide the young poet with an entry into the intellectual courtly society that sponsored theatre and literature, and could give him an insight into powerful decision-making circles. After the death of his father, Southampton had lived for some years as a 'royal ward' in the household of William Cecil, the queen's most favoured counsellor, who treated the boy like a son but also tried (in vain) to make use of him with regard to his matchmaking strategies. The young earl may well have been aware of the personal and political opinions of the leading Elizabethan statesman, who was responsible for the rigid anti-Catholic legislation. Since Southampton, moreover, became a close friend of the Earl of Essex, whom he idolised and in whose later conspiracy he was to play a significant role, Shakespeare could also expect that with Southampton as his patron, he would have access to Essex who, once he had become a Privy Councillor, possessed power and influence and, in the eyes of his contemporaries, seemed destined for even greater things.

Essex was notable for his religious tolerance of non-conformists; Puritans and especially Catholics. This may have prompted Shakespeare to pin his hopes on Essex in the late 1590s. In order to win over Southampton as a patron, Shakespeare used his poetic skills and flattery, to which the young earl was especially receptive.

Venus and Adonis was entered in the Stationers' Register in April 1593. In that year, Christopher Marlowe's narrative poem, *Hero and Leander*, probably the most impressive example of English Renaissance love poetry, was also published. Its notable characteristics are an outspoken treatment of erotic situations, the precise observation and description of natural beauty and a highly ornamental style. These same elements can be found in Shakespeare's *Venus and Adonis*, and although modern critics deem the work to be nothing more than 'a string upon which Shakespeare hung his rhetorical jewels'[98], it was eagerly devoured by the students at Oxford and Cambridge as well as the law students at the Inns of Court. The anonymous author of *The Return from Parnassus*[99], a play performed at Cambridge University, mocks the students' fascination and has the rapturous undergraduate named Gullio say:

> Let this duncified worlde esteeme of Spenser and Chaucer, I'le worshipp sweet Mr. Shakespeare, and to honoure him I will lay his Venus and Adonis under my pillowe.

The Cambridge scholar Gabriel Harvey (*c.* 1550-1631), a close friend of Edmund Spenser, stated that with this poem, Shakespeare had struck a chord with (academic) youth. According to Harvey, young people greatly enjoyed Shakespeare's *Venus and Adonis*, adding, however, that *The Rape of Lucrece* and his tragedy *Hamlet, Prince of Denmark*, had the wherewithal to please their wise elders.

The second edition of *Venus and Adonis* was published in 1594 and reprinted again in 1595. Further reprints appeared in 1596, 1599, 1602, 1610, 1617 and 1620. How Shakespeare's celebrated narrative poem found its way into print at all under the strict controls of Archbishop Whitgift is puzzling, for the archbishop campaigned heavily against erotic poetry influenced by Ovid. Did Shakespeare manage to outwit Whitgift once again, as he had in 1582 to obtain his marriage licence, when the archbishop was still the Bishop of Worcester? In any case, it is odd that the most senior representatives of the Anglican Church, with their fervent advocacy of strict discipline, propriety, decency, and morals should have permitted the printing of this frivolous and liberal narrative poem. As has been stated, Whitgift could not censor all texts himself, and used others to assist him. They may have been less than thorough in their task and the explosive power of the work may have gone unnoticed. Alternatively, the archbishop, who in the case of *Venus and Adonis* had actually issued the printing licence in his own hand, may have been asked by a member of the Privy Council to permit publication, presumably using a white lie as to the true content of the work. Since Shakespeare's first work of poetry was dedicated to Southampton, it is possible that Sir Thomas Heneage spoke out in favour of it from the ranks of the members of the Privy Council. Sir Thomas, as mentioned before, had married Southampton's mother, the dowager countess, and so had become the young earl's stepfather.

Sir John Fortescue may also have advocated publication. Sir John was the uncle of his namesake, John Fortescue, who belonged to the Catholic underground, and was the tenant of the eastern Blackfriars gatehouse in the 1590s, and indeed right up to the Gunpowder Plot of 1605. Shakespeare acquired this gatehouse in 1613. Sir John seems not only to have tolerated but also to have assisted and covered his relative's activities, i.e. harbouring priests in the eastern Blackfriars gatehouse. With his Catholic underground connections, Shakespeare must have known the tenant of this gatehouse and its special function. Unfortunately, it is no longer possible to determine which of these avenues finally led to the procurement of the printing licence for *Venus and Adonis*, but the explanation that the lubricious contents of this work completely escaped Whitgift and/or his staff does not appear plausible. Furthermore, the fact that Shakespeare's narrative poem was extremely popular in university as well as courtly and literary circles, particularly among London law students, and that it was frequently reprinted, suggests that there were forces in the Privy Council that supported its diffusion, even against the will and the interests of Archbishop Whitgift.

In his dedication to the 'Right Honourable Henrie Wriothesley, Earle of Southampton, and Baron Titchfield', Shakespeare's approach to the aristocrat is not only deferential, but also self-assured; for in addition to hoping to comply with Southampton's wishes, the author always had his sights on the world's judgment and expectations. The poet continues that he does neither know how to prevent that his unpolished lines would offend his lordship nor how the world would censor him as the author. Only if it pleased his lordship, would he consider himself highly praised, and would he vow to reap the benefits of all his idle hours until he could honour him (Southampton) with a 'graver labour.' But if this first child of his imagination should prove deformed, he was sorry that it had such a noble godfather.

Venus and Adonis was composed using six-line stanzas and the rhyme scheme ababcc. Edmund Spenser had used this pattern in *Astrophel*, an elegy on the death of Sir Philip Sidney that was written *c.* 1590 and published in 1595; Thomas Lodge had previously employed it in his erotic poem *Scilla's Metamorphoses* (1589).

In *Venus and Adonis*, the influence of Ovid, the Elizabethans' 'schoolmaster' in erotica and physical love, subjects that are generally treated with amazing frankness in Elizabethan poetry, is encountered at virtually every step of the way. Venus falls hopelessly in love with the beautiful Adonis. Her cheeks glow bright red with desire and longing, and she tries to whet the young man's appetite for the pleasures of carnal love. All that Adonis loves is the hunt, however. He has no more than a contemptuous smile to spare for the arts of love. The goddess's ferocious advances cause him to blush with shame, and he tries to resist her. But Venus is unrelenting, and is undaunted. She tears Adonis from his horse and takes possession of him.

> Backward she push'd him, as she would be thrust,
> And govern'd him in strength, though not in lust.
> So soon was she along as he was down,
> Each leaning on their elbows and their hips:

The goddess now initiates the love play. She strokes the young man's cheeks, and when he starts to scold her, she silences his lips with kisses. As the hungry eagle hastily devours its prey, so Venus seems to devour the young man, kissing not only his lips, but also his brow, his cheeks, and his chin. Adonis is practically her prisoner, a defenceless and shy victim of her desire. As if that were not enough, Venus immediately expects her partner to participate actively in the play, but he is by no means ready. The goddess attempts to use arguments: 'Thou wast begot; to get it is thy duty'. In this way, she shows him one of the ways which, in the Elizabethan view, it was possible to attain immortality, namely, to produce children and to live on through them. All this falls on deaf ears. Even the information that nature demands procreation proves fruitless with him.

> By law of nature thou art bound to breed,
> That thine may live when thou thyself art dead;
> And so, in spite of death, thou dost survive,
> In that thy likeness still is left alive.

Venus finally begs for a kiss from the shy boy and begins to insult him fiercely when he still fails to be seduced by her:

> Fie, lifeless picture, cold and senseless stone,
> Well-painted idol, image dun and dead.

Adonis rejects her importuning and insults and attempts to free himself. Venus then changes her strategy and offers to instruct him in love. The lesson is simple, and once learned, it is never forgotten. The young man answers that he does not know love and does not want to know it. It was, as he has heard, a life in death.

This is the first allusion to the tragic, fatal outcome of the poem. Death will overcome the handsome youth as he is out hunting, when a wild boar sinks its long, pointed tusks into his soft abdomen. With dark presentiments, Venus already anticipates her beloved's gruesome end. The boar's actual mortal blow is associated in her imagination with the act of carnal lust which before she had longed for in vain. After his death, the goddess performs a symbolic and ritual union with her dead lover by staining her face with his blood. The poet describes in detail how Venus gradually comes to a visceral 'understanding' of incontrovertible fate. She looks at the dead youth's pale lips and takes his cold hand in hers. She whispers a sad story in his ear, as if he could still hear her words of great sorrow. She lifts the lids from his eyes, which are now dark, like two burned-out lamps.

In *Venus and Adonis*, the elements of Catholic thought, to which Shakespeare alluded so frequently in his works, seem to have been temporarily abandoned. The Catholics appear to have reproached Shakespeare for his errant ways. In an essay significantly entitled *Saint Peter's Complaynt*, alluding to Rome, the Jesuit and poet Robert Southwell (born *c.* 1561, executed 1595) admonished the poets of England, ordering them to use their abilities for religious, rather than profane matters. Although a general exhortation, it seems to have been aimed primarily at Shakespeare. Christopher Devlin makes this claim in his biography, *The Life of Robert Southwell, Poet and Martyr* (1956). It has been disputed, but Devlin's assumption is backed by Southwell's dedication, which he used to make his main argument. Significantly, this dedication was not published until 1616 – the year of Shakespeare's death – for during the dramatist's lifetime, a dedication from an English Jesuit, and thus a traitor, would have been much too dangerous. Southwell's dedication read: 'To my worthy good cousin, Master W.S.' Devlin's interpretation is supported by the fact that Shakespeare was indeed an active member of the Catholic underground, yet his *Venus and Adonis* and *Titus Andronicus* seriously neglected the religious dimension of his work. Southwell's admonition appears to have had some effect, because Shakespeare's second narrative poem, *The Rape of Lucrece* (*Fig. 68*), treats his topic in a highly moralistic way. This poem was published in 1594, one year after *Venus and Adonis*. Field, the printer, produced it with the greatest care, and gave it the same title page emblem, the anchor of hope.

The Rape of Lucrece, which may be the poem the poet had announced one year previously as the 'more serious work', is divided into seven-line stanzas using the rhyme scheme ab abb cc. It is also based on a story by Ovid, and is dedicated to the earl. The wording of the dedication reveals that close ties of friendship had already developed between the poet and his high-ranking patron:

> The love I dedicate to your lordship is without end; whereof this pamphlet, without beginning, is but a superfluous moiety. The warrant I have of your honourable disposition, not the worth of my untutored lines, makes it assured of acceptance. What I have done is yours; what I have to do is yours; being part in all I have, devoted yours. Were my worth greater, my duty would show greater; meantime, as it is, it is bound to your lordship, to whom I wish long life, still lengthened with all happiness.

By 1640, *The Rape of Lucrece* had been re-published a total of seven times, and was exceeded in popularity only by *Venus and*

LVCRECE.

AN CHORA SPEI

LONDON.
Printed by Richard Field, for Iohn Harriſon, and are
to be ſold at the ſigne of the white Greyhound
in Paules Churh yard. 1594.

Fig. 68 – William Shakespeare, *The Rape of Lucrece* (1594). Title page of the first edition. After the publication of *Venus and Adonis*, Shakespeare was – as it appears – secretly admonished by the Jesuit Robert Southwell. The poet obviously followed this advice and authored a 'more serious' work. It deals with the honour of the noble Roman wife Lucrece, who kills herself after she is raped by Tarquin. This poem was also dedicated to the Earl of Southampton. The wording and tone of the dedication reveal that the poet and his noble patron had in the meantime become friends.

Adonis. The work is prefaced by a prose text under the title 'The Argument', summarising the contents and the essential elements of the plot. There is no doubt that it was written by Shakespeare, although it is his only text in prose, as Joseph Quincy Adams indicated in *A Life of William Shakespeare* (1930). Shakespeare's comprehensive twenty-eight-line exposé conveys a picture of a man who knew how to explain complicated matters in just a few, purposeful words. The wording is remarkably clear, precise and sophisticated, showing the author's skill in the composition of demanding texts.

The theme of *The Rape of Lucrece* is the virtue of a married woman. During the siege of Ardea by King Tarquin the Proud, high-ranking officers meet in the tent of the king's son, Sextus Tarquinius. After the meal, everyone praises the virtues of his own wife, and Colatanius surpasses all of the others with his paean of praise for the incomparable virtue of his wife, Lucrece. The soldiers steal back to Rome in secret, deciding to put their claims to the test, and it emerges that all the wives are pursuing their own pleasures – except Lucrece, who is found late at night at her spinning wheel. Overwhelmed by passion, Sextus Tarquinius steals into Lucrece's chamber, rapes her, and hurries away the next morning. Lucrece informs her father and her husband, and after requiring them to swear revenge, she stabs herself. The Romans determine to rid themselves of the monarchy altogether; the detested Tarquin dynasty is overthrown and banished, and thenceforward Rome is ruled by consuls.

In both *The Rape of Lucrece* and *Venus and Adonis*, Shakespeare predominantly uses imagery taken from nature. Thus, in describing Lucrece's immaculate beauty, Shakespeare writes:

> Her lily hand her rosy cheek lies under,
> Cozening the pillow of a lawful kiss;
> [...]
> Without the bed her other fair hand was,
> On the green coverlet; whose perfect white
> Show'd like an April daisy on the grass,
> With pearly sweat, resembling dew of night.
> [...]
> Her hair, like golden threads, play'd with her breath.

Tarquin the ravisher is compared to a hungry lion that first eyes its prey, then brutally carries out the deed:

> 'Lucrece,' quoth he, 'this night I must enjoy thee:
> If thou deny, then force must work my way,
> For in thy bed I purpose to destroy thee.'

The Rape of Lucrece not only offered Elizabethan readers an unusual example of virtuous female behaviour, but also a lesson about the consequences of grave dynastic wrongdoing. The example from Roman history seemed outwardly harmless, but it alluded to contemporary events. In boldly denouncing Tarquin's misdeeds, the poet uses evocative political metaphors. Sextus Tarquinius's infamous act is compared with that of a heinous usurper who overthrows the legitimate occupier of the throne.

The Rape of Lucrece is thus charged with political content, and Lucrece's death is ultimately not just a private matter; for the conclusion reveals that it was used as an exemplar by the polity. The dead Lucrece, still bleeding, is carried in a funeral procession through Rome in order to publicise Tarquin's dishonour. Moreover, the whole Tarquin family is condemned, with the consent and support of the Romans, to everlasting exile:

> The Romans plausibly did give consent
> To Tarquin's everlasting banishment.

For the English Catholics and Catholics-in-exile of the Elizabethan period, who suffered such persecution by the Crown and the Established Church, the expulsion of the tyrannical Roman family may have been comforting and – as expressed symbolically in the title emblem – an 'anchor of hope'. In the Renaissance, examples from the past were always used as patterns for the present. Furthermore, Shakespeare could be sure that the political rhetoric as well as the work's striking relevance to the present would be grasped by his patron and friend, the third Earl of Southampton.

THE LONDON THEATRES AND SHAKESPEARE'S ACTORS

During Elizabeth I's reign, a blossoming theatre culture developed, along with numerous venues and a staggering supply of new plays to amuse the London public. At the time, this was unique in Europe. One of Shakespeare's rival theatre companies premièred a total of thirty new plays in the 1594-95 season alone. Under James I, Elizabeth's successor, the English theatre continued to flourish. The American theatre historian T. J. King has counted no fewer than 276 dramas that were performed for the first time between 1599 and 1642 by professional actors on the English stage[100]. The well-known German Shakespeare scholar Ulrich Suerbaum succinctly describes the importance and popularity of this new cultural phenomenon as being 'theatre for every day, and theatre for every man'[101].

In the pre-Elizabethan period and even at the beginning of Elizabeth's reign, performances were generally held in the inner courtyards of London's five major inns, The Bell and the Cross Keys (both on Gracechurch Street), The Bull (in Bishopsgate), The Bell Savage (on Ludgate Hill) and The Boar's Head (in Whitechapel High Street). However, from 1576 on, independent theatres were founded that had permanent companies and were professionally managed. These were:

1576: The Theatre (Shoreditch)
1576: (The first) Blackfriars Theatre (Blackfriars)
1577: The Curtain (Shoreditch)
1587: The Rose (Southwark)
c. 1595: The Swan (Southwark)
1596: (The second) Blackfriars Theatre (Blackfriars)
1599: (The first) Globe Theatre (Southwark)
1600: The Fortune (Golding Lane, outside of Cripplegate)
c. 1604: The Red Bull (near Clerkenwell Priory)
1605: Whitefriars (Whitefriars)
1608: (The third) Blackfriars Theatre (Blackfriars)
1614: The Hope (Southwark)
1614: (The second) Globe Theatre (Southwark)
1617: Phoenix or Cockpit (St-Giles-in-the-Fields) [102]

Most of these facilities were established within a very short period of time and could hold very large audiences. The Theatre held approximately 1500 spectators, the Fortune and the Rose Theatre approximately 2400 each, and the Globe approximately 2100, although other estimates put its capacity at 3000. The Swan Theatre is said to have had a capacity of 3000, but new research suggests that this figure is too high. Incidentally, the Swan is the only London theatre of Shakespeare's time for which an interior view exists. All in all, it seems safe to assume that, at their peak, approximately 10,000 people visited the London theatres every day.

In other European cities, it appears that – with the exception of Antwerp, which had an impressive theatre-in-the-round (*Fig. 69*) – the construction of permanent theatres such as the Amsterdam Playhouse (1638), the Viennese Theatre (1651), the Dresden Theatre, the Theatre in Stockholm (1667), and the Nuremberg Theatre (1668) only began approximately half a century later. In Paris, the Hôtel de Bourgogne had a monopoly on the theatre productions, so the Parisian theatre scene was rather poorly developed and limited, whereas the London theatre experienced a boom between 1590 and 1624[103].

And yet in the first decade of Elizabeth's reign, the conditions for theatrical performances in the capital and provinces were far from ideal. One important, though indirect, reason for the theatre's sudden popularity was, paradoxically, the 'Bill against Vagabonds', passed in 1572. This law permitted only companies of travelling players who enjoyed the patronage of a nobleman to perform publicly. Offenders would be treated as vagabonds and faced stiff punishments. The actors therefore had to unite and appeal to noble patrons, which was apparently not too difficult. It was attractive for

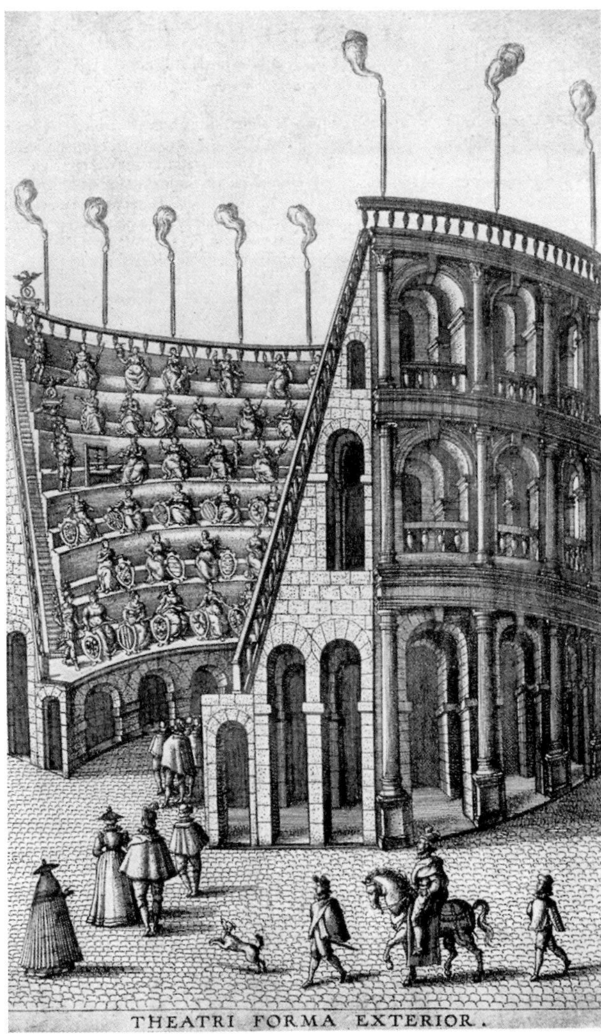

Fig. 69 – A view of the amphitheatre in Antwerp in 1594. Shown in the foreground is the entrance of Archduke Ernst.

representatives of high society, especially courtiers, to keep theatre companies, both for their personal entertainment and to enhance their reputations as patrons of the arts. They depended on how the actors spoke of them. As an example, Hamlet warns Polonius: 'Do you hear: let them be well used; for they [the actors] are the abstract and brief chronicles of the time; after your death you were better have a bad epitaph than their ill report while you live.' (*Hamlet*, Act II, scene 2).

In 1574 – when William Shakespeare had just turned ten-years-old – Elizabeth I gave a special gift to the actors of her favourite Lord Leicester, in the form of a licence to perform wherever they liked in London and its Liberties, as well as everywhere else in the kingdom. The only constraints were that no performances were allowed during 'common prayer' or during outbreaks of the Plague. Furthermore, the plays to be performed were subject to censorship by the Crown.

The opportunity associated with this permission was first recognised and exploited by James Burbage, a leading player in the Leicester's Men company. Approximately two decades later, Shakespeare was also to benefit from this historical change. Burbage was originally trained as a carpenter and was now obsessed by the idea of building a theatre in the capital, holding 3000 spectators, in which to perform plays. He faced a dilemma in respect of the site of the new theatre, for London's aldermen had a deeply rooted religious aversion to the theatre. Theatre productions with their elaborate costumes and props were anathema to the Puritan clergy and aldermen alike, for they were ultimately reminiscent of Roman Catholic rituals, of liturgical vestments and iconography. M. M. Reese, in *Shakespeare, His World and His Work* (1953, rev. new edition 1980), observed that Puritans could destroy the priestly vestments and accoutrements, but they were not able to silence the voices of drama. At that time, it was still possible for plays to represent Catholic doctrine and worship on the stage. Thus, it is not surprising that, in the eyes of the Puritans, the theatre was among the greatest evils of the age. Puritan pamphlets and sermons of the time cautioned strongly against the 'stage plays', though with little apparent success.

For these reasons, the Corporation of the City of London banned theatre performances and the construction of theatre facilities on its own territory, regardless of the royal licence, which had expressly permitted actors under aristocratic patronage to perform wherever they wished.

James Burbage was a fine actor with a keen business sense, and he also sensed what was feasible in this delicate situation. So, instead of confronting the aldermen, he looked for a suitable location outside the city boundaries. He found it in Shoreditch, where he established the first English theatre, and named it simply The Theatre. It was built, with the financial support of his brother-in-law, John Brayne, for about £650 on the site of a former monastery in Holywell, in the parish of St Leonard. Burbage had leased the site on which the building stood from the owner, Giles Alleyn, for a period of twenty-one years. Like Blackfriars and the other monasteries that were dispossessed and destroyed under Henry VIII, Holywell also belonged to the Liberties, which were outside the jurisdiction of the City of London. Other theatre managers and troupes followed Burbage's example and made use of former monasteries and convents so as to escape the reach of the puritanical aldermen of London.

Shakespeare probably spent the Plague years of 1592 to 1594 outside London. Like so many other Londoners, he may well have sought the safety of the countryside, where *Venus and Adonis* may have taken shape.

In 1594, when the epidemic had passed and the theatre companies were newly formed or were re-organised in the capital, Shakespeare had another stroke of luck. He and Richard Burbage joined a newly formed troupe of actors which would prove itself to be the best and the most professional in the country – the Chamberlain's Men. Shakespeare and the Chamberlain's Men would celebrate what were probably the greatest triumphs in the history of English theatre. Burbage, a brilliant young actor who had learned a great deal from Edward Alleyn, star of the Admiral's Men, was the son of the theatre builder and actor James Burbage and brother of Cuthbert Burbage, who managed the theatre's business affairs. By this time, Shakespeare had already attained great celebrity as a playwright and poet.

The patron of the Chamberlain's Men was Henry Carey, the first Lord Hunsdon, who had been Lord Chamberlain to Queen Elizabeth since 1585. William Kempe, John Heminge, Augustine Phillips, George Bryan, Richard Cowley and Thomas Pope formed the core of this new troupe, which took its name from its patron. These actors had previously been under the protection of Lord Strange and had been known under the name Strange's Men and/or Derby's Men. In 1593, Ferdinando Stanley became the fifth Earl of Derby and the patron of the Derby's Men troupe, but he died the following year under mysterious circumstances, forcing the company to seek other opportunities.

There is much to suggest that the Earl of Derby's death was an act of revenge by the Catholics. On behalf of the Jesuit William Holt and Sir William Stanley, Richard Hesketh had approached Ferdinando Stanley in 1592 to persuade him to lay claim to the English throne. Hesketh had promised him that Spain would come to his aid. Stanley, however, handed Hesketh over to the law, which found him guilty of high treason, and he was executed on 29 November 1593. Ferdinando Stanley died on 16 April 1594, just a few months later. The strange symptoms from which he suffered have now been interpreted as gradual poisoning.

Ferdinando Stanley was a Catholic, like the rest of his extended family. The request that had been made to him demonstrates this very clearly; but fearing that the plot would be discovered, he revealed the conspiracy in order to save his own life, and thus evidently provoked retaliation. It can be assumed that of the actors under his patronage most, if not all, were Catholic. So John Heminge and Augustine Phillips, who later became close friends of Shakespeare, and George Bryan, Richard Cowley, and Thomas Pope, could all have been clandestine Catholics, even if they pretended to support the State Church. Between 1608 and 1619, Heminge was active in his London parish of St Mary's Aldermanbury, though this does not prove that he was not a secret Catholic[104]. We know that Ellen Fortescue, wife of John Fortescue, the tenant of the eastern Blackfriars gatehouse, always informed the authorities that she regularly attended the Anglican service at St Andrew's, but it appears she did so to avoid being listed as a recusant. In reality, however, she and her entire family were Catholics, and she dedicated her life to the protection of the Catholic clergy.

Heminge (whose name was also variously spelled Heming, Hemminge or Hemmings) was a decidedly strong personality and absolutely reliable. This is made clear by the fact that Shakespeare selected him as one of his trustees when purchasing the eastern Gatehouse in Blackfriars (1613), and because it was Heminge who, some years after the playwright's death, along with Henry Condell carefully and conscientiously produced the First Folio Edition of the plays, since Shakespeare, by his death, was prevented from doing so. Heminge was not only an actor, but also the troupe's manager and their representative in dealings with the government. Ben Jonson's epitaph to Richard Burbage also sheds significant light on John Heminge, the great actor and performer of the Chamberlain's Men, which became the King's Men after the accession of James I. With characteristic irony, Jonson wrote:

> What need hee stand at the iudgment throne
> Who hath a heaven and a hell of his own.
> Then feare not Burbage heavens angry rodd,
> When thy fellows are angells & old Hemmigs
> [sic] is God.

The Chamberlain's Men undertook their first productions together with the Admiral's Men, who had previously celebrated great triumphs with the plays written by their inspired playwright Christopher Marlowe: *Tamburlaine the Great* (*c.* 1587), *Doctor Faustus* (*c.* 1588), *The Jew of Malta* (*c.* 1589), *Edward II* (*c.* 1592) and *The Massacre at Paris* (1593). For many years, Edward Alleyn, the star actor with the Admiral's Men, had impressed London theatregoers with his portrayals of Marlowe's heroes. Whereas the Admiral's Men lost their pre-eminent playwright when Marlowe died prematurely in 1593, the Chamberlain's Men, in 1594, won a genius, a man who could perform as both playwright and actor – William Shakespeare.

The joint productions of these two companies were performed in early June 1594 at the inconveniently located Newington Butts Theatre, south of the River and about a mile away from London Bridge. The plays included *Titus Andronicus*, *Taming of a Shrew*, and an early version of *Hamlet* (*Ur-Hamlet*). Only *Titus Andronicus* was obviously written by Shakespeare; the authorship of the other two plays is unclear. The author of *Ur-Hamlet* may have been Thomas Kyd. Only a short time later, the two companies separated again.

The Chamberlain's Men then performed at The Theatre in Shoreditch run by James Burbage, which put them in the privileged situation of possessing their own playhouse, the best Elizabethan actor (apart from Alleyn), Richard Burbage, and William Shakespeare as a playwright (and as an actor). After Marlowe's death, no English dramatist came close to Shakespeare's talent.

Like all other Elizabethan companies, the Chamberlain's Men performed repertory theatre. Like the other companies, it was tightly organised around a core of around nine, later twelve, permanent actors. These were also shareholders ('sharers') among whom all profits were divided. Up to his death in 1619, Richard Burbage was the troupe's undisputed star. In the title parts of the Shakespeare plays, he delivered unimaginably masterful performances and was highly acclaimed by the public.

Until his voluntary departure in 1599, William Kempe was the much-admired comedian of the Chamberlain's Men. He famously and spectacularly Morris-danced his way from London to Norwich. He performed the same dance on the Continent. The fact that, in 1601, Kempe met Sir Anthony Shirley, a representative of the Earl of Essex, in Rome casts a different light on his clownish antics. Just as Shakespeare may have used the poaching story in 1585 as a pretext for leaving Stratford in great haste, Kempe – who like Shakespeare was evidently also an Essex follower – could have staged all of this in order to leave England and travel to Rome on an important mission. It is improbable that he should have met Shirley, Essex's close friend and 'ambassador', by sheer coincidence.

As a comedian, Kempe had followed in the footsteps of his great predecessor, Richard Tarleton (d. 1588). His jokes often left the written text far behind. Hamlet's exhortation of actors, which in particular puts clowns in their place, was therefore probably equally aimed at Kempe.

> And let those that play your clowns speak no more than is set down for them; for there be of them that will themselves laugh, to set on some quantity of barren spectators to laugh too [...]. That's villainous, and shows a most pitiful ambition in the fool that uses it.
>
> (*Hamlet*, Act III, scene 2)

The group's leading men – Shakespeare and Burbage – selected Robert Armin as Kempe's successor. Armin was a particularly sensitive performer who could subtly convey melancholy as well as the finer points of tomfoolery. The troupe also had 'hired men' or 'hirelings' who were assigned smaller speaking parts for weekly wages, as well as 'boys' who were paid to play the female roles. In addition, paid extras would participate as needed, especially in plays that had crowd scenes. Where possible, actors would perform multiple roles in a single play, especially in times of need – such as the Plague years – when there was a shortage of actors.

In the winter of 1594-95, approximately half a year after their formation, the Chamberlain's Men performed, apparently with permission from the City Council, at the Cross Keys inn, which lay within the walls of the City of London. This concession from the city was unusual. When the Lord Strange's Men had performed in 1589 at the same place without the city fathers' permission, some of its members had ended up in prison. However, the Chamberlain's Men had in Henry Carey a patron who was especially powerful at Court and championed his actors. On 8 October 1594, Carey had written a personal note to the Lord Mayor of London asking that his troupe be allowed to perform their plays at the inn. In addition, the Chamberlain's Men had Shakespeare, whose patron, Southampton, was also influential and a passionate theatregoer. This all opened doors which would otherwise surely have remained closed to the players. The reputation of the Chamberlain's Men grew apace when they were allowed to perform before Her Majesty Queen Elizabeth I during Christmas, 1594. On 26 and 27 December 1594, the troupe entertained at the royal palace in Greenwich, performing two plays. A royal treasurer's receipt dated 15 March 1595 supplies the written proof that Shakespeare, along with Kempe and Burbage, performed there on the days mentioned. The payment was for £6-13s-4d (per performance) plus a premium (a royal tip) of £3-6s-8d to William Kempe, William Shakespeare and Richard Burbage for two performances at the palace (*Fig. 70*). It is highly likely that one of the two plays was Shakespeare's early comedy, *The Comedy of Errors*. The receipt is in the Public Records Office collection in London, and proves that Shakespeare, along with Kempe and Burbage, was a leading member of the Chamberlain's Men in the year that it was established[105].

After the death of their patron in 1596, The Chamberlain's Men were forced to change their name temporarily, for Henry Carey's son, George Carey, could not immediately take over the office of Lord Chamberlain. So, from July 1596, the troupe was called Lord Hunsdon's Men. It was able to resume its old name when Carey became Royal Chamberlain in March 1597.

Fig. 70 – Written evidence from 15 March 1595, showing that William Kempe, William Shakespeare and Richard Burbage, the leading actors in the Chamberlain's Men, were paid for performing two plays on 26 and 27 December 1594 before Queen Elizabeth I at the Royal Palace in Greenwich. The text does not mention which plays were performed, but it can hardly be doubted that they were written by Shakespeare, the dramatist for the Chamberlain's Men, who was already highly esteemed at this time.

Yet another change was in store for Shakespeare's troupe in 1596. There are indications that they were now no longer performing at The Theatre in Shoreditch, but at the Swan Theatre. It is conceivable that this move was connected with the squabbles which resulted when Giles Alleyn, who owned The Theatre, refused to let James Burbage extend the lease, which expired in 1597, because in this way he secretly hoped to acquire ownership of the theatre building.

The year 1597 brought further disaster for the Chamberlain's Men. They, like other troupes, were affected by the rigid sanctions imposed by the Privy Council after Thomas Nashe's highly explosive political satire, *The Isle of Dogs*, was first performed on 28 July of that year. The play was considered to be seditious and caused a great scandal. Three actors – including the co-author Ben Jonson – found themselves in prison. All theatres were closed, and Shakespeare's troupe was forced to go on tour in the provinces. After its return, it once again performed at a new location, The Curtain. The Chamberlain's Men apparently used this venue for a certain period of transition after the lease on The Theatre expired (1597).

In 1598, at William Shakespeare's instigation, the troupe staged the comedy *Every Man in His Humour*, which made its author, Ben Jonson, famous overnight. In that same year, Jonson had killed a fellow actor in a duel and been condemned to the gallows. He sought asylum from the Church, however, and was merely branded. In his London prison, which – like prisons throughout England at the time – was full to bursting with Catholics, he had been converted back into the old faith. Shakespeare may also have backed him for this reason. It is certain that Jonson was a lifelong, if not always uncomplicated, friend of Shakespeare's. By Jonson's own account, however, he converted back to Protestantism in 1610.

The complete edition of Ben Jonson's works, published in 1616, contains a list of the 'principal actors' who played parts in the individual productions of his plays. It shows that one of the leading players in *Every Man in His Humour* was Shakespeare himself. Other parts were played by William Sly, John Duke and Christopher Beeston. Much of the biographical information about Shakespeare collected and recorded in the seventeenth century by John Aubrey can be traced back to Beeston.

When James Burbage died in February 1597, he left his sons with substantial property holdings, but also with serious problems. To Cuthbert he had bequeathed The Theatre, a theatre building that was virtually worthless since the lease was due to expire that year. Richard inherited the great indoor theatre at Blackfriars, but performances were not permitted there. Confronted with this situation, the sons, in conjunction with the Chamberlain's Men shareholders, decided to build a new theatre on the south bank of the Thames in Maiden Lane in Southwark, not far from St Mary Overie, now known as Southwark Cathedral (*Fig. 71*). The Rose Theatre was nearby.

In December of the year 1598, the citizens of London were presented with an unusual spectacle. The capital's leading theatrical troupe arranged for The Theatre in Shoreditch to be dismantled and had the individual parts transported over London Bridge to Southwark, where it was rebuilt as a new theatre on leased land. Giles Alleyn, their former landlord, was so infuriated by what he considered to be the 'unseemly action' of the Burbages and their company that he instituted legal proceedings against them. The 1602 case of 'Allen v. Burbadge' describes the dismantling of The Theatre in detail. Cuthbert and Richard Burbage, a certain Peter Street (Street was the carpenter responsible for the construction of the new venue), William Smyth and around twelve other people, so the charge laid against them says, had assembled riotously, armed with swords, poniards, axes and similar forbidden weapons, between 8 and 20 December and had torn down The Theatre. Violently and just as riotously, they had then moved 'all the wood and timber' to Bankside, where they used the material to build a new theatre. Alleyn does not appear to have won his case, however.

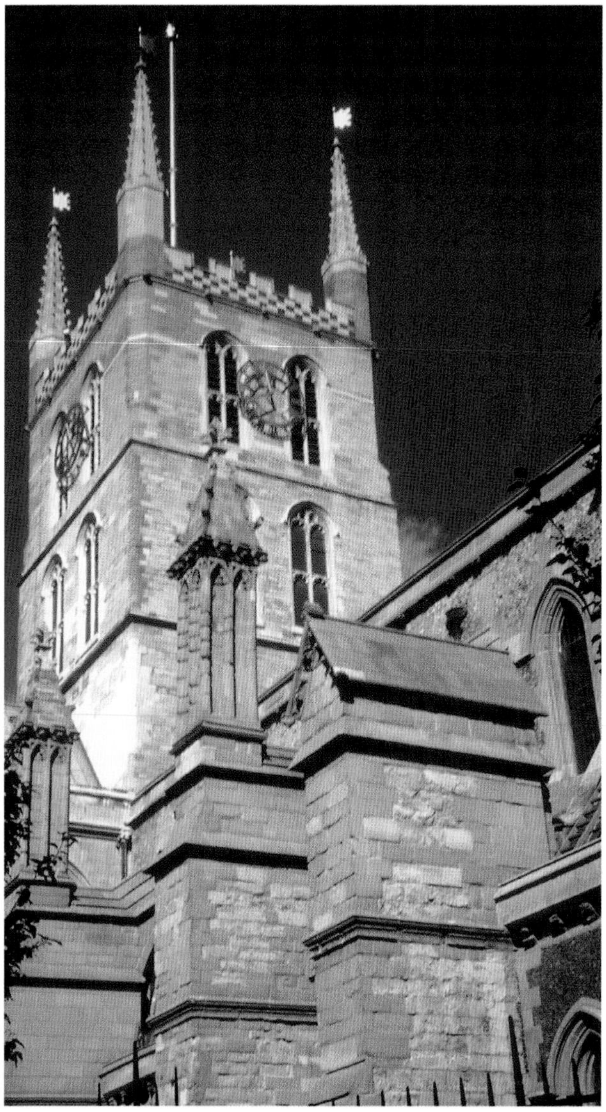

Fig. 71 – View of Southwark Cathedral today. It was formerly known as St Mary Overie.

A thirty-year lease was entered into with the new landowner, Nicholas Brend. Finance for the building was secured through shareholders. The Burbages bore half the costs, and in so doing acquired a fifty per cent share of the profits. The other half of the costs was shared by five members of the Chamberlain's Men – William Shakespeare, John Heminge, Augustine Phillips, Thomas Pope and William Kempe. Through the interim owners Willian Levison and Thomas Savage, they acquired profit shares of ten per cent each. As is clear from a later lawsuit, the contract was concluded around 21 February 1599.

In the spring of 1599, the new theatre constructed by Street was ready to open. In the prologue to *Henry V*, Shakespeare calls it 'this wooden O'. It was a round, open-air building and its name, the Globe, was as catchy as it was sophisticated. While other Elizabethan theatre companies foundered and sank without trace, the Chamberlain's Men were ideally situated. They owned a large, well-built, conveniently located and prestigious venue, a monumental theatre that was visible from a distance, and so became one of the capital's landmarks. For the owners, the theatre was a source of great profit. The Globe

Theatre was also to become the site of great thespian triumphs. The first Shakespeare play performed for an excited, socially broad-based audience was probably *Henry V*, a history which exudes optimism and offers a glimpse of the dramatist's political hopes and expectations (see p. 139 f.). A few years later, Shakespeare's great masterpieces, *Hamlet*, *Othello*, *King Lear* and *Macbeth*, among others, were also premièred at the Globe. However, between the first performances of *Henry V* and *Hamlet*, dramatic political events took place that – as it appears – not only marked the most decisive moment in William Shakespeare's life, but also caused him to turn to writing tragedies.

After the death of Elizabeth I in March 1603, the son of Mary, Queen of Scots ascended to the throne as James I of England. With this came the prospect not only of having the great honour of performing at Court, but also of being paid handsomely to do so. James himself now took over the patronage of what was by far the country's most important theatre company. The Chamberlain's Men thus became the King's Men in 1603. As the new king's servants and protégés, they had – according to the wording of the royal patent, issued on 19 May 1603 – the right to perform 'Comedies, Tragedies, histories, Enterludes, moralls, pastoralls, Stageplaies, and Suche others like as theie haue alreadie studied or hereafter shall vse or studie, as well for the recreation of our lovinge Subjectes, as for our Solace and pleasure'. The King's Men's right to public appearances applied to the Globe Theatre as well as to all the cities of the kingdom and other suitable places, including Liberties, universities, etc. The City of London was not specifically mentioned in the royal document, but it was nonetheless included.

For Shakespeare and his actors, markedly favourable conditions would have arrived with the regime change, especially if the new king had granted his Catholic subjects the tolerance that he had promised prior to his accession.

THE FIRST PHASE OF SHAKESPEARE'S DRAMAS: HISTORIES, COMEDIES, AND AN EARLY TRAGEDY

During the first phase of Shakespeare's theatrical career, which will be considered here as lasting until *c.* 1598, Shakespeare – with the exception of *Titus Andronicus* and *Romeo and Juliet* – only wrote histories, such as *Henry VI, Parts 1, 2, & 3*, *Richard III*, *King John*, *Richard II*, *Henry IV, Parts 1 & 2*, and *Henry V*, and comedies, such as *The Comedy of Errors*, *The Taming of the Shrew*, *Two Gentlemen of Verona*, *Love's Labours Lost*, *A Midsummer Night's Dream*, *The Merchant of Venice*, *The Merry Wives of Windsor*, *Much Ado About Nothing*, and *As You Like It*. To these should be added *Twelfth Night*, a comedy that was apparently premièred in January 1601 (see p. 162).

We owe great thanks to the schoolmaster, critic and Anglican clergyman Francis Meres (1565-1647) for his information about which of the dramatist's plays were written and performed by the late 1590s. Meres had studied at Cambridge, received his Master of Arts in 1591, and in 1597 lived in London, where he was a keen observer of the city's literary scene. He was particularly interested in the theatre and the plays that were thrilling their audiences. In 1598, this critic and cleric published the titles of the plays that had been performed, along with his own comparisons and assessments, under the title of *Palladis Tamia*. However, the work does not list all of the plays that Shakespeare had completed by then, omitting any reference to *The Taming of the Shrew*, *The Merry Wives of Windsor*, *Much Ado about Nothing*, and *As You Like It*. This may be because Meres only offers examples, but it also may be that some of the plays – such as *The Merry Wives of Windsor* and possibly *Much Ado about Nothing* – were not yet finished. Surprisingly, *Henry VI*, an early play, is not mentioned either, probably because it was no longer in the repertory by the time Meres settled in London in 1597. *Henry V* was not written until early 1599, so it couldn't be recorded in *Palladis Tamia*. Of Shakespeare's comedies, he mentions: *Gentlemen of Verona*, *Errors*, *Loue labors lost*, *Loue labours wonne*, *Midsummer night dreame* and *The Merchant of Venice*; and of the tragedies, *Richard the 2.*, *Richard the 3.*, *Henry the 4.*, *King Iohn*, *Titus Andronicus* and *Romeo and Iuliet*. Even for today's readers, these titles, despite the contemporary spelling, are easily identifiable. Only *Loue labours wonne*, a comedy that was probably intended as a counterpart to *Love's Labours Lost*, presents problems. To this day, the play has not been identified, or rather identifications of it are unconvincing. It is not even known if this is an as yet undiscovered play by Shakespeare or if it is actually another name for one of his works that is already known. There is a great deal to suggest that *Loue labours wonne* is not a missing work, but an early play which the dramatist revised and updated later, giving it a new name, probably for practical, as well as commercial, reasons. The Elizabethan public eschewed old or rehashed plays. By way of example, the Chamberlain's Men referred to the fact that *Richard II* was an old play and would fail to attract spectators when the conspirators of the Essex circle asked them to perform it at the Globe on the day before the planned rebellion. The troupe received extra payment from some of Essex's followers to stage the performance.

Which of Shakespeare's early comedies could be hiding behind the name *Loue labours wonne*? So far, the debate has included *Much Ado about Nothing*, *The Taming of the Shrew*, *Troilus and Cressida*, and *All's Well That Ends Well*. *Much Ado About Nothing* was probably not written until late 1599. In 1600, it was entered into the Stationers' Register, though it was not yet approved for publication. A version of *The Taming of the Shrew* had been printed by 1594 under the title *The Taming of a Shrew* and had been performed several times before that. It is, however, not clear whether – as mentioned above – Shakespeare is the author of this comedy. *Troilus and Cressida* was actually printed for the first time in 1609 as a 'new play' after it had previously been performed at the Globe Theatre, which had opened in 1599. *All's Well that Ends Well*, a comedy which a number of Shakespeare scholars have believed to be *Loue labours wonne*, is nonetheless probably ineligible, because Shakespeare apparently wrote the role of the clown, Lavache, for Robert Armin, who became William Kempe's successor in the Chamberlain's Men in 1599. The most likely candidate is the comedy *As You Like It*. So far, it has not entered into the discussion, though some scholars suspect it existed by 1593 and could have been revised towards the end of the decade. *As You Like It* deserves to be considered in this discussion, especially because of its subtle religious and socio-political references, which will be examined in greater detail later in the book.

The exact dates when Shakespeare wrote his dramas can no longer be determined today. The entries in the Stationers' Register, however, still act as a reliable source of reference for a *terminus ad quem*, the latest date at which a work could have been completed. The Register recorded titles which were complete and licensed by the Established Church, but which would not necessarily be printed.

HISTORICAL PLAYS

With the exception of *King John*, which takes place in the early thirteenth century, the historical dramas in the first phase of Shakespeare's theatrical career deal with the history of late fourteenth and fifteenth century England, including the bloodshed and vicissitudes of its wars and civil wars. They stretched from the reign of Richard II, who became king of England in 1377, at the age of ten, up to the Battle of Bosworth in 1485, where Richard III was defeated by his challenger, the Duke of Richmond, who as Henry VII subsequently established the Tudor monarchy.

Within the Elizabethan period, Shakespeare

conspicuously avoided plays about the Tudors, who governed until 1603. An exception is *Richard III*, a story in which the victor, Richmond, appears at the end in an extremely positive light. The ruling dynasty, however, was taboo, especially since the Tudor monarchs, namely Henry VIII, and then again, Elizabeth I, broke England's ties with Rome. The Catholics of England, including William Shakespeare, kept faith with the Pope as head of the Church, so the dramatist avoided the dangers and pitfalls inevitably associated with presenting this dynasty on the stage. It was not until the end of his career as a playwright, when the last Tudor ruler had been dead for approximately ten years, that Shakespeare became co-author of a play about the life and politics of Henry VIII. In co-operation with John Fletcher, he wrote what is known today as *Henry VIII*, which at the time bore the meaningful title, *All is True*. When this historical drama was first performed on St Peter's Day (June 29) 1613 at the Globe Theatre, it was interrupted by a disastrous fire. For whatever reason, Shakespeare was not present. His Globe Theatre property shares may have already been sold before the fire – perhaps in early March 1613 – so as to give him sufficient funds for his acquisition in Blackfriars. Even if by this time he had completely retired to Stratford, he could still have attended the Globe occasionally, especially as from 10 March of that year he owned his own house and rented it out to a tenant.

Even from today's perspective, the question of the aims William Shakespeare had in mind when he dramatised English history for the stage remains an interesting one. For several decades, the theory proposed in E. M. W. Tillyard's *Shakespeare's History Plays* (1944), namely that the so-called 'Tudor myth' is reflected in Shakespeare's histories, was accepted, with its perception that the plays upheld and glorified this English dynasty. In recent times, this theory has been strongly questioned. If the term 'Tudor myth' is to be used at all, then it only refers to the glorified picture which the dramatist paints at the end of *Richard III* of Richmond. Henry VII was a good and progressive ruler who had brought peace to a country wracked by civil war, the Wars of the Roses. By supporting his country's bold expeditions to the coasts of the New World, he had established the foundations for his future prosperity. He also contributed to the spread of Renaissance culture from the Continent, particularly that of the Italians, in England. It was he who brought the Italian sculptor Pietro Torrigiano (1472-1528) to England where this Italian artist established a new, realistic portraiture style, based on both life and death masks, for sculpture and funerary art[106]. Henry VII was, no doubt, a unifying figure and at the same time, he was the last great ruler of Catholic England at the beginning of modern times. Mainly because of this fact he was greatly revered by the Catholic population at the time of Shakespeare. It is significant that John Shakespeare when he applied for a coat of arms (seemingly supported by his son William) invoked the name of an ancestor who had served with distinction under Henry VII.

Since the young Shakespeare had apparently already written minor plays, including morality plays, while a 'schoolmaster in the country' in Lancashire and during 'the lost years', he might have already had one play or another – probably the *Henry VI* trilogy and *The Comedy of Errors* – either partially finished or completed when he came to London. Like Thomas Lodge (*c.* 1558-1625), who was engaged in literary activities over the course of his long, dangerous journeys and later, together with Robert Greene, wrote the play *A Looking Glasse for London and England* (1594), Shakespeare may have also used his extensive travels on the Continent to record his impressions, acquire historical and mythological material, and adapt it for the stage. Lodge, who had converted to Catholicism, was abroad in the Armada year of 1588, like many other English Catholics – Shakespeare most probably included. In 1591, Lodge sailed with the famous English sailor Thomas Cavendish on his ship to South America, where he visited the Jesuit library in Santos, Brazil. He was present when Cavendish negotiated the Straits of Magellan. A year earlier, he had sailed to the Canary Islands. During this trip, where he acted – according to his own accounts – as a soldier and sailor, his best work was written under what were sometimes extreme conditions in the open Atlantic, buffeted by heavy swells and storms. The manuscript of his work *Rosalynde*, *Euphues Golden Legacie* was spattered and dampened by the ocean spray. *Rosalynde* was a romance in the tradition of the novel *Euphues*, or *the Anatomy of Wit* by John Lyly, which was published in 1578. It reflected critically on such aspects of Elizabethan society as fashion, court life, religion, virtues, and vices, as well as friendship and love in particular. Lodge's romantic narrative was approved for print on 6 October 1590 in London. Shakespeare borrowed from this work for the plot of his early comedy *As You Like It*, though he added crucial characters. Lodge obviously tolerated this borrowing and raised no objections.

For his study of English history from the twelfth to the late fifteenth century, the budding dramatist had two important chronicles at his disposal: (1) *The Union of the two Noble and Illustre Families of Lancaster and York*, by Edward Hall (d. 1547); and the *Chronicles of England, Scotland and Ireland* (1577) by Raphael Holinshed (d. c.1580). Shakespeare used the second edition of the Holinshed Chronicle in which the politically offensive passages had been removed by the publisher, John Hooker *alias* Vowell. Other dramatists also used this popular version. The chronicles of Hall and Holinshed are the main sources for Shakespeare's English historical dramas. Since the second edition of the *Chronicles* was published during the 'lost years', the dramatist could have actually read them on those long journeys he undertook across the European mainland at this time.

In contrast to the chroniclers, who recorded the actions of famous individuals, dates and facts (political figures, reigns, wars, laws, decrees, etc.) in sober annals, Shakespeare based his histories on the formative historical processes, on the great historical decision-makers, their human strengths and weaknesses, on the interpretation of the historical event itself and on its practical application to the present. Thus the dramatist treated historical subject-matter not for the sake of the past, but to illuminate the problems and circumstances of his own time. The English history plays in Shakespeare's time had concrete, moral and didactic objectives as pointed out by Irving Ribner in 1957:

> (1) a nationalistic glorification of England;
> (2) an analysis of contemporary affairs, both national and foreign so as to make clear the virtues and the failings of contemporary statesmen;
> (3) a use of past events as a guide to political behaviour in the present;
> (4) a use of history as documentation for political theory;
> (5) a study of past political disaster as an aid to Stoical fortitude in the present;
> (6) illustration of the providence of God as the ruling force in human – and primarily political – affairs;
> (7) exposition of a rational plan in human events which must affirm the wisdom and justice of God [107].

Such an understanding of history shaped by its relevance to the present must have strongly affected the spectators of Shakespeare's historical plays. As the dramatist brought the fate of great historical figures to the stage, as well as emotionally stirring scenes that included harrowing experiences of suffering and death, it sharpened their perception of their own society, of contemporary political processes and the uses and abuses of power. The close relationship between the stage and politics in Elizabethan times is attested to by the fact that the Earl of

Essex's conspirators had Shakespeare's history, *Richard II*, performed directly before their attempted *coup d'état*, using Richard as an example of a ruler who was deposed because he had neglected his duties. In this way, Shakespeare's historical drama, treating as it did the most sensitive matter of the deposition of the rightful and anointed monarch, was used as a mirror for Elizabeth I. This was understood just as well by those in power as it was by the conspirators and their followers. The doyen of the Chamberlain's Men, the old actor Augustine Phillips (d. 1605), represented Shakespeare's troupe when it was interrogated on this subject. He was able to prove convincingly that the Lord Chamberlain's Men had only performed an old play because some courtiers had put pressure on them to do so. He was believed, and the troupe got off scot-free. When the Earl of Essex and his friend and right-hand man, the Earl of Southampton (Shakespeare's patron), were tried for high treason, Francis Bacon (1561-1626) played a major part in the prosecution and brought matters to a head. Using the bold but pithy phrase, 'from the stage to the state', he made it clear to the jury that the conspirators had exploited *Richard II* for their own purposes, and that they had used the dramatised deposing of a king who had neglected his duties as propaganda and as justification for their own cause.

HENRY VI

The *Henry VI* trilogy is considered to be Shakespeare's earliest historical drama. This work includes his first masterfully achieved scene, the death scene of Cardinal Beaufort in Part II (Act III, scene 3)[108], which was later admired by the German writers J. W. Goethe, A. W. Schlegel and J. Eichendorff. Eighteenth-century painters, especially Henry Fuseli and Sir Joshua Reynolds, were enthralled by it. Reynolds chose the death scene because for him it represented a morally instructive paradigm in the tradition of *ars moriendi*, the art of dying[109]. While the king as depicted by Reynolds stretches his arms towards heaven and calls upon the dying cardinal to give a similar sign of hope for salvation, the church dignitary, ravaged by his guilty conscience, tightly clutches the coverings of his deathbed. His facial expression is distorted, his gaze – averted from God, as it were – is directed downwards[110]. Shakespeare made his characters say:

> KING
> He dies, and makes no sign: O God, forgive him!
>
> WARWICK
> So bad a death argues a monstrous life.
>
> KING
> Forbear to judge, for we are sinners all.

Reynolds painted the devil behind the dying man's pillow, intending to place particular emphasis on the deeply religious message of both the text and the painting.

> KING
> O Thou eternal Mover of the heavens,
> Look with a gentle eye upon this wretch!
> O, beat away the busy meddling fiend
> That lays strong siege unto this wretch's soul,
> And from his bosom purge this black despair.

Reynolds' depiction of the satanic figure at Cardinal Beaufort's deathbed ignited violent criticism from his public. The figure was therefore omitted from engravings made from the painting.

It would not have occurred to the aristocracy and educated middle class of eighteenth-century England that when Shakespeare brought Cardinal Beaufort's 'wicked death' to the stage, alluding to his 'monstrous life', he was thinking of senior Protestant clerics who had been accused of, or had a reputation for, misdemeanours, either in recent memory or in Shakespeare's own day. Shakespeare could count on such allusions being well understood by his contemporaries, especially those who had kept the old faith.

For example, a seminary priest captured by the government spy Richard Topcliffe, and held by him under house arrest, asserted that the spy had made disparaging remarks about the allegedly loose morals of the Elizabethan Archbishop of Canterbury, Dr John Whitgift. When he was interrogated at his trial, the seminary priest Thomas Pormont, who was executed for high treason on 21 February 1592, stated that Topcliffe had declared:

> The Archbishop of Canterbury was a fitter councilor in the kitchen among wenches than in a Prince's Court; as for Justice Young, he would hang the Archbishop and three hundred more if they were in his hands.[111]

Pormont let his interrogators also know that Topcliffe had told him about his alleged intimate relations with Queen Elizabeth I and had boasted of it:

> Topcliffe said that [...] he himself was so familiar with Her Majesty that he hath very secret dealings with her, having not only seen her legs and knees but felt her belly, saying to her that it was the softest belly of any womankind. She had said unto him, 'Be not these the arms, legs and body of King Henry?' to which he answered 'Yea'. She gave him for a favour a white linen hose wrought with white silk.[112]

Just before the Jesuit priest was executed, Topcliffe put great pressure on Pormont and tried to coerce him into retracting his statements. Then he ensured that the Jesuit, dressed only in a shirt, would have to wait for two hours in the icy weather for his execution. He could not, however, force Pormont to recant.

Shakespeare's *Henry VI* was a great success from the outset, because it presented the eventful and bloody history of fifteenth-century England in such a personal and moving way. In Act 1, Scene 3 of the last part of the trilogy, Clifford meets the young Earl of Rutland, whose father had killed his own. Clifford is full of pitiless lust for vengeance. Rutland's tutor, a priest, tries to change his mind, but in vain: 'Ah, Clifford, murder not this innocent child, / Lest thou be hated both of God and man.'

Clifford, however, commands: 'Chaplain, away! Thy priesthood saves thy life.' His soldiers then drag the priest off. Ignoring young Rutland's pleas, Clifford is possessed by the thought of annihilating the House of York, to which the boy now in his clutches belongs:

> CLIFFORD
> Had I thy brethren here, their lives and thine
> Were not revenge sufficient for me;
> No, if I digg'd up thy forefathers' graves
> And hung their rotten coffins up in chains,
> It could not slake mine ire nor ease my heart.
> The sight of any of the house of York
> Is as a fury to torment my soul;
> And till I root out their accursed line
> And leave not one alive, I live in hell.
> Therefore – *(he lifts his arm)*

Rutland asks permission to pray, and prays to his murderer to be merciful: 'To thee I pray, sweet Clifford, pity me. / [...] / I never did thee harm: why wilt thou slay me?'.

> CLIFFORD
> Thy father hath.
>
> RUTLAND
> But 'twas ere I was born.
> Thou hast one son; for his sake pity me,
> Lest in revenge thereof, sith God is just,
> He be as miserably slain as I.
> Ah, let me live in prison all my days;
> And when I give occasion of offence
> Then let me die, for now thou hast no cause.
>
> CLIFFORD
> No cause!
> Thy father slew my father; therefore, die.
> *[Stabs him.]*

When Shakespeare wrote this disturbing Civil War scene, England was once more ravaged by internal strife, and the poet himself was probably still abroad in the ranks of the Catholic underground and Catholics-in-exile. Out of respect for their religious office, English priests were actually spared from the atrocities of the Wars of the Roses, as demonstrated in this scene. Under Elizabeth I, however, the priests of the old faith were treated as traitors and enemies of the state, and were publicly executed. Those who helped them were also traitors; they forfeited their assets and were sentenced to death.

The Elizabethan spectators, especially those who professed the Catholic faith and were therefore outcasts, deprived of their rights, and persecuted in their own country, could and must have related their own desperate situation to the misery of the Wars of the Roses, and the extermination of whole swathes of the population by their own compatriots. Shakespeare brought this to life for the stage by recreating the fate of individuals, in a manner that was both vivid and startlingly immediate.

RICHARD III

At the end of *Richard III*, a history that probably dates from 1592-93 and whose content bears a direct link with *Henry VI*, ending with the victory of Richmond (later Henry VII), Shakespeare seems to be encouraging the suppressed and despairing Catholic population of the Elizabethan era to take heart. In this historical drama, he drew a dark picture of the life and acts of Richard III, who may have been the most unscrupulous of English rulers, and is, at the very least, the most controversial. He is alleged to have eliminated all those who stood between him and the crown, including the princes in the Tower, his nephews, whom he was claiming to protect. Shakespeare's portrait of Richard is probably an even more negative account than is warranted by the historical figure. Richard's first biographer was none other than the English scholar, Lord Chancellor and later Catholic saint, Sir Thomas More (1478-1535). More's *The History of King Richard III* is not only considered to be the first great biography in English literature, but also strongly influenced Elizabethan historiography. The image of the hunchbacked villain encountered in Shakespeare's *Richard III* was first drawn by More and borrowed by the historians of the Tudor Age. Shakespeare thus came across it in the sources he used. More, who later became Henry VIII's chancellor, had, incidentally, written his biography of Richard in 1513, only four years after the death of Henry VII, who defeated Richard at Bosworth in 1485. More's account was therefore history written from the perspective of the victors. It would have pleased Henry VIII (1491-1547), who was the twenty-two-year-old second ruler of a new dynasty at the time. He had ascended the throne in 1509 as his father's successor. However, More's *Richard* was not published until 1543, after his death, and thus towards the end of Henry VIII's reign.

In Shakespeare's *Richard III*, the crown is immediately passed to the victor, Richmond, after the duel between Richard and his challenger. The educated members of the Elizabethan public knew that a new era had begun with the new ruler; that in historical reality, Henry VII had brought the divided nation together again and reunited it.

The bearer of the crown is Lord Stanley (later Earl of Derby). As in actual history, in Shakespeare's play Lord Stanley also changes sides on the battlefield of Bosworth, deserting King Richard and going over to Richmond's side. The historical figure who performed the symbolically important act of delivering the crown to Richmond was Baron Thomas Stanley (?1435-1504). The new king rewarded his change of allegiance with an earldom, creating him first Earl of Derby. The poet only needs a few lines in which to sketch in these highly dramatic events. At the end of Act V, scene 3,

Richard learns that Lord Stanley, along with his troops, refuses to obey his orders; by the beginning of Act V, scene 4, the king's situation is already hopeless. His despairing cry, 'A horse! a horse! My kingdom for a horse!' was already a familiar quotation in Elizabethan times, and was parodied by Shakespeare's contemporaries. While the outcome of the duel is still uncertain – 'The day is ours, the bloody dog is dead' (Richmond) – the spectator sees and hears what takes place. The stage directions read: '*Retreat, and flourish. Enter Richmond, Derby bearing the crown, with other Lords.*'

Richmond's concluding verses also contain a political agenda that the suppressed English Catholics of Shakespearean times may have likewise related to their own situation, for the victor announces that the insanity of the Civil War will come to an end, that the White and the Red Roses will be united, the country will be at peace and a new dynasty will be founded:

> Proclaim a pardon to the soldiers fled
> That in submission will return to us.
> And then, as we have ta'en the sacrament,
> We will unite the white rose and the red.
> [...]
> England hath long been mad, and scarr'd herself;
> The brother blindly shed the brother's blood,
> The father rashly slaughter'd his own son,
> The son, compell'd, been butcher to the sire,
> All this divided York and Lancaster,
> [...]
> O, now let Richmond and Elizabeth,
> The true succeeders of each royal house,
> By God's fair ordinance conjoin together!
> And let their heirs, God, if thy will be so,
> Enrich the time to come with smooth-fac'd peace,
> [...]

The conduct of Lord Stanley, particularly his desertion and his role of kingmaker, would have reminded the contemporary Catholic spectators of the conduct of someone of their own time with the same name and from the same family – Sir William Stanley, who had dramatically betrayed his country. In 1586, when English troops were assisting the Dutch against Spain, Sir William, as governor of the Dutch garrison town of Deventer, had handed over the city with 1200 soldiers, mostly Irish, to the Spanish. The English Catholics-in-exile celebrated him as their hero; the English government condemned him as a traitor. This inspired William Allen, founder of the Catholic college, to write the *Defence of Sir W. Stanley* (1587). Shakespeare's epitaph on the tomb of the Earls of Derby in Tong, Shropshire, which so far has not been convincingly assigned to any particular Stanley, can now be interpreted as an allusion to Sir William Stanley's action, which caused a great sensation at the time. The epitaph includes the following:

> The memory of him for whom this stands
> Shall outlive marble and defacers' hands.
> When all to time's consumption shall be given,
> Stanley for whom this stands shall stand in heaven.

Elizabethan theatregoers could explore the parallels between the historical and the contemporary 'deserter' Stanley even farther. If Baron Thomas Stanley had proved himself to be a kingmaker in 1485, then his relative, Sir William Stanley, had attempted to play this role in Elizabethan times. In conjunction with members of the leading ranks of the English Catholics-in-exile, he had chosen a Stanley as a possible successor to Elizabeth I. In 1593, together with the Jesuit Father William Holt, he arranged for Richard Hesketh to offer the crown, with Spain's support, to Ferdinando Stanley, later fifth Earl of Derby. Stanley had been the patron of the Lord Strange's men who had performed Shakespeare's early plays from 1592 to 1594 (see p. 116).

Sir William Stanley, the deserter of Deventer, was also to play an important role in the 1605 Gunpowder Plot (see p. 273).

RICHARD II

Among other things, it was his deeply rooted patriotism that induced the young Shakespeare to use examples from English history to censure contemporary iniquities. In *Richard II*, the dramatist appealed to the patriotic sentiments of his fellow countrymen. For those who attended the première, Shakespeare unveiled a unique 'historical monument' (written *c.* 1595) to England as a great, proud and admirable nation, celebrating 'this scept'red isle', 'this precious stone set in the silver sea', 'This other Eden demi-paradise'. On his deathbed, John of Gaunt, father of Bolingbroke, the future king of England, utters those incomparable words that still go to the heart of English national pride. Gaunt later deplores the sad condition of England during the reign of Richard II. Shakespeare thus criticises Elizabethan England. On the eve of the Essex Rebellion, *Richard II* was used by the conspirators as an instrument of political propaganda (see pp. 214 ff.). The eulogy, however, thrilled the playgoers, but they were also directed at a nation that had already laid the foundations for the future British Empire, with the establishment of numerous overseas trading companies[113]:

This royal throne of kings, this scept'red isle,
This earth of majesty, this seat of Mars,
This other Eden, demi-paradise,
This fortress built by Nature for herself
Against infection and the hand of war,
This happy breed of men, this little world,
This precious stone set in the silver sea,
Which serves it in the office of a wall
Or as a moat defensive to a house,
Against the envy of less happier lands,
This blessed plot, this earth, this realm, this England.
(Act II, scene 1)

It may be that, upon returning to England after long periods of absence, Shakespeare wrote this oft-quoted text, which idealises and even mythologises his contemporary reality, because he now had a basis for comparison. It was the view of an outsider, the reaction of somebody who, over the course of his long journeys, even as far as Rome, had surely suffered from homesickness and for whom the gradual approach to the island by ship (*Fig.* 72) was a lasting spiritual experience. This interpretation can be supported by the fact that in 1585, the year of crisis, the poet was forced to leave Stratford in a hurry, and that he, in the 'lost years' even used the name of his home town as a pseudonym several times (see p. 80–82).

***Fig.* 72** – The White Cliffs of Dover viewed from the sea.

KING JOHN

Histories like *Henry VI* and *Richard III* had captivated the Elizabethan public and held them in suspense. This power to enthral, however, was absent from the play *King John*, with the exception of a few scenes. None of Shakespeare's other historical dramas contain as many inconsistencies as this one, and none were so unpopular from the start. This could be the result of the fact that the historical figure of John was judged to be incompetent, even devious, as both man and monarch.

Uncertainty reigns with regard to the year in which this history was written; for a long time, it was believed to have originated between 1594 and 1597. However, the Shakespearean scholars J. Dover Wilson and E. A. J. Honigmann believed that it might date from 1590-91, since they thought that Shakespeare's play could have been the model for the anonymously-written *The Troublesome Raigne of John, King of England* (published 1591). Other scholars believed they could use internal evidence to date the play. For instance, Shakespeare's own suffering was said to be reflected in Constance's lament for her imprisoned son, Prince Arthur, and the prince's tragic death. In 1596, the poet lost his only son, Hamnet, Judith's twin, who was buried on 11 August 1596 in Stratford-upon-Avon, taking Shakespeare's great hopes for the future to the grave with him. Therefore, it may well be possible that the playwright demonstrates his own grief over the death of the young Hamnet in the mother's lament in Act III, scene 4 of *King John* for the loss of her son, which foreshadows the prince's actual death later (IV, 3), and which the dramatist describes with such extraordinary sensitivity:

> CONSTANCE
> Grief fills the room up of my absent child,
> Lies in his bed, walks up and down with me,
> Puts on his pretty looks, repeats his words,
> Remembers me of all his gracious parts,
> Stuffs out his vacant garments with his form;
> Then I have reason to be fond of grief.
> [...]
> O Lord! My boy, my Arthur, my fair son!
> My life, my joy, my food, my all the world!

If the poet actually wrote these lines in memory of his dead son, then this play could not have been completed before August 1596. *Richard II*, a history in which Shakespeare displays greater linguistic mastery than in *King John*, and whose characters are also portrayed with greater subtlety, would then have originated even later. As a contemporary source indicates, this is rather improbable.

On 7 December 1595, Sir Edward Hoby wrote a few lines to Robert Cecil, son and later successor to William Cecil, inviting him to his home. There, the writer added cryptically, King Richard would be presented. By 'Richard', he was not referring to Shakespeare's older play, *Richard III*, which was all too well known at the time, but it seems that he was referring to a new play, *Richard II*. In this way, Hoby could have even been making an allusion to Elizabeth I, who knew that (in her view) unpleasant parallels were drawn between herself and Shakespeare's Richard II. That is why she banned the scene depicting the deposition of Richard, represented by Shakespeare as a sovereign who had neglected his duties (Act IV, scene 1, lines 154-318). The deposition scene was not to be performed or published during the Elizabethan era. When Sir Edward invited Robert Cecil to his home in 1595, did he merely intend to entertain his eminent guest with a new historical drama, or was high politics involved? Or, to put it another way, did Hoby, like the Essex conspirators subsequently, use Shakespeare's history for similar political ends?

Robert Cecil's career advanced rapidly, and he eventually reached the highest political office. In 1596, two years before the death of his father, he was preferred over candidates put forward by his rival and opponent, the Earl of Essex, and

Fig. 73 – The Rialto in Venice, former marketplace of the Venetian Republic. There are many indications that Shakespeare must have been familiar with this square.

succeeded Sir Francis Walsingham as head of the spy network, which was especially important in terms of foreign and religious policy.

Contemporaries nicknamed Robert Cecil 'St Gobbo' because of the great power he wielded. With some certainty, the name can be traced back to Shakespeare's clownish character, Gobbo, in *The Merchant of Venice*. The marble statue of the hunchback on the Rialto in Venice, which the locals called 'Gobbo di Rialto', may have been Shakespeare's inspiration for the character and the name. On the Rialto, the old marketplace of the Republic of Venice (*Fig. 73*), Gobbo supports the marble pedestal on which the laws of Venice and the Doge's regulations were announced (*Fig. 74*).

Among other candidates for the post of spymaster-general, Essex had proposed William Davison, the former Secretary of State and Privy Councillor, to whom (as will be elaborated on later) Elizabeth handed over Mary Stuart's death sentence, and of whom she made a scapegoat, to be suitably punished, once matters had taken their inexorable course.

However, St Gobbo (i.e. Robert Cecil) triumphed across the board. In a letter written to his father from Lucca, Italy, William Davison's son refers to the events of 1595-96, particularly the succession to Walsingham. In it, he makes the cryptic statement that 'St. Gobbo' was a greater and more powerful 'saint' than 'St. Philip' or 'St. Diego'. In plain language, this means that Robert Cecil – from an English point of view – in terms of practical politics was much more important and influential than Philip II of Spain ('St. Philip') and James VI of Scotland ('St. Diego').

This assessment of the balance of power in the mid-1590s was correct, intelligent, and far-

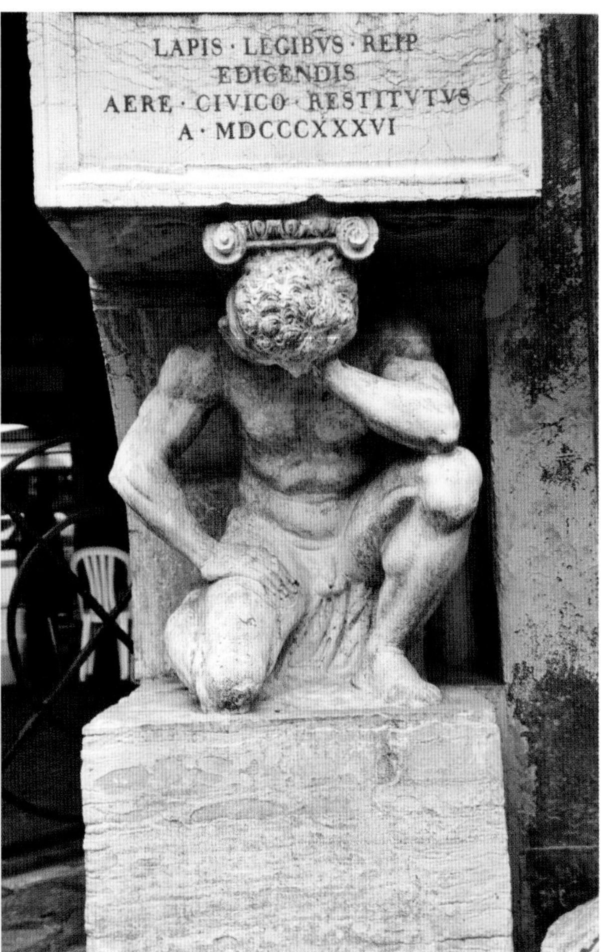

Fig. 74 – Gobbo di Rialto. Gobbo (the hunchback) can be found in the Rialto supporting the pedestal upon which the laws and statutes of the Venetian Republic were read out to the people. Shakespeare was probably inspired by this statue when naming his characters Launcelot Gobbo and Old Gobbo in *The Merchant of Venice*. After this play had been publicly performed, 'Gobbo' became the nickname for Robert Cecil, the politically powerful, hunchback son of William Cecil.

sighted. It was Robert Cecil who had prepared for the difficult regime change from Elizabeth to James, even while the queen was still alive, and therefore kept his hands on the reins of power both before and after her death. It was Cecil who had stood up to Essex and his supporters and, with Francis Bacon's support, after the failed *coup d'etat* in 1601 ensured that the man who had once been Elizabeth's favourite was found guilty of high treason, sentenced to death and executed, along with many of his fellow conspirators (with the exception of Shakespeare's patron, the Earl of Southampton). Afterwards, Cecil took over Essex's own plan, and began secret negotiations which secured the English throne for the Scottish king, James VI (see p. 222 f.).

Against the backdrop of this contemporary political context, Hoby's invitation to Robert Cecil could not merely have been a matter of a run-of-the-mill private dinner party followed by the performance of an historical play, but rather the staging of a drama which was new and fashionable, and above all extremely daring, because it contained allusions to the current, concrete political situation and even to the monarch herself.

Shakespeare used this history and his other historical dramas to influence the political consciousness of his contemporaries, those in high office and the general public. He himself – with a few notable exceptions – always remained in the background. Even more, he hid behind his characters, as it were, so as to remain faceless and escape prosecution. In this respect, he too led a clandestine existence.

Provided that Shakespeare had written *Richard II* after *King John*, he could have completed the latter, rather unpopular, history play, as early as 1595-6 as a kind of self-imposed exercise. If this is the case, he initially – for whatever reasons – held it back.

The (anti-Catholic) historical drama which was already in existence, *The Troublesome Raigne*, may have been the basis for Shakespeare's own work, though he must have made great changes. This was probably made all the easier because the Queen's Men, who had previously often performed this older, longer history play, were hardly present on the stages of the capital in 1591–92.

Not until 1596 – with the shock of Hamnet's death – could Shakespeare have added the deeply emotionally stirring scenes with and about Prince Arthur and/or have re-worked the entire play.

Considering his involvement with the Catholic underground, the young Shakespeare may have found it challenging to counter the interpretation of the life and death of King John from a Protestant perspective and eliminate anti-Catholic elements as far as possible. He certainly removed much that had previously shed a negative light on Catholicism, such as the dissolution of the monasteries that in the old play is presented as a comical scene, in which King John is poisoned, together with a monk who acts as his food taster. Shakespeare also cut out the monarch's actual death scene. His general intention of toning down this polemical Protestant drama is thus very obvious. It is particularly in evidence where the playwright seems to be alluding to a significant event in contemporary Elizabethan history.

In Act IV, scene 2, King John orders the killing of his nephew and rival, the young Prince Arthur, who is a pretender to the throne. Hubert de Burgh is to gouge out Arthur's eyes with red-hot irons, but he yields to the prince's entreaties (Act IV, scene 1). Later, John reproaches Hubert violently, because he believes that he has followed his orders. Elizabeth I had behaved in a very similar fashion towards Privy Councillor William Davison, former assistant to the principal spymaster, Sir Francis Walsingham. After the queen – following a long period of hesitation and indecision – had signed the death warrant of Mary, Queen of Scots, she handed it over to Davison, while suggesting that her wish was for the Scottish queen not to be executed publicly, but rather murdered in private. The death sentence was carried out on 8 February 1587, but Elizabeth likewise reprimanded Davison vehemently, holding him accountable, and had him thrown into the Tower for disobedience. He was not released until 1589. Davison, who was not guilty of anything, was nonetheless never reinstated, and was never again allowed to serve the queen, though Essex pleaded his cause to Elizabeth. The conduct of Shakespeare's protagonist in *King John* would obviously remind his contemporaries of Elizabeth's (not only in Catholic eyes) shabby treatment of Davison in this affair. For the English Catholics at home and abroad, a political beacon of hope had been extinguished with the death of Mary, Queen of Scots, who had a legitimate claim to the English throne.

In *King John*, Shakespeare makes even more conspicuous allusions to Elizabeth, her religious policies and her excommunication by the Pope in 1570. The Papal Anathema is pronounced on the English king by the Papal legate, Cardinal Pandulph of Milan. Like Elizabeth, John does not recognise Papal sovereignty, and he consummates the open break with Rome by not only quarrelling with the Papacy over the appointment of Stephen Langton as Archbishop of Canterbury, but by forcibly keeping him 'from that holy see'. In Act III, scene 1 there is a confrontation between the cardinal and the king in the presence of the French monarch, Philip, and the Austrian archduke:

> PANDULPH
> Hail, you anointed deputies of heaven!
> To thee, King John, my holy errand is.
> I Pandulph, of fair Milan cardinal,
> And from Pope Innocent the legate here,
> Do in his name religiously demand
> Why thou against the church, our holy mother,
> So wilfully dost spurn; and force perforce
> Keep Stephen Langton, chosen Archbishop
> Of Canterbury, from that holy see?
> This, in our foresaid father's name,
> Pope Innocent, I do demand of thee.[...]
>
> KING JOHN
> What earthy name to interrogatories
> Can task the free breath of a sacred king?
> Thou canst not, Cardinal, devise a name
> So slight, unworthy, and ridiculous,
> To charge me to an answer, as the Pope.
> Tell him this tale; and from the mouth of England
> Add thus much more, that no Italian priest
> Shall tithe or toll in our dominions;

But as we, under heaven, are supreme head,
So under Him that great supremacy,
Where we do reign, we will alone uphold,
Without th'assistance of a mortal hand:
So tell the Pope, all reverence set apart
To him and his usurp'd authority.

In this scene in the Shakespeare play, John shouts at the Papal legate, hurling at him a tirade against the selling of indulgences in Rome and the sinecures there, and reproaches him for the Church of Rome's deplorable situation, which, as is well known, did not become a decisive issue until the sixteenth century and led to the Schism. Previously, scholars have held this scene to be the only anti-Catholic passage in Shakespeare's treatment of the material. In reality, however, this is not the manifestation of an anti-Catholic attitude on the dramatist's part, but rather he is using King John as a covert representation of Elizabeth I, and the opinions voiced by King John reflect in large measure the viewpoint of Elizabeth. Shakespeare's intention was to derive solutions from the historical conflict to apply to similar problems in the present. The dramatist put words into the mouth of the Papal legate that must have sounded familiar to Elizabethan ears. The Catholics in the audience who were loyal to the Pope, and who thus experienced a conflict of loyalties after the excommunication of their monarch, would have inwardly agreed with the Roman cardinal; but the Protestants would have been indignant, and may even have demonstrated their displeasure loudly and openly.

When King John renounces the Pope, whom he no longer recognises and whose friends he would like to call his enemies, the cardinal answers by excommunicating him:

Then, by the lawful power that I have,
Thou shalt stand curs'd and excommunicate;
And blessed shall he be that doth revolt
From his allegiance to an heretic;
And meritorious shall that hand be call'd,
Canonized and worshipp'd as a saint,
That takes away by any secret course
Thy hateful life.

The parallels to the situation in which Elizabeth I found herself could not be overlooked. Cardinal Pandulph's words, 'Thou shalt stand curs'd and excommunicate', not only revived memories of the horrors of the Bull of Excommunication of 1570 (*'Regnans in Excelsis'*) whereby the queen had been excommunicated by Pope Pius V, but Shakespeare seems also to be alluding to the great, ever-present threat posed by Spain and the Pope.

The aims of the Spanish attack against England in 1588 were still fresh in the minds of Shakespeare's contemporaries. For Protestant England, Philip's Armada – despite the English victory – remained traumatic. Furthermore, Spain could be expected to despatch further fleets against England. Spain and England had been at war since 1585, and this situation lasted until 1604, a year after Elizabeth's death.

For the English Catholics, both in England and abroad, Philip, who was the English monarch's brother-in-law and the former consort of Queen Mary I, was not seen as a usurper, but as a liberator. He intended to depose the excommunicated English queen, release the country from the yoke of the Church of England, and return it to Catholicism. England would thus be governed by Spain and be once again subject to the sovereignty of Rome.

To Pope Sixtus V, the enterprise of reclaiming England for the Catholic cause was worth one million gold ducats. He immediately made half this huge sum available in cash; the other half was to be paid after the occupation of England or one of its famous ports. The Duke of Parma acted as Philip's representative, while the Pope was represented by William Allen, the founder of the Collegium Anglicum and close friend of the Jesuit Father, Robert Parsons, who was actually pulling the strings offstage. If the Spanish had been victorious, Allen would have been made Archbishop of Canterbury. Sixtus

Fig. 75a – Portrait of Elizabeth I. This official portrait of the queen dates from after the English victory against the Spanish Armada in 1588, and is therefore known as the Armada Portrait. Tellingly, the queen's right hand rests upon a globe. The English crown is positioned near her right elbow. The window in the upper left depicts a battle formation at sea.

Fig. 75b – Detail: The Spanish Armada

Fig. 75c – The right hand of the queen, resting on a globe.

had appointed him cardinal for this purpose on 7 August 1587. The two previous Bulls of Excommunication against Elizabeth I were confirmed and renewed by Sixtus. Thus, the English queen was not only permanently excommunicated, but – from the Catholic point of view – also robbed of her title, her rank and her very claim to the throne. Her subjects would now owe allegiance to the representative of the Spanish king (Parma) and the Papal legate (Allen)[114].

These conflicting positions are even represented in the royal portraits of Elizabeth I. In addition to the 1585 painting which was probably commissioned by Catholics, and was a retort to the coronation portrait, incorporating pictorial symbols to criticise the ruler (see *Fig. 20*), there are further portraits of the monarch extant which demonstrate the different political and religious positions. The famous Armada Portrait is a triumphant celebration of Elizabeth's victory over the Spanish fleet in 1588, glorifying her person and confirming her claim to greatness and the right to expansion through the depiction of the globe (*Fig. 75a*). In 1589, an engraving was made, supposedly intended also to glorify the monarch and the same historical event, but achieving the exact opposite. In contrast with the Armada Portrait, the neck, face, expression in the eyes and shape of the head, as well as the queen's lips, which are depicted as a straight line (*Fig. 76*), have a rather unpleasant effect on the viewer. It is significant that Elizabeth's crown, the most important symbol of her sovereign power and dignity, is not placed on *top* of her head, but *behind* it, apparently on the collar of her dress. Moreover, it is not placed symmetrically, but situated slightly to the right. In addition, the figures shown to the left, next to the plaque bearing the inscription, 'Eliza, Trivmphans', support the impression that this is most likely a criticism of the ruler and a questioning of the legitimacy of Elizabeth's reign. The crowned lion with a human face (probably an allusion to Henry VIII) is pushing a black figure towards the plaque, near where the 'E' of the queen's initials is located.

In *King John*, more obviously than anywhere else, Shakespeare made use of an historical example to pinpoint a burning contemporary issue: could and should the Elizabethan Catholics remain loyal to a queen whom Rome had excommunicated and proclaimed a 'heretic'? There seemed to be no way of resolving their crisis of conscience.

In *King John*, Shakespeare seems to point out a feasible solution – from the Catholic point of view. He makes use of an example from history, which is initially negative but eventually exemplary, to serve as a guideline for contemporary political conduct. In the end, John reconciles himself with Rome, and so in Act V, scene 1 he regains the English crown from the hand of Cardinal Pandulph, who again acts as the Pope's representative.

> PANDULPH
> [*gives back the crown*] Take again
> From this my hand, as holding of the Pope,
> Your sovereign greatness and authority.

If Shakespeare felt provoked by the play *The Troublesome Raigne of John, King of England*, which lauded Protestantism and ridiculed Catholicism, then this applied even more so to the short historical play *Kynge Johan* by the Protestant Bishop of Ossory, John Bale (1495-1563). Bale, known for his prolific, extremely polemical anti-Catholic writings defending and supporting the Reformation, had also used his history of King John for pro-Reformation purposes and argued strongly against Catholicism. His play, a short 'interlude' (an entr'acte) of no literary significance, was important insofar as it provided the first bridge between the medieval morality plays and the historical dramas of the Renaissance. It would seem that Shakespeare was unhappy about the strong anti-Catholic bias and pro-Protestant propaganda of Bale's *Kynge Johan*, the very first, though slight, English historical drama about King John, and of the two-part history (*The*

Fig. 76 – Eliza, Triumphans. A triumphal painting of Elizabeth I, created in 1589. Closer inspection revealed that this portrait also contains encoded negative signs. For instance, the crown is not positioned in the centre but to the right hand side of the head. Since the work is dated one year after the Spanish defeat, it could have been commissioned or influenced by disappointed Catholics.

Troublesome Raigne of John, King of England) about this unstable period under John's rule. Perhaps it was for this reason that he accepted the challenge of working on this historical material, to project a countervailing Catholic point of view. The result was no literary masterpiece; a play that was unpopular then as it is today.

HENRY IV

With his two-part history *Henry IV*, Shakespeare created a work that enjoyed enormous popularity among his contemporaries. The first part was probably written in late 1596. The play's attraction lay less in the historical setting than in the character of the knight, Sir John Falstaff, as rotund as he was bold, a comical figure who swept the Elizabethan public right off their feet and made theatrical history to a greater extent than any other of Shakespeare's characters. Falstaff's tall tales and amorous liaisons, his roguery and his bravado, and above all his cowardice, made him a great crowd-pleaser. The particular charm of the historical aspect of the play still lies in the scenes where the heir to the throne, Prince Henry, condescends to become involved with Falstaff and his cronies for a while, participating in the 'low life' of London, much to the king's consternation. In addition, the clash of opposing values, represented by the Scottish Hotspur and hero Henry Percy, on the one hand, and the lazy, cowardly Falstaff on the other, ensured that *Henry IV* would be a hit in Elizabethan times. If Percy stands for virtues such as chivalry and honour, Falstaff embodies every conceivable vice (alcoholism, gluttony, whoring, cowardice, dishonesty etc.), yet he still manages to get the upper hand in practically every situation (even those in which he is at a disadvantage) through his cunning and wiles. To the great astonishment of the prince, who defeats and fells Percy in a chivalric duel, Falstaff himself pretends to have killed the hero. What Sir John stands for is most expressly manifest in his thoughts on the nature of honour:

> FALSTAFF
> [...] Can honour set to a leg? No. Or an arm?
> No. Or take away the grief of a wound? No.
> Honour hath no skill in surgery, then? No.
> What is honour? A word. What is in that word?
> Honour. What is that honour? Air. A trim
> reckoning! Who hath it? He that died o'
> Wednesday. Doth he feel it? No. Doth he hear it?
> No.[...] 'Tis insensible, then? Yea, to the dead.
> But will it live with the living? No. Why?
> Detraction will not suffer it.
> Honour is a mere scutcheon: and so ends
> my catechism.

(Part 1, Act V, scene 1)

It is hardly possible to imagine a greater contrast between Falstaff and the ideal image of the Elizabethan gentleman, who ought to combine the qualities of a scholar, courtier and soldier in his person.

Elizabeth I had become so fascinated by the character of Falstaff that she wanted Shakespeare to write a comedy in which the popular knight falls in love. In his 'Epistle Dedicatory' to his work *The Comical Gallant* (1702), John Dennis wrote that he knew very well that this play 'hath pleas'd one of the greatest Queens that ever was in the world', and he continued: 'This comedy was written at her command'. In his 'Life of Shakespeare', prefixed to his 1709 edition of Shakespeare's works, Nicholas Rowe added: 'Queen Elizabeth was so well pleased with that admirable character of Falstaff in the two parts of *Henry IV* that she commanded him [Shakespeare] to continue it for one more play and show him in love'.

Yet the character of Falstaff initially caused many problems for his creator. The corpulent, drunkard knight who lodges with his cronies at the Boar's Head Tavern, whose purse is permanently empty, who is always threatened with debtor's prison, and who in the end does not even balk at holding up pious Canterbury pilgrims, was originally given the name of Sir John Oldcastle. Oldcastle was a religious dissident who was executed in 1417 as a heretic (*Fig. 77*) and was therefore commemorated as a Protestant martyr in John Foxe's *Book of Martyrs*, published in 1563. This work attained almost Biblical status when, in 1571, all English

Fig. 77 – Execution of Sir John Oldcastle, 4th Baron Cobham, the leader of the Lollards, in 1417. An illustration from the Protestant martyrology, known as *The Book of Martyrs*, by John Foxe (1563). In 1571, all the senior clergy and all the cathedrals in England were required to keep a copy of the book accessible to the public. Foxe's *Book of Martyrs* was the target of many attacks by the crypto-Catholics and English Catholics-in-exile. Shakespeare was accused of using Sir John Oldcastle as a comic figure in *Henry IV*. Lord Cobham and his family forced the dramatist to change the name, so Oldcastle became Falstaff.

cathedrals and the senior clergy in the country were ordered to make a copy of it accessible to the public. This fervently Protestant volume was a thorn in the side of the Elizabethan Catholics-in-exile and the clandestine Catholics and, as such, was frequently the object of their fierce polemical attacks. The surviving leader of the English Catholic missionary movement, Father Robert Parsons, as well as other dedicated Catholics, therefore attempted to ridicule the Protestant martyrs. Shakespeare was apparently acting in this vein by naming his comic villain Oldcastle, although he would later explain apologetically, 'this is not the [same] man'.

A descendant of the historical figure, then Lord Cobham, lodged a complaint. He objected that his ancestor was being ridiculed on the stage. Shakespeare was therefore compelled to change the name. The wordplay in 'my old lad of the castle' (*Henry IV*, Part 1, Act I, scene 2, line 47) still recalls the earlier name, but Oldcastle became Falstaff. The new name can be traced back to that of a rogue in Shakespeare's *Henry VI* (Part I), Sir John Fastolfe. The dramatist only had to change some letters, and Fastolfe became Falstaff.

Like many Catholics in Shakespeare's time, including Shakespeare himself, the historical figure of Sir John Oldcastle (*c.* 1370-1417), who from 1409 bore the title Lord Cobham, led a double life. For many years, he had been servant and friend to Henry V. Yet at the same time he was dedicated to the reformism of the Oxford theologian John Wyclif (*c.* 1330-1384), which was directed against the failings of the Church and against the papacy. In the year 1377, Pope Gregory had condemned his reforms as subversive of state and church. After Wyclif's death, his followers – known as the Lollards – who had been banished from Oxford, preached poverty and chastity to the people. The statute entitled *De heretico comburendo* (1401) proclaimed them heretics. Many were burned at the stake. Knights such as Sir John Oldcastle had also joined the movement. In 1414, Oldcastle staged a rebellion; when it failed, he was condemned as a heretic and was hanged and burned at the stake. Afterwards, the movement went underground, having its own priests, schoolmasters and books.

As a response to Shakespeare's distorted treatment of Oldcastle, now renamed Falstaff, the stage play *The first part of the life of Sir John Oldcastle the good Lord Cobham* was written jointly by the dramatists Munday, Drayton, Wilson and Hathaway in the course of the year 1599, probably at Lord Cobham's instigation. Incidentally, Anthony Munday (1560-1633) was not only a playwright, but also a well-known government spy who had made a name for himself through numerous anti-Catholic activities. In 1578, when William Shakespeare would have just begun his studies in Rheims, Munday was sent to France and Italy in order to spy on the exiled Catholics and students there. He was even received at the English College in Rome (founded in 1579) and collected material about the plans of his Catholic compatriots, which he published in 1582 under the title *The English Romayne Life*. Munday was also involved in the capture of the Jesuit Father Edmund Campion. The history, to which Munday made a significant contribution, and which was to depict the life of the Protestant martyr Oldcastle as it really was, would present not a glutton who indulged in his vices, not an aged roué who led young people astray, but a virtuous gentleman and a courageous martyr. The barbs against Shakespeare are obvious. Significantly, the play was first performed on 1 November 1599 (All Saint's Day) at the Rose Theatre. Henslowe, the owner of the theatre, was pleased. He paid the successful dramatists an extra ten shillings[115]. Twenty years later, Isaac Jaggard re-published it under Shakespeare's name, in order to turn a profit.

If William Shakespeare depicted the Protestant martyr Oldcastle on the stage in an unseemly manner, as a buffoon and a crook, then this was apparently the result – as a contemporary source suggests – of Parsons' influence, or it happened in collusion with him. The link between Parsons and Shakespeare is hinted at by the Elizabethan historian and cartographer John Speed, an avid patriot who had originally been a tailor. Speed refers to Shakespeare's treatment of the historical figure of Sir John Oldcastle. In his *History of Great Britaine* (1611), in which he polemically writes of 'this Papist and his Poet', the historian appears to be referring to Robert Parsons and William Shakespeare. Speed explains that N.D. [= Nicholas Doleman, a well-known alias for Robert Parsons], the author of *A Treatise of Three Conversations of England*, made a ruffian, bandit and rebel out of Oldcastle, and based this depiction on the authority of actors. This historical and religious context and Shakespeare's Catholic background now make it clear that the reference can only be to Parsons and Shakespeare. However, it can hardly have been a matter of the Jesuit using the dramatist for his own ends. At any rate, Shakespeare's character Falstaff / Oldcastle was a great success – no matter what the playwright's original intentions may have been.

At the end of *Henry IV*, the prince definitively and ruthlessly cuts his ties with the ruffian and rebel Falstaff, his former friend and companion, after he has ascended the throne as Henry V. He banishes Falstaff, who dies of grief. The brutal repudiation of his former friend in the famous 'rejection scene' has been considered a *non sequitur* by previous commentators, and has raised the question whether Shakespeare's Henry V really is the 'model king' he has long seemed. What has often been overlooked, however, is that the young prince only outwardly descends to the level of ruffians and drunkards, and is already inwardly distancing himself from their society at the beginning of the story. In his first monologue (Part 1, Act I, scene 2) it says:

> I know you all, and will awhile uphold
> The unyok'd humour of your idleness:
> Yet herein will I imitate the sun,
> Who doth permit the base contagious clouds
> To smother up his beauty from the world,
> That, when he please again to be himself
> [...]

HENRY V

Like Thomas Churchyard and John Norden[116], Shakespeare enthusiastically responded to the events of spring 1599, alluded to in the prologue to the fifth act of *Henry V*, namely the Earl of Essex's campaign in Ireland. In this patriotic history, whose prevailing mood is an almost effervescent and intoxicating optimism, the dramatist lifts the veil of his hidden existence in certain places, and in the prologue to Act II reveals for the first time his true feelings and political hopes:

> Now all the youth of England are on fire,
> And silken dalliance in the wardrobe lies:
> Now thrive the armourers, and honour's thought
> Reigns solely in the breast of every man:
> They sell the pasture now to buy the horse,
> Following the mirror of all Christian kings,
> With winged heels, as English Mercuries.
> For now sits Expectation in the air,
> And hides a sword from hilts unto the point
> With crowns imperial, crowns and coronets,
> Promis'd to Harry and his followers.

The enthusiasm manifested here for national feeling and political hopes can clearly be related to Essex. The earl, who was at the height of his powers in 1599, was not only England's commander-in-chief, leading a well-equipped army on an expedition to Ireland, but he also had excellent diplomatic and intelligence connections with many rulers and kings, including the Holy Roman Emperor and even the Shah of Persia. As he did during his earlier military operation in France in 1591, while in Ireland Essex would make many knights from among his followers and in so doing elevate men who had personally dedicated themselves to him. Such measures were certainly calculated, serving not least to strengthen the commander's political power. This is alluded to in *Henry V*, when in Act IV, scene 3 the king solemnly promises his men on the night before the decisive battle:

> For he to-day that sheds his blood with me
> Shall be my brother; be he ne'er so vile,
> This day shall gentle his condition
> ....

Incidentally, *Henry V* is – with the exception of the later work, *Henry VIII*, which occupies a special position – Shakespeare's last English historical drama. Later circumstances forced the playwright to resort to Roman history. *Julius Caesar* was written about six months after *Henry V*. This change of historical setting became necessary because John Whitgift, Archbishop of Canterbury, had issued a general ban on printing satires and epigrams, as well as dramas about English history, and had marked the implementation of this ban with a book-burning that he had arranged and performed on 4 June, 1599 at the London Stationers' company. A publication was only permitted if it had been authorised by a member of the Privy Council. Among the burned and repressed works were the epigrams of John Davies, Marlowe's elegies, a book about the fifteen joys of marriage, and

Willobie his Avisa, a narrative in verse in which a tavern-owner's wife is wooed unsuccessfully by a nobleman in the country *prior* to her wedding and *afterwards* – again in vain – by four foreigners. The last of these appears in the company of a close friend with the initials 'W.S.' Many scholars believe that this meant none other than William Shakespeare.

Shakespeare obviously complied with the archbishop's ban, and wrote no more plays about his country's history. With his more or less open homage to Essex in *Henry V*, he had already gone very far, although not without taking the appropriate precautions. The experienced London printer and publisher, James Roberts, who had been a member of the guild since 1564, evidently had strong business ties with Shakespeare's theatre company and had already produced numerous quarto editions of Shakespeare's dramas. Roberts had the play entered in the Stationers' Register with the note, 'to be staied'. This was nothing other than a 'blocking entry', meaning that the author and publisher wanted to hold back publication, hide the work from censors, prevent the printing of pirate copies, and, last but not least, stake Shakespeare's authorship of the work and what would later be called his copyright. These intentions were thwarted, however, and in 1600 an unauthorised quarto edition of the play had been published, with what was undoubtedly an incorrect reconstruction of the shortened text which was used by the company when on tour [117].

Shakespeare had also taken a great risk with the deposition scene in *Richard II*. The spectacular case of the Cambridge graduate and historian Dr John Hayward (*c.* 1564-1627) demonstrated how dangerous it was for Elizabethan authors to use persons or events from the history of England as a pattern or model for the present. On 21 February 1599, the first part of a book by Hayward on the life and reign of Henry IV was published which also describes the dethronement and death of Richard II. It contained a scholarly Latin dedication to the Earl of Essex. The queen immediately smelled high treason and assigned Francis Bacon to examine the matter. Bacon determined that a serious offence had occurred, although it was not high treason. Hayward was thrown into the Tower, where he was spared torture, but he evidently remained there until Elizabeth's death. All of this confirms how seriously the government took the taboo surrounding representations of English history. It was only under James I, whose succession to the throne Hayward had advocated in pamphlets, that he regained his standing as a professional historian.

Shakespeare's decision to represent in *Julius Caesar* the murder of a ruler on the open stage who had threatened to become a tyrant was at least as daring and dangerous as the forbidden representation of English history. In the Roman tragedy, however, the consequences of this bloody deed, the subsequent civil war, are demonstrated at the same time as a warning. The mood of the play is one of deep resignation and pessimism. This, in a way, appears to anticipate the state of mind that afflicted Shakespeare after the failure of the Essex rebellion in 1601, when he turned towards tragedy and was never to write any comedy again. The great turning point in Shakespeare's work is therefore closely related to the events of the day and the course of the poet's own life.

COMEDIES

In the comedies from the first phase of Shakespeare's theatrical career, the action takes place mostly in the Mediterranean, particularly in Italy (*Fig. 78*). The dramatist appears not only to be familiar with the names of the many Italian cities in which he stages the plots, but also with the places themselves, such as Venice (*Fig. 79*), Padua, Mantua, Verona, Pisa, Florence and Rome (*Fig. 60*). Shakespeare's

Fig. 78 – Map of Italy, Sardinia and Corsica by Cornelis Danckerts (II) dated 1640.

familiarity with the geography of northern and central Italy, his descriptions of journeys on land and sea around the Mediterranean, his recounting of disputes among the Italian city-states, his observation of the local atmosphere and his smattering of Romance languages, can be taken as indications that the poet was not merely drawing on graphic and literary sources, as has been previously accepted, but had himself visited Italy. In the meantime this has also been proved by new documentary evidence (see pp. 77–82). It is, therefore, quite conceivable that Shakespeare used the wealth of impressions and experiences garnered during the seven 'lost years' when he travelled on the Continent, in France, Italy and possibly Navarre and Spain, in the comedies he wrote in the 1590s.

THE COMEDY OF ERRORS

The Comedy of Errors was probably Shakespeare's first comedy. It is clear that the dramatist drew upon Plautus's *Menaechmi*. Even this otherwise cheerful Shakespearian play opens with a tragic scene, where the site of the impending execution of the merchant of Syracuse, Aegeon, recalls the spot where the execution of the Catholic priest William Hartley took place in Shoreditch in 1588 (see p. 88). This indicates that, even when writing comedies, Shakespeare did not lose sight of the persecution and execution of the priests of the Catholic Church. The allusion to an historical event is also useful proof in dating the play, making it at least probable that *The Comedy of Errors* was written shortly after 1588.

Fig. 79 – View of Venice in the sixteenth century, as Shakespeare could have seen it. Against the contemporary backdrop of the Doge's Palace and the Campanile, the artist Francesco Bassana depicts an event that occurred in 1177. The Pope thanks the Doge for negotiating the peace between himself and the German Emperor Frederick Barbarossa.

LOVE'S LABOUR'S LOST

Shakespeare's comedy *Love's Labour's Lost* was apparently performed in the presence of the queen after Christmas 1597 and published in a quarto edition in 1598. The title page reads: 'Newly corrected and augmented / by W. Shakespere' indicating that the play was not new at that time but had merely been revised and expanded by the author. It may have been written years before, performed in the private home of a nobleman and possibly printed in a 'bad quarto'. The similarities of many passages of this comedy to Shakespeare's narrative poems *Venus and Adonis* and *The Rape of Lucrece*, as well as to his sonnets, gave rise to the supposition that it was first performed at the country seat of the Earl of Southampton at Titchfield Abbey near Portsmouth (*Fig. 66*). For this reason, it is quite probable that the première of *Love's Labour's Lost* was actually staged at Titchfield, though not before 1593 and almost certainly not after 1595.

The play is based on an historical event which took place in 1578: the visit to Nérac by the French Queen Catherine de Medici (1519–1589) and her daughter Marguerite de Valois, the estranged wife of Henry of Navarre. Many researchers think that a lost account of this sensational event was used by the dramatist, but the probability of this is not very great, since no other copy of such an account has been found, nor is there any concrete indication that it ever existed. A book that must have been in Shakespeare's private library in New Place indicates his interest in the historical figure of Catherine de Medici. In *A Mervaylovs discourse vpon the lyfe, deedes, and behauiours of KATHERINE de Medicis* [...] by Henri Estienne, Catherine is condemned as a usurper who destroyed the French body politic. This interesting work cannot, however, be considered as a source for *Love's Labour's Lost*, since it appeared in 1575 in Heidelberg, three years before the ceremonial visit to Nérac.

There is always the possibility that Shakespeare heard of this spectacular journey while he was being educated at the English College in Rheims (1578–1580), since any major political events within the host country were of significance for the college. Furthermore, Robert Parsons, the close friend of the college founder, had good contacts with the highest circles in France, including Cardinal Guise, who in 1581-82 enabled Parsons to found an English college in Eu in Normandy. The visit of the two queens in 1578 had very concrete political goals, namely the reclaiming of the province of Aquitaine for France.

The conversion of Henry IV of France to Catholicism in 1593 caused a sensation all over Europe at the time. Elizabeth I was outraged and spoke of treason. She had earlier, when he was under serious threat from the Catholic powers, provided military support for the Protestant king, sending to Normandy an army of 4,000 men commanded by the Earl of Essex. Shakespeare may have written his comedy *Love's Labour's Lost* between 1593 and 1595. All previous discussions about the connection between Henry's conversion and the original date of the play[118] have disregarded the playwright's Catholicism, that of his patron Southampton and also the demonstrably tolerant position of the Earl of Essex towards the old faith.

Shakespeare obviously wrote his comedy about the King of Navarre and his Court after the king's conversion to Catholicism. He would have been able to learn more about the queens' visit to Nérac and the atmosphere of the Court in Navarre from Southampton, and possibly from Essex, who was extremely well informed about foreign affairs and to whom France was especially important. In the early 1590s, together with Anthony Bacon, brother of Francis Bacon, Essex had begun – secretly and in competition with both the powerful Cecils – to establish contact with the European courts and to gather all sorts of information. Consequently he had considerable knowledge of foreign affairs, and of France in particular.

It is significant that the official diplomatic mission to France in 1598, headed by Robert Cecil, virtually came to nothing. The (Catholic) Earl of Southampton, however, who belonged to the inner Essex circle and who had joined the delegation in order to travel round the Continent later, was very warmly welcomed by Henry IV.

The main characters in *Love's Labour's Lost* are based on historical figures, especially the King of Navarre, who seems indeed to have been modelled on the future Henry IV of France, one of the 'most attractive' and 'most gifted' ruling personalities of Europe at that time. In his biography *Der Traum Philipps II.* (The Dream of Philip II, 1951), Edgar Maass describes the appearance and personality of the king:

> Stocky, broad-shouldered, eyes sparkling with life, with a large, beaky nose and his characteristic short beard, he was full of energy, good sense, humour and kindness. Henry attracted people like a magnet ... (p. 164).

Maass says of the ruler's relationship with women:

> Henry was particularly favoured by women. The names of the beautiful Corisande de Gramont and the lovely Gabrielle d'Estrées are not forgotten. Henry only had particular difficulties with his own wife, Marguerite ... (p. 165).

Admittedly, Shakespeare emphasises a different aspect of the king. He sees him as a bookish, withdrawn individual who distances himself from women in order to discuss philosophy and morality in the company of like-minded courtiers. In this play, the French atmosphere is unmistakable, and the dramatist highlights the 'academies' formed in aristocratic circles in France and Italy at the time, where philosophical and literary topics were discussed. Shakespeare also seems to have in mind comparable coteries in his own country, such as those that surrounded Essex and Southampton. According to Joel Hurstfield (*The Queen's Wards*, London, 1958), the 'coteries' round Essex and Southampton may have been the academy run by Lord Burghley for his noble wards, such as Essex, Rutland and Southampton, at his house on the Strand. The young Southampton was particularly fond of literature and the theatre and, as a patron of the arts, he was a magnet for the literary figures and poets of his time. However, the Essex circle did not limit itself to patronage of the arts, but appears from the start to have had political interests and goals.

The most important characters in *Love's Labour's Lost*, after the king, are the courtier Berowne, based upon the historical figure of Marshal de Biron, and Longaville, based on the historical Duc de Longueville. Both men had fought on the side of Henry of Navarre in the French Civil War. The model for the courtier Dumain could have been the Duc de Mayenne, who had previously fought against the Protestant Navarre, but had been reconciled to him after he had converted to Catholicism. Biron was especially popular in England, due to his role as military adviser to the Earl of Essex. It was Biron who sent Elizabeth the sensational message from his king, Henry IV of France, that he was going to marry Marie de Medici after his marriage to Marguerite de Valois had been annulled in 1599. The marriage took place on 7 December 1600 at Lyon. This was designed to further strengthen the Catholic alliance, and caused great anxiety to the now aging queen.

The daughter resulting from this marriage, Henrietta Maria, later married Charles I of England. During the English Civil War, Henrietta Maria stayed for three weeks with Shakespeare's daughter Susanna in New Place[119]. Susanna Hall must have given the book about Catherine de Medici to her royal guest as a gift – as the handwritten inscription in Latin clearly indicates (see p. 315). This book from William Shakespeare's library is particularly informative about the life of the playwright, indicating his interest in contemporary French history. The religious conflicts between Catholics and Huguenots culminated in one of the most terrible bloodbaths in the history of France, the so-called St Bartholomew's Day Massacre on 24 August 1572. Catherine was known to have been responsible for the Massacre, and Henry of Navarre, who had married her daughter Marguerite on 18 August 1572, very nearly lost his life in the events. The handwritten annotations in the book, discovered by chance in the twentieth century, are very informative on this point (see p. 315).

On closer consideration, there also appear to be historical models for several of the minor characters in *Love's Labour's Lost*. Examples are Don Adriano de Armado, one of the so-called 'low comedy' characters, whom – much to the delight of his audience – Shakespeare portrays as a bombastic figure; Sir Nathaniel, a curate; and Holofernes, a schoolmaster who excels in classical (Latin) literature and grammar. The characters also include Dull, a constable, and Costard, a clown. The dramatist gives the clergyman and the schoolmaster lines containing allusions which can only be fully deciphered if they are considered within the religious and historical context of the time.

The First Folio Edition of Shakespeare's plays (1623), which was lovingly edited after his death by his friends and colleagues, John Heminge and Henry Condell, contains a version of *Love's Labour's Lost* in which it is evident that Holofernes is not identical to the schoolmaster Pedant, but is a separate character. Surprisingly, this is not highlighted by modern critics of Shakespeare, and is not mentioned at all in the commentaries. Moreover, in modern editions of the text, Nathaniel's speeches in the First Folio Edition are ascribed to Holofernes, and vice versa. Certain passages originally spoken by the schoolmaster, Pedant, and by Nathaniel have even been combined and put in the mouth of Holofernes[120].

This changes the meaning intended by Shakespeare, as shown by the following example in particular. In the First Folio Edition, Jaquenetta appears with greeting: 'God giue you good morrow M. *Person*.' Nathaniel feels that it is he who is being addressed and answers 'Master Person, quasi Person? And if one should be perst, Which is the one?' By 'perst', Shakespeare obviously means the word 'pursed' in the sense of 'to be provided with money'. The initiated among the Elizabethan audience would have realised exactly who was meant by this pun – the Jesuit father Robert Parsons (or Persons).

It is also worth noting that in the modern editions, it is not Nathaniel but Holofernes who answers, and that the original text has been revised. The wording of the Alexander edition (1951, reprint 1978) reads: 'Master Person, quasi pers-one? And if one should be pierc'd, which is the one?' The essay *Father Parsons in Shakespeare* (1915) by John Phelps sheds some useful light on this vexed question. Phelps spotted – as it seems for the first time in modern Shakespeare criticism – that 'Person' is an allusion to the surname of Father Robert Parsons or Persons[121]. His reading after this point is invalid, however, because it is based on the version 'pierc'd' and not 'perst' ('pursed'), as the First Folio Edition unmistakeably has it (*Fig. 80*). The untenable premise inevitably leads to an unsustainable interpretation. Phelps believed that Shakespeare alluded here to the 'piercing' of the arch traitor (Parsons), to entertain an audience who were familiar with this kind of torture. This has puzzled other scholars. For instance, in *Shakespeare's Religious Background*, Peter Milward speaks of 'a somewhat obscure jest'. In reality, at this point, the text deals with the pun 'Person'/'perst' (= 'pursed'), therefore with an allusion to the name of Parsons or Persons and to the fact that this historical figure was always well provided with funds collected by missionary priests from English Catholics. Parsons, as head of the English Catholic missionary movement and the most prominent English Catholic-in-exile, also received extensive financial support from the coffers of eminent foreign Catholic sponsors of his cause, including Philip II of Spain and the French Cardinal Guise.

Since the text of the plays in the First Folio Edition – as emphasised by the editors Heminge and Condell – was restored exactly as 'conceived' and written by Shakespeare and was therefore free from all alterations and distortions, it must be regarded as authentic, and should thus be consulted in cases of doubt.

That the passage is indeed a reference to Parsons (or Persons) becomes clear at the end of the scene. After Jaquenetta bids farewell to the schoolmaster with the words 'Sir, God save your life', Holofernes too turns to him, saying 'Sir you haue done this in the feare of God very religiously'. But when Holofernes is about to cite the words of a certain father ('and as a certaine Father saith') in support of what has been said, his interlocutor interrupts him abruptly. The schoolmaster clearly wants to prevent the name of this father being spoken (see *Fig. 80*): 'Sir tell not me of the Father, I do feare colourable colours'. He immediately brings the conversation back to the harmless subject of poetry.

132 *Loues Labour's loſt.*

ſhall want no inſtruction: If their Daughters be capable, I will put it to them. But *Vir ſapis qui pauca loquitur,* a ſoule Feminine ſaluteth vs.

Enter Iaquenetta and the Clowne.

Iaqu. God giue you good morrow M. *Perſon.*

Nath. Maſter Perſon, *quaſi* Perſon? And if one ſhould be perſt, Which is the one?

Clo. Marry M Schoolemaſter, hee that is likeſt to a hogſhead.

Nath. Of perſing a Hogshead, a good luſter of conceit in a turph of Earth, Fire enough for a Flint, Pearle enough for a Swine: 'tis prettie, it is well.

Iaqu. Good Maſter Parſon be ſo good as reade mee this Letter, it was giuen mee by *Coſtard,* and ſent mee from *Don Armatho:* I beſeech you reade it.

Nath. Facile precor gellida, quando pecas omnia ſub vmbra ruminat, and ſo forth. Ah good old *Mantuan,* I may ſpeake of thee as the traueiler doth of *Venice, vemchie, vencha, que non te vnde, que non te perreche.* Old *Mantuam,* old *Mantuan.* Who vnderſtandeth thee not, *vt re ſol la mi fa:* Vnder pardon ſir, What are the contents? or rather as *Horrace* ſayes in his, What my ſoule verſes.

Hol. I ſir, and very learned.

Nath. Let me heare a ſtaffe, a ſtanze, a verſe, *Lege domine.*

If Loue make me forſworne, how ſhall I ſweare to loue?
Ah neuer faith could hold, if not to beautie vowed.
Though to my ſelfe forſworn, to thee Ile faithfull proue.
Thoſe thoughts to mee were Okes, to thee like Oſiers bowed.
Studie his byas leaues, and makes his booke thine eyes.
Where all thoſe pleaſures liue, that Art would comprehend.
If knowledge be the marke, to know thee ſhall ſuffice.
Well learned is that tongue, that well can thee comend.
All ignorant that ſoule, that ſees thee without wonder.
Which is to me ſome praiſe, that I thy parts admire;
Thy eye *Ioues* lightning beares, thy voyce his dreadfull thunder.
Which not to anger bent, is muſique, and ſweet fire.
Celeſtiall as thou art, Oh pardon loue this wrong,
That ſings heauens praiſe, with ſuch an earthly tongue.

Ped. You finde not the apoſtraphas, and ſo miſſe the accent. Let me ſuperuiſe the cangenet.

Nath. Here are onely numbers ratified, but for the elegancy, facility, & golden cadence of poeſie *caret:* *Ouiddius Naſo* was the man. And why in deed *Naſo,* but for ſmelling out the odoriferous flowers of fancy? the ierkes of inuention imitarie is nothing: So doth the Hound his maſter, the Ape his keeper, the tyred Horſe his rider: But *Damoſella virgin,* Was this directed to you?

Iaq. I ſir from one mounſier *Berowne,* one of the ſtrange Queenes Lords.

Nath. I will ouerglance the ſuperſcript.

To the ſnow-white hand of the moſt beautious Lady Roſaline.

I will looke againe on the intellect of the Letter, for the nomination of the partie written to the perſon written vnto.

Your Ladiſhips in all deſired imployment, Berowne.

Per. Sir *Holofernes,* this *Berowne* is one of the Votaries with the King, and here he hath framed a Letter to a ſequent of the ſtranger Queenes: which accidentally, or by the way of progreſſion, hath miſcarried. Trip and goe my ſweete, deliuer this Paper into the hand of the King, it may concerne much: ſtay not thy complement, I forgiue thy duetie, adue.

Maid. Good *Coſtard* go with me:
Sir God ſaue your life.

Coſt. Haue with thee my girle. *Exit.*

Hol. Sir you haue done this in the feare of God very religiouſly: and as a certaine Father ſaith

Ped. Sir tell not me of the Father, I do feare colourable colours But to returne to the Verſes, Did they pleaſe you ſir *Nathaniel?*

Nath. Marueilous well for the pen.

Peda. I do dine to day at the fathers of a certaine Pupill of mine, where if being repaſt) it ſhall pleaſe you to gratifie the table with a Grace, I will on my priuiledge I haue with the parents of the foreſaid Childe or Pupill, vndertake your *bien vonuto,* where I will proue thoſe Verſes to be very vnlearned, neither fauouring of Poetrie, Wit, nor Inuention. I beſeech your Societie.

Nat. And thanke you to: for ſocietie (ſaith the text) is the happineſſe of life.

Peda. And certes the text moſt infallibly concludes it. Sir I do inuite you too, you ſhall not ſay me nay: *pauca verba.*

Away, the gentles are at their game, and we will to our recreation. *Exeunt.*

Enter Berowne with a Paper in his hand, alone.

Bero. The King he is hunting the Deare,
I am courſing my ſelfe.

They haue pitcht a Toyle, I am toyling in a pytch, pitch that defiles; defile, a foule word: Well, ſet thee downe ſorrow; for ſo they ſay the foole ſaid, and ſo ſay I, and I the foole: Well proued wit. By the Lord this Loue is as mad as *Aiax,* it kils ſheepe, it kils mee, I a ſheepe: Well proued againe a my ſide. I will not loue; if I do hang me: yfaith I will not. O but her eye: by this light, but for her eye, I would not loue her; yes, for her two eyes. Well, I doe nothing in the world but lye, and lye in my throate. By heauen I doe loue, and it hath taught mee to Rime, and to be mallicholie: and here is part of my Rime, and heere my mallicholie. Well, ſhe hath one a'my Sonnets already, the Clowne bore it, the Foole ſent it, and the Lady hath it: ſweet Clowne, ſweeter Foole, ſweeteſt Lady. By the world, I would not care a pin, if the other three were in. Here comes one with a paper, God giue him grace to grone.

He ſtands aſide. *The King entreth.*

Kin. Ay mee!

Ber. Shot by heauen: proceede ſweet *Cupid,* thou haſt thumpt him with thy Birdbolt vnder the left pap: in faith ſecrets.

King. So ſweete a kiſſe the golden Sunne giues not,
To thoſe freſh morning drops vpon the Roſe,
As thy eye beames, when their freſh rayſe haue ſmot.
The night of dew that on my cheekes downe flowes.
Nor ſhines the ſiluer Moone one halfe ſo bright,
Through the tranſparent boſome of the deepe,
As doth thy face through teares of mine giue light:
Thou ſhin'ſt in euery teare that I doe weepe,
No drop, but as a Coach doth carry thee:
So rideſt thou triumphing in my woe.
Do but behold the teares that ſwell in me,
And they thy glory through my griefe will ſhow:

But

Fig. 80 – Reproduction of a page of the First Folio Edition (1623). The original text of *Love's Labour's Lost* was later altered in several places. The word 'perst' (left: seventh line from the top) was replaced by 'pierc'd' in order to produce a negative allusion to the Jesuit priest Robert Parsons as a traitor. 'Perst', however, is obviously a variant of 'pursed' (= provided with money). Shakespeare is obviously referring to Parsons who was given a great deal of money by English Catholics that was exchanged in Florence and then sent to Rome, as was usual at that time.

Robert Parsons was considered to be the English government's worst traitor. Contact with him – or even careless mention of his name – was very dangerous. Incidentally, in his famous apologia *Execution of Justice in England* (1585), it is William Cecil, referring to the English Jesuits' 'seditious activity', who uses the phrase 'colourable colours'. Shakespeare brings this to mind in *Love's Labour's Lost*, and his schoolmaster is afraid because he is aware of the consequences. The dramatist thus evokes the two main protagonists of the early Elizabethan period, the bitter opponents Robert Parsons and William Cecil.

Cecil, as the initiator of the rigid anti-Catholic penal legislation, was particularly hated by the English Catholics. Shakespeare, entering into this controversy with the means at his disposal, apparently chose Cecil as the model for Polonius in *Hamlet*, ridiculing him as, among other things, 'so capital a calf' and 'fool'. In the closet scene (Act III, scene 4), Hamlet, although by mistake, kills Polonius as he would kill a rat:

QUEEN
What wilt thou do? Thou wilt not murder me?
Help, help, ho!

POLONIUS
[Behind] What, ho! Help, help, help!

HAMLET
[Draws] How now! A rat?
Dead, for a ducat, dead! [Kills Polonius with a pass through the arras].

Against the background of extreme anti-Catholic religious politics, it becomes understandable why even Shakespeare's noble prince is disrespectful to the dead Polonius. The dramatist seems not to have forgotten that it was Cecil, by then Lord Burghley, who in 1581 set the date for the execution of Edmund Campion. Nor that also, as a warning to others, he ordered that the convicted priests, Sherwin and Briant, should die with Campion, the one representing the English College in Rheims, the other representing the English College in Rome.

In Act V, scene 2 of *Love's Labour's Lost* Shakespeare appears to make further reference to contemporary events. In this passage some minor characters mime, to the amusement of their superior audience, the 'worthies' of antiquity. It is the small, bright, quick-witted page of Don Armado who plays Hercules. He is introduced with: 'Great Hercules is presented by this imp'. Even as a very small child Hercules had already accomplished glorious deeds. This 'Hercules', however, is then quickly and roughly ordered, with reference to his minority, to keep some state in his exit and vanish.

The term 'imp' has negative connotations. It could be a malicious sideswipe at the dwarfish Robert Cecil, who, in 1598, succeeded his father William Cecil upon the latter's death. In 1590, after the death of her chief spy, Walsingham, Elizabeth transferred Walsingham's official duties to Robert Cecil. From then on he became her 'principal secretary'. Nicknamed Gobbo, Cecil was said by both insiders and critics of government policy to be more influential than Philip II of Spain and James IV of Scotland (see p. 131). In the 1590s, there were two rival camps exerting great influence at the Court of Elizabeth I, that of Cecil, a powerful member of the government, and the circle around the Earl of Essex, which included Anthony and Francis Bacon, the Earl of Southampton, Shakespeare's patron, and Lord Mountjoy. This latter group was gaining influence and power in home and foreign affairs. Shakespeare belonged to the Essex camp (see pp. 118, 141 ff., 160, 200 and 219). In a comedy which was apparently performed for the first time in the Titchfield residence of the Earl of Southampton before members of the Essex circle, the oblique criticisms of their rivals were hardly unexpected, and were surely enjoyed by the select audience.

According to the First Folio Edition, it is the schoolmaster, Pedant, who appears as Judas. In the later variations, however, Judas is represented by Holofernes – with the additional statement that this refers to Judas Maccabæus. In this presentation, the ugliness of anti-Semitism among the English nobility at that time is fully exposed and is here criticised by Shakespeare:

HOLOFERNES	Judas I am -
DUMAIN	A Judas!
HOLOFERNES	Not Iscariot, sir. Judas I am, ycliped Maccabaeus.
DUMAIN	Judas Maccabaeus clipt is plain Judas.
BEROWNE	A kissing traitor. How art thou prov'd Judas?
HOLOFERNES	Judas I am,—
DUMAIN	The more shame for you, Judas.
HOLOFERNES	What mean you, sir?
BOYET	To make Judas hang himself.
HOLOFERNES	Begin, sir; you are my elder.
BEROWNE	Well followed: Judas was hanged on an elder.
HOLOFERNES	I will not be put out of countenance.
BEROWNE	Because thou hast no face.
HOLOFERNES	What is this?
BOYET	A cittern-head.
DUMAIN	The head of a bodkin.
BEROWNE	A death's face in a ring.
LONGAVILLE	The face of an old Roman coin, scarce seen.
BOYET	The pommel of Caesar's falchion.
DUMAIN	The carv'd-bone face on a flask.
BEROWNE	Saint George's half-cheek in a brooch.
DUMAIN	Ay, and in a brooch of lead.
BEROWNE	Ay, and worn in the cap of a tooth-drawer. And now, forward; for we have put thee in countenance.
HOLOFERNES	You have put me out of countenance.
BEROWNE	False; we have given thee faces.
HOLOFERNES	But you have outfac'd them all.
BEROWNE	An thou wert a lion, we would do so.
BOYET	Therefore, as he is an ass, let him go. And so adieu, sweet Jude! Nay, why dost thou stay?
DUMAIN	For the latter end of his name.
BEROWNE	For the ass to the Jude; give it him:-Jud-as, away.

Shakespeare's criticism of these vulgar anti-Semitic jibes manifests itself in the simple comment made by their target: 'That is not generous, not gentle, not humble.' Berowne and the rest of this high society have – as Shakespeare makes clear – behaved indecorously and practised none of the virtues associated with the ideal of the Renaissance courtier. Yet while the abuse and insults are put into the mouths of the representatives of the nobility of a different nation, the targets were the nobles at the court of Elizabeth I. A glance at the contemporary historical accounts of England indicates that Shakespeare may also have been thinking of members of the Essex circle, for example of Southampton, for whom he had already very clearly laid down rules of behaviour in the friendship sonnets, and even of Essex himself. Shakespeare had a keen interest in the rise of Essex, and he appears to be holding up a mirror to him, to aid his self-improvement – well in line with the famous Renaissance genre of 'mirrors for princes or magistrates'.

When *Love's Labour's Lost* was written, the fate of the physician to the queen, Dr Rodrigo Lopez, who had been accused of poisoning her, may still have hung in the balance, awaiting a verdict. As discussed in detail below in connection with *The Merchant of Venice*, it was

Essex who in blind over-zealousness ensured the prosecution and also the sentencing of the Jew, whose guilt in the eyes of many, including the queen, was not proven.

When English editors later ascribed the entire text spoken by a nameless schoolmaster to Holofernes, it was because they had understood the pun 'Person'/'perst' and had identified the reference to Robert Parsons. Their reworking meant – as it seems – that Holofernes became associated with the biblical traitor Judas Iscariot and, by extension, the arch-traitor Robert Parsons who was thus given the stigma of the English Judas. This interpretation, however, is not tenable because it contradicts the carefully edited First Folio text. In addition, this cannot have been Shakespeare's intention, as it contradicts the fact that he was a Catholic who must have known Parsons personally and did a great deal for the survival of the old faith, risking his life as well as incurring considerable financial expenditure for its survival (see pp. 56 ff., 77 ff. and 298 ff.).

THE TAMING OF THE SHREW

Allusions to actual situations in contemporary history are also to be found in *The Taming of the Shrew*. The action takes place in Padua. In one scene, there is a conversation between a character only referred to as Pedant, a schoolteacher, and Lucentio's servant Tranio, who poses as his master. Pedant declares he is a traveller from Mantua, who has stopped off in Padua on his way to change money in Florence. This information reveals Shakespeare's knowledge of northern and central Italian geography and his familiarity with currency exchange practices in the city of the Medicis. At that time, Florence was the place where currency from all Catholic countries intended for Rome was actually exchanged. Even though in Elizabethan times official funds could not be sent from England to Rome, large sums, however, flowed unofficially from the island into the papal coffers. The largest fundraiser among the English crypto-Catholics and Catholics-in-exile was none other than Father Robert Parsons. Henry Garnet, Superior of the English Jesuits, also sent him money which had been secretly collected in England. Parsons, too, depended on being able to exchange these large sums in Florence. Since Parsons was, like Pedant, a teacher, and the founder of several colleges, and since he had to change his money in the city ruled by the Medicis, Shakespeare again may have used this character to represent England's most feared and most hunted Catholic-in-exile. This interpretation explains why Pedant is heading for Rome, the place in which Parsons spent most of his time on the Continent and where, in 1610, he was buried in the crypt of the church of the English College (next to William Allen). Pedant greets Tranio with the words:

PEDANT
God save you, sir!

TRANIO
And you, sir; you are welcome.
Travel you far on, or are you at the farthest?

PEDANT
Sir, at the farthest for a week or two:
But then up farther, and as far as Rome.

(Act IV, scene 2)

In view of the strict censorship in force in England at that time, Rome could not have been the stated destination. So the cautious dramatist provides a quite different destination, namely Tripoli, deliberately not specifying which of the three cities of that name is meant. For security reasons such allusions had to be strongly disguised.

In *The Taming of the Shrew*, upbringing and education by private teachers play an important role. When Shakespeare's character Baptista Minola, a gentleman who resides in Padua, announces that he is to employ tutors to teach his daughters Katharina and Bianca, the dramatist may have been thinking of his own job in the household of the de Hoghtons. When he passes off the merchant's son Lucentio from Pisa, under the expressive pseudonym of 'Cambio', as a teacher from Rheims who has studied Greek, Latin and other languages there, he must have been thinking of William Allen's Collegium Anglicum which, at that time, was located there. In *The Taming of the Shrew*, there are also allusions to names of the classes in the humanities (Lower Studies) in Douai/Rheims, as there are in *As You Like It*. It was only because he had been educated there that Shakespeare was familiar with such details.

THE MERRY WIVES OF WINDSOR

We owe the comedy *The Merry Wives of Windsor* to the fact that Elizabeth I could not get enough of Falstaff. She demanded a comedy in which the portly, vainglorious, crafty, disreputable and inebriate knight played the part of an amorous philanderer (see p. 138). She is said to have raised this with her cousin George Carey, Lord Hunsdon. Hunsdon was the right person to approach, because at the time he held the office of Lord Chamberlain and was the patron of Shakespeare's acting troupe, the Chamberlain's Men. Shakespeare appears to have complied with the royal wish immediately. In the resulting comedy, *The Merry Wives of Windsor*, Falstaff attempts to court a Mistress Page and a Mistress Ford and as a result receives a sound beating. The play must have been written very quickly as, by 1597, it was already being performed at Windsor Castle.

The comedy contains numerous allusions to contemporary celebrities and events. We have already looked in detail at the satirical portrait of Justice Shallow, through whom Shakespeare attacks the puritan hardliner, Sir Thomas Lucy (see pp. 72 ff.). In this comedy, the dramatist also made fun of a German noble, the Count of Mömpelgart who in 1593 became Duke of Württemberg. Shakespeare called him simply 'Duke de Jamany'. This distortion of the name 'Germany', however, is due to the fact that it is pronounced by an irate French doctor, Doctor Caius, who is in love with Anne Page but learns that another suitor is preferred. When the host of the Garter Inn in Windsor asks Bardolph, a companion of Falstaff, 'Where be my horses?', he is told 'Run away with the cozeners ... like three German devils, three Doctor Faustuses'. But the host corrects him saying, 'They are gone but to meet the Duke, villain; do not say they be fled. Germans are honest men' (Act 4, scene 5). Nevertheless, *Love's Labour's Lost* does contain several distortions of names of leading French historical figures. Marshal Biron, for instance, becomes Berowne, the Duc de Longueville becomes Longaville, and the Duc de Mayenne becomes Dumain.

The Count of Mömpelgart had spent some days at Windsor Castle in 1592, where he became an object of ridicule. For a start, the English found his name practically unpronounceable. Mömpelgart was hoping to be knighted with the Order of the Garter, but his teutonic persistence greatly irritated the queen. However, the German count's persistence brought results, and in 1596 he was nominated for the order. The ceremony, which took place *in absentia*, was held on St George's Day, 23 April 1597 and it was on this occasion that the new play about Falstaff seems to have been performed. It was Shakespeare's thirty-third birthday.

THE MERCHANT OF VENICE

It is highly probable that Shakespeare's comedy *The Merchant of Venice*, which in many parts reads more like a tragedy, owes its origins to a contemporary event which stirred up strong feelings and caused turmoil in government circles, namely the indictment on serious charges of the queen's personal physician, Dr Rodrigo Lopez who, though a convert to Christianity, was still, in the eyes of many, a Jew. Lopez, who was from Portugal, entered Elizabeth's service in 1586. At that time, Lopez attended upon, and acted as translator for, the Pretender to the Portuguese Throne, Antonio Pérez. Spanish emissaries had dragged Lopez into a conspiracy to murder Pérez and later tried to gain his support for their plan to poison the English queen. While Elizabeth believed her personal physician was innocent, her favourite, Essex, was convinced of his guilt. He devoted his energies to gathering a body of evidence against Lopez, instigated proceedings against him and had him sentenced. Although the accused made strong protestations of innocence, he was sentenced to death on 7 June 1594, and died a traitor, being hanged, drawn and quartered. The large crowd present revealed its anti-Semitism and malice, delighting in the execution. For their part, the Admiral's Men players had helped to stoke up the anti-Semitic mood in the capital, already inflamed enough. During that year, Marlowe's *The Jew of Malta* was performed a total of fifteen times to full houses. In this play, a sensational tragedy about revenge, the Jew Barabas dreams up and commits appalling cruelties and at the end dies, with proverbial justice, in a grave which he himself has dug. It should be remembered that there were very few professing Jews in England at the time, as Jews had been expelled by Edward I in 1290 and were not readmitted into the country until 1655 when Cromwell tacitly rescinded the expulsion order.

Shakespeare did not publicly react to the Lopez affair. He nevertheless made it clear that he was referring to this event through allusions to, for example, the meaning of the name Lopez, which derives from the Latin 'lupus', a wolf. His play *The Merchant of Venice*, in which the Jew Shylock demands a cruel revenge on a Christian by insisting that the contract be fulfilled whereby he was promised a pound of flesh from around the heart of the merchant Antonio, could not have been written before 1596, since it refers to the defeat of a Spanish ship during the successful expedition to Cadiz by the Earl of Essex in July, 1596 (see pp. 197 and 218).

Unlike the atheist Marlowe, Shakespeare combines in his characterisation of the bloodthirsty Jew both religious and social issues which are only recognisable against the background of the Elizabethan religious conflict. It has been accepted by scholars[122] that he seems to have drawn on the medieval mystery plays, in particular the representations of the Last Judgement in which the personifications of Justice and Mercy do battle with each other for a human soul. Typically, the Virgin Mary often functions as an advocate of mercy.

According to this interpretation, Shylock would represent evil, even the devil himself, and has a proven right to the soul of the Venetian merchant Antonio. The name Shylock, which derives from the Hebrew 'shalach', was translated in the King James's Bible by the term used in English for the predatious sea bird, 'cormorant'. In Elizabethan times, a bird of prey was the symbol of a usurer, whose activities were regarded throughout the Middle Ages as despicable and sinful. That the usurer Shylock in *The Merchant of Venice* is made to assume the role of the devil is reinforced within the text. So in Act III, scene 1, Solanio says when he sees Shylock: 'for here he [the devil] comes in the likeness of a Jew'.

The wise lawyer, Portia, struggles to win the soul of Antonio back from the Jew. In her magnificent plea in Act IV, scene 1, she advocates clemency. At the same time, though without success, she appeals to Shylock, on behalf of Antonio, to show him mercy – very much in the manner of the Virgin Mary in the medieval mystery plays.

PORTIA
The quality of mercy is not strain'd;
It droppeth as the gentle rain from heaven
Upon the place beneath. It is twice blest;
It blesseth him that gives and him that takes.
'Tis mightiest in the mightiest: it becomes
The throned monarch better than his crown;
His sceptre shows the force of temporal power,

The attribute to awe and majesty,
Wherein doth sit the dread and fear of kings;
But mercy is above this sceptred sway;
It is enthroned in the hearts of kings,
It is an attribute to God himself;
And earthly power doth then show likest God's
When mercy seasons justice. Therefore, Jew,
Though justice be thy plea, consider this,
That, in the course of justice, none of us
Should see salvation: we do pray for mercy;
And that same prayer doth teach us all to render
The deeds of mercy.

Shakespeare contrasts Shylock's relentless quest for justice, based, as he sees it, on the Old Testament philosophy of revenge, with the Christian principle of mercy. As pointed out by Ernst Theodor Sehrt in *Vergebung und Gnade bei Shakespeare* (Forgiveness and Mercy in Shakespeare) (1952), he presents these problems on a new level, completely remote from the concept of the law and justice, and resolves them in a way that is most satisfactory to the Christian party. Shylock's tragedy is that while he does not associate mercy with justice, he is forced to practise it. As Sehrt observes, he stands squarely within the Christian interpretation of Jewish law, in which mercy is allegedly lacking.

The level on which Shakespeare discusses the controversy between Judaism and Christianity has nothing in common with the anti-Semitism of his contemporaries, as expressed so disturbingly in the case of Lopez. In contrast to Marlowe, whose protagonist in *The Jew of Malta* is a stereotypically cruel and vengeful monster, Shakespeare allows his Jew particular sensitivities and sentiments, and bestows human dignity upon him. Shylock's plea for fairer and more dignified treatment (Act III, scene 1) is made in order to shame his Christian fellow-citizens, for it is a moving appeal by a representative of a socially oppressed minority against discrimination on religious grounds. When the mocking Salarino in Act III, scene 1 enquires about the reason for the merciless revenge of the Jew on Antonio, Shylock replies:

He hath disgrac'd me, [...] scorned my nation,
thwarted my bargains, cooled my friends, heated
mine enemies.
And what's his reason? I am a Jew. Hath not a
Jew eyes? Hath not a Jew hands, organs,
dimensions, senses, affections, passions, fed with
the same food, hurt with the same weapons,
subject to the same diseases, healed by the same
means, warmed and cooled by the same winter
and summer, as a Christian is?
If you prick us, do we not bleed?
If you tickle us, do we not laugh?
If you poison us, do we not die?
And if you wrong us, shall we not revenge?
If we are like you in the rest, we will resemble
you in that. If a Jew wrong a Christian, what is
his humility?
Revenge. If a Christian wrong a Jew, what
should his sufferance be by Christian example?
Why, revenge. The villainy you teach me, I will
execute, [...].

Not only would the crypto-Jews and conversos living in England in Elizabethan times have felt that these words applied to themselves, but also the English Catholics, a much larger minority, who were threatened with extremely harsh and unjust punishment on account of their faith.

AS YOU LIKE IT

The central political and religious issue of Elizabethan times, is also a theme of *As You Like It*. As mentioned at the beginning of this chapter, the plot and characters of this comedy derive from the work of Thomas Lodge. Shakespeare added the significant characters Jaques, Touchstone, Audrey, William and Sir Oliver Martext. Martext (meaning 'he who marrs the text', obviously the Bible) is the name Shakespeare gives to an Anglican clergyman, whom he ridicules with surprising ferocity. The jester Touchstone and Celia intend to take their marriage vows before Martext. In Act III, scene 3, the text reads:

TOUCHSTONE
[...] Here comes Sir Oliver. -
Enter SIR OLIVER MARTEXT
Sir Oliver Martext, you are well met. Will you dispatch us here under this tree, or shall we go with you to your chapel?

However, before this can happen, the melancholy Jaques, who has been a secret observer of the scene, intervenes. He warns Touchstone about Martext and suggests that he should let a 'good' priest marry them.

JAQUES
And will you, being a man of your breeding, be married under a bush, like a beggar? Get you to church, and have a good priest that can tell you what marriage is: this fellow will but join you together as they join wainscot; then one of you will prove a shrunk panel and, like green timber, warp, warp.

By making Touchstone seriously consider this advice, the dramatist takes his criticism of the new Protestant clergy to extremes. The really inflammatory aspect of the situation is that the jester is allowed to think of the possible invalidity of a Protestant marriage as an advantage to himself. To an Elizabethan audience, Touchstone's aside may not only have provoked laughter, but also serious reflection:

TOUCHSTONE
[*Aside*] I am not in the mind but I were better to be married of him than of another: for he is not like to marry me well; and not being well married, it will be a good excuse for me hereafter to leave my wife.

During Shakespeare's time, all was not well with the Anglican Church. The monarch had learnt that all six ministers in one diocese were preaching conflicting messages from the pulpit. The Archbishop of Canterbury, John Whitgift, objected that it was impossible for him to fill 13,000 positions with clergy educated in the new theology. Thus he explained and apologised for the inadequacy of clergy serving the new religion. Although Elizabeth was surprised, she had some understanding of the difficulties facing her archbishop[123]. Shakespeare also seems to be touching on such problems in this passage.

The poet must have been fully aware of the considerable danger which attended the ridiculing of the new rites, since the law provided that priests and laymen were punished equally severely if they dared make fun of the new liturgy, the *Book of Common Prayer* (second edition, 1552)[124]. In this context, it is understandable that *As You Like It* and also *The Taming of the Shrew* were among the plays which were only printed for the first time in the First Folio Edition of 1623, seven years after Shakespeare's death.

It is also interesting that the philosopher 'the melancholy Jaques', who at this point is revealed as an adherent of the old faith, decides at the end of the play not to return to the Court with the rehabilitated duke, but rather to share the monastic life of the converted usurper.

In *As You Like It*, Shakespeare is not depicting a pastoral idyll, as is often assumed, but an almost ideal world to set against the false and corrupt world of the Court under Duke Frederick, who had come to power through the expulsion of his brother. It is an account of a community of outcasts, refugees and exiles who gather around the old, lawful duke. The members of this exiled community who, as stated at the end of the play, had endured 'shrewd days and nights' (V, 4), try to observe Christian values. They refuse to indulge in any violence, endure with patience the life of outcasts and practise many virtues, above all that of sharing. This is nowhere better expressed than in Act II, scene 7, where Orlando, starving and exhausted from a long march with his old servant Adam, falls with drawn sword upon the dining and philosophising party in the Forest of Arden, to take food by force. Despite his threat of violence, the intruder is invited in a friendly way by the duke to share the repast: 'Sit down and feed, and welcome to our table.' Orlando is amazed:

> Speak you so gently? Pardon me, I pray you:
> I thought that all things had been savage here;
> And therefore put I on the countenance
> Of stern commandment. But whate'er you are
> That in this desert inaccessible,
> Under the shade of melancholy boughs,
> Lose and neglect the creeping hours of time;
> If ever you have look'd on better days,
> If ever been where bells have knoll'd to church,
> If ever sat at any good man's feast,
> If ever from your eyelids wip'd a tear
> And know what 'tis to pity and be pitied,
> Let gentleness my strong enforcement be:
> In the which hope I blush, and hide my sword.

The duke explains that the group has indeed seen better days. He expresses himself cryptically, his speech requiring interpretation.

> True is it that we have seen better days,
> And have with holy bell been knoll'd to church
> And sat at good men's feasts and wip'd our eyes
> Of drops that sacred pity hath engender'd:
> And therefore sit you down in gentleness
> And take upon command what help we have
> That to your wanting may be minister'd.

It is noticeable that the duke is making a distinction, speaking, in contrast to Orlando, of the 'holy bell', which in those happier days had rung him and the others to church. This subtle difference may be taken to suggest that the country which the duke and his supporters had left, or rather had been forced to leave, now practises a different belief and that there – considered from the perspective of the exile community – the bells that ring to church are no longer 'holy'. By extension, this is a reference to the Protestant faith re-introduced under Elizabeth I.

This subtle allusion raises the question of whether Shakespeare had in mind an actual historical community which had been expelled or banned and obliged to flee from England. Considered in a historical and religious context, such a group, with hundreds of English emigrants, existed in Flanders, at that time the centre of English Catholics-in-exile, and as such, a thorn in the side of the English government.

On 11 October 1601, a government spy's report listed the haunts of the 'arch traitor' Father Robert Parsons – Douai in Flanders, Rome, Spain and above all England were named[125]. In Flanders, the report refers to a group of six or seven hundred people. Some were (trainee) priests, scholars and members of religious orders, others laypersons, pensioners and soldiers. Their leaders, reported the spy, were all dangerous and extremely vicious. Their names were all listed in a separate catalogue[126]. Parsons, states the report, was now determined at all costs 'to overthrow both the laws and State'[127].

Naturally, a completely different picture emerges from the perspective of the victims of persecution, the outcasts and their priests. There is constant stress on the fact that the English Catholics living in exile are peace-loving and practise their old beliefs in seclusion. The 'Rheims Report' compiled by the English College for the years 1579-80, draws attention not only to the subjects of Elizabeth I who had already spent many long years in prison or in hidden refuges, clad in rough sheepskins, always on hand when they were needed for the saving of souls. The report also describes those who were driven into exile from their homes (and from monasteries and convents), but who considered themselves fortunate 'merely' to have been expelled and not killed. The exact whereabouts of their safe place of exile were not divulged, due to the permanent danger of discovery by English government informers.

Since Shakespeare, as has been shown in Part I (pp. 45 ff.), probably received his academic education in Allen's Collegium Anglicum in Douai/Rheims, he may have wished to commemorate the numerous English Catholics-in-exile in Flanders, who, often with support from their relatives in England, lived in the vicinity of the college, or in the nearby forests, where they were free to practise the old faith. An indication of this seems to be the name of the scene where the action is taking place: 'Forest of Arden'. This does not appear to refer first and foremost to the Forest of Arden near Stratford-upon-Avon, but rather to the Ardennes, the forest in modern Belgium, Luxembourg and France. It is significant that the forty-six cures of the Department Ardennes belong to the diocese of Rheims (see 'Ardennes', *Encyclopedia Britannica*, 1899, II). There is, in fact, a triple significance in the name 'Arden' since it is also the maiden name of Shakespeare's mother. It was therefore possible to use the name without relating it too obviously to the politically dangerous scene of Flanders.

One of the most prominent English Catholics in Flanders at the time was Sir Thomas de Hoghton the Elder. As head of the family, he arranged for the rebuilding of the great estate of Hoghton Tower in Lancashire in the late 1560s, and left England for good because of his religious convictions (see p. 60). His brother, the covert Catholic Alexander de Hoghton, mentioned Shakespeare (as Shakeshafte) in his will. During his studies, Shakespeare may have met Sir Thomas Hoghton, who was probably one of the most outstanding personalities in the exiled community. As mentioned before, William Allen, founder of the English College, was among his closest friends. In Flanders, Sir Thomas was filled with a deep melancholy, lamenting his own fate and that of his Catholic compatriots. He longed to return to Hoghton Tower, about which he sought to express the pain of homesickness in heartfelt poems.

At Houghton High, which is a bower
Of sports and lordly pleasure,
I wept and left that lofty tower
Which was my chiefest treasure
To save my soul and loe the rest.

In view of this connection, it cannot not be ruled out that the melancholy Catholic Sir Thomas de Hoghton the Elder was the model for Shakespeare's 'melancholy Jaques', who as an outsider sharply criticises the pleasures of courtly society, including the popular sport of hunting.

As he approaches a stream in the forest, Jaques observes a stricken deer which expels a sigh so deep that his skin threatens to burst, and from whose eyes large tears well up to flow into the stream. The image of a 'weepinge Stagg' was a popular commonplace in the Renaissance, signifying both the pain of love and also a critique of hunting. In *As You Like It*, hunting is criticised, in contrast, for example, to the 'weepinge Stagg' represented on the Elizabethan painting *The Persian Lady* by Marcus Gheeraerts the Younger, in which it stands for the pain of love[128]. The occurrence is described to the (banished) duke by a nobleman:

To-day my Lord of Amiens and myself
Did steal behind him [Jaques] as he lay along
Under an oak whose antique root peeps out
Upon the brook that brawls along this wood!
To the which place a poor sequest'red stag,
That from the hunter's aim had ta'en a hurt,
Did come to languish, and indeed, my lord,
The wretched animal heav'd forth such groans
That their discharge did stretch his leathern coat
Almost to bursting, and the big round tears
Cours'd one another down his innocent nose
In piteous chase; and thus the hairy fool
Much marked of the melancholy Jaques,
Stood on th'extremest verge of the swift brook,
Augmenting it with tears.

In an illustration in his book *The Noble Arte of Venerie*, published in 1575, George Gascoigne shows what a hunting scene in Elizabethan times looked like. The Earl of Leicester can be seen kneeling beside Elizabeth I while at her feet lies a freshly killed deer. Leicester is presenting his queen with a sharp knife so that she can cut the first piece of venison. An occasion such as this took place during Shakespeare's childhood. In 1575, the monarch visited her favourite, Leicester, at Kenilworth Castle, Warwickshire, not far from Stratford-upon-Avon. There she was received with a show of great splendour and gaiety and indulged with amusements, including a deer hunt. The young Shakespeare may have been present as an onlooker with his father. The image of the killed deer at the feet of the queen may well have evoked mixed feelings among English Catholics.

In *As You Like It*, it is Jaques who philosophises about this pastime of the aristocracy and who strongly disapproves of it. He abuses those who 'fright the animals and [...] kill them up' as 'usurpers, tyrants, and what's worse'. In this remarkably modern critique, the sensibilities of the author are clearly manifested, showing the extent to which he really is 'our contemporary'.

The motif of the 'weepinge Stagg' used in this comedy has an additional meaning that seems to have been overlooked hitherto. The stricken, wounded and weeping deer may also symbolise the hunt for adherents of the old religion, and above all their priests. William Allen, the founder of the Collegium Anglicum in Flanders, was a keen observer of the plight of the Catholic English population at the time of Shakespeare as hundreds lived in exile not too far from his college. In his 'Answer to the libel of English justice' he provides us with a detailed description of their fate:

> If they [our fellows in the catholic faith through Christendom] might see all the prisons, dungeons, fetters, stocks, racks, that are through the realm occupied and filled with catholics; if they might behold the manner of their arraingment even among the vilest sort of malefactors; how many have been by famine, ordure and pestiferous airs pined away; how many by most cruel death openly despatched; how many have suffered proscription and condemnation to perpetual prison; how many have been spoiled and otherwise grievously punished by forfeiting to the Queen 100 marks [about £66] for every time they hear mass; how many gentlemen and others, persons of wealth, are wholly undone by losing thirteen score pounds by the year for not coming unto the heretical service; how many have lost all their lands and goods during life for flying out of the country for their conscience sake; [...] how many wander in places where they are not known, driven into woods, yea surely into waters [...] to save themselves from the heretics cruelty; how many godly and honest married couples most dear one to another by the imprisonment, banishment, flight of either party are pitifully sundered; how many families thereby dissolved; into what poverty, misery and mishap their children are driven; what numbers thereby run over sea into most desperate wars and fortunes, or by better luck and fortune go to the seminaries or other service to pass their time during their parents calamity[129].

In *As You Like It*, Shakespeare may well have used the pitiful image of the fatally wounded animal to express the plight of the English Catholics. There are many covert allusions in the text to the true reasons for the exile – voluntary or imposed – of the group living in the Forest of Arden. We learn that every day, people of prestige and importance leave the usurped dukedom, their homeland, in order to join the exile community in the Forest of Arden. Therefore the usurping duke raises an army so as to attack his brother, the banished rightful duke, imprison and kill him. The plan is that with the removal of the old duke, the exile community will be forced back under Frederick's rule. The usurper is already marching on the Forest of Arden with his troops, but is interrupted in his journey by an 'old religious man' and caused to undergo an internal and external transformation which leads him towards the path of righteousness.

The dramatist puts the exciting account of this completely unexpected conversion into the mouth of Jaques de Boys, the brother of Orlando and Oliver. The message in Act V, scene 4, with the sudden Damascene transformation of the duke from Saul into Paul, is directed not only at the members of the exiled community, but at the Elizabethan audience.

Fig 81 – Spanish soldiers looting the Dutch city of Mecheln (Malines). Engraving by Hogenberg dated 1572. Religious, political and military unrest forced the Collegium Anglicum to move from Douai to Rheims in 1578, and it did not return to Douai until 1593.

> JAQUES DE BOYS
> Let me have audience for a word or two:
> I am the second son of old Sir Rowland,
> That bring these tidings to this fair assembly.
> Duke Frederick, hearing how that every day
> Men of great worth resorted to this forest,
> Address'd a mighty power; which were on foot,
> In his own conduct, purposely to take
> His brother here and put him to the sword:
> And to the skirts of this wild wood he came;
> Where meeting with an old religious man,
> After some question with him, was converted
> Both from his enterprise and from the world;
> His crown bequeathing to his banish'd brother,
> And all their lands restor'd to them again
> That were with him exil'd.

Furthermore, the ducal usurper makes up his mind to leave the splendour of the court to 'put on a religious life'. This can only mean that he is going to join a religious order. The melancholy Jaques chooses to follow him.

Shakespeare here is describing a recurrent situation whereby the Jesuits in England, through sermons, conversations and rhetoric, caused many English Protestants to revert to Catholicism. Laymen such as Shakespeare himself, while a member of the Hoghton Secret Organisation in Lancashire and during the so-called 'lost years' of 1582-92, had surely also used his own mastery of language to persuade people back to the Old Religion

In view of this overlooked religious and political dimension of the play, it becomes clear that *As You Like It* is to be understood less as a pastoral on the model of Sir Philip Sidney's *Arcadia*, than as a didactic and uplifting simile devised to comfort the English crypto-Catholics and Catholics-in-exile. When viewed against the contemporary religious and poetical backdrop, it is amazing how many parallels can be spotted between the historical community of Elizabethan Catholics living in exile in Flanders and the community of exiles Shakespeare delineated in *As You Like It*. The playwright could have heard about this large group of catholics that had left England for religious reasons; he might even have met them.

Shakespeare's exiled duke presides over what can be conceived of as an almost perfect community, a utopian 'state' based on morality and decency. It shows up by contrast the world of the usurper, ruled by greed for power, money and property, where injustice, violence and murder are commonplace.

The English Catholics in Flanders, principally the teachers and students at the Collegium Anglicum, were exposed to threats and dangers similar to those faced by Shakespeare's exile community in the Forest of Arden. They were subject to constant surveillance by spies from the secret service of the crown, and were threatened by the regiment of soldiers sent by Elizabeth to support the Dutch Protestant revolt against Spanish Catholic rule. Allen's College had to be moved from Douai to Rheims because of the military conflict (*Fig. 81*). There were also plans to poison the college well and kill the students and teachers there. The English ambassador in Paris had advised his government to impose strict punishments on the parents of students at the English college.

In Shakespeare's comedy, however, immediately before the planned military attack, the usurper undergoes his miraculous conversion, the threatened disaster is averted, the exile community saved and the legitimate duke restored to power. 'Every of this happy number / That have endured shrewd days and nights with us', he declares in Act V, scene 4, 'Shall share the good'.

The English Catholics living in exile on the Continent, as well as the Catholics and crypto-Catholics in England, hoped for a comparable development at home in the 1590s. It was the decade during which the Earl of Essex and his circle became powerful and influential, and which led Catholics and Puritan non-conformists alike to believe that tolerance and religious freedom would eventually prevail. By writing his highly political comedy *As You Like It*, Shakespeare, an enthusiastic follower of Essex, obviously aimed at supporting these goals. The prevailing optimistic mood of this comedy (which may, indeed, be the play once called *Loue labours wonne*) arose from the hope Shakespeare must have cherished in the 1590s that religious tolerance and reconciliation were not merely utopian but actually achievable in his homeland, riven as it was by great religious tensions.

TWELFTH NIGHT

Shakespeare's comedy *Twelfth Night* marks the end of his first major creative phase. Experts agree that the play represents a clear turning point in his work. No explanation for this has yet been found, and none has really been sought. Dieter Mehl, for whom it is only the work that counts, sees no connections between Shakespeare's life and his literary output, and talks of a 'circumstance which we should not overemphasise' [130]. However, the reason for this change of direction will prove highly significant for an understanding of the poet's life and work will be analysed in more detail later.

Twelfth Night was performed on Candlemas, 2 February, 1602 in the Middle Temple law school[131]. This was noted in the diary entry for this date by a law student named John Manningham, who entered the legal profession in 1605. He writes that the play *Twelfth Night, or What You Will* was performed at the festivities, and that the play was very similar to *The Comedy of Errors* or *Menechmi* by Plautus. Manningham then reports in detail on the prank played on Malvolio, leaving no doubt that he had actually seen Shakespeare's comedy. However, the performance in the Middle Temple was probably not the première of *Twelfth Night*, which must have taken place on Epiphany (Twelfth Night or the Feast of Kings – 6 January): but in which year?

In *Twelfth Night*, Shakespeare alludes to interesting events that had apparently recently occurred, thus allowing for an approximate dating of the comedy. Fabian, Olivia's servant, explains that he would not miss the fun with Malvolio even for a pension of thousands. About the possible origin of such a large amount it is stated that it was: 'to be paid from the Sophy' (Act II, scene 5, line 197). One interpretation of 'Sophy' is the ship that, under the command of Sir Robert Shirley, sailed to Persia and returned to London in 1599, loaded with treasure. The cargo also contained valuable gifts from the Shah, presumably for Elizabeth I. Shakespeare and his contemporaries were obviously deeply impressed by the Persian luxuries. Since 'Sophy' was also the name of the Persian dynasty which ruled from *c.* 1500–1736, and furthermore was often used to refer to the Persian ruler himself ('Sophy' = 'Shah'), Shakespeare may have been linking it to him. Elizabeth I had first made contact with the Shah at the beginning of her reign through Anthony

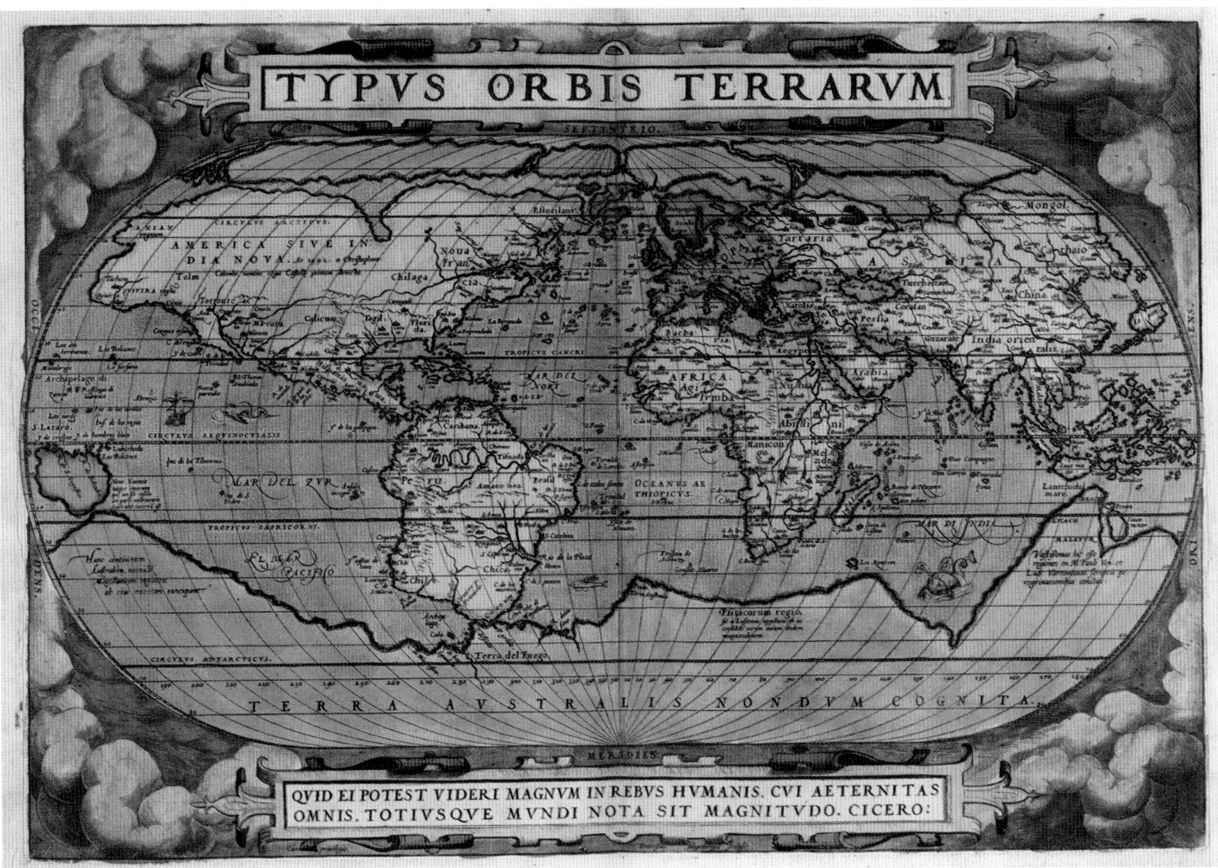

Fig. 82 – 'Ortelius' map of the world' (1575), produced six years after Mercator's famous first map of the world using his famous Projection (1569), and published in Richard Hakluyt's *Principal Navigations, Voiages, Traffiques and Discoveries of the English Nation* (1589). Hakluyt's work was reprinted in 1598, 1599 and 1600. Some editions produced in 1599 contain the so-called 'Wright-Molyneux Map'. This was created by the Cambridge mathematician Edward Wright, based on Mercator's map, with the aid of Emmerie Mollineux, Hakluyt's friend. In *Twelfth Night* (Act III, scene 2) Shakespeare refers to the 'Wright-Molyneux Map', and he must have owned or seen one of the rare 1599 editions of *Principal Navigations*. Maria says of Malvolio: 'He does smile his face into more lines than is in the new map with the augmentation of the Indies.'

Jenkins, who travelled to Persia between 1561 and 1564, opening it up as a trading centre for English merchants. Through Sir Anthony Shirley, Essex's 'ambassador' to Persia, Essex, the Essex circle and thus indirectly, William Shakespeare, enjoyed good connections with the country and its ruler, and were familiar with detailed descriptions of this remote and exotic land.

Some of the queen's subjects occasionally received pensions from overseas potentates (for example from Philip II of Spain or from the Pope). Shakespeare was aware of this. Therefore, the declaration by the servant Fabian about the practical joke which he would not be prepared to forgo even for the sake of a fabulous pension, may well have been a reference to the 'Sophy' or Shah of Persia who was surrounded by luxury and fairytale riches.

The second allusion refers to the Wright-Molyneux Map, the map of the world that had been expanded to include the West Indies and which appeared in 1599 in the famous *Principal Navigations* (1598-1600) by Richard Hakluyt, based on the first map of the world, by Mercator (*Fig. 82*). The map, new in England at the time, is mentioned by Maria in Act III, scene 2, so that the night of the Epiphany in 1599 can be ruled out as the possible date for the first performance, because Shirley did not return from Persia until later that year. Possible dates are 6 January 1600 at the earliest, and 1602 at the latest.

It was Leslie Hotson who located the crucial external evidence which indicated that *Twelfth Night* was first performed at Court on Epiphany, 1601. According to Hotson, the occasion for the performance was the visit of the Tuscan duke Don Virginio Orsino, whose name Shakespeare has used verbatim. The Italian duke would surely have been pleased with the sensitive literary portrait which Shakespeare painted of him.

The date of Epiphany, 1601 is consistent with the total context within which Shakespeare's life at that stage should be viewed. This lyrical comedy could not have been written after the tragic outcome of the Essex rebellion and the earl's execution on 25 February 1601. Shakespeare was deeply affected by these events, which within a very short time utterly demolished the carefully planned alternative policy of the Earl of Essex and his friends and advisers. If *Twelfth Night* was performed at the English Court in honour of the Italian Duke Orsino's visit, this must have taken place about four weeks before the Essex revolt, an event whose timing and outcome could not have been foreseen in early January 1601. Like many of his contemporaries, Shakespeare had pinned his political hopes on Essex. The failure of the earl's rebellion and his execution are not only the most important and momentous events in the final years of Elizabeth's reign, but also the most incisive influences in the life of Shakespeare as a writer. It is not, therefore, unreasonable to consider that this tragedy had such a profound impact on the playwright, causing what might be described as *a traumatic* effect which marked the end of the cheerful comedies and his turning to tragedy. This was a fundamental change of mood for which no convincing explanation has ever been put forward.

Significantly, *Twelfth Night* is one of the works which first appeared in print in the First Folio Edition of 1623. It is conceivable that the way in which the puritan Malvolio is mocked was considered to be too strong for the censor, and Shakespeare consequently withheld the comedy from publication. A more probable explanation is that it was not published because in it, Shakespeare fails to accord a Protestant minister due respect and makes fun of him, while treating a Catholic priest with deference. The play even contains explosive and extremely dangerous allusions to Catholicism and to both the leaders of the Jesuit missionary movement, Father Edmund Campion and Father Robert Parsons whom Shakespeare must have known. In *Twelfth Night* (Act IV, scene 2) the poet alludes quite openly to Campion and Parsons. Thus, Sir Toby Belch jokingly greets the clown Feste, dressed up as a curate, as 'Master Parson'. The gown and beard which the jester dons on stage turn him into a Protestant clergyman, a parson, much to the amusement of the audience. He can now acknowledge, under the protection of his clown's cap and Anglican clerical vestments: 'I, being Master Parson, am Master Parson'. Shakespeare's audience would have immediately recognised the intended pun on the name of 'Parson' (Parsons). They would have understood even more clearly the religion which the dramatist is deriding when Maria sneers at the behaviour of the puritan Malvolio:

> Yond gull Malvolio is turned heathen, a very
> renegado; for there is no Christian, that means to
> be saved by believing rightly, can ever believe
> such impossible passages of grossness.
>
> (Act III, scene 2).

While the clown Feste only disguises himself as a cleric of the Church of England in order to play a heartless game with the puritan Malvolio, who has been shut away because of alleged madness in a dark underground cell (reminiscent of the 'priest's holes' in which Catholic priests often had to be hidden), the secret marriage of his mistress to Sebastian is solemnly performed by a priest. Shakespeare lists him in the Dramatis Personae as 'Priest'. This could only mean a Catholic priest, because the term 'priest' was no longer used to denote Anglican clerics, who were called 'parson', 'vicar', 'curate', or 'reverend'. Just as in Elizabethan times numerous 'priests' lived hidden in stately homes owned by Catholics and disappeared into dark 'priest holes' during government raids, so the Catholic priest in *Twelfth Night* seems to dwell in the house of Olivia. He is characterised as a 'saintly man', in other words as a priest, and is shown profound respect. It is because the priest is part of the household that Olivia's secret Catholic marriage can be performed so quickly in the house chapel. The stage directions for Act IV, scene 3 are: '*Enter OLIVIA and Priest*'. To Sebastian, she explains:

> Blame not this haste of mine. If you mean well,
> Now go with me and with this holy man
> Into the chantry by: there, before him,
> And underneath that consecrated roof,
> Plight me the full assurance of your faith;
> That my most jealous and too doubtful soul
> May live at peace. He shall conceal it
> Whiles you are willing it shall come to note,
> What time we will our celebration keep
> According to my birth.

Later, in Act V, scene 1, the Catholic priest is called upon to bear witness. Cesario (actually Sebastian's twin sister, Viola, dressed in men's clothes), whom Olivia believes to be her husband because of the remarkable similarity between them, naturally finds the subject of getting married an uncomfortable one. Olivia is obliged to appeal to the priest: 'Father, I charge thee, by thy reverence,/ Here to unfold, though lately we intended. To keep in darkness what occasion now/ Reveals before 'tis ripe, what thou dost know'. The priest confirms that he has performed the ceremony, which he again describes in detail:

> A contract of eternal bond of love,
> Confirm'd by mutual joinder of your hands,
> Attested by the holy close of lips,
> Strengthen'd by interchangement of your rings;
> And all the ceremony of this compapt
> Seal'd in my function, by my testimony:

In printed form, such a detailed positive description of a Catholic wedding ceremony would certainly not have escaped the sharp eye of the censor. Nor would the Archbishop of Canterbury's censors have overlooked the allusions to certain situations in the life of Edmund Campion made by the clown Feste in the above scene, under the protective shield of folly and false identity.

Shakespeare makes Feste speak of the 'old hermit of Prague', an obvious allusion to Campion's life (almost) like a hermit at the Jesuit College in Prague before he led the English missionary movement together with Parsons. The Hapsburg Emperor Rudolf II who ruled from 1576 until 1612 lived in Prague where he attracted many scholars to his Court, as well as important members of the Catholic English aristocracy (some re-converted to Catholicism), much to the chagrin of Elizabeth I and her Privy Council, for whom Prague was the symbol of Continental Catholic power and splendour *par excellence*. So a reference in print to Campion in Prague would not have escaped the attention of the censors.

At this point in *Twelfth Night*, the dramatist went a step further, by alluding to the interrogation of Edmund Campion in the Tower of London on 24 September 1581. A certain Master Fulke was the interrogator. Campion was aware that his answers would be used against him in the imminent show trial which he (like all the other defendants of his time) had to endure without legal advice or representation. He knew that the outcome of the trial – as with all high treason trials at that time – was decided from the outset, and saw that his only chance lay in the written record of his statements. He therefore made constant requests for ink and paper which were refused. Shakespeare alludes precisely to the historical facts of the case when he speaks of 'the old hermit of Prague that never saw pen and ink'. This unusual passage in Act IV, scene 2, which opens with a greeting in Spanish ('Bonos dies'), is full of allusions to the contemporary Jesuit practice of ambiguous or evasive speech (equivocation).

Shakespeare makes his clown, who is disguised as an Anglican clergyman, say:

> for as the old hermit of Prague [Edmund Campion], that never saw pen and ink, very wittily said to a niece of King Gorboduc 'That that is is'; so I, being Master Parson, am Master Parson; for what is 'that' but that, and 'is' but is?

Recent research has revealed that this is an indirect affirmation of the rightful claim of the old (Catholic) religion[132], because King Gorboduc is a reference to none other than Elizabeth I[133]. Shakespeare here skilfully links this to the play *King Gorboduc*, or *Ferrex and Porrex*, written by the lawyers Thomas Norton (1532-84) and Thomas Sackville (1536-1608) and acted in the Inner Temple Hall on Twelfth Night 1561. In this tragedy the ancient British King Gorboduc is represented as a striking example of a failed monarch on the throne. The play would have been well-known to Shakespeare's contemporaries. Gorboduc brought chaos to his land, with a civil war that resulted in endless bloodshed and the destruction of the ruling aristocratic families. The presentation of the disastrous effects of this policy appears as harsh criticism of the rule of Elizabeth I, who, in the eyes of the two authors, had made wrong decisions – just like Gorboduc – and had thus caused the misery of the adherents of the old faith.

In view of the dangers inherent in the publication of plays with such highly inflammatory passages, it is not surprising that Shakespeare withheld works like *Twelfth Night* and *As You Like It*, i. e. did not obtain a license for them and would not let them be printed. It should not be overlooked, however, that in part this was also done to protect the texts from plagiarism, and keep them out of the hands of competitors.

AN EARLY TRAGEDY

ROMEO AND JULIET

When the Bodleian Library at Oxford University first acquired a copy of the First Folio Edition of Shakespeare's Plays (1623), highly prized even then, but now one of the most valuable books in the world, it was chained to shelves so that undergraduates also had the opportunity to read it. Much use was made of this offer, as the ragged and worn pages reveal. *Romeo and Juliet* was the Oxford students' favourite Shakespeare play, and was read with great enthusiasm, as the advanced degree of wear and tear shows, especially on those pages which contain the couple's farewell scene in Act III, scene 5.

About 200 years later, the Swiss artist Henry Fuseli (1741-1825) – whom his contemporaries were already calling 'Shakespeare's painter' – was similarly inspired by this scene, as his sensual and very modern-looking sketches show[134]. Goethe, who admired Fuseli, professed unlimited admiration for Shakespeare. In his famous speech '*Zum Shakespeares Tag*' [On Shakespeare's Day] (1771) he declared: 'The first page which I read of him [Shakespeare] made me his own for the rest of my life, and as I finished the first play, I stood like one who has been blind from birth and in an instant is given the gift of sight. I realised, I felt as alive as I had ever felt, my existence infinitely expanded [...].' Goethe's words read like a confirmation of the inscription on Shakespeare's monument: 'Sith all, that he hath writt, leaves living art, but page, to serve his witt.' The most recent filmed versions of *Romeo and Juliet* have also been enthusiastically received by young people all over the world.

When Shakespeare's famous tragedy appeared in print for the first time in 1597 in a quarto edition, the title page read: 'An Excellent conceited Tragedie of Romeo and Iuliet, As it hath been often (with great applause) plaid publiquely by the right Honourable the L. of Hunsdon his Seruants'. This significant advertising addition reveals a series of important details. The play is claimed to be 'of excellent quality' and frequently publicly performed by Lord Hunsdon's Men to great acclaim. This narrows down the actual date of the play, since this was the name of Shakespeare's theatre company only from July 1596 to March 1597. If, during these eight months, *Romeo and Juliet* appeared regularly on the playlist of the Hunsdon's Men, Shakespeare probably wrote it in the first half of 1596 – clearly *after* the history drama *King John*, which may have been revised in August 1596 after Hamnet's death, and before the comedy *The Merchant of Venice*, which alludes to the conquering of Cadiz in July 1596.

A second quarto edition appeared in 1599 under the title *The Most Excellent and Lamentable Tragedy of Romeo and Iuliet*, this time with the addition 'Newly corrected, augmented and amended: As it hath bene sundry times publiquely acted by the right Honourable the Lord Chamberlaine his Servants'. This suggests that the play was corrected, extended, improved and publicly performed several times by the Chamberlain's Men. Corrections and improvements were probably necessary because the text had to be adapted to the respective capacities of stage and actors. The allusion to the extension refers to the 700 lines added to the play before the second printing[135] – obviously by Shakespeare himself. It is correctly stated that the tragedy was performed by the Chamberlain's Men. This name was re-adopted from March 1597, and applied until 1603, when the troupe was renamed The King's Men.

Shakespeare's immediate and most important source for *Romeo and Juliet* was the poem, *The Tragicall Historye of Romeus and Juliet*, by Arthur Brooke, which appeared in 1562. The story of the star-crossed lovers was well-known and popular in the Italian Renaissance. Other authors had also adapted the theme. What Shakespeare discovered in Brooke was a strongly moralising version by a Puritan author, who intended it to be a cautionary tale for the young. Brooke was concerned to show, with a wagging finger as it were, the consequences of 'dishonest desire', disobeying parents and not heeding well-meant advice. In his eyes, the death of the pair of lovers was the correct punishment for the sins committed.

Shakespeare, who was thirty-two at the time, used this material to create one of the greatest tragedies in world literature. In contrast to the Puritan Brooke, he had the advantage of being familiar with the atmosphere and local colour of the original Italian setting of the action. This extends to those scenes in which the Catholic background of the play is especially prominent. An example of this is in the metaphorical language of the scene of the lovers' meeting, based on the custom of going on pilgrimages which had been abolished in England under Henry VIII. Others are the almost blind faith that the main characters have in a Franciscan friar, and the crucial role he plays in the action; the secret (Catholic) wedding, the Catholic forms of greeting and the invocation of Jesus, the Virgin Mary and the saints.

In *Romeo and Juliet*, Shakespeare was also influenced by the work of the Roman philosopher and dramatist Seneca, whose work was particularly highly regarded in the English Renaissance. Shakespeare had studied Seneca – and the other classical poets and historians – during his schooldays and academic education. So it is Fatum and Fortuna that set a tragic course for Romeo and Juliet, thwarting the well-meaning plans of Friar Laurence.

The close interweaving of Catholicism and the concept of 'fate' deriving from classical antiquity are obvious in the sentiments expressed by Romeo immediately before the

Capulets' ball, at which the crucial first meeting of the lovers takes place. When Benvolio in Act I, scene 4 – after the brilliant Queen Mab speech by Mercutio – warns the friends to leave and thinks they have already come too late, Romeo replies:

> I fear, too early: for my mind misgives
> Some consequence yet hanging in the stars
> Shall bitterly begin his fearful date
> With this night's revels and expire the term
> Of a despised life clos'd in my breast
> By some vile forfeit of untimely death.
> But He, that hath the steerage of my course,
> Direct my sail!

Romeo's speech ends in resignation to his fate, but is at the same time almost like a prayer. Further, a prayer-like spirit pervades the first meeting of the couple in Act I, scene 5. Romeo has already become aware of Juliet, seeing her from a distance like a celestial being: 'It seems she hangs upon the cheek of night / As a rich jewel in an Ethiop's ear – / Beauty too rich for use, for earth too dear!' He then approaches her, as a pilgrim approaches the image of his saint:

> ROMEO
> [*To JULIET*]
> If I profane with my unworthiest hand
> This holy shrine, the gentle fine is this:
> My lips, two blushing pilgrims, ready stand
> To smooth that rough touch with a tender kiss.
>
> JULIET
> Good pilgrim, you do wrong your hand too much,
> Which mannerly devotion shows in this;
> For saints have hands that pilgrims' hands do touch,
> And palm to palm is holy palmers' kiss.
>
> ROMEO
> Have not saints lips, and holy palmers too?
>
> JULIET
> Ay, pilgrim, lips that they must use in pray'r
>
> ROMEO
> O, then, dear saint, let lips do what hands do;
> They pray, grant thou, lest faith turn to despair.

In this play of words, Juliet has a fine command of well-wrought repartee. She explains to Romeo: 'Saints do not move, though grant for prayers' sake'. Romeo produces just as skilful a riposte with: 'Then move not, while my prayer's effect I take. [...] [*kissing her*].'

The game is still not at an end, and continues on a more metaphorical level, where now the idea of the forbidden and the sinful is introduced. Romeo continues: 'Thus from my lips, by yours, my sin is purg'd', and Juliet replies: 'Then have my lips the sin that they have took'. Romeo is quick to reply, questioningly: 'Sin from thy lips? O trespass sweetly urged!/ Give me my sin again [*Kissing her*].'

This first dialogue between Romeo and Juliet is structured like a Shakespeare sonnet and couched in the metaphorical language of the Catholic pilgrims. It shows how familiar Shakespeare was with the speech and customs of the pilgrims. The great shrines of English pilgrimage such as that of St Thomas à Becket in Canterbury, St Winefride's at Treffynnon (Holywell), North Wales, and at Walsingham in Norfolk, had been abolished decades before, so Shakespeare could not have become familiar with them in England, but only on the Continent – though scarcely as an outside observer. In his Catholic parents' home, he must have heard of a time in which pilgrimages to the shrines of the saints were a part of religious life in England. His father, John Shakespeare, stated clearly in his Borromeo Testament, that he honoured the Virgin Mary above all other saints, and he mentioned St Winefride by name as his patron saint.

It is Juliet's nurse who brings the lovers back to reality. Romeo now learns that his beloved is the daughter of the Capulets, who are in bitter conflict with his own family, the Montagues. Juliet also learns to her dismay: 'His name is Romeo, and a Montague;/ The only son of your great enemy.'

The action now moves quickly. Romeo and Juliet do not confide in their parents, but in the Franciscan friar and the nurse. Friar Laurence, is Romeo's closest confidant and adviser, to whom he confesses the torment of his love and seeks him out when he wants to marry Juliet in secret. Friar Laurence is found in the monastery garden with his herbs and replies to Romeo's morning greeting in Act II, scene 3 with the salutation 'Benedicite!'. After Friar Laurence has learned what business Romeo has come about, he reacts by invoking St Francis: 'Holy Saint Francis, what a change is here!' However he is prepared to perform the marriage ceremony as requested.

According to J. M. Raich in his *Shakespeares Stellung zur katholischen Religion* (Shakespeare and the Catholic Religion) (Mainz, 1884), Shakespeare's monk, although being a Franciscan, adopts a Benedictine rule, namely that monks should receive guests hospitably, in emulation of Christ, and with the salutation 'Benedicite'[136]. The same Latin salutation is used in *Measure for Measure*. The duke, disguised as a monk, says in farewell in Act II, scene 3: 'Grace go with you, Benedicite!' Raich is surprised that in both cases Shakespeare shows a remarkable knowledge of the religious life in cloisters. He finds it hard to explain how he could have acquired it in a country where the monastic orders had long since been banned[137]. We now know in which phases of his life Shakespeare must have met monks and that he admired the Order of St Benedict. It seems that he must have learned of the (first) reconstruction of an English convent in Brussels with great interest, and that this inspired him to portray a novice on the stage as the main female figure in *Measure for Measure* (see p. 265 f.).

Like Romeo, Juliet also confides totally in Friar Laurence. She is desperate, because – after her secret wedding to Romeo – she is being forced by her parents to marry Paris, and looks to Friar Laurence for help. Paris, whom Juliet meets in the monk's cell where he is discussing the date of their wedding, assumes his fiancée has come to make her confession there. Juliet, who is utterly dependent upon Friar Laurence's help, asks: 'Are you at leisure holy father now, / or shall I come at evening mass?' J. F. Bolton believes 'mass' is a spelling mistake and that 'evening mess' (supper) is intended; however, Raich rejects his English colleague's interpretation, mainly since each of the first three printed editions uses 'evening mass'.

The evening mass was peculiar to Italy. Raich reports that in some Italian churches, such as the Lateran Canons in Vercelli and Venice, and in the cathedral of Verona, an evening mass was held on certain days[138]. Raich believed that the fact that Shakespeare was familiar with this Italian custom was because he had travelled to Italy[139]. It is now known that Shakespeare visited Italy several times, especially Rome (see pp. 77 ff.). The allusions in the plays are now confirmed by external documentary evidence which gives them much greater weight.

Friar Laurence, comes to Juliet's rescue, initially helping her out of a desperate situation. However, the monk's strategy later leads to the tragic outcome of the play, through unfortunate inter-connections and coincidences.

Friar Laurence leads the life of a hermit, collecting herbs and flowers. The founder of his order, Saint Francis of Assisi, who was famous for preaching to the birds, could have been modelled on the old Catholic priest, John Frith, in Temple Grafton, whose 'chiefest trade' is – as a contemporary source tells us 'to cure hawkes that are hurt or diseased [i.e. needy Catholics]' It was Frith who, as has now been established, in problematic conditions must have performed the marriage of the eighteen-year-old Shakespeare to his bride Anne Hathaway under the forbidden Catholic rite.

As in many of Shakespeare's plays, in *Romeo and Juliet* the invocation or naming of various saints occurs quite naturally. The Virgin Mary is mentioned most frequently. Other saints who receive a mention in Shakespeare's dramatic work are St Peter, St Paul, St James the Elder, St Michael, St Stephen, St George, St Nicholas, St Patrick, St Benedict, St Francis, St Gregory, St Luke, St Martin, St Philip, St Crispin, St Denis, St Magnus, St Valentine, St Anna, St Clare and

St Katharine. Friar Laurence not only invokes the patron saint of his order, Saint Francis, but also Jesus and and the Virgin Mary. Protestant authors in Shakespearean times avoided mentioning the saints, especially the Virgin Mary, and mocked the way in which the Catholics honoured them. This was because in the Thirty-nine Articles of the Anglican faith, which represented the basis of the established religion, all this, as well as purgatory, indulgences, religious images and relics, are regarded as 'vainly invented' and 'repugnant to the Word of God'. Article 22 states:

> The Romish Doctrine concerning Purgatory, Pardons, Worshipping and Adoration, as well of Images as of Relics, and also Invocation of Saints, is a fond thing, vainly invented, and grounded upon no warranty of Scripture, but rather repugnant to the Word of God.

As has been shown, in his plays in the 1590s Shakespeare devoted himself to a re-working of English history in an attempt to exert influence on the official Protestant opinion of his time, and to use the extremely effective medium of the stage to correct it from a Catholic perspective. In the comedies of this period and in *Romeo and Juliet* he appears to be conveying his overwhelming impressions of the Mediterranean world with which he had become familiar on his journeys on the Continent. In his history plays, in his comedies, and above all in the early tragedy *Romeo and Juliet*, elements of the Catholic religion as well as a Catholic point of view are clearly displayed, and burning issues concerning the English recusants and English Catholics-in-exile are treated in covert form, mostly under the protective mask of irony, satire and jest.

AUTOBIOGRAPHY IN THE SONNETS: COURSE AND CONSEQUENCES OF THE RELATIONSHIP BETWEEN THE 'POET', 'DARK LADY' AND 'FRIEND'

William Shakespeare's sonnets, published in 1609, are probably the most personal of his writings[140]. Consequently, the literary critics of the Romantic Movement interpreted Shakespeare's poetry autobiographically, believing that with this approach they could contribute to a better understanding of his work as a whole. In his essays entitled *Über dramatische Kunst und Literatur* (Dramatic Art and Literature) (1808), August Wilhelm Schlegel charged Shakespeare's interpreters with showing an extreme lack of critical awareness, since none of them had thought of reading his sonnets as 'his autobiography', which 'quite obviously reflected real-life situations and moods'. Heinrich Heine wrote in his *Travel Pictures* (1828) that the sonnets are 'authentic documents of the circumstances of Shakespeare's life'. This judgement influenced the Scottish philosopher Thomas Carlyle, who claimed that the sonnets testify expressly into what deep waters Shakespeare had waded, and how he had struggled for his life. Late twentieth century research, however, strongly challenged Heine's and the Romantics' theories[141].

The most recent, interdisciplinary research into Shakespeare's sonnets is based on new, or rather, newly evaluated contemporary textual and visual sources, and newly discovered historical and biographical facts as well as expert assessments from the most diverse fields. All the new findings prove that Shakespeare's sonnets involve the literary processing of autobiographical facts, experiences and situations[142].

The sonnets can be divided into two parts, the 'friendship' and 'Dark Lady' sonnets (1-126 and 127-152). There are three central figures or characters: the 'Speaker' (here called 'poet'), the 'Friend'(a young man of noble birth who is a friend of the poet) and a young woman who appears to be a 'femme fatale'. Because of her appearance (and some negative character traits) she is known as the 'Dark Lady'.

There is a very close friendship and aesthetic connection between the 'Friend' and the 'Speaker'. This relationship appears to contain homoerotic features (although on closer consideration a homosexual relationship, can be ruled out). The Speaker's true love is the 'Dark Lady' and it is to her that he is passionately attracted. The Friend is also attracted to her, so that a three-way relationship develops, from which the poet is ultimately excluded. For centuries, there has been speculation that the protagonists could have been modelled on flesh and blood individuals, who aroused such turbulent emotions.

A. L. Rowse, an expert in Elizabethan history, culture and social history, had already declared convincingly in the 1960s that the 'Friend' in Shakespeare's sonnets could only refer to Henry Wriothesley, the young Earl of Southampton, friend and patron of the poet. This has now been confirmed. The 'friendship' sonnets deal with the relationship between the poet and his young friend and the various moods it engenders, ranging between harmony and jealousy, humiliation and conflict. Finely wrought and amazingly life-like portraits are created, describing the poet's emotional state as well as the appearance and behaviour of the friend.

In Sonnet 1, which familiarises the reader with the attractive appearance of the friend, the young man, who appears to be of considerably higher social standing, is asked repeatedly to perpetuate his image through procreation. Thus, in the first quatrain the poet says:

> From fairest creatures we desire increase,
> That thereby beauty's rose might never die,
> But as the riper should by time decease,
> His tender heir might bear his memory:

The third quatrain is praise and reproach in one:

> Thou that art now the world's fresh ornament
> And only herald to the gaudy spring,
> Within thine own bud buriest thy content
> And, tender churl, mak'st waste niggarding.

In a further sonnet, the poet asks the friend very directly to reproduce, in order to create a living monument, thereby ensuring that he will not be forgotten. Sonnet 3 says:

> Look in thy glass, and tell the face thou viewest
> Now is the time that face should form another,
> Whose fresh repair if now thou not renewest,
> Thou dost beguile the world, unbless some mother.
> For where is she so fair whose unear'd womb
> Disdains the tillage of thy husbandry?
> Or who is he so fond will be the tomb
> Of his self-love, to stop posterity?
> [...]
> But if thou live, remember'd not to be,
> Die single, and thine image dies with thee.

Taking the advice already given dozens of times is praised as 'wisdom' in Sonnet 11. Defiant rejection on the other hand is pilloried as 'folly'. A further conceit points out with wit and irony the dire consequences which threaten the whole of mankind if all men refused to become fathers. This tops the poet's argument thus far. His stubborn and repeated concern, that the friend must create a new plant from his own seed, is once again expressed and reinforced, this time from a demographic viewpoint.

> As fast as thou shalt wane, so fast thou grow'st
> In one of thine, from that which thou departest
> And that fresh blood which youngly thou bestow'st
> Tho mayst call thine when thou from youth
> convertest.
> Herein lives wisdom, beauty and increase:
> Without this folly, age and cold decay:
> If all were minded so, the times should cease,
> And threescore year would make the world away.

The aims of these powerful verbal warnings are in tune with the customs of the age and the Elizabethan obsession with immortality, which could be achieved in three ways: (1) by an expensive tomb bearing a true-to-life effigy of the deceased and by true-to-life portraits; (2) by the verses of a poet and (3) by begetting children.

These warnings also correspond to historical reality. Southampton's mother, the dowager countess, expressed regret at her son's reluctance to take a wife and fulfil his duty to produce an heir. She desperately sought a remedy. Like the poet, she asked the young earl to give up his bachelor's existence, marry, and sire children. As a result of his looks, status and wealth, Southampton was idolised by countless women, some of whom did not shy away from direct advances to him (see p. 108 f.). In spite of this, however, he remained adamant.

The statesman William Cecil had the same ambition at heart for young Southampton, though his intentions were not exactly selfless. After the death of Southampton's father, the second earl, Cecil adopted him as his ward and brought him up in his household. In 1590, Cecil wanted to marry off his foster-son, who was seventeen at the time, to his fifteen-year-old granddaughter Elizabeth de Vere, daughter of Edward de Vere, Earl of Oxford. The plan failed because Cecil's ward obstinately refused to be manipulated in this way. Another reason for Southampton's fierce resistance to Cecil's plans may have been that he had observed the sad example of de Vere, 17th Earl of Oxford, who had also been a ward in the household of the first minister. Cecil had practically forced him to marry his daughter. As was well known at the time, the marriage was an extremely unhappy one.

Lord Burghley (Cecil) punished Southampton harshly for this 'disobedience', demanding a large sum of money in compensation, which his foster-son could only raise by selling considerable amounts of land. Cecil was personally enriched by this, since the proceeds went directly to his private coffers.

The Elizabethan painting, *The Persian Lady* in the Royal Collection at Hampton Court, dating from the last decade of the sixteenth century, has played a crucial role in answering the frequently posed, but still unresolved question, as to the identity of the mistress in Shakespeare's sonnets, known as the Dark Lady (*Fig. 83a*)[143]. It was painted by Marcus Gheeraerts the Younger, the most fashionable portraitist of his day, and consists of three parts: a Latin inscription, the portrait of a lady and a sonnet in English. All three parts are closely linked.

Hitherto neither the subject of the portrait nor the author of the sonnet have been convincingly identified.

My investigations started with the anonymous sonnet in Gheeraerts's painting. This sonnet reads as follows (*Fig. 83b*):

> The restles swallow fits my restles minde,
> In still revivinge still renewinge wronges;
> her Just complaintes of cruelty vnkinde,
> are all the Musique, that my life prolonges.
>
> With pensive thoughtes my weeping Stagg I crowne
> whose Melancholy teares my cares Expresse;
> has Teares in Sylence, and my sighes vnknowne
> are all the physicke that my harmes redresse.
>
> My onely hope was in this goodly tree,
> which I did plant in love bringe vp in care;
> but all in vaine, for now to [o] late I see
> the shales be mine, the kernels others are.
>
> My Musique may be plaintes, my physique teares
> If this be all the fruite my love tree beares.

The crucial message is found in the third quatrain, in which the poet complains that the fruits of his love tree have been taken from him and now belong to 'others'.

Linguistic comparisons between Shakespeare's sonnets and plays and the anonymous sonnet have shown amazingly close parallels, indicating that they are by one and the same author. Literary comparisons, especially with Shakespeare's sonnets, also revealed consistent references, making it clear that the texts come from one and the same pen. The triangular relationship described in Shakespeare's sonnets can also be recognised in this sonnet, in which the poet mentions 'others' to whom the 'kernels' or 'fruite' of his love will belong.

In the Dark Lady sequence, which offers crucial information concerning the identity of

Fig. 83a – *The Persian Lady* by Marcus Gheeraerts the Younger, the leading portraitist of the last decade of the Elizabethan age, in the Royal Collection at Hampton Court is charged with emblematic content and depicts – according to recent interdisciplinary research (see p. 179) – Queen Elizabeth I's lady-in-waiting, Elizabeth Vernon, heavily pregnant and expensively dressed. Vernon, a cousin of the Earl of Essex, married Shakespeare's patron, friend and rival, the third Earl of Southampton, about ten weeks before the birth of her daughter Penelope. The portrait contains the text of a sonnet in a baroque cartouche in the bottom right corner which exactly corresponds to what is represented pictorially.

the speaker or poet, we are confronted with the poet courting his beloved with fervour. His strong urge for sexual fulfilment manifests itself clearly in his frivolous play with the different meanings of 'Will'. The poet repeatedly uses this word, simultaneously referring to his desire and his own forename. All this provides us with significant clues that we are dealing with Shakespeare himself here.

A. L. Rowse once casually claimed that the Elizabethan age was (massively) 'oversexed'. The notes and diary entries of the Elizabethan magus, the so-called 'doctor' Simon Forman, provides many examples. Forman kept an account of his own sex life – even specifying times of day. For this activity he coined the expression 'halec'[144].

Shakespeare's Dark Lady sonnets have to be read in the light of this contemporary background. Sonnet 135, for example, says:

Whoever hath her wish, thou hast thy Will,
And Will to boot, and Will in overplus;
More than enough am I that vex thee still,
To thy sweet will making addition thus.
Wilt thou, whose will is large and spacious,
Not once vouchsafe to hide my will in thine?
Shall will in others seem right gracious,
And in my will no fair acceptance shine?
The sea, all water, yet receives rain still,
And in abundance addeth to his store;
So thou, being rich in Will, add to thy Will
One will of mine, to make thy large Will more.
Let no unkind, no fair beseechers kill;
Think all but one, and me in that one Will.

Sonnet 136 revolves around the very same theme and once again harps upon the poet's first name:

If thy soul check thee that I come so near,
Swear to thy blind soul that I was thy Will,
And will, thy soul knows, is admitted there;
Thus far for love my love-suit, sweet, fulfil.
Will will fulfil the treasure of thy love,
Ay, fill it full with wills, and my will one.

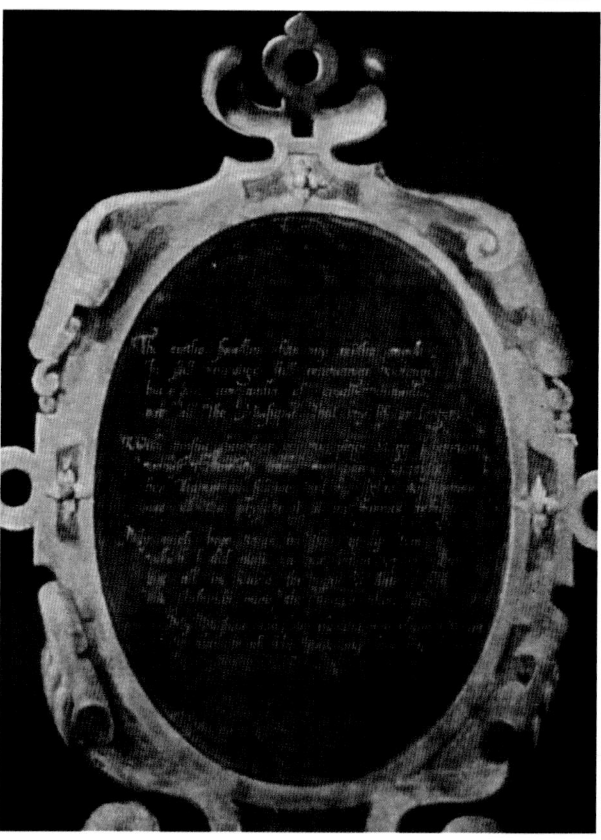

Fig. 83b – Text of the sonnet in the portrait of *The Persian Lady* by Marcus Gheeraerts the Younger. Linguistic and literary analysis has revealed that it must have been written by William Shakespeare, turning out to be the hitherto missing final sonnet of the 'Dark Lady' sequence. The poet laments the fact that the fruits of his love will belong to 'others'. He is obviously referring to the love triangle between Vernon, Southampton and himself, which ended with his exclusion, although he was the father of the unborn child as numerous clues were able to show (p. 168–185).

In things of great receipt with ease we prove
Among a number one is reckon'd none.
[...]
Make but my name thy love, and love that still,
And then thou lov'st me, for my name is Will.

The first two lines of the second quatrain are full of inventive word-play: 'Will will fulfil the treasure of thy love, / Ay, fill it full with wills [...]'. This wish is fulfilled. The Dark Lady becomes – in a purely physical sense – the lover of the poet. The closing couplet of Sonnet 138 states, ambiguously:

'Therefore I lye with her, and she with me, / And in our faults by lies we flattered be.'

As the 'Friend' is also hopelessly attracted to the Dark Lady, the poet fears he has lost him and that his beloved now possesses both of them. There are bitter arguments, in which the deceived poet fights off the urge to justify the wrong that the beloved has done to him.

Nevertheless, the poet falls into almost unconditional dependence upon his beloved. The text reveals that he is ready to accept everything – temporary withdrawal of love and affection, and even his rival – if the Dark Lady will only return to him in the end. This is illustrated in Sonnet 143, which recreates a situation which the poet must have observed in everyday domestic life, most probably at home in Stratford.

> Lo as a careful huswife runs to catch
> One of her feathered creatures broke away,
> Sets down her babe, and makes all swift dispatch
> In pursuit of the thing she would have stay,
> Whilst her neglected child holds her in chase,
> Cries to catch her whose busy care is bent
> To follow that which flies before her face,
> Not prizing her poor infant's discontent:
> So run'st thou after that which flies from thee,
> Whilst I thy babe chase thee afar behind;
> But if thou catch thy hope, turn back to me,
> And play the mother's part, kiss me, be kind.
> So will I pray that thou mayst have thy Will,
> If thou turn back, and my loud crying still.

A. L. Rowse quoted this sonnet in 1964 as evidence of a triangular relationship, or *ménage à trois*, and was convinced that 'The lady was in pursuit of Southampton'[145]. As we have seen, it was not unusual in Elizabethan times for women to set their caps at men. The Earl of Southampton, who appeared to many contemporaries, including Shakespeare[146], as a young Adonis, was among the most prominent male objects of attention. When Mrs Pranell, through Katharine Howard, made advances to him and alluded to the 'country pleasures' she had in store for him[147], we are reminded of the mousetrap scene in *Hamlet*, where the Prince of Denmark tries to shock Ophelia by referring to such 'country matters'. He asks, 'Lady, shall I lie in your lap?' and lies at Ophelia's feet. Afterwards he corrects himself: 'I mean, my head upon your lap?' and then follows this up with the question: 'Do you think I meant country matters?'

In the winter of 1597-98, Southampton had something other than 'country matters' on his mind. He was already engaged to Elizabeth Vernon but intended to leave her for two years in order to spend this time on the Continent. While Vernon gave free rein to her angry and tearful reaction, the queen made him wait for her permission to leave. It also emerged that a courtier named Willoughby had started a rumour, which was the latest gossip at Court, that Southampton was not the only man in his fiancée's life. The earl became quite violent with Willoughby, and a few locks of hair were even torn from his own head. He was in an unenviable position.

The Dark Lady sonnets reveal the identity of the other man in Elizabeth Vernon's life. The poet (Shakespeare) recognises in them that an intimate relationship between his beloved and his friend (Southampton) had already begun. In Sonnet 133, he describes the beginning of this three-way relationship.

> Beshrew that heart that makes my heart to groan
> For that deep wound it gives my friend and me!
> Is't not enough to torture me alone,
> But slave to slavery my sweet'st friend must be?

Later, there are concrete allusions to the fact that the three-way relationship is splitting into a two-way relationship – to the exclusion of the poet, who now seems to be driven mad by constant inner restlessness. In Sonnet 147, he confesses:

> My love is as a fever, longing still
> For that which longer nurseth the disease;
> [...]

Past cure I am, now reason is past care,
And frantic mad with evermore unrest;
My thoughts and my discourse as mad men's are,
At random from the truth vainly express'd;

In view of the blunt disclosure of such inner torment, it is quite understandable that Rowse, in his reading and analysis of this text, is led to make the surprising exclamation: 'How modern, how recognisable it all is! – like a modern novel, unlike anything else in Elizabethan sonnet-literature.'[148]

The Dark Lady sequence ends with abusive accusations and with the moral condemnation of the beloved. The relationship faces an imminent breakdown. Statements in Sonnet 153 like 'And all my honest faith in thee is lost' and 'For I have sworn thee fair – more perjur'd I, / To swear against the truth so foul a lie!' suggest that the Dark Lady is guilty of serious misconduct, even if the poet here – evasively – accuses himself of lying. There is probably a tactical reason for this evasion, as there is in other parts of the Dark Lady sequence. It is obviously a matter of necessary precautions. The evasiveness is also apparent, for example, when the poet repeatedly refers to 'others', although there is no doubt who is being referred to. The poet, who was of non-aristocratic origins and depended upon the favour of the Court, must have been very conscious, especially during the composition of the last, particularly delicate Dark Lady sonnets, that the poems' subjects belonged to influential Court circles or had family connections to them. He therefore leaves open the question which real facts of this painful three-way relationship lie behind the powerful expression 'so foul a lie'.

What really happened we can learn from the painting *The Persian Lady*, its true meaning becoming clear when viewed against its historical and biographical background. We now know how the triangular relationship ended, an ending ominously foreshadowed in the Dark Lady sequence. The poet was not only excluded once and for all and left isolated, but in the end also felt cheated of the fruits of his love:

But all in vaine, for now too late I see
The shales be mine, the kernels others are.

Linguistic, literary and scientific comparisons I have carried out with the help of experts have shown that the anonymous sonnet in the cartouche in *The Persian Lady* portrait belongs to the Dark Lady sonnets, and that these verses – unlike the Cupid poems, which were written and added by a different author – form in fact the final sonnet of Shakespeare's Dark Lady sequence.

The Persian Lady painting is a typical example of the emblematic art that began during the Renaissance and was extremely popular in Elizabethan England. Its basis was the idea that all outward appearances were full of secret references and hidden meanings, and replete with concealed spiritual references which were therefore capable of being 'revealed'[149].

Real events and interconnections, not immediately recognisable, also lie hidden behind emblems, as is shown in the case of Gheeraerts's painting, *The Persian Lady*.

On the left, next to the portrait of an elegantly dressed, very pregnant woman, there is a 'weepinge Stagg', a symbol of pain and separation, which applies to the writer of the new sonnet. The pain expressed in the picture is connected with the mysterious and unknown person in the centre of the image, who with her right hand on the head of the deer sheds pearls like tears. The deer's antler merges directly with the branches of a tree whose leaves are like bay leaves, and whose fruits are reminiscent of olives[150]. This discrepancy, however, yields a solution to the puzzle contained in the main part of the image: the tree bears false fruit. In other words, the pregnant young woman, to whom the 'goodly tree'/ 'love tree' alludes, carries false fruit. This gives us the key to one of the hidden messages of this emblematic painting.

The elegant, unknown woman – her most striking feature is that she is only 8-12 weeks away from giving birth[151] – wears an expensive white silk dress, which is actually a wraparound dress, patterned with flowers, fruits and leaves. This and the rest of the extravagant decoration on the garment would have been extremely expensive luxuries in Elizabethan times.

The Persian lady's clothing indicates that she moved in Court circles, in which 'Persian' dress was considered to be the height of elegance by status-conscious Elizabethan ladies around 1600. With this expensive gown, the unknown woman was emulating Queen Elizabeth I, whose legacy included around 3,000 garments of great value.

From Shakespeare's sonnets we learn that the Dark Lady also possessed high social status. She too is expensively dressed and makes use of the same costly cosmetics as her well placed contemporaries ('Why dost thou pine within and suffer dearth, / Painting thy outward walls so costly gay?' – Sonnet 146).

She carries her social position with confidence and this in itself inflicts humiliation on the poet ('Thine eyes I love, and they, as pitying me / Knowing thy heart torments me with disdain.' – Sonnet 132).

As with other Elizabethan and Jacobean emblematical paintings, there must have been a living model for *The Persian Lady*. Who was the mysterious, unknown woman? The Elizabethan lady in question would have had to have the following characteristics: since she was identical to the Dark Lady of the Sonnets, which were written in the last decades of the sixteenth century, more specifically between 1593 and 1599, she had to have been involved in an emotionally stormy triangular relationship, a relationship which must have been over at the time the portrait was painted. For, by then, as the new sonnet in the painting tells us, the poet had already been excluded.

The Dark Lady played a musical instrument, apparently the virginals (*Figs. 84 a-b*), since the first two quatrains of Sonnet 128 say:

How oft, when thou, my music, music play'st
Upon that blesed wood whose motion sounds
With thy sweet fingers, when thou gently sway'st
The wiry concord that mine ear confounds,
Do I envy those jacks that nimble leap
To kiss the tender inward of thy hand,
Whilst my poor lips, which should that harvest reap,
At the wood's boldness by thee blushing stand!

Furthermore, as the painting verifies, she must have been very attractive, her figure delicate. Her hands and fingers must, according to Gheeraerts's representation, have been slender, her hair long and dark, her skin pale[152], her eyes impressively large and dark. She must – as in the picture – have worn rich jewellery, mainly pearls, as well as valuable and elegant garments.

Apart from all that, there was another indispensable requirement to be fulfilled, namely that at the time the picture was painted she must have been 8-12 weeks away from giving birth. There is evidence that this is the portrait of a newly married woman. Her garment is adorned with symbols of marriage such as the flowers and fruits of a pomegranate. Furthermore, the thumb-ring she wears denotes marriage according to

Fig. 84a – Virginals belonging to Queen Elizabeth I. This or another of the queen's virginals, was played by Elizabeth Vernon, her lady-in-waiting. In the first of the Dark Lady sonnets (Sonnet 128), the poet is fascinated by the dexterity of the Dark Lady's fingers as she plays.

Fig. 84b – Parthenia or The Maydenhead of the first musicke that ever was printed for the Virginals by William Holo for Dorethie Evans [1611] (London). The title page of this first book of printed music for the virginals shows a noble young woman playing the instrument. An extract from *The Winter's Tale* (Act I, scene 2) shows that Shakespeare also used the noun 'virginal' as a verb. King Leontes describes the hand and finger movements of the queen as 'virginalling': 'still virginalling upon his palm?'[*9]

Catholic rites and is occasionally to be found in other contemporary portraits[153]. It can therefore be assumed that the unknown woman entered into marriage in this highly pregnant condition.

These criteria as well as the proximity to the Court evidenced by her dress, seriously restrict the number of possible subjects. It would seem reasonable to suspect one of Elizabeth I's ladies-in-waiting.

There were essentially three sensational affairs in which the queen's ladies-in-waiting were involved at the time when Shakespeare's sonnets were written, namely 1593–1599. In fact, only one is a serious candidate: the relationship between the Earl of Southampton and Elizabeth Vernon, cousin of the Earl of Essex and later Countess of Southampton. This affair took place in exactly this period[154].

The relationship between Southampton and Vernon had begun in 1595. In 1598, the pregnancy of the lady-in-waiting had caused a great scandal. All of this fits coherently into the timeframe outlined above.

The question of whether Vernon is actually the 'Persian Lady' and 'Dark Lady' was answered in *Das Geheimnis um Shakespeares 'Dark Lady'* (The Secret surrounding Shakespeare's 'Dark Lady'). The findings are the result of a careful study of the historical texts and pictorial sources, and of consultation with experts in different disciplines.

From this research, it has been established, among other things, that the future Countess of Southampton emerges from historical records as 'very feminine', 'strikingly emotional', 'doll-like' and 'pretty', and that Shakespeare's patron, the Earl of Southampton, who was twenty-two-years-old at that time, was infatuated and fascinated by her. When he took part in the Court festivities on the anniversary of Elizabeth I's coronation on 17 November 1595, he forgot protocol and etiquette so far as to exhibit little interest in the queen, instead paying almost exclusive attention to her lady-in-waiting, Elizabeth Vernon. He wooed her openly, to the intense and visible anger of the monarch. The love affair which ensued caused a great stir.

Events happened in a rush in the course of 1598. In January, Southampton revealed to Elizabeth Vernon that he intended to accompany Robert Cecil on a delegation to Paris and afterwards to travel on the Continent for two years. Vernon reacted with irritation and anger.

In the same month, a bitter quarrel broke out

Fig. 85a – Portrait of 'Elizabeth Wriothesley, née Vernon, Countess of Southampton, at her toilet' (*c.* 1600) by an unknown painter in the collection of the Duke of Buccleuch at Boughton House, Northamptonshire. The countess is standing and not yet fully dressed. She appears to be combing her hair. It has hitherto been overlooked that her facial features are are in agreement with those of the 'Persian Lady' and that the hair, the neck and the shape of the body also match. Furthermore, this portrait contains a more or less hidden, subtle and previously overlooked pictorial clue, hinting at the presence of a lover (see *Fig. 85b*).

between Southampton and the courtier, Willoughby. Willoughby apparently claimed that the earl's bride-to-be had had intimate relationships with another man. Following this, the relationship between Elizabeth Vernon and Southampton deteriorated to a very low point. In addition to ridicule, the earl also suffered greatly because the queen, as already noted, continued to refuse him permission to travel. At the end of January 1598, the crisis between Vernon and Southampton intensified even further, so that the planned wedding was delayed.

Finally, on 6 February, four days before the departure of the delegation, Southampton was granted permission to go with them. After sumptuous farewell banquets and theatre performances, the earl left for France on 10 February with Cecil's group.

In the summer of 1598, Vernon, who by that time was conspicuously pregnant, was dismissed from the Court and lived in Essex House, the London residence of the Earl of Essex, who was not only her cousin but also her guardian. Her pregnancy had caused a great scandal.

In late August 1598, Southampton secretly returned to London. After a clandestine meeting with his close and respected friend, the Earl of Essex, Southampton married his heavily pregnant bride, whom he had left behind in England in February that year.

In early September 1598, the queen finally learnt of the secret wedding, for which her permission had not been sought. Outraged, she carried out the extreme threat which she had made in anger, namely to assign the new countess 'the best-appointed Chamber in the Fleet' (London's Fleet prison). At the beginning of November, Southampton returned to London. On 8 November, the countess gave birth to her daughter, Penelope, in prison. The birth happened 271 days – almost exactly nine months – after Southampton's departure in February and around ten weeks after their marriage at the end of August.

Shortly afterwards, Southampton was also confined to the Fleet Prison. Through the mediation of the Earl of Essex, who was then still Elizabeth's favourite and thus very influential, the earl, his wife and the child were released at the end of November 1598.

This mass of historical and biographical facts, proofs and circumstantial evidence as well as the amazing coincidences of minor detail are all in perfect agreement with the many criteria that have to be fulfilled in order to be able to identify the unknown 'Persian Lady'. They allow us to conclude that the festively dressed pregnant woman in Gheeraerts's portrait is indeed the pregnant Countess of Southampton. This conclusion was confirmed by a forensic comparison between the subject of *The Persian Lady* and an authenticated portrait of the Countess of Southampton (*Fig. 85a*) [155], carried out by the present author and confirmed by the German BKA [= CID] expert Reinhardt Altmann. The shape of the head, hairline, forehead, eyes, shape and length of the nose, nostrils, shape of the mouth, upper and lower lips as well as the particularly pointed chin show striking resemblances[156].

The authenticated portrait of the Countess of Southampton which has been used for comparing the two portraits, contains a hidden and previously overlooked clue placed there by the painter (see *Fig. 85b*)[157].

The countess seems to have just risen, and still has sleepy eyes; she is dressing and attending to her toilette. Her outstretched left index finger points towards the skilfully placed face of a man on the outside of her sleeve at her right elbow.

Comparisons with the authenticated portraits of the Earl of Southampton reveal that this face does not have the features of the Countess's husband. The painter has doubtless hinted at the existence or even the presence of a lover. The elliptic oval shape of the head and the features of the face on the sleeve, above all the prominent, long nose, bear an amazing resemblance to those of William Shakespeare – as a comparison with the true-to-life facial features in the Chandos portrait, the Flower portrait, the Davenant bust and the

Fig. 85b – The face of a man can be seen on the right elbow of the countess's dress. The BKA criminologist Reinhardt Altman has confirmed that this face has features identical to those of William Shakespeare. This pictorial clue on an authentic painting of the Countess of Southampton is testimony, handed down to posterity, to an intimate relationship between her and Shakespeare.

Darmstadt Shakespeare death mask shows. The picture comparisons were again carried out by the BKA criminologist Reinhardt Altmann[158]. The investigation showed that we are dealing here with the first concrete pictorial allusion to an intimate relationship between the Countess of Southampton and William Shakespeare, one which carries particular weight because it is based on an authentic historical source.

Evidently the painter was aware of this relationship as an insider, and passed on his knowledge to posterity so skilfully disguised that his pictorial clue was able to remain hidden for more than four hundred years.

To summarize: *The Persian Lady* painted by Gheeraerts the Younger, obviously in close collaboration with William Shakespeare, the author of the new sonnet which is inscribed in the cartouche in this painting, is the heavily pregnant Elizabeth Wriothesley, née Vernon, cousin of the Earl of Essex, former lady-in-waiting to Queen Elizabeth I who, in late August 1598, married the third Earl of Southampton, Shakespeare's patron, friend and rival, thus becoming the Countess of Southampton. She meets all the requirements necessary for the identification. Because of the close correspondences between the pictorial representation *The Persian Lady* and the content of the sonnet written on this painting which ends the Dark Lady sequence, she is also Shakespeare's Dark Lady.

Penelope, first-born daughter to the Countess of Southampton and conceived out of wedlock, later married the Hon. William Spencer, who succeeded to the title of second Baron Spencer of Wormleighton in 1627. She was painted in adulthood as Lady Spencer by Paul van Somer (*c.* 1577/78-1622) (*Fig. 86a*)[159]. Her resemblance to William Shakespeare is striking, showing up in the outline of the shape of the head, in the area of the eyes as well as the expression of the eyes, in the area of the nose and chin, in the shape of the Cupid's bow lips, the shape of the mucous membrane of the upper lip, the ample mucous membrane of the lower lip and the drawn-in corners of the mouth, especially the right-hand corner of the mouth[160]. Additionally, symptoms of (a seemingly developing) disease can be discerned in Lady Penelope Spencer, née Wriothesley, which are also visible in the authenticated Shakespeare portraits and were diagnosed by medical specialists. This is the Mikulicz Syndrome, which manifests itself as a disorder causing swellings in the area of the tear

glands and a small caruncle tumour in the inner corner of the left eye.[161]

These findings confirm that there was an intimate relationship between the poet and the lady-in-waiting Elizabeth Vernon, who became Countess of Southampton in August 1598, and that William Shakespeare was actually the natural father of the child Penelope. They also show that the doubts indirectly expressed by contemporaries about Southampton's paternity of the child were well founded[162].

The family similarity is also discernible in portraits of Lady Penelope's children[163], especially in a portrait painted by Anthony van Dyck (1599-1641), which the German art historian Emil Schaeffer published in the early twentieth century in the volume *Van Dyck. Des Meisters Gemälde in 537 Abbildungen* (Van Dyck. Paintings by the Master in 537 Illustrations). Schaeffer identified the portrait as being that of Lady Penelope Spencer, née Wriothesley[164], but it must have been one of Lady Penelope's daughters (*Fig. 87*). For van Dyck (apart from a four-month stay in 1620) only worked in England after 1632, the dress of the lady corresponds to the fashion of the 1630s, and Penelope, born in 1598 and the oldest daughter of the Countess of Southampton, could not possibly be the subject on the basis of her age. This becomes clear, amongst other things, by comparing Van Dyck's portrait with the portrait of Penelope by Paul van Somer (*Fig. 86a*). The portrait in question apparently shows the Hon. Elizabeth Spencer, the older sister of

Fig. 86b –The head of Lady Penelope Spencer.

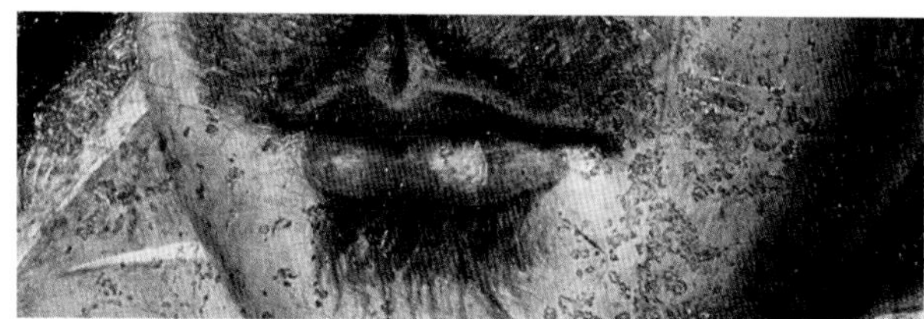

Fig. 86c – Mouth in the original Flower Portrait.

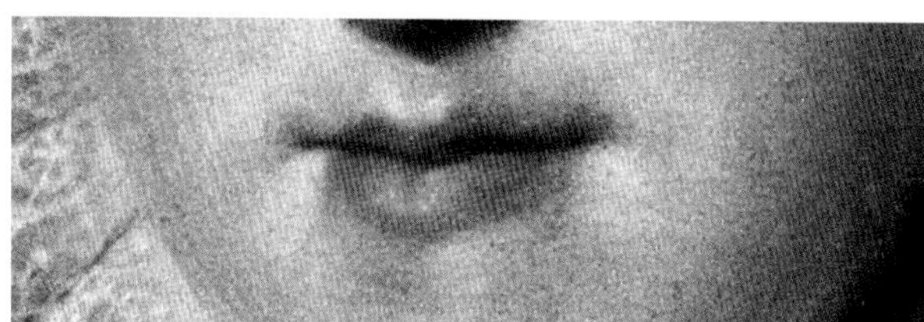

Fig. 86d – Mouth of Lady Penelope Spencer.

Fig. 86a – Portrait of Lady Penelope Spencer, née Wriothesley, by Paul van Somer (*c.* 1577/78-1622) in the collection of Earl Spencer at Althorp House, Northamptonshire. Lady Penelope was known for her beauty, intelligence and popularity. Penelope married William Spencer, later 2nd Baron Spencer, in 1616 or 1617 and is therefore an ancestor of the current ninth Earl Spencer and his three sisters, including Diana, Princess of Wales. The sombre colour of her dress seems to symbolise grief*[10]. Lady Spencer outlived her husband by thirty-one years. She died in 1667 at the age of sixty-nine. The portrait demonstrates the great similarities between herself and her biological father William Shakespeare. This can be seen in the shape of the face, the spacing between the eyes, the expression in the eyes, the shape of the nose and chin, the shape of the lips and the corners of the mouth, particularly in the right corner of Lady Spencer's mouth. (see *Fig. 86d*). Symptoms of disease can also be identified: the Mikulicz syndrome (particularly evident in the upper lid of the right eye), slight anomalies around the upper lid of the left eye, and what appears to be a small caruncle tumour in the inner corner of the left eye (*Fig. 86d* and *Fig. 63*).*[11]

Henry Spencer (b. 1620), later 1st Earl of Sunderland. She was born in 1618 and presumably named after her grandmother, Elizabeth Southampton, née Vernon. At the time she was painted (*c.* 1633-1638) she would have been around sixteen to twenty which corresponds to the age of the young lady represented by van Dyck (*Fig. 87*). This painting, released by Earl Spencer for auction in 1976, was acquired in 1977 by the Tate Britain Gallery in London. It is listed in the most recent catalogue of the gallery under the title '? A Lady of the Spencer Family'[165]. The English art historian, Sir Oliver Millar, has subsequently suggested that the portrait might be of the Hon. Elizabeth Spencer, which coincides completely with what is presented here.

On the basis of the Schaffer identification, in 1997 Reinhardt Altmann carried out a forensic comparison of the features of the subject painted by van Dyck with those of the Earl of Southampton, establishing that there was no similarity, only conspicuous differences. In a comparison with the portraits of William Shakespeare, however, there were surprising similarities[166].

Lady Penelope Spencer, née Wriothesley, led a happy married life at Althorp in Northamptonshire. (*Fig. 89*) In 1620, as stated earlier, her first son, the Hon. Henry Spencer (*Fig. 88*), was christened with the name of his (putative) grandfather Henry Wriothesley. If the present findings are correct, Lord Henry and his siblings were Shakespeare's grandchildren. The line of the Spencers leads from Lady Penelope Spencer, née Wriothesley, through Lord Henry Spencer down to the present ninth Earl Spencer[167]. It follows from this that he and his three sisters (Lady Elizabeth Sarah Lavinia, Lady Cynthia Jane and the late Princess Diana, d. 1997) must be descendants of William Shakespeare. The same applies to the English princes, William and Henry, the offspring of Princess Diana's marriage to Prince Charles, heir to the throne.

The new findings and discoveries not only revealed hitherto unknown historical and biographical connections, but also shed new light on Shakespeare's work, the sonnets as well as the plays.

Up until now the poet's moral condemnation of his mistress at the end of the Dark Lady Sequence has remained incomprehensible. Now we are able to understand the situation and what Shakespeare wanted to communicate to us when he wrote the final sonnet of this sequence, ending with the words 'so foul a lie' (Sonnet 152).

By making use of new or freshly-examined sources, and drawing on the work of a team of experts from different disciplines, it has become clear that the life of Elizabeth Vernon, Countess of Southampton, was indeed based on a lie. The father of her child, Penelope, was not the twenty-five-year-old Earl of Southampton, Shakespeare's patron at that time, but Shakespeare himself. After the death of her father in 1591, Elizabeth Vernon, through her cousin Essex, became lady-in-waiting to the queen. Shakespeare could have met the good-looking young woman in or shortly after 1592, by which date he was already a well-known London playwright.

As the historical documents prove, the Countess of Southampton hid her secret from the world and also, it seems, from her husband. However, Southampton appears to have shown indifference, and even an aversion, towards Penelope. This was in contrast to his contemporaries, particularly those in high places, who, as far as we know, consistently praised her outer and inner beauty, her radiance and her personality.

As the decoding of *The Persian Lady*, in combination with the autobiographical hints and information in Shakespeare's sonnets, has shown, the poet had obviously always understood the true situation. This must have been quite clear to him at the end of the turbulent triangular relationship which ended unhappily for him in 1598. Shakespeare undoubtedly knew, as did the child's mother, that he and not Southampton was Penelope's father, even if, understandably, he did not mention it openly.

Fig. 87 – A portrait from the collection of Earl Spencer, auctioned in London in 1977 and purchased by the Tate Britain Gallery. It was painted by Anthony van Dyck (1599-1641) and identified by the German art historian Emil Schaeffer in 1909 as being that of Lady Penelope Spencer, née Wriothesley*[12] but, in fact, it must be a portrait of one of Lady Penelope's daughters. She has been painted in a blue satin dress in the style of the 1630s. It is probably the Hon. Elizabeth Spencer, born in 1618, who was married three times and would have been the right age at the time when the portrait was painted. The English art historian Sir Oliver Millar suggested the same identification.*[13] Karen Hearn, the relevant curator at the Tate Britain, supported Sir Oliver's identification. She convincingly connects the portrait with the first marriage of Elizabeth in 1634. The similarities between Lady Penelope Spencer's daughter and William Shakespeare are striking as the image comparison, carried out by BKA specialist Altmann, has proved (see p. 180).

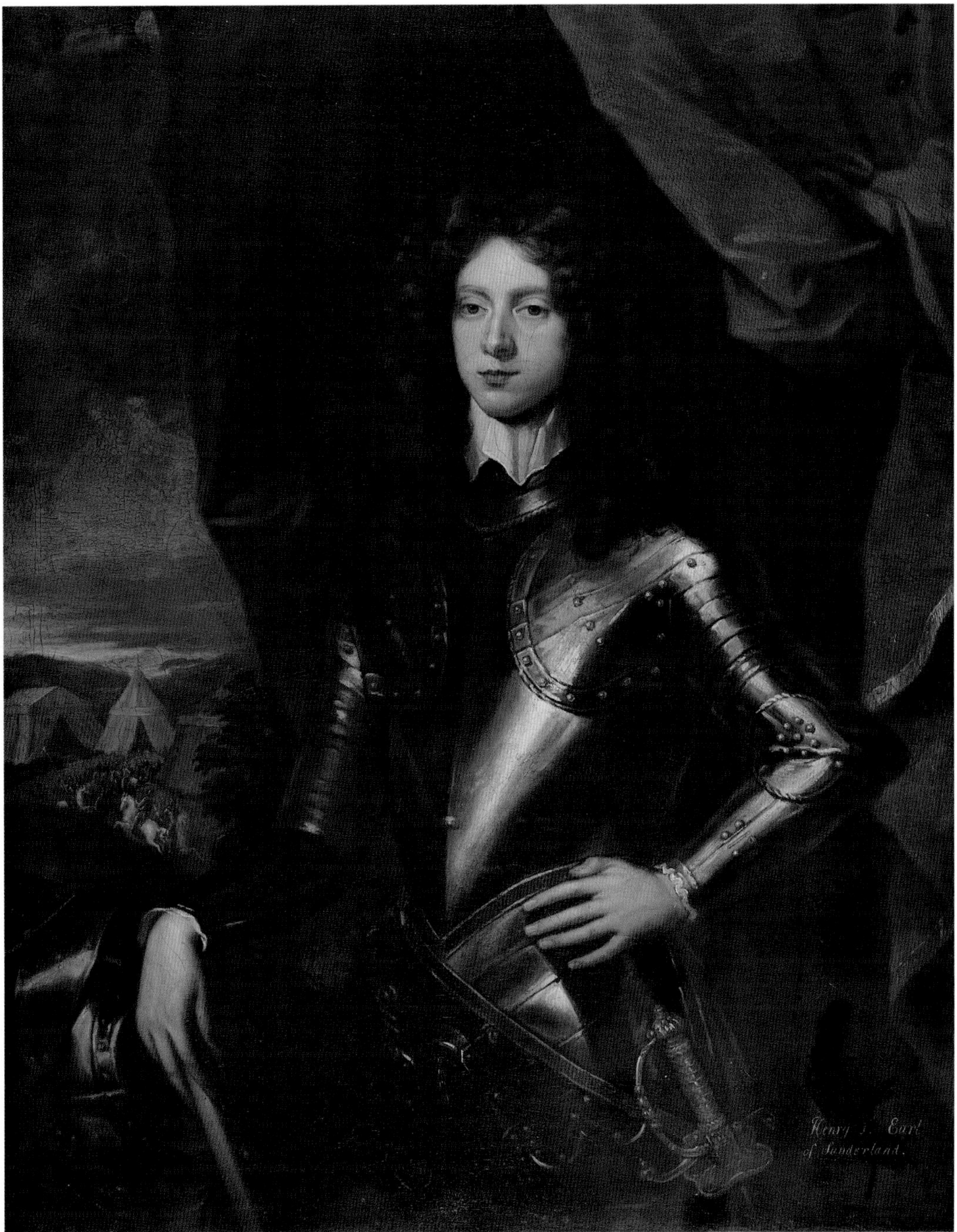

Fig. 88 – Portrait of Henry Spencer, first Earl of Sunderland. The eldest son of Baron William Spencer and Lady Penelope Spencer, née Wriothesley, was most probably named after the third Earl of Southampton, whom Penelope must have considered to be her father. Henry Spencer, whose facial features also resemble William Shakespeare (see outline of face, nose, left wing of the nose, mouth, lips and chin), was a great bibliophile. He married Dorothy Sidney, daughter of the Earl of Leicester. In 1641, his son Robert was born, who went on to study at Oxford, and embarked on the Grand Tour of France, Italy and Spain. He also created the Picture Galley at Althorp House, which remains practically unchanged to this day. During the Civil War (1642-1649), Henry Spencer supported Charles I, who made him first Earl of Sunderland. He died in battle at the age of just twenty-three. His heart was buried in the chapel of the Spencer family in St Mary's Church, Great Brington. This chapel also contains the elaborate baroque tombs of his parents, William and Penelope Spencer, created by the leading English sculptor of the time, Nicholas Stone.

Fig. 89 – Althorp House in Northamptonshire, the seat of Earl Spencer. Lady Penelope Spencer, née Wriothesley, and William Spencer, 2nd Baron Spencer of Wormleighton, led a happily married life here. As far as is known they had six children: Elizabeth (*Fig. 87*), Henry (*Fig. 88*) Robert, William, Alice and Margaret.

The lament arising from these facts is clearly articulated in the new sonnet, the closing sonnet of his Dark Lady Sequence. The poet complains that all his love and hope are in vain and that he has been cheated. He bewails the loss of his beloved ('this goodly tree'), but most of all the loss of his yet unborn child now belonging to 'others':

> My onely hope was in this goodly tree,
> Which I did plant in love bringe vp in care;
> but all in vaine, for now to[o] late I see
> the shales be mine, the kernels others are.

The search for the 'lost daughter' will become a dominant literary theme in his later work.

The Elizabethan dramatist and satirist John Marston (1576–1634), contributor to *Love's Martyr* (1601) and, like Shakespeare, an Essex supporter, presumably knew the poet well[168] and apparently knew something about this unhappy relationship. In 1598, precisely the year in which Shakespeare's relationship with Lady Elizabeth Vernon ended abruptly, Marston alludes to a colleague with the nickname 'Labeo', that is to say, somebody who had particularly noticeable lips. According to Marston, this person lamented that the lady he loved had turned to stone, and had become heartless and ruthless ('Labeo did complaine his loue was stone, / Obdurate, flinty, so relentlesse none'). Not only do the biographical facts fit his situation that year, but Shakespeare also had a bulging lower lip, as his authenticated portraits, particularly the Flower portrait, make clear (*Fig. 106*)[169]. On this evidence, the satirist Marston may have been cruelly and bluntly alluding to him. Moreover, at a later date when Shakespeare wrote his darker and most aggressive plays, a different contemporary used the nickname 'Labeo', obviously also with reference to the poet. On this occasion, the writer of the comment was trying to exert a moderating effect on him (see pp. 269–270).

By the end of the last decade of the sixteenth century, William Shakespeare had long since become one of the most prominent and celebrated writers, distinguished in his early history plays by his 'bombast' style, as Robert Greene spitefully puts it. The poet was also aware that his appearance was already very well known to his contemporaries, because of his frequent stage performances. He was not happy about the way in which he was obliged to 'market' himself, as the opening of Sonnet 110 can tell us: 'Alas, 'tis true I have gone here and there,/ And made myself a motley to the view,/ Gored mine own thoughts, sold cheap what is most dear.'

EARLY FAME

After the first, rather unflattering allusion to Shakespeare, by the jealous Robert Greene, refuted by the printer Chettle, there is a eulogistic reference apparently also to the author William Shakespeare in the allegorical poem *Colin Clout's come home againe* (1595) by Edmund Spenser (*c.* 1552–1599). Spenser, who lived in Ireland, appears to have written the first draft of this poem in December 1591, after an invitation from Sir Walter Raleigh (*c.* 1554–1618), to visit England in order to see 'Cynthia', that is Elizabeth I.

The allegory, which is dedicated to Raleigh, starts with a vivid description of the sea voyage from Ireland to England. Thereafter, Elizabeth and her Court are impressively described. This is followed by a bitter attack on the conspiracies and envy found at court, both of which Spenser experienced or observed.

The passage in which Spenser in all probability alludes to Shakespeare reads:

> And there, though last not least in *Aetion*,
> A gentler Shepheard may no where be found:
> Whose Muse, full of high thoughts invention,
> Doth like himselfe Heroically sound.

That this may well be a reference to Shakespeare is indicated by the fact that none of the other Elizabethan poets, dramatists and chroniclers who presented large, historical subjects in verse had a surname which sounded heroic[170]. This could only apply to the name 'Shakespeare'. Furthermore, Robert Greene, in his 1592 attack, had alluded to this name by using the expression 'Shake-scene' and calling Shakespeare's blank verse 'bombastic'. Spenser, next to Marlowe the greatest of the then established Elizabethan poets, was probably the first to fully recognise and appreciate the genius of the young Shakespeare.

This – as it appears – first great homage to Shakespeare's work – long before he had written his greatest masterpieces, *Hamlet*, *Othello*, *King Lear* and *Macbeth*, which Spenser did not live to see – was followed by countless expressions of appreciation and admiration.

Before Spenser's text appeared in print, it was expanded to include remarks about, among others, 'Amyntas', who was in fact the patron of the Shakespearean theatre company, Lord Derby (formerly Lord Strange), who died in 1594. Spenser may therefore have known the sensational stage plays from the early creative phase of the dramatist (up to and including 1594), as well as Shakespeare's narrative poems *Venus and Adonis* and *The Rape of Lucrece*, on which his early renown was largely founded.

In *Colin Clout's come home againe* Spenser nicknamed Shakespeare 'Aetion'. The Shakespeare scholar, Edmond Malone, made two attempts at interpreting this, unaware that it is a Greek name. The publisher of the *Shakspere Allusion-Book* (1932)[171] put this right, but did not determine which historical figure was alluded to. Apart from the mythological figure of the name 'Aetion' (being the father of Andromache, Hector's wife), it denoted also – according to English tradition – the famous Greek painter Aetion. This Aetion had painted a much-admired portrait of Alexander the Great[172] which was exhibited at the Olympic Games. It is he who is the most likely person of excellence from antiquity to have been invoked by Spenser in order to let his educated compatriots know of his high regard for Shakespeare. It has to be borne in mind that, in Elizabethan times, it was the painters who – as true and reliable chroniclers – were esteemed the most.

On 28 December 1594 Shakespeare's early comedy, *The Comedy of Errors*, was performed at Gray's Inn, one of the London Inns of Court. The eyewitness Henry Helmes reported: '[...] a Comedy of Errors (like to *Plautus* his *Menechmus*) was played by the Players'. By the 'players' he must have meant the newly-appointed Chamberlain's Men, who on the two previous days, 26 and 27 December, had performed with their leading actors Burbage, Shakespeare and Kempe, before the queen in Greenwich. The popularity of Shakespeare's *The Comedy of Errors* was demonstrated by the wild enthusiasm with which the play was received, especially by the women in the audience, resulting in brawls and riots which even spilled onto the stage. The guests from the Temple Inn left the hall in disgust[173]. Francis Bacon who, after studying at Cambridge had been trained at

Gray's Inn, and had since 1586 belonged to it as a bencher, was apparently among those present.

In his poetic obituary to Lady Helen Branch (1594) an author with the initials W HAR speaks of those young and brilliant authors who had put their 'silver quills' at the service of great men, who came, however, from foreign countries. His concern is to direct the attention of these authors to the events and personalities of their own country. Although the anonymous author initially uses the plural, he is actually aiming at a particular writer, namely the writer of *The Rape of Lucrece*: 'You that have writ of chaste Lucretia, / Whose death was witnesse of her spotlesse life: / Hither unto your home direct your eies, / Whereas, unthought on, much more matter lies.' He was directly addressing Shakespeare, whose poems *Venus and Adonis* and *The Rape of Lucrece* had been published in the years 1593 and 1594, with the famous dedication to the third Earl of Southampton. He requests that Shakespeare use his great literary talent to write about subjects closer to home, in which 'much more matter' lies.

The identity of the writer of Lady Branch's obituary is not clear. In 1815, Sir Egerton Brydges opted for Sir William Harbert[174]. But it could also have been Sir William Harvey. Harvey already knew the Southamptons, and in 1598 became the third husband of the mother of the third earl, familiar as Shakespeare's patron. He could therefore have been kept *au fait* by Southampton or his mother as each work appeared.

Michael Drayton (1563-1631) already a distinguished English poet, of whose personal life, in contrast to that of Shakespeare, we know very little, also in 1594 turned his attention to *Lucrece*. He points out that she had recently been revived in a different age. Here he is presumably referring to Shakespeare's work of the same name. He does this in order to describe a comparable chaste figure from English history, namely Matilda. However, Drayton's aim, for the most part, is to promote his own poem *Matilda*, since Shakespeare's *Rape of Lucrece* appeared in 1594, overshadowing his own work, which received little recognition.

In 1594, the Jesuit father and poet Robert Southwell, who was executed on 20 February 1595, delivered a moral appeal. In his poem with the expressive title *Saint Peters Complaint, with other Poemes* (1595) he laments that the cleverest and most subtle (English) heads are busy squandering their literary talent on works about Venus, 'Stil finest wits are "stilling Venus" rose'. This was a definite and obvious allusion to Shakespeare's *Venus and Adonis*.

The English poet Richard Barnfield (1574-1627) was ten years younger than Shakespeare, however, he admired him so much that his own works between the years 1594 and 1595, such as *The Affectionate Shepheard* and *Cynthia and the Legend of Cassandra*, contain many passages in which the resemblance to Shakespeare's verses, borders on plagiarism.

An epigram is included in *Epigrammes in the oldest cut, and newest fashion* (1599), in which the literary figure John Weever in 1595 addressed himself directly to William Shakespeare: 'Ad Gulielmum Shakespeare'. Weever's outspoken praise of the Bard is in places so fulsome that it borders on irony:

> Honie-tong'd Shakespeare, when I saw thine issue;
> I swore Apollo got them and none other,
> Their rosie-tainted features cloth'd in tissue,
> Some heaven born goddesse to be their mother

Adonis, Venus, Lucrece, Romeo and Richard are mentioned, and more Weever knows whose names he cannot recall.

Thomas Edwardes, a minor Elizabethan poet, takes a quite different approach in *L'Envoy to Narcissus* (1595). The original text of this poem, which is extremely important for Shakespeare's biography, is to be found in the library of Peterborough Cathedral. Edwardes refers indirectly to a series of prominent poet colleagues, all of whom are easy to identify since he names characters from their most important works. In the case of Spenser, whose poetic merits and influence he particularly highlights, the name is 'Collyn' (from the allegory *Colin Clout's come home againe*). 'Rosamond' refers to Samuel Daniel and his work of the same name. 'Amintas' to Thomas Watson, who published a Latin poem with this title in 1585, and 'Leander' to Christopher Marlowe, from his famous narrative poem *Hero and Leander*. Both Watson and Marlowe, as Edwardes informs us correctly, had already died by the time this poem was written. The jewel in the crown of this series of Elizabethan poets is, however, Shakespeare. We can identify him from the name 'Adon' from *Venus and Adonis*. The lines referring to Shakespeare read:

Amid'st the Center of this clime,
I have heard saie doth remaine,
One whose power floweth far,
That should have bene of our rime
The onely object and the star.

In this description, which is consistent with other statements by contemporaries, it is made clear that by 1595 Shakespeare was already the centre of literary life and that his influence was great ('whose power floweth far'). In the eyes of Edwardes, he should have been not just the subject of his rhymes but also the star ('of our rime / The only object and the star'). One does not have the impression that this is a case of flattery or excessive obsequiousness, but rather that Edwardes is merely making a factual statement, one that reflects the general opinion of Shakespeare in this early phase of his literary career.

Edwardes goes even further. He sets out for us some of the great poet's characteristics, to which until now Shakespearean research has paid surprisingly little attention. He states:

Well could his bewitching pen,
Done the Muses objects to us
Although he differs much from men
Tilting under Frieries,
Yet his golden art might woo us
To have honored him with baies.

Shakespeare's pen is described as 'bewitching'; the poet himself is somebody who 'differs much from men' and 'his golden art' leads us, 'to have honoured him with baies' [laurels]. Edwardes tries to explain why the great poet was so distinct from his fellow men: it is as a result of his dealings with the friars (in religious orders or monasteries), where he finds shelter. The term 'Tilting under Frieries' with reference to Shakespeare supports no other interpretation. This meaning has not been recognised hitherto, or perhaps there was a reluctance to do so. According to the *OED*, 'Tilt' is 'a covering of coarse cloth', and 'tilting' means 'the action of covering with a tilt or awning'. 'Tilting under Frieries' means 'pitching one's tent under the protection of monasteries' or 'lodging at friaries'.

All of this exactly fits the profile of the poet, established in this book on the basis of the new biographical evidence as well as special allusions in his works. The account by John Aubrey also shows that Shakespeare differed substantially and, in crucial ways from his colleagues and friends, for example, that he refrained from indulging in the excesses usual at that time (see p. 90). Shakespeare also demonstrates in his works a detailed appreciation of the different forms of monastic life which no longer existed in England during his lifetime.

Thomas Edwardes's poem *L'Envoy to Narcissus* (1595) can also now be taken as written proof that William Shakespeare took lodgings in monasteries. This fits in with the documentary evidence adduced here, demonstrating that during the 'lost years' (1585-92) Shakespeare spent seven years as 'an absolute interpreter of the puppets [= priests],' acting as an intermediary for the priests (see pp. 76–77), and went to Rome several times (see pp. 77 ff.).

Among all the evidence of Shakespeare's early fame in the 1590s, that of Francis Meres (1565-1657) is the best known, the best founded and the most important. Meres was educated at Pembroke College, Cambridge and later became an Anglican rector and schoolmaster, working from 1602 in Wing, Rutland. In his work *Palladis Tamia, Wits Treasury; being the second part of Wits Commonwealth*, which appeared in 1598, Meres deals with the literary achievements of his compatriots from Geoffrey Chaucer (*c.* 1340-1400) to his contemporaries. Of the total forty named authors from Elizabethan times, thirty are only mentioned once. They include Ben Jonson (*c.* 1572/73-1637), who at this time was only about twenty-five years old, and had just emerged as a writer. Another is Edward de Vere, Earl of Oxford (1550-1604), who was forty-eight at the time, and therefore almost twice as old as Jonson. He had long since passed his most creative and productive years, and yet he is only mentioned once by Meres.

The frequency of the references to the remaining ten Elizabethan authors provides information about their literary status and the importance which Meres attached to them in comparison with the literary authorities of Greek and Roman Antiquity. At the same time, it also testifies to the degree of their general popularity with the contemporary reader and/or audience.

Shakespeare is easily the most frequently mentioned author, being cited a total of nine times. Michael Drayton, on the other hand is referred to only five times, Spenser four times, Samuel Daniel likewise four times and Sir Philip Sidney three times. George Chapman similarly receives three mentions; Christopher Marlowe, George Gascoigne, William Warner and Nicholas Breton have two references each.

While Meres cites the works of the remaining authors only rarely, a total of fifteen titles by Shakespeare are named, though if both parts of *Henry IV* are counted separately, as they usually are, there are sixteen references.

These facts by themselves suffice to document the unique position of Shakespeare in Elizabethan poetry and drama of the 1590s. In addition, Meres draws up a 'league table' in which the English authors are allowed to compete on equal terms with writers of Greek and Roman antiquity and the Italian Renaissance so he can highlight their achievements, in particular those of William Shakespeare.

Just as the Greek language derived eloquence and fame from the Greek poets and thinkers (Homer, Euripedes, Aeschylus, Sophocles and Aristophanes), and the Latin language derived the same from the Roman poets and thinkers (Virgil, Ovid and Horace among others), so the English language – according to Meres – has been enormously enriched and wonderfully endowed with the jewels of splendid usage by the English poets Sidney, Spenser, Daniel, Drayton, Warner, Shakespeare, Marlowe and Chapman[175]. He goes on to say that, just as it was accepted that the soul of Euphorbus lived on in Pythagoras, 'so the sweete wittie soule of Ouid liues in mellifluous & hony-tongued Shakespeare'. This was proved by Shakespeare's narrative poems and privately circulated sonnets: 'witnes his *Venus and Adonis*, his *Lucrece*, his sugred Sonnets among his priuate friends, *& c.*'.[176]

In order to be able to judge, Meres must have been very familiar with both the classical authors and with the writers who were his contemporaries. In particular, he must have read thoroughly and appreciated Shakespeare's verses and sonnets. He had studied in Cambridge, where, as in Oxford, the ancient authors belonged to the canon, and yet contemporary authors were also appreciated – not least Shakespeare, as will be shown. His knowledge and judgement seem to be well-grounded. Since Shakespeare's sonnets, as Meres himself pointed out, were still not in print, as they were first published only in 1609, those Cambridge graduates especially interested in literature must have had private access to circulating copies, Meres included.

Later, Meres compares Shakespeare as a writer of comedy and of tragedy with the ancient classical authorities in these genres, explaining that just as Plautus and Seneca were considered by the Romans to be the greatest authors of comedy and tragedy, so the English regarded Shakespeare as the 'most excellent' writer for the stage in both genres (see p. 43).

Meres's list (see pp. 120–121), though not quite complete, is the most valuable evidence for Shakespeare's authorship in the 1590's. It goes without saying that he could only include those works that Shakespeare had written prior to 1598, the date of the publication of his *Palladis Tamia*. Neither Meres nor his contemporaries would ever have imagined that, about two and a half centuries later, William Shakespeare's authorship could be put into question. They knew the playwright, knew who he was, had seen him many times, had admired and revered him. The historical sources, still extant in large quantities, testify beyond doubt that William Shakespeare from Stratford-upon-Avon is the author of the great plays.

The most important documentary evidence comes from Shakespeare's funerary monument in Holy Trinity Church at Stratford-upon-Avon, erected in 1616-17, and the First Folio edition of Shakespeare's plays (see *Figs. 90 a–b*), published in 1623, both meant to be powerful and exclusive memorials which at that time were reserved for scholars and writers only.

The famous lines in Latin, engraved in black marble below the funerary bust, which is an exact likeness made on a one to one scale from the playwright's authentic death mask (as was customary at the time), 'focus on the prominent image of his personality, while at the same time recording for posterity that William Shakespeare [...] distinguished himself in life by abilities and talents that [...] place him on par with the greatest personalities of classical antiquity: Nestor, Socrates, and Virgil'[177].

The First Folio edition with its meticulously edited text, its dedication to two prominent noble patrons, its address to the general reader, its many verses of homage, and, above all, its accurate likeness of Shakespeare in copper, confirmed by Ben Jonson's most witty epigram, was 'designed to give expression to "a work/author identity related to name, respect and image" and to manifest an emphasised awareness of authors' copyright; thus escaping from anonymity'[178] Those, who today, hold the view that Francis Bacon, Edward de Vere, the Earl of Oxford, Christopher Marlowe, Henry Neville or any of the other candidates that have been put forward, wrote Shakespeare's works[179] are contradicted by the historical facts.

To take the claim of authorship by the Earl of Oxford as an example, he is only mentioned

To the Reader.

This Figure, that thou here ſeeſt put,
It was for gentle Shakeſpeare cut;
Wherein the Grauer had a ſtrife
with Nature, to out-doo the life :
O, could he but haue drawne his wit
As well in braſſe, as he hath hit
His face ; the Print would then ſurpaſſe
All, that vvas euer vvrit in braſſe.
But, ſince he cannot, Reader, looke
Not on his Picture, but his Booke.

B. I.

Fig. 90a – 'To the Reader' – epigram by Ben Jonson opposite the title page of the First Folio edition of Shakespeare's plays from 1623. As was customary in the Renaissance, engraved portraits were accompanied by names and texts, identifying the sitter and confirming his facial features. In conjunction with Shakespeare's authentic portrait and body of work, Jonson's epigram serves to express the 'work/author identity'. In these famous and witty lines, he attests 'to the engraver's accuracy in catching Shakespeare's looks', but admits that he is 'incapable of capturing his mind', taking up a familiar theme of his day: the 'theme of inexpressibility', thus showing 'his own very special reverence for the poet William Shakespeare' (see the author's book, *The True Face of William Shakespeare*, p. 44).

once by Meres, and then merely as a comedy writer. Oxford was a roué who left England in 1575 to spend a long time in Italy, where he dissipated his fortune, reputedly living in Florence in greater luxury than the Duke of Tuscany. By the end of his life he became impoverished, and subsequently lived on an annual pension of £1,000, granted to him by Elizabeth I[180]. While he was just a minor author, Shakespeare, on the other hand, was the most celebrated poet in England. By 1595, at the latest, he towered over all his colleagues and was almost unrivalled even at this early date; by 1598 he was ranked, as mentioned above, alongside the greatest literary figures of ancient times.

It is significant that both authors, Shakespeare and Oxford, are judged by one and the same contemporary writer (Meres) and in one and the same contemporary source (*Palladis Tamia*), which is in fact an evaluation or ranking of their respective literary achievements. What the Earl of Oxford had produced in literary terms by the age of forty-eight was, to say the least, poor and pathetic, and in the few years left before his death in 1604, he achieved little more. What William Shakespeare had already achieved by the time Oxford died (being only thirty-four) was a contribution to the English language and to literature that had virtually surpassed every measure. This is what his contemporaries, Francis Meres among them, recognised and handed down to posterity. The great masterpieces of Shakespeare were created after the execution of Essex in 1601, when he turned to writing tragedies. They were the foundation of his reputation for all time, even if it suffered a temporary eclipse when, during the English Civil War and under Oliver Cromwell, puritanical disapproval was expressed in violent attacks on Shakespeare, including his bust in Holy Trinity Church in Stratford [181].

The Anglican cleric and schoolmaster Meres, a graduate from the decidedly Protestant University of Cambridge, pays the (Catholic) poet and dramatist William Shakespeare perhaps the greatest compliment when he states that:

> As *Epius Stole* said, that the Muses would speake with *Plautus* tongue, if they would speak Latin: so I say that the Muses would speak with *Shakespeares* fine filed phrase, if they would speake English.[182]

MR. WILLIAM
SHAKESPEARES
COMEDIES,
HISTORIES, &
TRAGEDIES.
Publifhed according to the True Originall Copies.

LONDON
Printed by Ifaac Iaggard, and Ed. Blount. 1623.

Fig. 90b – Portrait engraving of William Shakespeare by Martin Droeshout the Younger on the title page of the First Folio edition (1623). This likeness was made from the original Flower portrait (1609) (see *Fig. 106*). It must have been commissioned by the editors John Heminge and Henry Condell, members of the King's Men and Shakespeare's close friends. The engraver did not incorporate all of the signs of illness, so forcefully and accurately depicted in the Flower portrait. He must have left them out deliberately (as, for example, the small caruncle tumour in the inner corner of the left eye) or reduced them as, for instance, the swelling on the upper left eyelid. There were three further editions of the Folio volume of Shakespeare's plays in the seventeenth century, in 1632, 1664 and 1685.

In 1600, only two years after the publication of Meres's *Palladis Tamia*, Cambridge University students performed the play *Returne from Pernassus* (Part I), which contains numerous direct allusions to Shakespeare and his literary work, especially to the lascivious narrative poem *Venus and Adonis*, about which the students at Cambridge were just as wild as their contemporaries in Oxford were about *Romeo and Juliet*. The undergraduate Gullio, in *Returne from Parnassus*, is entranced by Shakespeare's works, and above all by the lovelorn goddess Venus in *Venus and Adonis*. After quoting the opening lines from *Venus and Adonis*, he cries: 'O sweet Mr. Shakespeare! I'le have his picture in my study at the courte'[183].

Sometime between 1597 and 1603, an anonymous Shakespeare enthusiast scribbled at least fifteen times just on the title page of Francis Bacon's Essay, *Of Tribute, or giving what is dew*, in full or in part the name 'William Shakespeare', vertically and horizontally all over the page, now and again simply with individual syllables or letters of his name, for example 'will Shak', 'Shake', 'Shak', 'Sh' or 'h'. In addition, he neatly wrote out the titles of two well-known Shakespeare plays, which he probably rated especially highly: 'Rychard the second' and 'Rychard the third'. Only one other author's name, that of the Elizabethan author, Thomas Nashe (1567-1601), was added, though with the addition '& inferior places' suggesting that the writer did not particularly like this author. Nashe, who primarily portrayed Elizabethan low life, was a feared satirist. His co-authorship of the satirical and subversive play, *The Isle of Dogs*, after whose first performance the government closed all the theatres in the capital for some time, earned Nashe a long gaol sentence. He also wrote a novel about the fictitious travels of a Jack Wilton, published in 1594 under the title *The Unfortunate Traveler*, dedicated to the third Earl of Southampton. This tribute no doubt failed to win the earl's favour, in contrast to those of Shakespeare, who had that year already dedicated his second narrative poem to him, this time with a text from which it can be inferred that a friendly relationship existed between patron and poet.

The manuscript containing these interesting Elizabethan doodles is the property of the Duke of Northumberland. The identity of the author is unresolved. It could be that of a young man who came into contact with Shakespeare's work during his study at Oxford or Cambridge and was bored at home during the holidays. The publishers of the *Shakspere Allusion-Book* correctly assumed that this 'is probably one of the earliest evidences of the growth of Shakespeare's personal fame as a dramatic author'.[184] One might conclude, they think, that by 1597 English theatregoers and readers of Shakespeare's plays had begun to discuss the author, so that the name of Shakespeare would naturally cross the mind of an idle doodler.

Shakespeare's triumphal procession through the centuries, which – as we have seen – had already began in the first half of the last decade of the sixteenth century, was suddenly interrupted by the beginning of the English Civil War in 1642. The Puritans immediately ordered the theatres to close and subsequently demolished several of them. Under Cromwell, who ruled from 1649, the year in which Charles I was executed, until 1658, the rest were demolished. Cromwell's son and successor, Richard, continued his father's policy, but he resigned during 1659. When Charles II returned to England and came to the throne in 1660, the theatre was revived, and Shakespeare's plays were performed once more. It was Sir William Davenant (1606-68), Shakespeare's godson and possibly also his natural son, who not only adapted and staged the plays and greatly revered their creator but who also collected valuable Shakespearian mementos as did his friend and younger colleague, John Dryden. The admiration that Davenant had for Shakespeare was reflected in, among other things, his possession of certain mementos of the dramatist. These included not only the subsequently famed Chandos portrait, but also the Davenant bust. Dryden, who in any case had a particular fondness for all things Elizabethan, shared this love of Shakespeare. The lines of praise in verse, addressed to the painter Kneller who had painted the first, much valued copy of the Chandos portrait for him, bear vivid testimony to this.[185]

During the Civil War and under Cromwell, much evidence from the Shakespearean period was deliberately or unintentionally destroyed or damaged, as was, for example, Shakespeare's tomb monument[186]. That is why there are gaps in what are, nonetheless, still numerous early sources. It is as a result of these gaps that speculation flourished as to the authorship of the plays. Yet it should be noted that more is known about Shakespeare than about any of the other Elizabethan authors.

The wealth of tributes paid to the poet during his lifetime and after his death, can only be touched upon here. In his poetic homage which precedes the First Folio Edition of 1623, Ben Jonson called Shakespeare 'Sweet Swan of Avon', alluding to his hometown of Stratford-upon-Avon. He reminded his readers how profoundly Shakespeare's plays had impressed Queen Elizabeth I and King James I:

> Sweet Swan of Avon! What a sight it were
> To see thee in our waters yet appear,
> And make those flights upon the banks of Thames
> That so did take Eliza and our James!

In the first edition of Shakespeare's plays, the English poet Hugh Holland (d. 1633) is represented by a poem of eulogy entitled: 'Vpon the Lines and Life of the Famous Scenicke Poet, Master William Shakespeare'. Holland, who studied at Cambridge, had travelled on the Continent, where he had converted to Catholicism. He belonged to the circle of writers and poets who regularly met at the Mermaid Tavern, near Blackfriars. In his poem, he appeals to the audience which had applauded Shakespeare, and to all his brave British compatriots, making them aware of the fact that he who had 'made the dainty Playes, / Which made the Globe of heau'n [heaven] and earth to ring' was no more ('for done are *Shakespeares* dayes'). Holland points out that the 'bayes' (laurel wreaths), which now decorate Shakespeare's coffin, crowned him firstly as poet and then as King of the Poets. In this poem, the secret Catholic Holland refers to Shakespeare's fame with the term 'nuntius'[187] which was used rarely at that time. According to the *OED*, 'nuntius' can mean 'messenger', but in this instance, the meaning was similar to that of a papal emissary, a 'permanent official representative of the Roman See at a foreign court' (*OED*), Holland is thereby associating Shakespeare indirectly with Rome. He concludes that while the Bard's life-line is indeed at an end ('his line of life went soon about'), 'The life yet of his lines shall never out'.

The second edition of the Folio (1632) contains the poem: 'On Worthy Master Shakespeare and His Poems'. Its writer was a highly placed, anonymous admirer of the poet, with the initials I.M.S. He speaks of Shakespeare as the immortal poet, who succeeded in recreating vividly the events of the last thousand years, adding that although one can no longer enjoy Shakespeare as a person, since death has destroyed his body, one could enjoy him through his verse, for he breathes and speaks through his works and is therefore crowned with laurel that will never wither. This second Folio Edition also contains the effusive poem of homage by the young John Milton: 'An Epitaph on the Admirable Dramatic Poet, William Shakespeare.' Milton writes that the great poet with this 'invaluable book' has built himself such a magnificent monument that even kings would give their lives for it: 'And so sepulcher'd in such pompe dost lie, That kings for such a tomb would wish to die.' About twenty years after

Shakespeare's death, an anonymous poet expressed his deep sadness at the death of the Bard much more simply than Milton: 'I'll only sigh in earnest, and let fall / My solemn tears at thy great funeral, / For every eye that rains a show'r for thee / Laments thy loss in a sad elegy. [...] thy fame / Shall still accompany thy honoured name / To all posterity, and make us be / Sensible of what we lost in losing thee.'

It was Ben Jonson who may have paid the most moving and appropriate tribute; the English Shakespearean scholar T. J. B. Spencer in *Shakespeare as Seen by his Contemporaries* (1964) called them 'stirring words of praise'. Jonson, who probably knew Shakespeare better than any of his other colleagues with the exception of John Marston, who was well aware of the great importance and immense effect of his work, included the following words in his dedicatory poem written for the First Folio Edition:

> Triumph, my Britain, thou hast one to show
> To whom all scenes of Europe homage owe,
> He was not of an age, but for all time!

Many of Shakespeare's contemporaries tried to gain some personal advantage for themselves from his early fame – often by illicit means. The London bookseller and printer William Jaggard (1569-1623) published a collection of poems in 1599 under the title *The Passionate Pilgrime*, declaring the author to be 'W. Shakespeare', even though only five of the twenty poems came from his pen. This vexed Shakespeare, as recorded in *Apology for Actors* by the dramatist and actor Thomas Heywood (*c.* 1570-1641) written in 1612. Heywood strongly criticises Jaggard's piracy. In 1619, Jaggard's son Isaac (1595-1627) who was a profiteer like his father, even attributed to Shakespeare the stage play written from a Protestant viewpoint, *Sir John Oldcastle the good Lord Cobham* (1599) by the authors Munday, Drayton, Wilson and Hathaway. The work is an account of the Protestant martyr Oldcastle, whose name was (initially) borrowed by Shakespeare in *Henry IV* for his comic character, later named Falstaff (see pp. 138–140). Isaac Jaggard published the story *Sir John Oldcastle* in 1619 under Shakespeare's name, pre-dating it to the year 1600. By changing the name of the author to that of the Bard from Stratford-upon-Avon, who had died three years previously, he must have increased sales significantly.

IV. POWER POLITICS IN THE LATE ELIZABETHAN AGE AND SHAKESPEARE'S TURN TO TRAGEDY

THE RISE OF ROBERT DEVEREUX

The Reformation under Elizabeth I was a break with the past in social as well as religious terms. Most of the old-established Catholic nobility and aristocracy who had determined the destiny of England for hundreds of years were rapidly and effectively ousted by a new political class. Their representatives were drawn from the upper middle classes. They were university-educated and enjoyed immense power. They not only supported the introduction of the new religion, but rigidly enforced it without consideration for those who believed or thought differently. The traditional ideals of the Middle Ages (chivalry, loyalty, service etc.) were foreign to them; instead they practiced efficient 'realpolitik' The once powerful Norfolks and Howards had had their day and were executed as traitors. Now the Cavendishes and the Russells became powerful, and – above all – the Cecils, William and his son Robert. Nonetheless, in the final fifteen years of Elizabeth's reign, a representative of the ancient nobility, who embodied many of the traditional ideals, succeeded in rising to power. He was Robert Devereux (1566–1601), 19th Earl of Essex, and the second Devereux to hold this title. He was related on his father's side to famous noble families of the Middle Ages – the Dorsets, the Ferrers, the Rivers, and even the Plantagenets, who could trace their lineage back to Henry II, Richard the Lionheart and King John.

Robert was nine-years-old when his father died; only a year later, Elizabeth's favourite, Robert Dudley, Earl of Leicester – without the permission of the monarch – married the boy's mother, becoming his stepfather. This turn of events enraged the queen, but she had to resign herself to the situation. The young Earl of Essex became a ward in the household of William Cecil, the First Minister, as did the young Earl of Southampton at a later date. Placing fatherless or orphaned members of the nobility in the household of the most powerful man in the Privy Council was a shrewd move. It meant that the sons of the great noble families would be raised to be loyal to the Crown and would not fall into the hands of Catholic tutors in noble houses, or even priests of the Catholic Church. This solution also provided a very lucrative source of revenue for Cecil, enabling him to afford opulent mansions and palaces, such as Burghley House in the Soke of Peterborough and Theobald's Manor in Hertfordshire, which he purchased in 1563. Elizabeth's First Minister enriched himself partly at the expense of the young Earl of Southampton, Shakespeare's patron, who steadfastly resisted his foster father's plan – or, rather, orders – to marry him (Southampton) off to his (Cecil's) granddaughter. For this disobedience, he had to pay Cecil £5,000 in compensation, as noted by Henry Garnet, the well-informed future Superior of the English Jesuits[188]. The woman scorned was Lady Elizabeth de Vere, daughter of the Earl of Oxford. Oxford was another former ward of Cecil's, whom he had married off to his daughter. The marriage was particularly unhappy.

When his ward, Essex, was barely ten-years-old, Cecil sent him to Cambridge for a university education. Cambridge was chosen not only because the closest advisor of the queen had studied there himself, but mainly because the alternative – Oxford University – was still living up to its reputation of being a 'den of Catholics'. At the age of only fourteen, Essex gained his '*Magister Artium*' (MA). With his talent, he had the makings of a scholar; however he preferred the life of a nobleman, trained in the use of weapons, and devoted himself to the traditional sports of the nobility, above all hunting. In 1587 the Earl of Leicester introduced his stepson, Essex, to the Court. The English historian, Professor John E. Neale, paints the following graphic picture of the young earl:

> [...] tall, well-proportioned, with a strikingly handsome, open face, and soft, dreamy eyes. Mind and spirit matched his person. [...] a young aristocrat of irresistible attraction, impulsive and generous, the chivalrous, courtly knight of romance.[189]

Essex greatly pleased the queen. She supported and favoured him, perhaps also partly to provoke the jealousy of her favourite, Leicester. At any rate, Essex, rose rapidly. In the year he was presented at Court, he became Leicester's successor as Master of the Horse, and received the tidy sum of £1,500 per annum. The desire of the young man for fame and fortune led him to secretly join the expedition to Spain and Portugal (1589) under Sir Francis Drake and Sir John Norris, for the first time bringing down upon himself the queen's wrath.

But by 1591, when an English regiment was despatched to Normandy in support of Henry IV (then a Huguenot), Essex succeeded in persuading the queen, who had long hesitated, to grant him supreme command over the troops. Experienced officers were assigned to support this twenty-five-year-old commander, but were apparently unable to prevent one particularly reckless act of his. Essex left his infantry in Rouen and rode a hundred miles through enemy territory to seek out the French king, who was holding court at Compiègne. In accordance with his notions of chivalry, he entered the courtyard with great pomp on a splendidly caparisoned horse. The procession was led by six trumpeters; six stylishly dressed pages rode ahead of Essex; twelve squires and another sixty noblemen followed him. Henry was greatly impressed and struck up an immediate friendship with Essex. In this undertaking, Essex had put his own life and that of his companions at risk. He had to be escorted back to his base by his own troops, summoned for the purpose.

From a military standpoint, Essex's French expedition had basically achieved nothing. Elizabeth was once again angry about this, especially because her favourite had knighted twenty of his followers before he left France. The young man, however, succeeded once again in appeasing the queen with his charm.

In 1593, while only twenty-seven, Essex reached a rather important milestone in his political life when he was made a member of the Privy Council. In 1596, as the celebrated victor as commander of the army at Cádiz, the Spanish town which was conquered and destroyed, he was at the zenith of his power. He was favoured and trusted by the queen; the people cheered him on and celebrated him as their hero (*Fig. 91*).

Elizabeth, forever concerned about the balance of power, also promoted the career of Robert Cecil, the brilliant second son of William Cecil, Lord Burghley (*Figs. 92 a–b*). As early as 1590, she unofficially entrusted him with taking over the work of the deceased Francis Walsingham, former head of her network of spies; and in 1591, while Essex was in France, she appointed him to the Privy Council. In 1596, she again took advantage of the absence of her favourite, and officially assigned the vacancy left by Walsingham to Robert Cecil. Essex, who had nominated William Davison, was overruled.

The young Cecil and Essex represented diametrically opposed positions. Cecil followed the same domestic and foreign policy as his father, which can be summarised as strengthening the Established Church, and implementing an intolerant and rigid policy towards those of other beliefs, especially against the Catholics. Essex, on the other hand, showed himself to be open and tolerant on the question of religion. His radiant, alluring and still youthful appearance, his recklessness and his military achievements, coupled with his generosity and concern for his protégés and subordinates along with his

Fig. 91 – Portrait of Robert Devereux, Earl of Essex, after his victory at Cadiz in Spain. Fatherless, Essex was raised in the household of William Cecil and was sent to Cambridge at the age of ten. He graduated as Master of Arts at the age of fourteen. In 1587 his stepfather Robert Dudley, Earl of Leicester, introduced him at Court. The queen was very taken with his dazzling good looks. Essex became her favourite and experienced a rapid rise. His main political opponent was the intelligent but physically deformed (dwarfish) Robert Cecil. Cecil emerged the victor in the great power struggle at the end of the Elizabethan era. The historical depiction of the Earl of Essex as an incompetent statesman and military leader is a myth that was created and perpetuated by his enemies.

clemency towards those he had conquered, his classical education, and above all his chivalry, made him an icon of the people. Robert Cecil, on the other hand, had been delicate and frail from childhood, and was a hunchback, though with a keen intellect. He had a solid basis of knowledge, a sharp political mind and a shrewd understanding of the art of the possible in domestic and foreign policy. In contrast to his older half-brother, Lord Burghley, who was not very talented and had led a dissolute life on the Continent, Robert was his father's favourite and followed quite early in his footsteps.

Whereas the young Cecil fully backed the government, Essex and his followers represented the unofficial opposition. In his ambitious plans, Essex was supported by a pair of brothers who both proved to be very learned, intellectual and witty: Anthony (1558-1601) and Francis Bacon (1561-1626), the sons of Sir Nicholas Bacon (1509-1579), who had held high office under Elizabeth, including the post of Lord Privy Seal. Whereas Anthony Bacon would remain a true lifelong friend and supporter of the Earl of Essex, his brother, Francis, was almost entirely concerned with his own career. William Cecil, uncle of the highly gifted Bacon brothers, did everything in his power to ensure the rise of his son, Robert, preferably without competition, and thus made no effort to obtain high positions for his nephews, who associated themselves with Essex, the rising star.

After acting for about ten years on the Continent as an informer in the service of Walsingham and the Burghleys, Anthony Bacon returned to England in early 1592 – at about the same time as William Shakespeare. The dramatist, however, was on the side of those who were being spied upon by Bacon and numerous other informers. Bacon had been able to form connections in most of the great courts of Europe, and was disillusioned with his uncle, William Cecil, who paid him little and treated him badly. He now placed himself at Essex's disposal, introducing him to a network of

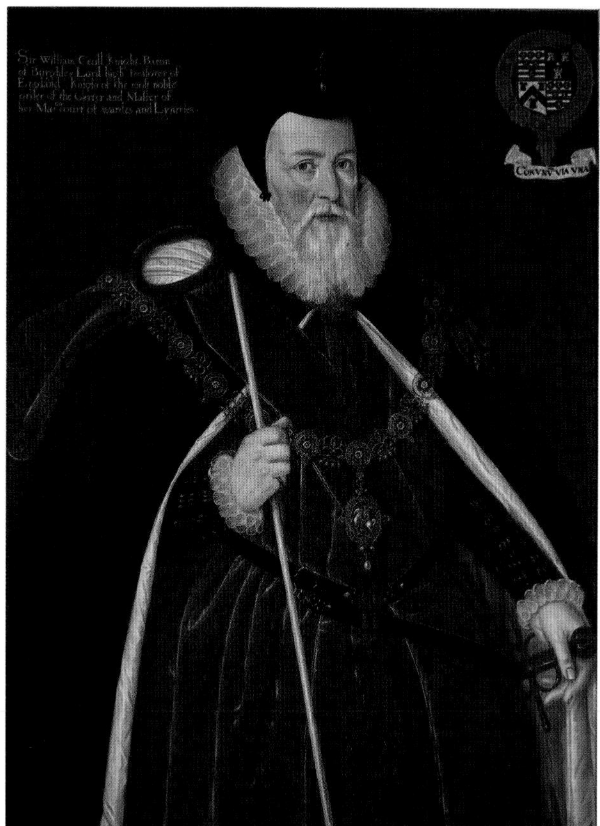

Fig. 92a – Portrait of William Cecil. William and his son Robert (*Fig. 92b*) were the leading figures in Elizabethan politics and enjoyed the full trust of the queen. William Cecil, the architect of Elizabeth I's new political strategy and religious policies, was a bitter opponent of the English Jesuit priest Robert Parsons and the English crypto-Catholics and Catholics-in-exile, who were trying to re-introduce Catholicism to England, initially by peaceful means, but increasingly by force of arms.

Fig. 92b – Portrait of Robert Cecil. Cecil became successor to the spymaster Francis Walsingham and continued the political work of his father. After successfully eliminating his enemy the Earl of Essex, he smoothed the ground for James VI of Scotland to accede to the English throne after the death of Elizabeth I.

information systems which substantially enhanced his (Essex's) political standing and decidedly strengthened his hand as a Privy Council member. This enabled Essex to provide the queen with more detailed and better targeted information on foreign affairs than could the Cecils. A circle of supporters that centred upon Essex was forming at Court which, in the second half of the 1590s, was to become a competent opposition force that had to be taken seriously. The government was worried about them and kept a wary eye on them. Although Essex remained her favourite, and was thus allowed certain liberties and a degree of impertinence, Elizabeth watched him closely, guided by her closest advisor, Cecil and his son, Robert, who were no friends of Essex. The queen feared that he was vying with her for popularity among her own subjects. His increasing power as a statesman with a multitude of connections abroad meant a weakening of the queen's own position. This was all the more important as it became clearer that the 'religious settlement' of the country had only been partially successful. The old faith continued to be practised, and Catholics as well as Protestants were very concerned about the future, as the queen had thus far failed to perform one of her most important duties – that of settling the question of the succession.

Francis Bacon – like his father – strove for high office, for power and influence. He was distinguished and extravagant, was deeply in debt and took other young men to bed, to the great displeasure of his puritanical mother, who loathed his lifestyle.

When the position of Attorney General became vacant, Essex used his personal and private connections with the queen to try to procure this high office for Bacon. The Cecils threw their power into the balance in order to prevent Bacon being offered the post. In 1594, after much prevarication over the matter, Elizabeth named Edward Coke to this high public office. Essex and Bacon were defeated, as was the courtier and diplomat Fulke Greville (1554-1628), who tried to mediate with the queen on behalf of Essex. The Cecils had won. In 1595, when the position of Solicitor General became vacant, William and Robert Cecil were again victorious, Essex and Bacon once more rebuffed. Essex generously gave his protégé a piece of land as compensation for the loss of the lucrative official position. Bacon sold the land for the considerable sum of £1,800. When compared to the £60 which Shakespeare paid in 1597 for his stately house in Stratford (New Place) and the £140 he paid in 1613 for the large eastern gatehouse of the old monastery of Blackfriars in London, it can be seen that this was a small fortune (£1,800 = about £250,000 in today's money). Essex's friend, the Earl of Southampton, was reported to be similarly generous. This background information would seem to support the story that Shakespeare received £1,000 as a present from his patron, Southampton.

After Essex failed in his mission as commander-in-chief of the Irish campaign of 1599, Bacon coolly, calculatingly and deliberately played a decisive role in the step-by-step destruction of the people's hero. This, despite the fact that Essex had done more for him than he had for anybody else.

It was Francis Bacon (*Fig. 93*), who, after consulting with his powerful cousin Sir Robert Cecil, Essex's greatest enemy, set the legal traps in the great propaganda trial after the Essex conspiracy and produced the decisive arguments against his erstwhile benefactor that sealed his fate and led to his condemnation. With a clear view to his own rise to power, he had already changed sides and was now working on behalf of Cecil. But it was only under James I, who – like himself – preferred boys, that Bacon achieved his ambitions. In 1607, he became Solicitor General, in 1617 Attorney General, in 1618 Lord Chancellor of England and first Baron Verulam, and finally in 1621, Viscount. In 1621, his enemies succeeded in getting him charged with accepting bribes. Bacon was impeached and admitted his guilt. The House of Lords sentenced him to a large fine and imprisonment in the Tower, and he was banished from Parliament and the Court. Although he was excused the fine, and spent only a few days in the Tower, his public career was ruined[190].

After the defeat of the Spanish Armada (1588) and the failure of all the plots of the English crypto-Catholics and Catholics-in-exile to re-introduce the old faith, the Catholic opposition, split into 'Spanish' and 'Scottish' parties[191], pinned their hopes in the 1590s on a natural solution to the problem, given the queen's advanced age. One party wanted the Spanish Infanta to succeed to the English throne, but the other favoured James of Scotland, son of Mary, Queen of Scots. The Cecils favoured the succession of the Infanta, although this did not mean that they changed their anti-Catholic domestic policy. The long war against Spain in the Netherlands that had begun in 1585 had so depleted the state coffers and cost so many English lives, that they had a strong desire to make peace with Spain. The Essex circle, however, favoured the Scottish king. Essex himself had in mind a military victory over Spain.

Fig. 93 – Francis Bacon in an engraving by William Marshall dated 1640. Francis and his brother Anthony were members of the Essex circle in the 1590s. Anthony spent many years on the Continent as a spy for William Cecil, but became a friend and ally of the Earl of Essex when he returned to England, and made his extensive network of spies available to him. Francis Bacon was generously supported by Essex, but he set the legal trap for Essex and Southampton when they were tried for high treason in 1601 that led to the execution of his former benefactor. Under James I, Francis Bacon, who had already been well known as an author of essays, attained high office, but was found guilty of corruption in 1621. This ended his political career.

SHAKESPEARE'S POLITICAL STANCE

On which side of the extremely polarised scene of Elizabethan politics did William Shakespeare stand? His career path hitherto shows that, due to his Catholic upbringing, employment in a Catholic household and in a Catholic secret organisation, as well as his connections with high-ranking representatives of the English Catholics-in-exile, he could not have sided with the government or the Established Church. So was he, therefore, necessarily a follower of the opposing Essex circle?

There is definite evidence to the effect that the playwright was, in fact, an enthusiastic follower of Essex, whose very name had served as a guarantee of religious tolerance in Catholic circles in the 1590s. Essex, moreover, was the closest friend and companion of the Catholic Earl of Southampton. And Southampton, to whom Shakespeare had dedicated his narrative poems in 1593 and 1594, was the poet's long-standing patron and friend (see p. 102 and pp. 112–113).

The stirring description of English youth and their eager expectations in the Prologue to Act II of *Henry V* is less of a representation of the situation in the year 1415, when Henry V fought the battle of Agincourt, than that of Shakespeare's own time. It reflects the emotions and high hopes pinned by the citizens of London, the persecuted Catholics, and, indeed, practically the whole population of England on the Earl of Essex. Just like Henry V in France, Essex as Elizabeth's Commander-in-Chief rode out to gain victory, fame and fortune in Ireland and to reward his supporters generously. Elizabeth forgave Essex his past misdeeds and in early 1599, offered him the command of the army in Ireland. His task was to crush the rebellion led by Hugh O'Neill, First Earl of Tyrone (1550-1616).

By bringing to life a great historical event, Shakespeare provides us with a realistic description of the atmosphere that prevailed in London in the spring of 1599 as the prologue to Act II in *Henry V* clearly shows (see pp. 141 ff.). This Shakespearian history play, however, contains

REGIVM IN ANGLIÆ REGNO APPELLATVM NONCIVTZ,
Hoc est nusquam simile.
Effigiauit Georgius Houfnaglius Anno 1582.

Fig. 94 – Nonsuch Palace near London in the year 1582; the queen's coach can be seen in the foreground. The palace, a place of unparalleled magnificence, was built by Henry VIII. It was destroyed by fire in 1668. Elizabeth was staying here when Essex returned from Ireland without permission on 28 September 1599 and pushed his way into her bedchamber to report to her in person.

even more concrete references to Essex. This is one of the few instances in the works of Shakespeare in which a contemporary is actually mentioned. In the prologue to Act V, the playwright speaks of 'the general of our gracious empress', and is thus specifically referring to the Earl of Essex, the beloved military leader, the learned courtier and favourite of Elizabeth I. Though the prologue is concerned with Henry V's victory in France, it alludes, however, to the most important current event, namely Essex's Irish campaign. The lords in *Henry V* relish in advance the triumphal procession of the king through London, with all the spoils of battle. Shakespeare hopes for a similar glorious return for Essex and endeavours to make his wishes felt through this example from English history and beyond – even by evoking the triumphal processions of the Roman emperors, especially those of Caesar. He writes:

But now behold,
In the quick forge and working-house of thought,
How London doth pour out her citizens!
The mayor and all his brethren in best sort –
Like to the senators of th' antique Rome,
With the plebeians swarming at their heels –
Go forth and fetch their conqu'ring Caesar in:
As, by a lower but loving likelihood,
Were now the General of our gracious Empress –
As in good time he may – from Ireland coming,
Bringing rebellion broached on his sword,
How many would the peaceful city quit,
To welcome him!

In Elizabethan reality, which Shakespeare as a writer of history plays principally had in mind, Essex was accompanied part of the way by a large cheering crowd as he set out on 27 March 1599 from London to Ireland. Since he could not (or perhaps would not) achieve the expected military triumph in Ireland and was even preparing to make peace overtures to O'Neill, resulting in an unauthorised truce and his plan 'to present Tyrone's demands to the English government'[192], the queen and the Privy Council could obviously not forgive him. That the tide would finally turn for the earl in 1600, that he would fall from grace and lead a *coup d'état*, and that he and many of his followers would be destroyed – none of this could have been predicted by Shakespeare when he wrote *Henry V* at the beginning of 1599, a play which included his remarkable eulogy for Essex, thus revealing his own political position.

On 28 September 1599, Essex, commander-in-chief of the English troops in Ireland, returned to London without permission and without prior announcement. He travelled practically day and night and rode directly to Nonsuch Palace (*Fig. 94*), where the queen was staying. Exhausted and dirty, still in his travelling clothes, he allowed himself to make a spectacular entry into the bedroom of the monarch, who was still undressed at the time. Essex kissed the hand and neck of the queen and then held a long audience with her. He could not have known that from this moment everything was to turn against him.

SHAKESPEARE'S HISTORICAL PLAY 'JULIUS CAESAR'

Shortly before Essex's return, Shakespeare's new play – *Julius Caesar* – appeared in the repertoire of the Chamberlain's Men. Since the government had forbidden the re-enactment of English history in order to prevent it from being used for political purposes, Shakespeare cleverly avoided this prohibition by resorting to the history of Rome. The censorship authorities had apparently not considered that other historical time periods, including the history of ancient Rome, could also be employed effectively as parallels for the present time. In any case, Shakespeare recognised this to be a huge loophole and exploited it. By referring to the case of Julius Caesar, he obviously tried again to influence the political fate of his country.

On 21 September 1599, the Swiss doctor, Thomas Platter the Younger, attended a performance of this play in the Globe Theatre, which had opened only in the spring of that year. We have him to thank for a vivid and charming description, in Swiss German, about the staging of a Shakespeare play during the lifetime of the dramatist, who may even have been present in person.

> On 21 September, after the mid-day meal, at about two o'clock, I went with my party across the water, and saw in the house with the thatched roof the tragedy of the first Emperor Julius Caesar, quite competently performed by about 15 people. At the end of the play, according to their custom, they danced exceedingly well, two got up in men's clothing and two in women's [*dancing*] wonderfully together[193].

Despite his great intellectual curiosity, Platter could not have known how daring Shakespeare's play really was. He was unaware of the political background and implications, and so could not have guessed that the play might be viewed as inflammatory, since it was about tyrannicide. The fact that it almost coincided with Essex's return from Ireland is startling.

Shakespeare apparently wrote his Roman tragedy in the summer of the year 1599, as it was not mentioned in Francis Meres's book *Palladis Tamia*, published in the autumn of 1598. *Henry V*, the great patriotic play, must have been created in early 1599. It was obviously the first play to be performed at the new Globe Theatre, which was now the home of the Chamberlain's Men. By the summer of 1599, the dissatisfaction and dismay of Elizabeth and the Cecil party over Essex's tactical manoeuvres in Ireland may well have become public knowledge. Shakespeare may even have had access to more insider information while he was writing *Julius Caesar*. Did he know that the Sword of Damocles was already suspended over his beloved general? Was Essex meant to recognise himself in the role of Brutus? If so, then the words of Cassius in Act I, scene 2 are addressed not just to Brutus but also to Essex:

> Men at some time are masters of their fates:
> The fault, dear Brutus, is not in our stars,
> But in ourselves, that we are underlings.

Just as the dramatist drew a parallel between Essex and Henry V, the victor of Agincourt, only six months earlier, he appears to have been suggesting once more a comparison between current and historical situations.

Shakespeare portrays Caesar as old, frail, deaf, overbearing and superstitious. He is merciless with petitioners who intercede for people who have been banished by him, just as Elizabeth showed no mercy to petitioners who interceded for their Catholic brethren who had lost their rights and property and/or were exiled. At that time the English queen, like Caesar, suffered from a series of physical failings. And, like Caesar, who – in the eyes of Brutus and his fellow conspirators – was guilty because his behaviour had become tyrannical, and because he threatened to abolish the Roman Republic in order to seize the crown, Elizabeth was also thought guilty of having made serious mistakes – not just in the eyes of Essex and his followers. She was now sixty-six-years-old, unmarried, and childless as far as anyone knew. Even in what was for the time old age, she had not named an heir. This was considered to be a serious dereliction of her duty as ruler. The queen steadfastly refused to settle the succession in the event of her death, and thereby ensure a peaceful transition of power; she may have had an eye to the fate of her half-sister, the Catholic Mary Tudor, who died eleven days after choosing her successor (see p. 20). By this refusal she risked her kingdom falling into chaos and civil war in a struggle for England's crown.

Fig. 95 – Ara di Cesare (Caesar's Altar) in Rome near the Rostra, the speakers' platform on the Forum Romanum, which was moved in 44 BC – when Caesar changed the lay-out of the Forum – from its previous position on the Comitium in front of the Curia to the opposite shorter side of the Forum, in the vicinity of the Regia. Here can be found the remains of the foundations of the Temple of Divus Julius. This was the site of the funeral pyre on which Julius Caesar's body was burned.
It is likely that William Shakespeare visited it when he stayed in Rome (in 1585, 1587, 1589 and 1613). Even today, flowers are still left at this ancient site where world history was made in Roman times. Shakespeare, who used the events surrounding the murder of Julius Caesar to point to parallels in his time and warn his countrymen of the consequences of similar acts, has also been associated with this site for centuries because of his tragedy *Julius Caesar*. Surrounded by his fellow-conspirators, Shakespeare's Brutus cries: 'Liberty! Freedom! Tyranny is dead!', and his Cassius utters the prophetic words: 'How many ages hence / Shall this our lofty scene be acted over / In state unborn and accents yet unknown!'

In *Julius Caesar*, Shakespeare dares to show the assassination of the Roman emperor on the open stage, and at times gives the impression that he justifies the act as the legitimate right of resistance to tyranny described in Renaissance statecraft teachings. In Act II, scene 1, Brutus calls upon his fellow conspirators to become Caesar's 'sacrificers', and not his 'butchers', to 'kill him boldly, but not wrathfully', and finally to offer him up as 'a dish fit for the gods' (*Fig. 95*).

The play *Julius Caesar* was political dynamite. Yet, as far as is known, Shakespeare was not called to account for his audacity, probably because his own standpoint could not be identified and because he hid, as the author, behind his historical figures. At the same time, his sympathies, at least at the beginning of the play, seem to lie with Brutus, who suffers on account of Caesar, and is troubled by inner conflicts because he selflessly represents the interests of ancient Rome: to him the common good matters more than anything else. The murder of Caesar, although justifiable in his own eyes, makes Brutus tragically guilty. However weak and fallible Shakespeare's Caesar was as a human being, this founder of the European monarchies was regarded by the Elizabethans as sacrosanct. Elizabeth was likewise old, weak and fallible; she too was an anointed sovereign. Moreover, in the eyes of her Catholic subjects, she bore the taint of excommunication. This weakened her position and made her vulnerable.

Julius Caesar triggered a heated and prolonged debate among Shakespeare's contemporaries. On 13 October 1600, about a year after *Julius Caesar* was performed on stage, a book was published entitled *An Historical collection* by William Fulbecke. It presented many examples from Roman history, from Livy to Tacitus, of quarrels, disturbances and massacres which yielded lessons for the present. The author deals very differently with Brutus, condemning him for plotting and participating in Caesar's assassination. Fulbecke represents a straightforward, loyalist standpoint: he holds that anyone who tries to create peace through bloodshed is merely pouring fuel on the fire. Further, he warns that anyone who commits 'the murder of a sovereign Magistrate' and then defends himself by arms can be compared to a man trying to cover himself 'from a shower of rain'. Just four months after the publication of Fulbecke's warnings, Essex and his followers chose the path of armed insurrection, with corresponding results.

The poet John Weever (1576-1632) who was born in Lancashire and educated in Cambridge, wrote the poem *The Mirror of Martyrs or the life and death of Sir John Oldcastle* (1601), in which he also expressed his reaction to *Julius Caesar*. He condemned the action of Brutus, but did so through a question:

> The many-headed multitude were drawne
> By *Brutus* speech, that *Caesar* was ambitious,
> When eloquent *Mark Antonie* had showne
> His virtues, who but *Brutus* then was vicious?

It is probable that Shakespeare's much-discussed play really encouraged Essex and his followers to begin their insurrection, but without new evidence this cannot be established with any greater certainty. It can be proved that the Essex conspirators used Shakespeare's *Richard II* as a tool for their purposes. They may have taken into consideration the new and even more daring Roman drama, but then, out of caution, rejected it immediately.

THE DOWNFALL OF THE EARL OF ESSEX

After his return to London, the reputation of Essex, the former shining hero and darling of the people, was gradually destroyed. This was probably the result of a prolonged strategy of attrition. In this, Elizabeth evidently let herself be persuaded by Robert Cecil and Francis Bacon. Essex was placed under permanent house arrest and suffered a great deal physically and mentally from this humiliation and disgrace. As part of the degradation, the men he had knighted had their knighthoods revoked. It seems that here not only Robert Cecil – nicknamed Gobbo (the hunchback)[194] – had a finger in the pie but also Francis Bacon, whom Essex had gone out of his way to protect in the 1590s.

The humiliation of Essex and his removal from political power, as well as the demotion of the officers and soldiers that he had knighted, deeply enraged his supporters, of whom Shakespeare was one. Not without reason, they suspected that Robert Cecil and his cronies were behind these intrigues, but for the time being their rage remained impotent.

In this dismal situation Shakespeare may have written Sonnet 66. For he uses this sonnet to pillory the political machinations and social conditions of his time, brought to light in all their ugliness by the current Essex crisis. If Sonnet 66 is viewed in the context of the events from the last quarter of 1599 onward, its strong social criticism and despairing tone may well be applied to the domestic scenario of England at that time.

An indication with regard to the time when this sonnet was written may be the numbering (sixty-six). The forceful accusations and allusions are aimed at the authorities, members of the Privy Council and even at the queen herself. Elizabeth, born on 7 September 1533, turned sixty-six-years-old three weeks before Essex's return from Ireland on 28 September 1599. Shakespeare may thus have been harping upon the number sixty-six, as it would have been on the minds of the queen's subjects after her birthday celebrations. This type of number game was very popular among Shakespeare's fellow citizens, as can be seen in the poet's political allegory, *The Phoenix and the Turtle*. The Essex circle also used numbers as code. For example, Essex was known by the number 2000, while Shakespeare's patron, the Earl of Southampton and Essex's fellow conspirator, was given the number 3000.[195] The English Jesuit priests at home and abroad, such as Father Robert Parsons and Father Henry Garnet, also made use of numbers as a code. For them, the Privy Council had the number 201 and Cecil the number 204. Since it was particularly important for priests living in hiding to know whether well-known Catholics were still in prison, they codified the expression 'still in prison' for security reasons, allocating it code 484[196].

Sonnet 66, which was first published in 1609 with all the other Shakespearian sonnets, had previously been privately circulated at the turn of the century in handwritten form. In it, Shakespeare castigates the authorities by invoking the terms merit, faith, honour, virtue, perfection, strength, wisdom, art, truth and good, in order to proclaim that these were being trampled underfoot. Every line in this poetical, political and philosophical masterpiece, as the German publisher and translator Ulrich Erckenbrecht succinctly remarks, strikes a blow like a whiplash[197].

Tir'd with all these, for restful death I cry:
As, to behold desert a beggar born,
And needy nothing trimm'd in jollity,
And purest faith unhappily forsworn,
And gilded honour shamefully misplac'd,
And maiden virtue rudely strumpeted,
And right perfection wrongfully disgrac'd,
And strength by limping sway disabled,
And art made tongue-tied by authority,
And folly, doctor-like, controlling skill,
And simple truth miscall'd simplicity,
And captive good attending captain ill –
Tir'd with all these, from these would I be gone,
Save that, to die, I leave my love alone.

Shakespeare could well have been referring in this sonnet to the situation in late 1599 as seen by Essex and his followers after his return from Ireland. Almost every line of this poem can be applied directly or indirectly to Essex. It begins with the melancholia that haunts the imprisoned commander, who is exhausted after the battles in Ireland, during his enforced isolation: 'Tir'd with all these, for restful death I cry'. The statement that in this country 'desert' (meaning a deserving person) is forced to be a 'beggar', appears to apply directly to Essex, as he provided a great service to the state, and, in the truest sense of the word, was reduced to begging, for the queen even denied him the renewal of the lucrative monopoly in the importation of sweet wine which had been Essex's main source of income. The statement that 'purest faith' was forsworn, indeed betrayed, is a clear reference to the dissolution and systematic extermination of Catholicism. This had led ever larger numbers of

Catholics, who refused to betray Rome, to flock to the cause of Essex in the 1590s. In the second quatrain, 'right perfection' is wrongly disgraced, while 'strength' is replaced by 'limping sway'. These could well be references to the great political rivals of the time, Essex and Robert Cecil. Essex's contemporaries saw in him the incarnation of their ideal image of courtier, scholar and soldier. Elizabeth was very old and weak; her chief advisor, William Cecil, was dead; and his son and successor, Robert Cecil, was a hunchbacked dwarf. For all the power the young Cecil possessed, his physical deformity made him fall painfully short of the Elizabethan ideal. The lines of the third quatrain also read like a commentary on the events of the years 1599–1600, that is, on the repression suffered not only by the arrested earl, his relatives and followers, but also by those writers and poets who sharply criticised the events of the day through historical parallels, and dedicated their works to Essex. Since Elizabeth was consulting Francis Bacon, Essex's former protégé, ever more frequently at that time, the sentence 'And art made tongue-tied by authority, / And folly, doctor-like, controlling skill' could also refer to him. It is well known that Bacon liked to pepper his speech with nuggets of wisdom. As would soon be brought home to them even more forcefully, he no longer took the side of Essex and his followers, but represented the interests of Cecil and the government. But first of all, Shakespeare's lines, especially the statement that 'art is made tongue-tied by authority' would have been aimed at John Whitgift, the Archbishop of Canterbury. Whitgift was the chief censor, who ruled the established church with an iron hand and brooked no resistance – as has been pointed out before (see p. 95). He even indulged in burning those books he considered inflammatory, and had their authors thrown in jail and/or banned them from publishing for life. The expression 'simple truth' could refer to what was probably the most burning issue of the last decade of the reign of Elizabeth I, that of her succession. Nobody dared broach this topic in the presence of the queen, not even Essex when he was still in her favour. He had, however, secretly used all his powers and his clandestine diplomacy to try to resolve the issue. Even the 'simple', anxious people ceaselessly wondered about the succession to the throne. Who, the poet appears to ask, was simple here, and who spoke the truth? In the last line of the third quatrain – 'And captive good attending captain ill' – the reference is clearer here than anywhere else in the sonnet; Shakespeare is describing none other than Essex, whose most striking character trait – as the sources show – was his goodness. It is an historical fact that Essex ('captive good') was placed under house arrest – most probably at the command of Robert Cecil ('captain ill') – after 28 September 1599, the date of his return from Ireland. Cecil was Essex's great opponent and enemy. He was, in every respect, the son of his father, representing an uncompromising stance that promised Catholics no mercy. He was the most powerful member of the Privy Council. Insiders held that, by 1596, his power was already greater than that of James of Scotland and Philip of Spain (see p. 131 f.). The situation at the turn of the seventeenth century evoked anger and indignation in all the followers of Essex. Shakespeare, in Sonnet 66, obviously refers to this, and joins those great authors, such as Petrarch, who criticised the political situation of their time[198]. The contents and form of Shakespeare's polemic have lost nothing of their immediacy over the last four hundred years. Thanks to the modernity of its expression and parallels with today's world, Sonnet 66 is the most admired and the most translated of all Shakespeare's sonnets[199].

Essex was to feel more sharply than ever Elizabeth I's capricious nature, guided as she was by Cecil and his circle, in the course of the year 1660 and in early 1601. His solitary confinement became a form of mental torture. On 12 May 1600 he complained in a letter to the queen he felt like 'a dead carcase' that was 'thrown into a corner' and was 'gnawed on and torn by the basest creatures upon earth'. Essex continued:

> The prating tavern haunter speaks of me what he lists; the frantic libeller writes of me what he lists; they print me and make me speak to the world, and shortly they will play me upon the stage.[200]

At court, Essex's name could no longer be mentioned. He was to be expunged from human memory. The earl's protectors, supporters and friends tried to counteract this move. On 2 February 1600, an engraving of Essex was put into circulation, showing him high on his horse wearing all his decorations (*Fig.* 96). In principle, this was nothing out of the ordinary. It was common at the time to distribute or sell one's own portrait attached to verses or other texts[201]. Many noblemen, and even commoners including authors like Edmund Spenser, had a likeness made of themselves, and distributed their picture as an engraving. However, the text attached to the picture of Essex alarmed the Crown. Not only were honour, prestige and wisdom emphasised in it, but also a claim that he was 'God's elect'. This was a clear indication that his followers and the people wanted Essex as their king. It was Dover Wilson who had already elaborated on this: 'There were two opinions among Essex's friends: one urged him to seize the crown at once by force; the other pointed out that if he only waited, and wisely became friends with the old Queen, the crown would fall into his lap.'[202] The English Shakespeare scholar was of the opinion that Shakespeare must have supported the second option. This would correspond most closely to what we know of the poet's personality as delineated in this book.

Six months after the reproduction and distribution of the Essex portrait, the startled government reacted to the provocation by forbidding the engraving and distribution of portraits. For this was the sole prerogative of the ruler. This prohibition was aimed principally at Essex, whose fame and popularity had long fuelled the suspicions of Elizabeth and her advisers.

Fig. 96 – The Earl of Essex on horseback, 1601. This copper engraving was circulated by his supporters and shows the earl asserting an almost limitless claim to power, in stark contrast to the position in which he actually found himself at that time. From late 1599 onwards, Essex was systematically diminished by his opponents, placed under house arrest and denied visitors. As a result his mental and physical powers waned. Influenced by the Cecils, Elizabeth thought that, although he was her favourite, Essex also represented a threat to her power as ruler of the State.

Much to the disapproval of the queen and her court, many of Essex's relatives and friends, including his mother, Lady Leicester, and the Earl of Southampton, stayed in a house adjacent to York House, where Essex was initially imprisoned. From there they could see into the

Fig. 97 – Elizabethan tavern. Late sixteenth-century woodcut. The negative aspects of the age – such as drinking – are strongly criticised by the Puritans. who also thought that taverns were hotbeds of subversion. In *Hamlet*, Shakespeare, too, condemns the vice of drinking.

A
Midſommer nights
dreame.

As it hath beene ſundry times publickely acted, by the Right honourable, the Lord Chamberlaine his ſeruants.

Written by William Shakeſpeare.

ALCIONE

Imprinted at London, for *Thomas Fiſher*, and are to be ſoulde at his ſhoppe, at the Signe of the White Hart, in *Fleeteſtreete*. 1600.

Fig. 98 – Title page of the first Quarto edition of the comedy *A Midsummer Night's Dream*, printed in 1600.

garden and make contact with Essex. However, Lady Rich, the earl's sister, was not able to do so. She was also under house arrest because she had published her letters to the queen when she was abroad. Essex was later permitted to return to his London residence, though he was still under house arrest and allowed only one servant.

On 25 March 1600, an incident occurred in the Mermaid Tavern on the west side of Bread Street (opposite St Mildred's Church) (*Fig.* 97) that was regarded by the regime as a riot and dealt with accordingly. Sir Edward Baynham and three other gentlemen – quite obviously Essex supporters – had eaten there and drunk late into the night while making inflammatory speeches. They then stormed outside, drew their weapons upon the watchmen in Friday Street and Saint Paul's Churchyard, and wounded them. They were overpowered and locked up. The tavern owner was not punished, as his guilt could not be established, but on 6 July 1600 the insurrectionists were fined £200 and sentenced to long prison terms. The owner of the Mermaid Tavern (which burned down in the Great Fire of London, 1666) was probably a friend of William Shakespeare. Thirteen years later, he was one of Shakespeare's trustees at the purchase of the eastern gatehouse of Blackfriars.

Shakespeare himself wisely kept a low profile during the year 1600. This was when he chose to publish the more harmless comedies he had written in the 1590s, steering attention well away from his politically dangerous works. The Stationer's Registry records on 23 August that *Much Ado about Nothing* was to be published, a play that had been publicly performed many times by the Chamberlain's Men; and on 8 October that *A Midsummer Night's Dream* was being prepared for publication (*Fig. 98*), a play that had also been given frequent public performances by the Chamberlain's Men. The

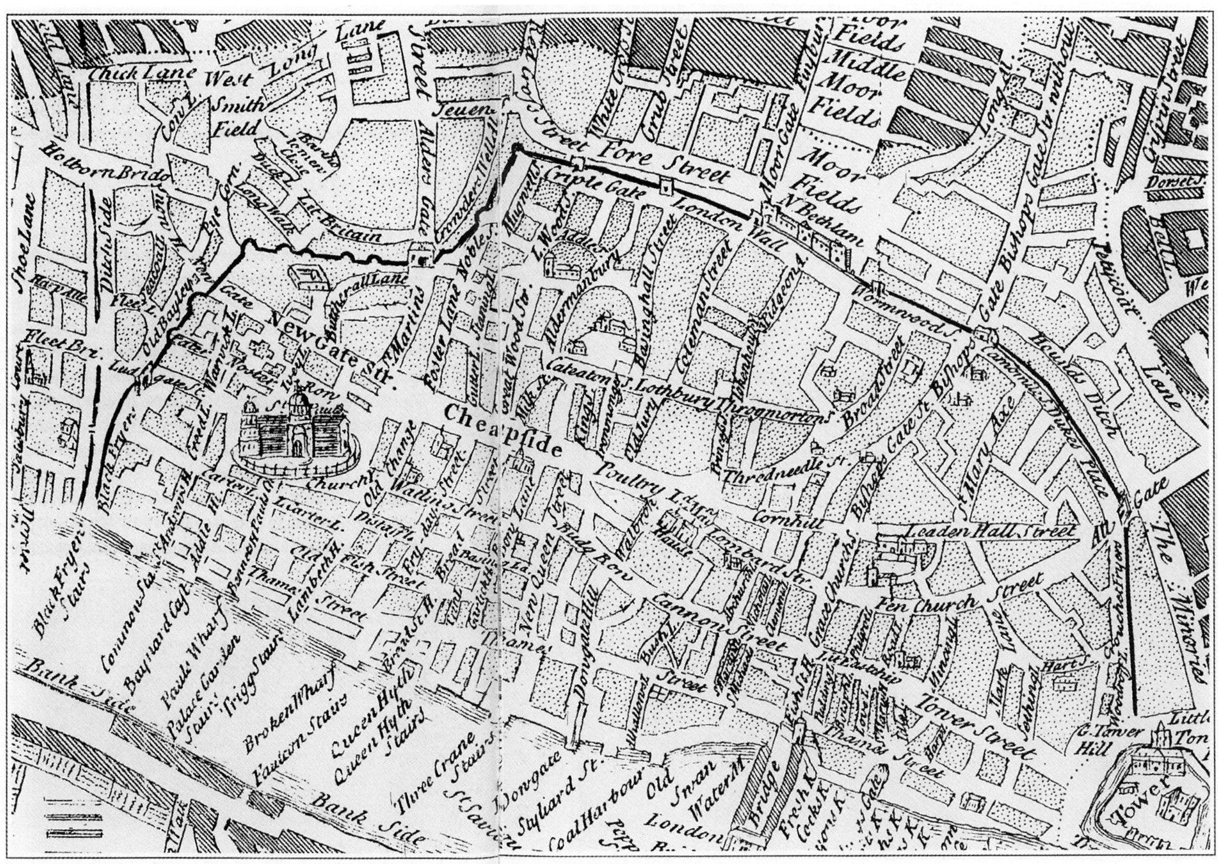

Fig. 99 – Map of London by Robert Dodseley dated 1744.

poet was well advised, following his praise of Essex in *Henry V* in March 1599 and the public performance of *Julius Caesar* in September of that year, to avoid confrontation with the censors and the government.

The Elizabethan historian, Dr John Hayward, was less careful, and met with the full fury of the government. Apparently, he had the same political leanings as Shakespeare and had probably – as has been suggested by research – used Shakespeare's *Richard II* as a source. His book, *Henry IV*, which contained a description of the deposition and eventual murder of King Richard II, was published in 1599. The reasons for the removal of Richard were mismanagement, corruption and a monstrous tax burden on the citizenry. In his hearing before the nobles of the kingdom on the 11 July 1600, Hayward was accused of having targeted the government, and the queen saw the book as a covert attack on her person. The author had unwisely dedicated his history to the Earl of Essex. Two days later, on 13 July, Hayward was thrown into the Tower of London. On the same day, the printer was required to answer for the printing of the dedication to Essex. Finally, on 20 July, the censor Samuel Harsnett (1561-1631), chaplain to the Bishop of Bancroft, was indicted since he had allowed the work to be passed. Harsnett, threatened with imprisonment, was able to show that he had not even read the book. One of the gentlemen of the bishop's household had requested his approval telling him that it was simply an extract from the English Chronicles, and displayed the author's wit. It appears that the censor had been duped, or perhaps he 'looked the other way', since Hayward had been a fellow student at Pembroke College, Cambridge. The Attorney-General, Edward Coke (1552-1634), who had been the Speaker of the House of Commons since 1593, also accepted Harsnett's explanation that he had not recognised the political motives of the book. Under James I and Charles I, Harsnett rose in the Anglican Church hierarchy to the post of Bishop of Chichester (1609) and eventually Archbishop of York (1629).

THE ESSEX REBELLION

In early 1601, Essex, in complete isolation and despair, appealed to James VI of Scotland and requested the dispatch of a fully empowered envoy. The Scottish king agreed and sent the Earl of Mar with a letter of encouragement to be delivered to Essex, which he carried in a little leather pouch around his neck. When the rumour reached Essex's supporters that their disgraced leader was to be taken to the Tower of London, they urged action and an attempt to free him. Was the prolonged emotional torture to which the earl's enemies subjected him perhaps intended, precisely to incite a rebellion, and thus provide a legal pretext for disposing of him once and for all?

On the morning of 7 February 1601 Essex received a messenger from the queen with a summons to attend a session of the Privy Council. His friends interpreted this as a move on the part of the government to seize the earl. Therefore, the decision was taken to attack and put an end to the 'regency' of Robert Cecil, though the queen was not to be harmed in the coup. Essex sent word officially that he was too sick to leave his bed.

The conspirators organised a performance of Shakespeare's *Richard II* at the Globe Theatre for the afternoon of 7 February. A template would thus be presented which they thought to emulate.

The next morning, about 300 men had assembled around the earl in the inner courtyard of Essex's house, when four high officials knocked on the door. They were permitted to enter, but their attendants had to wait outside. The officials in question were Sir Thomas Egerton, Lord Keeper of the Privy Seal; Sir William Knollys, Comptroller of the Queen's Household; Sir John Popham, Chief Justice of the Queen's Bench; and Edward Somerset, 4th Earl of Worcester. They were now in the power of Essex and Southampton. The mood was especially tense; cries such as 'kill them' and 'lock 'em up' were heard. Essex led the emissaries of the queen into his office and held them there. He ordered the crowd, who were about to head west with him towards Whitehall, to turn eastwards toward the City – contrary to his original intention. Essex hoped to be able to win the support of the citizens of London, so he marched with his men, not directly to the Palace of Whitehall, the seat of government, but first to the

Fig. 100 – Portrait of Robert Devereux, Earl of Essex. When Essex was executed for high treason on Tower Hill on Ash Wednesday, 25 February 1601, there was an outburst of grief and anger. It is said that the executioner was almost lynched by the people of London when he appeared in the streets. For the English population, especially the English Catholics, Essex had represented a future of religious tolerance. They, Shakespeare included, had pinned their hopes on him. Now they had all lost their political hero.

Fig. 101 – Portrait of Henry Wriothesley, third Earl of Southampton. Towards the end of the Essex Rebellion, Southampton, the closest friend and trusted companion of the Earl of Essex, and one of the leaders of the rebellion, took matters into his own hands. He stood on the roof of Essex House to negotiate a surrender with the representative of the Crown. He asked for the rebels to be allowed a free passage, but only the women and children (among them the Countess of Southampton and her daughter Penelope, then two-years-old) were to be released from the besieged residence. As an enthusiastic supporter of Essex, William Shakespeare must have observed events from a distance in great anxiety. Southampton's portrait, the so-called Tower Portrait, was painted to commemorate his time in the Tower of London, from which he was released by James I, in 1603. The painting contains many symbols, hitherto overlooked. For the origin of the black ribbon bows on Southampton's gloves see sub-chapter 'The origin of the sign of the Essex circle'. They seem to stand for those who participated in the Essex rebellion and were executed. The black and white cat cannot just be regarded as Southampton's pet but is, as it appears, a symbol of 'of ill-fortune' (John Horden, 'The Connotation of Symbols' *The Art of the Emblem. Essays in Honor of Karl Josef Höltgen*, New York, 1993, pp. 78-79) which may well be connected with the queen who, in the eyes of Southampton, was responsible for his ill-fortune. This interpretation can also be backed by the fact that the cat in Greek and Roman mythology stands for Diana, the ancient goddess of the moon, worshipped as the protector of virginity. 'Diana', however, was – as is well-known, one of the epithets of Elisabeth I – just like 'Gloriana', 'Astraea' or 'Cynthia'. The symbolism in this painting is discussed in detail in my book *The Secret Surrounding Shakespeare's Dark Lady*, pp. 76-78.

City of London. When the insurgents entered the city through Ludgate, they noticed that nobody was joining them. Essex wanted to speak to the people from the open-air pulpit by old St Paul's Cathedral, but the icy atmosphere blighted this plan, along with his hopes of winning the fearful crowd over to his cause. For in the meantime, the word had spread that Essex had been declared a traitor. The announcement by the earl that Lord Cobham and Sir Walter Raleigh had tried to assassinate him and that the English crown had been sold by Robert Cecil to the Spanish Infanta, was met without the slightest reaction. Essex's situation was hopeless. Many of his men had already crept away. The sweat rolled from his brow, as he and his remaining followers made their way along the 'very spacious street' of Cheapside (*Fig. 99*), 'adorned with lofty buildings' (Strype). His last hopes lay with Sheriff Smith, his friend, who had about 1,000 men of London's trained bands under his command. He entered the house of the sheriff in Gracechurch Street, but Smith was not at home – in order to gain time he had hurried to consult the Lord Mayor of London. Essex was eventually forced to signal retreat, but Ludgate had by now been locked and chained. Essex and his men hurried down to the Thames and were able to reach Essex's house by boat, barricading themselves in. Their prisoners had been freed in the meantime. They quickly destroyed any incriminating evidence – including the letter which Essex had received from James VI of Scotland in early 1601.

Led by the Lord of the Admiralty, the queen's troops marched out, and artillery was also drawn up. Resistance seemed futile. The cries of women and children rang from the house. The position of the insurgents was desperate.

It was Southampton, Shakespeare's patron (*Fig. 101*), who courageously took the initiative and – standing high above the crowd on the roof of Essex's house – negotiated with Robert Sidney, once a supporter of the Essex circle, who had been sent to parley on behalf of the government. Southampton demanded free passage in return for the rebels' surrender and acceptance of trial at Court. Sidney replied that a subject had no right to force conditions upon a sovereign. However, the women and children were allowed to leave Essex's besieged residence. They included not only the Countess of Essex and Lady Rich and her children, but also the Countess of Southampton and her daughter Penelope, who was now twenty-seven months old. Where Penelope's biological father – William Shakespeare – was at this time we do not know. As it seems he kept well in the background, whether as a hidden participant or only a spectator, we will probably never find out. As an Essex supporter, he must have endorsed the initial goal of the rebels, namely the removal of the advisors to Queen Elizabeth, who were Essex's enemies. Yet, as can be deduced from his literary work, for Shakespeare the act of rebellion was obviously unacceptable except as a measure of last resort. All the same, on the eve of the rebellion, his theatre company had played a major role in setting the mood. The outcome of the Essex Rebellion had grave consequences for Shakespeare and the English crypto-Catholics, as will be shown later. The dramatist must have followed the events with great anxiety, because it involved people with whom he had had a very close relationship in the 1590s and – in the case of the Countess of Southampton – seemingly still had. The authenticated portrait of the countess with its hidden miniature image of Shakespeare on her sleeve, dating *c.* 1600, tells its own story of the love affair (see *Figs. 85a* and *b*).

THE TRIAL OF ESSEX AND SOUTHAMPTON FOR HIGH TREASON

The surrender of the conspirators was unavoidable. Both leaders were tried quickly. The verdict was a foregone conclusion, as was the case in all trials of this type. Nobody was more aware of this than the chief defendant, Essex, who wore black for the trial, anticipating the outcome of the proceedings. Essex and Southampton were both found guilty of high treason and were sentenced to death.

Fig. 102 – The Tower of London. This most impenetrable of all English medieval fortresses has, throughout its history, been used as a Royal palace, a prison, a place of execution, a mint and an observatory. It has housed the Royal armoury, the State Archives, a Royal menagerie and – to this day – the Crown Jewels. When Shakespeare came to London in 1592, the Tower had been used since time immemorial as a prison, the largest and most feared in England. One of the dungeons was known as Little Ease. It consisted of an unventilated hole only four feet square. This is where Edmund Campion, the Jesuit missionary priest and former Oxford don who had been celebrated as the 'Cicero' of England, was kept in 1581 before his execution. Southampton's father, the second Earl of Southampton, also spent time in the Tower for his Catholic beliefs. The third earl himself must have been conceived in the Tower (see p. 105).

During the trial there was an incident that almost brought about a complete reversal of the situation when, instead of Essex and Southampton, their opponent, Robert Cecil, might have stood accused of the same crime. Essex disclosed to his dumbfounded judges that Mr Secretary (meaning Cecil) had sold the succession to the English throne secretly to the Spanish. Cecil, who had been eavesdropping on the trial from 'behind the arras' (tapestry), quickly emerged from his hiding place, fell to his knees and asked that he be allowed to clear himself of this libellous accusation. He was given the stand immediately, and declared that the informant on whose testimony the accusation was founded was Sir William Knollys, the earl's uncle. Knollys was called as a witness and his testimony exonerated Cecil on the spot. The witness declared that the minister had once mentioned a book to him whose author had placed the claim of the Spanish Infanta to the English throne above all other pretenders. This denial could have been pre-arranged in a conversation between Cecil and Knollys. Essex had already shouted out this – by no means unfounded – accusation on the day he led the rebellion in the streets of London. So Cecil and his followers knew the chief argument of his opponent and had time to work out a strategy for exonerating themselves. The evidence of Sir William Knollys, another of Elizabeth's close advisors and, indeed, one of the very government representatives whom Essex had imprisoned in his house on the day of the rebellion, was decisive. The fact that the Attorney General Edward Coke was satisfied with this explanation shows that it was not in the interest of the Crown to examine the facts too closely, for they would have shown that Essex's accusation was correct. Instead, Coke reverted to the main charges, screaming insults at the chief defendant and shaking an accusing index finger at him. He claimed, without evidence, that Essex had not only wanted to capture the Tower of London, but also the Palace of Whitehall, and that he had wished to seize the person of the queen, and even make an attempt on her life. But it pleased God that he, Essex, who strove to be Robert I of England, would now be Robert the last Earl of Essex. It was Bacon who then coldly and calmly interrupted Coke's emotional tirade to shift the attack on to a different and more effective plane, as soon became evident. He made it clear that the events initiated by Essex on 8 February 1601 were, from a judicial standpoint, an armed uprising. When Essex interrupted him and stated that he had only wanted to act against his private enemies, Bacon retorted that Essex had hoped for the support of the citizens of London. Bacon's reference to the horrific example, well known in

Elizabethan England, of the Duke of Guise, who successfully incited the people of Paris against Henry III so that the latter had to flee secretly, did not miss its mark. According to Bacon, Essex had the same intention, but had been unsuccessful. Nonetheless, this was high treason. Thus the fate of Essex and Southampton was sealed. They were condemned to death as traitors. Robert Cecil, who had heard every word from his hiding-place behind the tapestry, had reason to be pleased with the work of his cousin Francis Bacon. He intervened, however, in the case of Southampton, whose death sentence he subsequently had commuted to life imprisonment in the Tower (*Fig. 102*), apparently because of the entreaties of the young earl's mother and wife.

SHAKESPEARE'S 'RICHARD II' – AN INSTRUMENT OF POLITICAL PROPAGANDA

Shakespeare's theatre company, the Chamberlain's Men, who, by special request of the conspirators, had staged a performance of the dramatist's *Richard II* at the Globe Theatre on the day before the failed rebellion, were now in a dangerous situation. Essex's supporters had used Shakespeare's play to get themselves in the right mood for the rebellion and to give each other encouragement. The performance included the banned deposition scene that Hayward had used and that had landed him in the Tower of London. The old actor in Shakespeare's company, Augustine Phillips, later convincingly claimed in defence of his colleagues that they had not wanted to perform the play, but did so only at the insistence of certain noblemen and for extra payment. So the Chamberlain's Men escaped unscathed, as did the playwright. It seems that, apart from their patron, the Lord Chamberlain, they must have had other high-ranking protectors in the Privy Council.

Some cryptic remarks by Privy Council member Sir John Fortescue about an anonymous dear friend, who could even have been Shakespeare, have been passed down from the time after the death of Essex, These remarks indicate that both Fortescue and the person he addressed were secret Catholics. Sir John, who was also Keeper of the Royal Wardrobe, could have warned his nephew, John Fortescue of danger ahead (see p. 96). The latter, who lived with his family in the eastern gatehouse at Blackfriars, immediately opposite the Wardrobe, is known to have harboured and protected numerous Catholic priests whom he also helped to escape. In his official functions and to the outside world, however, John Fortescue kept his religious beliefs well hidden at all times. Shakespeare, who purchased the eastern gatehouse at Blackfriars in 1613, must have known both the uncle and the nephew. Moreover, since Sir Nicholas Fortescue, the head of a branch of this family living near Stratford, who also harboured priests – was a patient of the playwright's son-in-law, Dr John Hall, Shakespeare would seem to have been acquainted with Sir Nicholas as well.

On 27 May 1602, Sir John Fortescue alluded meaningfully and with great caution to 'the frailty of the time'. This echoes Hamlet's more radical observation: 'The time is out of joint'. Fortescue claimed that he found it a comfort to be old and weak – as old as the queen and as weak as the times. He mentioned Mary Tudor and quoted the Bible, saying that whoever cometh in the eleventh hour to the vineyard, shall receive the same payment as the one who had laboured throughout the day (the Parable of the Labourers in the Vineyard). The term 'vineyard' or 'vineyard of the Lord' was used by Jesuit missionaries when speaking of the land in which they operated, i.e. England. They referred to themselves as 'labourers' in the English vineyard. The encoded observation of Privy Council member Fortescue makes sense only when placed in this context. Referring to the Parable of the Labourers in the Vineyard, he said he would make it clear to his son (who may well have stood for the youth of England) that he should embrace this cause when the time came.

About three and a half years later, that time seemed to have come for the sons of the Catholic gentry from the Midlands. Their assassination attempt, the famous Gunpowder Plot (1605), intended to destroy the whole English Parliament and the royal family by blowing them up, was foiled at literally the last minute.

Not without cause, the queen, in the final years of her life, constantly suspected danger to the state at every step. She also thought Shakespeare's play *Richard II* to be dangerous, and recognised that it contained a message concerning her own position. This is shown by her remarks in connection with the delicate task the jurist and antiquarian William Lambarde (1536-1601) had carried out. Since January 1601, Lambarde had been charged 'with the care of the records that be reposed in the Tower of London'. On 4 August 1601 he presented to the queen his *pandecta* (digest) of these documents. Nobody else was allowed to see them before. The conversation started in a rather relaxed fashion. When opening the book, the queen remarked jovially, 'You shall see that I can read'. She then carried on to read out the epistle and the title 'with an audible voice', demanding of Lambarde to explain certain meanings, which he did. She then continued, in a still jovial manner, 'she would [even] be a scholar in her age'. Suddenly, however, the queen 'fell upon the reign of King Richard the Second', bluntly confronting Lambarde with the question: 'I am Richard the Second, know ye not that?' Lambarde must have been extremely baffled and embarrassed. Of course, he knew that the Earl of Essex and his circle had compared Elizabeth with Richard (and why). However, he reacted wisely and evasively: 'Such wicked imagination was determined and attempted by a most unkind gentleman, the most adorned creature that ever your Majesty made'. Neither Lambarde nor the queen mentioned the name of Essex. Elizabeth's answer was cryptic: 'He that will forget God will also forget his benefactors'. Then she continued: 'this tragedy was played forty times in open streets and houses'. That was a clear allusion to Shakespeare's history play *Richard II* which the conspirators had performed on the eve of Essex's rebellion. The enormous number of performances in the open streets of the capital as well as in private houses, was astonishing and greatly disturbed Her Majesty – the more so because they had obviously taken place after the execution of the Earl of Essex to keep his ideals and memory alive. The queen must have been informed about these activities by her spies. The performances were acts of disobedience (and even insult) to the monarch, but obviously Elizabeth could not stop them. As a result, she seems to have become obsessed with the idea to learn more about the historical King Richard II, even about his portraits. For she asked Lambarde 'whether he had seen any true picture or lively representation of the countenance of King Richard'. The antiquarian replied that he knew 'none but such as be in common hands'. But the queen had not listened to him. She continued that one portrait had been presented to her. This was probably the image of Richard II that is still being kept at Westminster Abbey. All of a sudden, the queen seemed in haste. Being called to prayer, she 'put the book in her bosom', said 'Farewell, good and honest Lambarde', and disappeared. Lambarde died on 19 August 1601, only fifteen days after this audience[203].

Yet, unlike Hayward, Shakespeare was never called to account for his explosive history play. That was probably due to the fact that *Richard II* was not a new play and contained no dedication to Essex, although the Essex conspirators had used the play for their own ends, Elizabeth however, was applying a double standard. As the ruler of the state she must have noticed that Shakespeare's historical drama *Richard II* was inflammatory and that the play continued to be performed in the streets and houses of the capital. As a lover of the theatre, she would consider Shakespeare, the star playwright, to be indispensable. As mentioned above, the dramatist must have had powerful advocates in the Privy Council, and he had kept a low profile during the difficult year 1600 when Essex was kept under house arrest and when it was dangerous to show loyalty to him. General Mountjoy too remained untouched, although he had been one of the leaders of the Essex conspiracy and had even secretly negotiated with James VI of Scotland. As Essex's successor in Ireland, Lord Mountjoy, however, was also equally indispensable to the queen. The other conspirators were either condemned to death or were allowed to buy their freedom, as it suited the Crown.

THE EXECUTION OF THE EARL OF ESSEX AND THE CAUSES OF HIS DOWNFALL

Essex was executed by the sword inside the Tower on the Green on 25 February 1601. As the executioner held high the head of the victim and cried out 'Look, the head of a traitor!' a vigorous voice rose from the crowd shouting that he was lying. The people were both sad and angry. Later, the executioner was a hair's breadth from being lynched by an angry mob in the streets of London.

On the eve of the execution of her former favourite, the queen allowed herself to be entertained in her palace in Richmond. She attended a performance by Shakespeare's theatre company[204]. Shakespeare himself was presumably not present.

The day Essex died was Ash Wednesday, the beginning of Lent. Southampton's death sentence had – as has already been mentioned – been commuted to life imprisonment in the Tower. When James VI of Scotland ascended the English throne, Southampton was released and his old rights were restored. Francis Bacon, who had done so much to bring about the downfall of both Southampton and Essex, was now one of the first to congratulate the earl and declare his loyalty to him.

Why did Essex fall irredeemably into disfavour with Elizabeth after his interrupted Irish campaign? Why was he isolated, cut off from all outside connections, humiliated and ignored? Why did he have to die? The answer to these questions, which are critically important for the life and work of William Shakespeare, cannot be given without re-examining the traditional picture of Essex, the queen's favourite in the last decade of the sixteenth century, and revising his role in the political power struggle of the time. In *The Polarisation of Elizabethan Politics. The Political Career of Robert Devereux, 2nd Earl of Essex, 1585-1597*, the Australian historian Paul E. J. Hammer comes to the conclusion that the traditional image of Essex which portrays him as a political lightweight, a gambler and an incompetent military leader, even as 'the playboy of the western world' is not merely inaccurate, but worse: it is a caricature, in urgent need of revision[205].

Francis Bacon and his friend of many years, Thomas Phelippes, introduced Essex to the world of espionage, after the death of Walsingham in the year 1591. The English government, isolated from the rest of Europe, was very much dependent on the procuring of secret service intelligence. Bacon and Phelippes recommended William Sterrell (alias Henry St Main), who would then be paid by Essex in order to spy on the English Catholics-in-exile in Flanders and inform him about their plans. Essex passed this information to the queen, thereby demonstrating his commitment in the area of national security. He distanced himself from Roger Walton, showing that he (Essex) realised the dirty game the agent was playing. Walton was a shady agent provocateur who wheedled dangerous statements from his fellow countrymen and then denounced them.

It was only after the return of Anthony Bacon, who had spent over ten years as a spy on the Continent, and was now offering his services to Essex, that Elizabeth's favourite, with the help of Anthony Bacon, began to build a solid network of informants, in order to keep the queen up-to-date with events in Europe. Through his contacts, Anthony Bacon facilitated the secret co-operation between Essex and James VI of Scotland regarding James's succession to the English throne. As was well known, this topic that profoundly concerned Elizabeth I's subjects could not be raised in the queen's presence. The intermediary was Dr Thomas Morrison an agent of Anthony Bacon whom he had met in France. James, who had secretly taken all the necessary steps to become Elizabeth's successor, proved willing to negotiate with the English Catholics, signalling tolerance towards them. This tolerance was demonstrated by an incident that had occurred in 1592. A document was found on a Scottish ship which indicated a Spanish offer to James, and incriminated three Scottish Catholic earls. Elizabeth reacted in an uncontrolled manner, urging the Scottish king to treat the Catholic noblemen concerned with the utmost severity. James, however, responded evasively. While Essex's representative, Dr Morrison, befriended the leader of the Catholic Scottish nobles, the Earl of Huntly, Elizabeth, helped by the Cecils, began to create a pro-English Protestant 'party' in Scotland.

The alliance between Essex and the Scottish king had to remain secret. It grew even stronger because James hated the Cecils from the bottom of his heart, since he blamed William Cecil for the death of his mother, Mary, Queen of Scots. In internal affairs, Essex too was to become increasingly the opponent of the Cecils. The elder Cecil, who was grooming his son, Robert, to be his successor, saw Essex, the shining hero of the people, as the main stumbling-block to his son's rise to power. Robert Cecil, however, was totally eclipsed by Essex.

By 1594, Elizabeth's favourite had gained such esteem and importance as a statesman that King James VI assigned him the function of representing his interests in England. This put Essex in a difficult position as he knew that, in order to be able to strengthen and secure the Scottish king's claim to the English throne, James would have to be receptive to the wishes of the Pope and the Spanish king, all of which ran contrary to the interests of the English government. The Scottish king was known to have visited Italy in late 1591, in order to demonstrate how important his pro-Catholic relationships were to him. In Florence, he gave alms of five crowns to a completely penniless English Catholic.

While Essex – with a constant eye on the Scottish succession to the English throne – secretly supported the apparently pro-Catholic policy of James, he was ordered by Elizabeth to provide instructions for the English Protestant agents who were to be despatched to the centres of English Catholics in Rheims or Douai and in Rome. Like many of his fellow countrymen, Shakespeare included, Essex was thus also forced to lead a double life.

During the 1590s, the earl's popularity and the number of his supporters increased rapidly. The brutal oppression and persecution of the Catholics evidently caused Essex great unease. In the early 1590s he asserted himself on behalf of loyal – but anti-Spanish – English Catholics, thus gaining many supporters in Catholic circles. Furthermore, Essex came from Staffordshire, a county which had remained largely Catholic or had converted back to Catholicism. Many of the earl's relatives, friends and acquaintances were Catholic. Burghley, described by Hammer as 'the Architect of the Repression', was the initiator of the harsh anti-Catholic penal laws that forced so many Catholics into exile, ruined them financially and even took them to prison or the gallows. Essex, on the other hand, stood for tolerance and the relief of the distressed English Catholics, although outwardly he appeared to be a very steadfast Protestant.

When the English spy Anthony Standen, a close friend of Anthony Bacon, who had been working for Walsingham in Italy and Spain, was unmasked and brought back to England in June 1593, Burghley shunned him. Essex, however, gave him a friendly reception. Under the protection of the earl, Standen was able to practise his Catholic beliefs – presumably even in

Essex's London residence. This news spread like wildfire amongst the English Catholics-in-exile on the other side of the Channel, reaching Venice by October 1593. Essex had even praised the bravery of the Jesuit priest, John Gerard, who had been hideously tortured by his English captors. Essex's attitude caused a sensation, given the fact that Jesuits were considered to be traitors. Gerard had been trained at the same time as Shakespeare at the English College in Douai or Rheims. He was, like Shakespeare, born in 1564 and like him, had visited Rome and lived there at the pilgrim's hospice of the English College. They may even have eaten at the same table in Rheims. It is thus well within the realms of possibility that it was Shakespeare who had informed Essex – through Southampton, or directly – about the bravery of the Jesuit under torture. Essex is supposed to have spoken out in a similarly positive way about Father William Weston.

Around this time, the English Catholics sent the earl an anonymous book in the hope that he would support it and pass it on to the government. Among other things it contained the proposal for a (special) Catholic oath of loyalty. The work, called *A Conference about the next Succession to the Crowne of England* (1594), was written under the pseudonym of 'R. Doleman' who was in fact none other than Robert Parsons, a leading figure among the English Catholics-in-exile. He ironically thanks the earl for the help his 'friends' had received from His Lordship (Essex). In his reference to his 'friends', Parson seems to have been alluding to his high-ranking Spanish allies who supported his struggle against Protestantism in England, and saw Essex as their enemy on account of his anti-Spanish position.

The Earl of Essex's more or less covert pro-Catholic position also allowed him to nurture friendly relations with Henry IV, King of France. The former Henry of Navarre had turned Catholic in 1593. The pro-Catholic politics of the English earl opened doors, not only in Spain but throughout Europe, for the secret service agents he deployed and paid.

In the final decade of the sixteenth century, Essex had not only developed into a prudent and far-sighted politician and statesman with clear aims and with powerful and influential friends, he had also bravely tackled the most important issue of the day, the succession to the throne, without actually betraying the queen. His reputation as the queen's best commander spread rapidly, especially after his victory at Cádiz in the year 1596. No other Elizabethan statesman could boast of a comparable network of spies, extending from the British Isles throughout the European continent and as far as Persia. When Essex was sent to crush the Irish Rebellion in 1599, he was by far the most powerful subject of the queen and the most loved by the people.

In Ireland, to the annoyance of Elizabeth, Essex showed himself to be patient rather than aggressive, evidently in order to lay the foundations for talks with the Catholic rebel leader O'Neill. The Irish leader was concerned mainly with obtaining a guarantee to allow the Catholic religion to be practised in his country, as can be gleaned from his later written demands. This was something that Protestant England could not possibly accept. An ill wind was now blowing in Essex's direction from London. His opponents sensed their chance to do him harm. That was why he interrupted his Irish campaign in September 1599, and crossed back to England in such haste. He seemed at first to have succeeded in appeasing the queen, but it did not take long for her to completely change her mind. She realised that Essex had once again disobeyed her explicit orders, thus apparently putting himself above her. On 15 November 1599, Elizabeth had a long talk with her godson, Sir John Harington, who had been knighted by Essex in Ireland and had accompanied him on his return. Before she did so, she had threatened Harington with imprisonment in the Fleet Prison. In this discussion she gave her anger free rein: 'By God's Son, I am no Queen; that man is above me'[206]. It can hardly be doubted that Elizabeth's Secretary of State and chief advisor Robert Cecil (and presumably also Francis Bacon) had decisively contributed to the fact that the queen had come to such a dangerous conclusion with regard to Essex.

The falsified picture of Essex as an incompetent commander-in-chief and politician that has entered history was created by Essex's opponents, chief among them Robert Cecil, who not only wanted to demote him and remove him from his position as the queen's favourite, but also to destroy his positive image for ever. The evidence of those who had known and loved Essex, who could judge him and his achievements, painted a totally different picture of him. One of these contemporaries was – as has been mentioned before – William Shakespeare.

SHAKESPEARE'S ELEGY 'THE PHOENIX AND THE TURTLE'

Shakespeare's encoded allegorical poem *The Phoenix and the Turtle* was described by the famous English literary critic I. A. Richards (1893-1979) as 'the most mysterious of English poems'[207]. A convincing solution to this mystery has only recently been put forward[208]. The poem appeared in Robert Chester's *Love's Martyr or Rosaline's Complaint*[209] shortly after the execution of the Earl of Essex (1601). As only fifty copies were printed of this work, it was thought to have been produced for a 'closed group of people' who 'obviously were able to keep the secret'[210]. This group probably consisted of the friends and supporters of the Earl of Essex, as indicated by the number of copies and the date of publication. It was probably printed by Richard Field, Shakespeare's Stratford schoolmate and friend[211].

The Phoenix and the Turtle is a poem of sixty-seven lines, divided into thirteen quatrains and five triplet stanzas. The number of lines may well be an allusion to the age of the queen, who in February 1601 was sixty-seven-years-old. The last fifteen lines are the actual Threnos or lament. The poet appears to be referring here to the fifteen-year relationship between Elizabeth and Essex, which began in 1587 when the earl was presented at Court and ended with his death in 1601. This allegorical elegy is in every way different from Shakespeare's other literary work. That is why Shakespeare's authorship of this poem has been questioned from time to time. However, as there is clear evidence as to its source, these doubts have proved to be unfounded.

Shakespeare's elegy obviously alludes to contemporary personalities and events. But what were these events, who were the 'Phoenix', who the 'Turtle', who the 'eagle' and who the 'crow', who the 'shrieking harbinger', who the 'fiend' himself? Furthermore, who were the birds with 'chaste wings', who the 'fowl of tyrant wing', and finally, who the bird chosen to be the herald of these sad happenings? These questions can only be answered if asked in the context of the tumultuous and stirring political events at the end of the Elizabethan era and the bitter struggle for power.

Since the Essex rebellion and its consequences were by far the most dramatic political events of the time; since Shakespeare, a secret Catholic, was a confessed follower of Essex; and since the Earl of Southampton was the poet's friend and patron, Shakespeare, in *The Phoenix and the Turtle*, may well have been referring to this decisive historical event and its protagonists, Essex and Southampton, encoding them allegorically as 'Phoenix' and 'Turtle'.

Shakespeare must have written his elegy immediately after the death sentence had been imposed on both leaders, i.e. at a time when he could not have known that Southampton's punishment would be commuted to a life sentence. It seems obvious that he wanted to offer to Essex and Southampton *through literature* what would be denied to them as executed traitors, namely, a solemn funeral procession and a requiem mass, said by a priest 'in surplice white'. It appears that the poet intended to create a memorial for his friends through a political allegory written in a code that has remained unbroken for more than four hundred years.

The other characters in Shakespeare's allegorical poem can also be identified within the context of political events at the end of the Elizabethan period. '[T]he bird of loudest lay / On the sole Arabian tree', selected by the poet to serve as the herald who announces this sad news to the world (see lines 1 and 2), is probably Sir Anthony Shirley, who lived at the Court of the Shah of Persia where he had been made very welcome as 'ambassador' of Essex. Shirley later led negotiations at the Court of Emperor Rudolf II in Prague to forge an alliance against the Turks. His account of these journeys was printed in London in October 1600, although without permission from the censors. For this reason, all copies were immediately seized and burned and the printers, Blore and Jaggard, had to pay a fine. The fact that the government decided to take this step, despite its generally great interest in reports from distant lands, shows that it believed the contents of the work to be politically dangerous. As emissary of the Earl of Essex in Persia, Shirley, in 1601, spent some time in Rome, among other places. There he had a meeting with the famous former comic actor of Shakespeare's theatre company, William Kempe.

Kempe had left the Chamberlain's Men – as it seemed – unexpectedly in 1600 in order to Morris-dance his way from London to Norwich in nine days[212]. He wrote about this extraordinary feat in *Kemp's Nine Days' Wonder. Performed in a Dance from London to Norwich* (1600) with a picture of himself on the title page, performing a dance step. In 1601, Kempe travelled around the Continent with his act, spending some time in Italy and Germany. Given the particular circumstances of the time, it appears that Kempe merely used his spectacular performance as a pretext for travelling without official interference, his actual destination being Rome, where he met Anthony Shirley, Essex's confidant. It can be assumed that the two men exchanged important information, for it is rather unlikely that Kempe and Shirley met in Rome purely by chance.

After his return to London in September 1601, Kempe reported on his meeting with Shirley, who felt it was far too dangerous to come back to England after the death of Essex. There is evidence that Shirley was still in Venice in May 1602, but he felt that he was being persecuted there by the very people from whom he had expected help. In this precarious situation, Shirley petitioned the French king, Henry IV, to send a letter to his consul in Cairo in order to allow him (Shirley) to make another trip to Persia, but his hopes were dashed. Henry was told by Sir Henry Wotton (1568-1639), the English ambassador to Venice, that Elizabeth and her Privy Council had already sent letters discrediting Shirley.

Wotton, who himself had previously worked for Essex on the Continent, had clearly not intervened on the side of Shirley. He (Wotton) is the source of the famous definition of an ambassador – a man sent abroad to lie for his country. The real reason for Shirley's unfortunate situation was the fact that he had been commissioned by Essex[213] but, to all appearances, he was not ready – unlike Wotton – to compromise, or switch allegiance to the anti-Essex pro-government camp.

The 'shrieking harbinger' of the evil foe, who is not allowed to come close to (his own) troop (see stanza 2), reminds us so strongly of Francis Bacon (*Fig. 93*), who destroyed his former patron, Essex, in such an underhand manner in the trial for high treason, that the poet can only be referring to him. Behind the 'fiend' seems to be none other than Robert Cecil (*Fig. 92b*), Essex's arch enemy. His supporters must be the 'fowl[s] of tyrant wing' (see stanza 3). All of them are excluded from the assembly.

When the poet includes the eagle, the 'feather'd king', he may well have been thinking of James VI of Scotland (*Fig. 113*), who was accepted as successor to Elizabeth I not only by the Essex circle, but also by many English Catholics because they associated him with religious tolerance.

The expressions 'priest in surplice white' and the 'requiem' in the fourth stanza clearly show that the poet had a Catholic ceremony and a Catholic priest in mind, with a Catholic funeral procession and a requiem mass for the dead. The white colour of the priest's surplice appears to symbolize the innocence of the victims, who had died for their political or religious convictions.

The mention of an old 'crow' (see stanza 5) who is ordered to take part in the funeral procession can refer only to Queen Elizabeth herself. Essex had once talked of her dismissively as a 'cadaver'. The poet actually commands that she be present, emphasizing the former close relationship between the queen and Essex. In his eyes it is obligatory for her to pay her last respects to the dead man.

The two main figures, 'Phoenix' and 'Turtle' (= Essex and Southampton) first appear in stanza 6 (*Figs. 91* and *101*). They are two distinct, but inseparable, friends ('Two distincts, division none' – stanza 7), and, as stated in stanza 13 are 'Co-supremes and stars of love', who – flaming in each other's sight – have fled this world.

In the actual lament, it is stated that beauty and truth have now turned to ashes, and that at the urn of the phoenix and the turtle, (only) those who are themselves 'either true or fair'[214] can say the prayer for the dead.

In reality only Essex had been executed. Dying on Ash Wednesday, in 1601, in Shakespeare's poem he can be identified with the phoenix, also called the fire bird. And it seems as if the poet hoped for his return, phoenix-like, from the ashes.

Shakespeare's inspiration for the imagery of the phoenix may have come from the epitaph on the famous double tomb of the two first bishops of Ghent, Cornelius Jansen (1510-1576) and Guillaume-Damase van der Linden (1525-1588) in the Church of St John (later St Bavo's Cathedral) of Ghent in Flanders (*Figs. 103*). This site was already a tourist attraction in his day, and Shakespeare must have known Flanders well from his time on the Continent. During his 'lost years' (1585-1592), the poet may well have visited this tomb. The names of these prominent Catholic bishops must have been known to the students at the Collegium Anglicum in Douai and in Rheims. Before he became the first Bishop of Ghent in 1560, Jansen had been professor of Catholic Theology at the University of Louvain; he was the author of commentaries on the Gospels, and had represented Philip II at the Council of Trent. Van der Linden was one of the most eminent Catholic theologians of the seventeenth century.

On 10 September 1599 the Swiss doctor, Thomas Platter the Younger, with his travelling companions visited the town of Ghent and its magnificent St John's Cathedral. In his travel diary, he noted that he saw in it a set of tomb inscriptions on marble for two bishops. He wrote down one of the Latin inscriptions[215] and translated it into Swiss German. On 13 January 2002, the present author also visited this place, and found the second inscription[216] mentioned by Platter. Their English translation reads:

THIS IS A PHOENIX WITHOUT COMPARE:
THIS GRAVE CONTAINS THE ASHES OF TWO PHOENIXES
OF THE TRUE RELIGION.

And:

THESE WHO DURING THEIR LIFE
WERE INCLINED TO ONE ANOTHER,
ARE ALSO IN THEIR DEATH
NOT SEPARATED.

It appears perfectly reasonable to see a connection with the two friends, Essex and Southampton, who – after their rebellion – were both condemned to death. Just like Jansen and van der Linden, they were inseparable in life. Shakespeare must have assumed that they would also be reunited in death. In his eyes, Essex and Southampton could also have been 'Phoenixes of the true religion'. For the latter was a Catholic, and the former a protector of Catholics.

Fig. 103 – The emblem of a phoenix above the double tomb of the first two Bishops of Ghent, Cornelius Jansen and Guillaume-Damase van der Linden, in St Bavo's Cathedral, Ghent. This impressive tomb was visited by many European travellers in the late sixteenth century, including Thomas Platter the Younger, who stayed in Ghent on 10 September 1599 before setting sail to England where, on 26 September 1599, he caught a glimpse of Queen Elizabeth I at her palace of Nonsuch (see *Fig. 94*) – only two days before the spectacular visit of the Earl of Essex. The famous phoenix emblem could have been Shakespeare's inspiration for the image of the phoenix in his political allegory *The Phoenix and the Turtle*.

Shakespeare could have learned at first hand from his former mistress about the circumstances leading to the commutation of the sentence of his former patron from execution to life imprisonment. Elizabeth Vernon, who became the Countess of Southampton in 1598, probably continued to have intimate relations with the poet while Southampton was in the Tower (*Figs. 85a* and *85b*). In the hour of her greatest need, the countess begged Robert Cecil to pardon her husband, and actually moved him to clemency. Southampton's mother also beseeched Cecil for mercy for her son.

Only a few days after he had visited the tomb of the two Catholic bishops in Ghent, Thomas Platter crossed to England, where he attended a performance of Shakespeare's *Julius Caesar* at the Globe Theatre in London on 21 September. His subsequent report is one of the most important eye-witness accounts of how a Shakespeare play was performed during the lifetime of the playwright.

THE VICTORY OF ROBERT CECIL

With the failure of the Essex rebellion, the hopes of the English Catholics were also doomed to failure. The political power of Robert Cecil became almost absolute. Once his bitterest enemy was out of the way, however, Cecil actually adopted some of the policies of his dead opponent and carried on secret negotiations with James VI of Scotland, whom he had hitherto firmly rejected as Elizabeth's successor. He was thus preparing for the transfer of power, so that he might secure a strong position for himself under the new king. When Elizabeth I lay on her deathbed in March 1603 (*Fig. 104*), Cecil obtained her approval for her successor to the throne. He thereby legalised his arrangement, and sent for James VI of Scotland (*Fig. 113*). Cecil, who has often been celebrated as the architect of the smooth transfer of power, was in fact a pragmatist. He had unscrupulously reaped the harvest of a whole decade of hard and difficult work by Essex and his closest friends.

In view of the historical and biographical context just described, it is not surprising that Shakespeare – unlike many other poets – never mentions the death of the queen in his writings. From his pen flowed no hymn to the dead sovereign, no lines of lament over the death of a queen who had determined the fate of the country for almost half a century and who had also ensured that the theatre – its authors, actors and audiences – was able to operate with relatively little hindrance. Shakespeare even refused to praise the dead monarch when anonymous verses called upon him to do so:

You Poets all brave *Shakspere, Johnson, Greene*,
Bestow your time to write for Englands Queene.
Lament, lament, lament you English Peeres.
Lament your loss possest so many yeeres.
Returne your songs and Sonnets and your sayes:
To set foorth sweete *Elizabeth[a]'s* praise.[217]

Indirectly, Henry Chettle also invited the silent Shakespeare to commemorate the dead queen. In his own elegy on Elizabeth's death – *Englande's Mourning Garment* – he writes: 'Shepherd, remember our *Elizabeth*'[218]. Chettle's allusion to 'Shepherd' – like Edmund Spenser's before him – refers to Shakespeare, as the following line reveals: 'And sing her Rape, done by that *Tarquin*, Death'. This was clearly an allusion to Shakespeare's famous narrative poem, *The Rape of Lucrece*, written in 1594.

Shakespeare's silence can be explained by the fact that he was a secretly practising Catholic, involved in the Catholic underground. He was thus all too conscious of the sorrow and distress that the queen's religious policy had imposed on those of her subjects who had remained Catholic or had returned to Catholicism. The poet's silence can also to be explained by the fact that Elizabeth, through Robert Cecil, Edward Coke, Francis Bacon and others of their political ilk, brought about the downfall of the popular, generous, skilled and religiously tolerant statesman and commander-in-chief Essex, the bearer of hope for the English crypto-Catholics and many of the English Catholics-in-exiles. In addition, Shakespeare and many of his contemporaries recognised the strategy whereby the earl was virtually provoked into rebellion, so that he could be accused of treason and condemned to death.

By coincidence, the extravagant young nobleman Essex – who until then had been more inclined to live a life emulating the chivalric ideal of the Middle Ages – began his serious foreign and domestic career in exactly the same year in which Shakespeare, after seven years activity in the service of English Catholicism and its priests, came to London and started his own career as a dramatist and poet. The general optimism and positive world view of Shakespeare during this decade, especially in his earlier comedies, may well have been influenced by the very promising political advancement of the Earl of Essex. In any case it is unthinkable that Shakespeare, who announced his enthusiastic support for Essex in March 1599, would not have shared the expectations that so many of his fellow Catholics had of Essex. If the poet, in his elegy *The Phoenix and the Turtle*, mourns Essex's death, this is another indication of his close and deep connection with this outstanding Elizabethan statesman, whom so many of Elizabeth I's subjects followed – often blindly and unconditionally.

Fig. 104 – The original wax effigy of Queen Elizabeth I. This accurate likeness of the queen was produced after her death and is kept at Westminster Abbey. Her facial features are identical to those on her funerary sculpture.

THE TRAUMA OF WILLIAM SHAKESPEARE

The terrible and breathtaking political events that occurred between 28 September 1599 and

25 February 1601 left deep emotional scars on Shakespeare, as his later works vividly show, if viewed in their historical and biographical context. The beginning of his pessimism emerges for the first time in *Julius Caesar*, the Roman tragedy which must have been written in the summer of 1599, when Essex's enemies at Court, especially Robert Cecil, Elizabeth's right hand man, and the ambitious careerist and former protégé of the earl, Francis Bacon, may have started to plot the downfall of the queen's favourite. After the failure of the Essex rebellion in February 1601, Shakespeare never again wrote a comedy. What followed are tragedies and problem plays and – at the end of his literary career – romances and one more history play. In the tragedies, scepticism, pessimism, world-weariness and cynicism predominate. Significantly, the first of the plays mirroring Shakespeare's deep political and religious resignation, in which disgust with present political conditions is often expressed, is *Hamlet*. The relationship between Hamlet and Essex is discussed in more detail in the following chapter. The fact that the play is set on foreign soil cannot mask that the dramatist was pointing to conditions in his own country – as scholars have long since acknowledged.

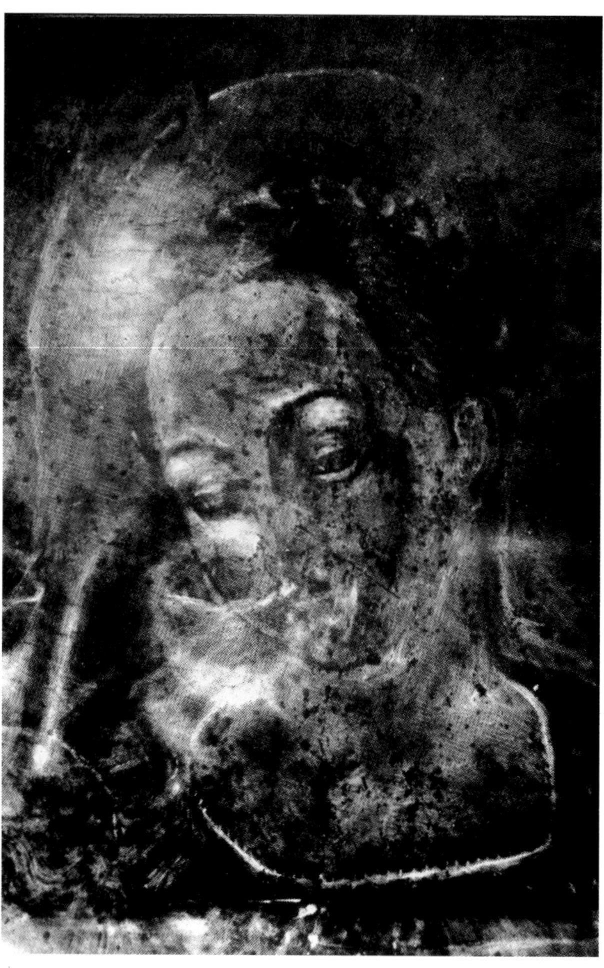

Fig. 105 – Madonna and Child with St John – Detail: Mary. X-ray image by the Courtauld Institute, London (1966). The original of this x-ray image is no longer extant.

Evidence that Shakespeare kept the memory of Essex alive well after his death can be seen not only in the new edition of Chester's anthology, published in 1611 which contained the political allegory *The Phoenix and the Turtle*, recalling the events of 1601. Further evidence of the freshness of this memory can be found in the so-called Flower portrait, created during the reign of James I. This authenticated portrait of the poet painted from life[219], which has already served to clarify an unanswered biographical question (see p. 317 f.), contains an interesting visual clue. It has previously been overlooked that the dramatist had himself portrayed in the year 1609 – eight years after the execution of Essex – wearing a pointed collar that was rather unusual for the time (*Fig. 106*). This collar resembles the one worn by Essex in one of the most famous portraits in oils (*Fig. 100*). This may well be interpreted as a display of the inner bond between them that extended beyond death. Shakespeare had his portrait painted over one of the Madonna[220], presumably a painting he had inherited from his devoutly Catholic mother who died in 1608. The possession of such a picture in Protestant England meant mortal danger – just like the possessing of rosaries and Jesuit testaments. The fact that Shakespeare's portrait merges with one of the Madonna and Child may have protected the underlying picture from destruction, and could well be thought of as a further sign of the poet's religious conviction. The wearing of the distinctive collar, as worn by the Earl of Essex, allows him to display his political allegiance once again.

Fig. 106 – Portrait of William Shakespeare (original of the Flower Portrait) dated 1609. Shakespeare had this portrait painted on top of a late fifteenth or early sixteenth-century painting of the Madonna and Child, which he presumably inherited from his mother, who died in 1608. The symptoms of illness, already visible in the Chandos Portrait (*Fig. 63*), are even more prominent here. There are also new signs of disease. For the authentication of this portrait see the present author's book, *The True Face of William Shakespeare*, parts III and IV). It is significant that Shakespeare had himself painted wearing a collar very similar to the one worn by the executed Earl of Essex in one of his final portraits (*Fig. 100*).

THE ORIGINS OF THE ESSEX CIRCLE'S SYMBOL

In another portrait of Robert Devereux, Earl of Essex, painted in 1597 and now preserved in the National Gallery in London, he is shown in the ceremonial robes of the Order of the Garter (*Fig. 107*). The portrait contains another significant detail that apparently links it to Shakespeare, Southampton and probably the whole Essex circle, namely the bows on his shoes. We see the same bows in the two most famous portraits of Southampton. In the portrait of the earl, also in the National Portrait Gallery collection, two white ribbon bows adorn his belt (*Fig. 65*) and two dark ones his shoes, as Dr Martin Nickol has pointed out in his expert report of 11 July 2002. And in the so-called Tower portrait of Southampton in Boughton House, black bows in a distinctive pattern adorn the cuffs of his gloves, looking like black crosses that are particularly prominent against the white background (*Fig. 101*). They look as though they signify membership of a particular group, and appear to commemorate the conspirators around Essex and Southampton[221]. The courtier and diplomat, Sir Henry Lee (1530-1610), who from 1571 onwards organised court tournaments and who was very influential in establishing the romantic Elizabethan ideal of chivalry to which Essex and his supporters keenly aspired, commissioned a portrait of himself with these bows on his shoes (*Fig. 108*). Lee, who lived in Ditchley near Woodstock in Oxfordshire, was the doyen of the Essex circle and one of its central figures. He served as patron and sponsor of the portrait painter, Marcus Gheeraerts the younger[222], who painted members of Essex's circle as well as their wives and mistresses, often including cryptic emblematic allusions as, for example, in the case of *The Persian Lady*. In Gheeraerts's painting, depicting the former lady-in-waiting, Elizabeth Vernon, who in late August 1598 in a highly pregnant condition had married the third Earl of Southampton, the emblem on the thumb ring worn by the countess resembles a four-leaved clover, and is reminiscent of the bows or crosses on the portraits of the Earls of Essex and Southampton[223]. The baroque cartouche containing the new Shakespearian sonnet depicts this symbol three times, to the left and right of the centre as well as on the top[224]. It is, however, somewhat adapted to suit the style of the setting. It also adorns the sculpted figure of the kneeling

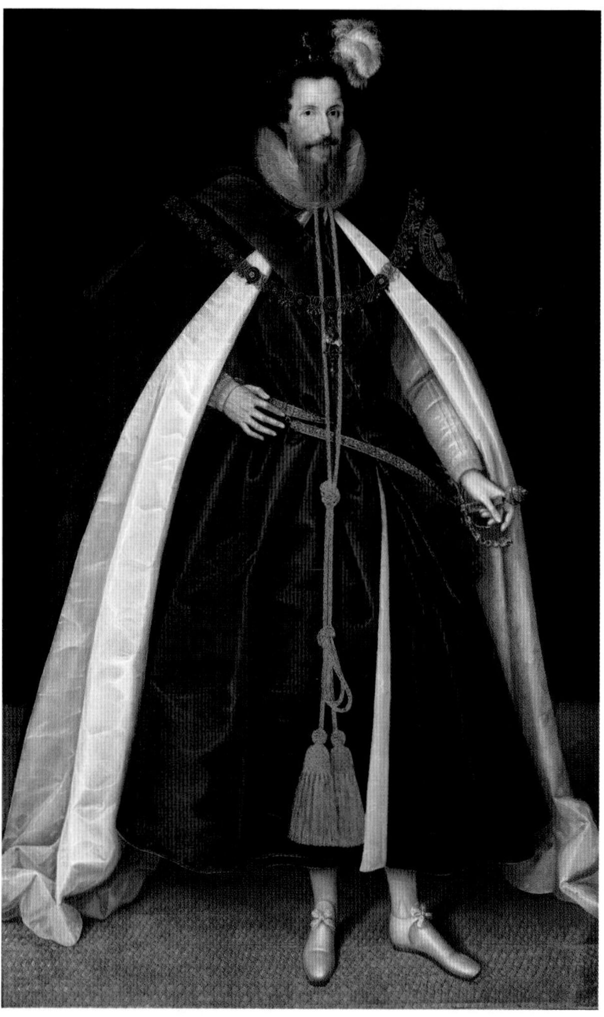

Fig. 107 – Portrait of the Earl of Essex in all his glory (*c.* 1597). The earl wears the robe of the Order of the Garter and shoes decorated with bows identical to those found in several portraits of the Earl of Southampton (*Figs. 65* and *101*), and also in several other contemporary portraits (*Figs. 108–113*). These bows seem to tell us that their wearers are the members of a special group. All indications are that this is the Essex circle and that these particular bows are the sign or emblem of the earl's followers.

Fig. 108 – Portrait of Sir Henry Lee (1530–1610). Lee was an important member of the Court of Queen Elizabeth I, as he arranged the tournaments and revived the romantic ideal of chivalry, to which Essex and Southampton aspired. In the 1590s, he was a central figure in the Essex circle and patron of the portraitist Marcus Gheeraerts the Younger. This painting dates from 1602, one year after the Essex Rebellion, and contains the motto *Fide et constantia*. Lee is also portrayed with the emblem of the Essex circle on his shoes.

Fig. 109 – Portrait of Mary Sidney, Lady Wroth. This portrait was probably painted by Marcus Gheeraerts the Younger and contains a total of five bows, which are in accordance with those in the portraits of the Earl of Southampton (*Figs. 65* and *101*), the Earl of Essex (*Fig. 107*) and *The Persian Lady* (*Fig. 83a* – on the thumb ring). Lady Wroth was the niece of the poet Sir Philip Sidney (1554–1586), and the daughter of Robert Sidney (1563–1626), awarded the titles of Viscount Lisle, Baron Sidney and Earl of Leicester by James I. Sidney – like Francis Bacon – was originally a member of the Essex circle, for whom Essex tried to procure high office. After the failed rebellion on 8 February 1601, Sidney was sent by the Crown to Essex House to negotiate the surrender of the rebels.

third Earl of Southampton at the family tomb in St Peter's Church in Titchfield[225]. This symbol can be seen a total of five times in the 1620 portrait of Mary Sidney, Lady Wroth (*Fig. 109*), one on each arm, one on her neckline, and one on each shoulder. It may be surprising at first to learn that this emblem is used, again on both shoes, in a 1604 portrait of the heir to the

English throne, Prince Henry (*Fig. 110*), eldest son of James I, as well in a portrait dating from 1603 that probably portrays his sister, Princess Elizabeth, the later Queen of Bohemia (*Fig. 111*). It should be realised, however, that Essex, Southampton and their circle enjoyed the favour of James I, since they had secretly paved the way for his succession, and had obtained his agreement that as king of England he would show tolerance towards the Catholics. Furthermore, it can be assumed that James I's Catholic queen, Anne of Denmark, who secretly employed Catholic priests, brought up her children in the old faith, and shared the

Fig. 110 – Portrait, dated 1604, of Prince Henry, son of James I and heir to the throne, at the age of ten. The talented Prince, a sponsor of the arts and literature, became the patron of the playwrights George Chapman and Ben Jonson and of the Admiral's Men, the main rivals to the Chamberlain's Men. He was also a friend and advocate of Sir Walter Raleigh (*Figs. 112*). It appears that Prince Henry and his siblings, Princess Elizabeth and Prince Charles, were initially raised according to the old faith, practised by their mother Queen Anne, who secretly employed two Catholic priests. The prince died in 1612 at the age of eighteen, allegedly of typhoid. In this portrait he is wearing bows which conspicuously resemble those seen in the portraits of Southampton and Essex and their followers.

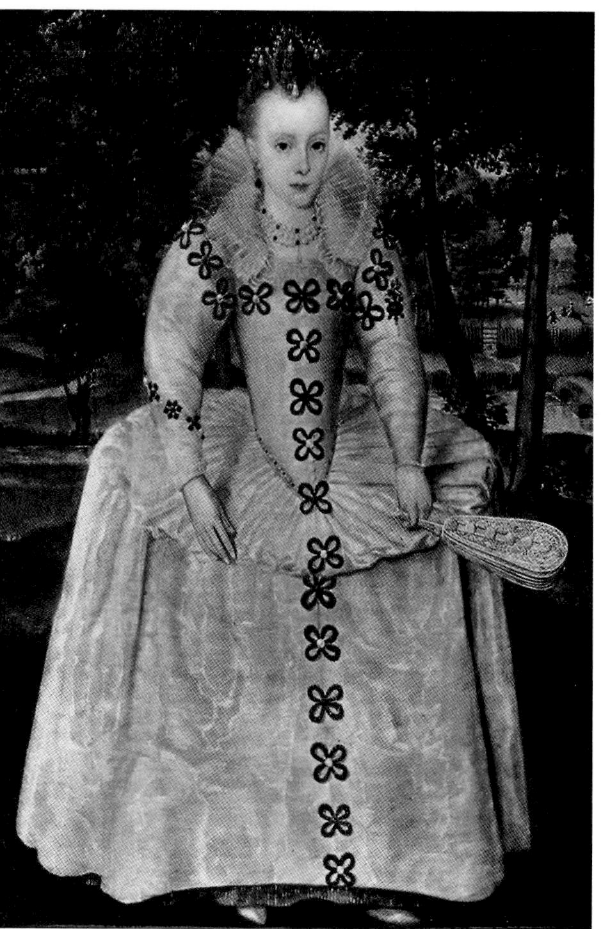

Fig. 111 – This portrait, dated 1603, apparently by Marcus Gheeraerts the Younger, is thought to depict Princess Elizabeth, daughter of James I, who, in 1612, married Frederick V, Elector Palatine of the Rhine, who resided in Heidelberg and later became King of Bohemia (the Winter King). The identification has been made on the basis of a strong family likeness, particularly to Prince Henry. The princess's dress is covered with a stylised bow motif which reminds us strongly of the bows on the portraits of members of the Essex circle. One of these bows on the lower sleeve of her right arm is in complete agreement with the emblem depicted in the portraits of Essex and Southampton.

Fig. 112 – Double portrait of Sir Walter Raleigh and his son from 1602. This Elizabethan seafarer, courtier, politician, poet and historian was the queen's favourite in the 1580s. He fell out of favour when he had an affair with her lady-in-waiting, Lady Elizabeth Throckmorton, and married her. At court, Raleigh was eclipsed by Essex, who also became Raleigh's political rival. On the day of the Rebellion, Essex announced in the streets of London that Lord Cobham and Sir Walter Raleigh aimed to kill him. It has been suggested that the character of Don Armado in *Love's Labour's Lost* is an attempt by Shakespeare to ridicule Raleigh. In September 1601, Raleigh showed Marshal Biron and his entourage the sights of London and Westminster, including the tombs in Westminster Abbey. Raleigh also wore black when Biron and his delegation appeared at Court the next day, dressed entirely in black and without their decorations, as a symbol of solidarity with the executed Earl of Essex. Both father and son are wearing the symbol of the Essex circle. After Essex's execution, Robert Cecil adopted almost all of the policies of his former political enemy – apart from that of religious tolerance – and Raleigh fully supported him in this.

objectives of the supporters of Essex. The Earl and Countess of Southampton were friendly with King James's children, especially with Princess Elizabeth[226], so that it is not surprising that she wore bows that resembled those of Southampton. In one place, the bow is perfectly reproduced, at the end of the princess's right sleeve.

It appears remarkable that the emblem can even be made out in the double portrait of Sir Walter Raleigh and his young son (*Fig. 112*), as Raleigh was one of Essex's opponents. In view of the fact that this portrait, now in the National Portrait Gallery in London, was painted in 1602, a year after the execution of the Earl of Essex, when the most powerful Elizabethan statesman, Robert Cecil, had adopted some of the policies of his tragically failed opponent and had secretly negotiated with James of Scotland, it is plausible that Raleigh may have adapted to the circumstances. In the portrait of James I painted by Daniel Mytens the Elder in the robes of the Order of the Garter in 1621, he also wears the ribbons in question on his shoes (*Fig. 113*), though it was twenty years since the Essex rebellion. Perhaps it was Southampton, Essex's former friend and fellow conspirator, and Shakespeare's former patron, who reminded the king of the events of the year 1601. Because of his leading role in the Essex circle, Southampton enjoyed James's special favour. Neither the meaning nor the origin of this visual symbol was previously known, but it may now well be interpreted as a distinguishing mark of the Essex supporters.

In the course of my research into Shakespeare's life, his origins and his appearance, I came across the seal of the town of Stratford (*Fig. 114*), which the bailiff has been allowed to carry since the town was granted the status of a Borough in 1553. John Shakespeare also carried it when he served as Bailiff of Stratford in 1568. On this seal, there is a symbol in three places that bears great resemblance to the bows in the portraits mentioned above.

My observation was examined by the expert Dr Martin Nickol, who had made a considerable contribution to the interpretation and identification of visual symbols in the Elizabethan portrait *The Persian Lady* in the Royal Palace of Hampton Court. In his expert opinion of 11 July 2002, Nickol first mentions three occurrences of a symbol on the seal of Stratford that can be interpreted as a 'cross-like symbol, as a clover leaf or a bow': two 'on the middle of the seal, grouped with three lion heads', and one at the 'beginning and end of the inscription around the edge of the seal'. On the basis of portrait analysis, in my book on The Dark Lady, as well as 'comparative studies of botanical works of the sixteenth and seventeenth centuries' and 'portraits and paintings of this time in the Tate Britain and the National Gallery in London', Nickol found that the claim that the symbol on the seal represented a cross was rather unlikely, and the clover leaf lacked 'heraldic and other iconographic associations'. In his expert opinion, the three symbols appeared to be 'the stylised representation of a flexible object such as a bow made of cloth or rope'. In his comparison of the pictures, Nickol determined that the symbol on the seal corresponded with the following signs and symbols: (1) with the bow on the portrait of Lady Penelope Spencer, née Wriothesley[227], (2) with the 'ring on the thumb of the right hand' in *The Persian Lady*, (3) with the 'glove cuff' on the Tower portrait of the Earl of Southampton by John de Critz painted in 1603, (4) with the bows on Southampton's belt in the portrait entitled 'Henry Wriothesley, third Earl of Southampton (Montacute)', and (5) with the bows on the shoes worn by the earl in the same picture. In his summary, he states: 'as for the interpretation of the three symbols on the seal before us, it fits most closely with a representation of a bow'. This corresponds 'as much to the state of art at the time in question as to the fact that we are dealing with three similar symbols that are

Fig. 113 – Portrait of King James I by D. Mytens (1621). James was secretly chosen and supported by Essex and his circle in the 1590s to succeed Queen Elizabeth I. He promised the Catholics religious tolerance, but failed to keep his word. Under his rule, the Catholic population of England was further deprived of rights and oppressed. The sons of the Catholic landed gentry in Warwickshire and the surrounding counties, who had already endured harsh punishments under Elizabeth I, opposed James and were supported by the English Catholics-in-exile. They plotted to blow up Parliament at the Opening of Parliament on 5 November 1605, and could have killed the royal family as well as the members of parliament. The Gunpowder Plot conspirators were sentenced to death and executed in a particularly cruel fashion. The anti-Catholic penal laws were made even harsher as a consequence. This was the period when Shakespeare wrote one of his darkest tragedies, featuring a Scottish king: *Macbeth*. James I, too, wears the emblem of the Essex circle on his shoes. At this time, as the Earl of Southampton was still alive and playing a prominent role at Court, he may have helped to keep the memory of Essex fresh for the king. It was twenty years since the earl's execution.

depicted on the same seal with slight differences.' With regard to the clover leaf on the thumb ring in *The Persian Lady*, Nickol came to the conclusion that it was more likely to be 'a stylised shape of a bow in metal', rather than 'an actual representation of a four-leafed clover', and concludes: 'Thus the result of the comparison leaves no doubt that the symbols on the seal of the town of Stratford and the bows in the portraits investigated are in agreement'[228].

Fig. 114 – Imprint of the seal of Stratford-upon-Avon, dating from 1553 when the town became a Borough. This seal would have been carried by John Shakespeare, when William was still a young boy. In its centre (right and left) and on its edge (top), the present author discovered three bows (serving as emblems) which, in her view, greatly resembled the ones depicted in *Figs. 107* to *113*. The German expert Dr Martin Nickol, botanist at the University of Kiel, who, among other things, has examined plants and flowers in early modern paintings, carried out detailed (partly microscopic) comparisons between the bows in the seal of Stratford and the ones in the above-shown portraits of members of the Essex circle. In his assessment, Nickol came to the conclusion that all the bows are in perfect agreement. This result strongly suggests that the sign or emblem of the Essex circle could have been based on the seal of Stratford. If this proves to be true, it may well be that it was Shakespeare's idea to employ it for this particular purpose.

These results show that in all these cases virtually the same symbol is used, a symbol which seems to be the secret distinguishing mark of the members of the Essex circle and their relatives. Furthermore, it appears that none other than William Shakespeare, who had a particularly close affinity with his home town and who even used its name as a pseudonym (see pp. 77–82: 310), could have thought of using the ribbon, found on the seal of Stratford and tied in a rather inconspicuous bow, as a secret symbol of the Essex supporters. Through his father, the dramatist could have become familiar with the bows and lion heads on Stratford's official seal when he was still a child. In *Hamlet* it is his father's seal that gets the hero, who is sent to England, out of trouble at times of great danger (see *Hamlet*, Act V, scene 2).

In conjunction with numerous indications of Shakespeare's involvement as a supporter of Essex, these findings reveal that the poet must have played a greater and more important part in this circle than could hitherto be assumed. This could also account for the fact that it was the tragedy of the Earl of Essex that caused such a traumatic effect on the playwright and that his life and works change so dramatically after the rebellion failed.

THE SECOND PHASE OF SHAKESPEARE'S DRAMAS: TRAGEDIES AND PROBLEM PLAYS

TRAGEDIES

After the failed uprising of 1601 and the execution of the Earl of Essex, Shakespeare wrote no more comedies but only tragedies and problem plays. Very late in his creative life he turned to a new genre, the romance. After that, Shakespeare co-authored a final English history play, which however, has to be regarded as an exception (see pp. 296–297 and 306–309).

HAMLET

In the marginalia of a copy of the works of Geoffrey Chaucer (first edition, 1598), the English scholar Gabriel Harvey (the brother of William Harvey, who discovered the circulation of blood) deals briefly with Shakespeare's narrative poems, remarking how they fascinated the youth of the time. Harvey also mentions Shakespeare's tragedy *Hamlet, Prince of Denmark*. According to him, the nature of this play was capable of appealing to wiser heads. A few lines earlier, he refers to the Earl of Essex, who spoke in praise of 'Albion's England'. Harvey talks about Essex in the present tense, implying that he was still alive when *Hamlet* was performed, though this is unlikely. It could, however, be expected that the play would contain references to the earl and the events that surrounded him. The theory that the character of Hamlet is based on the Earl of Essex, and that Shakespeare's play is an attempt to understand him, is by no means new. John Dover Wilson (1881–1969), one of the most prolific and stimulating English Shakespeare scholars of the first half of the twentieth century, put this forward in *The Essential Shakespeare* (1932).

The sources tell us that the execution of Essex in 1601 was greatly regretted, and not only in England. As shown by the decoding of Shakespeare's allegorical poem, *The Phoenix and the Turtle*, the dramatist grieved deeply for Essex (see pp. 219–222), but this was not the only sad loss he experienced that year. Like his hero, Hamlet, Shakespeare also lamented the death of his father, John Shakespeare, who died on 5 or 6 September 1601 and was buried in Stratford-upon-Avon on 8 September. The loss of his own father must have added to Shakespeare's deeply-felt grief at that time, and the poet may well have used *Hamlet* to express it.

Further unexpected events occurred during this year of mourning that kept the memory of Essex alive. On 5 August 1601, Roger Manners, fifth Earl of Rutland, Lord Sandys, Lord Cromwell and Sir William Parker – all conspirators in the Essex Rebellion – were released from the Tower of London upon paying a huge surety, in some cases amounting to many thousand pounds each. They were then placed under house arrest in their private residences. Roger Manners was made to pay a fine of £30,000, but this was later reduced to £10,000 because he had testified against his friend, the Earl of Southampton, during the latter's trial. Francis Manners was the brother of the fifth Earl of Rutland, whom he succeeded in 1612. He was released against the sum of £1,000[229].

The Earl of Southampton, however, had to serve his term of life-long imprisonment in the Tower. He was only released and fully reinstated when James VI of Scotland became James I of England in 1603 (*Fig. 115*). The painting commissioned by Southampton, Shakespeare's patron, to commemorate his stay in the Tower (*Fig. 101*) contains many significant symbols.[230] For instance, the cat in the painting does not represent a domesticated pet, but is 'a symbol of ill fortune'[231], darkness and death[232], and here it seems to be an allusion to Elizabeth I, who was, as Southampton and his friends saw it, responsible for the earl's sufferings. Another important feature is that the Bible is not only closed and tied with a ribbon, but it is shown upside down[233]. These pictorial symbols are obviously meant to show that Southampton rejected the new religion. Years later, however, under the influence of James I, Southampton converted to Anglicanism.

On 7 September 1601, the French Marshal Biron arrived in England. Biron was accompanied by twenty French nobles and caused a stir when he appeared at Court on 14 September, since he and his entourage were clothed entirely in black, wearing no decorations or insignia at all. Sir Walter Raleigh (*Fig. 112*) had accompanied Biron around the sights of London, including the famous tombs in Westminster Abbey, but when he heard about the black garments that the guests of the State were intending to wear at the royal audience the following day, he rushed to London

Fig. 115 – Triumphal arch constructed to celebrate the coronation of James I in London on 15 March 1604. A festive procession took place a year after the coronation – it had been postponed due to the Plague – and Shakespeare's theatre company, dressed in red livery, also took part. As James I was now their patron, the troupe was renamed the King's Men. Shakespeare probably also took part in the procession. At this time, the Catholics were still expecting their plight to improve under the new king.

in the middle of the night to acquire plain, black silk clothing and a black saddle. What had happened? Biron and his entourage were openly displaying their mourning for Essex in a show of public solidarity; out of sympathy for him they laid aside their own insignia.

On 15 September 1601, Essex was the main topic of discussion between the queen and her distinguished French guest, a close friend of the French King Henry IV. Elizabeth blamed her favourite for his ingratitude, his rash actions and his refusal to beg for mercy. According to contemporary reports, the queen is said to have kept Essex's head, which she showed to her French guests[234].

In the following weeks, the queen displayed obvious signs of distress. She refused to dress and left her usual rich meals untouched, only eating small amounts of 'manchet and succory pottage'. In his *Last Elizabethan Journal* G.B. Harrison reports:

> Every new message from the City doth disturb her, and she frowns on all the ladies. She walks much in her privy chamber, and stamps with her feet at ill news, and thrusts her rusty sword at times into the arras [tapestry] in great rage. ... she always keeps a sword by her table.[235]

The tapestry at which the queen thrust her sword would no doubt have featured historical figures in its design. This compulsive behaviour indicates that Elizabeth was greatly troubled, and may well have been suffering from inner turmoil, which can only be accounted for by the downfall of Essex and his execution, breathtaking events which the queen, led by Robert Cecil, had brought about and for which she was legally and morally responsible. Could it be possible that when the queen's sword stabbed at a tapestry (or a special figure in that tapestry) her mind was on one man in particular – Marshal Biron? The French marshal had dared to display his sorrow for Essex in such a public fashion and, in so doing, had harshly criticised the behaviour of the English queen and her court in the Essex affair. Is it a mere coincidence that Biron was executed for high treason in Paris in 1602, less than a year later, and that he died in exactly the same way as Essex? The accusation of treason against Biron came like a bolt from the blue, and the French king, Henry IV, made short work of his former friend, showing him as little mercy as Elizabeth had shown her close friend. Elizabeth must have regarded the way Biron expressed his sympathy for Essex as an unforgivable affront, and would easily have been able to use her well-established network of spies in France to fabricate evidence against him to destroy him. Essex's French friend was executed on 31 July 1602[236].

When Elizabeth opened Parliament on 27 October 1601, she was so physically and emotionally drained by the year's events that she fell to the ground but was caught at the last moment by some gentlemen.

A few days later, on 2 November, Sir Edward Hoby – apparently out of loyalty to Essex – attempted to persuade Parliament to reduce the severity of the anti-Catholic laws. In his opinion, the laws were like a thorn bush, vicious but barren of fruit. While Hoby spoke of 'the need of the time' to amend the laws, Sir John Fortescue, a member of the Privy Council and a secret Catholic, used – with suitable care – the phrase 'the weakness of the time' to give voice to the general feelings of hopelessness that prevailed. Shakespeare is not known to have publicly expressed a political opinion, but reacted in his own way to these unprecedented contemporary events.

All indications are that Shakespeare started writing *Hamlet* during the course of the fateful year of 1601, when Essex was mourned both in England and abroad. *Hamlet*, the most performed, most read and most studied of Shakespeare's tragedies, must have been completed by July 1602, since it was entered by James Roberts in the London Stationers' Register on 26 July 1602, just five days before Biron's death. The play was printed with the following comment:

> James Robertes. Entred for his Copie vnder the handes of master Pasfield and master Waterson warden A booke called the Revenge of Hamlett Prince Denmarke as yt was latelie Acted by the Lord Chamberleyne his servantes.[237]

Hamlet was performed in London, at England's two universities and elsewhere, but because of its inflammatory political content Shakespeare and his actors seem wisely to have decided against performing the play at Court. The first Quarto edition appeared in 1603 (*Fig. 116*), but it appears that this edition was an unauthorised transcript of a stage performance because it contains numerous errors and distortions. One year later (1604) a second Quarto edition was published. Heminge and Condell used the text of this edition in 1623 when they published the First Folio Edition, but cut 200 lines from it.

Is *Hamlet* Shakespeare's response to Essex's dilemma and death? Should the play, written towards the end of the Elizabethan age, be considered a literary memorial to the tragic Elizabethan hero? The striking literary, historical and biographical connections indicate that the answer is a resounding 'yes'. The play makes numerous references to the tragic events of the Essex affair. Thus the (idealised) depiction of Hamlet by Ophelia in Act III, scene 1 can be applied to Essex:

> The courtier's, soldier's, scholar's, eye, tongue, sword;
> Th'expectancy and rose of the fair state,
> The glass of fashion and the mould of form,
> Th'observ'd of all observers –

Moreover, the description in *Henry IV* (Part 1, Act IV, scene 1) of the heir to the throne dressed for battle could have been an even earlier verbal depiction of the Earl of Essex. It is significant that it is Sir Richard Vernon who speaks these words of praise. Vernon was the surname of Shakespeare's Dark Lady of the sonnets, who was a cousin of Essex, and at the same time his ward. Sir Richard goes even so far as to compare his subject to 'an angel dropp'd down from the clouds':

> All furnish'd, all in arms;
> All plum'd like estridges ...
> Glittering in golden coats, like images;
> As full of spirit as the month of May
> And gorgeous as the sun at midsummer;
> Wanton as youthful goats, wild as young bulls.
> I saw young Harry with his beaver on,
> His cushes on his thighs, gallantly arm'd
> Rise from the ground like feathered Mercury,
> And vaulted with such ease into his seat
> As if an angel dropp'd down from the clouds
> To turn and wind a fiery Pegasus,
> And witch the world with noble horsemanship.

Essex had proved his superiority in 'noble horsemanship' especially during the tournaments to mark the anniversary of Elizabeth's ascension

THE

Tragicall Hiſtorie of

HAMLET

Prince of Denmarke

By William Shake-ſpeare.

As it hath beene diuerſe times acted by his Highneſſe ſeruants in the Cittie of London : as alſo in the two Vniuerſities of Cambridge and Oxford, and elſe-where

At London printed for N.L. and Iohn Trundell. 1603.

Fig. 116 – Title page of the first Quarto edition of *Hamlet*, dated 1603. It is thought to be an unauthorised transcription of a stage performance. The text contains errors and is corrupt in places. The emblem on the title page*[14] is a reference to Horatio's words in Act V, scene 2: 'And flights of angels sing thee to thy rest!'. This text is similar to a prayer twice repeated by Essex on his scaffold, and it appears that the artist was making a direct reference to this. The victim (Hamlet/ Essex) is portrayed as a tied up fish. The arrow penetrating the body of the fish transmutes into plant- or flower-like forms, thrusting upwards towards a dove and to heavenly angels. The dove is a well-known symbol of the Holy Ghost, while the fish is an ancient Christian symbol, which, based on Matthew 4:19, was used as a secret symbol among the early persecuted Christians by which they recognised each other. The fish in this emblem also seems to represent persecuted Christians, namely the adherents of the old faith whom Elizabeth I tried to eradicate within her own lifetime.

to the throne when he had won almost every competition. Here Shakespeare seems to have had in mind an image of Essex similar to the engraving of the earl, produced and circulated in 1600 by an artist belonging to the Essex group, or closely related to it. It depicts the great popular hero – with the obvious aim of restoring to the earl the standing which his supporters desired for him, but which Essex had already irredeemably lost (*Fig.* 96). In view of such allusions, it is not surprising that Shakespeare's historical play *Henry V*, in which the playwright – as has been mentioned before – openly and enthusiastically refers to Essex, was entered in the Stationers' Register on 27 May 1600 by the printer James Roberts with the comment 'to be staied', meaning that it should not be printed.

In contrast to Essex, at least until he proved himself on the battlefield, Shakespeare's Prince Henry, much to his father's displeasure, had distinguished himself mainly through his youthful excesses in the London taverns, and the company he kept with Falstaff.

Shakespeare could also have been thinking of Essex when he wrote *Coriolanus*, probably in 1608. In Act II, scene 1 the messenger reports:

> I have seen the dumb men throng to see him and
> The blind to hear him speak; matrons flung gloves,
> Ladies and maids their scarfs and handkerchers,
> Upon him as he pass'd; the nobles bended
> As to Jove's statue and the commons made
> A shower and thunder with their claps and shouts.
> I never saw the like.

Just like Essex, Hamlet is also popular with the people, and the Danish prince, like the earl, is characterised by melancholy and indecision. Essex lived in fear that his enemies were plotting to kill him, and Shakespeare's protagonist finds himself in the same position, as the king plots to have Hamlet killed in England, a fate that the hero narrowly escapes. Dover Wilson identified many parallels – both positive and negative – between the personality traits of Essex, the noble

Elizabethan statesman and military commander, and Hamlet, Shakespeare's tragic hero. The positive similarities include:

> ... his courtesy, his kindness to inferiors, his intellectual virtues, his passion for drama, his interest in spiritualism, his open and free nature, his nobility of bearing, his piety, his bravery, his genius for friendship, his brilliant wit, his love of field-sports, of hawking and horsemanship ...[238].

And the negative parallels are as follows:

> ... his moods of profound melancholy, his touch of insanity, his dangerous impetuosity, his frequent talk of suicide, his coarseness, his brutality and callousness to women, his ruthlessness towards those he hated, his theatricality, and above all his complete inability to think out a continuous line of action[239].

After the terrible revelations recounted by the ghost of his father in Act I that made 'each particular hair [of the hero] to stand an end, / Like quills upon the fretful porpentine' (*Fig. 117*), Hamlet declares that the time is 'out of joint' and laments that 'ever I was born to set it right'. The prince is not, however, referring to Denmark as described by the ancient Danish chronicler Saxo Grammaticus, whose book *Gesta Danorum* was by then four hundred years old, and described a time and civilisation which was already very remote for the Elizabethans. Instead, Hamlet is referring, as is seems, to late Elizabethan England, ruled by a queen who had been excommunicated by the Pope (her claim to the throne therefore being disputed by the Vatican and by the English Catholics), a queen who – after her 'sister' Mary, Queen of Scots, had been sentenced to death – would have looked with favour upon her clandestine assassination.

In *Hamlet*, King Claudius ascends to the throne after deviously murdering his brother. Events in the play, such as Laertes' rebellion in Act IV, scene 5, also appear to mirror the events,

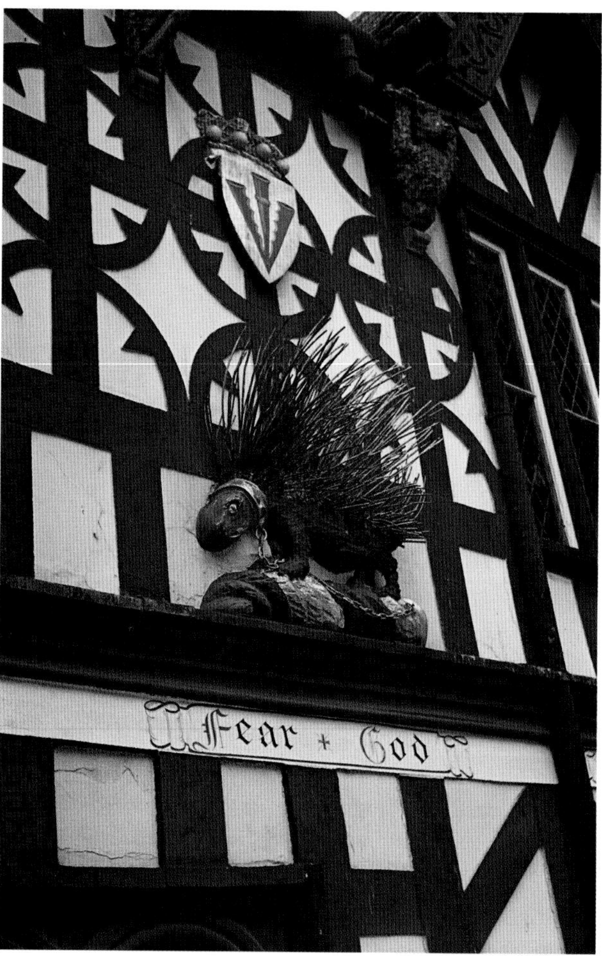

Fig. 117 – The Porcupine at Leicester's Hospital in Warwick, the handsome building erected by the queen's favourite, the Earl of Leicester, for the veterans of his campaigns. Horst Oppel*[15] suggests that Shakespeare, as a child, saw this heraldic animal when he visited Warwick, since he refers to it in *Hamlet* Act I, scene 5, where the ghost of Hamlet's father proclaims that he 'could a tale unfold whose lightest word / Would harrow up thy soul [...]', and make 'Thy knotted and combined locks to part, / And each particular hair to stand an end, / Like quills upon the fretful porpentine.'

reactions and atmosphere of 1601, after the failure of the rebellion and the execution of the Earl of Essex.

Essex already wore black when on trial for high treason (see p. 212), and Biron's French delegation also wore black when received at Court. From his first appearance on stage in Act I, scene 2, Shakespeare's Hamlet is similarly dressed in black, significantly saying of himself:

> 'Tis not alone my inky coat, good mother,
> Nor customary suits of common black,
> Nor windy suspiration of forc'd breath,
> No, nor the fruitful river in the eye, ...
> Nor the dejected haviour of the visage,
> Together with all forms, moods, shapes of grief,
> That can denote me truly. These, indeed, seem;
> For they are actions that a man might play;
> But I have that within which passes show –
> These but the trappings and the suits of woe.

Scholars have long assumed that when Hamlet describes Denmark as a state in which something is 'rotten', he is obviously referring to Shakespeare's own country. When he remarks, 'Denmark's a prison', he again may well have thought of England. To the countless Catholics of the time, crammed into England's prisons, wasting away in appalling and inhuman conditions, England would have indeed seemed to be one large prison. On Sundays, people would visit friends and relatives in jail, to bring them food and clothing and to comfort them. Simon Forman, an Elizabethan astrologer who practised medicine without a licence and was consequently persecuted and thrown into prison, wrote about the conditions in Elizabethan jails. Forman treated a large number of patients and he was a keen observer of people and events. His detailed records give us an insight into daily life in Elizabethan times, including the complaints and difficulties experienced by many, also his own. Forman treated many Catholics. His female companion dedicated a great deal of her time to visiting imprisoned Catholics, languishing in prisons near her home.

Thus Shakespeare's audience would immediately have understood what was meant when Hamlet, in Act II, scene 2, said that, within the great prison that is the world, 'in which there are many confines, wards, and dungeons, Denmark [i.e. England] being one o' th' worst'. Not only the Catholics, but all of Elizabeth I's subjects in the late 1590s would have known, either from their own bitter experience or that of those close to them, that the ports were under close observation, that no one was permitted to enter or leave the country without permission, and that every person entering or leaving was thoroughly checked. Huge numbers of Elizabeth's roughly five million subjects – whatever their social class – were at risk of being spied upon and denounced. All of the queen's subjects must have known that recusants were only permitted to travel within a five-mile radius of their home, that the prisons were full of Catholics, that Catholic priests were being hunted down as traitors and hanged, drawn and quartered when caught, and that anyone who helped them was subject to the same fate. As mentioned before, the main political aims of the Earl of Essex, which he pursued secretly, were to solve the open question of the succession, to achieve toleration of the old faith and to relieve the unbearable hardships of the English Catholics. Essex, however, had in mind only those parts of the Catholic population who had remained loyal to the queen and were not supported by the Spanish king. He paved the way for the Scottish king who, before he became king of England, had promised to tolerate Catholicism. This is why the earl, who had long been the hero of the English people, was also the hero of large numbers of the Catholic population, Shakespeare included. William Cecil, however, was despised and hated by all English Catholics because they knew that he bore the chief responsibility for the harsh anti-Catholic penal legislation under Elizabeth I.

In the Denmark that Shakespeare describes in *Hamlet* – obviously a cipher for England – spying, denunciations and murders are rife. Claudius hires Hamlet's friends from the University of Wittenberg as spies; Polonius orders a spy to follow Laertes and instructs him on how to catch the 'carp of truth' with a 'bait of falsehood', and even uses his daughter Ophelia to learn Hamlet's inner thoughts and feelings. Hamlet knows that he is being spied upon, betrayed and drawn into a net, but sets a trap himself with the aim of proving the king's guilt. Polonius, and even the king, stoop so low as to creep into the queen's bedchamber and hide behind the tapestry to eavesdrop upon a conversation between a mother and her son. Polonius is accidentally killed by Hamlet as he is eavesdropping 'behind the arras'.

Shakespeare's model for the role of Polonius, whom he constantly ridicules, was William Cecil, Elizabeth's chief counsellor and the most important member of the Privy Council until his death in 1598 (*Figs. 23* and *92a*). In Act III, scene 4, Polonius is killed by Hamlet like a rat: '[*Draws*] How now! a rat? [...] [*Kills Polonius with a pass through the arras.*]' Hamlet, who portrays his own role as that of a 'scourge and minister', thought he had been killing the king and shows no sign of grief or regret. In fact, he makes fun of the dead man:

> Indeed this counsellor,
> Is now most still, most secret, and most grave,
> Who was in life a foolish prating knave.

This behaviour is uncharacteristic of Hamlet, who is a sensitive and magnanimous prince and usually eschews violence[240], and the play suggests no real motivation for the hero's unscrupulous action. A key to this riddle, however, could be provided by Shakespeare's involvement in the Catholic underground and with Catholics-in-exile. English Catholics, at home and abroad, were well aware of the fact that William Cecil was responsible for their suffering. Hence he was their main target. Robert Parsons in particular, the Jesuit priest (nicknamed 'hell hound' by English government spies), who together with Edmund Campion had led the Catholic missionary movement, never missed an opportunity to attack and revile Cecil's religious policies in his writings. According to the geographer and historian John Speed, Shakespeare was Parsons' poet (see p. 140). The way in which the playwright portrays Polonius demonstrates rather clearly what Speed must have meant by this.

In order to be able to caricature William Cecil, Shakespeare must have heard and read about him, his policies and his demeanour a great deal. Details about Elizabeth's influential first minister would have been available to him via the Catholic network, both in England and abroad. Shakespeare, his family and his friends had felt at first hand the effects of Cecil's religious policies, especially the anti-Catholic penal laws he had initiated. When in London, the playwright would have been given the opportunity to observe Cecil during his frequent performances at Court with the Chamberlain's Men. In addition, he could have gained considerable insider knowledge from the queen's lady-in-waiting, Elizabeth Vernon, later Countess of Southampton, who had been his mistress for many years, but probably also from Vernon's cousin and friend, Lady Penelope Rich, who was the sister of the Earl of Essex. Finally, Shakespeare could have obtained a great deal of information about William Cecil from his patron, friend and later rival, Henry Wriothesley, the Earl of Southampton, who was Essex's best friend, and had – just like him – lived as a ward in Cecil's household during his childhood.

Polonius loses his life while secretly overhearing the conversation between Hamlet and his mother in the queen's privy chamber. Eavesdropping behind (arras) tapestries at Court and during trials was very common in the Elizabethan and Jacobean ages. Even kings and queens would listen in secret. When Edmund Campion was being interrogated in the residence of the Earl of Leicester, Elizabeth secretly eavesdropped and then made an unexpected entrance. The royal family and also the king himself listened clandestinely when Henry Garnet was placed on trial for high treason. Robert Cecil eavesdropped behind a tapestry when Essex and Southampton were tried for high treason. When, during this trial, Cecil himself was accused of treachery by Essex, he immediately stepped forward and dropped to his knees, asking the jury if he could present a witness to refute the allegations (see p. 213).

Why Elizabeth repeatedly stabbed at the tapestry in her private apartments, eight months after Essex had been executed, we cannot know for certain, but it appears that this behaviour was provoked by Biron's visit. The queen seems to have suspected eavesdropping. If so, she may well have thought of Robert Cecil, who had advised her during the Essex affair and was now the most powerful English politician. For it is very likely that Elizabeth later regretted following Cecil's advice, especially after Biron and his entourage had tried to shame and even humiliate her in public.

In Sonnet 66, Shakespeare denounces the unbearable state of affairs as it manifested itself at the end of 1599 (see pp. 205–206). In *Hamlet*, the playwright's criticisms are even harsher. His Danish prince touches a most painful subject: the cause of the disease of his country, which serves, however, as a cipher for England.

Only in five of his thirty-seven dramas does Shakespeare use medical metaphors and references to disease to describe the inner condition of the State and its people. Most of these medical metaphors are employed for the very first time in *Hamlet*. Subsequently they appear in *Troilus and Cressida*, *Macbeth*, *Coriolanus* and *The Winter's Tale*. In *Hamlet*, Shakespeare uses an astounding variety of realistic descriptions of illnesses in order to portray the decay and rottenness in Denmark/England, mentioning foul-smelling diseases, sharp pains and stabs, blisters on the forehead, a boil, an abscess, a chilblain (having developed into a raw wound), pleurisy, consumption, a stroke and a malignant mole (probably skin cancer). He mentions scars, being 'sicklied o'er with the pale cast of thought', ulcers, the poison of deep pain and the deadly breath of the Plague[241]. A more negative inventory is hard to imagine. *Hamlet*, Shakespeare's first great play after his turn to tragedy, clearly demonstrates how deeply and painfully involved Shakespeare must have been in the events of the day.

In Act III, scene 1, both, Claudius and Polonius, are eavesdropping behind the tapestry and overhear those things which, in the eyes of Hamlet, they should be ashamed of. This cunning device is used by Shakespeare to list the outrages committed by the State. In reality, Shakespeare is criticising the English government, especially the queen's closest adviser, Robert Cecil, who was virtually ruling the State as the queen's health increasingly deteriorated. Hamlet's famous monologue strongly reminds us of Essex, who – after he had been humiliated and deprived of power – was demoralised, deeply melancholy and on the brink of suicide. Like Essex, Hamlet reflects upon his options, and on their consequences, asking himself whether it would be 'nobler in the mind' to endure the 'slings and arrows of outrageous fortune' or to bring an end to the misery by means of (armed) resistance:

> To be, or not to be – that is the question;
> Whether 'tis nobler in the mind to suffer
> The slings and arrows of outrageous fortune,
> Or to take arms against a sea of troubles,
> And by opposing end them? To die, to sleep –
> No more; and by a sleep to say we end
> The heart-ache and the thousand natural shocks
> That flesh is heir to. 'Tis a consummation
> Devoutly to be wish'd. To die, to sleep;
> To sleep, perchance to dream. Ay, there's the rub;
> For in that sleep of death what dreams may come,
> When we have shuffled off this mortal coil,
> Must give us pause. There's the respect
> That makes calamity of so long life;
> For who would bear the whips and scorns of time,
> Th'oppressors wrong, the proud man's contumely,
> The pangs of despis'd love, the law's delay,
> The insolence of office, and the spurns
> That patient merit of th'unworthy takes,
> When he himself his quietus make
> With a bare bodkin? Who would these fardels bear,
> To grunt and sweat under a weary life,
> But that the dread of something after death –
> The undiscover'd country, from whose bourn
> No traveller returns – puzzles the will,
> And makes us rather bear those ills we have
> Than fly to others that we know not of?
> Thus conscience does make cowards of us all;

> And thus the native hue of resolution
> Is sicklied o'er with the pale cast of thought,
> And enterprises of great pitch and moment,
> With this regard, their currents turn awry
> And lose the name of action.

It can hardly be overlooked that many references in this monologue would also point to the immense suffering of the English Catholics at that time – as William Allen, president of the Collegium Anglicum, had already described it in the 1580s (see p. 158) and as it presented itself – even more drastically – after the tightening of the anti-Catholic legislation in the course of the 1590s.

At the end of the play, Hamlet receives the full military honours of 'a peal of ordnance' (a gun salute) and martial music, as we are told in the stage directions. This is striking, because Hamlet, unlike his father and Fortinbras, was no army commander and had not fought in any war. Hamlet hardly gives a single thought to military matters anywhere in the play. One cannot help thinking that Shakespeare is using this military ceremonial to pay tribute to his idol, Essex. As one of Essex's supporters and followers, the playwright would have known that Essex regarded such rituals very highly, and that upon his execution, this honour had been withheld. In his elegy, *The Phoenix and the Turtle*, written in reaction to the sentence of death imposed on Essex and Southampton, Shakespeare holds an imaginary funeral procession for his friend(s) and an imaginary requiem with a priest 'in surplice white' (see pp. 219 and 221). In *Hamlet*, a Catholic prayer is said for the dead prince, who also receives full military honours:

> Let four captains
> Bear Hamlet like a soldier to the stage;
> For he was likely, had he been put on,
> To have prov'd most royal; and for his passage
> The soldier's music and the rite of war
> Speak loudly for him.
> Take up the bodies. Such a sight as this
> Becomes the field, but here shows much amiss.
> Go, bid the soldiers shoot.

If this extract is a reference by Shakespeare to the dead Earl of Essex, then the sentence 'For he was likely, had he been put on, / To have prov'd most royal' can be read as an allusion to the uprising of 8 February 1601, indicating that Shakespeare too – as most of his compatriots – wanted Essex to be Elizabeth's successor. For it seems that the playwright believed that the skill and character of Essex (just like those of Hamlet) would have made him an extremely fine leader of the state, although neither of them was given the opportunity to prove this.

The procession ordered by Fortinbras echoes that of the French Marshal Biron in memory of Essex. Thus Shakespeare once more pays his last respects to his dead political hero by literary means, a hero who had carried the hopes of so many with him.

In *Hamlet*, Catholic thought and ritual are depicted quite openly and brazenly. The dramatist here presents his main character in deep despair and depression. Hamlet's desire to commit suicide is against God's law (in reality it is against the law of the Catholic Church). When Laertes complains about the meagre rites at his sister's funeral, the (Catholic) priest has to tell him that the circumstances of Ophelia's death were dubious. English Catholics during Shakespeare's lifetime sometimes steadfastly and demonstratively defied the authorities and maintained their lavish funeral rites, despite the fierce sanctions with which they were threatened. This can be demonstrated by the Catholic funeral in May 1605 of the recusant Alice Wellington, who had been excommunicated by the Anglican Church. This funeral was a deliberate public gesture of disobedience against the State and the Anglican Church, and was punished accordingly (see p. 271).

At the very beginning of the play, Hamlet invokes the aid of 'Angels and ministers of grace' when he encounters a ghost. In his book, entitled *Of ghostes and spirites walking by nyght, and of strange noyses, crackes, and sundry forewarnynges, which commonly happen before the death of menne, great slaughters & alteration of kyngdomes*, published in Latin in 1570 in Geneva and appearing in an English translation by R.H. in London in 1572, Ludwig Lavater (1527-1586) made it quite clear that 'the appearance of the souls of the dead' was 'Papist doctrine', according to Protestants. How closely Shakespeare stuck to this doctrine becomes particularly apparent when the appearance and behaviour of the ghost as well as Hamlet's reaction to it, are compared with Lavater's remarks[242]:

> And whersoeuer these spirits be, they say, that they endure punishment. Besides that soules do not appeare, nor answeare vnto euery mans interrogatories, but that of a great number they scantlie appeare vnto one. And therefore they teache. Whensoeuer such visions of spirits are shewed, men should vse fasting and prayer or euer they demaund any question of them. ... Besides this, shrift, and massing shoulde bee vsed ere we question with them: farther, that we should not giue credite as soone as we heare but one signe, but waite to heare the same thrice repeated ... for otherwise the Diuell may delude and deceyue vs, as he doth very often.

'Moreouer', the author continues, 'popishe writers teache vs to discerne good spirits from euill by foure meanes'. He explains:

> First they say that if he be a good spirit, he will at the beginning, somewhat terrifie men, but againe soone reuiue and comforte them. ... Their second note is to discry them by their outward and visible shape. For if they appeare vnder the forme of a Lyon, beare, dog, tode, serpent, catte, or blacke ghoste, it may easly be gathered that it is an euill spirit. And that on the other side good spirits do appeare vnder the shape of a doue, a man, a lambe, or in the brightnesse, and clere light of the sunne.
>
> We must also consider whether the voice whiche we heare be sweete, lowly, sober, sorowfull, or otherwise terrible and full of reproch, for so they terme it.
>
> Thirdly we must note, whether the spirit teache ought that doth varie from the doctrine of the apostles, and other doctoures approued by the Churches censure: or whether he vtter any thing that dothe dissent from the faith, good maners, and ceremonies of the church, according to the canonicall rites or decrees of councels, & against the lawes of the holy Church of *Rome*.
>
> Fourthly we must take diligent heede whether in hys words, deeds, and gestures, he do shew forth any humilitie acknowledging or confessing of his sinnes & punishments, or whether we heare of him any groning, weeping, complaint, boasting, threatning, slaunder or blasphemie. For as the begger doth reherse his owne miserie, so likewyse doo good spirits that desire any helpe or deliuerance. Other signes also they haue to trie the good angels from the bad: but these are the cheefe.

It can easily be recognised that, directly or indirectly, *Hamlet* observes or considers nearly all of these distinctions.

The ghost in *Hamlet* rues the fact that he has lost his 'life', 'crown', and 'queen' and that he was carried off in 'the blossoms of sin', 'Unhous'led' and 'unanel'd' (without communion given the dying man and without the last rites). In his most famous tragedy, Shakespeare does not shy away from mentioning these deeply Catholic doctrines, concepts and rites, and he even refers to two Catholic sacraments by name. His protagonist learns that the ghost of his father is 'confined to fast in fires'. This Catholic concept of the afterlife (purgatory) had already been rejected by Edward VI.

Furthermore, mention should be made of the fact that the (Catholic) prayer, spoken by Horatio for the dead prince in Act V, scene 2 – 'And flights of angels sing thee to thy rest' – is very similar to the prayer that Essex twice repeated on the scaffold: 'And when my soul and body shall part, *send thy blessed angels to be near unto me which may convey it to the joys of heaven.*'[243] Edmond Malone, an eighteenth-century Irish Shakespeare scholar living in England, was the first to notice this similarity. In his well-known book, *The Essential Shakespeare*, first published in 1932, John Dover Wilson also mentions this and comments that Horatio's prayer 'grates upon our religious sensibility'[244].

Shakespeare's ghost scenes and lighting effects had already been compared with Jesuit drama in the early seventeenth century. For instance, the Oxford graduate and government spy, John Gee, wrote in a report published in 1624 that Jesuit actors had developed such great skill and ability, that if they were to form a theatre company, they would not only provide competition for the big London theatres – such as the Globe – but that they would cause such venues to close. He takes a sideswipe at this religious order, stating that the Jesuits extract too much money from their 'spectators', and that scenes like the ghost scene in *Hamlet* or the use of a lantern to represent the moon in *Pyramus and Thisbe*, (referring to Shakespeare's *A Midsummer Night's Dream*) were available at much less expense in other theatres[245].

It was because of the political climate of the time that Shakespeare was willing to risk much more open references to Catholicism in *Hamlet* than in his other works. Between Essex's death in 1601 and the change of sovereign in 1603, supporters of the old faith showed their strength, decisiveness and readiness to resist or even topple the regime. There were increasing signs of open rebellion. Catholics-in-exile and clandestine Catholics in England had got wind of the fact that Robert Cecil was acting behind the back of the aged queen and had adopted the plan of Essex to secure the English throne for James VI of Scotland. They would, of course, have realised in advance that with Cecil as his advisor and first minister, James was unlikely to change the anti-Catholic penal laws. This new political situation could and would not be accepted by the underground Catholic leadership.

In early March 1603, security in London was heightened for fear of an uprising by 'Papists' and other 'malcontents'. The Catholic Sir Edward Baynham, who in March 1600 together with three other gentlemen had rioted in Friday Street and Saint Paul's Churchyard in London, wounding the watchmen (see p. 208), expressed on 17 March 1603, just seven days before the queen's death, a conviction shared by most of his Catholic compatriots, that he would rather lose his life than let the Scottish king enter England, and that forty thousand Catholics were ready (in London) to prevent this happening. On the very same day, the Privy Council pronounced its support for James as the future king of England. These events help explain the increasing number of largely overt references to Catholic doctrine in Shakespeare's *Hamlet*, a play written in memory of the Earl of Essex. They also make it quite clear that the English Catholics rejected James VI of Scotland as their king – obviously because the Scottish monarch's ideas were now in line with Robert Cecil.

Between 1601 and 1603, i.e. from the writing of *Hamlet* to Queen Elizabeth's death and / or the arrival of the new monarch, Shakespeare remained conspicuously silent[246]. Seemingly he was a passive observer. This would allow him to come to terms with events. During this period, he moved from Southwark, where he was near the Globe Theatre, and lodged in Silver Street (inside the north-west corner of the City wall) with the Mountjoys, a family of immigrant French Huguenots. This was a cunning move by Shakespeare. At a time when friends and acquaintances of the dead earl were under particularly close observation, Shakespeare, as a secret Catholic and a supporter of the earl, could receive no better protection than to live among foreign Protestants who had been offered a new homeland and protection by the English Crown, and therefore enjoyed the complete trust of the authorities. Sir Francis Walsingham, the former head of the spy network who had died in 1590, had been Elizabeth's ambassador in Paris between 1570 and 1573. He had witnessed the St Bartholomew's night massacre and had offered many Huguenots protection in his Paris residence.

In 1601, Shakespeare was not only in danger because he had been an acquaintance of the Earl of Essex, but also because *Hamlet* was much more politically subversive than *Julius Caesar*. Whereas Talbot, in the first part of *Henry VI* (Act IV, scene 1), invokes God and St George, the Patron Saint of England, for help on the battlefield, Hamlet, in Act I, scene 5, calls upon St Patrick, the Patron Saint of Ireland. This was open provocation. As far as is known, *Hamlet* was never performed at Court in the reign of Elizabeth I, and understandably so. Essex had negotiated with Irish Catholic rebels and had even arranged a truce with their leader, Hugh O'Neill. The Irish were allies of the English Catholics-in-exile, led by Robert Parsons, and supported by Spain, against the English government. Hamlet's exclamation 'By Saint Patrick' can therefore be regarded as a hidden reference to Essex's pro-Catholic tendencies.

Shakespeare's English historical plays, as well as *Julius Caesar* and *Hamlet*, the plays he wrote just before and just after the Essex rebellion, show that the playwright could be considered as a kind of 'unseen stage manager' behind the scenes, attempting to influence the politics of his age. His instruments of magic, the 'magic cloak' and 'wand' as Prospero put it, were the spoken word and printed text. These he used to recreate the world on the stage – the macrocosm and the microcosm. He depicts active participants and passive victims in historical situations; Machiavellian schemers, who break the rules and laws according to their own needs, or simply because they enjoy doing so; but also courageous individuals who rebel against the despotism of the authorities, and act to bring down failed rulers and tyrants alike, to restore the disturbed order of state and society. A study of Shakespeare's plays written during the period in which he turned to tragedy shows that the playwright was indeed more deeply involved in the political events of his time than was previously thought when little or nothing was known about his activities in the Catholic underground.

In *Hamlet*, Shakespeare expresses the full measure of his grief at Essex's death. Horatio, to whom the hero opens his heart, even telling him that Claudius had been planning a cowardly attempt on his life, is perhaps reminiscent of Southampton, Essex's closest friend. 'What a king is this?', asks Horatio. Southampton could have said the same of Elizabeth, in view of what was done or caused to be done in her name between 28 September 1599 and 25 February 1601. Shakespeare, whose history, *Richard II*, had played such an important role in the Essex Rebellion, now prudently disappeared from the immediate vicinity of the Globe Theatre, to move in with the Huguenots. Augustine Phillips, the oldest member of the Chamberlain's Men, was to be interrogated by the authorities. Phillips, who died in 1605, had been a member of the troupe since its inception in 1594.

Living with the Mountjoys, Shakespeare must have had numerous opportunities to see the ladies of the Court, who came to the Mountjoy residence to have their headdresses made up. This is where he might have frequently met Elizabeth Wriothesley (née Vernon), the Countess of Southampton, whose husband was imprisoned in the Tower. Had she – once more – become Shakespeare's mistress? The fact that Shakespeare's likeness appears on the Countess's sleeve in an authenticated portrait of her dating from this time (*Figs. 85a* and *85b*) is a strong indication that the relationship had been rekindled at this time or had never ceased. The constant comings and goings between Silver Street and the Court would have given Shakespeare plenty of opportunity to send and receive news. For the remainder of Elizabeth I's reign, Shakespeare the Catholic became more inconspicuous and withdrawn and lived perhaps a more secret existence than ever before. As an author he remained silent.

What did Shakespeare do during this period of silence after writing *Hamlet*? It is well documented that in 1602, the playwright made important property acquisitions in Stratford

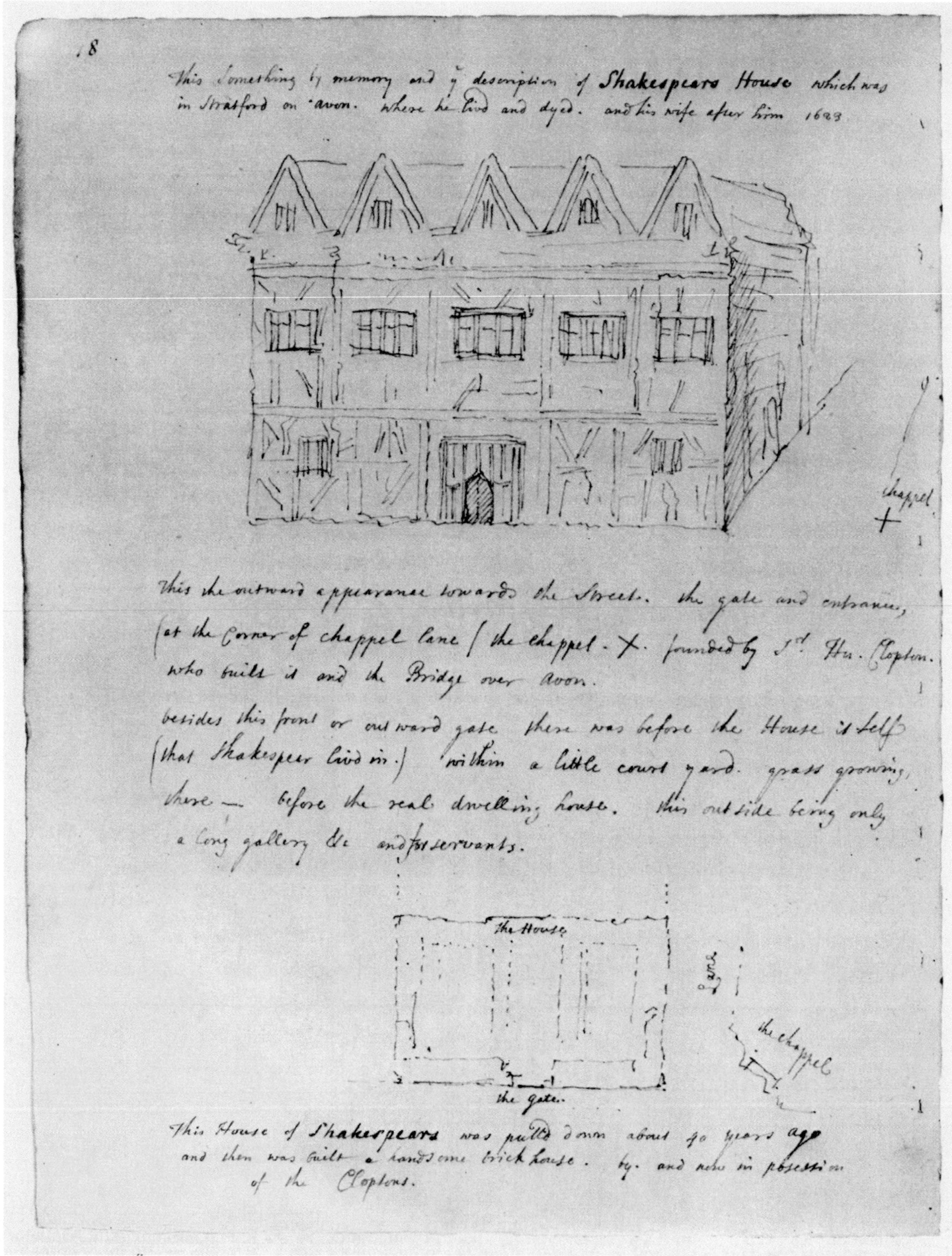

Fig. 118 – Sketch of Shakespeare's Stratford residence, New Place. It was over sixty feet wide and roughly seventy feet deep. The main entrance was on Chapel Street. This wing of the house was occupied by the servants' quarters. This sketch by the English antiquary George Vertue (1737) shows that New Place had three stories, five gables and a sizeable inner courtyard. It also had ten grand chimneystacks. The Chapel Street entrance led, via a wide pathway, across an inner courtyard planted with symmetrical lawns, to the main wing of the house, in which the family's living quarters and bedrooms were to be found. Shakespeare's study and library were probably also housed here. The sketch was drawn from memory and contemporary descriptions.

which, given the size and importance of these transactions, would have occupied much of his time. Since 4 May 1597, Shakespeare had been the owner of New Place (*Fig. 118*), described in a source dating from 1540 as a 'praty [pretty] howse of brike and tymbar'. New Place was situated in a prominent location, directly opposite the Guild Hall and the Grammar School (*Figs. 119 a–b*). The poet had purchased the property from the Catholic William Underhill, who lived in Ettington Park, about five miles south-east of the town (*Figs. 120 a–b*) and who, in 1592, had been named, along with William's father, John Shakespeare, on the list of Stratford recusants. Apart from Old College, a former Crown property and home of Stratford's wealthiest citizen, John Combe, the landowner and moneylender (*c.*1560-1614), New Place was the largest, grandest and most attractive house in Stratford. It is very likely that Underhill – like many other Catholic landowners – was forced to sell his property quickly and at a low price, in order to pay the exorbitant fines levied upon him by the Anglican Church. The sources which show that Shakespeare purchased the house for £60 may well be accurate, therefore, although many scholars have thought the sum far too low, since the same residence had previously been sold for twice that amount. This large financial transaction and the necessary preparations for it were certainly undertaken personally by Shakespeare, meaning that he must have been present in Stratford in late April or early May 1597. To complete the purchase, it is likely that the poet rode to Ettington Park (*Figs. 120 a–b*). When William Underhill was murdered by his own son Fulke, the sale needed to be reconfirmed[247]. Fulke Underhill was executed and the estate passed to another of Underhill's sons, Hercules. Hercules Underhill signed a supplementary deed to complete the sale, and this may have required Shakespeare to pay another visit to Ettington. But it is also possible that Shakespeare was represented in the sale by one of his brothers (Richard or Gilbert) or even by his relative and friend, Thomas Greene, a lawyer who became town clerk of Stratford in 1603 and who lived in New Place.

Shakespeare's new Stratford residence had a ground plan of over sixty feet wide (in Chapel Street) and roughly seventy feet deep (along Chapel Lane). The maximum height was twenty-eight feet (northern gable). The main entrance was situated on Chapel Street. This part of the building was occupied by the servants' quarters. A sketch by the antiquary George Vertue, made in 1737, shows that New Place had three stories,

Fig. 119a – Corner of Chapel Street and Chapel Lane in Stratford-upon-Avon, where Shakespeare's house, New Place, once stood. The half-timbered building in the background is the famous inn, The Falcon; on the left is the Guildhall and the former Grammar School.

Fig. 119b – Former interior courtyard of New Place, containing a well. The garden can be seen in the background.

Fig. 120a – The site of Ettington Park, seat of the Underhills of Warwickshire, roughly five miles south-east of Stratford which was remodelled in High Victorian Gothic style in 1858. Like numerous other families of the English gentry, the Underhills remained followers of the old faith. Sir William Underhill was listed, like John Shakespeare, in the Stratford list of recusants in 1592. They were neighbours of Shakespeare's friend and executor Thomas Russell, who lived in Alderminster. Russell's stepson Leonard Digges, son of the prominent London astronomer Thomas Digges, was one of Shakespeare's greatest admirers, and knew the dramatist personally. It was Digges who first mentioned Shakespeare's funerary monument ('thy Stratford Moniment') in one of the many poems paying tribute in the First Folio Edition of 1623. Headed 'To the Memorie of the Deceased Authour Maister W. Shakespeare', it concludes by asserting 'Be sure, our Shake-speare, thou canst neuer dye, / But crown'd with Lawrell, liue eternally.'*[16]

five gables, and a sizeable inner courtyard (*Fig. 118*). Furthermore, it had no less than ten fireplaces[248]. The Chapel Street entrance led, via a wide pathway across an inner courtyard planted with symmetrical lawns, to the main wing of the house, in which the family's living quarters and bedrooms were to be found. Shakespeare's study and library were also probably housed here.

After acquiring the title to New Place, the poet made many structural changes to the fabric to meet his requirements. He sold a superfluous consignment of bricks to the town. He had the gardens of the property, particularly the terrace, elaborately laid out. In the centre of the terrace he placed a fascinating octagonal structure (*Fig. 121a*), which I photographed from a number of angles in the summer of 1996. On the side facing the garden, there was a badly weathered and seemingly illegible inscription, while the other seven sides featured relatively well-preserved scenes of figures in relief. In summer 2002, when I decided to reproduce some views of this weathered stonework, I set about deciphering the inscriptions on it. When the images were greatly enlarged, I was able to make out certain letters and words, which gave me the key to the text as a whole. It is the monologue of the melancholy Jaques from Shakespeare's comedy *As You Like It* (*Figs. 121b* and *121c*) about the seven ages of man. Each of the seven ages is impressively illustrated (*Fig. 121d*). The decoding of the inscription suddenly offered answers to other

Fig. 120b – Entrance to Ettington Park. In 1597, Shakespeare purchased New Place from Sir William Underhill, the owner of this country seat. The playwright (or a representative) probably rode to Ettington in April/May 1597 in order to negotiate and conclude the sale. Just after the contract was signed, Sir William was poisoned by his son Fulke. The patricide was convicted and executed. Shakespeare (or his representative) was no doubt required to travel to Ettington once more, to confirm the sale with Fulke's younger brother Hercules Underhill, who had inherited the estate.

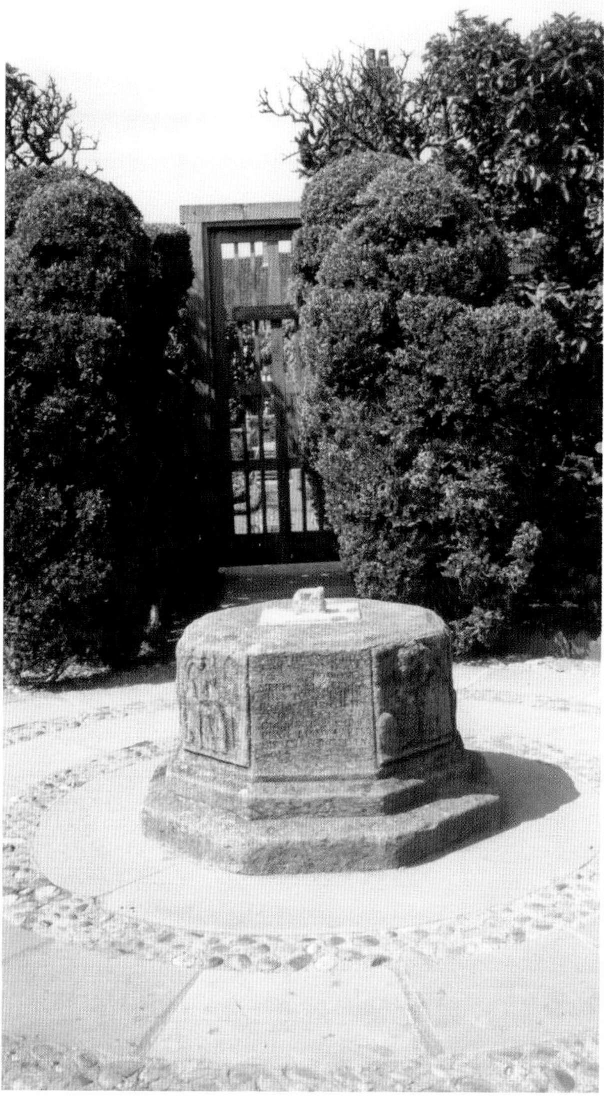

Fig. 121a – Octagon on the terrace of the garden of New Place, photographed by the present author in the summer of 1996. On the side facing the garden, there is an inscription; the other seven sides feature scenes of figures in relief. According to the expert opinion of the paleographer Dr Sebastian Scholz, from the Academy of Science and Literature in Mainz, who compared the inscriptions below Shakespeare's funerary bust and on the (original) stone slab covering his grave to the one on the octagon, the latter was even more accurate. He concluded that nothing contradicted the assumption that this monument was created around the year 1600. It had served as a base which at one time bore a decorative or functional object, now lost. Shakespeare himself – we may assume – had commissioned it after the purchase of New Place (1597) when the garden of the property, especially the terrace, was elaborately laid out.

open questions concerning Shakespeare's life.

The monument is likely to have been created in the years immediately after Shakespeare completed the purchase in 1597. Shakespeare himself – we may assume – had commissioned it precisely for the newly laid–out garden at New Place. In traditional symbolism an octagon stands for 'regeneration', 'happiness', 'resurrection', 'paradise regained', and the 'perfection of the cosmos'[249]. It recalls the eight points of the compass and wind directions[250], and this shape was adopted for churches dedicated to our Lady, and also for crowns, candelabras, and baptismal fonts[251].

I asked Dr Sebastian Scholz, an expert on inscriptions at the Academy of Science and Literature in Mainz, to compare the octagon inscription with those below the poet's funerary bust and on the stone slab covering his grave. Dr Scholz's palaeographic report of 22 July 2002, supported my hypothesis about the octagon's date of origin. He also noted that the craftsmanship of the octagon's inscription had been carried out even more carefully than those on the gravestone and the marble tablet below the funerary bust. Concluding his report, he stated that those who claimed that the octagon and its inscription 'could not date from soon after 1597' bore the onus of proving it. From a palaeographical point of view there was nothing to contradict the assumption that the monument had not been made 'soon after the purchase of the property'.

This Renaissance monument in the garden of New Place, bearing a quotation from the pen of Shakespeare, who had his own words carved and illustrated in stone, shows that the prominent burgher of Stratford was prepared to proclaim his status as a playwright even here, in his home town, despite being well aware of the fact that the Puritans, always hostile to the theatre and to image-making, had grown in power and influence.

To be precise, the octagon is merely the pedestal of a monument, and at the time bore some decorative or functional object, now lost. This may well have been a sculptured figure, of

ALL THE WORLDS
A STAGE AND ALL
THE MEN AND WOMEN
MERE PLAYERS
THEY HAVE THEIR
EXITS AND THEIR
ENTRANCES AND
ONE MAN IN HIS TIME
PLAYS MANY PARTS
HIS ACTS BEING SEVEN
AGES

Figs. 121b and ***121c*** – Badly weathered and illegible inscription of the octagon. While preparing the German edition of my Shakespeare biography in the summer of 2002, I set about deciphering the inscription. Certain letters and words, which I could make out, gave me the key to the text as a whole. It is the monologue of the melancholy Jaques from Shakespeare's comedy *As You Like It* (Act II, scene 7).

the kind so much admired in the Renaissance. But it could also have been a sundial. In the notes that the English antiquary Robert Bell Wheler made in New Place on 26 September 1758, he mentions that there was 'In ye Wilderness [the neglected garden of the property] a Stone-Dyal'[252]. This suggests that the sundial may once have stood on the richly decorated octagon.

For advice on this question, I consulted Professor Edmund Buchner, former President of the German Archaeological Institute in Berlin, who excavated the sundial of the Emperor Augustus in Rome. Based on my photographs from 1996, Buchner looked into the matter. His expert report of 14 September 2002 revealed some surprising new aspects. Around 1600, Buchner said, there was a type of (octagonal) free-standing sundial, which was placed upon a plinth and probably – as in New Place – secured by pinning. This could have been the type of sundial that stood in Shakespeare's garden. Professor Buchner also helpfully drew my attention to the historic octagonal 'block sundial' on Mont St Odile[253] in Alsace, which corresponds closely in time and style to the octagon in New Place, as I was able to confirm for myself on the spot in Alsace in September 2002.

An eight-sided sundial of this type (*Fig. 122*), like a modern 'global clock', should make it possible to tell the time not only locally, but also in several other places all over the world – obviously in a more symbolic sense. Such a device was in keeping with the global consciousness of the early modern age. Shakespeare, too, thought globally. In *Twelfth Night* he alludes to a new world map, showing 'both the Indies', and published in a very limited edition in England in 1599. He gave his new theatre, which opened in the same year, the imposing name 'The Globe'. And, inspired by a shipwreck near the Bermudas in 1609, he chose to set the scene of his grand finale, *The Tempest*, in the New World.

Since Shakespeare had a liking for sundials (see quotation below) and since such a time-measuring device was found in the grounds of New Place in the eighteenth century, it can safely be assumed that this kind of free-standing sundial stood on his octagonal pedestal in the garden of New Place decorated with seven reliefs and the quotation from *As You Like It*.

Fig. 121d – View of the octagon from above: The sixth age of man (centre, foreground).

Fig. 122 – Historic octagonal 'block sundial' on Mont St Odile in Alsace. According to the expert opinion of Professor Edmund Buchner, former President of the German Archaeological Institute in Berlin, this type of free-standing sundial was typical of the period around 1600 and could have stood on the octagonal base in the garden of New Place. Another option was a free-standing sculpture. But since a stone sundial had been found in the 'wilderness' of the garden of New Place in the eighteenth century which, however, went missing again, it is safe to assume that an impressive octagonal block sundial with a globe on top once decorated Shakespeare's terrace, standing on the octagonal pedestal (secured by pinning). Such a device was in keeping with the global consciousness of the early modern age. Shakespeare, too, thought globally. In *Twelfth Night* he even alludes to a new world map, showing 'both the Indies', and published in a very limited edition in England in 1599 (see p. 249). The playwright gave his new theatre in Southwark, which opened in the same year, the imposing name 'The Globe'.

In *Henry VI* (Part 3, Act II, scene 5) Shakespeare's King Henry, all alone on a battle field, philosophises on the 'grief and woe' of the world, longing for the 'happy life' of 'a homely swain', so that he could 'sit upon a hill ...

> To carve out dials quaintly, point by point,
> Thereby to see the minutes how they run -
> How many makes the hour full complete,
> How many hours brings about the day,
> How many days will finish up the year,
> How many years a mortal man may live.

When I examined the frescoes on a wall of the White Swan inn in Stratford on 28 July 2001 and afterwards went to the garden of New Place again, I was very surprised to find that the monument was no longer there. In its place stood a tall sculpture by a contemporary American artist. On 9 January 2002, I checked the site once more to make sure I had not been mistaken. Sure enough, where I had photographed the octagon in 1996, there was a work, dated 1999, by the American sculptor Greg Wyatt (*Figs. 123a* and *123b*) with an inscription taken from *The Tempest* (Prospero's epilogue). There was no indication of the whereabouts of the Renaissance octagon.

In answer to my enquiry, the Birthplace Trust in Stratford-upon-Avon informed me on 16 May 2003 that the octagon had been 'damaged by vandals on more than one occasion', and was now being stored, 'in several pieces', in the

Fig. 123a – Front view of a sculpture by the American artist Greg Wyatt, created in 1999. This sculpture was placed on exactly the spot where the Renaissance octagonal monument stood which, in all probability, was commissioned by Shakespeare himself.

Fig. 123b – Rear view of the sculpture by Greg Wyatt. In the background are the lawns of the garden of New Place and the Memorial Theatre.

Garden Department of the Trust on the outskirts of Stratford. When I enquired further on 28 May 2003, Professor Stanley Wells, Chairman of the Birthplace Trust, sent me excerpts from the minutes of 1925 to 1929, showing that an American couple, Mr and Mrs Cass Gilbert, had donated a sundial to the Trust for the terrace at New Place. The estimated cost was £185. The first design, from 1927, was thought to be 'too large'. Mr Osborne of the Stratford Guild was asked 'to proceed on the basis of a smaller, slightly changed design'. In April 1929, Alderman Bullard thanked the Gilberts 'for their gift of a sun dial'. The minutes show that the gift consisted only of the sundial. This must have been mounted on the old pedestal. The Trust, and probably the Gilberts themselves, almost certainly knew about Wheler's mentioning of a stone sundial in New Place, first cited in Charlotte Stopes's *Shakespeare's Environment* (1918). So, thanks to the Gilberts' donation, the Shakespeare monument was restored or completed in 1929.

As shown by a photograph, published in the 1989 booklet *Stratford-upon-Avon. Shakespeare's Town* by Dr Levi Fox, Director Emeritus of the Shakespeare Birthplace Trust, the Gilberts' sundial was still extant in or shortly before 1989 (*Fig. 124*). Its style, however, differs greatly from that of the (octagonal) free-standing sundial of the Renaissance. Between 1989 and 1996, it must have been damaged by vandals, and was therefore removed.

In July 2003, when I visited the Garden Department of the Birthplace Trust, I found the octagon easily accessible, in an open tool shed (*Fig. 125a*), and saw that it had been severely damaged. The rim of the plinth was lying in fragments, but the monument itself was still in one piece. Its inscription 'ALL THE WORLDS A STAGE ...' had, obviously intentionally, been

Fig. 124 – The octagonal monument in the garden of New Place, photographed before, or in, 1989. Picture quotation from the booklet *Stratford-upon-Avon. Shakespeare's Town* by Dr Levi Fox, OBE, MA, FSA, Director Emeritus of the Shakespeare Birthplace Trust, published by Jarrold Publishing, Norwich, in 1989 (p. 24). The sundial on the base must be the one donated to the Birthplace Trust by the American couple Mr and Mrs Cass Gilbert, replacing the lost original which had been found somewhere in the overgrown garden of New Place in 1758, but was not preserved. This can be concluded from the minutes of 1925 to 1929, kept at the Birthplace Trust. At the present author's request, the relevant extracts of these minutes were sent to her by Professor Stanley Wells, Chairman of the Birthplace Trust, in May 2003. According to the minutes, the first design, from 1927, was thought to be 'too large'. Mr Osborne of the Stratford Guild was asked 'to proceed on the basis of a smaller, slightly changed design'. This must have happened. For in April 1929, Alderman Bullard thanked the Gilberts 'for their gift of a sun dial'.

almost entirely erased, except for two or three letters that could barely be made out, but were enough to recognise that this was precisely that side of the octagon where the inscription had been (*Fig. 125b*). The relief figures, too, were badly damaged.

The octagon from the garden of New Place brings into focus new aspects of Shakespeare's private and literary existence. It reveals a man who had a refined and elegant lifestyle, a predeliction for symmetry in choosing the highly symbolic octagonal form, and also expertise in the commissioning of stone carving, all of which shows his love of the pictorial or fine arts, demonstrated also in his literary work, as, for instance, in *The Winter's Tale* (Act V, scene 3). Not least, it reveals his self-confidence as an author, and his knowledge of the influence his texts exerted on the visual arts.

In the epilogue to the first (German) edition of this book I expressed the hope that this precious piece of visual and written evidence from Shakespeare's own lifetime, so closely tied to his personal life and country home, which is an historical monument testifying to his authorship of the plays and his role in inspiring visual art, might be returned to its original site. Now I would like to add that I hope the octagon may be restored as far as is possible and thus be preserved for posterity, and, furthermore, that it may be placed once again on the spot that Shakespeare himself must have chosen for it.

On 1 May 1602, Shakespeare purchased a large tract of land in the district of Old Stratford. This was an estimated 107 acres of arable land, and a further twenty acres of pastureland. The vendor was Squire William Combe (1551-1610) of Warwick. Combe's wealthy nephew, John Combe of Stratford, who had inherited a coat of arms from his father, played an important role in the sale. Shakespeare and John Combe were acquainted, and may even have been friends. When John Combe died in 1614, leaving his estate to his nephew, Thomas Combe, Shakespeare dedicated a tomb inscription to

Fig. 125a – The original octagon, formerly found on the terrace of the garden of New Place, now in the Garden Department of the Shakespeare Birthplace Trust – badly damaged. A written communication from the Trust of 16 May 2003 revealed that it 'was damaged by vandals on more than one occasion and is now in several pieces and is in storage in ... [the] Garden Department, at The Hill, on the outskirts of Stratford'. When the author visited the Garden Department in July 2003, she found the octagon, easily accessible, in an open tool shed, still in one piece (apart from the plinth). Most of the reliefs representing the Seven Ages of Man from Shakespeare's *As You Like It* had been severely damaged. Some of them were no longer recognisable. The inscription had been completely destroyed.

Fig.125b – View of that side of the octagon where Shakespeare's lines 'All THE WORLDS A STAGE' were inscribed as photographs taken by the author in 1996 can prove (see *Figs. 121 a* and *b*). The inscription is now completely erased. Only a few, hardly recognisable letters tell us that it was once there.

him, which made ironic reference to his usury and his coat of arms. It read:

> Ten in the hundred must lie in his graue,
> But a hundred to ten whether God will him haue?
>
> Who then must be interr'd in this Tombe?
> Oh (quoth the Diuell) my *John a Combe.*

John Combe remembered Shakespeare in his will, bequeathing him the sum of five pounds. Shakespeare would later mention Thomas Combe in his own will. Like William and John Combe, William Shakespeare was also at this point entitled to call himself a Gentleman, and, as shown on the title deeds, possessed a family coat of arms, inherited from his father who had died in 1601 (*Figs. 16* and *17*). Shakespeare himself was not present for the transaction – presumably as a precaution in these dangerous times. He was represented by his brother, Gilbert Shakespeare, but Shakespeare must personally have instigated the acquisition of such a large amount of land, and this means that he must have been in Stratford, Old Stratford and maybe even in Warwick in early 1602.

About five months later, on 28 September 1602, Shakespeare purchased a cottage in Chapel Lane, directly opposite his garden at New Place, which he had significantly enlarged through further purchases[254] (*Figs. 141 a–b*). Significantly, he was not present for this purchase either. E.K. Chambers (1866-1953), the eminent English Shakespeare scholar, states that this property was probably intended for Shakespeare's gardener:

> And in the same year he [Shakespeare] acquired, for the use of his gardener, one may suppose, a cottage in Chapel Lane [...].[255]

During this long period of silence in his creative life, Shakespeare was busy with his personal affairs, but remained inconspicuous. This may be because times were dangerous for Essex supporters, but also because, as the author of *Hamlet*, Shakespeare wished to keep a low profile. He seems to have been content to await political developments at a safe distance.

This is when Shakespeare took steps to create an existence for himself independent of patrons and public, of princes and populace alike. Having spent two years in the household of a Catholic nobleman in Lancashire (as an illegal teacher and protector of priests) and seven years on the Continent (working to assist the priests and lodging in monasteries), Shakespeare probably knew better than most that the Catholic English gentry offered protection to priests, and had even constructed special hiding rooms for them. The considerable and lucrative purchases of property he made in 1602 enabled him to be financially independent, and adopt a lifestyle almost similar to that of the gentry. The aforementioned small cottage in Chapel Lane may well have been intended for his gardener – as Chambers suggested – but this gardener appears to have had additional duties in Shakespeare's residence, as will be seen later (see p. 326).

On 7 February 1603, two years after the performance of *Richard II* in the Globe Theatre which was the prelude to the Essex uprising of 8 February 1601, Shakespeare made his comeback as London's star playwright, only six weeks before the death of the queen. When Elizabeth I died on 24 March 1603, many famous writers of the time honoured her with verses, but Shakespeare remained silent. Even the Earl of Oxford, who had been in poor health for some time, had lost his fortune and was living on a pension granted by the queen, composed at least some lines of prose. Elizabeth I had ruled in England for forty-four years, and Shakespeare's unprecedented career as a dramatist would hardly have been possible without the queen's love of the theatre. In contrast to his reaction after Essex's death, Shakespeare dedicated not a single line of verse to the dead queen, even when asked to do so. During this period, or at least towards its end, Shakespeare was probably working on *Troilus and Cressida*, one of his 'problem plays', which contains some echoes of *Hamlet*. He may also have started working on *Othello*, a tragedy about jealousy, in which, taken to extremes, the manipulation of feelings end in destruction and chaos.

OTHELLO

Othello was performed at Court on 1 November 1604 (All Saints Day). James VI of Scotland had been James I, King of England, for nineteen months. Shakespeare probably wrote the play early in 1604. He found the story of Christophero Moro and Disdemona [sic], which ends tragically due to the machinations of the scoundrel Alfiero, in a popular collection of tales called *Hecatommithi* by Giovanni Battista Giraldi, known as Cinthio. In Shakespeare's play, Moro became Othello, and Alfiero became Iago. The name changes are not without significance. Iago's name may have been derived from Santiago (St James). If the 'Sant' is removed, this leaves 'Iago'. Santiago de Compostela in the Spanish province of La Coruña, where the relics of St James the Great had been kept since the ninth century, was one the greatest places of pilgrimage in Europe and attracted many English Catholics. Robert Cecil employed a spy named Hans Owter to inform him of events there. Owter was paid 400 ducats a year. One ducat was then the equivalent of five shillings and six pence i.e. more than £100 a year. In a list of the names of Cecil's spies throughout Europe, including where they were stationed and the sums they were paid[256], Santiago is abbreviated to 'St. Jago'. Cecil drew up this document in early 1598, before his diplomatic voyage to France, on which he was joined by the Earl of Southampton, Shakespeare's patron. Elizabeth's First Minister did this in order to ensure that his spy network would function as usual in his absence.

Southampton probably never knew that one of his best friends, Sir Charles Danvers, who with his brother Sir Henry Danvers was also staying at the French Court, was discreetly spying for

Robert Cecil and informing him of events in Italy. In his list, Cecil notes that 'Sir Charles Danvers doth very discreetelye advertise mee of all Italien occurrents'. Charles Danvers must have been a double agent, however, since he was executed in 1601 as a member of the Essex Conspiracy.

One of Cecil's best informers and recruiters on the continent was Sir Horatio Palavicino (*c.*1540-1600), a rich Italian merchant from an aristocratic family[257] which had fallen out with the Pope. Palavicino worked for Walsingham, and later Robert Cecil. He emigrated to England, where he converted to Anglicanism and was knighted. In the eyes of all Catholics, not just English Catholics, Palavicino was a devil (Beelzebub) who had betrayed the Pope. The Protestants welcomed him, precisely because he had betrayed the 'Anti-Christ' (the Pope). Palavicino, however, was accused of other nefarious things by the Catholics. As early as 1578 he was active as a merchant in the part of the Netherlands that was allied with England, and in due course became a spy and intermediary between the opposing camps, with a hand in all sorts of dubious and dirty business. Working for Robert Cecil, Palavicino is thought to have supported the rebel O'Neill in Ireland by supplying him with victuals, in order to give strength to Essex's enemies. As a supporter of the Earl of Essex, Shakespeare must have been aware of these facts or rumours, and therefore it may well be that the character of Iago is based upon the Italian spy Palavicino. Until now, no convincing motive has been found for the extreme malice of this Shakespearian character. Shakespeare's Iago is possessed simply by the desire to do evil. Samuel Taylor Coleridge spoke of the 'motiveless malignity' of this character. By the time Shakespeare wrote *Othello*, Palavicino had been dead for four years.

It was already very clear by 1604, a year after ascending the throne, and one year before the Gunpowder Plot, that James I had no intention of honouring his earlier promise to improve conditions for his Catholic subjects. It cannot therefore be ruled out that the name of Shakespeare's character Iago is also meant as a reference to the new king's name. As early as the 1590s, English Catholics had referred to James of Scotland as 'St Diego' (see p. 131).

KING LEAR

Shakespeare's tragedy *King Lear*, which is, after *Hamlet*, his most important literary work, was performed before King James I and his family in the palace of Whitehall on Boxing Day 1606, also known as the Feast of Stephen, the great martyr. The protagonist of this tragedy is one of the most outstanding and archetypal figures of world theatre, and can be compared to the heroes of Greek tragedy and the Bible.

The play was first printed by Nathaniel Butter in 1608 in a quarto edition, and was sold in St Paul's Churchyard at the 'Pide' or 'Pied Bull'.

Shakespeare must have started writing *King Lear* in 1605. A hint to this effect is given in the play itself: in Act I, scene 2, Gloucester mentions both a solar and a lunar eclipse that had recently occurred. In fact, there were two such eclipses in September and October 1605.

Shakespeare's main source for *King Lear* was an old play about a King Leir, entered in the Stationers' Register in 1594, printed in May 1605, and entitled *The True Chronicle of King Leir and his three daughters, Gonerill, Ragan and Cordella.* Other important sources were Holinshed's *Chronicles*, Spenser's *Fairie Queene*; John Higgins' narrative poem in *The Mirror for Magistrates*; Sidney's *Arcadia*; and above all, one of Michel de Montaigne's (1533–1592) famous essays entitled *Apology for Raymond Sebonde*, translated by John Florio (*c.*1554–1625), as well as the true story of Sir Brian Annesley, and Samuel Harsnett's *A Declaration of Egregious Popish Impostures*.

In the sources used by Shakespeare, the story of King Lear and his daughters ends well. Cordelia does not die, at least not straight away. Holinshed's version states that 'This Cordeilla after hir father's deceasse ruled the land of

Britaine right worthily during the space of fiue yeeres, in which meane time hir husband died, and then about the end of those fiue yeeres, hir two nephews Margan and Cunedag, sonnes to hir aforesaid sisters, disdaining to be vnder the gouvernment of a woman, leuied warre against hir...'[258]. Cordelia is taken prisoner by them and takes her own life in prison.

Much has been written about the influence of Montaigne on Shakespeare[259]. The greatest similarity with Montaigne's work can be found in *Hamlet*, where as many as fifty-one parallels have been noted. In *King Lear* there are twenty-three similarities, and in *The Tempest* a further seven.

When Shakespeare wrote *King Lear*, he was living more or less in hiding in the house of the Huguenot family, the Mountjoys. On his desk he would have had the aforementioned sources, including Florio's 1603 translation of Montaigne's *Essays*, which includes *Raimond Sebonde*. Shakespeare's former patron, Southampton, had once accommodated Florio in his household, and it is possible that the Italian scholar had presented him with the book.

Montaigne's sceptical view of the world and people and his accurate observations, aphorisms and judgements made a deep impression on Shakespeare. The French philosopher's writings expressed exactly how the playwright must have felt after his bitter experiences of 1599, 1600, and above all 1601 as well as the disenchantment and disappointment that followed the change of government in 1603. Montaigne's remarks about religion were particularly relevant to Shakespeare. Until now, Shakespearian research has ignored the fact that, in *Raimond Sebonde*, the French philosopher had expressed disapproval and regret about the legally imposed change of religion in England, and thanked his creator that he himself by the grace of God had been enabled to adhere to the old forms of belief without fear and struggle of conscience. This and Montaigne's concrete references to the situation in neighbouring England must have been avidly read by Shakespeare as he lived under the roof of his Huguenot landlord Mountjoy, whose family regarded him highly. Shakespeare would have read in Montaigne: 'Nothing is more subject unto a continuall agitation then the laws'[260]. And furthermore:

> I have, since I was borne, seene those of our neighbours, the English-men, changed and re-changed three or foure times, not only in politike subjects, which is that some will dispense of constancy, but in the most important subject that possibly can be, that is to say, in religion: whereof I am so much the more ashamed, because it is a nation with which my countriemen have heretofore had so inward and familar acquaintance.[261]

In France, Montaigne wrote, he had observed that former capital offences were later made legal. Since in times of great change, anything was possible, the French philosopher feared that the adherents of the old religion might one day appear as offenders against earthly and divine majesty[262]. This was already the case in England. What answer did Montaigne have to this problem? Shakespeare must have been fascinated. Here was an author whose thoughts very much echoed his own. Hitherto, according to Montaigne, philosophy had no solution to offer, other than to obey the law, but this was no solution at all. He asks:

> What will Philosophie then say to us in this necessity? That we follow the lawes of our country, that is to say, this waveing sea of a peoples or of a Princes opinions, which shall paint me forth justice with as many colours, and reforme the same into as many visages as there are changes and alterations of passions in them.[263]

The following passage Shakespeare must have felt addressed him directly:

> I cannot have my judgement so flexible. What goodnesse is that which but yesterday I saw in credit and esteeme, and to morrow to have lost all reputation, and that the crossing of a river is made a crime?[264]

While Shakespeare must have fully agreed with Montaigne, he would have dismissed Harsnett's *A Declaration of Egregious Popish Impostures.* It is true that he adopted some names and parts of that text, but adapted them and used them for his own purpose. Harsnett was the government censor who, in 1599, approved Hayward's book about Henry IV, despite the fact that it contained a dedication to the Earl of Essex. This action almost landed him in prison. In 1603, he appeased the authorities by printing *A Declaration*, an anti-Catholic treatise which included a vehement attack on the Jesuit practice of exorcism. It is certain that Shakespeare read this treatise. Kenneth Muir, the English Shakespeare scholar, has identified numerous textual similarities between Harsnett and King Lear[265]. For example, in Act IV, scene 1, Shakespeare uses the same names that Harsnett used for the five devils who have possessed Edgar (disguised as Tom o'Bedlam):

> Five fiends have been in poor Tom at once; of lust,
> as Obidicut; Hobbididence, prince of dumbness;
> Mahu, of stealing; Modo, of murder;
> Flibbertigibbet, of mopping and mowing, who
> since possesses chambermaids and waiting-women.

At first sight, it would seem that Harsnett's treatise had an influence on Shakespeare. But, just as in Act IV, scene 3 of *Macbeth*, in which Malcolm, the eldest son and heir of King Duncan, accuses himself of terrible vices even though he is actually flawless, Edgar only pretends to be possessed by devils. In this very scene, he proves himself to be the guardian angel and protector of his blind father, Gloucester. His true thoughts and feelings are shared with the audience in the monologue at the start of Act IV, scene 1:

> Yet better thus, and known to be contemn'd,
> Than still contemn'd and flatter'd. To be worst,
> The lowest and most dejected thing of fortune...

Whereas Harsnett attacks and vilifies the Jesuits and Catholic clergymen working secretly in England, Shakespeare takes their part – though he does so indirectly, using hidden references in order to protect himself. The example of Edgar is to demonstrate their miserable and tragic situation in a way that inspires sympathy. His animal nakedness and his suffering are able to move the reader and/or the audience almost as much as the tragedy of the main character, King Lear.

Like the priests, Edgar is persecuted by the authorities, forced to disguise and conceal himself. Neither Edgar nor the priests were able to escape by sea from the official ports, as these were all under strict surveillance.

The Cinque Ports – Hastings, Hythe, Sandwich, Romney and Dover – had been administered since Norman times by a governor, the Lord Warden and Admiral of the Cinque Ports and Constable of Dover Castle, who was one of the most powerful figures in England. Until 1599 this was the tenth Lord Cobham, who was succeeded by his son, the eleventh Lord Cobham. The Cobhams kept an extremely close watch on the ports. No English subject, of whatever social class, and no foreign citizen could leave or enter England without a valid *laissez-passer*. In 1604, control of the Cinque Ports passed to Henry Howard, who had been created Earl of Northampton by King James I. Howard was a secret Catholic, but he had not only managed to come to terms with life under the rule of the new king; he had even forged a political career for himself. In 1608, Howard became Lord Privy Seal, and in 1612, Chancellor of Cambridge University. However, he was mistrusted by the Catholic population, particularly since he was a member of the jury who had found Henry Garnet, the Superior of the English Jesuits, guilty of high treason. It is unclear whether or not the strict harbour controls were relaxed for Catholics and fleeing priests under Howard's control. What is known, however, is that he was in the pay of Spain before 1613, and influenced James I's pro-Spanish policies.

The sealing and monitoring of the ports were measures introduced by the English government in order to try to halt the flow of English seminary priests into the country, which had greatly increased in the late 1570s. This measure was accompanied by the creation of an English international spy network under the control of Francis Walsingham. He was aided by Thomas Phelippes, a cryptographer who deciphered secret writings and codes; by Judge Young; Richard Topcliffe, the chief spy; and Norton, the master torturer[266]. The tight harbour controls were also intended to stop the flow of correspondence between the Papists, which was often smuggled in and out of the country through the Cinque ports[267].

The correspondence between Jesuits shows that for English Catholics-in-exile, particularly those conspiring with Spain and Ireland, the Welsh port of Milford Haven offered a chance of avoiding detection. It is significant that the characters in Shakespeare's later play *Cymbeline*, in particular the heroine Imogen, make their way to Milford Haven, and it is there that the arrival of Lucius from Rome is awaited in Act III, scene 4.

In his book, *Shakespeare's Religious Background* (1973), Peter Milward, SJ, an English Shakespeare scholar living in Japan, has already drawn attention to the similarity between the situation of Edgar in *King Lear* (Act II, scene 3) and the situation of Catholic priests in England during Shakespeare's time. According to Milward, the persecuted priests would also have been able to say:

> I heard myself proclaim'd;
> And by the happy hollow of a tree
> Escap'd the hunt. No port is free; no place
> That guard, and most unusual vigilance
> Does not attend my taking. Whiles I may scape
> I will preserve myself: and am bethought
> To take the basest and most poorest shape
> That ever penury in contempt of man
> Brought near to beast. My face I'll grime with filth,
> Blanket my loins, elf all my hair in knots,
> And with presented nakedness outface
> The winds and persecutions of the sky.
> [...] Poor Turlygod! poor Tom!
> That's something yet. Edgar I nothing am.

Close parallels are drawn with the plight of the Jesuit priests Edmund Campion and Robert Southwell. After Campion had come to England with Parsons and the other missionary priests in 1580, he wrote to the Father-General of the Jesuits, giving him the following description of his situation: 'I cannot long escape the hands of the heretics; the enemy has so many eyes, so many tongues, so many scouts and crafts. I am in apparel to myself very ridiculous; I often change my name also ... . Threatening edicts come forth against us daily.'[268] Fifteen years later, in a petition to Elizabeth I in 1595 entitled *An Humble Supplication to Her Maiestie*, Southwell, a distant cousin of William Shakespeare who had criticised *Venus and Adonis*, painted a shocking picture of the plight in which he and his fellow priests found themselves. Milward also justly believed that this petition provided Shakespeare with a model for the character of Edgar. Southwell wrote:

> We are made the common theme of every railing declaimer, abused without hope or means of remedy, by every wretch with most infamous names; no tongue so forsworn but it is of credit against us; none so true, but it is thought false in our defence .... So heavy is the hand of our superiors against us, that we generally are accounted men whom it is a credit to pursue, a disgrace to protect, a commodity to spoil, a gain to torture, and a glory to kill.[269]

Even if Shakespeare had not been a Catholic, he would probably still have spoken out on behalf of the 'poor afflicted', just as he spoke out on behalf of other minorities. The famous speech by Shylock in *The Merchant of Venice* demonstrates that the noble merchant Antonio and his fellow Christians in Venice (for which read London) do not act in a very Christian manner when they bombard him with insults; Antonio even spits on Shylock. Even in Shakespeare's early play *Love's Labour's Lost*, Shakespeare reprimands the nobles at the Court of Navarre (perhaps suggestive of the English Court) when they use an actor playing the part of Judas Maccabaeus to demonstrate their anger at Judas Iscariot.

The parallels between the events in *King Lear* and the political and religious reality of the Elizabethan and Jacobean ages are striking. The injustices, the evil machinations, the treachery, cruelty and death in this tragedy are clearly a reflection of life at the time of Shakespeare. Referring to a letter, written by Henry Garnet to Robert Parsons in 1594, Milward drew our attention to the notorious case of Thomas Fitzherbert, who offered £5,000 to Topcliffe, the equally infamous government spy, to hunt down Fitzherbert's own father and uncle ruthlessly, and persecute them to death[270].

Many aspects of *King Lear* which hitherto have remained obscure, or which have previously defied interpretation, acquire clearer contours and, in many cases, even a new and different meaning when viewed against the actual context of contemporary history and the extremely harsh conditions under which Shakespeare as an adherent of the old faith had to live and work. Above all, it becomes apparent why and how the playwright developed so great a sympathy for human suffering, and such immense sensitivity to what human beings are capable of doing to each other.

MACBETH

'Fair is foul and foul is fair'. This memorable chiasmus, pronounced at the end of the first scene of *Macbeth*, is not only the *leitmotif* of Shakespeare's darkest tragedy, it is also the central message, criticising, as it seems, the period and the government. In the Middle Ages and the early modern period, the words 'fair' and 'foul' carried religious connotations, and these concepts are both central to *Macbeth*, a work that has at its core the concerns of a medieval morality play.

In *Macbeth*, Shakespeare depicts a character who sells his soul to gain a crown, but – unlike in morality plays – he is not redeemed or rescued at the end by the grace of God. Shakespeare bases the story on Holinshed's *Chronicles*, published in 1577. His protagonist, the eponymous medieval Scottish king, is initially honourable and courageous, heroic, and worthy of the title and honours heaped upon him by King Duncan. During the course of the play, Macbeth – under the influence of the witches, the powers of darkness (in the biblical sense) – becomes a cold-blooded, murdering monster, a tyrant who steps over corpses, orders the killing of innocent women and children, and behaves like the spawn of the devil.

At the play's end, Macbeth is a man devoid of all human feelings. At the start he is close to his wife, with whom he shares his joy at the honours and the advancement he achieves (see Act I, scene 5). But later, when news comes that his wife is dead, his reaction is almost one of indifference. Her death is an inconvenience to him and he states laconically that 'she should have died hereafter'. Imprisoned within the hell that is himself, Macbeth broods upon his utterly meaningless life. What eventually awaits him is not mercy and redemption – as in a morality play – but nothingness:

MACBETH
I have almost forgot the taste of fears.
The time has been my senses would have cool'd
To hear a night-shriek, and my fell of hair
Would at a dismal treatise rouse and stir
As life were in't. I have supp'd full with horrors;
Direness, familiar to my slaughterous thoughts,
Cannot once start me.

[*Re-enter* SEYTON]

Wherefore was that cry?

SEYTON
The Queen, my lord, is dead.

MACBETH
She should have died hereafter;
There would have been a time for such a word.
To-morrow, and to-morrow, and to-morrow,

Creeps in this petty pace from day to day
To the last syllable of recorded time,
And all our yesterdays have lighted fools
The way to dusty death. Out, out, brief candle!
Life's but a walking shadow, a poor player
That struts and frets his hour upon the stage,
And then is heard no more: it is a tale
Told by an idiot, full of sound and fury,
Signifying nothing.

(Act V, scene 5)

Many Shakespeare scholars regard as a *non sequitur* the transformation of the main character from a courageous and virtuous hero, richly rewarded by his king, into a regicide and a heartless, murderous tyrant who knows perfectly well that his evil actions will cost him the most precious thing he possesses: his soul.

As with *Hamlet*, the key to this hitherto unsolved problem lies in the events of the time. If *Hamlet* is Shakespeare's response to the events of early 1601, then *Macbeth* could be seen as his perception of England at the start of the reign of James I. Previous research has shown that there are a number of indications that the play was written in 1606, one year after the Gunpowder Plot.

Since it was very dangerous to make critical allusions to living people, and especially to the king himself, it is no surprise that Shakespeare couches them very subtly. An example can be found in the speech of the drunken Porter (Act II, scene 3), who enjoys a kind of jester's licence to do as he pleases; Shakespeare could therefore not be held accountable for the sometimes confused statements of this character. The Porter breaks the news that a farmer has hanged himself because he was expecting a good harvest. Edmund Malone, the eighteenth-century Irish Shakespeare scholar, was the first to point out that this is a reference to the wheat glut of 1606, when the price of wheat fell drastically. This particularly threatened the existence of small-scale farmers. Shakespeare was a landowner, and would also have been affected by the low price of wheat. In 1602, the playwright had purchased a large tract of land in Stratford, and on 24 July 1605 he procured the right to levy tithes on lands in neighbouring villages for £440: in Old Stratford, Welcombe, and Bishopton. In a year of normal harvests, these rights would have provided an income of about £60. This indirect reference to the low wheat prices in 1606 and their devastating consequences for small-scale English farmers reveal that *Macbeth* was, in all probability, written in this year.

The repeated references to the terms 'equivocator' or 'equivocate' must – as has long been thought – also refer to an event of 1606, namely the great show trial of Henry Garnet, the Superior of the English Jesuits, who was accused of high treason and participation in the Gunpowder Plot. The accusations against Garnet included 'equivocation', the act of concealing or remaining silent about certain facts, or of expressing oneself ambiguously. There was much public discussion which particularly centred on this point at the time. Garnet stated that he and others had the right to answer with ambiguous or veiled remarks, if the questions were aimed at delving into one's thoughts. This highly topical reference can be found in Act II, scene 3, where the Porter's ramblings in fact refer to the main action of the play, in which the host Macbeth, spurred on by Lady Macbeth, has just murdered his sovereign lord, the king ('I have done the deed' – Act II, scene 2). Since the drunken porter sees himself as the porter of hell-gate or of the devil, who speaks in the name of Beelzebub, then the murderer's castle must be the true site of hell, where 'Beelzebub' (i.e. Macbeth) and the 'other devil' (i.e. Lady Macbeth) reside:

PORTER
Here's a knocking indeed! If a man were porter
of hell-gate, he should have old turning the key.

[*Knock*]

Knock, knock, knock! Who's there, i' th' name
of Beelzebub? ...

> Knock, knock! Who's there, in the other devil's name? Faith, here's an equivocator, that could swear in both the scales against either scale; who committed treason enough for God's sake, yet could not equivocate to heaven: O, come in, equivocator. ... Knock, knock; never at quiet! What are you?
> But this place is too cold for hell. I'll devil-porter it no further.

Shakespeare's text, too, is ambiguous in some places. The Porter refers to the 'equivocator' (i.e. Garnet), who committed his 'treason' 'for God's sake'. Shakespeare thereby obviously implies that the Jesuit did all of this for his faith. Hence the line 'Yet [he – Garnet] could not equivocate to heaven' could carry the meaning that the Superior of the English Jesuits 'could not compromise with heaven', i.e. could not in the end renounce his Catholic faith to save his life[271]. On the other hand this line could also have slightly negative connotations, indicating that the playwright did not fully approve of Garnet's language or actions. It is recorded that Garnet's executioner believed that, at the last moment, the Jesuit priest was hoping for a royal intervention and a pardon. This would also have been witnessed by the crowd. It was surely observed by the Catholics who were present. As shown by Jesuit writings, they came to be blessed by the condemned priests, whom they worshipped as martyrs even before their execution. After their deaths, they would collect relics of the dead priests or dipped their cloths in their blood. It is possible that Shakespeare had such scenes in mind when, in Act II, scene 2 of *Julius Caesar*, he had Decius interpreting Calpurnia's dream of Caesar's death as a positive sign of renewal, and predicting that 'great men shall press / For tinctures, stains, relics, and cognizance'. It was not just members of the lower and middle classes who attended the executions of Catholic priests in London; there is historical evidence that nobles also attended these events, for the same reasons. Even a French ambassador in London who – according to contemporary sources – often travelled in his coach down what is today Oxford Street to the place of execution at Tyburn, now Marble Arch, in order to be blessed by the priests who died a martyr's death.

It may well be that Shakespeare – like many other English Catholics – attended Garnet's execution on 3 May 1606, especially since it did not take place outside the city, at Tyburn, but on a scaffold erected in front of St Paul's Cathedral, quite close to where he lived in Silver Street. In his work Shakespeare always placed a great deal of importance on death scenes and the medieval concept of *ars moriendi* (the art of dying)[272]. In *Macbeth* (Act I, scene 4), Malcolm, on the basis of information from an eyewitness of the execution of a traitor, states that: 'nothing in his life / Became him like the leaving it; he died / As one that had been studied in his death / To throw away the dearest thing he owed, /As 'twere a careless trifle'. The eyewitnesses of Garnet's execution and those who heard about it at secondhand would have found precisely this *ars moriendi* lacking in the way he met his death (see p. 275). Shakespeare may have had this in mind when he wrote that he (Garnet) 'could not equivocate to heaven'.

The connections of *Macbeth* with the Gunpowder Plot (1605) and Garnet's trial (1606) have been mentioned and used by past Shakespeare scholars mainly to date the play. It seems to have been overlooked that this tragedy – from the Catholic point of view of the playwright – contains numerous, albeit allegorically veiled references to the precarious political and religious situation in England in the early reign of King James I. Shakespeare's inspiration for the character of Macbeth was – as it appears – not so much the historical figure of the medieval Scottish king, as James I himself.

It has of course not been lost on commentators that in *Macbeth*, Shakespeare probably made use of a Scottish historical theme precisely because a Scottish king had succeeded Elizabeth to the English throne. It has even been mooted that Shakespeare wrote the play as a tribute to James I, not only because it concerned Scottish history, but because the play broached the subject of witchcraft. James I was known to be fascinated by witchcraft, and had even written a book about it.

In the 1590s, as mentioned before, many of Elizabeth I's subjects – Essex and his followers, but also a great part of the Catholic English population – looked to the Scottish king with hope and expectation, thinking that James would relieve their plight. They were soon disappointed. The king's proclamations that the anti-Catholic penal laws would remain unchanged were in stark contrast to his earlier statements. The secret Catholics in England, the Catholics-in-exile and even the powers in Rome, accused James of breaking his word and of treachery. There was much anger, particularly among the sons of the Catholic gentry in the Midlands who had suffered particularly badly under the anti-Catholic legislation and had sustained great financial losses. A little over two years after James I's coronation, their pent-up fury was vented in the Gunpowder Plot, which very nearly became the most devastating act of assassination in English history. As a result of the Gunpowder Plot, official anti-Catholic measures became even more draconian. The Catholics must have regarded James I as a fallen angel, as Lucifer himself. Within a very short period, their plight became even worse than it had been under Elizabeth I. It is telling that the Catholic conspirator, Guy Fawkes, used words very similar to those used in *Hamlet* to justify his actions. At his trial, Fawkes said: 'a dangerous disease required a desperate remedy'[273], thus apparently echoing the words of Claudius in *Hamlet* which may have been a reference to the Essex rebellion: 'Diseases desperate grown / By desperate appliance are relieved / Or not at all' (Act IV, scene 3). Under James I, pro-government dramatists were deployed even more effectively than under Elizabeth to write plays about contemporary history favourable to the Protestant authorities. An entry in the Stationers' Register dated 20 April 1607 records the printing of Thomas Dekker's allegorical play *The Whore of Babylon*, in which the virtues of Elizabeth I are praised and the 'scarlet whore of Rome' is accused of treachery and bloodshed. Leading figures from the Elizabethan age were represented in the play, including Edmund Campion – portrayed, however, from a Protestant point of view. Much to Dekker's irritation actors who did not like the content of the plays 'ruined' the lines and altered their meanings. The accuracy of the historical content of his plays was closely examined by critics. They accused him of having falsified his historical account of the Elizabethan age. Dekker's defence was to claim that he was writing as a dramatist, not as a historian[274].

These increasing religious-political tensions are also the context of Shakespeare's tragedy *Macbeth*, written, as it appears, one year earlier, at a time when playwrights were virtually being recruited by the Court to spread Protestant propaganda. If Dekker's allegorical drama *The Whore of Babylon* can be regarded as toeing the government's anti-Papist line, then Shakespeare's Scottish play – on closer inspection – contains strong hidden criticism of the tougher religious policies under the new monarch, resulting in the deepening of the gulf between Protestants and Catholics.

In *Macbeth*, the protagonist is initially a hero and brilliant military leader, but becomes the very embodiment of evil. 'There's no art / To find the mind's construction in the face: / He was a gentleman on whom I built / An absolute trust.' These words of King Duncan in Act I, scene 4 refer to a remorseful traitor who has been executed. Ironically and tragically, the truth of his words is confirmed in the course of the play, since they also apply to Macbeth, who at this point is honoured and favoured by Duncan, but who will later murder him. Is Shakespeare – as a former Essex supporter – also writing these words on behalf of the Earl of Essex, so to speak, to remind his Catholic audience of the trust that Essex and those who followed him placed in James of Scotland, a trust which later proved to be misplaced?

There can be no doubt that in *Macbeth* Shakespeare reaches the culmination of the representation of evil in his work. The play also marks the end of a creative period against a background which Shakespeare and his Catholic contemporaries must have regarded as dark and absolutely hopeless, as can be proved by numerous historical facts (see. pp. 271–278). Shakespeare's *Macbeth* closes the series of four great tragedies. After *Macbeth*, the playwright wrote only dark and bitter tragicomedies or problem plays, until, it seems, another turning point in his life fundamentally altered the tone of his work yet again.

PROBLEM PLAYS

TROILUS AND CRESSIDA

The first documentary evidence for Shakespeare's problem play *Troilus and Cressida* is an entry by James Roberts in the Stationers' Register, dated 7 February 1603. As with *Henry V*, this seems to be a 'blocking entry', intended as a precautionary measure. Roughly six months earlier, Shakespeare's *Hamlet* was entered in the same register, also by Roberts, with the same intention. Next to the entry is written 'as yt is acted by my lord chamberlen's Men'; but this must have been a routine addition, as there is no evidence to indicate that the play was performed by the Chamberlain's Men at this time. The play did not appear in print until 1609, in a Quarto edition, and was next reprinted in 1623 in the First Folio Edition. Shakespeare's sonnets were also published in 1609 (*Fig. 126*). There is a connection between these two publications: both works could be a message to the Earl and Countess of Southampton. In the sonnets, the 'Dark Lady' (i.e. Elizabeth Wriothesley, née Vernon) is unfaithful to the 'Speaker' (i.e. the poet), and the central theme of the problem play *Troilus and Cressida* is the infidelity of the heroine.

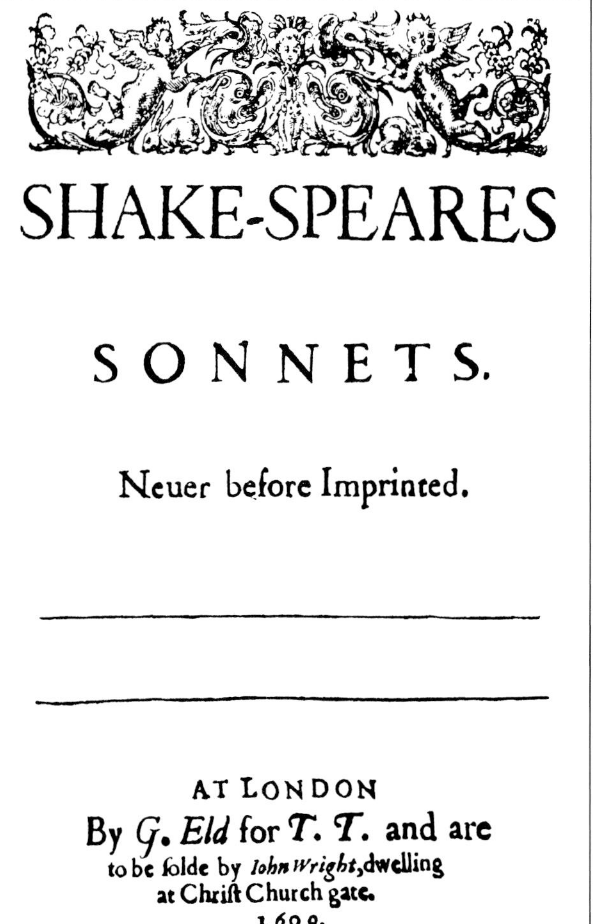

SHAKE-SPEARES

SONNETS.

Neuer before Imprinted.

AT LONDON

By *G. Eld* for *T. T.* and are
to be folde by *Iohn Wright*, dwelling
at Chrift Church gate.
1609.

Fig. 126 – Title page of the first edition of Shakespeare's sonnets from the year 1609. They were apparently published by the author himself, one year after the death of his mother.

Something highly unusual happened during the printing of the Quarto edition of *Troilus and Cressida*. The title page of the play was mysteriously altered. The (adjusted) words 'As it was acted by the Kings Maiesties seruants at the Globe' were removed and replaced by the text: 'Excellently expressing the beginning of their [Troylus' and Cresseid's] louves [...].' The play also begins with a most remarkable address to the reader entitled 'A neuer writer, to an euer reader. Newes' [A never writer to an ever reader. News]. No one but Shakespeare could have written this, as no one else would have had the right and freedom to interfere with the printing process and insert this correction. And a correction was necessary, because *Troilus and Cressida* had never actually been performed by Shakespeare's theatre company, the King's Men. What is more, the preface to the play implied that this was a new work which had never been seen on stage and so had never been applauded. The astonished reader is told, furthermore, that when the author is gone and his plays are no longer available, people will 'scramble for them'. He also writes that 'a new English Inquisition' will begin. By 'inquisition', the writer seems to be referring to censorship. The exact wording is:

> Eternal reader, you haue heere a new play, neuer stal'd with the Stage, neuer clapper-clawed with the palmes of the vulger ... And beleeue this, that when hee [Shakespeare] is gone, and his Commedies out of sale, you will scramble for them, and set vp a new English Inquisition. ... Vale.

This unusually direct address to the reader bears no signature or initials, but ends with the Latin salutation '*Vale*' (farewell), and could also only have been written by and printed with the approval of the writer.

These facts – and the play itself – have understandably presented an incomprehensible puzzle to Shakespeare scholars which again – as it appears – can only be solved by considering the historical and biographical context in which the play was written. Shakespeare began *Hamlet* in 1601 as a literary monument to the Earl of Essex, who was executed in February of that year, and he obviously completed the play in the first half of 1602. Between 1601 and 1603, Shakespeare withdrew from public view, and did not publish any new works. *Troilus and Cressida* must have been the first play written by Shakespeare after this period of silence.

Shakespeare probably wrote the play weeks or months before it was entered in the Stationer's Register. The fact that it was neither printed nor performed means that Shakespeare deliberately withheld it from his audience, and in particular the queen. *Hamlet*, Shakespeare's grand 'obituary' to Essex, would therefore have been the last work by the playwright that Queen Elizabeth I could have seen or read. It is also possible, however, that the queen never saw *Hamlet* as there is no record that it was ever performed at Court.

Shakespeare's theatre company, too, were masters of evasiveness. His actors would not give private performances, even to powerful senior statesmen, if they hated them because of their political or religious views – as Robert Cecil, the most powerful man in the Privy Council, learned to his cost when he tried to hire the Chamberlain's Men to perform a play for important guests at his private residence. The actors were nowhere to be found, and Cecil only managed to track down Richard Burbage. The Chamberlain's Men were obviously engaged in passive resistance.

Troilus and Cressida has many thematic similarities to *Hamlet*. In Act III, scene 1 of *Hamlet*, the prince reprimands Ophelia and accuses women of promiscuity, perversion and depravity, and the passage can be interpreted in the light of the hurt feelings experienced by Shakespeare in 1598 when his mistress Elizabeth Vernon, who was heavily pregnant with his child, married the Earl of Southampton, his patron and friend[275]. These themes, and especially infidelity, are taken even further in *Troilus and Cressida*. In Act V, scene 2, the Trojan Troilus witnesses Cressida's infidelity, which might be another reference to the infidelity of Shakespeare's own mistress, whom he immortalised in his sonnets about the Dark Lady. Troilus can only watch as Cressida deceives him and passes a love token that she herself received from him (Troilus) on to his Greek rival Diomedes.

Shakespeare found this negative image of the world of the Greeks and Trojans among his medieval and early modern sources. In the poem *The Testament of Cresseid* by Robert Henryson (also known as Henderson: *c.* 1425 – *c.* 1500), published in 1593, Cresseid is a victim of leprosy when she meets Troilus for the last time. In Shakespeare's time, this image would have had even more negative connotations. It is significant and informative that Shakespeare is here reflecting the political circumstances of the time. This sheds light on the meaning of Ulysses' speech in Act I, scene 3, which has always been taken to echo the author's own opinion:

O, when degree is shak'd,
Which is the ladder to all high designs,
The enterprise is sick! How could communities,
Degrees in schools and brotherhoods in cities,
Peaceful commerce from dividable shores,
The primogenity and due of birth,
Prerogative of age, crowns, sceptres, laurels,
But by degree, stand in authentic place?
Take but degree away, untune that string,
And, hark, what discord follows!

If this speech refers to the Essex rebellion, in which Southampton played a significant role, then Shakespeare cannot have supported Essex's attempt to make the citizens of London rise up against the government, the act which finally brought about his downfall. This does not mean, however, that the poet had abandoned his hero. Both *The Phoenix and the Turtle* and, in particular, *Hamlet* demonstrate how sincerely Shakespeare mourned his dead leader.

In her book *Shakespeare's Imagery and what it tells us* (1935), Caroline Spurgeon explains how *Hamlet* and *Troilus and Cressida* contain very similar imagery, both being notable for their repeated, accurate descriptions of the disease, rot and decay in the body politic. She notes that the two plays were written very close together in terms of time and mirror the suffering, pain, disillusionment, horror, and feeling that nature itself is out of joint that Shakespeare must have felt as he wrote these plays. The intensity of the emotions is fiercer here than in any other of his works[276].

The events of Shakespeare's private life explain why the sonnets, in which he describes the highly passionate love triangle between the Speaker, the Dark Lady and the Friend, were published in the same year as *Troilus and Cressida* – and a year after the death of Mary Shakespeare, William's mother. When Shakespeare writes '*Vale*' in *Troilus and Cressida*, the forty-five-year-old poet is saying farewell and drawing a definitive line under this relationship. It was at about this time that Southampton converted to Protestantism, in acknowledgement of the favours that James I had granted him. The Catholics were bitter about this decision, and Shakespeare surely felt it more keenly than anybody.

MEASURE FOR MEASURE

A record from the Revels Office, the office responsible for performances and festivities, reveals that *Measure for Measure* was performed on St Stephen's Day (26 December) 1604 at Court. The text contains references to the peace negotiations between England and Spain which were held between 9 and 27 August 1604 in Somerset House in London. These negotiations ended the war fought by England and the Protestant Netherlands against Spain which had begun in 1585. These clues, and the fact that the theatres were closed until April 1604 after the serious outbreak of Plague in 1603, strongly suggest that *Measure for Measure* was premièred between August and December 1604. It is, however, possible that Shakespeare began writing the play early in 1604, probably immediately after he had finished *Othello*. His main source was the two-part play *Promos and Cassandra* by George Whetstone, who himself found the story in Giovanni Battista Giraldi Cinzio's collection of tales called *Hecatommithi* (1565) and who used the plot once again in prose romances *Heptameron of Civil Discourses* (1582).

More than any other of Shakespeare's problem plays, *Measure for Measure* interweaves the tragic, comedic and satirical elements of tragicomedy. The structure and much of its content demonstrate how deeply Shakespeare must have been involved in the Catholic underground movement. With the exception of *Hamlet*, Catholic concepts are more overtly stated in this play than in any other of Shakespeare's dramas. It was because of this, no doubt, that the play posed problems for many of Shakespeare's critics in earlier times. For Samuel Taylor Coleridge (1772-1834), the English poet, critic and philosopher, the escape of Angelo the villain at the end of the play was an offence to his sense of justice[277]. The fact that he is even shown compassion and forgiveness so enraged the poet Algernon Charles Swinburne (1837-1909) that he exclaimed that justice had been dealt a blow; it had been ravished, insulted, and struck in the face[278].

Deviating from his source, Shakespeare sets the play in Vienna, under the rule of a duke. Individual scenes take place in Court, a brothel, a monastery, and a prison.

The heroine's name is Isabella, a name which, for many reasons, was very meaningful to Shakespeare. Isabella was the name of the wife of Archduke Albert, who became governor of the Spanish Netherlands in 1596. Thomas Platter's travel writings contain a sketch of a pyramidal structure in which the name Isabella appears three times, alongside the names Carolus, Philippus and Albertus. Prominent Spanish and French (Catholic) queens were called Isabella. Before the Dissolution of the Monasteries by Henry VIII, there was a convent in Wroxall, north of Stratford, the name of the prioress in the early sixteenth century being Isabella Shakespeare. She seems to have been a relative of John Shakespeare's Wroxall ancestors[279].

The novice Isabella in *Measure for Measure* desires nothing more than to be accepted into the Order of Saint Clare, and is regarded as a saint even by the roughest and most corrupt of her fellow men. In Act I, scene 4, Lucio gives this description of her:

> I hold you as a thing ensky'd and sainted.
> By your renouncement an immortal spirit,
> And to be talk'd with in sincerity,
> As with a saint.

As pointed out by R.W. Chambers in *Man's Unconquerable Mind* (1939), Isabella herself uses expressions which give her the aura of a Christ-like martyr. She explains to Angelo in Act II, scene 4:

> ... were I under the terms of death
> The impression of keen whips I'ld wear as rubies,
> And strip myself to death as to a bed
> That longing have been sick for, ere I'ld yield
> My body up to shame.

These words are reminiscent of the numerous Catholic priests and clergymen, often very young men who had just completed their divinity studies and had been ordained, who when captured by government agents refused to renounce their faith, preferring a martyr's death. Whereas in *Hamlet* the hero sarcastically tells Ophelia to 'get thee to a nunnery' (Act III, scene 1) – a nunnery at this time could also mean a brothel – Isabella describes convent life as almost idyllic:

> But with true prayers
> That shall be up at heaven and enter there
> Ere sun-rise, prayers from preserved souls,
> From fasting maids whose minds are dedicate
> To nothing temporal.
>
> (Act II, scene 2)

When Shakespeare – perhaps in his study above the shop of the Huguenot hairdresser Mountjoy, in Silver Street in the shadow of St Olave's Church – wrote these words for his heroine, he could have been recalling an event from a few years earlier, which caused a sensation in Catholic circles of the time. On 20 November 1599, reports reached London that an English convent for the genteel class of woman, eventually housing sixteen nuns, had been founded in Brussels[280]. The founding of the convent had been made possible by the previously mentioned Archduke Albert of Austria (1559-1621). He gave the English nuns £2,000 to enable them to buy a building.

On 4 November, the daughter of Sir John Berkeley, sister of Sir Nicholas Pointz, was appointed abbess by the Archbishop of Malines (Mecheln) and invested in a grand ceremony. On the following Sunday, Lady Mary Percy, Mistress Dorothy Arundell and six other noble English ladies were also invested. Dorothy Arundell was probably a relative of Thomas Arundell, the Catholic brother-in-law of Shakespeare's patron, the third Earl of Southampton, who was also a Catholic. Shakespeare may well have learned of this grand opening of an English convent in Flanders through a private source – namely through his patron and/or his wife with whom in 1600 the poet still must have had very close contact (*Figs. 85 a–b*).

This grand ceremony began early in the morning and lasted until two in the afternoon, and was attended by the Infanta and the Archduke, the entire Court and the Papal Nuncio. The eight English nuns were decorated with jewels and dressed like brides, and were led into the church by the Infanta and other ladies of high standing. At the end of the festivities, the Infanta, who had acted as sponsor for the sisters, embraced each one of them. The ceremony culminated in a banquet for a hundred people, hosted by the Infanta. According to contemporary accounts, this ceremony was the grandest in a hundred years. It is not difficult to see the thematic connection with Shakespeare's heroine Isabella, who is set on becoming a nun – an option no longer available in Shakespeare's England – before she is obliged to accept the hand of the duke.

The character of Isabella in *Measure for Measure* has been much criticised. In *The Jacobean Drama* (1936), the Marlowe and Shakespeare scholar Una Ellis-Fermor holds that Isabella is the personification of pitiless, unimaginative and self-obsessed virtue.

Angelo's name alone is suggestive of his character, that of an unblemished hero. He is chosen by the duke to preside over government affairs while he himself is away.

As the duke's representative, Angelo ensures that the rules and laws are strictly obeyed in order to eradicate loose customs in Vienna, especially sexual offences. He closes the brothels and sentences to death the young gentleman, Claudio, whose betrothed is with child by him. The famous chiasmus in *Macbeth*, 'Fair is foul and foul is fair', might well refer to Angelo. He is captivated by the virtuous novice Isabella, who has come to his house to plead for her brother's life. Angelo offers to spare Claudio in exchange for Isabella's virginity (see Act II, scene 4). From Isabella's point of view, this would mean eternal damnation, and she recognises her hopeless situation as a woman: 'To whom should I complain? Did I tell this, / Who would believe me?' She knows that she is powerless against the slanderous account of events that Angelo will give, and Angelo is confident in the success of his villainous plan:

> Who will believe thee, Isabel?
> My unsoil'd name, the austereness of my life,
> My vouch against you, and my place i' the state,
> Will so your accusation overweigh,
> That you shall stifle in your own report.

Slander and false witness – mainly by informants and government spies – were very common in trials against Catholic priests. In Sonnet 125, Shakespeare makes a clear and unmistakeable reference to the hated informants: 'Hence, thou suborn'd informer! a true soul, / When most impeach'd stands least in thy control.'

Faced with his imminent execution, Claudio pleads with his sister to accept Angelo's offer and thus save his life, and his description of life after death contains several concepts from Catholic doctrine (rivers of fire, by which he means purgatory, wailing and deepest hell). This speech is also reminiscent of Hamlet's famous monologue in Act III, scene 1 ('To be or not to be'), and of Hamlet's fear of 'something after death', his fear of the 'undiscover'd country, from whose bourn / No traveller returns', as a result of which he would prefer 'those ills we have', than to 'fly to others that we know not of':

CLAUDIO
Ay, but to die, and go we know not where;
To lie in cold obstruction and to rot;
This sensible warm motion to become
A kneaded clod; and the delighted spirit
To bathe in fiery floods, or to reside
In thrilling region of thick-ribbed ice;
To be imprison'd in the viewless winds,
And blown with restless violence round about
The pendent world; or to be worse than worst
Of those that lawless and incertain thought
Imagine howling: 'tis too horrible!
The weariest and most loathed worldly life
That age, ache, penury and imprisonment
Can lay on nature is a paradise
To what we fear of death.

Isabella makes it clear to her brother that she could never do what Angelo has asked of her. She reprimands Claudio and even accuses him of fornication, suggesting that it would be best if he died quickly:

O, fie, fie, fie!
Thy sin's not accidental, but a trade.
Mercy to thee would prove itself a bawd:
'Tis best thou diest quickly.

The situation seems hopeless, but the audience and the reader know that the duke has not really left the city, but is instead secretly observing and guiding events. In order to remain undetected, he has disguised himself as a monk named Lodowick. In Shakespeare's time there were officially no monks or priests in England. Before the Dissolution of the Monasteries by Henry VIII, monks, monasteries and abbey-churches had been very common, particularly in London. In the Elizabethan and Jacobean ages, the only places in which monks and nuns could be found were in hiding or in prison. Yet monks play an important role in many of Shakespeare's dramas. The playwright brings them to the stage because they were banned in real life, and in so doing he reminds the audience of their existence and provides a tribute to them. In Sonnet 70, the narrator, engulfed in a bitter autumn wind, mourns the ruins of the monastery chancel, 'bare ruin'd choirs where late the sweet birds sang'; 'birds' refers to the monks. In Shakespeare's plays, monks appear as advisors to those in need and in danger. They are wise and knowledgeable, charitable, sympathetic, understanding and generous. They can help and guide the way when the situation looks hopeless and conflicts seem to defy resolution. The English vernacular of the time contained many derogatory terms applied to members of monastic orders – for example the rhyme 'a friar a liar' – but none of these expressions can be found in Shakespeare's works.

In *As You Like It*, when the usurper is already marching on the community-in-exile in the Forest of Arden (Ardennes), bent on destroying it, it is an old religious man (i.e. a monk or friar) who converts him and, in a long speech, even persuades him to restore the dukedom to his brother, the rightful ruler. The usurper then enters a monastery himself. In *Romeo and Juliet*, Friar Lawrence's plan is initially helpful, but goes disastrously wrong because of one unpredictable detail. In *Measure for Measure*, the duke, disguised as Friar Lodowick, saves the situation at the last minute by showing Isabella a way out and saving Claudio from death. In the end, the duke reveals himself and – in a gesture of forgiveness – shows mercy rather than following the letter of the law. He even shows mercy to Angelo, who has committed so many evil deeds.

ALL'S WELL THAT ENDS WELL

The text of *All's Well That Ends Well* first appeared in the Folio edition of 1623. There is no entry for the play in the Stationers' Register, but it is possible to determine approximately when the play was written. It is commonly thought that

Shakespeare wrote the part of the clown Lavache for Robert Armin (*c.* 1568–1615), a new comic actor in his company. Armin was the successor to William Kempe, who left the Chamberlain's Men in 1599, so the play could not have been written before 1599. The play also contains many thematic, linguistic and structural similarities to *Measure for Measure*, and the two plays also have somewhat similar characters. These facts have led to broad agreement that *All's Well* was written at about the same period as *Measure for Measure*. The latter, however, was probably created somewhat earlier.

At this time, Shakespeare would surely have been unable to write a light-hearted comedy such as those he wrote in the 1590s before the downfall of his hero, the Earl of Essex, and his politics of religious tolerance. He took Boccaccio's amusing story about Beltramo de Rossiglione and Giglietta de Narbone, and transformed it into a 'dark comedy' or 'problem play', featuring the characters of Bertram and Helena.

Helena is the orphaned daughter of the famous doctor Gerard de Narbon, who is brought up in the household of the Countess of Rousillon. She loves the young Count Bertram, the son of her foster mother, but is in despair, believing he is beyond her reach because of the difference in their status. When Bertram moves to Court as the ward of the ailing King of France, Helena follows him. She has acquired some medical knowledge from her father, and assures the king that she can heal his festering wound. As a reward, Helena is permitted to choose a husband from among the young men in the Court. When the king is restored to full health by Helena's treatment, she chooses Bertram as her husband, but he protests forcefully. So as not to anger the king, he eventually agrees to the match, but directly after the marriage he secretly travels to Florence with his friends.

The determined young woman then disguises herself as a pilgrim, and makes a pilgrimage to the shrine of St James, which astonishingly in this play is to be found in Florence! Shakespeare is clearly referring to James the Apostle and martyr, also known as James the Great – Shakespeare calls him 'Saint Jaques le Grand' – whose shrine is in the Spanish town of Santiago de Compostela. By alluding to this Catholic pilgrim city, situated in the land of England's greatest enemy (Spain), Shakespeare risked attracting the attention of the censors, and could have been interrogated and imprisoned, like many writers before him, the more so since Santiago de Compostela was on Robert Cecil's list of places to be spied on (see p. 253). To protect himself, Shakespeare pretends that the shrine is in Florence where, in fact, there were two ancient churches dedicated to St James, San Jacopo tra i Fossi in the Via dei Benci, and San Jacopo Sopr' Arno. It is, however, unlikely that Shakespeare is referring to either of these churches, since there was no shrine to 'Saint Jaques le Grand' in the city.

The situation in which the 'pilgrim' Helena finds herself in Act III, scene 5 is described very realistically, and suggests that Shakespeare himself – perhaps during the 'lost years' (1585-1592) – found himself in a similar situation when travelling to Rome. Outside the city walls, Helena meets some female Florentines, one of them a widow who is also a landlady who offers accommodation to pilgrims, approaching them at the city gates. She is accompanied by her daughter Diana, and her friends Violenta and Marianne. Helena soon discovers that Bertram has declared his love for Diana, which she does not reciprocate:

> WIDOW
> Look, here comes a pilgrim: I know she will lie
> at my house; thither they send one another: I'll
> question her. God save you, pilgrim! whither are
> you bound?
>
> HELENA
> To Saint Jaques le Grand.
> Where do the palmers lodge, I do beseech you?

WIDOW
At the Saint Francis here beside the port.

HELENA
Is this the way?

WIDOW
Ay, marry, is't.

[A march afar]

Hark you! they [Bertram and the French nobles] come this way.
If you will tarry, holy pilgrim,
But till the troops come by,
I will conduct you where you shall be lodged;
The rather, for I think I know your hostess
As ample as myself.

HELENA
Is it yourself?

WIDOW
If you shall please so, pilgrim.

As soon as Bertram and his attendants have paraded past the women with their drums and flags, the widow quickly returns to her offer:

Come, pilgrim, I will bring you
Where you shall host: of enjoin'd penitents
There's four or five, to great Saint Jaques bound,
Already at my house.

Once again, Shakespeare makes it clear that he is referring to the shrine of St James which his pilgrims wished to visit. He could be certain that English Catholics would immediately understand which pilgrimage site he was alluding to, and that the Protestant censors would not at once recognise it. Nevertheless, he took care never to enter the play in the Stationers' Register, or to publish it as a Quarto edition. It was first published in 1623, seven years after Shakespeare's death. There is no evidence that the play was ever performed prior to 1642, when the Puritans closed the London theatres. There is also no indication that it was even performed during the Restoration period, after 1660. It appears that the very first performance did not take place until 7 March 1741 in the Goodman's Fields Theatre in London, where David Garrick, the famous eighteenth-century Shakespearian actor, made his stage debut in that same year[281]. Shakespeare ensured that *All's Well That Ends Well* was not published until well after his death, because this play also demonstrates his Catholicism very clearly.

In *Romeo and Juliet*, the playwright uses the expression 'pilgrim' as part of his elaborate metaphorical texture woven around the subject of love, and in so doing surrounds the first tentative meeting between the protagonists with a religious aura. Elsewhere in his works, Shakespeare uses several distinctly Catholic metaphors, and does so without any hint of irony. In *The Two Gentlemen of Verona*, there is a conversation between Julia and her chambermaid Lucetta, in which Julia asks her maid to tell her how she can win the love of Proteus 'with [her] honour' (Act II, scene 7).

LUCETTA
Alas, the way is wearisome and long!

JULIA
A true-devoted pilgrim is not weary
To measure kingdoms with his feeble steps;

When Shakespeare describes a pilgrim's determination to travel right across the kingdom, despite his 'feeble steps', he again gives the impression that he is on familiar ground.

Helena finally wins back her husband by using a ruse similar to the one devised by the duke in *Measure for Measure*, when, disguised as a monk, he comes to protect Isabella. In *All's Well That Ends Well*, Helena uses the 'bed trick', and pretends to be Diana, who has a tryst with Bertram.

Shakespeare wrote these problem plays in the same period in which he wrote the four great tragedies. It is not surprising, therefore, that the problem plays and the tragedies contain parallels that are so characteristic of the dramatist. Caroline Spurgeon, the American Shakespeare scholar, believed that – in comparison to the imagery of his contemporaries – Shakespeare's images express his own deep-seated likes and dislikes, his interests, mental associations, mindset and opinions[282].

There are essential differences, however, between the tragedies and the problem plays. The latter contain many crude scenes from everyday life and common situations, which are transferred directly to the stage. In *Hamlet*, female vices and transgressions are denounced and judged in moral terms through the hero's tirades, but in *Troilus and Cressida* Shakespeare places these vices before us, showing them with vivid immediacy. In so doing, he satisfies his audience's curiosity and love of sensationalism. Furthermore, the settings of the problem plays are often those associated with 'low life' characters, though they are also frequented by aristocrats, whether in disguise or not – for example, the ruler himself in *Measure for Measure*. As Shakespeare reached the pinnacle of his creativity and wrote his finest plays, he embraced the whole of the social spectrum, as well as the widest range of emotions, whether positive or negative.

TIMON OF ATHENS

Timon of Athens was written between 1605 and 1609, at the very end of the series of Shakespeare's tragedies and problem plays. This play has been considered as one of the most puzzling of Shakespeare's dramas. At the start of the play, the protagonist Timon is a generous and kind philanthropist, but during the course of the action he turns into a bitter and merciless misanthrope, who heartlessly orders and finances the military destruction of his home city of Athens, along with all of its citizens, women and children. On the eve of the World War I in 1913, the English artist and dramatist Wyndham Lewis (1882-1957) created images inspired by Shakespeare's *Timon of Athens*, which exactly capture the cold and military atmosphere of the play, and Timon's contempt for human life[283].

The highs and lows of Shakespeare's life are also mirrored in the further course of his works. This play, however, marks the peak of Shakespeare's pessimistic image of man and the world. It seems to be expressing once again, and even more vehemently than in *Troilus and Cressida* and the other problem plays, the deep disgust the playwright must have felt at the tightening of the anti-Catholic legislation as well as the worsening and humiliating treatment of his Catholic countrymen during the first decade of the new century.

The intensity of Shakespeare's negative feelings did not go unnoticed by his contemporaries. Thomas Freeman, an Oxford graduate and gentleman who lived in London and was active as a playwright between 1607 and 1614, alludes to Shakespeare, Samuel Daniel, John Donne and others in a two-part collection of epigrams published in 1614 under the titles *Rubbe and a Great Cast* and *Runne and a Great Cast*. Epigram 84 of his collection may well be taken as a reference to the raging misanthropy of Shakespeare's Timon and the deplorable contemporary state of affairs that must have caused it. Freeman, who recognises the futility of such anger, appears to offer constructive criticism and help. The epigram is about the nature of courage and is addressed '*Ad Labeonem*'. This is a reference to Shakespeare's nickname ('Labeo'), first used by the dramatist John Marston (1576-1634) in 1598, and alluding to Shakespeare's prominent lips[284]. In places, Freeman's advice is even more direct: 'Believe me *Labeo*, this were fortitude, / Ouer thy selfe to get a victory'. Freeman tells 'Labeo' that true courage is not demonstrated through 'active' undertakings, but in strength of disposition and the ability to bear injustice. The right way, he says, is not to fight 'Beast-like furious', or to be too mild, but to find the middle ground between the extremes. To overcome hurt feelings and to conquer one's own emotions was to demonstrate true power and would be a triumph worthy to be remembered. Freeman recommended fortitude in the face of suffering, and was thus in line with a contemporary school of thought which drew upon the example of the 'good old Stoicks' of Antiquity.

It is likely that Shakespeare received this and similar advice, and it would be fair to say that it may well have contributed to the 'inner peace' that the dramatist demonstrates in his later works.

THE PLIGHT OF THE CATHOLICS UNDER JAMES I: DISAPPOINTMENT AND RESISTANCE

In 1603, James I succeeded Elizabeth, and the plight of English Catholics and their priests worsened. This was hardly what they had been expecting. During the last years of Elizabeth's reign, the Scottish king had repeatedly made it clear to Essex and Catholic negotiators that, as king of England, he would grant religious tolerance. Therefore the Catholic English population had great expectations. In addition, as the son of Mary, Queen of Scots, it was believed that James would show compassion to the followers of his mother's faith.

For these reasons, soon after Elizabeth's death in 1603, numerous English Jesuits and priests returned to the country. In many areas, recusants dared to acknowledge their Catholicism and attend Mass more or less openly. But the English Catholics were quite wrong in their expectations of James and his administration. None of the anti-Catholic penal laws were abolished or relaxed, and they continued to be applied with as little mercy as under Elizabeth's rule.

It was not long before criticisms of the king, the State and the Anglican Church followed. These criticisms often came from actors, or more precisely from playwrights, who were not afraid to use the stage to express their anger. On 28 March 1605, Harrison wrote:

> It is much observed that the players do not forbear to present upon their stage the whole course of this present time, not sparing either King, State or religion, in so great absurdity and with such liberty as any would be afraid to hear them.[285]

Confrontations between the representatives of the State Church and the Catholic population were common. On 23 May 1605, an Anglican clergyman in Allen's Moor, near Hereford, refused burial to the recusant Alice Wellington, because she had been excommunicated by the Anglican Church[286]. The Catholics of the region reacted with open anger. They buried the body according to Catholic rites at six o'clock in the morning in the local cemetery. Those present carried torches and weapons.

The Bishop of Hereford was informed of these events and immediately gave orders for the one hundred people who attended the funeral to be seized and thrown into jail. While the prisoners were being escorted to Hereford by the constables, the column was attacked by between forty and fifty armed men. They held a spear to the chest of the High Constable and gave him the choice of releasing the prisoners or seeing his own entrails. He chose the first option.

This victory for the recusants was not without its consequences. The leaders were later identified and brought to trial in London. When they were tried on 20 June 1605 in the Star Chamber at Westminster, the Lord Chancellor used the opportunity to denounce the large numbers of Papists and Papist priests entering the country – in particular the Jesuits, whom he referred to as 'agents of the Pope'. He complained that these traitors were skulking everywhere, all over the country, and were trying to persuade the king's subjects to acknowledge a foreign power, namely the Pope, as their spiritual leader. He also denounced the negligence of many magistrates who allowed so many priests and Jesuits to overrun the country.

The Lord Chancellor took this opportunity to quote one of James I's speeches, in which the king had clearly quashed the earlier, premature and much-publicised hopes of the Catholic population that he would follow a policy of tolerance. The Lord Chancellor reported that the king had spoken of the 'folly' of the Catholics' hopes. Harrison writes:

> Moreover also he showed that Papists in divers parts do brag that they are in good hope of a toleration, to which he added a speech of his Majesty concerning the folly of Papists how they are so besotted, yea and more than bewitched, to suppose any such matter[287].

The new king's true attitude towards his Catholic subjects had, however, become clear as early as spring 1604. The French ambassador to the English court had made himself the advocate of the oppressed and deceived English Catholics. As a consequence, he had to experience some unpleasant scenes. On 1 April 1604, James I received from him a petition entitled *A Supplication to the King's Most Excellent Majesty*, written by the seminary priest Colleton. On reading the petition, the king became furious, threw it to the ground and trampled it underfoot[288].

On 10 February 1605 James I once more asserted his negative attitude towards the Catholic faith. He stated that the Papists' hopes for tolerance were in vain, 'declaring that he never had any such intention'. He said that the Catholic population had one year in which to accept the new religion; if they did not, he would further tighten the laws against them and have them executed[289].

James I had been playing a double game: to ensure that he won the throne, he had promised the Protestants that he would retain Anglicanism as the established Church, and he had told the English Catholics that they would be able to practise their religion freely. In the late 1590s, he had even made overtures to the Pope and the Spanish King[290]. Once the throne was his, he no longer cared about his promises to the Catholics.

The famous Gunpowder Plot, planned for 5 November 1605, was an attempt by Catholics to blow up the English parliament buildings, thereby killing not only all of the Members of Parliament, but also King James I and his queen, who would have been present for the State Opening of Parliament, due to be held on that day. The attack was planned by Robert Catesby, Guido (Guy) Fawkes, Sir Everard Digby, Robert Winter, Thomas Winter and others, as a Catholic act of revenge to destroy the centre of power and bring about the collapse of the Protestant regime. The conspirators came from the old established Catholic gentry throughout Warwickshire including Stratford itself – and Gloucestershire, and they had often met in the residences of these families. It was later discovered that one such meeting-place had been a secret room in Clopton House, Stratford (*Fig. 127*). The Cloptons were the most important upper-class family in the area, and fiercely rejected the new religion. The family's impressive tombs can still be seen in the Holy Trinity Church in Stratford.

The Gunpowder Plot was discovered at the very last moment, and the conspirators were gradually traced, arrested and brought to the Tower of London – apart from Catesby and Percy. Catesby was killed by an explosion at Holbeach House, the property of his friend Stephen Littleton.

Guido (Guy) Fawkes – his real name was John Johnson – was captured *in flagranti* in the basement of the old House of Parliament, with the barrels of gunpowder. Fawkes was brought before the king the following day. When the monarch asked him how he could carry out 'so hideous a treason against his children' and so many innocent souls, Fawkes answered that a dangerous disease required a desperate remedy, obviously using an argument from *Hamlet* as has already been mentioned (see p. 261). Fawkes, however, took this opportunity to tell some Scots to their faces that he had intended to

Fig. 127 – Secret priest's chamber in Clopton House, the Stratford residence of the Cloptons, who belonged to the Catholic gentry of Warwickshire. The Gunpowder Plot conspirators met in this room and hatched a plan, very nearly successful, to blow up parliament, the king and the royal family at the State Opening of Parliament on 5 November 1605.

blow them all the way back to Scotland. It goes without saying that the conspirator was also referring to the king himself[291].

Fawkes came from the Continent, where he had worked for Sir William Stanley, the English commander and deserter of Deventer. Sir William was one of the leaders of the militant wing of English Catholics-in-exile. When the Gunpowder Plotters were tried for high treason on 27 January 1605, Attorney-General Coke assumed that Fawkes had visited the Spanish Court on the orders of Sir William and other Catholics-in-exile, and had there met Christopher Wright – another of the conspirators. Together, the two had attempted to persuade the Spanish King to send an army to Milford Haven in Wales, where they would be met and supported by an army of English Catholics. Coke had previously attempted to uncover a conspiracy, put together in 1601 and 1602, not implemented at the time, but resumed at a later date[292], between Henry Garnet, the Superior of the English Jesuits, and the Gunpowder Plot conspirators Catesby, Tresham and Thomas Winter on the one hand, and the Spanish King on the other.

Twenty days after the Gunpowder Plot, during the night of 25 November 1605, Catholic priests caused much unrest in Southwark. The authorities arrested three suspected Catholic clergymen and searched them for letters. This incident mirrored the atmosphere among the population, and must have been part of the reason for the unusually large-scale security precautions on the days when the Gunpowder Plot conspirators were executed.

On the morning of 27 January 1606, eight of the key conspirators were taken by boat from the Tower of London to Westminster, where they were brought before the Star Chamber. The trial was secretly watched by Queen Anne and her son Henry, Prince of Wales. It is thought that the king may also have secretly attended the trial.

The most important charges in the long bill of indictment read out by Edward Coke were that the accused – together with Catesby and Percy, who were already dead, the two Wrights and Tresham, and in collaboration with the three Jesuits Henry Garnet, Oswald Tesimond (alias Greenway) and John Gerard – had committed high treason by conspiring against the king, the queen and Prince Henry, in order to cause rebellion, resistance and a bloodbath in the kingdom, to undermine and overthrow the government and 'the true worship of God'.

They also faced accusations that they had asked foreigners to enter the country and wage a war against the king. It was here that Coke mentioned the military invasion planned by the English Catholics-in-exile. He emphasised the extreme clemency of the king, who had decided that in punishing the accused he would not exceed the usual punishments set down in law, and would not invent new forms of torture. Only the prescribed punishment for high treason would be used. In his summing-up, Coke described the punishments in great detail:

> ... first, after a traitor hath had his just trial, and is convicted and attainted, he shall have his judgment, to be drawn to the place of execution

from his prison, as being not worthy any more to tread upon the face of the earth whereof he was made: also for that he hath been retrograde to nature, therefore is he drawn backward at a horse-tail. And whereas God hath made the head of man the highest and most supreme part, as being his chief grace and ornament, he must be drawn with his head declining downward, and lying so near the ground as may be, being thought unfit to take benefit of the common air; for which cause also he shall be strangled, being hanged up by the neck between heaven and earth, as deemed unworthy of both or either; as likewise, that the eyes of men may behold, and their hearts condemn him. His bowels and inward parts taken out and burned, who inwardly had conceived and harboured in his heart such horrible treason. After, to have his head cut off, which had imagined the mischief. And lastly, his body to be quartered, and the quarters set up in some high and eminent place, to the view and detestation of men, and to become a prey for the fowls of the air. And this is a reward due to traitors, whose hearts be hardened; for that it is a physic of state and government, to let out corrupt blood from the heart.' Sir Edward Coke (Westminster Hall, Court of Star Chamber, 27 January 1606)[293].

After reading several admissions of guilt, Lord Chief Justice Popham instructed the jury to reach a verdict. The jury left the court and returned a short time later to record a guilty verdict for all of the accused[294].

Sir Everard Digby faced a separate charge. As motives for his involvement in the conspiracy, Digby named: (1) his great affection for Catesby, (2) his (Catholic) religion, for which he had risked all[295], (3) the broken promise (of the king) to the Catholics[296] and (4) the fear of even harsher laws against recusants[297]. When Digby pleaded for mercy for his wife and children and other relatives, Coke quoted Psalm 109: 'Let his wife be a widow, and his children vagabonds, let his posterity be destroyed.'

The treatment of Digby and others demonstrate that Coke, Lord Chief Justice Popham and the jury were primarily bent on revenge. The punishments were more cruel and merciless than we can imagine today. The motives of the conspirators were given no consideration. Although Robert Cecil – whom James I had rewarded that year, 1605, for his services by naming him Earl of Salisbury – touched upon the accusation that His Majesty had broken a promise towards the recusants, he quickly dropped it again. Instead of answering it, he used the opportunity to thank Lord Mounteagle, whose warning letter had uncovered the conspiracy, for his loyalty to his king and country.

On 28 January, one day after the trials, Cecil received an anonymous threatening letter from Catholics stating that five men had been given the sacrament (meaning Confession and Absolution) in order to kill him (Cecil), because he had used the conspiracy to eradicate the memory of the Catholic religion through banishments, massacres, imprisonment and other means[298].

The executions of the Gunpowder Plotters were particularly inhuman[299]. On 30 January 1606, Sir Everard Digby, Robert Winter, John Grant and Thomas Bates were dragged on hurdles to the scaffold erected in front of St Paul's, and were executed after making speeches to the crowd. They were hanged, drawn, beheaded, and quartered (*Fig. 128*). Since there was a fear of unrest, the city council had ordered a sentry to be posted in front of the entrance of every house in the streets through which the condemned men were to be dragged.

On the following day, 31 January, Thomas Winter, Rookwood, Keyes and Guido (Guy) Fawkes were executed. Presumably for security reasons, they were not dragged to the same place of execution, but were taken from the Tower to the old Palace of Westminster. Differences were made in the way they were executed. Winter, for example, who expressed regret for his actions but proclaimed that he would die a true

Fig. 128 – The Gunpowder Plot conspirators. Frontispiece of Johann Theodor and Johann Israel de Bry, *Warhafftige und eygentliche Beschreibung der allerschrecklichsten vnd grawsamsten Verrätherey so jemals erhört worden/ wieder die Königliche Maiestat/derselben Gemahl vnnd junge Prinzen / sampt dem ganzen Parlament zu Londen in Engeland ...* (True and real account of the most terrible and cruel treachery that has ever been heard of against His Royal Majesty, his Consort and the young Princes as well as the whole Parliament in London, England ...) *Gedruckt zu Franckfurt am Mayn ... Im Jahr* 1606 (Printed at Frankfurt upon Main ... in the year 1606).

Catholic, was cut down shortly after he was hanged, and while he was still alive. He was then – according to sources – 'quickly despatched'. Rookwood also regretted his crime, but prayed to God to bless the king and his family and make them into good Catholics. He was left hanging until he was almost dead, and was then finished off in the usual manner.

The heads of those executed on 30 and 31 January were displayed on London Bridge as a deterrent. The heads of Catesby and Percy were placed on the roof of the Parliament building. The quartered limbs of all the executed men were displayed at London's gates.

On the morning of 23 December 1605, the first of the Gunpowder Plotters had been executed, nearly one month earlier. His name was Francis Tresham. His case had been heard before the others, probably because the government hoped that he would give incriminating evidence against Henry Garnet, Superior of the English Jesuits. Tresham died a long and painful death, lasting two hours. He had previously made a written declaration and sworn that his earlier statement, namely that Henry Garnet had known that Thomas Winter was a member of the conspiracy, had been false. Nonetheless, the government made every effort to track down Garnet, who was suspected to have been behind the plot. They managed to do this on 30 January 1606.

After eight days of searching Hindlip House, the residence of Master Habington in Worcestershire, the judge, Sir Henry Bromley, found the entrance to a small hidden chamber, in which Henry Garnet and Edward Oldcorne (*alias* Hall) were hiding. The hiding-place was so small that the priests could scarcely move. They had received food, candles, books, quill pens and paper through a hole in the chimney. When the Sheriff's men found them, they thought they were ghosts, and fled. A short time later, both priests were arrested.

Garnet and Oldcorne were brought to the London Gatehouse prison on 12 February 1606. Directly after their capture, they were treated remarkably well. Garnet was accommodated in the house of Sir Henry Bromley, who was believed to have Puritan sympathies. He ate his meals with Sir Henry and his family. On Candlemas Day, a great dinner was prepared, and all of the guests, including the Jesuit Oldcorne, doffed their caps to toast the king's health. A burning candle bearing the word 'Jesus' was brought in. 'Mary' was written on the reverse. Garnet asked to see the candle. When it was given to him, he took it in his hand, went to Oldcorne and said that he was lucky to be able to hold a holy candle on Candlemas.

When Garnet was finally taken away, he bade farewell to the women of the house in such a friendly manner that Sir Henry feared that they might have been converted to Catholicism by the Superior of the Jesuits. Sir Henry's suspicion was not unfounded, and the fact that at the aforementioned dinner, Lady Bromley had a burning candle brought into the room bearing the name 'Mary' is a distinct sign of her Catholicism, proving that she had indeed been converted to the old faith by Garnet. It appears that Sir Henry did not notice the word 'Mary', for its significance would certainly not have been lost on him if he had seen it[300].

On 28 March 1606, Garnet was tried for high treason at the Guildhall in London[301]. The judges included Sir Leonard Halliday, the Lord Mayor of London, Sir John Popham, Lord Chief Justice, Sir Christopher Yelverton, a judge from the King's Bench, Robert Cecil and the (Catholic) Earl of Northampton, who enjoyed the favour of the king, but was later to apologise to the Catholics for his role in Garnet's trial. Sir Edward Coke once again acted as Crown prosecutor. The spectators included many courtiers and ladies. King James himself was there privately.

The first charge was that Garnet had conspired with Catesby and Greenway. Garnet answered forcefully that he was not guilty of this charge. Coke used the remainder of the trial, which lasted only one day, to defame and humiliate Garnet with polished phrasing, and finally to place him on a par with common criminals. Garnet, he said, was a man of many names. He was an Englishman and a gentleman by birth. He had been educated at Westminster and Oxford and had initially worked for the printer Tottel as a corrector (copy-editor or proofreader). He was now being 'corrected' by the law. Coke stated that his current employment was as a Jesuit and a Superior. The latter title was certainly accurate, for his diabolical treason surpassed that of all his predecessors. Garnet was 'a doctor of Jesuits', said Coke – which meant that he was a Doctor of five D's: 'of dissimulation, of deposing of Princes, of disposing of Kingdoms, of daunting and deterring of subjects, and of destruction'.

Coke's other charges included Garnet's preaching of the Jesuit doctrine which taught that rulers could be deposed; his technique of 'equivocation' (the art of concealing and distorting the truth, or of speaking with double meanings); and his acknowledgement of the authority of the Pope above the sovereignty of kings and princes. To the charge of 'equivocation', the accused responded that

> if a man be brought before a lawful judge to be examined he must answer all things truly which that judge had cognizance to inquire of: but if he be examined before one who hath no authority to interrogate, or be asked concerning something which belongeth not to the cognizance of him who asketh, as what a man thinketh etc., he is not bound to answer, and may equivocate[302].

Concerning the authority of the Pope, Garnet told the judges that this was not his doctrine but that of the Church. Concerning Jesuit teaching, according to which excommunicated monarchs may be deposed, Garnet explained that this only applied to formerly Catholic kings, 'fallen away from the See of Rome'. This teaching did not affect 'his Majesty' (James I), for he had never been a member of the Catholic Church. The accused added that he knew 'that all quiet Catholics had ever a better opinion of the King than of the late Queen'. This statement is astonishing for Garnet, unlike Edmund Campion, in general remained remarkably reticent and answered many of the accusations with silence. One explanation could be that the Jesuit had secretly been in contact with the queen, Anne of Denmark, who was a clandestine Catholic and kept two priests (see p. 278), another that the king was present privately.

Only after he was sentenced – the judges returned after only fifteen minutes and imposed the death penalty – did the Superior of the English Jesuits, back in the Tower, compose a document, in which he referred to the (medieval) Doctors of the Church, as well as Aristotle and other philosophers, to point out that every law has to fulfil one important condition: it has to be just. The law which banned Catholic priests from entering England and preaching (the true religion), was no law. Those sentenced under this law were truly martyrs. To fall foul of an unjust law, said Garnet in conclusion, could not be considered high treason.

On 3 May 1606, Garnet was dragged on a hurdle from the Tower to a scaffold in St Paul's Churchyard. Contemporary sources state that the deacons of St Paul's Cathedral and Winchester Cathedral were present. These important Protestant dignitaries urged the condemned man to unburden his conscience and admit his treason to the world. The Jesuit priest asked them not to pester him any longer.

In his address to the people, Garnet mentioned the Gunpowder Plot and admitted that he had insulted the king, and for this he was sorry. He was guilty insofar as he had kept the plan secret. Treason against the king and the State were to be condemned, and he too would have despised the deed, had it been successfully carried out. He deeply regretted that Catholics had ever conceived such a cruel plan[303]. In the last minutes of his life and on the ladder to the gallows, he prayed. The Recorder of London present at the execution thought that Garnet's actions and his look showed that he hoped for a pardon from the king. The Recorder, however, wished him 'not to deceive himself, nor beguile his own soul', telling him: 'he was come to die, and he must die'. Furthermore he required him 'not to equivocate with his last breath'[304]. There are indications that the monarch had encouraged Garnet's hopes. In fact, the only act of mercy shown to him by King James I was that he, 'by the King's express command', was not – as was customary – cut down from the gallows while still alive, so that the rest of the gruesome and inhuman execution rituals were performed when he was already dead.

The Jesuit priest John Gerard, who – after Garnet – headed the wanted list and who had managed to escape the Tower of London in 1597, evaded the authorities once more. He had been educated at the Collegium Anglicum in Rheims and was of the same age as William Shakespeare. Gerard used the shelter and protection of the eastern gatehouse of Blackfriars in London. There the Catholic tenant John Fortescue and his family harboured priests and helped them to escape. With the aid of Fortescue, John Gerard reached the Continent unscathed. This gatehouse had been employed for these purposes by the Catholic underground – decades before the Gunplowder Plot and continued to be a buttress of English crypto-Catholicism. It was acquired by Shakespeare in 1613.

The Gunpowder Plot caused a further deterioration in the already desperate plight of the English Catholics. Robert Cecil used the almost unlimited powers granted to him by the king in order, among other things, to pursue the Catholics with more vigour than ever before. Drawing upon early seventeenth century sources, G.B. Harrison states that Cecil was 'an extreme enemy to the Catholics'[305]. In 1604, James I granted Cecil the title Viscount Cranbourne, and in 1605 made him Earl of Salisbury. These honours were no doubt in recognition of the services Cecil had rendered James I in his accession to the throne, and of his relentless persecution of the Catholic population.

A few months before the foiled Gunpowder Plot, Shakespeare made his largest acquisition in

Stratford. He must therefore have stayed for some while in his home town, and experienced the seething atmosphere in Warwickshire. We lack the historical evidence to know whether or not Shakespeare was aware of what the plotters were up to in their secret meetings. It is unlikely, however, that he would have approved of this terrible attack by radical Catholics.

Again – as in 1602 – Shakespeare used a time of crisis to purchase land in Stratford and in so doing made himself independent of the theatre, and the favour of patrons and the public. As mentioned above, on 24 July 1605, he acquired a share of tithes worth £440 from the town of Stratford. The holder of the deeds was Ralph Hubaud (or Huband), who had inherited them from his brother, Sir John Hubaud, in 1583. Sir John had been Constable in Kenilworth, in the manor of the Earl of Leicester, the queen's favourite. Ralph Hubaud died shortly after the purchase, and from an inventory of his assets in January 1606 it emerged that Shakespeare still owed him £20. The entry read: '[£ 20] Owing by Mr. Shakespre [sic].'[306]

This could represent the remainder of the purchase price that Shakespeare had not yet paid. Shakespeare's total expenditure on property and land must by this point have exceeded £900 pounds[307].

After the condemnation and execution of the Gunpowder Plot conspirators and Henry Garnet, Parliament drafted and passed an Oath of Allegiance Act in late 1606. As part of this oath, the king's subjects had to swear not to use 'equivocation', 'mental evasion' or 'secret reservation'. Rome reacted quickly, and in January 1607 Pope Paul V advised Catholics in England not to take the oath[308].

This situation led ever more Catholic parents to send their sons to the English Catholic colleges abroad. In February 1606, the increased number of Catholic youths attending these institutions on the Continent was brought to the attention of the House of Commons. It had emerged that within the previous two years, 2,000 boys under sixteen years of age had been sent to be educated on the European mainland. Fearing Catholic conspiracies, the government and Parliament pressed for more vigilant surveillance and an intensification of the persecution and punishment of Catholic priests, Jesuits and recusants. One of these measures was the Oath of Allegiance, which, however, was counter-productive, leading ever larger numbers to take advantage of a Continental Catholic education.

In 1613 Parliament decided to ban Catholics from carrying weapons. This represented a further degradation and exclusion of those who adhered to the old faith. They could now be identified by their appearance, and were indeed outcasts in their own land. In the same year, the Crown came close to passing a sumptuary law whereby Catholics would have been forced to wear red caps and coloured stockings.

Faced with such humiliation, the Catholic population of England must have found it sheer effrontery that Anne of Denmark, wife of James I, secretly practised her Catholic faith and kept two priests who said Mass in the Royal chapel and elsewhere.

William Shakespeare was silent on all this. But his silence was due neither to agreement nor to apathy, compliance, or laziness. He remained silent in order to continue his secret work more effectively.

With silence he also reacted to those great events which had inspired his fellow writers to heightened, euphoric literary productivity: the demise of Queen Elizabeth in 1603, and the sudden death of the heir to the throne, Prince Henry, in 1612 at the age of eighteen.

Where Shakespeare must have stood on the religious questions that deeply divided the English nation of his day is also revealed by the concrete measures he took in 1613 to strengthen the old faith. They can be regarded as his legacy to the Catholic underground. His actions not only endangered his life and those of his friends and colleagues; they also placed his family in grave jeopardy.

V. SHAKESPEARE'S LATE WORKS: TALES OF THE SUPERNATURAL AND FINAL RECONCILIATION

THE BLACKFRIARS THEATRE

As early as 1576, a theatre was set up in a building on the site of the former monastery of Blackfriars. The Children of Windsor performed there under the direction of the organist and choirmaster Richard Farrant (*c.* 1530–1580), of St George's Chapel, Windsor, who had leased the building. When Farrant died, his widow tried to sublet the playhouse to the writer and dramatist John Lyly (*c.* 1554–1606) and the theatre manager Henry Evans (active *c.* 1582–1608). Mrs Farrant got into legal difficulties, and the space was eventually used privately by the owner, Sir William More, until 1596.

Lyly and Evans also ran child actor groups. We know that for a long time, before 1584, Lyly was in the service of Edward de Vere, 17th Earl of Oxford (1550-1604). In 1584, de Vere's actors, the Oxford's Men, made their debut at Court. The company's author and their paid member, was Lyly himself. From 1585 until 1589-90, de Vere's players performed in the provinces and no longer appeared at Court. In 1602, they merged with the Worcester's Men. Thus the Oxford Men ceased to exist as a separate company. The only well-known actors among them were John and Laurence Dutton, who performed respectively from 1571 and 1575 until 1591. In 1583, John moved to the Queen's Men. The Oxford Men may well have performed at the Theatre in Shoreditch in 1580.

In *Palladis Tamia* (1598) Francis Meres describes Oxford as a writer of comedies, but does not mention the titles of any of his plays. This is probably connected to the fact that, as far as is known, they were never printed, and Meres knew of them only from hearsay. By the late 1590s, impoverished and dependent on a pension granted to him annually by the queen, Oxford was no longer active on the London literary and political scene. Shakespeare, on the other hand, whose works were admired at Court, at both the universities and by the public at large, must have been known personally to Meres, who lived in London from 1597 – not least because the playwright was still acting on the stage at that time. The fact that Meres lists in detail all the Shakespeare plays that had been performed hitherto shows how familiar he was with the dramatist's works. The comedies of the Earl of Oxford are no longer even mentioned in contemporary English literary history. *The Oxford Companion to English Literature* (1932, reprinted 1985) attributes about fifteen poems to de Vere, including, 'Love compared to a tennis playe' which may have been an allusion to his famous quarrel on the real tennis court with Sir Philip Sidney in 1579. Oxford certainly contributed to *The Paradyse of Daynty Devises* (1576), an anthology which is modelled upon its famous predecessor, *Tottel's Miscellany* (1557), and which – as is remarked in a standard work of twentieth-century literary history – contains a few good poems, but is otherwise very monotonous[309].

In 1596, James Burbage, owner of The Theatre in Shoreditch, paid £600 for a part of the More building in Blackfriars, in order to open a second theatre there. However, the influential residents of the former monastery area, which had now become a wealthy neighbourhood, succeeded in putting a stop to these plans by successfully petitioning the Privy Council. The petitioners included Sir George Carey, the second Lord Hunsdon, who became Lord Chamberlain in 1597, a post which until a year earlier had been held by his father Sir Henry Carey, the first Lord Hunsdon. As Lord Chamberlain, George Carey automatically became the patron of Shakespeare's theatre company. Another petitioner was one of the wealthiest and most respected printers and publishers in London – and, moreover a good friend of William Shakespeare: Richard Field of Stratford-upon-Avon, who only a few years earlier had printed Shakespeare's narrative poems *Venus and Adonis* (1593) and *The Rape of Lucrece* (1594).

When James Burbage died in 1597, his plans were shelved for three years. It was not until 1600 that his son Richard set up a theatre in Blackfriars, which, with the help of his friend, William Shakespeare, he succeeded in letting. He did so by copying the tactics of the previous tenant, Farrant, whose announcements always advertised performances as taking place in a 'private house'. Burbage signed a twenty-one-year lease with Nathaniel Giles and his Children of the Chapel, for which he was paid a yearly rent of £40. The 'Chapel' in question was the Chapel Royal, founded in the twelfth century as part of the king's household. The Children of the Chapel choristers were first formed under Henry IV, who in 1401 appointed a chaplain to educate the boys. In the late sixteenth and early seventeenth centuries, the often forcibly recruited choristers of the Chapel Royal made a name for themselves, primarily for the musical 'interludes' (lyric dramas) they performed.

Neither Burbage nor his friend Shakespeare seemed to have considered the fact that the children's choir at Blackfriars Theatre, who had a competent manager in Henry Evans, posed serious competition to them, and might affect their income. The 'Theatre Battle' which ensued from this situation, joined by Ben Jonson on one side, and John Marston and Thomas Dekker on the other, is alluded to by Shakespeare in *Hamlet*. In the discussion between Rosencrantz and Guildenstern (Act II, scene 2), where Hamlet speaks about the arrival of the actors, the prince wants to know why they are so itinerant, when it would be much better for them to have a fixed venue in which to perform. He continues:

> ... but there is, sir, an eyrie of children, little eyases, that cry out on the top of question, and are most tyrannically clapped for't. These are now the fashion, and so berattle the common stages—so they call them—that many wearing rapiers are afraid of goose quills and dare scarce come thither.

Surprised by this new item of information, Hamlet wants to know more and asks shrewd and perspicacious questions

> What, are they children? who maintains 'em? how are they escoted? Will they pursue the quality no longer than they can sing? Will they not say afterwards, if they should grow themselves to common players—as it is most like, if their means are no better—their writers do them wrong, to make them exclaim against their own succession?

To this barrage of questions Rosencrantz answers:

> Faith, there has been much to-do on both sides; and the nation holds it no sin to tarre them to controversy. There was, for a while, no money bid for argument, unless the poet and the player went to cuffs in the question.

This passage illustrates very clearly how Shakespeare reacts to current affairs, especially when they have a bearing upon his own material existence. The playwright takes this opportunity to raise on the stage a problem that he and his actors face in real life – much to the amusement of his audience, who were aware of the dispute, were hungry for gossip about it, and, as unaffected bystanders, found it good entertainment.

One of the most famous child stars of the Children of the Chapel, the handsome Nathan Field (1587–1620), later became a leading actor of the King's Men, so Hamlet's (i.e. Shakespeare's) assessment of the situation proved to be accurate. Field – referred to as 'Nat' or 'Nid' – was the son of the puritanical minister John Field, ironically a

Fig. 129 – Portrait of the playwright Ben Jonson by Gerard Honthorst. In the 1590s, Jonson, who had attended Westminster School, worked for his stepfather as a mason. He fought as a soldier in Flanders, then joined a travelling theatre company. From 1597, he lived in London and worked as an actor and playwright. In 1598, he killed a fellow actor in a duel and saved his life by seeking sanctuary from the Church. He nevertheless received a prison sentence. While in prison, Jonson converted to Catholicism. It is only after this time that he became friends with Shakespeare, whose theatre company performed Jonson's *Every Man in his Humour* in 1598 with Shakespeare himself playing a leading role. Jonson's next play, *Every Man out of his Humour*, was performed in the newly opened Globe Theatre in 1599. Later in their lives, Shakespeare and Jonson fell out. This is indicated by the fact that Jonson is not named in Shakespeare's will. In 1610, under the influence of James I, Jonson had reconverted to Protestantism. He did, however, contribute most important verses to the First Folio edition of Shakespeare's plays, among them an epigram to accompany the famous Droeshout engraving. Both image and text served to authenticate Shakespeare's facial features as well as his authorship of the plays.

bitter opponent of the theatre and its actors. He attended St Paul's School and was forcibly inducted into acting while still a child. His brother Theophilus later became a bishop, and another brother, Nathaniel, a printer. From 1616, the year of Shakespeare's death, Field and Richard Burbage headed the cast of the King's Men's actors. Burbage died three years later on 13 March 1619, and was carried to his grave in the presence of large crowds. Famous contemporaries, among them Ben Jonson, commemorated him in elegies and obituaries. Shakespeare's co-author, John Fletcher (1579-1625) referred to the event in his *Elegy on the death of the famous actor Rich: Burbage*, which contains the line, 'Hee's gone & with him what a world are dead'[310]. Field survived Burbage by only a year. Burbage's successor was Joseph Taylor (1586-1652). Taylor was an admirer of Shakespeare and knew the famous playwright personally; he is said to have played Hamlet 'incomparably well'[311].

The Children of the Chapel, who from 1605 were under the direction of Robert Keysar (active 1605-1613), were temporarily forbidden to appear during that year due to the production of the scandalous, politically provocative satire *Eastward Ho!*, a joint production by the dramatist George Chapman, Ben Jonson (*Fig. 129*) and John Marston. The play contained anti-Scottish passages, and was thus seen as an affront to James I. Marston fled to the Continent, and Chapman was sentenced to a short term in jail, where he was joined voluntarily by Jonson.

The children's troupe were allowed to appear again shortly afterwards, but their name was changed from Children of the Chapel to Children of Blackfriars – presumably because the English queen and wife of James I, Anne of Denmark, had withdrawn her patronage from them. A new scandal engulfed them only three years later. This was the end of the Children of Blackfriars. Keysar had rehearsed with them the play *The Conspiracy and Tragedy of Charles Duke of Byron* by George Chapman (*c.* 1560-1634), in which there are daring references to contemporary French politics and French manners. The protagonist, Charles Biron, Marshal of France, was the man who, only a few months after the execution of the Earl of Essex, had caused a sensation at the English Court. King Henry IV had had Biron executed on 31 July 1602, in Paris, because he was supposed to have negotiated the partition of France with Spain and Savoy. The French ambassador was so outraged that he lodged a complaint with the English government, and achieved the play's immediate withdrawal. Some of the boy actors were thrown into prison, and Chapman himself only narrowly escaped the same fate.

Richard Burbage now had a problem. He urgently needed a new tenant for his theatre. So – presumably in consultation with his friend Shakespeare – he devised a totally different solution. He decided to manage the Blackfriars Theatre himself, as yet another venue, in addition to the Globe.

On 9 August 1608, Richard Burbage, his brother Cuthbert, William Shakespeare, John Heminge, Henry Condell, William Sly and Thomas Evans formed a syndicate to rent the Blackfriars Theatre. Each of the seven members of this alliance – who designated themselves as 'Housekeepers' – signed separate twenty-one year contracts, in which each agreed to pay one- seventh of the yearly rent of £40 to the syndicate, which then went to Richard Burbage as the owner. The contracts were valid retrospectively from 1607, and the agreement continued until the theatre was closed in 1642.

The new King's Men Theatre was housed in a large hall whose longer sides ran from north to south. It measured 66 by 46 feet (*c.* 20 by 14 metres), had a paved stone floor, a candlelit stage and three galleries. There were seats for 600 to 700 spectators. Unlike the Globe, the Blackfriars Theatre could be used in winter.

Like the Globe Theatre, the new playhouse of the King's Men was a great success. There it was that Shakespeare's late plays were performed, to enthusiastic public acclaim. The Blackfriars

Theatre quickly developed into the most popular venue in London. It was also the most elegant. The fashionable area in which it was situated, however, created further difficulties for it, because the residents were angered and annoyed by the noise and the traffic jams caused by carriages that blocked the streets right up to St Paul's Churchyard.

To silence the complaints of local residents and the Corporation of London once and for all, three years after Shakespeare's death the King's Men asked the king to renew their license to perform in Blackfriars. James granted this right again for both houses, Blackfriars and The Globe in Southwark. In the case of the Blackfriars Theatre, it was – evidently for legal protection – once again confirmed that it was a matter of a 'private house'.

In 1631, some residents of Blackfriars sought to resolve the dispute their own way, offering to buy the so-called 'private house'. In order to add more substance to their offer, they enlisted the support of William Laud, the former Bishop of Bath and Wells, who was Bishop of London from 1628 to 1633. Neither this nor a bid of £2,900 for the building from judges in Middlesex in 1633 had the desired result. The offer by the judges cannot have been taken seriously by the King's Men, especially since their own estimate was that the Blackfriars Theatre was worth £21,900[312].

The theatre of the King's Men in Blackfriars – like all other theatres – was closed by the Puritans in 1642 and stood empty for some years; many people, however, remembered its former glory. In his *Miscellania* (1653), the English dramatist Richard Flecknoe (died *c.* 1678) describes the great sadness he felt when passing the deserted playhouse where no longer 'a Play-bil on the Gate' was seen and 'no Coaches on the place, nor Doorkeeper at the Play-house door, with his Boxe like a Churchwarden desiring you to remember the poor Players'[313]. In view of the great fame which Shakespeare had already enjoyed while he was

Fig. 130 – A modern view of the Playhouse Yard on the site of the former Blackfriars monastery.

alive, it is not at all surprising that Flecknoe, standing in front of the playwright's closed down Blackfriars Theatre, should remember the glorious days of Shakespeare's theatre, now for ever lost.

> Poor House that in the dayes of our Grand-sires,
> Belongest unto the Mendiant Fryers:
> And where so oft in our fathers dayes
> We have seen so many of Shakspears Playes[314]

It must have given the representatives of the Puritan regime special satisfaction to shut down this particular theatre. In 1655, after it had stood dark for thirteen years, the Blackfriars theatre made famous by Shakespeare's works fell victim to demolition. On this site where Queen Hermione, unjustly accused of adultery, and Imogen, wrongfully suspected of sexual

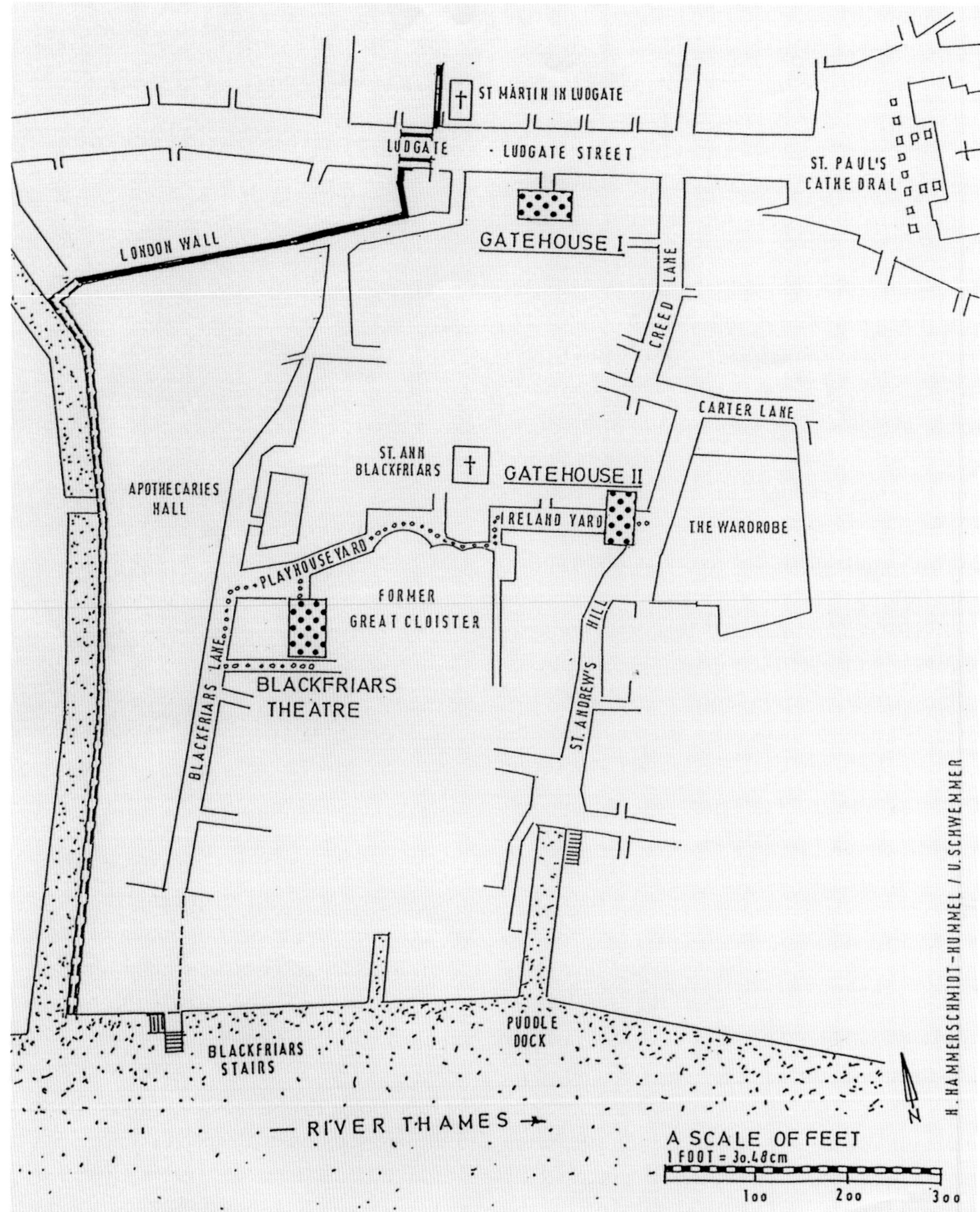

Fig. 131 – Architect's drawing of Blackfriars monastery near St Paul's Cathedral, produced in 1998 by Udo Schwemmer based on research results by H. Hammerschmidt-Hummel. The area of land occupied followed the line of the old city wall from Ludgate Hill or Ludgate Street in the north to the banks of the Thames in the south. This map does not merely show the exact, hitherto unknown location of the northern and eastern gatehouses for the first time, but also the exact, hitherto unknown location of the Blackfriars Theatre. The theatre stood south of Playhouse Yard (*Fig. 130*), near Blackfriars Lane in the western part of the grounds. It was about 250 yards from the eastern gatehouse which was bought by Shakespeare in 1613[*17]. The main entrance of the Blackfriars Theatre was to the north, just opposite Apothecaries' Hall (*Fig. 163a*). A forecourt is still visible here today.

Fig. 132a – Apothecaries' Hall, north of Playhouse Yard on the site of the former Blackfriars monastery in London (*Fig. 130*). The building is still used by The Worshipful Society of Apothecaries of London. It was rebuilt after the Great Fire (1666) in its original style, and is an impressive example of the elegant architecture of Blackfriars in the early seventeenth century.

Fig. 132b – The great hall of Apothecaries' Hall. It measures 60 x 30 feet and so gives us an idea of the interior of the Blackfriars Theatre, whose external measurements were 66 x 46 feet.

impropriety, had first taken the audiences by storm; where the actors first created Shakespearean roles, to thunderous applause; where the rich and famous mixed with lesser mortals to witness world-class theatre – here small dwellings were built for the God-fearing, Bible-thumping subjects of the Lord Protector, the leading Puritan, Oliver Cromwell.

Until recently, the exact site of the theatre on what had once been monastery land could not be determined with any accuracy, but – due to results of new research results – its location has now been established[315]. The building was situated south of what is still called Playhouse Yard (*Fig. 130*), just off Blackfriars Lane in the western part of the site, about 600 feet (*c.* 200 metres) from the eastern Gatehouse, as shown in the architect's drawing, based on the present author's research (*Fig. 131*)[316]. The main entrance was on the north side, diagonally across from the Apothecaries' Hall (*Figs. 132 a–b*), where even today, tracing the road layout, a kind of forecourt can be made out. On a map of London published in September 1666, shortly after the Great Fire that burned the city to the ground, a footpath is drawn in, running from Shakespeare's eastern gatehouse, past the Blackfriars Theatre to the landing-stage of Blackfriars on the Thames (*Fig. 133*). This might have been the old escape route for persecuted Catholic priests, who found refuge in the eastern gatehouse and were able to disguise themselves in the theatre, and thence escape by rowing-boat to the ships at Gravesend (see p. 84).

THE THIRD PHASE OF SHAKESPEARE'S DRAMAS: ROMANCES AND A LATE HISTORY

In the last phase of Shakespeare's life and work, the former incidences of strong aggression and invective (see p. 270 f.) have disappeared, despite the fact that the situation of English Catholics had worsened. This may have been due to the well-

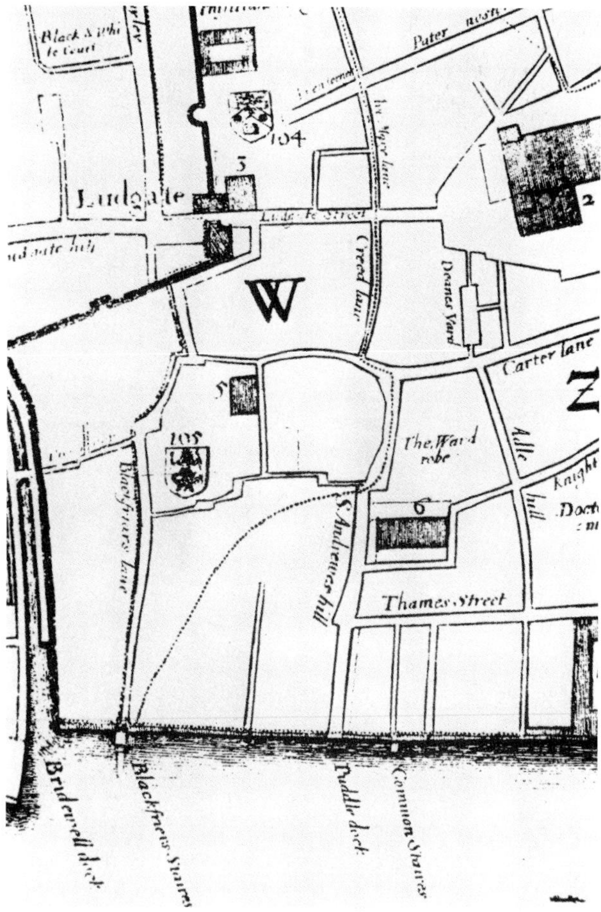

Fig. 133 – The area around Blackfriars in 1666. Section of a London map completed in September 1666 by John Leake, roughly three months after the Great Fire and engraved by the famous Wenceslaus Hollar. The map shows a path descending from the north, entering the grounds of the former monastery just at the point where Shakespeare's eastern gatehouse once stood. It leads past the south side of the Blackfriars Theatre and ends at Blackfriars Stairs, the landing stage on the Thames. This may well have been the old escape route used by numerous Catholic priests, Jesuits and other persecuted adherents of the old faith who wished to enter or leave the country in secret.

meaning advice of his colleagues, but also suggests that the poet's outlook may have mellowed. In the later plays, the romances *Pericles, Cymbeline, The Winter's Tale* and *The Tempest*, Shakespeare's dark mood lightens again and a conciliatory note is struck. Supernatural forces intervene in the troubled fate of Shakespearian heroes, and even tragic and seemingly insoluble conflicts have a happy ending. This new attitude can certainly be explained by the changes in Shakespeare's private life and circumstances. It appears that the poet was already working on plans he was to put into effect at the end of his literary career (see pp. 298–303).

ROMANCES

PERICLES, PRINCE OF TYRE

Shakespeare's romance, *Pericles, Prince of Tyre* was not only the favourite Shakespearean play of the Victorian era, it was greatly admired by the subjects of James I and was performed frequently. A Quarto edition appeared twice in 1609 in Shakespeare's name. Further editions followed in the years 1611, 1619, 1630 and 1635. The title page of the first edition promised adventure, vicissitudes of fortune, coincidences and strange happenings that would befall the hero, Pericles, and his daughter Marina. The subtitle read: 'The Late, And much admired Play, Called Pericles, Prince of Tyre. With the true relation of the whole Historie, aduentures, and fortunes of the said Prince: As also, The no lesse strange, and worthy accidents, in the Birth and Life, of his Daughter Mariana [sic].' Information was added to the effect that this drama had often been performed by His Majesty's actors (the King's Men) at the Globe Theatre. As a seal of quality, the name of its famous author, William Shakespeare, was given, though apparently he was not the only contributor. The English Shakespeare scholars Park Honan and Katherine Duncan-Jones showed in 1998 and 2001 that Shakespeare's co-author was the insignificant, minor writer George Wilkins (active 1603-1608). Wilkins owned an inn with a brothel attached and was known to be violent to women, so he had an unsavoury reputation[317]. Duncan-Jones draws some wide-ranging conclusions from this fact (see p. 317). Shakespeare may well have received the inspiration for some of the brothel scenes via his contact with Wilkins. However,

Fig. 134 – Tomb of the English poet John Gower (*c.* 1325-1408) in Southwark Cathedral. Gower is a character in Shakespeare's later play *Pericles*.

what the playwright is demonstrating here is the triumph of virtue over vice.

It is noteworthy that the heroine's name in the original title is 'Mariana' and not – as it later became – 'Marina'. 'Mariana' is an expanded form of 'Maria'. This name is unlikely to have appeared by chance or through a misprint on the title page in 1609, the year in which Shakespeare had a valuable old Madonna portrait over-painted with his own portrait (the original Flower portrait, authenticated in 1995 and again in 2006). Although the cult of the Madonna was deeply disapproved of by English Protestantism, the dramatist chose the name of the mother of Jesus for two of his female characters (see *Love's Labour's Lost* and *Twelfth Night*). This was not without danger. 'Mariana' is the name of a character in *Measure for Measure*, a problem play that, because of its 'Catholic' content, remained unpublished until seven years after Shakespeare's death.

Pericles was not included in the First Folio edition published in 1623 by John Heminge and Henry Condell, although the text was listed on 20 May 1608 in the Stationers' Register (of the London Printers and Booksellers Guild) and – as mentioned – was printed twice only a year later. In the Second Folio Edition of Shakespeare's plays, which appeared in 1632, one would also search in vain for *Pericles*. It was not published until the second printing of the third Folio edition in 1664. Heminge and Condell must have known about Shakespeare's collaboration with Wilkins, who probably produced Acts I and II. Did they decide against including the play because they feared that the setting and Shakespeare's co-author would damage posterity's image of the Bard?

Pericles was written between 1606 and 1608. Zorzi Giustinian, the Venetian ambassador to the Court of James I, between 5 January 1606 and 23 November 1608, had attended – as recorded in the *Calendar of State Papers, Concerning Venice* – a performance of a drama with this title at the English Court. This must have been Shakespeare's *Pericles*. The date of the première can even be narrowed down further. Since this romance had been announced in the Stationers' Register in May 1608, it was probably written in the winter of 1607-08 or in early spring 1608.

Shakespeare had no direct source for *Pericles*, a play with which he virtually created a new genre – the romance. The plot is laid out in a contrapuntal fashion. It contains a religious sub-structure rather like that of certain medieval miracle plays, in which virtue and purity are praised, and which always include supernatural phenomena such as miracles, visions and resurrections. The counterpoint here is the world of vice and sin, most clearly depicted in the brothel scenes. The protagonist, Pericles, stoically bears his tribulations and the vicissitudes of his many (almost archetypal) sea voyages, from which he is eventually saved through the grace of God and is reunited with his family. These trials can ultimately only be understood in the Christian context. Through the device of using a narrator in the person of the medieval English poet John Gower (*c.* 1325-1408) (*Fig. 134*) who describes, accompanies and comments on the events like a Greek chorus, the dramatist appears to be harking back to the Middle Ages. Shakespeare was no doubt also looking back on his own eventful life and the many dangerous enterprises in which he had been involved. We may well assume that the theme of the 'lost daughter' played such a prominent part in *Pericles*, as it does in *The Winter's Tale* and *Cymbeline*, because this subject had preoccupied the playwright since he had also 'lost' a daughter (see pp. 168–185).

Marina, daughter of Pericles, has been brought up by Cleon, Governor of Tarsus, after the presumed death of her mother. She only just escapes an assassination attempt planned by her stepmother, Dionyza, but is then ambushed and kidnapped by pirates who take her to a brothel, where her virtues shine through even more brightly. The setting is described by Shakespeare with dramatic, unsparing realism.

The brothel-keeper, 'The Bawd', orders his servant, Boult, to appraise the 'new arrival' and note her identifying features – hair colour, appearance, height, age and state of virginity. Boult had already inquired about this last characteristic when she was delivered. Marina's virginity is a treasure that is to be auctioned off to the highest bidder.

The first visitor to the establishment is Lysimachus, Governor of Mytilene. Marina is presented to this distinguished and high-ranking guest as an unsullied and unequalled rarity. The governor wants to commit what he himself terms a 'deed of darkness' with her, but the innocent young woman succeeds in narrating her story to Lysimachus with such well-chosen words that he is deeply moved, undergoes a transformation, and now perceives her as the embodiment of virtue ('a piece of virtue'), promising to protect her from now on. Terms such as 'deed of darkness' and 'piece of virtue' emphasise the fact that this is the classic battle between Good and Evil (as in the miracle and morality plays of the Middle Ages), in which Good always triumphs.

CYMBELINE

The play's original title, *The Tragedy of Cymbeline*, was no doubt what led the editors of the First Folio edition to assign it to the tragedies, but later editors all agreed that in terms of setting and content, it is a romance. The exact date when it was written is not known. The astrologer Simon Forman, who died on 8 September 1611, remarked, in his *Bocke of plaies and Notes herof & formans for Common pollicie*, that he had attended a production of *Cimbalin, King of England*, but gives no date[318]. It can be assumed that the romance was written in 1609-10 for the more sophisticated audience of the Blackfriars Theatre, a so-called 'indoor theatre' in which Shakespeare's theatre troupe performed from 1608 onwards.

Cymbeline, King of the Ancient Britons under the rule of the Roman Emperor Augustus, instigated by his second wife, wants to shake off the Roman yoke, by force if necessary, and bluntly conveys his intention to Caius Lucius, a general sent from Rome. Cloten, Cymbeline's crafty stepson, whose mother would prefer him to rule in place of his stepfather, speaks out likewise for the freedom of Britain and against Rome. He pursues Cymbeline's married daughter, Imogen, and tries to rape her. Her husband, Posthumus Leonatus, an impoverished nobleman whom Imogen married against her father's will, has been banished to Italy.

Shakespeare took great liberties with this tale of Ancient Britain. Historical accuracy and the authenticity of the events and the characters were clearly less important to him than using the story to convey a message. In a way *Cymbeline*, too, echoes the great debate in the England of Shakespeare's time for and against breaking away from Roman Catholicism, reminding us of Shakespeare's *King John* where this topic plays a prominent part. Like the protagonists in other later plays, Cymbeline is made to undergo a moral purification. It is significant that the man who had dared to stand against the might of Rome, and even defeated the Romans on the battlefield, would eventually voluntarily subjugate himself to Roman rule once more, so that the Roman and British flags would henceforth fly side by side as symbols of friendship and freedom. Shakespeare also mentions that Cymbeline and his successors would henceforth have to pay tribute to the Roman emperor. The question, however, is whether the playwright was, in fact, hinting at the tribute which all Catholic countries had to pay to the Pope as head of the Roman Catholic Church, and which was still being paid secretly by the English crypto-Catholics and Catholics-in-exile (see pp. 147 ff.; 151). Seen in this light, the closing scene of *Cymbeline* can be interpreted as a kind of wishful thinking on the part of the playwright, stemming from his own faith.

The funeral dirge that Cymbeline's sons, Guiderius and Arviragus, strike up in honour of the deceased Cloten, could almost be seen as a foretaste of Shakespeare's own farewell, of the tranquil inner harmony with which he distanced himself from the world and its cares only a few years later: his retirement to the refuge or perhaps even the sanctuary of New Place. It might even be interpreted as an imaginary lament, presaging the poet's own death:

> Fear no more the heat o' the sun,
> Nor the furious winter's rages;
> Thou thy worldly task hast done,
> ...
> Fear no more the frown o' the great;
> Thou art past the tyrant's stroke;
> Care no more to clothe and eat;
> ...
> Fear no more the lightning flash,
> Nor the all-dreaded thunder-stone;
> Fear not slander, censure rash ...

'The frown o' the great', 'tyrants' stroke', 'lightning flash', and also 'slander': the English Catholics, of whom Shakespeare was one, had had bitter experience of all of these.

THE WINTER'S TALE

In *The Winter's Tale*, Shakespeare turns once again to material that Robert Greene had used in his novella *Pandosto, or the Triumph of Time* (1588, reprinted 1607). It might be recalled that shortly before his death, Greene spoke disparagingly of the fast-moving young man on the make on the London theatre scene, revealing his great envy of his brilliant young colleague. The Elizabethan astrologer and theatregoer, Simon Forman, attended a performance of *The Winter's Tale* on 15 May 1611[319]. In the basement of Somerset House in 1842, the English scholar Peter Cunningham (1816-1669) found two accounts books from the Revels Office, one of which, for the year 1611-12, contained the entry: 'The Kings Players on 5 November 1611. A play called ye winters nightes Tayle'. Since it is almost certain that parts of this late Shakespearean work were influenced by Ben Jonson's *Masque of Oberon* – the Jonson play was performed at Court on New Year's Day, 1611 – *The Winter's Tale* was probably written in early 1611. At that time, Shakespeare was presumably already spending most of his time in Stratford.

The play is set in Sicily and Bohemia, two important Catholic kingdoms on the Continent. The kingdom of Sicily was a Spanish possession at the time. In 1442, Alfonso V of Aragon had brought about the reunification of Sicily with the kingdom of Naples.

Departing from his source, Shakespeare switched the rulers of Sicily, which he calls Sicilia, and Bohemia. Critics have been astonished that the dramatist provided Bohemia with a coastline, but a glance at a map of Europe in the second half of the sixteenth century shows that the combined territories of Bohemia and Austria had a coast, the Gulf of Trieste on the Adriatic, so Shakespeare was not completely wrong in attributing a coast to Bohemia. In 1382, Trieste had voluntarily become a vassal of the Austrian Duke Leopold III of Styria.

The unity of Bohemia and Austria was clearly demonstrated to the outside world in the sixteenth century, when Emperor Rudolf II, who ruled from 1576 to 1612, chose to reside in Prague, the capital of Bohemia. Rudolf had been brought up at the Spanish court, became king of Hungary in 1572, and king of Bohemia in 1575. In 1609, the Catholic emperor granted religious freedom and privileges for the Protestant Bohemian nobility. Under his rule, Prague became a cultural and scientific centre. As a tolerant Catholic ruler, a lover and patron of the arts and sciences, Rudolf must have particularly appealed to Shakespeare. The leader of the English Catholic missionaries, Edmund Campion, whom the sixteen-year-old Shakespeare had most probably met in Lancashire, must also have been impressed by Rudolf, whom he would have seen in Prague, where he spent many years prior to 1580, living at the Jesuit college, now the Clementinum, on the Charles Bridge, with a view of the Hradschin Palace. The gifted, educated and sensitive Thomas Arundell, brother-in-law of the third Earl of Southampton, Shakespeare's patron, and an ardent follower of the old faith, was also captivated by Rudolf, and fought bravely for him against the Turks. In recognition of his outstanding services, Rudolf made Arundell a count of the Holy Roman Empire on 14 December 1595. At the behest of his wife, Arundell then returned to England, but just as his ship approached the shore, it ran into a huge storm and was wrecked. He was washed ashore, alive, near Aldeburgh on the Suffolk coast, but had lost all his possessions. Nevertheless, he could count himself lucky to have survived at all. Sources state that he stood 'extremely cold & wett upon the shore'[320], just as Hamlet does when, in a letter to the king, he wrote: 'High and mighty, You shall know I am set naked on your kingdom' (Act IV, scene 7).

In February 1596, Arundell wrote to Cecil, assuring him that he had never visited Rome and had never been associated with the Papists or supporters of Spain. When Cecil presented this letter to his queen, she was absolutely furious, mainly because the emperor of the Holy Roman Empire had bestowed upon Arundell the title of count of the Empire. She had Arundell thrown into the Fleet prison, and wrote to Emperor Rudolf informing him that she did not wish foreign monarchs to bestow titles on her subjects. Although Arundell sent letters to

Elizabeth from prison in which he submitted tempting plans offering the prospect of earning great wealth in the East Indies, Elizabeth was in no hurry to forgive him. He was finally released from prison in mid-April, but only on condition that he did not appear at Court.

Since Shakespeare had been close to the Earl of Southampton in the mid-1590s, he probably learned of Arundell's fate directly from his patron. He must also have recognised the real reason for the ruler's displeasure with Arundell. She knew Arundell to be a Catholic, in addition to which he had received one of the highest honours from the most powerful Catholic ruler on the Continent, so she made an example of him, to prevent any future recurrence.

In *The Winter's Tale*, Shakespeare clearly refers back to the 1590s and to personal experiences, in which Arundell's brother-in-law, the Earl of Southampton, and his wife played important roles.

In the decisive first scenes of this romance, the dramatist portrays King Leontes' growing mistrust of his wife, Queen Hermione and his best friend, King Polixenes of Bohemia, a mistrust that would deteriorate into intense jealousy. Leontes is convinced that Hermione has betrayed him with his best friend. He accuses her of breaking their marriage vows, and has her thrown into prison. While there, Hermione gave birth to a daughter, whom Leontes slanders as the 'Bastard of Polixenes'. He abandons the child in the wilderness, where she is supposed to die. His fear that his son Mamillius may also not be his own 'flesh and blood' is dispelled, however, when he recognises in the child's features his own face as a boy. Shakespeare's former patron, the Earl of Southampton, played a prominent role at the Court of James I, and probably continued to frequent the theatre as he had done in his youth, or to see performances in the residences of the nobility, including his own, Southampton House. Was the searching eye of Leontes an invitation to Southampton to examine the facial features of his eldest daughter, Penelope? In contrast to Leontes, he would not have recognised his own face in Penelope's features, but rather that of his former friend, William Shakespeare – if he had not known this truth already.

Only two years after the publication of the sonnets (1609) that cast a light on the *ménage à trois* between the poet, Elizabeth Vernon and Southampton, a fact that, at this time, must have been very embarrassing for the earl and his wife, Shakespeare again hints at this three-way relationship. When *The Winter's Tale* was performed for the first time, Penelope was twelve-years-old. According to the testimony of her contemporaries, she was beautiful, virtuous, intelligent and popular. The pain that his seed or fruit ('the kernels') belonged to 'others' (i.e. the Earl of Southampton and the Countess of Southampton), as stated in the new sonnet in the cartouche of the painting *The Persian Lady*, still must have rankled very badly with Shakespeare.

Yet even in *The Winter's Tale*, the situation does not take a tragic turn. At the end, the king is full of remorse, and has one more extraordinary experience. The lifelike statue of Queen Hermione that is about to be unveiled is miraculously brought to life. Peter Milward, in his book *Shakespeare's Religious Background*, considered this scene not only to be Catholic in its concept, but even to contain concrete references to the Catholic cult of Mary, banned in the England of Elizabeth's reign. As in the previous romances, bad luck turns into good luck in *The Winter's Tale*. The suffering is over, the 'lost daughter' is found again, the king and queen who have long been separated are reunited.

THE TEMPEST

The last play written entirely by Shakespeare is *The Tempest*. It was performed at Court on All Saints' Day, 1 November 1611 and was apparently written that year, probably immediately after *The Winter's Tale*. The playwright's original inspiration for this work came from the great shipwreck of 1609 off the Bermudas. One of the nine ships in the Virginia fleet, *The Sea Venture*, under the command of Sir Thomas Gates and Sir George Somers, became separated from the rest of the fleet in a hurricane. The ship was shipwrecked and its crew stranded on the coast of one of the Bermuda islands. Among the reports of the disaster, in which Shakespeare found details of the violent storm and the animal and plant life of the West Indies, there are letters by William Strachey dated 15 July 1610, which were published in 1625 in *Purchas His Pilgrims*, an anthology of travel and discovery literature of the Elizabethan-Jacobean period. The letters were already being circulated in London by 1610-11. Other reports of the catastrophe which, as first-hand accounts, sold like hot cakes in London, included Sylvester Jourdains' *Discovery of the Bermudas* and the official report of the Virginia Company *The True Declaration of the Estate of the Colonie in Virginia*, both of which were printed in 1610. The playwright knew that he could enthral his audience with these scenes depicting the exotic New World and its inhabitants. The Elizabethan seafarer Martin Frobisher had brought back from his expedition to North America (1576-1578), not only fish and furs, but even a captured Eskimo, to be exhibited in London. One of the guests who stayed at the 'Belle Sauvage' (Savage's Inn) on the north side of Ludgate Hill, opposite the site of the former Blackfriars monastery (*Fig. 131*), in whose inner courtyard plays were regularly played before the establishment of the permanent theatre, was the native American princess, Pocahontas, who lodged there in 1616-17. This exotic creature, whose story is nowadays commercially exploited by Walt Disney, could be marvelled at in the flesh by Shakespeare's contemporaries in the English metropolis. The name of the monster, Caliban, is an anagram of canibal (from the Spanish caníbal for caríbal), the name by which the Caribs, the original inhabitants of the Caribbean, were known. This must have attracted people in their droves to the Globe and the Blackfriars theatres. Exoticism, foreign lands, luxury items and stimulants held such an attraction for the English public of the time, that even level-headed lexicographers occasionally so far forgot themselves as to make enthusiastic reference to their own experiences. Thus, John Bullokar notes in *An English Expositor*, a dictionary of difficult words published in London in 1616, at the end of the entry for 'Crocodile', that he himself had seen a stuffed crocodile in London.

The Tempest continues to deal with the themes that had preoccupied Shakespeare in his previous plays, and through which he tried to influence the political events of his time – sovereign authority, usurpation, banishment and the re-establishment of order under a just and fair ruler.

After a terrible tempest on the high seas which destroys their ship, King Alonso of Naples and his son Ferdinand, his brother Sebastian and Antonio, the ducal usurper of Milan, are beached on an enchanted island, where live Prospero, the rightful duke of the northern Italian city-state, with his daughter Miranda. Prospero is a magician, governing his realm by means of his magic cloak and wand.

Shakespeare's romance has often been read as a kind of an autobiographical document[321]. The identification of Prospero with Shakespeare is compelling, and cannot be dismissed out of hand. Marc Chagall depicted this graphically in his illustrations for the play[322].

The Tempest is the last play to have been written by Shakespeare alone, his final work, *Henry VIII*, having most probably been composed in collaboration with John Fletcher. In this play, Shakespeare, the famous and celebrated star, takes his leave from the contemporary theatre with a grandiose gesture. He also bids farewell to the political stage, upon which, like Prospero on his island, he had exercised invisible influence. In Prospero's words of farewell in Act IV, scene 1, Shakespeare could equally have been speaking of himself:

> Our revels now are ended. These our actors,
> As I foretold you, were all spirits, and
> Are melted into air, into thin air.

Moreover, when Shakespeare makes Prospero look back at this point on the vanity and mighty splendour of that great stage, the world, his own thinking which is, deeply rooted in his religion, the old religion that is, becomes apparent:

> And, like the baseless fabric of this vision,
> The cloud-capp'd towers, the gorgeous palaces,
> The solemn temples, the great globe itself,
> Ye all which it inherit, shall dissolve
> And, like this insubstantial pageant faded,
> Leave not a rack behind. We are such stuff
> As dreams are made on, and our little life
> Is rounded with a sleep.

In Gonzalo's description of Utopia in Act II, scene 1, Shakespeare returns to the themes that so preoccupied him in his earlier history plays, those of the rule of the sovereign and government, and modes of living together with one's fellow human beings. Here they are exemplified by an ideal, utopian community. This too is a kind of leave-taking. In his final philosophical reflections on society, the playwright leaves us in no doubt that the perfect form of government is only a utopian dream. Should *The Tempest* therefore be interpreted as Shakespeare's political testament? Gonzalo begins his discourse with the question: 'Had I plantation of this isle, my lord – [...] / And were the king on't, what would I do?' The answer is:

> I' th' commonwealth I would by contraries
> Execute all things; for no kind of traffic
> Would I admit; no name of magistrate;
> Letters should not be known; riches, poverty,
> And use of service, none; contract, succession,
> Bourn, bound of land, tilth, vineyard, none;
> No use of metal, corn, or wine, or oil;
> No occupation; all men idle, all;
> And women too, but innocent and pure;
> No sovereignty –
> ...
> All things in common nature should produce
> Without sweat or endeavour. Treason, felony,
> Sword, pike, knife, gun, or need of any engine,
> Would I not have; but nature should bring forth,
> Of its own kind, all foison, all abundance,
> To feed my innocent people.
> ...
> I would with such perfection govern, sir,
> T' excel the golden age.

It is well-known that the playwright's vision of Utopia is similar to that of Montaigne's in his *Les cannibales* (1580). The French philosopher's *Essays* were published in an English translation in 1603, but Shakespeare may also have read them in the original since, as certain passages in *Henry V* demonstrate, he was clearly proficient in French. He could have learned his French in Rheims. Besides, Montaigne's translator was the scholar John Florio, who lived in England (*c.* 1554-*c.* 1625), and whom Shakespeare probably knew personally through his friend and patron, the Earl of Southampton, as Florio was a tutor to the young earl, and lived in the Wriothesley household.

Just as Sir Thomas More (*c.* 1477-1535) in his *Utopia*, published in 1516, had the England of his day in mind, so the playwright here uses Gonzalo's speech to criticise the political, social and economic conditions of Elizabethan and Jacobean times. His vision of an ideal commonwealth must also be viewed, however, against the backdrop of Renaissance thinking which was greatly preoccupied with these ideal worlds and 'the deep yearning for a renewal of all the conditions necessary of life'[323]. Among the best known examples of such 'islands' humanist scholars and writers created for themselves 'mostly in remote countryside' are the Medicis' Villa Careggi, Rabelais' Abbey of Thélème,

Thomas More's garden and the Villa of Pietro Bembo in Padua. The Scottish poet, John Barclay (1582-1621) who wrote *Euphormionus Satyricon* (*c.* 1603-1607), a satire about the Jesuits in the form of a picaresque novel, and the popular *Romance Argenis* (1621) which, in the guise of an allegory, refers to real people and events, even implemented an idea of Pope Paul V. He exchanged the court of James I of England for a house with a large garden below the Vatican, in order to renew the idyll of *Georgica* here until his death (1621) and to dedicate his free time to his bees and his flowers'[324].

At the end of *The Tempest*, Prospero relinquishes a similar idyll, the solitude of his island where – free from the burden of power – he could dedicate himself to study and the upbringing of his daughter. He does so in order to return to his duties as ruler. His creator, Shakespeare, goes in the opposite direction, returning to life in the country – perhaps in the hope of making the garden of New Place in Stratford with its ornamental fountain, its impressive octagon on which a sundial stood, and its mulberry tree into a small-scale realisation of that idealistic concept of the Renaissance period that he knew from literature or experience, but that had hitherto been denied to him.

The final reconciliation between former warring parties or brothers is similar to the storyline of *As You Like It*. However, the union between Ferdinand and Miranda is what crowns and completes the reconciliation in *The Tempest*. In Act V, scene 1, the entrance to Prospero's cell, where the young couple are playing chess, is opened before the eyes of King Alfonso and his companions. To Alfonso, who believed his son was lost at sea, this appears to be a miracle. Even the now remorseful usurper, Sebastian, also talks of an astounding miracle, and Miranda – who until then has known only her father, Ferdinand, Ariel and Caliban – speaks in amazement of the 'goodly creatures' of this 'brave new world'.

Shakespeare may have found inspiration for the chess scene in the so-called Paradise Room in the Palace of Hampton Court. This room contained a gallery of beautiful paintings, an exquisitely ornate throne beneath a star-studded canopy inlaid with precious stones, and a valuable table, covered by a tapestry worth over fifty thousand crowns, embroidered with pearls and precious stones. Thomas Platter the Younger from Basel saw this room with his own eyes on 27 September 1599, and wrote a description. On the table, there stood a 'very beautiful chess set with pieces beautifully carved out of ivory'[325]. Platter found even more to report. In another room, he discovered a portrait of 'Ferdinandi, the Spanish prince's portrait when he was ruler at the age of eight'[326]. The subject was clearly the Spanish Prince Ferdinand who had been brought up by his grandfather, Ferdinand of Aragon. In 1556, Ferdinand succeeded his brother, Emperor Charles V, and ruled until 1564. He had become King of Bohemia and Hungary in 1526, and in 1531 had been elected King of the Romans. Before he became Emperor of the Holy Roman Empire, he was Charles V's deputy in the Holy Roman Empire, and strove to achieve a compromise with the Protestants. Because of his involvement in the Catholic underground and his relationship to Robert Parsons, Shakespeare must have been well aware of the history of this dynasty, which, through the marriage between Philip of Spain and Mary, for some time exercised great influence in England.

The valuable and striking childhood portrait of Ferdinand in Hampton Court is also mentioned in the travel writings of Hentzner, a German visitor to England[327]. Further, Ferdinand was a member of the Order of the Garter. Therefore he himself (or his uncle, Philip of Spain), could have brought the picture to England.

The assumption that the Hampton Court treasures inspired Shakespeare to create the chess game scene in *The Tempest* and to give the king's son a Spanish name, gains added credibility when his secret Catholicism is taken into account. Moreover, Robert Parsons, with whom the Bard must have had close contact, was a frequent visitor to the Spanish court at the time of Philip II.

The Spanish connections set up in this particular play, Shakespeare's theatrical swan-song, so to speak, may contain a hidden message. The prospect of the Scottish king, James VI, succeeding to the English throne was a promising one in the 1590s, but once James had acceded to the English throne, in 1603, it proved catastrophic for the English Catholics. Writing just one year after Parsons' death in 1610, was Shakespeare now backing the Spanish horse, as Parsons had? Ferdinand (Ferrante in Italian) was the name of a prominent King of Naples who ruled between 1458 and 1494, and was a son of Alfonso V of Aragon. It is important to note that the kingdoms of Sicily and Naples belonged to Spain at this time. Shakespeare, therefore, had selected a Spanish setting for his play, but perhaps believed that the censors would not recognise this at first glance. If necessary, he could claim ignorance. Ferdinand I's court in Naples enjoyed a high reputation on the Continent as a centre of the culture of the Italian Renaissance and of humanism. It is significant that King Ferdinand's father was called Alphonse or Alfonso, a name that is little different, except for a missing 'f', from Alonso, the name given by Shakespeare to his King of Naples.

Another Ferdinand, a member of the Medici family, was a cardinal until 1589 and ruled as Grand Duke of Tuscany between 1587 and 1609. In 1600, he married off his niece, Maria de Medici, mother of the future English queen, Henrietta Maria, to Henry IV of France, who had converted to Catholicism seven years earlier. Shakespeare may have heard about the Florentine ruler, his contemporary, during his 'lost years', or may even have seen him in person.

The assumption that Shakespeare might have noticed the portrait of the young Spanish Prince Ferdinand and the aforementioned chess set at Hampton Court is by no means implausible. The dramatist was very receptive to the visual arts, and in *The Winter's Tale* he praised the great talent of a student of Raphael, Guilio Romano, mentioning him by name. From time to time, he had the opportunity to visit the interior of English royal palaces in London and elsewhere, and admire their art treasures, especially when acting in plays performed at royal palaces. These treasures were described in detail in E. Law's three volume *History of Hampton Court Palace* (1885-1891). It was Hans Hecht, a former editor of Platter's account of his journey to England, who drew our attention to the fact that Law mentioned how often Shakespeare had spent time at Hampton Court[328].

Even as an ordinary subject, the dramatist would have found it by no means impossible to visit the palaces. The great palaces of the monarch could be visited even by foreign tourists if they had the appropriate recommendations. As one of many examples, the Basel physician, Thomas Platter the Younger, even had the pleasure of seeing the queen in person on 26 September 1599 at Nonsuch Palace, describing the scene as follows:

> After we waited there a while, some time between twelve and one o'clock, there came many men with white staffs, afterwards many nobles, important men from an inner chamber, following them came the queen towards us, alone and unaccompanied, she moved still straight-backed and upright, sat down in the audience room in a chair overlain with many red, damask and gold-embroidered cushions; the cushions were lying almost down to the floor, so low was the chair under a baldachin that was attached most beautifully up there on the dais.

Platter continued:

> She was most wonderfully dressed in a totally white satin gown, embroidered with gold, and wore a whole bird of paradise as a feather headdress, inlaid with expensive precious stones. She wore around her neck a string of large round pearls, had handsome gloves and a fine ring

> worn over them, and although she was already 74 years old, she looked rather young still, as if she were not older than twenty years.[329]

Platter was wrong about one thing. At that time, Elizabeth was not seventy-four, but only sixty-six-years-old. The fact that she, indeed, appeared young even as an old woman, or was made up to look young, is attested by the well-known painting that depicts her around 1600 with her retinue in front of the northern gatehouse of Blackfriars.[330]

A LATE HISTORY

HENRY VIII

Although Shakespeare appeared to have put the grand finale of his literary career in London behind him, in early 1613 he co-authored a late work, *Henry VIII*. He wrote it most probably with John Fletcher (*Fig. 135*)[331], who was born in December 1579 in Rye (Sussex), and died in August 1625 in London. Fletcher was son of a vicar who had attended the execution of Mary, Queen of Scots, as a chaplain, and later became Bishop of Bristol and then Bishop of London. He later fell out of favour with Queen Elizabeth and died impoverished in 1596. John Fletcher was an unusually prolific dramatist. Together with Sir Francis Beaumont (1584-1616), who came from an old established noble Leicestershire family, he wrote at least thirteen other plays. Fletcher shared not only his London apartment with Beaumont, but also a mistress, probably their maidservant.

The ostensible occasion for Shakespeare's late history play was apparently the wedding of the daughter of the English king, Elizabeth (1596–1662), to the young Elector Palatine, Frederick V (1596–1632), who resided in Heidelberg, and who, in 1619 became king of Bohemia (known as 'the Winter King'). This great event took place in London in February 1613. The King's Men performed fourteen plays altogether at Court, however, there is no clear entry for *Henry VIII* – for example in the *Chamber Accounts*[332]. The play was certainly available and offered for performance at the wedding celebrations, but was not accepted. The subsequent report of the event, *The Magnificent Marriage of the Two Great Princes Frederick Count Palatine and the Lady Elizabeth* (1613),

Fig. 135 – Portrait of the playwright John Fletcher who wrote many plays. This prolific Jacobean writer was the son of an Anglican clergyman who acted as chaplain at the execution of Mary, Queen of Scots, and who later became Bishop of Bristol and then of London. The bishop fell from Elizabeth's grace, however, and died in poverty in 1596. Together with Sir Francis Beaumont, who came from an old-established noble family in Leicestershire, Fletcher published more than thirteen additional plays. He most probably co-authored *Henry VIII* with Shakespeare, which was known at the time as *All is True*. Whereas Shakespeare was responsible for the parts of the play written from a Catholic point of view – he even made Catherine of Aragon into the secret heroine of the play – Fletcher would have written the ones from a Protestant point of view.

recorded laconically and dismissively that the performance was dropped, to be replaced by greater attractions which were in preparation ('it lapsed contrarie, for greater pleasures were preparing')[333].

The title under which *Henry VIII* was announced and performed at the time is significant. It read: *All is True*. When *All is True* was finally performed on St Peter's day (29 June) 1613 in the Globe Theatre – this seems to have been the première – a fire broke out in the building, and the theatre was burnt down to become rubble and ashes.

In *Henry VIII* or *All is True*, as in his earlier histories, Shakespeare pursues concrete moral and politically motivated didactic objectives. For the playwright, three points were particularly important: (1) the fall of Cardinal Wolsey, which he connects to the fall of Lucifer; (2) a positive re-assessment of Catherine of Aragon – who was cast aside by Henry VIII in favour of Anne Boleyn and experiences in this play her 'death dream' as a transfiguration and exaltation[334], and (3) a reminder to his compatriots that under Henry VIII, the great watershed – the separation of England from Rome – was created, with all its well-known consequences.

Henry VIII was not the first play in which Shakespeare portrayed a queen on the stage whose suffering was a forcible reminder of that of Catherine of Aragon; this theme had already been used in *The Winter's Tale*. Through Hermione the poet appears to commemorate the former Spanish princess and English queen, the daughter of Ferdinand and Isabella of Castille and Aragon. Even the building (the Blackfriars Theatre) in which Shakespeare's romance, *The Winter's Tale*, was performed and in which the innocent queen was forced to defend herself in the play, was identical with the one in which the great divorce trial against Catherine of Aragon was held between 31 May and 23 July 1529: the Great Hall of Blackfriars. The positive light in which Shakespeare presents Catherine, the 'secret heroine' of the play, elevating her above the mere historical figure, makes his religious and political standpoint in this last play abundantly clear.

VI. SHAKESPEARE'S LEGACY TO THE CATHOLIC UNDERGROUND AND RETURN TO STRATFORD

PURCHASE OF A HOUSE IN BLACKFRIARS

As has been shown in the preceding chapters, William Shakespeare's origin, upbringing and education, his early employment in Lancashire and his journeys on the Continent are – in conjunction with many references and peculiarities within his literary work – all able to prove that the playwright must have professed the old (Catholic) faith. There is now further documentary evidence to this effect. For, at the end of his most successful career as a dramatist in London, Shakespeare made a significant contribution to strengthening the Catholic underground in England.

On 10 March 1613, for the sum of £140, Shakespeare acquired a building in the grounds of the former Blackfriars monastery in London. The vendor was a certain Henry Walker. The dramatist paid £80 in cash, and on the following day he closed the transaction with a mortgage deed for the remaining £60 (*Fig. 136*). The mortgage was to be paid off on the following St Michael's day (Michaelmas), 29 September 1613. The fact that the deed describes him as 'William Shakespeare of Stratford-vpon-Avon in the countie of Warwick, gentleman' shows that, at this time, he no longer lived in London but in Stratford, and employed the title 'gentleman', which he inherited from his father. The purchase and mortgage deeds show that the building Shakespeare acquired in Blackfriars consisted of a house with a plot of land behind it, which was used as a garden. One side – probably the west side – was enclosed by an old brick wall. The storehouse, cellar, and loft were referred to separately in the deed of sale. The property was directly opposite the royal armory ('The Wardrobe') on the street that led to Puddle Dock on the Thames. An unusual feature of the building was that it was built partly over a large gateway, through which a path led directly to one of the main parts of the monastery grounds (*Fig. 137*). The deeds legally ensured unrestricted access to the acquired property through the large gateway, the normal entrance, and through an inner courtyard.

The acquisition of the gatehouse in Blackfriars was probably financed by the dramatist from the sale of his Globe Theatre property shares. He may have relinquished the shares in 1612 or early in 1613 at the latest, since such a momentous transaction would have had to be put in train well in advance. As we know that the reconstruction of the Globe after the fire on 29 June 1613 cost about £1,400, the value of the theatre before its destruction can be estimated. The money Shakespeare had released to purchase the house in Blackfriars may have been more or less sufficient. The fact that Shakespeare's name was never mentioned in the report about the fire (see pp. 123 and 307) indicates that by then he had sold his shares in the property and no longer lived in London.

The acquisition of the house in Blackfriars differed significantly in at least two respects from all the other property purchases that Shakespeare had made. Firstly, he was buying a property in London, where it seems that previously he had always lived as either a tenant or a lodger. Secondly, Shakespeare bought this house together with three trustees, William Johnson, John Jackson and John Heminge.

There has been much speculation over the reasons for the acquisition of the property. The American Shakespeare biographer, Samuel Schoenbaum, thought it was merely an 'investment', an opinion shared by the English historian A.L. Rowse; but this is hardly a satisfactory explanation. Robert Bearman of the Stratford Birthplace Records Office, on the other hand, fully recognised the uniqueness of this business transaction, standing in stark contrast to the rest of Shakespeare's purchases, all of which were made in or around Stratford. But Bearman did not have a conclusive explanation to offer either.

In Elizabethan times, London rapidly became not only a stronghold of English Protestantism, but of Puritanism as well. When Edmund Campion, having been out of the country for years, returned to England as a Jesuit missionary, he noted and regretted the spread of Protestantism. Catholics living in London were in much greater danger than those who lived, for example, in Lancashire or Warwickshire. They were subject to many more raids by the authorities. However, as a dramatist and actor Shakespeare was obliged to live in the capital. His actors lived in London, and the Globe and the Blackfriars Theatre were situated there. Only in England's capital could he exercise his brilliant literary talent to the full. Yet, apart from the gatehouse in Blackfriars, Shakespeare chose not to buy property in or near London. He never intended to live there with his family in a grand house, let alone spend his old age there. The dramatist, a loyal Catholic, had amassed property in a place where he felt safer from the clutches of the government or the church, namely in his home town of Stratford-upon-Avon. This is demonstrated by the acquisition of New Place (1597); the acquisition of another 127 acres of farmland, as well as a cottage (1602); and his purchase of a share in rights to the tithes of Stratford (1605).

As far as is known, neither Shakespeare nor his family ever lived in the London house. The dramatist bought it after he had settled his affairs in London and had firmly established himself once more in Stratford. The property is specifically mentioned in his will, however, as well as the tenant who was living there, John Robinson. The reasons behind this purchase in Blackfriars are not the only enigma. It is not obvious, either, why Shakespeare chose to make the purchase together with three trustees. Leslie Hotson, the twentieth-century Canadian-born Shakespeare scholar who made some important discoveries about the details of Shakespeare's life, carefully investigated the lives of the trustees. He discovered that William Johnson was the owner of the Mermaid Tavern. This tavern was located in Cheapside, not far from St Paul's Cathedral and Blackfriars. Its actual address, though, was Bread Street (*Fig. 54*) which led down from the imposing main shopping street of Cheapside to the Thames (with a landing stage at Queenhithe Dock). The Mermaid Tavern, the Mitre Tavern (which was also in Bread Street), and the Boar's Head in Eastcheap (Falstaff's 'local') were among the most famous inns in London, but the Mermaid eventually outstripped the other two. Literary circles met regularly at the Mermaid Tavern, including – as is well known – Shakespeare and his colleagues. The witty travel writer Thomas Coryat (1577-1617) also frequented the Mermaid, where he met many of Shakespeare's friends, and apparently Shakespeare himself. As Hotson's investigations have proved, Coryat was acquainted with another of Shakespeare's trustees, John Jackson. He studied in Oxford, but did not graduate, which at this time could indicate that he had refused to take the Oath of Supremacy. Coryat was highly esteemed by his contemporaries, mainly because of his sense of humour. He was in demand at Court and later became a member of the household of Prince Henry, heir to the throne. In 1608, he travelled on the Continent and described his journey. In 1612, a year before Shakespeare bought the house in Blackfriars, he set out on a new journey – this time to the Middle East and India. We are grateful to Coryat for his information about the monthly meeting of a small group of young aristocrats, lawyers, actors and playwrights who were interested in literature. Francis Beaumont, John Fletcher, Ben Jonson and William Shakespeare also attended these meetings, at which the discussions were heated and amusing. The dramatist Beaumont provides a lively description of them:

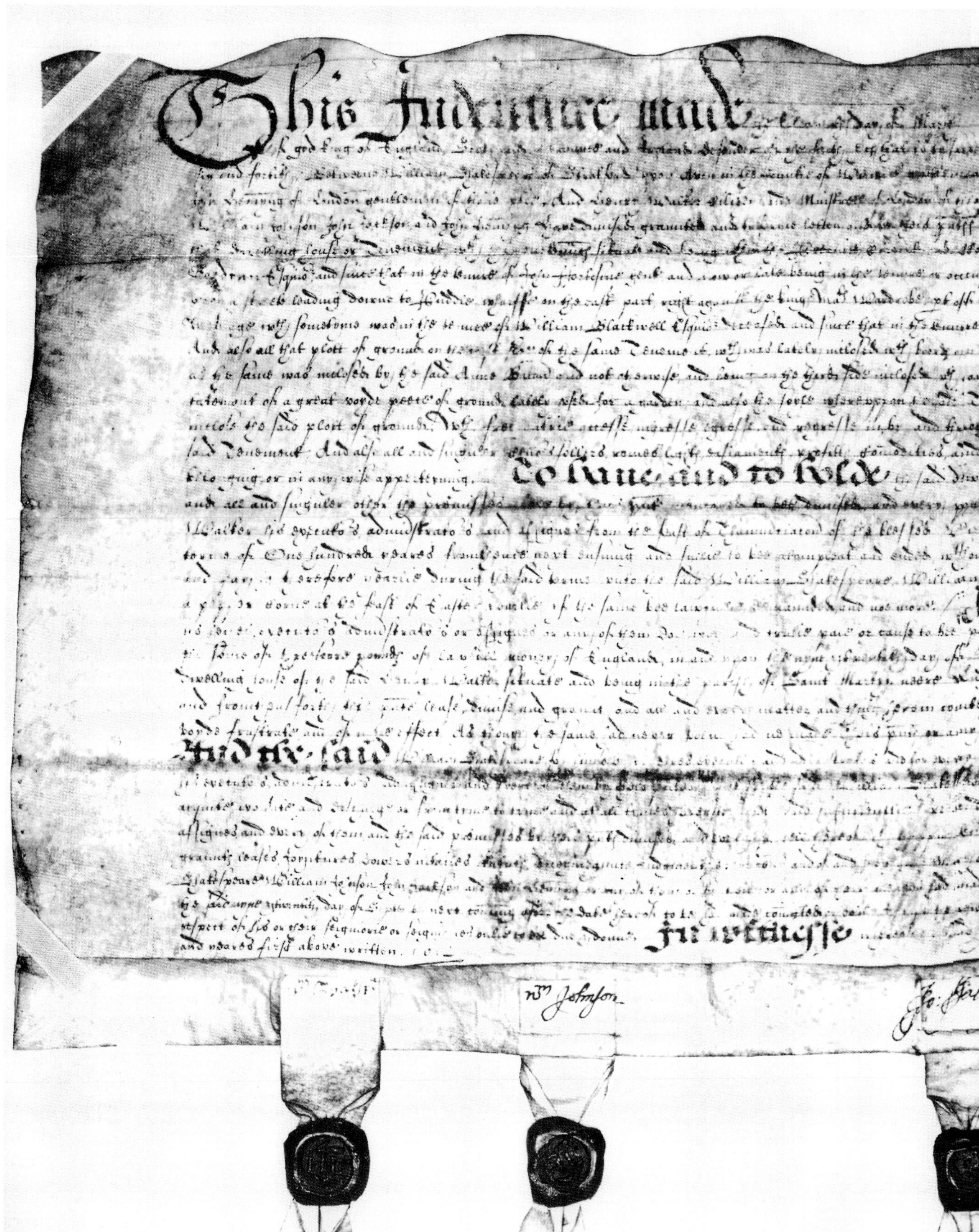
This Indenture made
To have and to hold
And the said
In witnesse
Wm Johnson

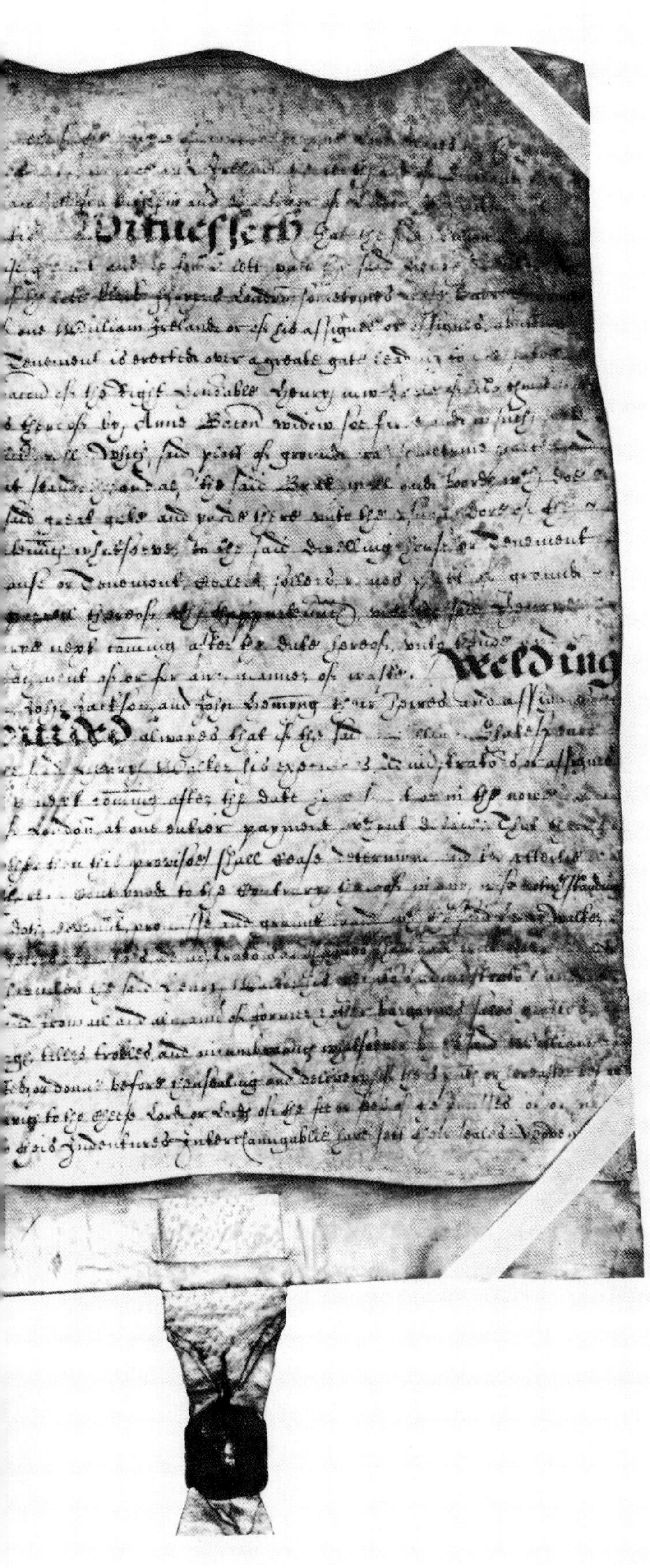

What things have we seen
Done at the Mermaid!
Heard what words that have been
So nimble, and so full of subtile flame,
As if that every one, from whence they came,
Had meant to put his whole wit in a jest
And had resolv'd to live a fool the rest
Of his dull life.[335]

The favourite drink on such occasions was probably 'Sack' or 'Seck', wine from Spain, or perhaps Rhenish wine from Bacharach ('backrag'), or wine from Hochheim on the Main ('hockamore' or 'hock') both from Germany[336].

Followers of Essex who participated in the Rebellion also gathered at the Mermaid Tavern, as well as the Gunpowder Plot conspirators, who mostly came from Warwickshire. These circles, with whom Shakespeare – as we have seen – was either directly or indirectly involved, overlapped to a large extent.

As Hotson's researches revealed, Shakespeare's trustee, John Jackson, who likewise frequented the Mermaid Tavern, was obviously a shipping magnate from Hull. Thomas Coryat may have travelled on one or more of his ships.

Fig. 136 – Deed, with seals and signatures, documenting the purchase of the eastern gatehouse on the site of the former monastery in Blackfriars by William Shakespeare on 10 March 1613. The playwright's signature can be seen above the first seal on the left. Shakespeare's trustees were William Johnson, the owner of the Mermaid Tavern, John Jackson, the shipping magnate, and John Heminge, who dealt with the business affairs of the King's Men. By purchasing this gatehouse, Shakespeare acquired a building used by the Catholic underground to provide accommodation for persecuted priests. The various professions of the trustees reveal that here we are dealing with an almost perfect division of labour among these English crypto-Catholics.

Fig. 137 – Remains of a wall in Ireland Yard, which apparently belonged to the eastern gatehouse of Blackfriars, purchased by Shakespeare in 1613.

Shakespeare's third trustee, John Heminge, was the famous actor and business manager of Shakespeare's theatre company. In 1623, with Henry Condell, he compiled, edited and published Shakespeare's plays.

This detailed information about Shakespeare's trustees still does not answer all the open questions. But a thorough study of the documents concerning the history of this gatehouse in Elizabethan and Jacobean times shows that when Shakespeare acquired it, the building had already been in use for several decades to harbour Catholic priests as well as members of Catholic orders, and help them to escape. Now it becomes clear why Shakespeare has bought this particular house and also why he chose the form of a trust when purchasing the building[337]. For the trust, a typical instrument of English law[338], would have ensured that its members, a group of persons with a fiduciary duty, would continue using Shakespeare's gatehouse exactly as he wished, even after his death, and thus fulfil his purpose in purchasing the property.

In 1586 Richard Frith, who was living in Blackfriars at the time, reported that the estate had various back entrances, alleys, secret vaults and hiding-places in which 'Papists' had been sought in the past, although without success, since the full extent of the building's hiding-places was unknown.

There is information that, particularly in the 1590s, there was a constant coming and going of priests in this house. Throughout the next decade, the house was frequently suspected of providing a hiding place for Catholic priests.

Richard Topcliffe, the most dangerous government spy as far as the Catholics were concerned, was always well informed. He issued a veiled warning to the tenant of the gatehouse, John Fortescue, as well as to his uncle, Sir John Fortescue – a member of the Privy Council who was also in charge of the Wardrobe, across the way – that they were storing up grave trouble for themselves. But Sir John's position on the Privy Council was obviously so strong and secure at the time that he was immune to Topcliffe's attacks.

Nonetheless, in 1598, there was a large-scale raid on the gatehouse by government officials. The tip-off apparently came from William Udall, who had spoken of the house's secret corridors, connected to secret passageways which led down to the Thames. Ellen Fortescue, the wife of the then absent tenant, confessed to being a recusant. However, she denied harbouring priests. She succeeded in convincing the authorities of her innocence in this respect, especially since the raid was unsuccessful. In reality, however, Mrs Fortescue had several priests hidden in her house even during the search – among them a priest named Joseph Pollen. This information came from the English Jesuit, Oswald Greenway, who visited the gatehouse on the day after the raid and learned that the priests had been able to disappear into their bolt holes in the nick of time. In order to protect his family after this incident, John Fortescue wrote to the Earl of Essex, assuring him that he never broke the laws of Her Majesty, whereby it was forbidden to hide, provide for, or aid and abet priests or Jesuits ('harboring, maintaininge or abbetting ether prist or Jesuit'[339]). That was obviously a white lie. Since the correspondence was directed at Essex, who was tolerant of Catholics and even covertly supported their cause, Fortescue could be assured that, should his case ever be brought before the Privy Council, he would be protected by his uncle and by the Earl of Essex.

Shakespeare's gatehouse played a very important role during and immediately after the Gunpowder Plot of 1605. Before the attack, the Jesuit father John Gerard wanted the main conspirators – Catesby, Percy, Winter and Digby – to stay there, but the stalwart Mrs Fortescue wouldn't allow it because – so she said – she disapproved of Catesby's way of life. When the plot failed and the hunt began for the rest of the plotters, John Gerard escaped through this gap to freedom. Wearing a wig and a false beard, he made for St Omer south of Calais, to the English college founded by Robert Parsons in 1593, the main bridgehead of the exiled Catholics on the Continent. Fortescue and his family followed suit, since he considered his life and theirs to be in serious danger. His son, George, who was born in 1578 and probably received his basic academic education in Rheims or Douai, studied at the Collegium Anglicum in Rome from 1609.

Against this background, Shakespeare's acquisition of the eastern gatehouse in Blackfriars, together with three trustees, must be seen in a completely different light. The dramatist had bought a clandestine gathering place for fugitive Catholics who received shelter and help there, and were then escorted to the Blackfriars landing stage on the Thames to be safely taken, first by boat and then by ship, to the Continent. The whole thing also operated in reverse: Catholic priests and adherents secretly returning to the country could evade the strict surveillance in the ports, and make a discreet landfall. By purchasing this house Shakespeare had acquired what might also be called the most important institution of English crypto-Catholicism – with the clear intention of making an essential contribution to the survival of the old faith which in England was threatened by extinction.

The task of the trustees Johnson, Jackson and Heminge was obviously to act in Shakespeare's interest and fulfil the purpose of the purchase. Their various professions, which were only fully revealed in the twentieth century, were an almost perfect division of labour among these English crypto-Catholics. Shakespeare himself provided what the fugitive priests needed most: a safe and secret building with many hiding places where they could lodge. Johnson, the landlord of the Mermaid Tavern, could supply them with food. Jackson, the shipping magnate, could arrange their transport to the Continent, and Heminge, the actor and business manager of the King's Men, could deal with the administrative side of the operation. The Blackfriars Theatre had all the equipment for disguising the priests with different clothing, wigs, false beards, and so on, to save them from capture or, at least, to make it more difficult[340].

At this time, many fugitive English Catholics, who had fled to the Continent, found shelter at the English College in St Omer in France (see *Figs. 34 a–c*).

Another building in the old monastery grounds of Blackfriars was also used by the Catholic underground. This fact first came to light through a serious accident. On the afternoon of 5 November 1623 (Gregorian calendar)[341] at about 3.00p.m., somewhere between 200 to 300 people had gathered for a secret Catholic religious service, held in an attic on the third floor of another Blackfriars gatehouse. People had turned out in large numbers to hear the prominent Jesuit father, Robert Drury, who was preaching that day. Drury had been rector at the St Omer College for three years, and was now working as a missionary priest in the Catholic underground in England. The believers were listening to Drury's words while, directly below them, Father Wittingham (alias Redyate) was in the priest's room, preparing a sermon. Suddenly a supporting beam on the third floor broke and collapsed. A detailed report of this disaster, entitled *The Doleful Evensong*, was recorded, according to Catholic sources, by the Puritan Rev. Samuel Clarke. More recent research suggests the author was Thomas Goad. The chronicler wrote:

> The floor whereon that assembly stood or sat, not sinking by degrees, but at one instant failing and falling by the breaking asunder of a main sommier or dormer of that floor; which beam, together with joices and plancher thereto adjoined, with the people thereon, rushed down with such violence that the weight and fall thereof brake in sunder another far stronger and thicker sommier of the chamber situated directly underneath, and so both the ruined floors, with the people overlapped and crushed under or between them, fell (without any time of stay) upon a lower third floor, being the floor of the said Lord Ambassador's withdrawing chamber ... [342]

The report revealed that the catastrophe, which was also known as 'Fatal Vespers', killed ninety-nine people, including both Jesuit fathers. Many people sustained serious injuries. It seems that those who survived were not prosecuted. However, the Bishop of London refused the dead burial in the cemeteries and churches of London. They were therefore buried in a mass grave in an inner courtyard behind the collapsed building. Only a few of the dead, being of noble birth, were allowed to be buried in London's churches.

The Puritans immediately interpreted the disaster as divine punishment. The professor of divinity and prominent Jesuit father, John Floyd, emphatically rejected this theory. In that same year, he composed a pamphlet entitled *A Word of Comfort to the English Catholics*[343], which was printed in St Omer.

At the time, it was suspected of being an anti-Catholic act of sabotage, given the date of 5 November, although according to the long-standing Julian calendar the event had occurred on 23 October. Amidst the ruins, the exact cause of the accident was never established. It is, however, certain that the spacious upper floor was known to a few Protestants as one of the principal meeting-places for the Catholics of the capital[344]. Some have surmised that this was the very gatehouse in Blackfriars that Shakespeare had acquired, but in the course of my research into written and pictorial sources, and in collaboration with an architect, I discovered that the gatehouse in which the disaster occurred could not possibly have been the one bought by Shakespeare. The fateful building was the northern gatehouse, while Shakespeare's house was the eastern gatehouse of the monastery (see *Fig. 131*). The two buildings had different functions for the English crypto-Catholics. Unlike Shakespeare's gatehouse, a clandestine gathering place for priests and other fugitive Catholics who were trying to escape, the gatehouse in which the tragedy occurred was the secret pastoral care centre for crypto-Catholicism in the English capital. It contained priests' rooms and rooms in which Catholic divine services were offered. It was here where, on a regular basis, confessions were held and Masses were said. The two gatehouses (Gatehouse I and Gatehouse II) are marked on a map of the Blackfriars monastery site (*Fig. 131*).

The catastrophe in the northern gatehouse (Gatehouse I) in the former monastery grounds of Blackfriars also revealed that the building very close to St Paul's Cathedral housed the chief secret Catholic church in London. This is a further pointer to the importance of the eastern gatehouse (Gatehouse II) as a place of shelter for hunted priests and Catholic believers. Without this second gatehouse, which enabled the Catholic clergy to come and go unnoticed (*Fig. 133*), the religious services and pastoral care offered by Gatehouse I could not have been maintained. Believers who attended Mass on the third floor could have felt fairly secure because they enjoyed the protection of the French ambassador, who resided on the imposing first floor, the *belle étage* of the elegant Gatehouse I. The ambassador's residence had a secret exit which led directly to the Catholic church on the third floor. The many churchgoers from outside used a concealed side-entrance of the building.

Fig. 138 – Queen Elizabeth and her entourage on the way to St Paul's Cathedral after the victory over the Spanish Armada in 1588. In the background of this contemporary copper engraving, the entrance of the northern gatehouse of the former monastery of Blackfriars can be made out, consisting of two arches of a vault behind and partly above which there is a three storey building, erected in typical Renaissance style. Unlike Shakespeare's eastern gatehouse, which offered an escape route to persecuted Catholic priests, the northern gatehouse housed a secret Catholic centre, with a church on the third floor. There was a secret passage within the building that gave the French Ambassador, who lived on the first floor, direct access to this church. It was during Mass on 26 October 1623 (according to the Gregorian calendar, this was 5 November, the anniversary of the Gunpowder Plot) that a beam collapsed in the floor of the room used as a church, and ninety-nine people died, including the important guest, the Jesuit priest Robert Drury, who had been rector of the English College in St Omer.

Incidentally, at the time of the accident, the ambassador was not at home; he was visiting the Venetian ambassador.

An engraving dated 1588 shows what the author has identified as the northern gatehouse[345], a handsome edifice in the Renaissance style. In the foreground (*Fig. 138*), Elizabeth I is shown on her way to St Paul's Cathedral to attend a Service of Thanksgiving after the victory over the Spanish Armada. The same subject was used in a painting of which the entire upper part was later cut off. It was painted circa 1600 and is attributed to the painter Robert Peake the Elder[346]. Comparison with the engraving makes it clear that the second and third storeys – the floors used as priests' rooms and the secret church – are the parts of the picture that were cut out. The ambassador's residence is clearly recognisable on the first floor. Well-dressed, wealthy people are depicted crowding at the windows, watching the procession of Elizabeth I and her attendants. The engraving shows that at the windows of the upper storeys there is no one watching; not a soul eager to see the queen. It now does make sense that this valuable painting was so badly mutilated.

From what has been said above, it is safe to say that when Shakespeare purchased the eastern gatehouse in Blackfriars, he most certainly intended to make a considerable contribution to strengthen the Catholic underground and preserve what was left of the old religion.

THE GLOBE THEATRE FIRE

On 29 June 1613, a good four months after Shakespeare's house purchase in Blackfriars, the first Globe Theatre, erected in 1599, caught fire and rapidly burned to the ground. The day of the week was a Tuesday, according to the Julian calendar. Shakespeare's and Fletcher's *Henry VIII* was playing at the time, which was then significantly entitled *All is True*. Fletcher, or perhaps an additional co-author, may have been responsible for the part of the play that was written from a Protestant point of view, with Shakespeare obviously writing from the Catholic perspective.

Sir Henry Wotton (1568-1639) wrote the most detailed report of the event, to his nephew, Sir Edmund Bacon, on 2 July 1613. Wotton, who had studied in Oxford, travelled around the Continent and had been in the service of Essex purveying news to him from the Continent, wrote about a new play by the King's Men, that described 'some principal pieces' from the reign of Henry VIII and furthermore, brought unusually monumental and majestic pomp to the stage. Thus, Wotton added somewhat ironically, greatness had been, if not ridiculed, at least made conceivable for the spectators.

Wotton then wrote about the Maskers scene in the play, which took place in the house of Cardinal Wolsey, and in which the monarch himself participated. At the entrance of the king, a cannon, stuffed with paper and other materials, was fired. One of these discharges fell on to the thatched roof of the theatre, and from a smouldering spark a conflagration rapidly took hold. In less than an hour, the entire theatre was destroyed. The burning trousers of one of the spectators was extinguished by another quick-witted theatregoer with a bottle of beer he was carrying. The novelty of bottled beer, incidentally, was the recent invention of Alexander Nowell, headmaster of Westminster School and later the dean of St Paul's Cathedral.

It was very fortunate that, despite the fact that there was a full house, not a single person died. There would have been well over 2,000 spectators[347], some of whom were in the upper circle of the theatre, but sufficient exits and emergency exits must have existed for all to leave safely.

In 1613, the performance of a drama about Henry VIII was a risky undertaking, even though the Tudor dynasty had died out in 1603 with the death of Elizabeth I. As heir to the Tudors, James Stuart fully accepted the Church of England which they had founded. The fact that this explosive play was performed, or premièred, on 29 June, St Peter's Day; the feast of St Peter, a saint who aroused diametrically opposed feelings and emotions for supporters and enemies of the Pope respectively, reminding them of Rome, the See of the Catholic pontiff. Henry VIII and his daughter, Elizabeth, however, had broken with Rome.

The cannons that had caused the devastating fire had been fired for the Maskers scene when Henry and Anne Boleyn first meet each other at the house of Cardinal Wolsey (Act I, scene 4). Anne and other guests were already on the stage as the king, dressed as a shepherd, entered with sixteen torchbearers. The meeting of Henry and Anne is imminent. In view of the fact that this history play was premièred on St Peter's day, in addition to its delicate historical subject matter and also the crucial scene of the play in which the misfortune happened, it cannot be ruled out that this was a deliberate act of anti-Catholic sabotage.

An anonymous contemporary ballad entitled *A Sonnett upon the pittiful burneing of the Globe playhowse in London*[348] was composed immediately after the fire and appears to contain certain hints. It strikes a strong Puritanical note of secret satisfaction and malicious glee. Each of the six stanzas ends with the refrain, 'Oh sorrow, pittiful sorrow, and yett al this is true', an ironic reference to the alternative title of the play *All is True*. We are then given a series of details, such as the fact that 29 June 1613 was a brilliantly sunny day, so that rain, which might have extinguished the fire, was not to be expected. People rushed out of the building, their eyes smarting, blinded by the smoke, leaving hats, swords and other personal belongings behind. The author of the anonymous ballad names none of the aristocratic members of the audience, but mentions the leading actors of the King's Men: Burbage, Condell and Heminge, Shakespeare's closest friends. The fact that the dramatist is not named implies that he was not present. Most probably, he had sold his shares in the Globe Theatre in late 1612 or early 1613 (see p. 123).

The Puritan authorship of the ballad is suggested by the disparaging mention in verse of two of the leading actors in Shakespeare's theatre company, who were the big stars of their day:

Out runne the knightes, out runne the lordes,
And there was great adoe;
Some lost their hattes, and some their swordes;
Then out runne Burbidge too;
The reprobates, though druncke on Munday,
Prayd for the Foole and Henry Condye.
Oh sorrow, pittiful sorrow, and yett all this is true.

By 'reprobates', the author certainly meant the actors. The anonymous ballad writer claims that the actors had still been drunk on Monday, the day before the performance. 'Heminges', the business manager of the King's Men, his name rhyming with 'druncken Flemminges' in verse three, is mocked for his stammer: 'Then with swolne eyes, like druncken Flemminges,/ Distressed stood old stuttering Heminges./Oh sorrow, pittifull sorrow, and yett all this is true.' The Puritanism of the author becomes even clearer in verse five when he delivers a warning to all the actors ('stage-strutters') and prophesies for them a fate similar to that of the actors at the Globe Theatre:

Be warned, you stage-strutters all,
Least yow againe be catched,
And such a burneing doe befall,
As to them whose howse was thatched
[...].

Like a self-appointed punitive judge, the anonymous writer continues to castigate the actors, demanding that they 'forebeare [their] whoreing, breeding biles.'

Considering these facts, it is very likely that the Globe Theatre fire was the work of Puritan fanatics, not only because they hated the theatre and its actors, but also because of the covertly Catholic tendency of the play and the date of the first performance.

Shakespeare was the main author, but apparently was not present at the performance.

Everything he had to tell us had already been said through the scenes and subject matter he chose to contribute to this play, and also through comments in the Prologue to this, his last dramatic work:

> I come no more to make you laugh: things now,
> That bear a weighty and a serious brow,
> Sad, high, and working, full of state and woe,
> Such noble scenes as draw the eye to flow,
> We now present. Those that can pity, here
> May, if they think it well, let fall a tear;
> The subject will deserve it. Such as give
> Their money out of hope they may believe,
> May here find truth too. Those that come to see
> Only a show or two, and so agree
> The play may pass, if they be still and willing,
> I'll undertake may see away their shilling
> Richly in two short hours. Only they
> That come to hear a merry bawdy play,
> A noise of targets, or to see a fellow
> In a long motley coat guarded with yellow,
> Will be deceived; for, gentle hearers, know,
> To rank our chosen truth with such a show
> As fool and fight is, beside forfeiting
> Our own brains, and the opinion that we bring,
> To make that only true we now intend,
> Will leave us never an understanding friend.
> Therefore, for goodness' sake, and as you are known
> The first and happiest hearers of the town,
> Be sad, as we would make ye: think ye see
> The very persons of our noble story
> As they were living; think you see them great,
> And follow'd with the general throng and sweat
> Of thousand friends; then in a moment, see
> How soon this mightiness meets misery.

Here Shakespeare speaks directly to his audience and openly expresses his own mood, something he very rarely does in his writings. An exception, however, is the Prologue to Act V of *Henry V*. In the Prologue to *Henry VIII* he makes it quite clear to the audience that what they can expect by this play (with the significant title *All Is True*) will be no cause for joy. For now truths would be told which still seemed incredible, even after eighty years. Shakespeare is, of course, referring to Henry VIII's marriage to Anne Boleyn, after he divorced Catherine of Aragon and broke with Rome in 1533. His characters, so Shakespeare announces, will give the audience food for thoughts, furrow their brow, make them sad and even cause pain in them. There will be no more laughter, only sorrow, pity and tears. Whereas the fate of Queen Catherine will bring tears of pity to the viewer, the fall of Wolsey, the penultimate Catholic cardinal[349] to serve as Archbishop of Canterbury, will make them aware of how unstable power and greatness are, and how abrupt their end can be. For the Elizabethans, Wolsey's great advancement and sudden fall were a perfect exemplar of the fickleness of Fortune. Shakespeare pays tribute to the fallen Wolsey, Catherine's adversary, by granting him a long closing monologue in Act III, scene 2:

> Farewell! a long farewell, to all my greatness!
> This is the state of man: to-day he puts forth
> The tender leaves of hopes; to-morrow blossoms,
> And bears his blushing honours thick upon him;
> The third day comes a frost, a killing frost,
> [...] I have ventured,
> Like little wanton boys that swim on bladders,
> This many summers in a sea of glory,
> But far beyond my depth: my high-blown pride
> At length broke under me and now has left me,
> Weary and old with service, to the mercy
> Of a rude stream, that must for ever hide me.
> Vain pomp and glory of this world, I hate ye:
> I feel my heart new open'd. O, how wretched
> Is that poor man that hangs on princes' favours!
> There is, betwixt that smile we would aspire to,
> That sweet aspect of princes, and their ruin,
> More pangs and fears than wars or women have:
> And when he falls, he falls like Lucifer,
> Never to hope again.

Due to the outbreak of fire during Act 1, scene 4 the audience at the first performance never got to hear these words, but they did hear the Prologue, whose meaning they would have understood only too well. Shakespeare was preparing them for an account of the historical events from a Catholic perspective. The Anglicans and Puritans could have been aware of this intention, as this historical drama belonged to the selection of plays that had been put forward for performance by the King's Men on the occasion of the royal wedding in February 1613, but was rejected. The Catholic perspective of many passages in *All is True* may have displeased the censors, and the young German bridegroom, Frederick, would also have found it quite disturbing.

When looked at in this context, clearly not only radical Puritans, but also Protestants would have had reason to try to prevent the performance of *All is True*. Both factions may have been angered by a history of Henry VIII of which Catherine of Aragon was the covert heroine. This makes the possibility of arson on St Peter's Day, 1613 even more likely. If this was a deliberate attack by militant Puritans or Protestants, they would have taken into account not just considerable property damage (the cost to rebuild the theatre amounted to £1,400) but, what was worse, also the loss of many lives. Since the Gunpowder Plot of 1605, the government had been increasingly prepared to use violence to impose religious and political order.

The *Annals* of the English chronicler John Stow, continued by Edmund Howes, record that many acts of sabotage and arson with devastating consequences occurred in many English churches during the year 1614[350]. This historical source tells us to what extent the propensity to violence had already increased at that time. It does, however, not indicate who was responsible for these terrible attacks. But it appears, that they were carried out by militant Puritans rebelling against those aspects of the Anglican liturgy that had been taken directly from Catholic ritual.

The Globe Theatre was rebuilt in the spring of 1614 and was back in business by 30 June 1614 at the latest. The scholar John Chamberlain (1553-1637) wrote to a friend that the New Globe was the prettiest theatre ever in England. When the Civil War broke out in 1642, all theatres were closed by the Puritans. The New Globe was demolished only two years later. Thanks to the initiative of the late actor and director, Sam Wanamaker, a replica of the Globe Theatre was constructed near the original site on the South Bank and completed in 1997[351]. Today it is among the biggest attractions of the English capital.

RETURN TO STRATFORD

There are many reasons why Shakespeare prematurely ended his triumphant dramatic career in London. After a long stay on the Continent, mostly in Rome, he finally retired to his home town and his family in Stratford (*Fig. 139*). Shakespeare's intellectual and creative powers may have been exhausted after such an intensive, scarcely imaginable period of creativity and performance, often under severe pressure of time and other difficult conditions. John Aubrey reported that Shakespeare was beginning to suffer from health problems even at the beginning of his career in Shoreditch. Modern medical specialists have been able to identify in the authenticated portraits of Shakespeare clearly recognisable symptoms of disease (as shown in my book *The True Face of William Shakespeare*, 2006, for the first time).

A decisive blow that, apart from his serious illness, seems to have caused Shakespeare's premature retirement and return to Stratford, must have been the additional severe government measures that led to the further deterioration of the deplorable state of the Catholic population of England. Although it was never passed, a bill was introduced in parliament in the year 1613 forcing followers of the old faith to wear red caps and coloured stockings, thereby marking them out, making it easy to distinguish them from the rest of the population and brand them as outcasts. In the same year, however, another bill did pass and had more or less the same effect: Catholics were banned from carrying weapons. This was supposed to prevent attacks by the followers of the old faith, but in an age where it was customary and honourable for men to wear rapiers and daggers, this meant a further degradation and humiliation of male English Catholics.

Shakespeare seems to have responded to this shabby treatment of his fellow Catholics with a kind of 'inner immigration', retreating to his own private world in Stratford. Before he left, he settled his business affairs in London, including what might be called his religious legacy: the purchase of the eastern gatehouse in Blackfriars.

During Shakespeare's most active and creative phase as a London dramatist and poet, 1592-1612, he obviously had not had time to visit Rome. However, the entries for the year 1613 in Pilgrim book No. 282 of the English College in Rome include the name 'Ricardus Stratfordus'. This is reminiscent of the pseudonym 'Arthurus Stratfordus' that Shakespeare used in 1585. Again the name of the town of Stratford replaced his last name, and for his first name he took the name of both his grandfather (Richard Shakespeare from Snitterfield) and his brother Richard who died in February 1613. In the Elizabethan and Jacobean era, it was common for persecuted Catholics to use the names of relatives, especially grandparents. They are a hidden indication of family affiliation. All this strongly suggests that the person thus listed could only have been William Shakespeare from Stratford-upon-Avon. At the end of his brilliant literary career, the playwright thus appears to have visited Rome once again – probably for the last time. 'Richard Stratford' stayed in the English hospice for eight days, as he had done on his first known visit to Rome in 1585. He did not supply the customary information regarding month and date of arrival, probably for security reasons. From the other entries on this page, however, it can be inferred that he was there in October 1613.

While in Rome, Shakespeare would surely have visited the crypt of the English College (*Fig. 48*), the final resting place of William Allen and Robert Parsons, the leading English Catholics-in-exile, whom he had much to thank for. Parsons, who died in 1610, was buried at his own request next to his friend Allen, who had died in 1594. It was Napoleon who destroyed this burial place and had the lead caskets of the exiled Catholics melted down. In English historiography of the early seventeenth century, Allen and Parsons, like Edmund Campion, were considered to be arch-rebels and traitors. Carlton's publication, *A Thankful Remembrance*, published in 1627, eleven years after Shakespeare's death, contains an engraving entitled 'Rebellion, the effect of Monasteries'. The engraving depicts Parsons and Campion (*Fig. 140*). From 1613 at the latest, possibly even earlier, Shakespeare chose to live the life of a well-to-do gentleman residing with his family in New Place, a handsome mansion with extensive grounds. (*Figs. 141 a–b*). The title 'gentleman' had been granted to his father, due to services performed by an ancestor under Henry VII, because of his own standing as a Stratford magistrate, because of his 'Landes and tenementes of good wealth' and because he had married 'the daughter of a gentleman'.

There was a sundial installed in the garden at New Place (*Fig. 141a*). Sundials are referred to in several of Shakespeare's plays (see among others AYL, II, 7 and 3H6, II, 5).

In the garden at New Place, also stood a mulberry tree that was said to have been personally planted by Shakespeare. The tree was cut down in the eighteenth century and its wood made into mementos. It was probably planted in May 1609, because on 1 May in that year many thousands of mulberry saplings were planted in England, having been imported from France for the purpose of feeding silkworms, bred for silk production.

John Aubrey reports that the poet visited his family in Stratford once a year. Aubrey remembers hearing that Shakespeare left £200-300 each time he visited, and also deposited some money with his sister who lived there.

Fig. 139 – The Shakespeare Hotel in Stratford-upon-Avon. Shakespeare's handsome residence, New Place, on the corner of Chapel Street and Chapel Lane, would have looked very similar.

After deducting his family's living expenses, he must have used these large amounts to buy land in the vicinity of Stratford[352]. The sister whom Aubrey mentions was Joan Hart, who had a very close relationship with the playwright. Joan was remembered generously in his will, receiving the handsome sum of £20, as well as Shakespeare's entire collection of clothing, and above all the right to live in his house in Henley Street for the rest of her life, in return for a peppercorn rent of just one shilling a year. It was Joan's descendants who, in 1757, found John Shakespeare's Borromeo Testament in the rafters of this house.

On his annual trips home to Stratford, about which Aubrey reported and which almost certainly occurred in summer, Shakespeare was in the habit of breaking his journey by staying the night in Oxford. The route from London was the highway that led eventually to Chester in the north-west, one of the four major highways leading to and from the English capital. The other three led to Dover in the south, Bristol in the west, and Berwick-on-Tweed in the north. As a gentleman, Shakespeare owned his own horse, as is apparent from Sonnet 50, and so might have used it for the journey; but if pressed for time, he could have taken the mail coach or used post horses. The coach horses were changed at staging posts, so that Shakespeare could make the 110-mile trip from London to Stratford in one day, or just over twelve hours. For example, if he left London at 6.00 a.m., if everything went well and he only took short breaks, he could have reached Stratford at about 6.30 p.m., or slightly later if he took longer breaks. Such calculations are based on comparisons with

Fig. 140 – Illustration from the anti-Catholic pamphlet *A Thankfull Remembrance*, written by Carleton in 1627. It depicts the Jesuit priests Robert Parsons and Edmund Campion, and also shows Campion hanging from the gallows in front of a monastery and church. The subtitle 'Rebellion the effect of Monasteries' makes it clear that the monasteries were regarded as hotbeds of rebellion by the Protestants. As the present author has been able to show, Shakespeare took lodgings at monasteries when travelling. This can only have been on the Continent since all English monasteries had been destroyed under Henry VIII (see Chronology: 1536 and 1537–1539).

information in contemporary sources. The Swiss traveller Thomas Platter reports that his party first sailed on the return trip from London to Gravesend and from there rode with the post horses to Dover. This final forty-four-mile stretch of the trip took five hours[353].

Shakespeare, however, would normally break his journey at Oxford as pointed out above. The university city is about fifty-six miles from London, and the playwright evidently did not travel all the way to Stratford in one day, but spread the journey over two days. Travelling in this way meant that he could use his own horse. He probably relished these trips, not only because they meant seeing his family and friends in and around his home town, to which he remained attached throughout his life, but also because of the interesting break in Oxford.

Sonnet 50 dates from the 1590s, like the other sonnets. It is addressed to the 'Friend' (the Earl of Southampton), and in it the mood of the poet is all projected on to his horse:

> How heavy do I journey on the way,
> When what I seek, my weary travel's end,
> Doth teach that ease and that repose to say
> 'Thus far the miles are measured from thy friend!'
> The beast that bears me, tired with my woe,
> Plods dully on, to bear that weight in me,
> As if by some instinct the wretch did know
> His rider loved not speed, being made from thee.

The same empathy was no doubt brought to bear in later years, too, when the poet was exposed to the elements on the long ride to Stratford. In Sonnet 34 he speaks of clouds and the rain whipping his face. Even though Shakespeare was famous by the time this sonnet was written, he was still working his way up financially and socially. By the end of his highly lucrative career his horse was surely no longer a 'wretch', but a fine steed befitting his position and status.

In Oxford, where the poet usually lodged, he was (as Aubrey tells us) both highly esteemed and extremely popular. He stayed in 'The Crown' (*Fig. 142*) an inn run by John Davenant, whose wife Jane Davenant was strikingly beautiful and intelligent. These visits may have had their consequences. The Davenants' son, the dramatist Sir William Davenant (1606 –1668), who was William Shakespeare's godson, never denied the rumour that he was not merely the godson but also the natural son of the great playwright from Stratford-upon-Avon. At any rate, this is what the well-informed John Aubrey, who had known William Davenant and his friends personally, noted in his *Brief Lives*[354]. Aubrey drew upon reliable information from the actor William Beeston, whose father, Christopher Beeston, was a member of the Chamberlain's Men and who, for example, had acted with William Shakespeare in the comedy *Every Man in His Humor* by Ben Jonson, performed in 1598.

Fig. 141a – Garden of New Place. Shakespeare spent the last years of his life in Stratford, and in fine weather would probably have spent many hours in his garden in contemplation or talking to friends. At the end of *The Tempest*, Prospero abandons his idyll on the enchanted island in order to resume his duties as Duke of Milan. Shakespeare, however, chose otherwise. He returns to New Place and his garden, which even today radiates something of that peaceful atmosphere the poet seems to have created for himself, thus pursuing an ideal of the humanists in which gardens have always played such an important role.

There is a story, not necessarily to be dismissed as a mere anecdote, that one day young William Davenant heard that Shakespeare was arriving for a visit, and rushed home from school to welcome the famous guest. Along the way he met the vicar, who asked him where he was off to in such a hurry. He answered truthfully, 'To see my Godfather.' The minister, who had heard the rumour about Shakespeare's paternity, rebuked him by saying, 'have care that you don't take *God's* name in vain'.

Fig. 141b – Fountain in the garden of New Place.

Fig. 142 – View of The Crown Inn in Oxford today. When Shakespeare was alive, the inn was run by John Davenant and his attractive wife Jane. The poet returned to Stratford each summer, and is said to have stayed at this inn on his way home. William, the Davenants' son, was Shakespeare's godson, but he may even have been his biological son. This rumour was never denied by Sir William Davenant, who later became a playwright himself, and was a great collector of Shakespeare memorabilia.

Fig. 176 – Hall's Croft in Stratford-upon-Avon. This Stratford residence was the home of Shakespeare's son-in-law Dr John Hall, a respected and popular physician, his wife Susanna (née Shakespeare) and his daughter Elisabeth. Dr Hall also ran his practice from here. After Shakespeare's death in 1616, the family moved to New Place.

Due to her allegedly intimate relationship with William Shakespeare, Jane Davenant has sometimes been a candidate for the role of the Dark Lady. But this suggestion was unsustainable even before the Countess of Southampton was identified as Shakespeare's mistress (see pp. 168 ff.).

In Elizabethan times, it was not considered a stigma to have fathered illegitimate children. In the higher social classes, 'bastards' were openly acknowledged by their natural fathers, who would provide for their education and often leave them a generous inheritance[355].

It is against this background that we must view Shakespeare's lament in the new sonnet, in the cartouche of the painting *The Persian Lady* created in 1598. Having lost his only (legitimate) son, Hamnet, in 1596, Shakespeare could not reconcile himself to losing his yet unborn child along with his mistress and his friend (see pp. 182–185).

During Shakespeare's long absences from Stratford, he was represented by a relative, John Greene (1575-1640). Greene, a lawyer employed by the Stratford Corporation, lived in New Place and represented Shakespeare's interests as a householder and landowner. The fact that in 1609, by giving notice to his landlord, he was preparing to move from New Place to his own house, indicates that he was making room for Shakespeare, the master of the house, who sometime between 1609 and 1613 finally moved back to Stratford in order to live in New Place from then on.

Shakespeare's oldest daughter Susanna must also have lived in New Place until 1607. After her marriage on 5 June, 1607 she moved to nearby Hall's Croft (*Fig. 143*), home of her husband, Dr John Hall. Their daughter Elizabeth, Shakespeare's granddaughter, was apparently born in Hall's Croft on 18 February 1608 and was baptised three days later in the parish Church of Stratford. Judith, the playwright's younger daughter, probably lived in New Place until the beginning of 1616. She married Thomas Quiney (1589–*c.* 1662) on 10 February of that year, barely two months before the death of her father. A few weeks later, Quiney would be the cause of the Shakespeares' most embarrassing scandal (see p. 318). Hamnet Shakespeare, Judith's twin brother, who would have been the

Fig. 144 – Entry for Hamnet Shakespeare, the poet's eleven-year-old son, in the register of deaths of Stratford-upon-Avon, dated 11 August 1596.

heir to Shakespeare's estate, did not live to move with his family into their mansion opposite the Stratford Guildhall. It was a hard and bitter blow to the dramatist and his family when Hamnet died at the tender age of eleven. In *King John*, Shakespeare may have used a mother's lament for her dead son to create a literary memorial for his own child (see p. 130). Hamnet was buried in Stratford on 11 August 1596 (*Fig. 144*). The cause of his death is not known.

Anne Shakespeare survived her husband by seven years. Her original wish, to be buried in Shakespeare's grave, was not granted. When she died in 1623, she was buried in a plot next to the poet.

Shakespeare's Stratford residence, New Place, contained a study, or library. This is known due to an unfortunate incident that occurred in 1637. The sheriff of Stratford and his men forced their way into the house and searched William Shakespeare's former 'study of books', as it is referred to in the sources. Susanna, Shakespeare's recently widowed daughter, who lived there with her husband after the death of her father (1616), and then alone after the death of her husband in 1635, later claimed that 'diverse bookes' and 'other goods of greate value' were seized.

Six years later, in 1643, Shakespeare's daughter must have removed a book from her father's library in order to present it as a gift to an important guest, Henrietta Maria, the Catholic wife of King Charles I. It was entitled, *A Mervaylovs discourse vpon the lyfe, deedes, and behauiours of Katherine de Medices, Queene mother....* It was written by Henri Estienne and printed in Heidelberg in 1575. There is an unequivocal indication on the title page that the queen had received this copy from her friend, Susanna Shakespeare, because it contains the handwritten Latin note: 'Liber R: Gracei [?gratiae causa] ex domo amicae D. Susanne Hall', which translates into English as, 'Book of the Q[ueen]: [?with gratitude] from the house of her friend D. Susanne Hall.' Because the American Shakespeare biographer Samuel Schoenbaum mistakenly transcribed the words 'ex domo' as 'ex dono', the clear meaning 'from the house of D. Susanne Hall' went undetected[356].

In 1643, the second year of the Civil War, when Charles I was forced to move his Court to Oxford, Henrietta Maria returned from France to England. She landed at Milford Haven in Wales and travelled thence to Oxford, staying in Stratford-upon-Avon along the way. In Elizabethan and Jacobean times, Milford Haven, a somewhat secluded port, played a prominent part in the invasion plans of the English Catholics in exile. It is significant that it features frequently as the destination of land and sea journeys in Shakespeare's *Cymbeline*. The Roman general Caius Lucius also lands there in the play. Maria Henrietta was the daughter of Maria de Medici and Henry IV of France and Navarre who in 1593, to the horror and anger of Elizabeth I, renounced his Protestant faith and converted to Catholicism with the famous words 'Paris is worth a mass'. Susanna Hall had chosen this particular book from her father's library, obviously knowing very well that it would bring great pleasure to the queen, as Estienne's book described the life of Catherine de Medici, who was responsible for the 'Blood Wedding' of Paris, in which Henry of Navarre was almost killed.

This book was auctioned at Sotheby's in 1973 and is now included in the Shakespeare Birthplace Trust Library. The Latin inscription is documentary evidence that it was once a part of Shakespeare's collection in New Place; this was previously overlooked merely because of a mistake in the transcription. Since Shakespeare's busy son-in-law, the physician Dr John Hall, was – as can be proved by his will – no great book-lover[357], it is unlikely that he was the original purchaser.

New Place was later acquired by the Cloptons, who had it rebuilt in 1702 in the neoclassical style. Nobody, not even the city of Stratford, took steps to prevent the Anglican clergyman Francis Gastrell, the last owner of this historic building of national interest, from tearing it down in 1759.

ILLNESS AND LAST WILL AND TESTAMENT

ILLNESS

Shakespeare's contemporaries always believed that the actor and playwright exited the stage of life much too early. This can be seen in a tribute to the playwright, written by 'I.M.', an anonymous poet – possibly John Marston – for the First Folio Edition of Shakespeare's plays and entitled '*To The Memorie Of M. W. Shake–speare*':

> Wee wondred (Shake-speare)
> that thou went'st so soone
> From the Worlds-Stage,
> to the Graues-Tyring-roome.

What happened at New Place in the spring of 1616? Tradition has it that Shakespeare was consorting with his fellow poets and dramatists, Michael Drayton and Ben Jonson (*Fig. 129*) a few days before his death, that he drank too much and caught a fever. This was recorded by the Reverend John Ward, Vicar of Holy Trinity Church in Stratford, 1661-1663. Yet there are no contemporary reports of this happening. Even the otherwise loquacious Ben Jonson said nothing about it. Shakespeare, however, particularly detested drunkenness. His plays contain numerous passages in which inebriation is caricatured or fiercely condemned (always, as it seems, with pedagogical intent). Many instances of this could be quoted, but may just one example suffice. In *Hamlet* Act I, scene 4, the prince denounces excessive drinking in Denmark, mentioning that even the king 'drains his draughts of Rhenish [wine] down'. In reality, however, Shakespeare has in mind his own countrymen and criticises them severely for this vice:

> This heavy-headed revel east and west
> Makes us traduc'd and tax'd of other nations:
> They clepe us drunkards, and with swinish phrase
> Soil our addition; and indeed it takes
> From our achievements, though perform'd at height,
> The pith and marrow of our attribute.

According to John Aubrey, Shakespeare would not be 'debauched' and when invited to wrote that he was 'in pain' (see p. 92). Ward's claim that Shakespeare's death resulted from excessive drinking, is thus implausible. John Payne Collier's assertion, made in 1844, that there was utmost 'uncertainty' with regard to the cause of Shakespeare's (untimely) death, was not to be challenged for around 150 years[358]. Recent British research has tried to throw some light on the subject of Shakespeare's last illness, an illness from which he may have died.

It has always been presumed that the dramatist would have been treated by his son-in-law, Dr John Hall, during his last illness. Hall, a celebrated physician, was running a big practice in Stratford. He kept diaries in Latin about his patients, their illnesses, and his treatments and cures. Captain James Cooke, a naval doctor, received these books personally from Susanna Hall after John Hall's death. He translated parts into English and published them as: *Select Observations ON ENGLISH BODIES OR, Cures both Empericall and Historicall* (1657).

Unfortunately, since the entries begin in 1617, Cook's edition records nothing about Shakespeare's last illness before his death on 23 April 1616. Hall must have treated his father-in-law, however, as he is known to have looked after his wife Susanna and his daughter Elizabeth.

In her book, *John Hall and his Patients* (1996), Joan Lane points out that in Hall's 'casebook' a few cases were listed that had occurred before

1617[359]. Nonetheless, it is safe to assume that Hall kept a regular patient diary before 1617, too, and that the book containing entries referring to his most famous patient, William Shakespeare, must either have been lost or destroyed.

Lane calls attention to the typhus epidemic that raged through Stratford in 1616-17[360]. She seems to be suggesting that Shakespeare was another of its victims. Indeed Hall speaks of it in an entry dated July 1617, noting that the burning, vicious, unbroken and persistent fever affecting the twenty-eight-year-old Lady Beaufou was the 'new fever' that had afflicted many townspeople[361]. That the epidemic was raging during the year of his death does not amount to proof that Shakespeare succumbed to typhus[362]. If it had been the cause of death, Cooke would surely not have failed to mention it[363].

In her biographical study *Ungentle Shakespeare* (2001), Katherine Duncan-Jones even claims that Shakespeare contracted syphilis sometime between 1604 and 1608 in the seedy area of Clerkenwell around Turnmill or Turnbull Street and Cow Cross[364]. She bases her assumption on Shakespeare's professional and, most likely, personal contact with the dramatist and brothel-owner George Wilkins, whom he may have met through Stephen Belott, the son-in-law of the Mountjoys of Silver Street. Wilkins owned an inn and brothel on the corner of Turnbull Street and Cow Cross, outside the city walls, north-west of Aldersgate. Duncan-Jones based her theory on general metaphorical allusions to this illness in *Troilus and Cressida* and in the sonnets[365]. Yet Duncan-Jones produces neither external references nor concrete evidence to substantiate this thesis. Merely because there are allusions to syphilis in Shakespeare's plays, and because the dramatist was acquainted with a brothel-owner, does not mean that Shakespeare himself had contracted the disease. It is true that the poet must have been to a certain extent promiscuous as becomes apparent from his literary work, especially his Dark Lady sonnets, but also from the new discoveries about his personal life presented in this book (see pp. 174–185). However, this applied to most of his contemporaries (see, for instance, the private life of Simon Forman, p. 172), and was, so to speak, a common phenomenon of his time.

The new research results concerning the authenticated likenesses of Shakespeare from his lifetime and immediately after his death have thrown new light on the poet's illnesses, also his last one[366]. The likenesses in question are the Chandos Portrait (*Fig. 63*), created sometime between 1594 and 1599; the original Flower Portrait (*Fig. 106*) painted in 1609; the Davenant bust (*Fig. 1*), created in *c.* 1613, and the Darmstadt Shakespeare death mask (*Fig. 147*), which according to Professor Michael Hertl, an expert on death masks and the physiognomy of the sick, was taken from Shakespeare's face – one or possibly two days after he had died. The Chandos and Flower portraits both reveal a large swelling on the upper left eyelid and left temple, which the ophthalmologist, Professor Walter Lerche, diagnosed as Mikulicz Syndrome[367]. The Flower portrait reveals a more advanced stage of the disease, since the swelling is twice as large as that on the Chandos portrait. This particular sign of illness must have been removed on the Davenant bust, obviously by the finder William Clift. But its former location can still be made out clearly[368]. It can also still be seen on the death mask, although in a different form[369]. Another sign of illness in both portraits is a swelling in the nasal corner of the left eye which Professor Lerche interpreted as a small caruncular tumour. This swelling must have grown quite large and extensive by the end of Shakespeare's life. For in the nasal corner of the left eye of an old marble copy of the Stratford bust in Charlecote, I discovered a trilobate swelling which the original Stratford bust no longer shows – obviously because it had been painted white in the late eighteenth century and stayed like that for many decades. When, in the mid-nineteenth-century, this paint was taken off, the pathological symptom must have been removed. The Darmstadt Shakespeare death mask was then re-examined in this particular location. There was an 'almond-shaped slit' (Professor Hertl) and an underlying cavity with three craters beneath it, made visible by applying photogrammetry at the Technical University of Darmstadt[370]. In extent and form, these craters were very similar to the trilobate swelling on the marble copy of the Stratford bust in Charlecote. Thus it became clear that the sculptor of the Stratford bust must have faithfully depicted this sign of illness from his model (the death mask), and that the artist who created a copy of Shakespeare's funerary bust in marble had also done so. This deformity can still be traced on the Davenant bust (see Fig. 064 of my book *The True Face of William Shakespeare*). The left eye of the death mask still shows an appalling deformity in this location. In contrast to the right eye, which is normal, the swollen left eyeball of the mask protrudes from its socket. The poet would probably have been unable to open this eye at all in the last few months of his life.

Furthermore, the pathologist, Professor Hans Helmut Jansen[371] and the dermatologist Professor Jost Metz[372] provided expert opinions on the clear, almost circular swelling in the central forehead region both in the Flower portrait and on the death mask. In conjunction with the Mikulicz Syndrome and the caruncular tumour in the corner of the left eye, this could be interpreted as a chronic skin sarcoidosis, a systemic illness which, after a very protracted course, proves to be fatal. There is a recognisable progression of the disease symptoms, starting with the Chandos portrait, moving on to the Flower portrait, then to the Davenant bust, and ending with the death mask. The medical experts were only able to make their diagnoses because of the remarkable truth to life of the paintings, bust and mask. Based on these findings, William Shakespeare had been 'a sick man for many years' (Hertl), suffering from severe pain and exhaustion as a result of his progressive disease. It can, however, not be excluded that his death may have been accelerated by an acute infection.

LAST WILL AND TESTAMENT

In January 1616, Shakespeare composed his will (*Fig. 145*), in the presence of his notary, Francis Collins, as he may have felt the end approaching. He revised it in March and signed it on 25 March 1616. We may well assume that there was a particular reason for this revision. On 10 February 1616, his thirty-one-year-old daughter Judith had married the twenty-seven-year-old vintner and tavern-owner, Thomas Quiney. Shakespeare's faith in his new son-in-law, however, was soon to dwindle. Quiney came from an important Stratford family. His father, Richard Quiney, a friend and neighbour of the poet, was a town councillor in 1588 and Bailiff of Stratford in 1592. In 1598, he had written to Shakespeare about an urgent matter (see p. 92 f.). In February 1616, a few weeks before the poet's death, Thomas Quiney severely compromised his father-in-law. Thomas and Judith had married during Lent and without an Episcopal licence. The pair were summoned before the church tribunal in Worcester and excommunicated by default. This, however, cannot be considered as the true reason for Shakespeare's annoyance, for, as a Catholic, he could even have advised the couple not to appear before the tribunal. The real reason, however, must have been the fact that on 26 March 1616, just six weeks after his marriage to Judith Shakespeare, Thomas Quiney was summoned to appear before the church tribunal in Stratford, also called Bawdy Court, where he had to confess that he had impregnated Margaret Wheeler, who had died in childbirth just eleven days earlier. The mother and child are listed in the register of deaths in Stratford under the date of 15 March 1616. The hasty marriage to Judith Shakespeare indicates that Quiney wanted to avoid marriage to the impoverished Margaret Wheeler. The Reverend John Rogers, the vicar who presided over the Bawdy Court, imposed a stiff penalty on Quiney. This was only discovered in the mid-twentieth century in the

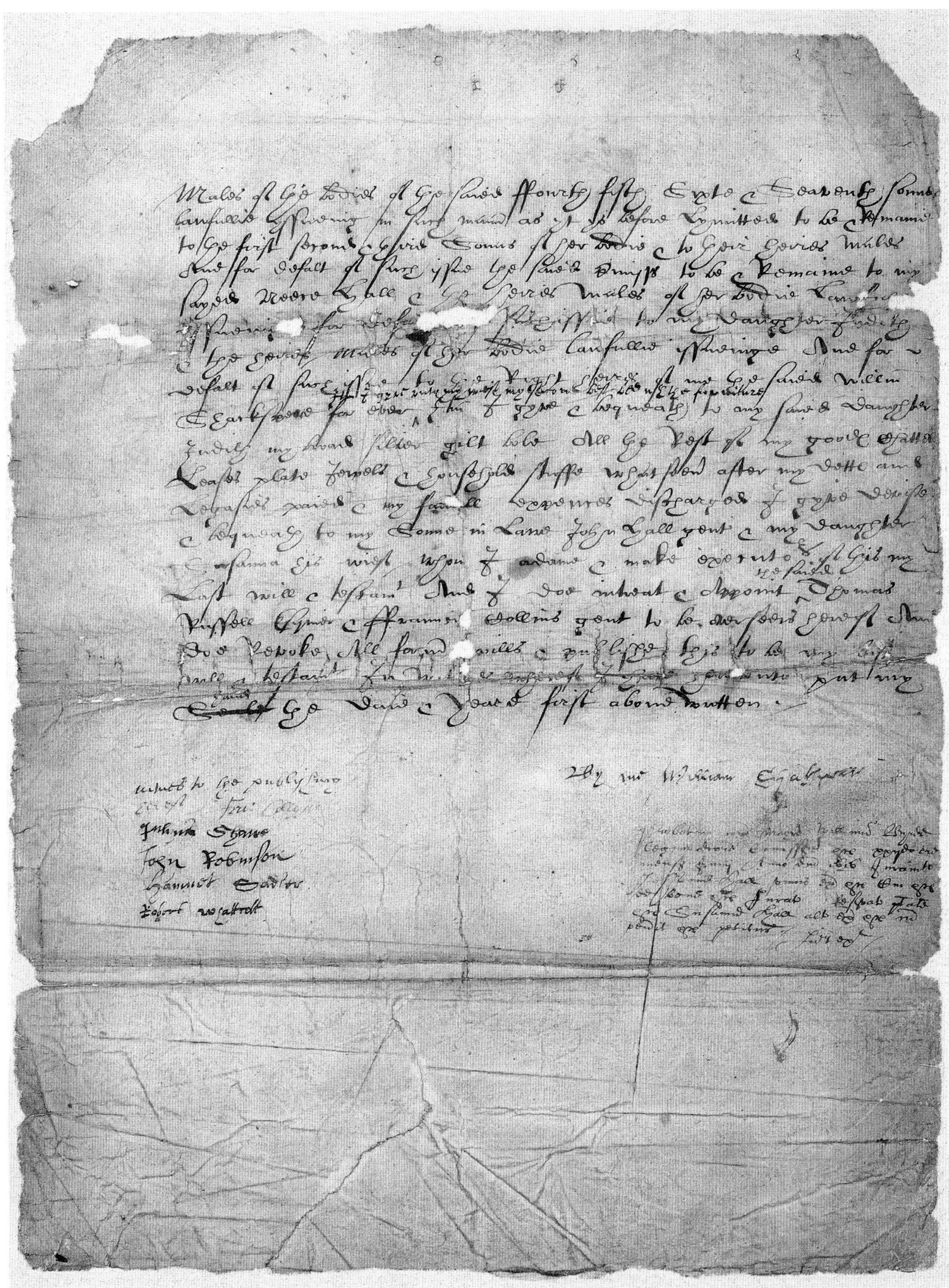

Fig. 145 – Extract from Shakespeare's will. This is the third page and is signed: 'By me William Shakespeare'.

Kent County archives in Maidstone in a document dated 26 March 1616. Clothed only in a penitent's shirt, the offender was to do public penance for three consecutive Sundays in the Stratford church[373]. Quiney was able to avoid this punishment by offering a donation of five shillings to the poor of the town. Rogers accepted the offer, but Quiney still had to confess his guilt before the vicar of Bishopton, but was allowed to do so fully clothed. During the next session of the Bawdy Court, he had to report that he had indeed made his confession.

The misconduct of the tavern-owner, his embarrassing sentence and his easy escape from it were the talk of Stratford for weeks and a heavy blow for the Shakespeares. The disgrace that Quiney had indirectly brought on his and his wife's family had unfortunate consequences for Judith, as far as her inheritance was concerned. With the revision of his will on 25 March 1616 the poet inserted a clause to the effect that there was now a 'discharge of her marriage porcion' of £100.[374]. This disgraceful family affair might even have contributed to the poet's sudden death.

Thomas and Judith had three sons who were named Shaksper, Richard and Thomas. Shaksper Quiney was born in 1616, and died the following year. Richard lived from 1618 until 1639, and Thomas lived from 1620 until 1639. This is where Judith's line came to an end. The list of material bequests made by William Shakespeare to his dependants was relatively short. However, they have given rise to some surprise and misunderstanding.

Shakespeare's second daughter Judith inherited £150, but only on certain conditions. There was – as mentioned above – a discharge of her portion of £100. The remaining £50 was only to be paid if Judith made over her inheritance from the Rowington estate to her sister, Susanna, or her heirs. This was the cottage with land on Chapel Lane that Shakespeare had purchased in 1602. Judith would inherit another £150 if she had living descendents three years after the date of the will. Since this proved to be the case, she must also have received this substantial sum. Her father also bequeathed to her 'my silver and gilt bowl'. The bowl is mentioned twice in the will, and appears to have some special significance.

Shakespeare's sister, Joan Hart, inherited £20. She lived in the parental home in Henley Street, which now belonged to her brother William. Under the terms of the will, she received the right to live there for the rest of her life as long as she paid the peppercorn rent of one shilling per annum. Joan also inherited Shakespeare's clothes. Shakespeare bequeathed £5 to each of her sons, William, Michael and Thomas Hart.

Elizabeth Hall, Shakespeare's eight-year-old granddaughter, inherited the dinner service and silverware – probably partly of gold or silver – with the exception of the bowl bequeathed to Judith.

Shakespeare's wife, Anne, née Hathaway, inherited the poet's 'second best bed' with its accoutrements. The will, and the first codicil that the poet added in the revision, states 'Item I give unto my wife, my second-best bed, with the furniture'[375]. This provision is the one that has created the most puzzlement. Chambers explains that Mrs Shakespeare would not only be endowed with an old bed but that, as Shakespeare's wife, she would automatically have inherited one third of his estate according to the laws of the time. The gatehouse in Blackfriars was excluded, as now becomes perfectly clear (see pp. 298–303). Chambers thought that the bed was an heirloom from Anne Hathaway's family. Katherine Duncan-Jones thought the opposite, namely, that Shakespeare had begrudged his wife the best bed and that he therefore fobbed her off with the second-best bed, which Duncan-Jones took to be a guest bed[376]. There is, however, a more plausible explanation that has not been considered so far, and will be discussed later.

Susanna, the dramatist's oldest daughter, was his chief heiress. His entire fortune went to her, including New Place, the house in Henley Street, the house in Blackfriars and eventually the small property from the Rowington estate, minus all other possessions that had already been otherwise disposed of in the will.

After the family inheritance had been settled, there followed bequests to his friends. These have not aroused much comment in the past. Yet they have some interesting features, and will repay a closer look. This part of the will begins with an act of charity. Shakespeare set aside the considerable sum of £10 for the poor of Stratford, which is in fact half of the sum the poet left his sister Joan.

Of those who are mentioned by name in the will, the first is Thomas Combe, who inherited Shakespeare's sword. This important symbolic act has been overlooked hitherto. Among other things, a sword symbolised 'power', 'protection', 'authority', 'leadership', 'justice', 'courage' and 'strength'. In hagiography it is the attribute of the Archangel Michael, the English St Alban, the saints Paul, Peter and James the Apostle (St James of Compostella)[377]. Shakespeare was presumably alluding to some of these attributes when he bequeathed his sword to the young Thomas Combe. The symbolism of the sword makes it clear that the poet had assigned a special role to Combe.

Thomas Combe (1589-1657) was the younger son of Thomas Combe (d. 1609) who, like Shakespeare, had acquired the right to tithes in Stratford. In 1648, he was the Sheriff of Warwickshire and from 1648 until his death, town clerk and chronicler of Stratford. Like his brother, William Combe (1586-1667), the young Thomas had studied law at the Middle Temple in London. Starting on 14 November 1608, his time there overlapped with Shakespeare's last productive years in the capital. The playwright's relationship with the Combe family was consolidated over a legal wrangle. It was Katherine Duncan-Jones who first drew attention to the fact that Shakespeare's friendship with his relative Thomas Greene ended over a land enclosure dispute in Stratford, and he was therefore left out of Shakespeare's will[378]. William Combe wanted to force through the enclosures against the will of the town of Stratford, and his brother supported him in this. Greene, who was on the town's side, had tried – in vain – to win Shakespeare over to his side in the fight against the Combes. However, to assume that Shakespeare supported the enclosures would be to jump to conclusions. The more obvious assumption is that Shakespeare did not want to act against the Combe brothers because they were actually secret Catholics. When Thomas Combe called the Stratford councillors 'dogs and curs' and 'Puritan knaves'[379], this could be an indication of his Catholicism. The recusant list for the year 1640-41, moreover, in which they were recorded as William and Thomas Combe, residents of Old Stratford, shows that both had even confessed to being Catholics[380].

These facts suggest that at that time the twenty-seven-year-old lawyer, Thomas Combe, was Shakespeare's confidant at the time. He may have been a torch-bearer in the struggle to defend beleaguered Catholicism in the area, and perhaps even beyond. Combe's fighting spirit, acumen and power of judgement were well known to Shakespeare, and might have caused him to bequeath his sword to him to mark his special role.

When Shakespeare's will is viewed against the backdrop of his involvement in crypto-Catholicism, new explanations emerge for many of the other, hitherto puzzling bequests, which can now be convincingly accounted for.

With the exception of Thomas Combe, those who were remembered in Shakespeare's will, and who were not family members, can be divided into three groups. All received money, though in relatively small amounts. For some, the intended purpose of the bequest was stated. One legatee was paid in gold.

Group one: Shakespeare names two of Stratford's leading lights, Squire Thomas Russell and the lawyer and gentleman, Francis Collins. Russell received £5, but Collins receives £13–6s–8d, mainly for his services as a notary.

Thomas Russell (1570-1634) was one of Shakespeare's closest friends and obviously enjoyed his absolute confidence. Russell is named immediately after Thomas Combe, and received the largest sum of all the non-family members apart from the notary. He married Katherine Bampfield in 1590, and was thus in close contact with the Willoughbys. This fact supports the opinion that with the initials 'W.S.' in his satirical poem *Willobie his Avisa* (1594) Henry Willoughby is referring to Shakespeare, especially as in Willoughby's satire an experienced young man gives his friend some useful advice, and Shakespeare had been considered an authority on matters of love ever since the publication of *Venus and Adonis* in 1593. After the death of his first wife, Russell married the widow of Thomas Digges, a prominent London astronomer and mathematician. Her son, Leonard Digges, was a great admirer of Shakespeare. We encounter him in 1623 as the author of one of the many poems paying homage to the dramatist in the First Folio Edition. It was entitled, 'To the memorie of the deceased author, Maister W. Shakespeare' and mentions the poet's funerary bust in the church at Stratford, ending with the verses: 'Be sure, our *Shake-speare*, thou canst never dye,/ But crown'd with Lawrell, liue eternally.'[381]

Francis Collins (d. 1617) was a Stratford lawyer and notary who held the position of deputy town clerk from 1602 to 1608 and, as Thomas Greene's successor, became town clerk of Stratford in April 1616. Shakespeare must have known him well because, as his will testifies, Collins also enjoyed the poet's complete trust. In the last paragraph of the will, Shakespeare asks Collins and Russell to act as 'overseers', having already appointed Susanna and her husband, Dr John Hall, as executors earlier in the will.

Group two: The first to be named was Mr Richard Tyler, who inherited 26 shillings and 8 pence for a ring. Tyler was dropped from the will in the revision, however, and was replaced by Hamnet Sadler, who would now receive the money for a ring in his (Tyler's) place. After Hamnet Sadler, the gentleman William Reynolds was bequeathed 26 shillings and 8 pence for a ring. Next comes Shakespeare's eight-year-old godson, William Walker, for whom the poet sets aside 20 shillings in gold. The young Walker, however, does not belong to this group, which continues with the gentleman Anthony Nash. Like Sadler and Reynolds, Nash receives 26 shillings and 8 pence. His brother, John Nash, is also bequeathed 26 shillings and 8 pence. The original addition 'in gold' was later crossed out.

Richard Tyler (1566-1636) was probably one of Shakespeare's school friends. Two of his daughters were named Judith (born 1593) and Susanna (born 1597). The poet could have crossed him out because in March 1616 he was accused of embezzling public money. However, in 1618 he participated in choosing new trustees for the eastern gatehouse in Blackfriars, now in the possession of Shakespeare's daughter Susanna[382].

Hamnet Sadler (died 1624), the Stratford baker whose bakery stood on the corner of High Street and Sheep Street, was a very close friend of the poet. Sadler and his wife Judith were Catholics and also the godparents of the twins, Judith and Hamnet Shakespeare. At Easter 1606, the first Easter after the Gunpowder Plot, they featured together with Shakespeare's daughter Susanna on the recusant list, having refused to take communion in the Anglican Church.

William Reynolds (1575-1633) was the son of William and Margaret Reynolds, wealthy Stratford landowners who died in 1613 and 1615 respectively. In 1604, the parents had been suspected of harbouring priests. William, the son, had increased his parents' property holdings and became one of the biggest landowners of Stratford. In 1619, he was one of the leaders of the anti-Puritan rebellion in Stratford, which was to prevent the appointment of the Puritan vicar and zealot, Thomas Wilson[383].

Anthony and John Nash were the sons of Thomas Nash, who died in 1587. Nash had become wealthy through the purchase of tithe rights in Stratford. Anthony and John Nash were Shakespeare's neighbours and friends. Elizabeth Hall, the poet's granddaughter, would later marry Anthony Nash's son, Thomas (1593-1647). Shortly before his death in 1637, Elizabeth's father, Dr Hall, bequeathed his books to his son-in-law – as well as New Place, though Dr Hall's widow Susanna would later have this part of the legacy overturned. Anthony Nash served as a witness to the signing of the contract for Shakespeare's major land purchase in Old Stratford in 1602, and again to a contract signed in 1614. He later bore the title 'gentleman', which he had probably purchased. When he died in 1622, he was one of the richest men in Stratford. Another witness to the contract in 1602 was Anthony's brother John Nash. Like Shakespeare, John had also acquired tithe rights in Stratford. He had the same anti-Puritanical convictions as Thomas Combe, who had inherited Shakespeare's sword, and William Reynolds, the son of steadfast Stratford recusants. John Nash commanded the anti-Puritan rebellion in 1619 and was arrested as its leader.

These facts and their historical context make it quite clear that Shakespeare had made bequests to a circle of like-minded people, who evidently supported the same secret goal of strengthening the Catholic underground. The rings that Sadler and Reynolds were to purchase with their legacies were therefore obviously not only 'memorial rings', as was generally assumed, but must have had further important symbolic functions such as 'to give power, to swear loyalty, to bind those involved'[384]. Not everyone in the four-man group was granted a ring, only Sadler and Reynolds, with whom Shakespeare was close friends and whose families, like his own, distinguished themselves through their courage in resisting the new religion[385]. Shakespeare's contemporaries were far more capable of reading subtle symbols and signs than can be imagined today in a world generally reduced to simple signs or pictograms.

Since it can be ruled out that Shakespeare bequeathed 26 shillings and 8 pence to the people in Group two simply for the money's sake (with the exception of Sadler these men were among the richest citizens of Stratford) or to buy them a memorial ring, there must have been a completely different reason for this bequest. Considering the poet's Catholic faith, the purpose of these legacies may have been similar to that behind Alexander Hoghton's will, and behind Shakespeare's purchase of the building in Blackfriars: to ensure the survival of the oppressed and officially non-existent Catholic religion in the region, linked to the practically nationwide network of the Catholic underground.

Group three: This is the group that includes Shakespeare's actor colleagues and friends, such as the King's Men's business manager, John Heminge; the star actor of the troupe, Richard Burbage; and the long-standing actor, Henry Condell. Shakespeare also bequeaths 26 shillings and 8 pence to each of them for rings.

Altogether, there were seven bequests of 26 shillings and 8 pence, and one of 20 shillings. This amounts to a total of £10–6s–8d.

In the case of Heminge, Burbage and Condell, too, the rings almost certainly had another purpose than to serve as mere memorials. With these rings, Shakespeare was probably laying claim to the symbolic loyalty of his three closest friends, as well as handing power to them – but in a completely different area. The preservation and protection of his intellectual property and the careful and conscientious preparation of the publication of his plays, must have been one of the poet's predominant concerns. For all he wanted to communicate to his contemporaries or to be handed down to posterity, he had said or encoded in his literary work. It appears that all this was prudently taken care of in his will as well.

As a measure of special precaution, Shakespeare appointed three of his closest friends to this task, so that his aims would still be fulfilled if one, or even two of them, died prematurely. This happened in the case of

TO THE MOST NOBLE
AND
INCOMPARABLE PAIRE
OF BRETHREN.

WILLIAM
Earle of Pembroke, &c. Lord Chamberlaine to the
Kings moſt Excellent Maieſty.

AND

PHILIP
Earle of Montgomery, &c. Gentleman of his Maieſties
Bed-Chamber. Both Knights of the moſt Noble Order
of the Garter, and our ſingular good
LORDS.

Right Honourable,

Hilſt we ſtudie to be thankful in our particular, for the many fauors we haue receiued from your L.L. we are falne vpon the ill fortune, to mingle two the moſt diuerſe things that can bee, feare, and raſhneſſe; raſhneſſe in the enterprize, and feare of the ſucceſſe. For, when we valew the places your H.H. ſuſtaine, we cannot but know their dignity greater, then to deſcend to the reading of theſe trifles: and, while we name them trifles, we haue depriu'd our ſelues of the defence of our Dedication. But ſince your L.L. haue beene pleas'd to thinke theſe trifles ſome-thing, heeretofore; and haue proſequuted both them, and their Authour liuing, with ſo much fauour: we hope, that (they out-liuing him, and he not hauing the fate, common with ſome, to be exequutor to his owne writings) you will vſe the like indulgence toward them, you haue done

A 2 *vnto*

The Epiſtle Dedicatorie.

vnto their parent. There is a great difference, whether any Booke chooſe his Patrones, or finde them: This hath done both. For, ſo much were your L.L. likings of the ſeuerall parts, when they were acted, as before they were publiſhed, the Volume ask'd to be yours. We haue but collected them, and done an office to the dead, to procure his Orphanes, Guardians; without ambition either of ſelfe-profit, or fame: onely to keepe the memory of ſo worthy a Friend, & Fellow aliue, as was our SHAKESPEARE, *by humble offer of his playes, to your moſt noble patronage. Wherein, as we haue iuſtly obſerued, no man to come neere your L.L. but with a kind of religious addreſſe; it hath bin the height of our care, who are the Preſenters, to make the preſent worthy of your H.H. by the perfection. But, there we muſt alſo craue our abilities to be conſiderd, my Lords. We cannot go beyond our owne powers. Country hands reach foorth milke, creame, fruites, or what they haue: and many Nations (we haue heard) that had not gummes & incenſe, obtained their requeſts with a leauened Cake. It was no fault to approch their Gods, by what meanes they could: And the moſt, though meaneſt, of things are made more precious, when they are dedicated to Temples. In that name therefore, we moſt humbly conſecrate to your H.H. theſe remaines of your ſeruant* Shakeſpeare; *that what delight is in them, may be euer your L.L. the reputation his, & the faults ours, if any be committed, by a payre ſo carefull to ſhew their gratitude both to the liuing, and the dead, as is*

Your Lordſhippes moſt bounden,

JOHN HEMINGE.
HENRY CONDELL.

Fig. 146 a–b – Dedication by the editors of the First Folio edition (1623), John Heminge and Henry Condell, the eminent actors of the King's Men, who had been Shakespeare's long-standing close friends and colleagues, to the Earls of Pembroke and Montgomery. Heminge and Condell call to mind how much the two lords enjoyed Shakespeare's plays. They make it quite clear that they had 'but collected them, and done an office to the dead, to procure his Orphanes, [as] Guardians without ambition either of self-profit, or fame: onely to keepe the memory of so worthy a Friend, & Fellow aliue, as was our *Shakespeare* ...'.

Richard Burbage, who died in 1619, and could thus not participate in this work. Heminge and Condell, however, were alive and obviously in good health and were to become the 'executors' of Shakespeare's literary legacy. That the poet himself must have planned the printing of his plays can be shown clearly in the dedication to the Earls of Pembroke and Montgomery (*Figs. 146 a–b*) and the general prefatory note (*Fig. 146c*) in the First Folio Edition of 1623. These are the texts with which Heminge and Condell prefaced their most valuable first edition of Shakespeare's dramatic work. As stated in the dedication to the two earls, fate did not grant Shakespeare the privilege 'to be exequutor to his owne writings'. The editors' address to the

To the great Variety of Readers.

Rom the moſt able,to him that can but ſpell There you are number'd.We had rather you were weighd. Eſpecially, when the fate of all Bookes depends vpon your capacities : and not of your heads alone, but of your purſes. Well ! It is now publique, & you wil ſtand for your priuiledges wee know : to read, and cenſure. Do ſo,but buy it firſt. That doth beſt commend a Booke, the Stationer ſaies. Then,how odde ſoeuer your braines be, or your wiſedomes, make your licence the ſame,and ſpare not. Iudge your ſixe-pen'orth, your ſhillings worth, your fiue ſhillings worth at a time, or higher, ſo you riſe to the iuſt rates, and welcome. But, what euer you do, Buy. Cenſure will not driue a Trade, or make the Iacke go. And though you be a Magiſtrate of wit, and ſit on the Stage at *Black-Friers*, or the *Cock-pit*, to arraigne Playes dailie, know, theſe Playes haue had their triall alreadie, and ſtood out all Appeales ; and do now come forth quitted rather by a Decree of Court, then any purchas'd Letters of commendation.

It had bene a thing, we confeſſe, worthie to haue bene wiſhed,that the Author himſelfe had liu'd to haue ſet forth, and ouerſeen his owne writings ; But ſince it hath bin ordain'd otherwiſe,and he by death departed from that right,we pray you do not envie his Friends,the office of their care, and paine, to haue collected & publiſh'd them ; and ſo to haue publiſh'd them, as where (before) you were abus'd with diuerſe ſtolne, and ſurreptitious copies, maimed,and deformed by the frauds and ſtealthes of iniurious impoſtors, that expos'd them : euen thoſe, are now offer'd to your view cur'd, and perfect of their limbes; and all the reſt, abſolute in their numbers, as he conceiued thē.Who,as he was a happie imitator of Nature,was a moſt gentle expreſſer of it.His mind and hand went together: And what he thought, he vttered with that eaſineſſe, that wee haue ſcarſe receiued from him a blot in his papers. But it is not our prouince,who onely gather his works, and giue them you, to praiſe him. It is yours that reade him. And there we hope,to your diuers capacities, you will finde enough, both to draw, and hold you : for his wit can no more lie hid, then it could be loſt. Reade him, therefore ; and againe, and againe : And if then you doe not like him, ſurely you are in ſome manifeſt danger, not to vnderſtand him. And ſo we leaue you to other of his Friends, whom if you need,can bee your guides : if you neede them not, you can leade your ſelues,and others. And ſuch Readers we wiſh him.

A 3 *Iohn Heminge.*
Henrie Condell.

Fig. 146c – 'To the great Variety of Readers' – Address from the editors of the First Folio Edition, John Heminge and Henry Condell, to the readers, in which they let the public know: 'It had bene a thing, we confesse, worthie to haue bene wished, that the Author himselfe had liu'd to haue set forth, and ouerseen his own writings; But since it hath bin ordain'd otherwise, and he by death departed from that right, we pray you do not envie his Friends, the office of their care, and paine, to haue collected & publish'd them ...'

reader is just as clear:

> It had bene a thing, we confesse, worthie to haue bene wished, that the Author himself had liu'd to haue set forth and overseen his owne writings; But since it hath bin ordain'd otherwise, and he by death departed from that right, we pray you do not envie his Friends, the office of their care, and paine, to haue collected & publish'd them.

The First Folio Edition was surely created under most difficult and stressful conditions. Today it is considered to be the most important book in world literature.

Shakespeare seems to have left nothing to chance. He may have lived long enough to see the preparations for the magnificent complete Folio edition of the literary work of his friend and fellow-playwright, Ben Jonson, which appeared in 1616. This kind of publication had hitherto been reserved for the Bible and theological works, and hugely enhanced the prestige of drama, which had previously been regarded as the poor relation of poetry.

The many and meticulous provisions in Shakespeare's will that have puzzled scholars in the past coalesce into a coherent and meaningful picture when viewed in the light of his clandestine Catholicism and obviously lifelong efforts to support the Catholic underground. They now illuminate the poet's true concerns, concerns which he could not openly address.

In Shakespeare's last will and testament, the following items stand out:

(1) His small 'copyhold tenement' in Chapel Lane opposite New Place which the playwright acquired in 1602, about which, however, he is deliberately vague.

(2) His 'wearing apparel' his sister Joan was to inherit.

(3) His large silver-gilt bowl (the testator speaks of his 'broad silver and gilt bowl' and then a second time of his 'broad silver-gilt bowl') that was to go to Judith.

(4) His 'second-best bed with furniture' for his wife, Anne.

(1) The small property in Chapel Lane may have been used as accommodation for a priest disguised as a gardener. If this was the case, it would have been a brilliant strategy to harbour and maintain a priest over a long period of time. It would also have been an additional precautionary measure to keep the priest outside New Place, but very close to it, providing ready access for him. Shakespeare seems to have learned from the bitter experience of the Catholic landed gentry who secretly kept Catholic priests and members of holy orders inside their grand residences where they were frequently discovered in raids. The 'copyhold tenement' in Chapel Lane had already been in Judith's possession, but she was now obliged to transfer it to her sister Susanna in order to gain access to the remaining £50 of her inheritance.

According to tradition, in the last years of his life Shakespeare was cared for by a Benedictine monk and received from him the last rites of his Church in his dying hours. This Benedictine monk and priest may have been David Baker, known as Father Augustine, who, after his late ordination in Rheims in 1613-14, returned to England, 'disappeared' and was not heard of again until 1620[386]. Since the motto of Father Augustine's order was *Ora et labora* (pray and work), gardening in Shakespeare's spacious garden would have been an ideal second job for him. This Benedictine monk was a learned man, and it is possible that while conversing with him, perhaps in the garden of New Place, Shakespeare could realize his dream of 'Idyll of the *Georgica*' which he alludes to in Gonzalo's vision of Utopia in *The Tempest* and elsewhere.

(2) By 'wearing apparel' Shakespeare may actually have referred to vestments worn by a priest when saying Mass. This reminds us of Alexander de Hoghton's will of 1582, in which the testator speaks of 'play clothes' in a similar meaning.

(3) The silver-gilt bowl could in reality have been a ciborium, or a vessel, similar to the one in the collection of the Birthplace Trust in Stratford (see *Fig. 182* in the German edition of this book).

(4) The 'second-best bed with furniture' probably meant the secret bed and furniture that was kept available for priests who needed sanctuary. It was probably a bed in a secret chamber, or priest-hole like those in noblemen's houses. The furniture could have been a table and chair. Further items in this room could have been a Catholic Bible, breviary, catechism and similar objects that, for reasons of safety, priests could not carry with them. It was strictly forbidden by law to harbour or support priests or members of holy orders, and anyone in breach of this law would be severely punished (see p. 27 ff.). John Fortescue, the long-standing tenant of the eastern gatehouse of Blackfriars, must have been well aware of this because he was, so to speak, professionally engaged in this dangerous task. With an aldermen's and sheriffs' raid safely behind him, he emphasised the penalties for such behaviour in a letter to the Earl of Essex (see p. 302 f.). Viewed against the dangerous religious times Shakespeare lived in, it now appears that Anne Shakespeare's 'second-best bed' was neither an heirloom from her own family, as Chambers has claimed, nor a simple guest bed, as other Shakespeare scholars have suggested, but rather a place of accommodation and shelter where persecuted priests could stay in safety.

In summary, the above-mentioned items in Shakespeare's will that have hitherto seemed odd or puzzling were very probably all needed for the secret practice of Catholicism at New Place. For security reasons, these objects would – so it seems – have been distributed amongst close family members such as Joan Hart, Judith Quiney and Anne Shakespeare.

Susanna, Shakespeare's principal legatee, was spared involvement in all this, possibly out of consideration for her husband, who had Puritan leanings, and who would therefore not have hidden such objects in his house, despite his religious tolerance. Furthermore, Susanna had to administrate the most important but dangerous heritage: Shakespeare's eastern gatehouse in Blackfriars. As early as 1618 a new contract, with two new trustees, was signed. This contract contains passages that confirm the existence of a secret arrangement between William Shakespeare and his trustees. For Jackson, Heminge and Johnson now act according to their loyalty to their late friend, i.e. 'in performance of the confidence and trust in them reposed by William Shakespeare deceased late of Stretford aforesaid gent'[387]. They 'conveyed and assured [their trusteeship] according to the true intent and meaning of the last will and testam[en]t of the said William Shakespeare'[388]. The reference by the trustees in the 1618 contract to 'the true intent and meaning' of Shakespeare's will is evidently an allusion to hidden intentions and also, perhaps, to the inventory that was attached to Shakespeare's will and was still extant when the Stratford schoolmaster, Reverend Joseph Greene, found this document in 1747. However, like so much else relating to Shakespeare's life and religion, this has disappeared[389].

John Hall and Susanna Shakespeare had entered into a mixed marriage. This was not unusual in Elizabethan and Jacobean times. The marriages of Sir Philip Sidney and Frances Walsingham, or Sir Thomas Heneage and the second Countess of Southampton, are other examples. These marriages were harmonious for the most part since religious tolerance was practised on both sides. An important aspect of such a marriage was that it could offer protection. So, for example, the respected physician Dr John Hall was able to protect not just Shakespeare's daughter Susanna and his granddaughter Elizabeth but also the other members of the Shakespeare family. This protection was badly needed. Stratford became ever more Puritan from the first decade of the seventeenth century onwards. The local Puritans achieved a clear victory when a new vicar, the Puritan zealot Thomas Wilson, was appointed to Stratford in 1619. But this provoked, as has already been mentioned, an anti-puritan rebellion, led by John Nash with the support of William Reynolds, which was to prevent Wilson from taking up his appointment. These two men were very close friends of Shakespeare.

Shakespeare's direct line from his marriage to Anne Hathaway died out with his granddaughter Elizabeth in 1670, since she remained childless even from her second marriage. Elizabeth had first married Thomas Nash, whose father Anthony was a close friend of John Shakespeare, her grandfather. Her husband died in 1647, and in 1649 she married Sir John Bernard and lived with him as Lady Bernard at Abington, the estate he inherited. New Place was bequeathed by Lady Bernard to a distant relative. It was bought back again by the Cloptons, the family of the original owner, in the early eighteenth century.

In 1756, New Place came into the possession of the Protestant minister, the Reverend Francis Gastrell. He disliked inquisitive visitors, so in 1758 he had the mulberry tree that Shakespeare had planted cut down. A year later, he became so furious that he had the entire estate demolished. The public outcry came too late. The reason given by Gastrell was harassment by the many tourists who wanted to see Shakespeare's home. That appears to have been merely an excuse. It seems that this Anglican clergyman, on thorough inspection of New Place, stumbled upon something that must have outraged him. His inspection may well have been prompted by the earlier discovery of the Borromeo testament in John Shakespeare's home in Henley Street in 1757. It is likely that he found equipment and items that left no doubt that Shakespeare and his family had secretly practised the Catholic faith. Naturally, this is only a hypothesis, but one that contains a high degree of probability given all that we know about Shakespeare's involvement in English crypto-Catholicism and the many allusions to the old faith in his works.

From today's standpoint it seems utterly inexplicable that Shakespeare's property could be completely destroyed. His work had enjoyed a revival since the Restoration and his tomb and last home were the destination of many pilgrimages. In 1769, only ten years after the demolition of New Place, the great Shakespearean actor and director David Garrick (1717-1779) organised a Shakespeare Jubilee festival in Stratford. The Jubilee drew the world's attention to Shakespeare's literary work, his home town, and the many historical traces of him that survived there.

DEATH AND BURIAL

DEATH

Shakespeare died at the age of fifty-two at New Place, surrounded by his family. According to the Julian calendar then in use, the date of his death was Tuesday, 23 April 1616. This date is engraved on the black marble plaque beneath his funerary bust in Holy Trinity Church in Stratford-upon-Avon:

> OBIIT AÑO DO^I 1616
>
> AETATIS • 53 DIE 23 AP^R

His age at death is stated incorrectly. In fact he was exactly fifty-two-years-old on the day of his passing, not fifty-three as stated in the inscription. Consequently, he died on the same day of the month of April on which he apparently has been born. Coincidentally, the dates of his birth and death fall on the day of England's patron saint, St George. This correspondence could only enhance his already almost saintlike reputation as a national icon.

It was either on this day or on the following day that his death mask (*Fig. 147*) was taken, possibly by Shakespeare's son-in-law, Dr John Hall. It is also possible that an official plaster-moulder may have performed the work. The sculptor used the death mask as the model for Shakespeare's funerary bust in the church of Stratford. The original death mask is on permanent loan from the city of Darmstadt to the Hesse *Land* and University Library in Darmstadt Castle and is now exhibited there in a secure showcase[390].

Shakespeare, at the end of his life, apparently received the ministrations of a Benedictine priest, as has already been referred to before. The many pieces of evidence adduced here that Shakespeare must have been a practising Catholic lends credence to this story, as it does to the tradition that it was a Benedictine monk who contributed to William's education. The Benedictine who would have administered the last rites to the dying poet could have been – as mentioned above – David Baker or rather, Father Augustine. Baker, with a reputation as a 'master of the spiritual life' and of religious meditation, had connections with the extensive Fortescue family who were so prominent in the Catholic underground. What further helps to identify him is that we know that all of the six other English Benedictine monks – the total English membership of the order at this time – were engaged on other tasks. Baker had lived for many years on the estate of Sir Nicholas Fortescue at Cookhill. Sir Nicholas, like most of his numerous relatives, including the former tenant of the eastern gatehouse in Blackfriars, John Fortescue, was an ardent Catholic. Nicholas Fortescue was a patient of Shakespeare's son-in-law, Dr John Hall, so direct contact could have been made and maintained in this way[391].

Shakespeare mentions a John Robinson in his will, his tenant in Blackfriars. A John Robinson is also a witness to the will and is obviously the same person. Was this 'tenant' – Ian Wilson also calls him an 'guardian' – not only the organiser of Shakespeare's gatehouse at Blackfriars, but also perhaps the person who circumspectly and discreetly prepared Shakespeare for his final journey and assisted the Benedictine monk? Was it he who made an inventory – now lost – of the items in the room in which Shakespeare died, and

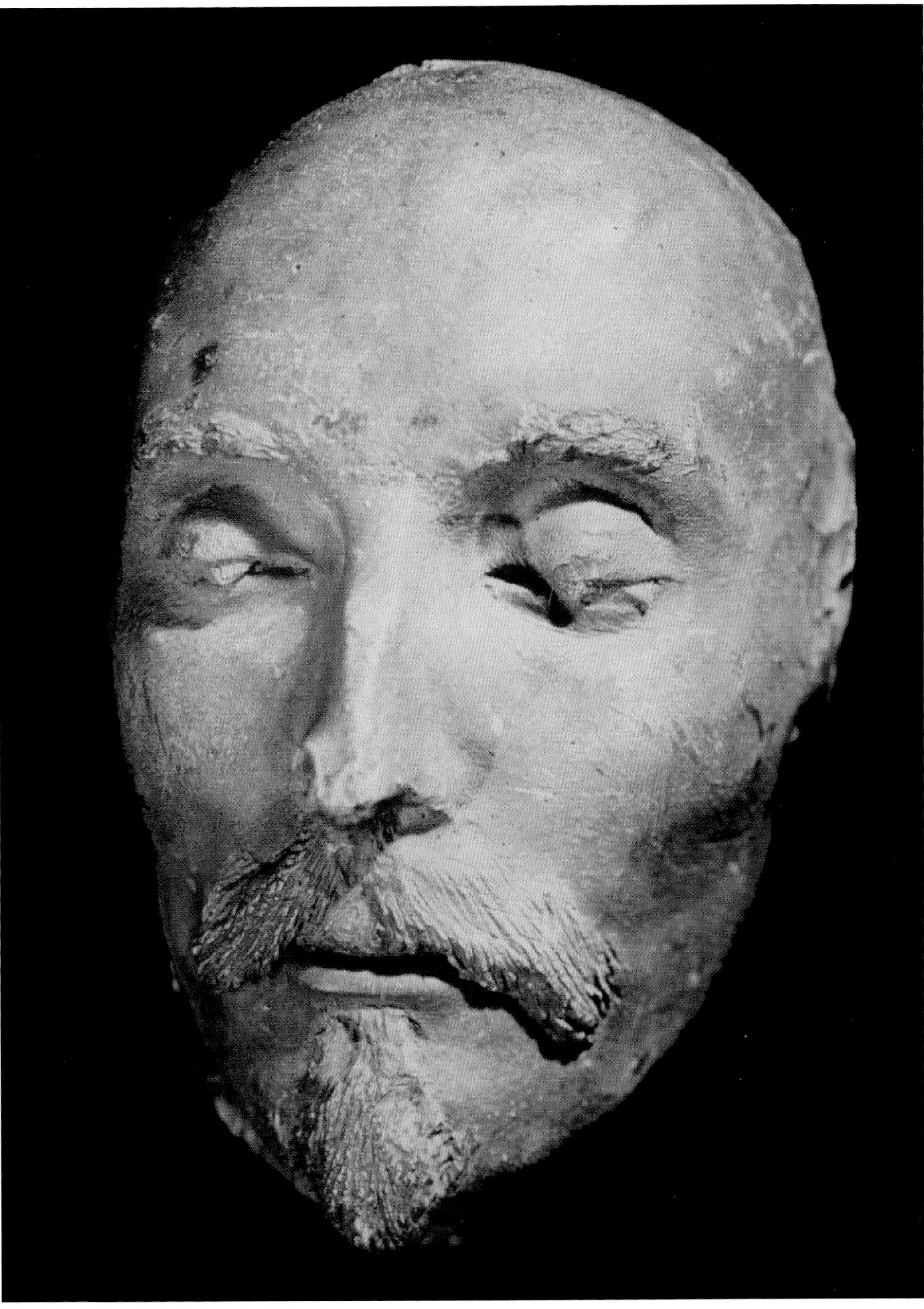

Fig. 147 – Shakespeare's death mask. The authenticity of this mask was proved for the first time by the present author in 1995 with the help of experts from the German Bureau of Criminal Investigation (BKA = CID) and two professors of medicine.*[18] Further scientific investigations and medical assessments, carried out between 1996 and 2005, have since confirmed these findings (see *The True Face of William Shakespeare*, parts III and IV). This mask was used by the sculptor Gheerart Janssen the Younger when he was creating the bust for Shakespeare's funerary monument in the Holy Trinity Church in Stratford*[19]. It is owned by the City of Darmstadt and kept as a permanent loan in the Hesse *Land* and University Library in the castle of Darmstadt.

who organised a secret Catholic burial ceremony? John Robinson, like John Fortescue, was a devout Catholic. In 1599, he was reported to the authorities for harbouring a priest (Richard Dudley), but he got off lightly, possibly because of protection in high places. Robinson's son, Edward, was educated in Parson's English College in St Omer. He went on to study at the Collegium Anglicum in Rome and became a priest.

While Dr John Hall evidently tried to ease the poet's tremendous suffering before his death, Father Augustine, if it was him, seems to have provided Shakespeare with the comforts of his religion, and performed the last rites, including extreme unction. Robinson could have been the man who discreetly took over all the remaining work that was necessary for the poet to perfect his *ars moriendi*. How important the 'art of dying well' in hope of salvation really must have been for Shakespeare, is stressed in many of his plays.. The death scene of Cardinal Beaufort in *Henry VI* is just one example (see p. 125 f.).

Perhaps it was Robinson who took the death mask to London and entrusted it to Gheerart Janssen the Younger to be used as the model for Shakespeare's funerary bust. Janssen was commissioned by the family to design the playwright's imposing tomb monument in Holy Trinity Church in Stratford. A late seventeenth-century source confirms the theory put forward here that Shakespeare was a practising Catholic. The written record of this can bear close scrutiny. The two friends, William Fulman (1632-1688) and Richard Davies (d. 1708), both Protestant ministers and Oxford graduates, collected together in the late seventeenth century a series of interesting and enlightening details about Shakespeare's life. Fulman's earlier, vague information is augmented by Davies' better knowledge of Shakespeare's life. Davies tells us, in sober and matter-of-fact style, that the poet died as a 'papist'. His choice of the word 'papist', which was a term of denigration and even abuse in Protestant England, shows his own unsympathetic attitude to Catholicism. It goes without saying that Davies would not have relied on sources of information that he deemed untrustworthy and that he, as a Protestant minister, would not have pointed out Shakespeare's Catholicism without sufficient evidence.

The entry in question, reproduced here as a printed facsimile (*Fig. 148*), was obviously written in two different hands. In it we recognise the finer lines of Fulman's script which appear at the beginning of the text, and the heavier hand of Davies that completely fills the gaps that Fulman had left blank, no doubt expecting to make later additions. The sentence that ends the entry is clearly visible and reads: 'He dyed a papist'[392].

In his book *The Essential Shakespeare* (1932), however, the English Shakespeare scholar John Dover Wilson prematurely consigned Davies' claim to the realms of legend, and did his best to justify doing so, though without success:

> As for 'dying a papist', that is just the sort of story a parson of the time would delight in crediting, and circulating, about 'one of those harlotry players' who, by amassing wealth acquired in infamy, had taken upon him to become a great person. I do not believe it ...[393]

Dover Wilson attempted a balancing act with regard to *The Tempest*, stating that he saw in the play 'no signs whatsoever of any "papistry"'[394], while admitting, none the less, that Shakespeare might have undergone a 'conversion', yet 'certainly not a doctrinal one, hardly a religious one'[395]. However, Dover Wilson does not specify to what Shakespeare might have been 'converted'.

Long before Dover Wilson, the English Shakespeare scholar Sir Sidney Lee had indicated in his standard work, *A Life of William Shakespeare* (1898), that Davies' account was an 'irresponsible report' and had rejected it as 'idle gossip.' There is no question, claimed Lee, but

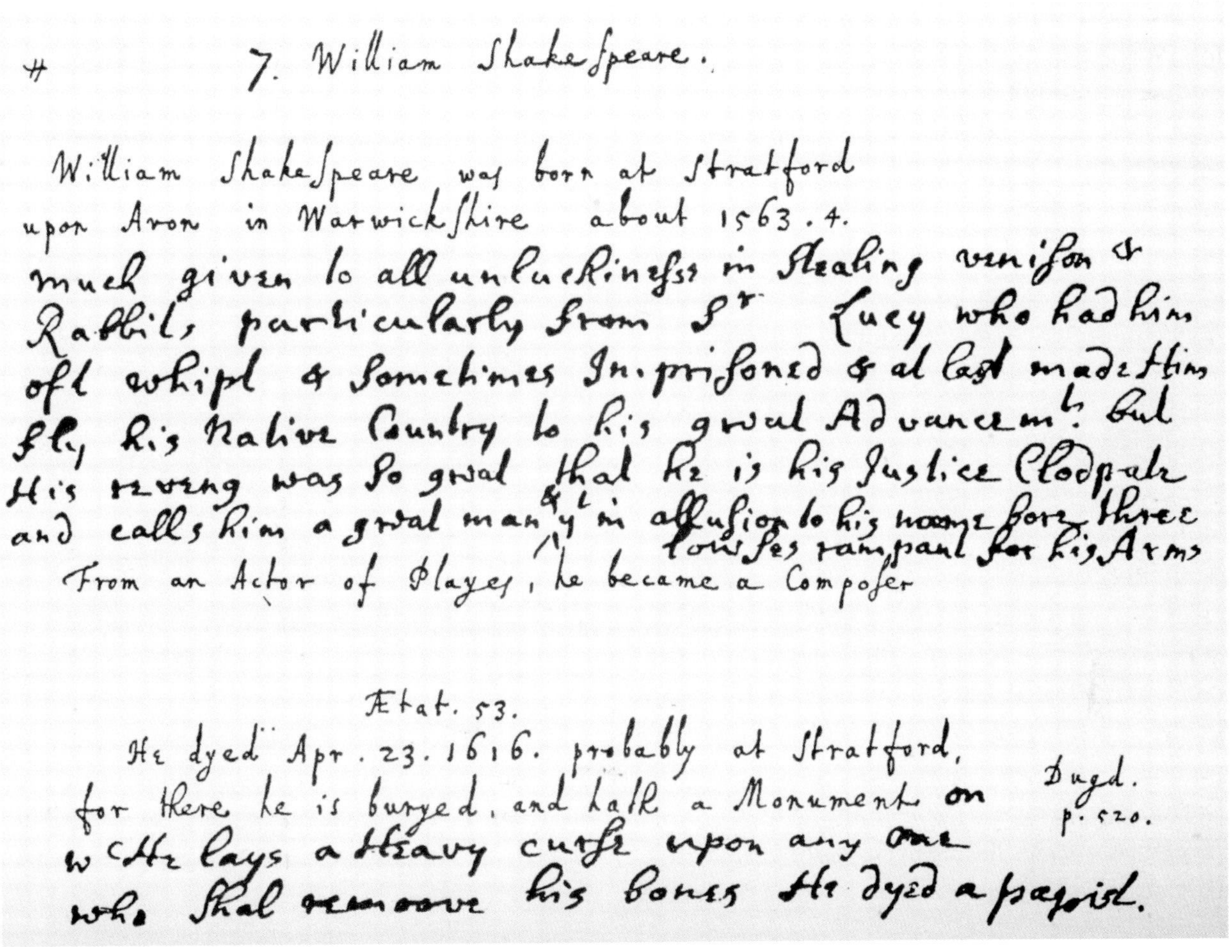

7. William Shakespeare.

William Shakespeare was born at Stratford upon Avon in Warwickshire about 1563.4.
much given to all unluckinesse in stealing venison & Rabbits, particularly from Sr Lucy who had him oft whipt & sometimes Imprisoned & at last made him fly his Native Country to his great Advancemt. but His reveng was so great that he is his Justice Clodpate and calls him a great man & yt in allusion to his name bore three lowses rampant for his Arms
From an Actor of Playes, he became a Composer

Ætat. 53.
He dyed Apr. 23. 1616. probably at Stratford, for there he is buryed, and hath a Monument on wch He lays a Heavy curse upon any one who shal remoove his bones He dyed a papist.

Dugd. p. 520.

Fig. 148 – Biographical entry by the Anglican Clergyman Richard Davies about William Shakespeare, containing the testimony: 'He dyed a Papist'. Davies added his testimony to the writings of his friend William Fulman, who died in 1688. Both men had studied theology at Oxford University. This most valuable written source from 1688 or slightly later is able to stand up to close examination.. It is easy to see that it is written by two distinct hands. The thin and fine writing belongs to Fulman, the thicker is that of Davies. The statement that Shakespeare died a Papist can be found at the bottom of the text. There is no reason to doubt its veracity.

that William Shakespeare had been a 'conforming member of the Church of England' until the very end of his life. Lee, however, did not produce any evidence for this. E.K. Chambers, one of the most eminent English Shakespeare scholars of the first half of the twentieth century, in another standard biographical work, *William Shakespeare: A Study of Facts and Problems* (1930), still being much referred to in our time, took a completely different line:

> I am not so certain as was Sir Sidney Lee that we can, without more ado, 'dismiss as idle gossip the irresponsible report', or that it 'admits of no question' that Shakespeare 'was to the last a conforming member of the Church of England'[396].

And he continued:

> How did Sir Sidney know that Davies was irresponsible or a gossip? What little is recorded of him suggests that he was a man of scholarly attainments. It was by no means unusual for a seventeenth-century Catholic to be buried in his parish church[397].

From an historian's point of view, the notes made by Archdeacon Davies must be regarded as perfectly authentic seventeenth-century source material that cannot be dismissed because we might or might not like their content. Davies' additions to the entry of his friend Fulman were obviously made conscientiously and to the best of his knowledge. So there is no real reason that they should not be accepted, especially since the writer could not have a personal interest in Shakespeare being a Catholic. At this time, many people who had known Shakespeare personally were still alive. Davies was the vicar of Sapperton, a village in Gloucestershire, not far from Stratford. Fulman had already been the vicar of Meysey Hampton as early as 1669. He was like John Aubrey, an antiquarian and, moreover, a noted scholar. Fulman's publications include *Academiae Oxoniensis Notitia* (1665); volume one of the *Rerum Anglicarum Scriptorum Veterum* (1684), and *The Works of Henry Hammond* (1684). He had also begun a collection of biographical notes about the English poets[398].

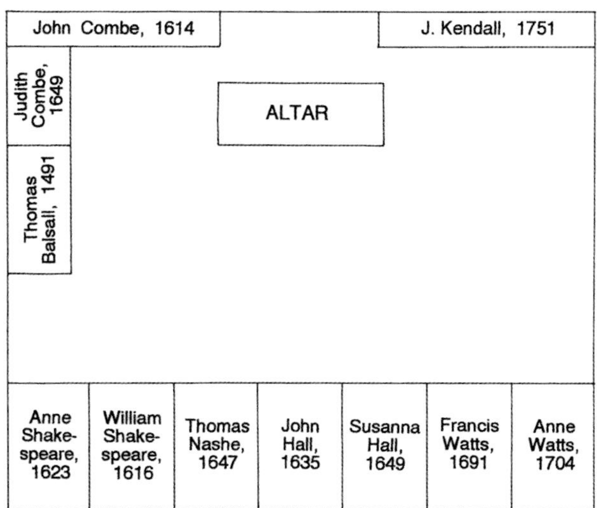

Fig. 149 – Plan of the tombs of William Shakespeare and his family in the chancel of Holy Trinity Church, Stratford-upon-Avon.

BURIAL

William Shakespeare was buried on 25 April 1616 in front of the altar on the left side of the chancel of Holy Trinity Church, Stratford-upon-Avon. The date of the burial, like the date of his baptism, is documented in the parish register of Holy Trinity Church.

Shakespeare may well have had a costly, elegant, and elaborate funeral. Since the poet had inherited the title of 'gentleman' and a coat of arms, he would have had a 'heraldic funeral.' In Elizabethan and Jacobean times, such funerals were reserved not only for royalty, the nobility, archbishops, bishops and knights, but also for 'gentlemen-at-arms'[399]. There would have been a solemn street procession displaying the dead man's coffin, coat of arms and decorations, as well as his helmet and a funerary sword which would have been made for the occasion. The chief mourners – Dr John Hall and his wife Susanna, Shakespeare's widow, his daughter Judith and her husband Thomas, and his eight-year-old granddaughter, Elizabeth Hall, would have complied with the dress regulations prescribed for their rank. The procession would have consisted of six yeomen carrying the coffin covered with a pall, accompanied by four other pallbearers and a herald with an entourage. All of these would have worn the customary black hooded cloak with a fur collar[400]. The cost of Shakespeare's funeral must have been significant. This is why the poet specifically mentioned them in his will and decreed that they should be deducted from the inheritance.

The College of Arms would have been responsible for arranging funerals of this type. It supervised funeral practices throughout the country, ensuring that the strict rules of etiquette were observed and that only those whose social status entitled them to these honours actually received them.

Shakespeare's mortal remains were committed to the earth deep beneath the stone floor of the chancel in Stratford parish church (*Fig. 149*). On the stone slab covering the poet's grave, a stonemason chiselled the following verse (*Fig. 150*):

Fig. 150 – Inscription on the stone slab covering the grave of William Shakespeare. Expert analysis has shown that this inscription and the one beneath the playwright's funerary bust, in Latin and English (*Fig. 153c*), are, as far as their typography is concerned, in agreement with the inscription on the octagon in the garden at New Place (see *Fig. 121b*), though the one on the octagon is even more accurate.

GOOD FREND FOR IESVS SAKE FORBEARE,
TO DIGG THE DVST ENCLOASED HEARE.
BLEST BE YE MAN YT SPARES THES STONES,
AND CVRST BE HE YT MOVES MY BONES

As far as is known, this imprecation has so far had the desired effect. The poet himself evidently devised it because he wanted to protect his earthly remains above all against transfer to the anonymity of the charnel-house.

The depth of the grave, a good seventeen feet if traditional reports are to be believed, afforded additional protection for Shakespeare's bones.

The family commissioned Gheerart Janssen and sons[401] to erect a costly monument in typical Jacobean style. It was placed on the left wall of the chancel, only a couple of yards from the grave (*Figs. 190* and *191a*). The monument is surmounted by a square stone tablet on which the poet's coat-of-arms is depicted (*Fig. 19*), as well as his helmet with crest. Presumably the Janssens were given the customary year in which to complete the project.

Shakespeare's funerary monument belongs to a certain type of contemporary monuments which was typical of those commemorating prominent divines, scholars, poets, writers, historians, astronomers and other outstanding personalities in Elizabethan and Jacobean times. They always accurately portrayed the image of the deceased. Gheerart Janssen Jr., the son of the master who had since died, made such a bust of William Shakespeare (*Fig. 153b*), based on the death mask

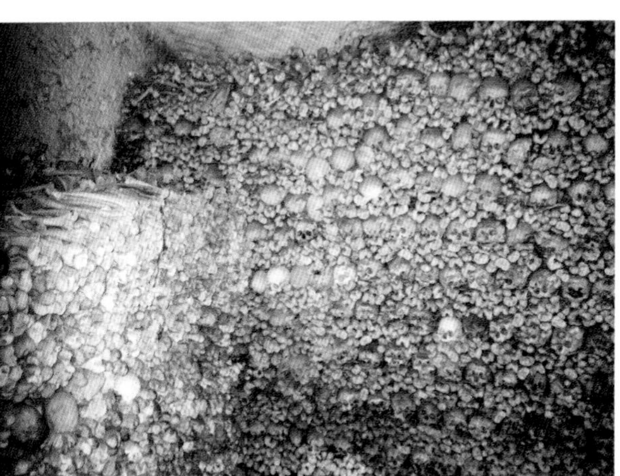

Fig. 151 – Collection of human bones in St Michael's chapel, belonging to St Catherine's Church, Oppenheim on the River Rhine near Mainz. In this charnel-house, human bones and skulls are piled up against the wall. Until the eighteenth century, Holy Trinity Church in Stratford had a similar charnel-house. An old sketch of Holy Trinity shows two side-chapels attached to the church (see Fig. 4a in the German edition of this book). The building on the right has a large door, accessible from outside: this would certainly have been the charnel-house. Shakespeare must have been familiar with it. It is very likely that he, as a child or later in life, had seen the moving of bones from old graves to the charnel-house.

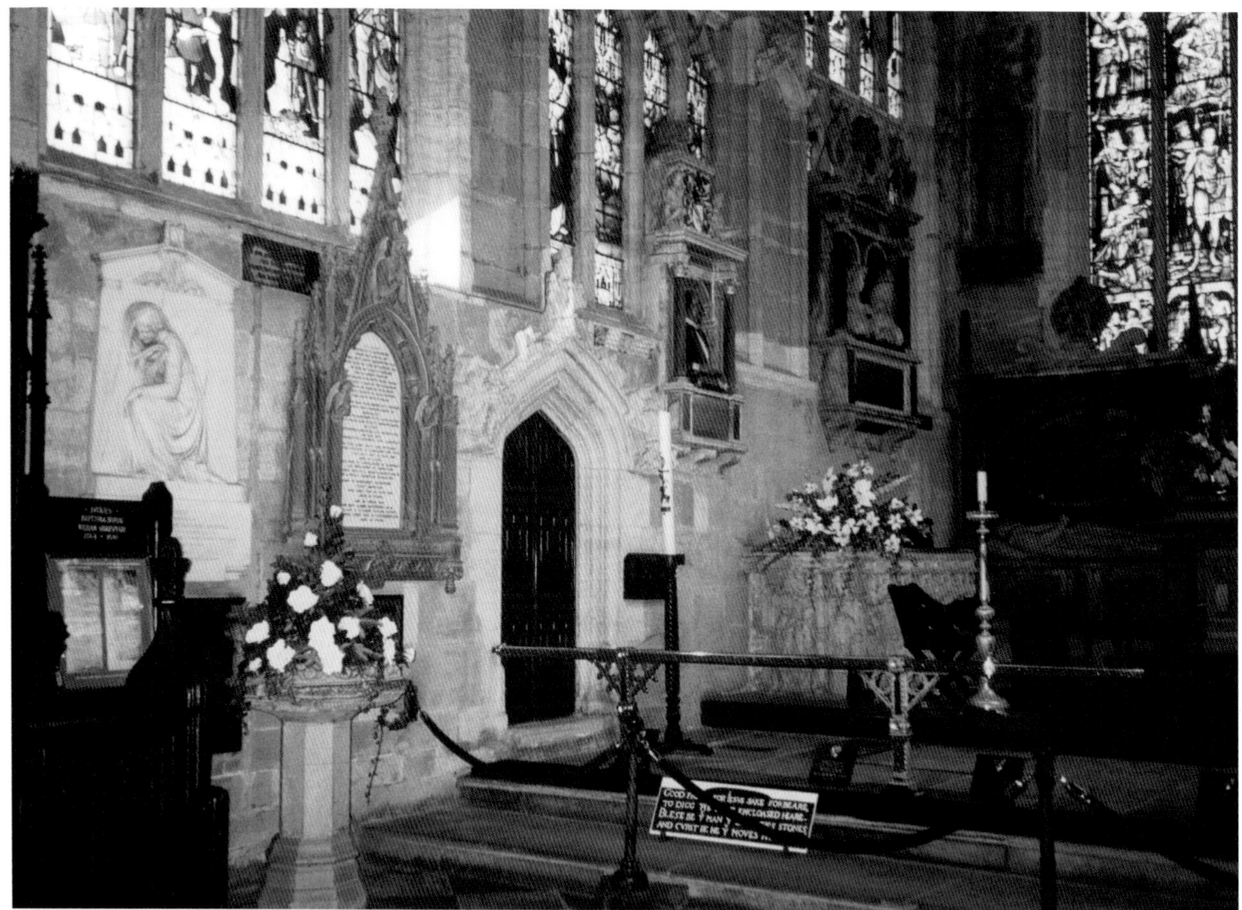

Fig. 152 – Left wall of the chancel in Holy Trinity Church, Stratford-upon-Avon, with Shakespeare's funerary monument, built in typical Jacobean Renaissance style. Front left: copies of extracts from the registers of birth and deaths of 1564 and 1616, showing the poet's name. Next to it there is the old, restored baptismal font from the time of Shakespeare.

now in Darmstadt (*Fig. 147*). Shakespeare's funerary bust experienced a number of vicissitudes, described in what follows.

The monument was mentioned in the 1623 Folio Edition[402] and was probably erected in 1616 or 1617. It survived the Puritan iconoclasm during the Civil War, though not without suffering considerable damage. A report from the mid-eighteenth century mentions that it was in pitiful shape[403]. The nose was broken off, the original moustache was missing, the head had an 'indentation'[404] in the back and as late as 1911, it appeared to be sitting only loosely in place[405], as if it had been violently knocked to the ground. The bust had undergone some makeshift repairs, but no one knew exactly what the original statue looked like, and therefore how to restore it. The nose and moustache did not match those first reproduced in an engraving of Shakespeare's monument in Sir William Dugdale's *Antiquities* (1656), taken from a sketch made in 1636[406], and discovered in the nineteenth century. Compared to the head in the Dugdale engraving, which quite reliably reproduces the features of the poet's funerary bust, the expression of the bust's face must later have been altered to the disadvantage of the poet. Afterwards it looked coarse and dull, not suggestive of genius[407].

Below the original, brightly painted limestone bust of Shakespeare there was a black marble plaque with an inscription in Latin and English (*Fig. 153c*). As was customary in the Renaissance,

Fig. 153a – Shakespeare's funerary monument in Holy Trinity Church, Stratford-upon-Avon, the bust of which is a copy (see *The True Face*, pp. 127 f.). It belongs to a certain type of tomb which in the Elizabethan and Jacobean ages was strictly reserved for scholars (theologians, historians, mathematicians, etc.), but also for poets and writers. Such a funerary monument consists of a true-to-life likeness of the deceased, normally a bust, which depicts his facial features accurately, and inscriptions recounting his life and outstanding achievements. Whereas Shakespeare's gravestone and the curse upon it are very famous all over the world, the inscriptions on the marble plaque beneath his funerary bust have received relatively little attention, although they clearly document Shakespeare's genius and place him on par with the greatest authors of classicial antiquity. Thus the Latin text tells us that Shakespeare had the judgement of Nestor, the genius of Socrates and the art of Virgil.

Fig. 153b – William Shakespeare's original funerary bust by Gheerart Janssen the Younger, based on the Darmstadt Shakespeare death mask (*Fig. 147*). The London sculptor was most certainly given a year in which to complete the tomb and its sculpture, as was usual at that time. This means that the monument must have been erected in 1616 or in 1617 at the latest. Shakespeare's '*Stratford* Moniment' is referred to (as far as we know) for the first time in Leonard Digges' poem 'To the memorie of the deceased Authour Maister W. Shakespeare', which appeared in the 1623 First Folio Edition. Shakespeare's funerary bust – just like his death mask – has had a rather fateful history. It survived the Puritan iconoclasm of the Civil War, but was badly damaged and afterwards repaired in a kind of makeshift way.[*20]

the inscription conveys extremely significant information about the personality of the deceased and the way that he had distinguished himself in life[408]. The English inscription reads:

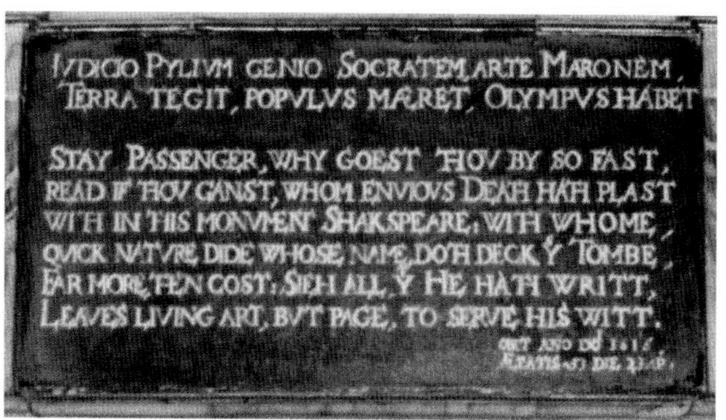

Fig. 153c – Latin and English inscription below Shakespeare's funerary bust in Holy Trinity Church, Stratford-upon-Avon. This contemporary text is an authentic historical source, giving testimony to Shakespeare's unique position as a playwright and an intellectual (see *Fig. 153a*). The Latin text must have been written by an educated person, probably a scholar, who must have been very familiar with Shakespeare's outstanding achievements.

STAY PASSENGER, WHY GOEST THOV BY SO FAST,
READ IF THOV CANST, WHOM ENVIOVS DEATH HATH PLAST
WITH IN THIS MONVMENT SHAKSPEARE: WITH WHOME,
QUICK NATVRE DIDE WHOSE NAME DOTH DECK YS TOMBE,
FAR MORE THEN COST: SITH ALL YT HE HATH WRITT,
LEAVES LIVING ART, BVT PAGE, TO SERVE HIS WITT.

The Latin inscription above the English one is a piece of historical evidence *par excellence.* It describes the deceased as having been 'an ingenious creator of a literary work'[409], who can be measured against the greatest authors of classical antiquity: Nestor, Socrates and Virgil. We do not know who authored this inscription, but what we do know of him is that he must have been highly educated. In addition, he must have known the poet William Shakespeare and his work very well. It is possible that it was the learned Benedictine monk, Father Augustine Baker who, as church historian, may have been aware of the various and complex meanings of 'maronem'[410]. But whosoever created this text, one thing must have been absolutely clear to him: William Shakespeare had achieved for England the equivalent of what the celebrated Roman poet Virgil, who was later known as 'Father of the Occident', had done for the Roman empire, which in the sixteenth and seventeenth centuries had been held in greatest esteem by educated Englishmen, including Shakespeare. The Latin original of the inscription reads:

IVDICIO PYLIVM, GENIO SOCRATEM, ARTE MARONEM
TERRA TEGIT, POPVLVS MAERET, OLYMPVS HABET.

This translates as follows:

HE WHO HAS
THE JUDGEMENT OF NESTOR,
THE GENIUS OF SOCRATES,
THE ART OF VIRGIL;
THE EARTH ENCLOSES,
THE PEOPLE SORROW,
OLYMPUS POSSESSES.

Fig. 154 – Tower of Holy Trinity Church, Stratford-upon-Avon, framed by weeping willows.

AFTERWORD

Why write another Shakespeare biography?

Because, as this book seeks to show, many valuable new insights into Shakespeare's life, times and work can be gained on the basis of historical facts and authentic written or pictorial sources. Often by mere coincidence, I have made discoveries on facets as diverse as Shakespeare's religion , the identity of his 'dark lady', his outer appearance, his illnesses, and the most probable cause of his death, through the discovery of new documentary evidence and by applying interdisciplinary research methods from fields including medicine, physics, botany, criminology, architecture, history of art, archaeology, palaeography, jurisprudence, theology, historiography, linguistics, and cultural and literary studies.

This book provides the reader with completely new results, offering conclusive answers to many of the unresolved problems of the Bard's life and literary career, viewed against the backdrop of the turbulent times he lived in. Shakespeare's religion has been a source of speculation for hundreds of years,, however, new evidence revealed here shows that he was a Catholic and also a member of the Catholic underground movement. Not only do these findings cast new light on Shakespeare's upbringing, schooling, academic education, marriage, whereabouts during the 'lost years', mistress and religion, but also on his moral qualities and ethical principles, his intellectual and highly politically-motivated personality as well as his cultivated lifestyle and impressive appearance (see the Davenant bust, Fig. 1). In addition, they allow us unexpected insights into Shakespeare's plays, many of which have topical political implications showing how the poet's life and literary work were closely linked to the often dramatic historical events of the period.

This work, to a considerable extent, challenges received opinions on the subject. It aims to demonstrate, on the basis of this cross-disciplinary approach, that the new knowledge of Shakespeare's secret Catholicism is the most important key to productive research on his biography, and that very close connections and links can be established between his life, his writing, and the historical events of his time. It also wants to show that this complex interplay places the chronology of the plays in a new perspective, and that, moreover, it can improve our grasp and understanding of the conditions under which they originated and were received.

This new approach reveals that Shakespeare was a highly political playwright, who not only reacted to the turbulent events of his time, but also tried (often successfully) to influence them. However, only with the background of his secret Catholicism in mind can we identify his political stance, and make sense of his sudden and abrupt switch from writing plays about ruling figures in English history to dealing with a central event of Roman history, the murder of Julius Caesar. Again, it is only when we take into account the whole complex inter-relationship of contemporary history, biographical details, and literary production that it becomes clear why – with equal abruptness – the dramatist ceased to write comedies, undergoing the sudden turn to tragedy that has previously defied (convincing) explanation. This biography illuminates and explains this turn to tragedy against the background of power politics prevailing at the end of the Elizabethan era, an element that now proves to be essential to our understanding of the poet's life and work. The momentous events of high politics are more clearly reflected in Shakespeare's works at this point than in any other phase of his literary career.

Numerous pieces of visual evidence from the time of Shakespeare, many of them previously neglected, are interrogated and used in this book as new, important and informative historical sources. The images (portraits, drawings, busts, death masks etc) of this time are executed in such a true-to-life manner that today's identification specialists can identify the persons portrayed, and medical experts are able to diagnose their illnesses and assess their progressive pathological states as well as their stage of pregnancy. Numerous paintings of the time, especially those whose purpose is emblematic, are full of hidden messages, allusions, and meanings, which in many cases have previously escaped attention because their value as historical sources was not recognised.

With the help of specialists, monuments, paintings, inscriptions, legal documents, diaries etc have been investigated. The results have contributed substantially to the resolution of crucial open questions of Shakespeare biography, including the identity of the sonnets cycle's Dark Lady. We can now marvel at authenticated portraits of the heroine of some of the most romantic and vitriolic love poetry ever written.

This Shakespeare biography is the fruit of a decade of research labours into different aspects of Shakespeare's life. It is an updated version of the original edition, which was published in German in 2003. New documentary evidence concerning the identification of Shakespeare's Dark Lady was first presented in my book *The Secret Surrounding Shakespeare's 'Dark Lady'. Uncovering a Mystery* (published in German in 1999). Most of the external documentary evidence that Shakespeare had been a clandestine Catholic was first established in my book *The Secret Life of William Shakespeare. Poet and Rebel in the Catholic Underground* (published in German in 2001). In the summer of 2006, Chaucer Press published an English translation of my book *The True Face of William Shakespeare. The Poet's Death Mask and Likenesses from Three Periods of His Life.* This established the authenticity and lifelikeness of three works of art and a death mask representing Shakespeare and, much to my surprise, turned up evidence that the poet is likely to have died of a skin sarcoidosis, an immune system disorder, which as a systemic disease leads to death normally after many years.

The account given by this book accords with many earlier insights and conjectures from the rich canon of Shakespearian biography, which are now carried forward, expanded, and – not least – verified. Many previous advances have been absorbed into the present book, although only the most important works can be listed below.

For many years *A Life of William Shakespeare* (1898, German translation 1901) by Sir Sidney Lee, co-founder of the *Dictionary of National Biography*, was regarded as the standard work. It was followed in 1923 by the knowledgeable *Life of William Shakespeare*, by the American expert Joseph Quincy Adams, and in 1930 the Oxford scholar Sir Edmund [E.K.] Chambers produced his major, comprehensive, and influential two-volume work, *William Shakespeare. A Study of Facts and Problems.* Particularly indebted to Chambers was another English scholar, John Dover Wilson, who in 1932 published his provocative study *The Essential Shakespeare* (German version 1953), which often departed from traditional critical approaches, and was the first to consider *Hamlet* in its historical context. Another well-researched and stimulating two-volume work, *Shakespeare. Man and Artist*, by the English antiquary Edgar I. Fripp, appeared in 1938. In the jubilee year of 1964, the Oxford historian A. L. Rowse produced his *William Shakespeare. A Biography*, with its wealth of informative historical detail. It was in 1970 that the English novelist Anthony Burgess published a lively and readable Shakespeare biography, where he frequently filled in the gaps in the familiar story with fictional elements. In the same year, Samuel Schoenbaum, the American Shakespeare specialist, began to bring out his ambitious biographical accounts, with a rich basis of material and including many impressive reproductions of historical documents: *Shakespeare's Lives* (1970, 2nd edn. 1991);

William Shakespeare. A Documentary Life (1975); *William Shakespeare. A Compact Documentary Life* (1977, 2nd, expanded edn. 1987, German version 1981); and *William Shakespeare. Records and Images* (1981). In these books, the author brought together practically all the information and insights available at that time concerning Shakespeare's life. Just when it seemed that no new sources could possibly emerge, the English Shakespearian scholar E. A. J. Honigmann came out with the sensational findings of his book *Shakespeare. The 'Lost Years'* (1985, 2nd edn. 1998), which followed the trail of Shakespeare to the aristocratic Catholic household of the de Hoghtons of Hoghton Tower, Lea Hall in Lancashire. Honigmann emphasized that the Jesuit and Shakespeare scholar Peter Milward 'saw more clearly than any predecessor ... that Shakespeare's biographers must take a detour into Lancashire'. Honigmann was the first to record the family tradition, handed down by word of mouth through the generations, that as a young man Shakespeare had lived for two years with the de Hoghtons. Sir Bernard de Hoghton, the present head of the family, confirmed this tradition to the present author in November 2002.

While Ian Wilson in his 1993 book, *Shakespeare. The Evidence*, greeted Schoenbaum's work as the 'soundest study of the available documentation', he found the author disappointingly reluctant to formulate conclusions and assessments. Wilson himself freely aired some of the problems of Shakespeare biography – including for example Shakespeare's religious inclinations and his 'curious purchase' of a gatehouse on the Blackfriars site in London. He queried Schoenbaum's 'established' view that Shakespeare's property acquisition at Blackfriars was purely for investment purposes, posing the crucial question of why Shakespeare would choose to invest precisely in a 'notoriously Catholic Gatehouse'.

There is much factionalism amongst Shakespeare biographers over numerous vexed questions – paramount among them his religion. The latter question, however, had already been dealt with in the 19th century (see J. M. Raich, *Shakespeare's Stellung zur katholischen Religion* [Shakespeare and the Catholic Religion], 1884, and H. S. Bowden, *The Religion of Shakespeare*, 1899). In the 20th century Heinrich Mutschmann and Karl Wentersdorf published their major work, *Shakespeare und der Katholizismus* (1950) (*Shakespeare and Catholicism*, 1952), which was to influence Peter Milward whose own seminal book on the subject – *Shakespeare's Religious Background* – appeared in 1973. All this research was principally based on internal evidence, deriving from Shakespeare's plays and emphasising the playwright's familiarity with Catholic thoughts and rites.

After the original publication of my Shakespeare biography in German in 2003, in which new *external* evidence was presented, especially with regard to Shakespeare's Catholicism, other British and American studies on the life of Shakespeare have appeared which consider the possibility that the poet might have been a Catholic or had Catholic leanings or sympathies.

Richard Wilson's research concerning Shakespeare's 'possible' Catholicism and the poet's connection to the de Hoghton family in Lancashire, were publicised in various newspapers in the late summer of 1999. In his book *Secret Shakespeare*, published in 2004, he accuses 'the current critical establishment' of being 'deeply invested in building a Protestant canon' and provides 'close reading of the plays to illustrate the influence of the shaded, secretive, dangerous, hidden life of the English Catholics on Shakespeare's work' (publishers' description). In the summer of 2003, Michael Wood's powerful BBC documentary series *In Search of Shakespeare* was broadcast and the accompanying book, in which he deals with some of Shakespeare's 'Catholic leanings', was published simultaneously. In 2004, Stephen Greenblatt's study *Will in the World* appeared and received worldwide press attention. Greenblatt, who tried to fill the numerous gaps in the poet's biography by using his own imagination, suspects 'Catholic sympathies' in Shakespeare, but thinks that the poet's overall motives were essentially worldly. In his book, *Shakespeare. The Biography*, published in 2005, Peter Ackroyd stresses that four of six Stratford schoolmasters had 'Catholic sympathies'. Peter Milward, however, wrote about 'Shakespeare's Jesuit schoolmasters' (*The Month*, April 2000). Moreover, Lady Clare Asquith, who examined Shakespeare's plays closely, taking into account the harsh environment English Catholics experienced under the Tudors, found many examples of 'coded Catholic language' in Shakespeare's dramatic work – following Milward's *Shakespeare's Religious Background*. Her subsequent study, *Shadowplay. The Hidden Beliefs and Coded Politics of William Shakespeare*, also appeared in 2005. In her article 'The Catholic Bard: Shakespeare & the "old religion"', *Commonweal* (17 June 2005), she pointed out: 'Ever since a seventeenth-century Protestant clergyman, Richard Davies, remarked that "William Shakespeare dyed a papist," Shakespeare's religion has been a thorny subject for scholars and biographers. Protestant England would much rather he had not died a papist.'

When reading the proofs, Peter Milward drew my attention to A. Keen and R. Lubbock, *The Annotator* (1954). Keen had already mooted that Shakespeare might have been a student at Douai (see Milward's 'History of William Shakeshafte', *Renaissance Pamphlets* 56, April 2006). Milward, who holds that John Shakespeare (with William) received his Borromeo testament from Campion at Sir William Catesby's house at Lapworth, in *Shakespeare the Papist* (2005, p. 183) also suggests that the entry in the diocesan register of Worcester in November 1582 may have been after the event of marriage, recording what Anglicans would have seen as a 'pre-contract' but Catholics would have recognized as a marriage ceremony which could already have taken place in the summer of 1582. In 'Religion in Arden' (*Shakespeare Survey*, 2001, p. 118) he concludes that Shakespeare's model for the exiled duke in *As You Like It* may have been William Allen, president of the English College at Douai/Rheims. Milward too sees *Twelfth Night* as a turning-point in Shakespeare's dramatic production, as the last of his 'happy comedies' (see his *Shakespeare the Papist*, p. 119). He drew my attention to Francis Edwards's article 'The Plot that never was and never ends', *Folio Magazine* (Autumn 2005). According to Edwards, the exposure of the Gunpowder Plot 'at the last minute' seems to have been carefully plotted by Robert Cecil, who must have been aware of the activities of the plotters for a long time beforehand. In *Shakespeare's Religious Background* (pp. 32 and 255) the Shakespeare expert had already pointed out that Hamlet's 'By Saint Patrick!' refers to St. Patrick's Purgatory in Ireland which was regarded as a gateway to Purgatory and is described in Holinshed's *Chronicles*. In *Religious Controversies in the Elizabethan Age* (1977, nn. 610-621), he clarified that the Elizabethan censor Samuel Harsnett, in his *Declaration*, would have undertaken the task of refuting the exorcizing activities of the Jesuits at the request of Richard Bancroft, Bishop of London, owing to the recent discovery of a 'Book of Miracles' attributed to the Jesuit William Weston. As to Shakespeare's patron and friend, the Catholic Earl of Southampton, Milward, interestingly, sees in the Italian scholar John Florio a spy for William Cecil planted in Southampton's household, just as Macbeth keeps a 'servant fee'd' in the houses of his nobility.

ACKNOWLEDGEMENTS

It is my British Publisher, John Maxwell, Managing Director of Caxton Publishing and Chaucer Press, London, to whom I owe deep and special thanks. Only due to his great personal commitment this publication was made possible – at a time when yet again we are seeing forceful but ungrounded 'revisions' of Shakespeare's identity and authorship.

The highly commendable efforts of John Maxwell as well as the generous understanding of my German publisher Dr Annette Nünnerich-Asmus, Director of Philipp von Zabern Verlag, Mainz, have enabled the English translation of this book to be published by Chaucer Press only about fifteen months after the launch of my study *The True Face of William Shakespeare. The Poet's Death Mask and Likenesses from Three Periods of His Life,* also by Chaucer Press. Thanks to them, the new historical and biographical findings and the new insights presented in *The Life and Times of William Shakespeare* are now giving the English-speaking readership access to Shakespeare's life and literary career – viewed against the backdrop of the turbulent political and religious times he lived in.

I would also like to express my most sincere thanks to Caxton's Trade Director, Terry Price, to whom I first presented the project at the Frankfurt Book Fair in 2004. Soon afterwards we had an extremely fruitful meeting at 20 Bloomsbury Street, London, where I was given the opportunity to introduce my Shakespeare biography as well as my book on Shakespeare's authentic images to John Maxwell and his team. What followed was a wonderful and most exciting collaboration. To Caxton's Sales & Marketing Director, Finbarr McCabe, Beth Macdougall, Director of MGA Publishing Consultancy, and MGA's Bethan Jones I owe great thanks for their untiring efforts and energetic contributions on behalf of the project as well as their marvellous assistance and help.

I should like to offer my great gratitude to Victoria Huxley for her meticulous editing of the text. Her care has been admirable and her collaboration has been both very efficient and pleasant. I want to thank Rachel Burgess most heartily for her impressive jacket design and lay-out, but also for her wonderful patience with me. My thanks also goes to the Ingrid Lock, who carefully built the index of this book, and to Dr Barbara Schwepcke, Publishing Services, for her advice.

To Emeritus Professor Alan Bance of the University of Southampton (kindly recommended to me by Professor Roger Paulin at Cambridge University) I owe a special debt of gratitude. He most carefully executed and/or revised the English translation of the vast text and captions of the book, the first draft of which was provided by American Pie/Interlegal Translations, London. I have gained enormously from working with him, our exchanges have been extremely fruitful, and I shall always remember his assistance in solving difficult problems. I also owe special thanks to Graham Nattrass, former Head of West European Collections at the British Library in London, for his most thorough revision of the English translation of the book's extensive chronology and his kind and most valuable help.

I shall never forget that this book was inspired by Emeritus Professor Rüdiger Ahrens, OBE, British Studies, University of Würzburg, founder and editor of *Anglistik. Proceedings of the German University Teachers of English.* To him I would like to offer my sincere thanks.

In January 2007, the English Shakespeare scholar Peter Milward, Emeritus Professor of English at the Sophia University in Tokyo, took the trouble to read the proofs of this book for which I owe him deep and special thanks. Between January and February 2007, we had a most fruitful exchange of thoughts. Since it was not possible to integrate Professor Milward's valuable comments and suggestions in the main body of the text at this stage, I have briefly summarized them in the 'Afterword'.

I also owe great thanks to the British journalist and writer Tom Templeton for his wonderful editorial assistance shortly before the book went to press.

However, it is to my husband, Dr Christoph Hummel, and my daughter, Anna Corinna Hummel, I owe my deepest debt of gratitude. Without their help, support, understanding and constructive criticism, this book could hardly have come about. They raised my spirits at difficult times.

In view of the large numbers of people involved in the project, I hope I may be excused for listing in alphabetical order the names of those I also wish to thank. The reader will be able to gauge from this list the wide range of scientific disciplines which contributed to the results achieved, or made them possible in the first place.

I would like to thank the owners of private collections who kindly allowed me to view their paintings, provided me with useful illustrative material for my research, and gave me permission to reproduce the paintings in my book:

Her Majesty Queen Elizabeth II

The Marquess of Bath, Longleat House

The Duke of Buccleuch, Boughton House

The Duke and Duchess of Devonshire, Chatsworth

Sir Edmund Fairfax-Lucy, Bt., Charlecote Park

Sir Bernard de Hoghton, Bt., DL, Hoghton Tower

Viscount De L'Isle, Penshurst Place

The Earl of Mar & Kellie, Lord Erskine of Alloa Tower

The Duke of Portland, Montacute

The Marquess of Salisbury, Hatfield House

The Earl Spencer, Althorp

The Marquess of Tavistock, Woburn Abbey

I would also like to thank those who assisted me in my research and investigations, gave me valuable suggestions, stood by me with help and advice, read my manuscript critically and allowed me to use numerous pictures and maps or helped me gain access to them. Without their help and support, this book would not have been possible:

Eileen Alberti
Archives Assistant, Photographic Collection, Records Office, Shakespeare Birthplace Trust, Shakespeare Centre, Stratford-upon-Avon

Elizabeth Allen CBIOL MIBIOL
Qvist Curator, Hunterian Museum, The Royal College of Surgeons of England, London

Reinhardt Altmann, EHK
Former Forensic Expert (Imaging Identification), German Bureau of Criminal Investigation, Wiesbaden

Margherita d'Ayala Valva
Antella, Florence

Matthew Bailey
Picture Librarian, National Portrait Gallery, London

Jörg Ballerstaedt
Director, German Bureau of Criminal Investigation, Wiesbaden

Valentina Bandelloni
Scala Group, Picture Library, Antella, Firenze

John Baskett
Former Chairman, Works of Art Committee, Garrick Club, London

Theodor Bauer
Department of Maps and Paintings, Bavarian State Library, Munich,

Dr Robert Bearman
Head of Archives, Records Office, Shakespeare Birthplace Trust, Shakespeare Centre, Stratford-upon-Avon

Bernd Becker
Chief Restorer, Hesse *Land* and University Library, Darmstadt

Peter Benz
Former Mayor of Darmstadt, Darmstadt

Professor Peter Berle
Gynaecologist, former Head of the Gynaecological Clinic at the Dr. Horst-Schmidt Clinics, Wiesbaden

Alessandra Biagianti
Archivio Fratelli Alinari, Firenze

Tom Bishop
Information Services Manager, Library, The Royal College of Surgeons of England, London

Dr Heinrich Boge
Former President of the German Bureau of Criminal Investigation, Wiesbaden

Denise Bontoft
Permissions Assistant, The Random House Archive & Library, Rushden

Vivien Bradley
Imaging Services, Bodleian Library, University of Oxford, Oxford

H. O. Brooks
Former Verger, Holy Trinity Church, Stratford-upon-Avon

Professor Dr. Edmund Buchner
Archaeologist, former President of the German Archaeological Institute, Berlin

Anthea Pelham Burn
Conservator, Garrick Club, London

Anthony Butcher
Former Chairman, Works of Arts Committee, Garrick Club, London

Louise Bythell
Bridgeman Art Library, London

Christine Campbell
Reproductions, British Library, London

G. C. Cannell
Sub Librarian, The Parker Library, Corpus Christi College, Cambridge

David Carter
Supervisor, Althorp, Northamptonshire

Andrew Cohen
Film Producer, BBC, London

Caroline Cole
Penshurst Place, Penshurst, Tonbridge, Kent

Pater Dr. L. Collin
St Bavo's Cathedral, Ghent

Sian Cooksey
Picture Library Assistant, Royal Collection Enterprises, Windsor Castle, Windsor

Dr Tarnya Cooper
Curator, Sixteenth Century, National Portrait Gallery, London

Joseph Coughlan
Manager and Bursar, Venerable English College, Rome

Joe Cowell
Keeper of the Royal Collection, Hampton Court Palace, Surrey

Tina Craig
Deputy Head of Library and Information Services, Royal College of Surgeons of England, London

Dr Jane Cunningham
Librarian, Courtauld Institute of Art, Somerset House, London

John M. Deasy, B.A.
Historian, Mainz University

Annick Degouy
Assistant, Douai Town Archives, Douai

Christian Derosne
Administrative Assistant, Douai Town Archives, Douai

Ann Dickson
Curator, Dulwich Picture Gallery, London

Christiane Dinger
Department of English Philology, Mainz University

Frances Dominy
Secretary to Earl Spencer, Althorp, Northamptonshire

Barbara Donovan
Secretary to the Rector, Venerable English College, Rome

Vincent Doom
Curator, Douai Town Archives, Douai

Margarethe Drewsen
Translator, Munich

Prue Dunne
Royal Shakespeare Company, Stratford-upon-Avon

Dr Rolf Dieter Düppe
Physicist, Institute for Photogrammetry and Cartography, Technical University, Darmstadt

SUE EDWARDS
Picture Gallery, Althorp, Northamptonshire

ANN-MARIE EHRLICH
Director, Art Archive, London

CHARLIE ELLIS
Picture Research Department, Bridgeman Art Library, London

ULRICH ERCKENBRECHT
Shakespeare translator, Muriverlag, Kassel

PROFESSOR KLAUS FAISS
Linguist (English studies), Department of English Philology, University of Mainz

SIR EDMUND FAIRFAX-LUCY
Charlecote Park, Warwickshire

GARETH FITZPATRICK, B.SC.
Director, The Living Landscape Trust, Boughton House, Kettering, Northamptonshire

AUDE FITZSIMONS
Assistant Librarian, Magdalene College, Cambridge

THE FITZWILLIAM MUSEUM, CAMBRIDGE

SUE FLETCHER
Photographic Services, Windsor Castle, Windsor

PATRIZIA FOGLIA
Civica Raccolta delle Stampe Achille Bertarelli, Castello Sforzesco, Milan

SUSIE FORSTER
Picture Researcher, National Portrait Gallery, London

DR GOTTHARD FUCHS
Theologist, Wiesbaden

TOM GILLMOR
Library Picture Researcher, Mary Evans Picture Library, London

BRIAN GLOVER
Former Director of the Royal Shakespeare Company Collection, Stratford-upon-Avon

THE REVD. MARTIN GORICK
Vicar, Holy Trinity Church, Stratford-upon-Avon

DR J.M.N.T. GRAY (CANTAB)
Physicist, University of Manchester

RIMA GRAY, B.A.
Manchester

HEINZ GRUBER
Portrait Collection, Picture Archive, Austrian National Library, Vienna

DR YORCK ALEXANDER HAASE
Former Chief Director, Hesse *Land* and University Library, Darmstadt

PROFESSOR WOLFGANG HACH
Former Director of the William Harvey Clinic, Bad Nauheim, Surgeon, Institute of Angiology, Frankfurt am Main

DR C. DE HAMEL
Librarian, The Parker Library, Corpus Christi College, Cambridge

Robin Harcourt Williams, M.A., F.S.A.
Librarian and Archivist to the Marquess of Salisbury, Hatfield House, Hatfield, Hertfordshire

SUSAN HARRIS
Printed Book Photographic Permissions, Bodleian Library, University of Oxford, Oxford

HERTA HARTMANN
Retired Senior Teacher, Wiesbaden

MECHTHILD HAWELLECK
Hesse *Land* Library, Wiesbaden

KAREN HEARN
Curator, Tate Britain Gallery, London

DR ULRICH HECKER
Academic Director, Institute of Botany, Director of the Herbarium, University of Mainz

PROFESSOR MICHAEL HERTL
Supernumerary Professor of Pediatrics, University of Heidelberg, Expert on the Physiognomy of the Sick and Death masks. Former Medical Superintendent of the Children's Clinic at Neuwerk Hospital, Mönchengladbach

MAUREEN HILL
Hampton Court Palace, Surrey

WALTER HOFFMANN
Mayor of Darmstadt

THOMAS DE HOGHTON
Hoghton Tower, Hoghton near Preston, Lancashire

THE REV. PETER L. HOLLIDAY
Vicar, formerly of Holy Trinity Church, Stratford-upon-Avon

PROFESSOR KARL JOSEF HÖLTGEN, OBE
Professor of English Literature, Department of English and American Studies, University of Erlangen-Nürnberg

DR KORT VAN DER HORST
Curator of Manuscripts, University Library, Utrecht

DAVID HORTON-FAWKES
General Manager, Althorp, Northampton

DAVID HOWELLS
Curator, Royal Shakespeare Company Collection, Stratford-upon-Avon

GEOFFREY HOWARTH
National Trust Severn, Tewkesbury

GERTRUD HÜTHER
Library of the Department of English Philology, University of Mainz

ANNA CORINNA HUMMEL
Student, St Andrews University, Scotland

EVA-MARIA HUMMEL
Pharmacist, Aachen

ERIKA INGHAM
Senior Archive Assistant, Heinz Archive and Library, National Portrait Gallery, London

PROFESSOR HANS HELMUT JANSEN
Former Medical Superintendent of Pathology, Darmstadt City Hospital

PAUL JOHNSON
Image Library Manager, Public Record Office, Kew, Richmond

ANDREAS KAHNERT
Photographer, Hesse *Land* and University Library, Darmstadt

CHRISTOPHER KENNEDY
Former Churchwarden, Holy Trinity Church, Stratford-upon-Avon

DR KLAUS ULRICH KERSTEN
Former President of the German Bureau of Criminal Investigation, Wiesbaden

COUNT FRANZ EUGEN VON KESSELSTATT
Kesselstatt Castle, Föhren near Trier

COUNTESS LOUISETTE VON KESSELSTATT
Kesselstatt Castle, Föhren near Trier

KAVOOS KIANY
Legal Manager, Public Record Office, The National Archives, Kew, Richmond

JAMES KILVINGTON
Picture Library, National Portrait Gallery, London

PROFESSOR BERND KOBER
Head of the Institute for Radiology, Darmstadt City Hospital

KRISTINA E. KOCH, M. A.
Assistant in the English and Romance Studies Department, University, Kassel

P. GERWIN KOMMA SJ
Rector, Pontificium Collegium Germanicum et Hungaricum, Rome

KARL-HEINZ KRATZ
Head Librarian, Hesse *Land* and University Library, Darmstadt

FATHER DR ROBERT LACHENSCHMID SJ
Collegium Germanicum, Rome

KARLA LEMM
Dip. Librarian, Library of the Department of English Philology, University of Mainz

PROFESSOR WALTER LERCHE
Former Medical Superintendent of the Eye Clinic at the Wiesbaden *Land* Capital Hospital, Wiesbaden

RUI LINNARTZ
Restorer, Hesse *Land* and University Library, Darmstadt

CHARLES LISTER
House Manager, Boughton House, Kettering, Northamptonshire

DARREN LOMAS
Printed Books & Journals, The British Library, London

CATHARINE MACCLEOD
Curator, Seventeenth Century Collections, National Portrait Gallery, London

MAIRI MACDONALD
Deputy Head of Archives, Records Office, Shakespeare Birthplace Trust
Shakespeare Centre, Stratford-upon-Avon

PAUL M. R. MAEYAERT
Viu de Llevata, Belgien

LIZ MANN
Permissions Manager, Academic Division, Oxford University Press, Oxford

MARILYN MASTERS
Principal Accounts Team Leader, Bodleian Library, University of Oxford, Oxford

GERDA MARON
The British Council, Berlin

FRAN MATHESON
Photographic Researcher, Tate Publishing Ltd, London

HANNA MATTHEWS
Assistant Secretary to Earl Spencer, Althorp, Northamptonshire

MARIE MCFEELY
Rights and Reproductions Officer, National Gallery of Ireland, Dublin

TIM MCGUFFOG
Photographer, Lancaster University, Lancaster

PROFESSOR HANS-JOACHIM MERTENS
Department of Law, University of Frankfurt am Main

PROFESSOR JOST METZ
Medical Superintendent of the Dermatological Clinic of the *Land* Capital Hospital, Wiesbaden

ALISON MILES
Picture Library, Tate Enterprises Ltd, London

GUSTAV MILLER
Engineer, Würzburg

DEANA MITCHELL
Former Secretary, Royal Shakespeare Company Collection, Stratford-upon-Avon

TOM MORGAN
Head of Rights & Reproductions, National Portrait Gallery, London

RICHARD MORTIMER, MA, PHD, FSA, FRHISTS
Keeper of the Muniments, Westminster Abbey, London

ROBIN MYERS
Hon. Archivist, Archive of the Worshipful Company of Stationers and Newspaper Makers, London

DIANE P. NAYLOR
Devonshire Collections, Chatsworth, Bakewell, Derbyshire

DR. MARTIN NICKOL
Head of the Botanical Gardens, Kiel University

HANNAH NEALE
Curator, Abbot Hall Art Gallery, Kendal, Cumbria

CHARLES NOBLE
Deputy Keeper of the Devonshire Collections, Chatsworth, Bakewell, Derbyshire

DR GEORG NOLTE-FISCHER
Chief Director, Hesse *Land* and University Library, Darmstadt

ANGELIKA OBERMEIER
Department of Maps and Paintings, Bavarian State Library, Munich

PETRA OSSWALD
Photographic Laboratory, Mainz University

EMERITUS PROFESSOR KURT OTTEN
British Studies (Literature), University of Heidelberg, Visiting Fellow, Clare Hall, University of Cambridge

MARLIES PICHLER
Schwabe & Co. AG Verlag, Basel

ANDREW PINSENT
Venerable English College, Rome

JO PHILLIPS
Information Assistant, Shakespeare's Globe, London

SHELAGH PHILLIPS
Permissions Department, Oxford University Press, Oxford

CHRISTINE REYNOLDS
Assistant Keeper, The Muniment Room & Library, Westminster Abbey, London

MARCUS RISDELL
Librarian and Archivist, Garrick Club, London

CAITRIONA ROE
Assistant, National Gallery of Ireland, Dublin

PROFESSOR GERD ROHMANN
British Studies (Literature), University of Kassel

STEPHEN ROPER
Reproductions (Western Manuscripts), British Library, London

AMANDA RUSSELL
Senior Picture Researcher, The National Photographic Library, London

EMERITUS PROFESSOR WALTER SALMEN
Mujsicoogy, University of Freiburg

DR CLAUDIO SALSI
Direttore, Civica Raccolta delle Stampe Achille Bertarelli, Castello Sforzesco, Milano

CHARLES SAUMAREZ SMITH
Director of the National Portrait Gallery, London, former Director, National Portrait Gallery, London

DR SEBASTIAN SCHOLZ
Palaeography, Academy of Science and Literature, Mainz

EDITH SCHUÉ
Head of the Photographic Laboratory, University of Mainz

NICHOLAS SCHOFIELD
Chief Archivist, Venerable English College, Rome

UDO SCHWEMMER
Architect, Wiesbaden

MICHAEL SCOTT
Photographic Department, Folger Shakespeare Library, Washington

CHANTAL SERHAN
Department of Prints and Drawings, British Museum, London

GEORGE E. SHIERS
Charlecote Park, former Head Teacher of Mathematics, Grammar School, Stratford-upon-Avon

BERNHARD SIMON
Archivist, Trier City Archive

T.J.K. SLOANE OBE, RN
Commander, Armourers & Brasiers' Company, London

RODNEY TODD-WHITE
Photographer, Photographic Services, Windsor Castle, Windsor

HELEN TROMPETELER
Picture Librarian, National Portrait Gallery, London

TONY TROWLES, DPHIL.
Librarian, The Muniment Room & Library, Westminster Abbey, London

EMERITUS PROFESSOR CLAUS UHLIG
British Studies (Literatur), University of Marburg

ALISON WALKER
Art Archive, London

TRACEY WALKER
Picture Library, Manchester City Galleries, Manchester

HORST WASSMUTH
Jurisprudence, Wiesbaden

WERNER WEGMANN
Chief Librarian, Hesse *Land* and University Library, Darmstadt

LAVINIA WELLICOME
Curator, Woburn Abbey, Bedfordshire

EMERITUS PROFESSOR STANLEY WELLS
Former Director of the Shakespeare Institute, Stratford-upon-Avon, Chairman of the Shakespeare Birthplace Trust, Stratford-upon-Avon

SARAH WICKHAM
Assistant Archivist, Lambeth Palace Library, London

JOHN B. WILLIAMS
Hall Manager & Beadle, The Worshipful Society of Apothecaries, Blackfriars Lane, London

PROFESSOR JOHANN-DIETRICH WÖRNER
President of the Technical University, Darmstadt

PROFESSOR DR HUBERT WOLF
Theology, University of Münster

MICHAEL WOODS
Reproductions, British Library, London

PROFESSOR BERNHARD WROBEL
Director of the Institute of Photogrammetry and Cartography, Technical University, Darmstadt

EMERITUS PROFESSOR DIETER WUTTKE
German Studies and Head of the Centre for Renaissance Studies, University of Bamberg, former Member of the Institute for Advanced Study in Princeton, Visiting Fellow, CASVA, National Gallery of Art, Washington

R. C. YORKE, M.A.
Archivist, The College of Arms, London

PROFESSOR HANS-LUDWIG ZACHERT
Former President of the German Bureau of Criminal Investigation, Wiesbaden

JÖRG ZIERKE
President of the German Bureau of Criminal Investigation, Wiesbaden

PROFESSOR CLEMENS ZINTZEN
Former President of the Academy of Science and Literature, Mainz

Hildegard Hammerschmidt-Hummel
April 2007

FOOTNOTES

FOOTNOTES FOR CAPTIONS

PART I.

*1 See Snowden Ward and Catharine Weed Ward, *Shakespeare's Town and Times* (London, *c.* 1896), p. 165 – Fig. 14.

*2 This drawing can be found in the copy of the Third Folio Edition of Shakespeare's plays (1664), housed at Colgate University in Hamilton, NY. The artist used the back of the original title page of the 1663 edition, which was afterwards inserted in the 1664 edition. A second original page was also inserted in this edition. On the back of the latter there are the following verses, based on the famous lines by Ben Jonson in the first folio edition and marked with the initials 'D.J.': 'This figure that thou there seest put/ It was for Shakespeare's Consort cut...' (see Fig. 90a). Next to this poem the name 'Anne Hathaway' has been handwritten – seemingly by a different person. This identification of the lady in the portrait has never been fully accepted by Shakespeare researchers. Samuel A. Tannenbaum published the picture and text in *Shakespeare Association Bulletin* (April, 1942) and added a question mark to the title: 'A Portrait of Anne Hathaway?'. – Fig. 15a.

*3 See Roy Strong, The English Icon (London, 1969), No. 12: 'Mary I' (1544), No. 13: 'Lady Jane Grey' (*c.* 1545), No. 11: 'Elizabeth I' (c.1546), No. 46: 'Anne, Lady Penruddocke' (1551), No. 65: 'Mary I' (1554), No. 67: 'Jane Fitzalan, Lady Lumley' (1563), No. 72: 'Elizabeth Fitzgerald, Countess of Lincoln' (1560). The centre parting hairstyle and bonnet date back to the 1540s, but the ruff was still being worn in the 1570s. – Fig. 15a.

PART III

*4 See p. 355, footnote 47: *The First and Second Diaries of the English College, Douay*, p. 14. – Fig. 59.

*5 See the forensic report by Reinhardt Altmann, expert at the German Federal Bureau of Criminal Investigation (BKA=CID), 'Report on images relating to art-historical research [...] SHAKESPEARE (File reference: BKA Wiesbaden, ZD 15 – 1170/95 – appendix: 1 folder of images)' of 3 May 1995, pp. 4-5 of text section pp. 1-10, and nos. 1-2 of image folder containing nos. 1-21. – Fig. 62a.

*6 See my article, 'Identifying Richard Burbage and (?) William Shakespeare in Henry Peacham's Stage Drawing of Shakespeare's *Titus Andronicus*', in *Shakespeare & Pictorial Art*, ed. Joachim Möller (forthcoming). – Fig. 62a.

*7 See Altmann, 'Report on images relating to art-historical research [...] SHAKESPEARE ...', image folder No. 1. – Fig. 62b.

*8 See Altmann, *op. cit.*, image folder No. 2. – Fig. 62c.

*9 E. W. Naylor comments: 'Thus, in Shakespeare's mind, the word 'virginals' clearly pictured the action of musical fingers on a keyed instrument': *An Elizabethan Virginal Book* (London/New York, 1905), p. 149 – Fig. 84b.

*10 The cut is similar to that of the dress worn by Queen Anne in a portrait, also by Paul van Somer, in the Windsor Castle collection, and reproduced by Roy Strong in *The English Icon* (London, 1969), p. 26, fig. 19. – Fig. 86a.

*11 See the literature cited in note 186, in which the relevant forensic and medical findings are presented. – Fig. 86a.

*12 See *Van Dyck. Des Meisters Gemälde in 537 Abbildungen* (Van Dyck: the Master's Paintings in 537 Illustrations, Stuttgart/Leipzig, 1909), p. 410. – Fig. 87.

*13 See the text on the website of Tate Britain, Van Dyck, Sir Anthony 1599-1641, 'A Lady of the Spencer Family', *c.* 1633-8 (www.tate.org.uk – May 2001), compiled by the relevant curator, Karen Hearn. – Fig. 87.

PART IV

*14 It is noticeable that the starting point of the composition is the human head at the bottom of the design (centre), flanked by two *putti*. At the top, the design culminates in the head of a cat, placed above what looks like a dove. These motifs may well refer to Elizabeth and Essex, who emerged as victor and vanquished respectively from the most dramatic political event of the time, the Essex rebellion and its outcome. In the so-called Tower Portrait of the Earl of Southampton, painted to commemorate his time of tribulation in the Tower, the queen, too, appears to be alluded to in the form of a cat with deadly claws (Fig.101). This point is discussed at length in *Das Geheimnis um Shakespeares 'Dark Lady'* (The Secret of Shakespeare's 'Dark Lady'), pp. 74ff. Compared to the revised and expanded 2nd Quarto edition of 1604 (Q2), which retained the title emblem of Q1, the contemporary relevance and political explosiveness of the text of the first edition are most striking. In the eyes of the fratricidal king, Hamlet is a somewhat inscrutable enemy of the state, who must be eliminated in order to free it: 'Our Letters are vnto the King of England, [...] / Hamlet loose his head, for he must die, / There's more in him than shallow eyes can see: / He once being dead, why then our state is free.' Significantly, these sentences were omitted from the later editions – most probably because the dangerous parallel to Essex could hardly be overlooked. At the same time, the ending of Q1 was shortened considerably: for example, the whole of the last page is missing, so that Horatio's (Catholic) prayer, identical with the prayer Essex repeated twice on the scaffold, was cut. It goes without saying that such important clues with regard to the faith of Essex as well as Shakespeare, who at this time was nearly forty, proved to be extremely dangerous. When the text of Q2 was reprinted in Leipzig in 1825, the German publishers commented on the missing page, but – astonishingly – thought that 'the loss' was 'of comparatively small importance'. – Fig. 116.

*15 'Shakespeare und das elisabethanische Drama', in Horst Oppel/Kurt Schlüter, *Englische Dichtung des 16. und 17. Jahrhundert* (English 16th and 17th Century Literature) Frankfurt am Main, 1973), pp. 34-81, p. 71, fig. on p. 70. – Fig. 117.

*16 Leonard Digges also prefaced a volume of Shakespeare's poetry, published in 1640, with a long poem in praise of the late poet, full of allusions to his plays, character and theatres (see note 381). – Fig. 120a.

PART V

*17 See *Die verborgene Existenz des William Shakespeare*, 'Exkurs I: Zur Lage des Blackfriars Theatre' (Excurse I: [New Evidence] Concerning the Site of the Blackfriars Theatre), pp. 150-153. – Fig. 131.

PART VI

*18 See under footnote 186 for my earlier publications on this subject. In a chapter devoted to the Darmstadt Shakespeare Death Mask in his book *Totenmasken. Was vom Leben und Sterben bleibt* (Death Masks: what is left after Life and Death) (Stuttgart, 2002), Michael Hertl, professor of medicine and expert on death masks, comments on these findings, summarizing: 'William Shakespeare (1564-1616), author of 38 plays, 154 sonnets, and various minor works: since 1995 there has been no doubt that here we possess an authentic likeness of him. It is his original death mask (fig. 73). [...] The trail leading to the final proof was a long one. In the end, forensic and medical experts were called upon to help, and the last links in the chain of evidence are now in place' (p. 121). – Fig. 147.

*19 The vicissitudes the mask was exposed to during its history are outlined in my book *The True Face of William Shakespeare*, pp. 99-118. – Fig. 147.

*20 See *The True Face of William Shakespeare*, pp. 118-128. – Fig. 153b.

FOOTNOTES FOR TEXT

I. CHILDHOOD AND YOUTH

1 This is not the original document, but a careful copy, made in 1600 by an official scrivener, which can be regarded as completely reliable. This copying of documents was ordered by the government and was also performed in other locations. The practice ensured that entries could be safely preserved on robust parchment. Once the copy was complete, the originals were not deemed worthy of retention.

2 See E. K. Chambers, *William Shakespeare. A Study of Facts and Problems*. 2 Vols. (Oxford, 1930, repr. 1951), I, p. 11.

3 Lee is one of the two editors of the famous Dictionary of National Biography: Leslie Stephen and Sidney Lee, *The Dictionary of National Biography: From the Earliest Times to 1900*, 22 vol. (London, 1908, repr. 1949–1950).

4 See H. Hammerschmidt-Hummel, *Die verborgene Existenz des William Shakespeare. Dichter und Rebell im katholischen Untergrund* (The Secret Life of William Shakespeare. Poet and Rebel in the Catholic Underground), (Freiburg im Breisgau, 2001), p. 175.

5 Coincidentally, the two families became related through marriage in 1615, when Spencer's heir married William Shakespeare's illegitimate daughter. This means that the ninth Earl of Spencer, and his three sisters, including Princess Diana, are descendants of Shakespeare (see Pt. 3, subchapter: Autobiography in the Sonnets: Course and Consequences of the Relationship between the 'Poet', 'Dark Lady' and 'Friend').

6 It is commonly believed that the potato was introduced into Europe by Sir Walter Raleigh, who probably planted it on his estate in Ireland between 1586 and 1588. See H. Hammerschmidt, *Die Importgüüter der Handelsstadt London als Sprach- und Bildbereich des elisabethanischen Dramas* (The Import Commodities of the City of London and their Impact on the Life-Style, Language, and Dramatic Literature of Elizabethan England) (Heidelberg, 1979), pp. 88–89. Coffee, tea and chocolate were introduced to London in around 1650, and quickly became familiar commodities in Britain. See H. Hammerschmidt, 'Frühphasen der englischen Handels- und Kulturgeschichte der Neuzeit und ihre linguistischen, literarischen and bildküünstlerischen Implikationen' (Early Stages of English Trade and Cultural History and their Linguistic, Literary and Art-historical Impact), in: *Anglistentag 1980 Giessen*. Papers and reports presented at the annual symposium of the German society for English studies, edited by Herbert Grabes (Grossen-Linden, 1981), pp. 397–417, pp. 403–404.

7 An illustration of gloves dating from Shakespeare's time, showing the mark of the glover (or an emblem of the owner) can be found in Park Honan, *Shakespeare. A Life* (Oxford, 1998), pp. 240–241, fig. 6.

8 Reproduced by Levi Fox, *Historic Stratford-upon-Avon* (Norwich, 1986), p. 31.

9 H. Snowden Ward and C. Weed Ward, *Shakespeare's Town and Times*, (London, *c.* 1896).

10 'Wheler Miscellaneous Papers', ii, n. 39, as quoted by Charlotte C. Stopes in *Shakespeare's Environment* (London, 1918), p. 120.

11 See also the engraving in E. A. G. Lamborn and G. B. Harrison, *Shakespeare: The Man and his Stage* (Oxford/London), p. 56. The engraving by Hoefnagel is from 'Female Costume – Gentry', Nonesuch Palace, 1582.

12 The importance of this unique Elizabethan wall painting has been appreciated by many researchers, yet it has never before been suggested that the people depicted in this scene could actually be local residents, let alone that they could be John and Mary Shakespeare. Norman Scarfe writes the following about the general cultural and historical background of such wall paintings (and their endangerment in Protestant times) and mentions some unique features of this painting in the White Swan Hotel: 'In Shakespeare's day it was natural and commonplace to act out scenes of ancient local history [...] and also to enact guild pageants, the scenes of religious history. Such stories had for centuries appeared to people in paintings all over the walls and in the windows of their churches, some of the murals being painted as late as the reign of Mary Tudor [...]. Obliterated by whitewash in the circumstances of Elizabeth's church settlement, they may still have appeared on some secular walls. At Stratford, in the Rother Market, round the corner from the Shakespeare's house, in a tavern known as the King's Hall, and now the White Swan Hotel, a wall-painting of about 1560 depicts scenes from the Apocryphal story of Tobias and the Angel [...]. – The picture is singularly like the coloured sketch for a stage-set. Appropriately prophetic, it shows a sort of proscenium-stage, with the young Jew Tobias in the costume fashionable in the days of Shakespeare's youth, being sent off from Nineveh to collect his father's money in Media. To be actually translated into the language of the theatre, the theme had to wait for James Bridie in the 1930s. But the mere fact that it was painted on a wall just round the corner from Shakespeare's home is interesting. It is an example of one form of stimulus that was certainly present in a Stratford tavern in the days when the young dramatist's mind was being formed. The strength of the stimuli may perhaps be measured by the range and wisdom and poetry of Gaunt's advice to the banished Bolingbroke in

contrast with the prosy commandments Tobias received from his father in the Apocryphal Book of Tobit.' 'Shakespeare, Stratford-upon-Avon and Warwickshire', in: *Shakespeare: A Celebration, 1564–1964*. Ed. T. J. B. Spencer (Harmondsworth, 1964), pp. 15–29, pp. 25–26.

13 The administrative and judicial duties of the Justices of the Peace expanded very greatly in the second half of the sixteenth century. In Lambarde's *Eirenarcha* (1581), their duties are described in great detail in over 600 pages. Of the 309 relevant bye-laws listed, 133 date from before 1485, before the start of the Tudor dynasty, 60 were introduced between 1485 and 1547, 39 between 1547 and 1558, and 77 were introduced between 1558 and 1603. The Justices of the Peace were, so to speak, the long arm of the central government in London. On a local level, they performed almost all government functions. For this reason, in retrospect they were often referred to as 'the Tudor maids-of-all-work'.

14 See D. Harrison, *The First and Second Prayerbooks of Edward VI* (London, 1968), p. 392.

15 See Snowden Ward and Catharine Weed Ward, *Shakespeare's Town and Times* (London, *c.* 1896), p. 127.

16 See Sidney Lee, *A Life of William Shakespeare. Illustrated Library Edition* (London, 1899), p. 151.

17 See Michael Davies, 'Die Zerstöörung des englischen Katholizismus durch die anglikanische Liturgiereform' (The Destruction of English Catholicism by the Anglican Liturgical Reforms), *Una Voce Korrespondenz* (March/April, 2002), pp. 89–112, p. 94.

18 See J. J. Dwyer, *The Reformation in England* (London, 1962), p. 21.

19 Chapter B.II.2 of *Die verborgene Existenz des William Shakespeare* (The Secret Life of William Shakespeare) states: 'In 1580, a large-scale Jesuit mission to England began, led by the Jesuit priests Edmund Campion and Robert Parsons. Fifty-one priests from Rheims and Rome were sent to the country. The Pope strictly forbade the leaders to make political statements, speak out against the English Queen, or lend an ear to seditious remarks about the Queen. [......] The priests of the movement were given the task of converting lost souls back to Catholicism, of tending to the pastoral needs of the Catholic faithful – especially in country districts – and of setting a good example for others to follow'. (pp. 28-29) [Extract translated by Peter Bajorek]

20 See Henry Foley, *Records of the English Province of the Society of Jesus*. 7 Vols. (London, 1877–1882, repr. New York/London, 1966), II, 'Father Thomas Cottam', pp. 145–177, p. 149.

21 This line is unlikely to be a reference to the social problem of 'enclosure'. The process was certainly very topical in Shakespearian times, when arable land was being converted to pasture on a grand scale. However, this problem mainly affected tenant-farmers who were summarily evicted by their landlord, and thus plunged into poverty and forced to live off charity from the town and district. Whatever their plight, though, they were not deprived of rights, and neither were they outlawed or criminalised as a group. In fact, the authorities tried to resolve the problem by creating the Poor Law. In addition, Shakespeare was at no time a victim of the problems resulting from enclosures.

22 Snowden Ward and Catharine Weed Ward write the following about the seats of noble families in the region surrounding Stratford: 'The old halls and mansions within a few miles of Stratford have many a bit of interesting history and legend, more than one blood-stained floor, and haunted room, and secret passage, and priest's hiding chamber, to tell of those turbulent and intolerant days of which we often speak as the "good old times".' *Shakespeare's Town and Times*, p. 28.

23 A Borromeo Testament is described in depth in my book *Die verborgene Existenz des William Shakespeare* (The Secret Life of William Shakespeare): 'These texts consisted of fourteen paragraphs and were composed by the Cardinal of Milan, Carlo Borromeo. [...] They were printed under the official title of *The Contract and Testament of the Soule*, and enabled English Catholics to profess their Roman Catholic faith in oral and written form. It was a clearly worded testamentary provision which affirmed that, before his death, the signatory had expressed a wish to receive the sacraments of the Roman Catholic Church (Confession, Communion, Last Rites).' (Chapter B.II.2.b, endnote 124). [Extract translated by Peter Bajorek]

24 Edwin H. Burton and Thomas L. Williams, eds., *The Douay College Diaries, Third, Fourth, and Fifth, 1598–1654*. With the Rheims report, 1579–80. Catholic Record Society, x–xi (London, 1911), II, p. 562.

25 At the start of the English Civil War (1642) the Puritan aldermen of London closed all the theatres in the capital. Roughly ten years later, under Oliver Cromwell's Protectorate, the theatres were demolished.

26 Gerard was born in 1564, the same year as Shakespeare, and was sent to Douai by his parents in 1577 (see his entry in the *DNB*, volume VII).

27 According to Michael Davies, 'Oxford had lost all its leading scholars, since they would not accept the Acts of Supremacy. They preferred to emigrate to Louvain.' 'Die Zerstörung des englischen Katholizismus durch die anglikanische Liturgiereform' (The Destruction of English Catholicism by the Anglican Liturgical Reforms), *Una Voce Korrespondenz* (March/April, 2002), pp. 89-112, p. 95.

28 See Davies, 'Die Zerstörung des englischen Katholizismus.', p. 93. According to a complaint in the year 1577, the

number of Catholic recusants living in Oxford was so great that there were not enough government informers to report all of those who refused to attend Anglican divine services. (See Davies, pp. 93-94)

29 See Schoenbaum, *William Shakespeare. A Documentary Life*, p. 37, and S. Lee, *A Life of William Shakespeare* (1901), p. 9 and p. 10, note 1. Lee correctly identifies the error as having been introduced by the Shakespearean scholar James Orchard Halliwell-Phillipps in his book *Life of William Shakespeare* (1848). Halliwell-Phillipps at one point refers to a sale price of £4 and at another point to a price of £40. The second figure is obviously the correct one.

30 Between 1561 and 1628, a skilled builder could earn 10 to 12 pence per day, and the labourers employed under him would earn between 6 and 8 pence. This equates to a maximum annual income of about £18 for the former and £12 for the latter.

31 The Queen's Bench/King's Bench was, and still is, one of the three divisions of the High Court of England based in London. The two others were the Court of Common Pleas and the Court of Exchequer. These courts constituted the foundations of the English justice system. All three courts sat in Westminster Hall. Unlike the Justices of the Peace, who were laymen drawn from the upper middle classes and minor nobility, the judges were all qualified legal experts, and were appointed and dismissed by the monarch. The Court of Chancery was also located in Westminster. It is here that quick and cheap justice was dispensed, and injustices resulting from overly strict application of the Common Law were resolved. The Court of Chancery also sat outside the fixed times and gained in importance during the fifteenth and sixteenth centuries.

32 For more about Campion's trial and execution see chapter B.II.2a of my book *Die verborgene Existenz des William Shakespeare* (The Secret Life of William Shakespeare).

33 Schoenbaum, *William Shakespeare. A Documentary Life*, p. 38.

34 Schoenbaum elaborates: 'This time the Council ordered commissioners in every shire to ferret out and report all those who gave sanctuary to seminary priests, Jesuits, or "fugitives", and "all such as refused obstinately to resort to the church".' *William Shakespeare. A Documentary Life*, p. 38.

35 There are no official and accurate statistics from the reigns of Elizabeth I and James I concerning the number of Catholic priests and faithful who fled the country, were executed or died in overcrowded prisons as a result of torture, hunger or the cold. The imprisonment, trials and executions of Catholic priests in England were meticulously documented in the English colleges on the Continent, however.

36 See Schoenbaum, *William Shakespeare: A Documentary Life*, p. 42.

37 See ibid., p. 43

38 A concise account can be found in Peter J. Helm *England under the Yorkists and Tudors 1471–1603* (London, 1968, repr. 1972), p. 341.

39 See *Correspondence of the Reverend Joseph Greene. Parson, Schoolmaster and Antiquary (1712–1790)*. Ed. Levi Fox (London, 1965), pp. 157–158.

40 In 1748, Greene had a dispute with the elementary schoolmaster Mr Smith, who used the rooms at the end of the classroom, 'ye Rooms at ye End of ye Grammar School', as he saw fit. He claimed that this right had been given to him 24 or 25 years previously by one or two members of the council. Greene, the schoolmaster, regarded this as an infringement of his own privileges and successfully brought a complaint against Smith before the Lord of the Manor, the Duke of Dorset, and the Stratford Town Council. The legal basis for this decision was the unamended Foundation Charter dated 1553. The wording of this Charter was very strictly complied with, and even the schoolmaster's salary had not changed in over two hundred years since the school had been founded by Edward VI. The Charter also stated that no change could be made with regard to the school buildings. In 1748, Greene therefore maintained that 'the building where the Free-School now is' had been used for education since 'time immemorial'. 'School Affairs', in: *Correspondence of the Reverend Joseph Greene. Parson, Schoolmaster and Antiquary (1712–1790)*, pp. 153–157.

41 Thomas Nashe (1567–1601), an Elizabethan author, writes: 'A rodde for the Grammar boy, he dooth but wrangle about words' (*Pasquil's Apol.*, I, C, III, 1590). In *The Spectator* in 1711, Sir Richard Steele (1672–1729) writes of the 'many Heart-aches and Terrors, to which our Childhood is exposed in going through a Grammar-School.'

42 Ben Jonson (1572/73–1637), the English playwright and actor, was a colleague and friend of Shakespeare. His plays, too, were extremely popular. Both authors were often mentioned in the same breath by their contemporaries and later generations.

43 According to G. Anstruther, *The Seminary Priests – A Dictionary of the Secular Clergy of England and Wales 1558-1850* – I Elizabethan 1558-1603 (Gateshead, 1968), Debdale was martyred on 6 October 1586. The year 1585 was a particularly important one for English Catholicism and was also a turning-point in Shakespeare's life. In 1585, the twenty-one-year-old father of three disappeared, only to re-appear in London seven years later as a successful, confident and much-envied playwright.

44 The pressure of student numbers in Allen's College in Douai/Rheims was only reduced when other colleges were founded on the Continent, for example in Rome (1579), Eu (1581/82), Valladolid (1589), Seville (1592) and St Omer (1593).

45 This paragraph is taken from the author's book, *Die verborgene Existenz des William Shakespeare* (The Secret Life of William Shakespeare), Chapter C.I.3. [translated by Peter Bajorek]

46 Thomas Platter, *Beschreibung der Reisen durch Frankreich, Spanien, England und die Niederlande 1595–1600* (Travels in France, Spain, England and the Netherlands 1595-1600). On behalf of the Basel Historical and Antiquarian Society. Ed. Rut Keiser. 2 volumes. (Basel/Stuttgart, 1968), II, p. 857.

47 The supporting documents are to be found in *The First and Second Diaries of the English College, Douay, and an Appendix of Unpublished Documents*, introd. Thomas Francis Knox (London, 1878, repr. Farnborough 1969), pp. 8, 9, 14 and 30. They are described in chapter C.I.3 of my book *Die verborgene Existenz des William Shakespeare* (The Secret Life of William Shakespeare) pp. 89 f.

48 We may well assume that these deletions occurred after Napoleon had abolished the college and ejected the teachers and students, and the school records were taken to England. For at this time it was – despite the Catholic Emancipation Act of 1829 – still an awkward fact that the sons of important English families had been educated and brought up in Douai or Rheims. Thus the deletions could have occurred for national and patriotic reasons, as well as religious ones. It was only just over sixty years ago that, based on George Santayana, William R. Inge, Dean of St Paul's, wrote in his book *England* (repr. 1937) the following revealing sentence: 'The Englishman, he [Satayana] says, living in and by his inner self, can never really be a Catholic. "... if he becomes a Catholic at heart, he is no longer the man he was. Words cannot measure the chasm which must henceforth separate him from everything at home".' Unfortunately, the present author was not able not inspect the originals of the Douai records. These manuscripts are now kept in the Archive of Westminster Cathedral, but are in very poor condition and in danger of decay, as I learned in July 1999 when I contacted Father Ian Dickie in order to examine these valuable sources.

49 When Professor Klaus Faiss, Professor of Linguistics in the Department of English at the University of Mainz, Germany, read my manuscript and studied the scenes in question of *Henry V* in July 2002, he offered two explanations for the errors in Shakespeare's French shown in this extract from the play and in other extracts: 'a) Shakespeare's knowledge of French is flawed, and no better than the French of other English people at the time. Thus the poet did not necessarily learn French in Rheims. b) Shakespeare learnt or heard French in Rheims, but introduces errors in order to keep his time in Rheims a secret. See also the scene in which Katherine learns English.' Faiss mentions, in particular, the example of Shakespeare's use of 'à les' instead of 'aux' (used since the thirteenth century) and the fact that a Frenchwoman uses the wrong gender for the definite article, '*le possession*'.

50 Marlowe is quoted by A. L. Rowse in *William Shakespeare. A biography*. (New York, 1964), p. 115.

51 E.A.J. Honigmann, Shakespeare. *The 'Lost Years'* (Manchester, 1985, repr. 1998), pp. 28–30. Sir Bernard de Hoghton, the head of the de Hoghton family, confirmed the existence of this oral family story to the present author during a telephone conversation in November 2002.

52 A bill was passed in the twenty-third year of Elizabeth's reign whereby '[...] every person that shall keep a schoolmaster which shall not repair to church, or be allowed [licensed] by the bishop of the diocese where such schoolmaster is kept, shall forfeit for every month £10; and such schoolmaster shall be disabled to be a teacher of youth and shall be imprisoned without bail for one year.' '23 Eliz., chap. 1', quotation from Thomas Francis Knox's Historical Introduction to *The First and Second Diaries of the English College, Douay, and an Appendix of Unpublished Documents*. Published by Fathers of the Congregation of the London Oratory (London, 1878), p. lxviii.

53 Honigmann writes: 'In the hundreds of Elizabethan wills that I have seen I have not come across any other in which annuities grow in this way.' He continues: 'As I see it, the will is unclear and eccentric where the annuities are concerned, and could have caused all kinds of trouble'. *Shakespeare: The 'Lost Years'* (1985), p. 26.

54 Hammerschmidt-Hummel, *Die verborgene Existenz des William Shakespeare* (The Secret Life of William Shakespeare), pp. 96–97.

55 See also chapter II of ibidem.

56 E.A.J. Honigmann, *Shakespeare. The 'Lost Years'* (1985), p. 136.

57 This summary comes from chapter C.II of my book *Die verborgene Existenz des William Shakespeare* (The Secret Life of William Shakespeare). In total, eleven members were to receive a full annuity, even after de Hoghton's death. See p. 99.

58 Ibid., p. 98.

59 The original text is contained in the entry 'Thomas Pounde of Belmont' in Volume III (p. 623) of Henry Foley's seven-volume *Records of the English Province of the Society of Jesus*, which was published in London between 1877 and 1882 and reprinted in New York and London in 1966.

60 George Townsend and Stephen R. Cattley, eds., *The Acts and Monuments of John Foxe*. 8 vols. (London, 1837–1842).

61 See also chapter B.II.2.a of my *Die verborgene Existenz des William Shakespeare* (The Secret Life of William Shakespeare). I consulted Klaus Faiss, an expert in English linguistics and the history of the English language at the University of Mainz, Germany, about my conclusions. He checked my comparisons and agreed that there was much convincing evidence to attribute this poem to Shakespeare.

II. SHAKESPEARE'S MARRIAGE, FLIGHT AND THE 'LOST YEARS'

62 See Schoenbaum, *William Shakespeare. A Documentary Life*, p.72.

63 See ibid., p.62.

64 See H. Hammerschmidt-Hummel, *Das Geheimnis um Shakespeares 'Dark Lady'. Dokumentation einer Enthüllung* (The Secret of Shakespeare's 'Dark Lady'. Uncovering a Mystery) (Darmstadt, 1999), p.118.

65 'William Shakespeare was born at Stratford upon Avon in Warwickshire about 1563.4. much given to all unluckiness in stealing venison & Rabbits particularly from Sr Lucy who had him oft whipt & sometimes Imprisoned & at last made Him fly his Native Country to his great Advancemt. but His reveng was so great that he is his Justice Clodpate and calls him a great man & yt in allusion to his name bore three lowses rampant for his Arms.' Richard Davies, quoted by Oscar James Campbell and Edward G. Quinn, *A Shakespeare Encyclopaedia* (London, 1966, repr. 1974), 'Lucy, Sir Thomas (1532–1600)'. See also Fig. 46.

66 See Charles Percy, MS. Letter in Public Record Office, Domestic State Papers, Elizabeth, Vol. 275, No. 146. *The Shakspere Allusion-Book: A Collection of Allusions to Shakspere from 1591 to 1700*. Compiled by C. M. Ingleby, L. Toulmin Smith and F. J. Furnivall. Re-edited, revised and re-arranged, with an introd. by John Munro (1909), re-issued with a pref. by Edmund Chambers. 2 Vols. (London/Oxford, 1932) I, 86–87. Percy was also a follower of the Earl of Essex, and accompanied him in Ireland and on his fateful march into London in February 1601. It was he who arranged for *Richard II* to be performed by the Chamberlain's Men. This performance took place on the day before the uprising on 7 February 1601 with the purpose of encouraging the conspirators of the Essex Rebellion.

67 'He had, by a Misfortune common enough to young Fellows, fallen into ill Company; and amongst them, some that made a frequent practice of Deer-stealing, engag'd him with them more than once in robbing a Park that belong'd to Sir *Thomas Lucy of Cherlecot*, near *Stratford*. For this he was prosecuted by that Gentleman, as he thought, somewhat too severely; and in order to revenge that ill Usage, he made a Ballad upon him ...' Campbell/Quinn, *Shakespeare Encyclopaedia*, 'Lucy, Sir Thomas (1532–1600)'.

68 In *Shakespeare Versus Shallow*, the Canadian-born Shakespeare scholar Leslie Hotson proposes the theory that Shakespeare's character Shallow is actually a satirical portrait of William Gardiner (1531–1597), the Justice of the Peace in Southwark. His coat of arms also depicted three pickerels ('luces'), as he was related by marriage to the family of Sir Thomas Lucy. Two contemporary sources mention the escalating tensions between Sir Thomas and William Shakespeare, and the fact that Shakespeare retaliated with a mocking ballad against Sir Thomas makes it much more likely that the playwright actually based his character on Sir Thomas Lucy.

69 Campbell/Quinn, *Shakespeare Encyclopaedia*, 'Barnes, Joshua (1654–1712)'.

70 Campbell/Quinn, *Shakespeare Encyclopaedia*, 'Lucy, Sir Thomas (1532–1600)'.

71 To my knowledge this was first suggested by A. L. Rowse in *Shakespeare the Man* (New York et al., 1973), pp. 59–60. In *William Shakespeare. A Documentary Life*, Schoenbaum discusses this source and rejects Rowse's theory, though he does not give convincing grounds for this rejection. He states, without any evidence, that the encounter between Roberto and the stranger does not take place in 1592, but in Roberto's past. He asserts that the 'morals' which the stranger claims to have written are examples of 'pre-Shakespearian drama'. If Shakespeare wrote these pieces, as we must assume, when he was 'in his younger yeares a schoolmaster in the countrey', i.e. while he was a private tutor in Lancashire, then they would in fact have to be classed as 'pre-Shakespearian drama'. Schoenbaum furthermore assumes that in this scene, Greene is portrayed as the younger man. In reality, however, he was six years older than Shakespeare. This argument, too, is not convincing because it is Roberto (as the older man) who initiates the conversation, confidently questions the stranger (who turns out to be an actor), and judiciously weighs him up.

72 See *Die verborgene Existenz des William Shakespeare* (The Secret Life of William Shakespeare), The Epilogue. There these findings were first presented.

73 Ibid., pp. 153 ff.

74 Cf. Michael L. Carrafiello, *Robert Parsons and English Catholicism, 1580-1610* (London, 1998).

III. SHAKESPEARE'S RISE AS A PLAYWRIGHT IN LONDON

75 (Oxford, 1998), p. 92.

76 (London, 1999), p. 79.

77 (London, 1970), pp. 77–78.

78 (London, 2004), pp. 162-63.

79 William Harrison, *An Elizabethan Journal. Being a Record of those Things most Talked of during the Years 1591–1594*, (London, 1928), p. 266.

80 See ibid. p. 86.

81 Ibid., p. 83.

82 Ibid., p. 84.

83 The relevant page of Aubrey's manuscript, which is held in the Oxford Bodleian Library, was reproduced in E. K. Chambers, *William Shakespeare. A Study of Facts and Problems*. 2 vols. (Oxford, 1930), I, p. opposite p. 252.

84 See 'Given at Our Manor of Richmond, the 18th of October, 1591, in the 33rd year of Our reign.', Harrison, *An Elizabethan Journal... 1591–1594*, p. 76.

85 Ibid., p. 87.

86 See also H. Hammerschmidt-Hummel, *Das Geheimnis um Shakespeares 'Dark Lady'* (The Secret Surrounding Shakespeare's 'Dark Lady'), pp. 87–88.

87 G.B. Harrison, *An Elizabethan Journal. Being a Record of those Things most Talked of During the Years 1591-1594* (London, 1928), p. 220.

88. William Harrison writes: 'The Lord Strange's Players now begin to play at the Rose Theatre on the Bankside, and act this day Friar Bacon.' *An Elizabethan Journal...* 1591–1594, p. 103. Unless stated otherwise, all information regarding the plays performed at the Rose Theatre has been gleaned from Harrison's Journal for the years 1591-94.

89 W. W. Greg, ed., *Henslowe's Diary*. 2 Parts (London, 1904-1908); R. A. Foakes, *The Henslowe Papers*. 2 Vols. (London, 1977).

90 The play on which Greene collaborated with Thomas Lodge *A Looking-Glass for London and England* (*c*. 1590) was performed four times during this period. The now lost play *Titus and Vespasian* played a total of seven times, but there are no records of its authorship. There is a faint possibility that it was an early version of Shakespeare's *Titus Andronicus*.

91 Subtitled *Conteigning fiue apparations with Their Inuectiues against abuses raigning*.

92 *The Shakspere Allusion-Book*, comps. Ingleby, Toulmin Smith and Furnivall, I, p. 4.

93 Franciscus Lang, *Dissertatio de actione scenica*, (1727); *Abhandlung über die Schauspielkunst* (On the art of acting). Transl. and ed. by Alexander Rudin (Bern/Munich, 1975), p. 170. Similar rules exist for the knees, hips, shoulders, arms, elbows and hands.

94 See Reinhardt Altmann, 'Assessment of pictorial material for art-historical research, re: SHAKESPEARE', reference German Federal Bureau of Criminal Investigation Wiesbaden, ZD 15 – 1170/95 (3 May 1955), text section, pp. 1-10: picture file appended, pp. 1-21 (Bildgutachten in der kunsthistorischen Forschung, hier: SHAKESPEARE, Aktenzeichen Bundeskriminalamt Wiesbaden, ZD15 – 1170/95 (3. Mai 1995), Textteil: S. 1-10, Anlage: 1 Bildmappe, S. 1-21). See also the present author's summary in her article 'Shakespeare-Forschung – kriminologisch. Henry Peachams Bühnenzeichnung zu 'Titus Andronicus" (Criminology and Shakespeare research. Henry Peacham's stage drawing of *Titus Andronicus*.), *Neue Zürcher Zeitung* (17/18 June 1995).

95 The identification test was performed by Reinhard Altmann, then senior forensic expert at the German Federal Bureau of Criminal Investigation (BKA=CID). The results of this test proved that seventeen facial features of the Droeshout engraving, the Chandos portrait and the Flower portrait are in agreement. See Altmann, 'Assessment of pictorial material for art-historical research, re: SHAKESPEARE', text section p. 5-7, image section p. 4–7. They thus also proved that all three images depict the very same person: William Shakespeare. Signs of illness in the Shakespeare portraits, first noticed by the present author in 1995, were diagnosed at the author's request by medical experts in 1995 and 1996, and again in 1997 and 1998. Since they were evened out or even omitted by the engraver, it became clear that the engraving was made from the (original) Flower portrait and not vice versa as scholars had previously assumed. Shakespeare's close friends and colleagues John Heminge and Henry Condell made sure that the accuracy of the engraved portrait of Shakespeare was vouched for – as was usual at the time – by another close friend of Shakespeare's, the dramatist Ben Jonson. Heminge and Condell placed Jonson's lines opposite the frontispiece picture in the First Folio (see *Figs. 90 a–b*)

96 See *Calendar of State Papers (Rome) I, Elizabeth, 1558–1571*, p. 265–266.

97 See Rowse, *The Elizabethan Renaissance: The Life of the Society*, p. 152.

98 Campbell/Quinn, *Shakespeare Encyclopaedia*, 'Venus and Adonis'.

99 There are a total of three 'Parnassus' plays by an unknown author: *The Pilgrimage to Parnassus*, *The First Part of the Returne from Parnassus* and *The Second Part of the Returne from Parnassus*. They were written between 1598 and 1602 and performed at St John's College in Cambridge. They are classified as 'University plays', written by students.

100 See T. J. King, 'Shakespearean staging, 1599–1642,' in *Shakespearean research opportunities: Department of English, Berkeley, Cal.* 5–6 (1970/71), pp. 30–35.

101 Ulrich Suerbaum, *Das elisabethanische Zeitalter* (The Elizabethan Age) (Stuttgart, 1989), p. 400.

102 See Joseph Quincy Adams, *Shakespearean Playhouses. A History of English Theatres from the Beginnings to the Restoration* (Gloucester, Mass., 1960).

103 See Klaus Heitmann, 'Das französische Theater des 16. und 17. Jahrhunderts' (French Theatre of the 16th and 17th centuries), *Neues Handbuch der Literaturwissenschaft* (New Literature Handbook),

Vol 9: *Renaissance und Barock*, Part 1. Ed. August Buck (Frankfurt a. M., 1972), pp. 272–310, p. 277.

104 It is known that in England at the time, many priests publicly celebrated 'heretical' services, after performing Mass in private. Michael Davies, 'Die Zerstörung des englischen Katholizismus...', p. 100.

105 This receipt was discovered by H-P [sic] in the nineteenth century in the Public Record Office, and published in his *Illustrations of the Life of Shakespeare* (1874). It was stored under 'Public Record Office, Exchequer, Pipe Office, Declared Accounts, E. 351/542, f. 107v'.

106 See my publications: 'Zur Rolle der Totenmaske in der Porträtplastik der Renaissance' (The Role of the Death Mask in portrait sculpture of the Renaissance), in: H. Hammerschmidt-Hummel, 'Neuer Beweis für die Echtheit des Flower-Porträts und der Darmstädter Shakespeare-Totenmaske. Ein übereinstimmendes Krankheitssymptom im linken Stirnbereich von Gemälde und Gipsabguß' (New Proof of the authenticity of the Flower Portrait and the Darmstadt Shakespeare Death Mask. Signs of illness on the left-hand side of the forehead in the portrait and on the plaster-cast), *Anglistik. Mitteilungen des Verbandes Deutscher Anglisten* (Sept. 1996), pp. 115–136, pp. 118–123. See also my book *The True Face of William Shakespeare* (London, 2006), where all these topics are discussed. See in particular Part III, 'Tests of Identity and Authenticity on the Basis of New Research Methods and Expert Assessments', pp. 38-80.

107 See Irving Ribner, *The English History Play in the Age of Shakespeare* (Princeton, 1957), p. 26. For Shakespeare's history plays seen in the light of the times see also Lily B. Campbell, *Shakespeare's Histories. Mirrors of Elizabethan Policy* (San Marino, 1947).

108 See Horst Oppel, *Shakespeare. Studien zum Werk und zur Welt des Dichters* (Heidelberg, 1964), pp. 9-27.

109 See *Die Shakespeare-Illustration (1594-2000). Bildkünstlerische Darstellungen zu den Dramen William Shakespeares: Katalog, Geschichte, Funktion und Deutung.* Mit Künstlerlexikon, klassifizierter Bibliographie und Registern. 3 Teile. Kompiliert, verfasst und herausgegeben von H. Hammerschmidt-Hummel. Mit 3100 Abb. (Wiesbaden: Harrassowitz Verlag, 2003), I, p. 25-26 (Illustrations of Shakespeare 1594-2000: artists' work on Shakespeare's plays: catalogue, history, function and interpretation. With a lexicon of artists, classified bibliography, and indices, 3 parts, compiled, authored and edited by H. Hammerschmidt-Hummel. With 3100 figs. (Wiesbaden, 2003), I, pp. 25-26.

110 See also my contribution 'Boydell's Shakespeare Gallery and its Role in Promoting English History Painting', in the *The Boydell Shakespeare Gallery*. Eds. Walter Pape and Frederick Burwick in collaboration with the German Shakespeare Society (Bottrop, 1996), pp. 33–44.

111 Harrison, *An Elizabethan Journal... 1591–1594*, p. 104.

112 Ibid. p. 104.

113 See H. Hammerschmidt, *Die Importgüter der Handelsstadt London als Sprach- und Bildbereich des elisabethanischen Dramas* (The Import Commodities of the City of London and their Impact on the Lifestyle, Language, and Dramatic Literature of Elizabethan England) (Heidelberg, 1979), pp. 49ff.

114 See 'The miraculous victory atchieved by the English Fleete, under the discreet and happy conduct of the right honourable, right prudent, and valiant lord, the L. Charles Howard, L. high Admirall of England, &c. Upon the Spanish huge Armada sent in the yeere 1588. for the invasion of England, together with the wofull and miserable successe of the said Armada afterward [...]. Recorded in Latine by Emanuel van Meteran in the 15. booke of his history of the low Countreys', in: Richard Hakluyt, *Voyages & Documents*. Selected with an introduction and a glossary by Janet Hampden (London/Oxford/New York/Toronto, 1958, repr. 1965), pp. 358–398, p. 367.

115 See G. B. Harrison, *A Last Elizabethan Journal. Being a Record of those Things most talked of during the years 1599–1603* (London, 1933), pp. 48–49.

116 In response to this event, Churchyard published the poem *The Fortunate Farewell to the most forward and noble Earl of Essex*, and Norden wrote A prayer for the prosperous proceedings and good success of the Earl of Essex and his companies.

117 Campbell/Quinn, *Shakespeare Encyclopaedia*, 'The Life of King HENRY the Fifth'.

118 This debate is concisely summarised by Ursula Sautter in her introduction to the English-German dual language version of William Shakespeare, *Love's Labour's Lost. Verlorene Liebesmühe.* (Tübingen, 1999), pp.50 ff.

119 See Ward/Weed Ward, *Shakespeare's Town and Times*, p. 28.

120 First Folio Edition: 'Ped. You find not the apostraphas, and so misse the accent. Let me superuise the cangenet. / Nath. Here are onely numbers ratified, but for the elegancy, facility, & golden cadence of poesie caret: Ouiddius Naso was the man. and why in deed Naso, but for smelling out the odoriferous flowers of fancy? the ierkes of invention imitarie is nothing: So doth the Hound his master, the Ape his keeper, the tyred Horse his rider: But Damosella virgin, Was this directed to you?' Modern Shakespeare editions read: 'Holofernes. You find not the apostrophus, and so miss the accent. Let me supervise the canzonet. Here are only numbers ratified, but for the elegancy, facility, and golden cadence of poesy, caret. Ovidius Naso was the man. [...].'

121 *Archiv für das Studium der neueren Sprachen und Literaturen* 133 (= N. F. 69) (1915), pp. 66–86.

122 See Campbell/Quinn, *Shakespeare Encyclopaedia*, 'The Merchant of Venice'.

123 See Neale, *Queen Elizabeth*, p. 350.

124 If a member of the clergy refused to use the new liturgy or made negative comments about it, he was stripped of his stipend for a year and jailed for six months. If a clergyman repeated an offence he could be deprived of all income and sentenced to a year in jail. Laymen who criticised the liturgy or tried to obstruct its use were threatened with similar harsh punishments. See Michael Davies, *Die Zerstörung des englischen Katholizismus durch die anglikanische Liturgiereform*, pp. 95–96. This was normal practice from the start of Queen Elizabeth's reign and predated the harsh anti-Catholic penal laws introduced from the 1570s onward.

125 '[...] I will make the first head at Douay and in Flanders, the second, middle and chief head, at Rome, the third and worst in Spain, the heart of the hell-hound Cerberouse [a reference to Parsons] I reckon to be in England, and the other parts and members dispersed all over [...]'. Henry Foley, *Records of the English Province of the Society of Jesus*. 7 Vols. (London, 1877–1882, repr. New York/London, 1966), pp. 732–733.

126 The report about the situation in Flanders reads: 'To begin with Flanders. This party reckons me thereabouts six or seven hundred, the one half priests, scholars, and religious, the other laymen, pensioners, and soldiers, the names of the chief of them [...] your honour shall receive a catalouge here inclosed, of all which the most dangerous and pernicious are these few following'. Foley, *Records*, VI, p. 733.

127 Foley, *Records*, VI, p. 741.

128 See my book *Das Geheimnis um Shakespeares 'Dark Lady'* (The Secret of Shakespeare's 'Dark Lady'), p. 39.

129 William Allen, quoted from Thomas Francis Knox, "Historical Introduction", *The First and Second Diaries of the English College, Douay, and an Appendix of Unpublished Documents*, ed. by Fathers of the Congregation of the London Oratory, with an Historical Introduction by Th. F. Knox (London, 1878), pp. lxviii-lxix.

130 'Zum Verständnis des Werkes' (About the play), in: Shakespeare, *Twelfth Night or What you will – Was ihr wollt* (Reinbek bei Hamburg, 1967), pp. 136–153, p. 136.

131 Mehl assumed that the perfomance took place at the Feast of Epiphany. This would have been 6 January. See 'Zum Verständnis des Werkes', ibid., p. 13.

132 See C. Richard Desper, 'Allusions to Edmund Campion in Twelfth Night', *Elizabethan Review* 3.1 (1995), pp. 37–47, p. 41.

133 See my book, *Die verborgene Existenz des William Shakespeare* (The Secret Life of William Shakespeare), p. 35–36.

134 See figs. 1875-1877 in Part 3 of *Shakespeare-Illustration* (The Shakespeare Illustrations), ed. H. Hammerschmidt-Hummel. See also 'Geschichte, Funktion und Deutung bildkünstlerischer Werke zu den Dramen William Shakespeares' (History, function and meaning of artistic depictions of William Shakespeare's Dramas), sub-chapter 'Der Shakespeare-Maler Johann Heinrich Füssli' (Shakespeare's painter Johann Heinrich Füssli').

135 See Campbell/Quinn, *Shakespeare Encyclopaedia*, 'Romeo and Juliet'.

136 Raich, Shakespeare's *Stellung zur katholischen Religion* (Shakespeare and the Catholic Religion) (Mainz, 1884), p. 118.

137 Ibid., p. 120.

138 Ibid., p. 121.

139 Ibid., p. 121. The accuracy of Shakespeare's reference to 'evening mass' at Verona was also confirmed by F.S. Bowden, *The Religion of Shakespeare* (London, 1899).

140 This does not include the two Cupid Sonnets Nos. 153 and 154, which – as is generally accepted among Shakespeare researchers – were not written by Shakespeare.

141 In his essay 'Die Ordnung der Shakespeare-Sonette. Zur Situation der Forschung' (The arrangement of the Shakespeare Sonnets: on the state of research) Wolfgang Weiss summarised the three most common positions: '1. The sonnets are poetic records of experiences and relationships from Shakespeare's life. 2. The sonnets depict Shakespeare's inner feelings, but are not necessarily based on real events. 3. The sonnets are to be considered solely as a literary work. Autobiographical interpretations are unproductive and misleading.' *Shakespeares Sonette in europäischen Perspektiven. Ein Symposium* (Shakespeare's Sonnets from a European Perspective. A Symposium). Ed. Dieter Mehl und Wolfgang Weiss (Münster/Hamburg, 1993), pp. 4–19, p. 6.

142 See chapters II and III of *Das Geheimnis um Shakespeares 'Dark Lady'* (The Secret of Shakespeare's 'Dark Lady').

143 This painting is discussed in great detail in Ibid., pp. 36-79.

144 See A. L. Rowse, *The Casebook of Simon Forman. Sex and Society in Shakespeare's Age* (London, 1974). 'Halec' is mentioned, for example, on p. 76, p. 77 and p. 111.

145 A.L. Rowse, *Shakespeare's Sonnets* (New York, 1964), p. 297.

146 Shakespeare wrote an obsequious dedication to Southampton in his 1593 narrative poem *Venus and Adonis*.

147 Rowse, *The Elizabethan Renaissance: The Life of the Society*, (London, 1971) p. 152.

148 Rowse, *Shakespeare's Sonnets*, p. 309.

149 Arthur Henkel und Albrecht Schöne, eds. *Emblemata. Handbuch zur Sinnbildkunst des XVI. und XVII. Jahrhunderts* (Emblemata. A Handbook of Sixteenth and Seventeenth Century Emblematic Art) (Stuttgart, 1967, spec. ed. 1978), p. xv.

150 This was established in a report by the Head of the Herbarium at the University of Mainz, Dr Ulrich Hecker, whom I consulted while researching for my book, *Das Geheimnis um Shakespeares 'Dark Lady'* (The Secret of Shakespeare's 'Dark Lady'). See Part III, 'Die *Pictura*: Identifizierung der dargestellten Unbekannten' (The *pictura*: identifying the unknown subject of the painting), p.140, n. 20.

151 This is the diagnosis provided in a report by the gynaecologist Professor Peter Berle, at that time Head of theGynaecological Clinic at the Wiesbaden City Hospital. See *Das Geheimnis um Shakespeares 'Dark Lady'* (The Secret of Shakespeare's 'Dark Lady'), p. 44. The lady's condition was also confirmed by Professor Wolfgang Hach, at that time Head of Department at the William Harvey Clinic in Bad Nauheim, who identified several other indicators of the woman's advanced stage of pregnancy.

152 Her pallid complexion could be linked to her pregnancy.

153 Percy Macquoid writes: 'English ladies at this time are occasionally represented in portraits as wearing their wedding rings on the thumb. [...] This fashion originated from the Catholic ritual of marriage [...].' 'The Home: Furniture: Food and Drink: Domestic Customs: Christenings, Weddings, Funerals', in: *Shakespeare's England. An Account of the Life & Manners of his Age* (Oxford, 1916, repr. 1966), pp. 119–152, p. 145.

154 Other pre-marital affairs and pregnancies in courtly circles can be excluded due to the time frame (see *Das Geheimnis um Shakespeares 'Dark Lady'*, p. 55–56). What can also be absolutely ruled out is the affair between the Earl of Oxford and Anna Vavasour in 1580, though it is still mentioned in connection with the Persian Lady. See Wolfgang Riehle, 'Zur aktuellen Frage nach der Identität der 'Persian Lady' (On the Question about the Identity of the 'Persian Lady), *Anglistik* (March 2002), pp.139–151. Riehle – apparently without consulting any relevant specialists – tries to prove that Marcus Gheeraerts' 'Persian Lady' is Anne Vavasour. He postulates that Sir Henry Lee had his beloved Anne Vavasour painted in her pregnant state, as the 'Persian Lady', in the 1590s by Gheeraerts, *post factum* [after the event], in order to commemorate her pregnancy in the year 1580. Expert analysis, however, shows great differences between the facial features and neck of the 'Persian Lady' and an authenticated portrait of Anne Vavasour. See the present author's response in *Anglistik* (September 2002), pp. 227–230.

155 This painting has been produced several times in the past. The original is in the collection of the Duke of Buccleuch, K.T., at Boughton House in Northamptonshire.

156 The details can be found in *Das Geheimnis um Shakespeares 'Dark Lady'*, p. 66.

157 I discovered this hidden pictorial clue in 1997 and – for the first time – drew the reader's attention to it in *Das Geheimnis um Shakespeares 'Dark Lady'* (see pp. 68–70).

158 See *Das Geheimnis um Shakespeares 'Dark Lady'*, pp.68–70.

159 The portrait hangs in the Spencer Gallery in Althorp, on the left next to the great staircase. It is catalogued as number 34.

160 See the seventeen matching facial features in the Shakespeare portraits (Droeshout engraving, Chandos portrait, and Flower portrait) identified by the BKA [= CID] expert Reinhardt Altmann in 1995, which were used to identify the subject of the portrait. In addition, he employed the Trick Image Differentiation Technique to confirm his findings. See Altmann, 'Bildgutachten in der kunsthistorischen Forschung [...]' (Assessment of pictorial material for art-historical research), 3 May 1995.

161 See my publications on the subject in endnote 186.

162 See *Das Geheimnis um Shakespeares 'Dark Lady'*, p. 84ff.

163 The present author ascertained this on a visit to Althorp on 10 September 2002. The Supervisor, Mr David Carter, and Ms Sue Edwards kindly showed her Earl Spencer's collection of paintings and answered all her questions.

164 Emil Schaeffer, *Van Dyck. Des Meisters Gemälde in 537 Abbildungen* (Van Dyck. Paintings by the Master in 537 Illustrations) (Stuttgart/Leipzig, 1909), p. 410.

165 Richard Humphreys, *The Tate Britain Companion to British Art* (London, 2001), p. 37, No. 21.

166 See *Das Geheimnis um Shakespeares 'Dark Lady'*, p. 91 and fig. 16, p. 95.

167 See *Das Geheimnis um Shakespeares 'Dark Lady'*, p. 115.

168 See Katherine Duncan-Jones, *Ungentle Shakespeare. Scenes from his Life* (London, 2001), p. 208.

169 The protruding lower lip is covered with plaque in some places, as ascertained by Prof. Michael Hertl, an expert in facial signs of illness. See 'Gutachterliche Stellungnahme: Zu den Krankheitserscheinungen auf den Porträts und an der Totenmaske von William Shakespeare' (Expert opinion: Evidence of illness in portraits of Shakespeare and on his death mask) (15 August 1997). See also H. Hammerschmidt-Hummel, *The True Face of William Shakespeare* (London, 2006), p. 76.

170 See *The Shakspere Allusion-Book*, I, p. 3.

171 Unless other sources are given, the examples in this chapter come from the *Shakspere Allusion-Book*, I.

172 See J. Lempriere, *A classical Dictionary; containing a copious account of all the proper names mentioned in ancient authors [...]* (London, 10th ed., 1818), 'Ætion'.

173 See *The Shakspere Allusion-Book*, I, p. 7.

174 See ibid., I, p. 14.

175 Meres literal quotation reads: 'As the Greeke tongue is made famous and eloquent by *Homer, Hesiod, Euripedes, Aeschilus, Sophocles, Pindarus, Phocylides* and *Aristophanes*; and the Latine tongue by *Virgill, Ovid, Horace, Silius Italicus, Lucanus, Lucretius, Ausonius* and *Claudianus*: so the English tongue is mightily enriched, and gorgeouslie invested in rare ornaments and resplendent habiliments by sir *Philip Sidney, Spencer, Daniel, Drayton, Warner, Shakespeare, Marlow* and *Chapman*.' Quoted from *Shakspere Allusion-Book*, I, p. 46.

176 Quoted from ibid., I, p. 46.

177 H. Hammerschmidt-Hummel, *The True Face of William Shakespeare. The Poet's Death Mask and Likenesses from Three Periods of His Life* (London, 2006), p. 41.

178 Hammerschmidt-Hummel, *The True Face of William Shakespeare*, p. 44.

179 In the mid-nineteenth century Delia Bacon, the daughter of a failed American pioneer with very little education, came up with the erroneous supposition that her English namesake, Sir Francis Bacon, must have written the works of William Shakespeare. She also claimed – again erroneously – that Shakespeare had been an uneducated country bumpkin. See also *Die verborgene Existenz des William Shakespeare. Dichter und Rebell im katholischen Untergrund* (Freiburg i. Br., 2001), p. 165–175.

180 See G.B. Harrison, *A Jacobean Journal. Being a Record of those Things most Talked of During the Years 1603–1606* (London, 1941, repr. 1946), p.147. One reason why the queen did not abandon Oxford was that he had supplied her with luxuries and novelties from Italy, such as gloves and perfume.

181 Cf. Hammerschmidt-Hummel, *The True Face of William Shakespeare*, pp. 125-26.

182 Quoted from *Shakspere Allusion-Book*, I, p. 46.

183 Quoted from ibid. I, p. 68.

184 See ibid., I, p. 41.

185 See Hammerschmidt-Hummel, *The True Face of William Shakespeare*, p. 87.

186 See ibid., pp. 125-127, and also my essays 'Ist die Darmstädter Shakespeare-Totenmaske echt?' (Is the Darmstadt Shakespeare Death Mask Genuine?), *Shakespeare-Jahrbuch* 132 (1996), pp. 58-74. 'Neuer Beweis für die Echtheit des Flower-Porträts und der Darmstädter Shakespeare-Totenmaske. Ein übereinstimmendes Krankheitssymptom im linken Stirnbereich von Gemälde und Gipsabguß' (New Evidence for the Authenticity of the Flower Portrait and the Darmstadt Shakespeare Death Mask. A Matching Symptom of Illness in the Area of the Forehead of Painting and Plaster Cast'), *Anglistik* (September, 1996), pp. 115-136; 'Shakespeares Totenmaske und die Shakespeare-Bildnisse 'Chandos' und 'Flower'. Zusätzliche Echtheitsnachweise auf der Grundlage eines neuen Fundes' (Shakespeare's Death Mask and the Shakespeare Portraits 'Chandos' and 'Flower'. Additional Proofs of Authenticity on the Basis of a New Find', *Anglistik* (March, 1998), pp. 101-115; 'What did Shakespeare Look Like? Authentic Portraits and the Death Mask. Methods and Results of the Tests of Authenticity', in: *Symbolism* 1 ed. Rüdiger Ahrens (New York, 2000), pp. 41-79.

187 'If tragedies might any prologue have, / All those he made would scarce make one to this, / Where fame, now that he gone is to the grave/Death's public tiring-house the (nuntius) is; [...].' William Shakespeare, *Mr. William Shakespeares Comedies, Histories, & Tragedies*. Published according to the True Originall Copies (London, 1623, reprint – ed. Helge Kökeritz. Introduction by Charles Tyler Prout, New Haven/ London, 1954).

IV: POWER POLITICS IN THE LATE ELIZABETHAN AGE AND SHAKESPEARE'S TURN TO TRAGEDY

188 'The young Erle of Southampton refusing the Lady Veere payeth 5000li of present payment.' *Stonyhurst MSS., Angl.* Vol. I, n. 82, quoted from: G. P. V. Akrigg, *Shakespeare and the Earl of Southampton* (London, 1968), p. 39.

189 John E. Neale, *Queen Elizabeth I of England* [1934] (Garden City, New York, 1957), p. 316.

190 In addition to his official duties, Bacon found the time to publish numerous works on wide-ranging topics,

including the natural sciences, philosophy, history and education. His works had great influence on the style of English prose. His collection of essays, which he added to after 1597, was very popular. In 1605, he published *The Advancement of Learning*, in 1620 *Novum Organum*, in 1620-23 *Instauratio Magna*, and 1626 saw the posthumous release of *New Atlantis*.

191 'The political situation, which arose from the fact that Elizabeth was about to die leaving no lawful heirs of her body, divided Catholics into two camps, which supported rival candidates for the English crown. Thus arose the Spanish party and the Scottish party.' Edwin H. Burton and Thomas L. Williams, eds., *The Douay College Diaries, Third, Fourth, and Fifth, 1598–1654*. With the Rheims report, 1579–80. Catholic Record Society, x–xi (London, 1911), I, 'Introduction', p. vii-xxx, p. xiv.

192 'Robert Devereux, Earl of Essex (1566-1601)', ed. from Emery Walker's 'Historical Portraits' (1909), publ. in: http://www.britannica.com/bio/lords/essex2rd.html.

193 Platter, *Beschreibung der Reisen* (Travel diaries), II, p. 791. [Extract translated by Joyce Shorthall-Stevenson]

194 See p. 131.

195 This is known from a letter dated 19 January 1598, written by the spy Rowland Whyte to Sir Robert Sidney.

196 See Foley, *Records*, IV, p. 49.

197 *Zweite, erweiterte Ausgabe Shakespeare sechsundsechzig. Variationen über ein Sonett* (The second, extended edition of Shakespeare 66. Variations on a sonnet) (Kassel, 2001), p. 216.

198 See Kurt Flasch, "Hall dir im Lorbeerkranz. Haupt- und Staatsaktionen: Neue Editionen von Dante und Petrarca" (See the conquering hero comes. High-level drama: new editions of Dante and Petrarch), *Frankfurter Allgemeine Zeitung* (15 May 2002): "Petrarch's political intervention took place in three main areas: he supported Cola di Rienzo's attempts to topple the order of the Roman state; he criticised the corruption and the policies of the Avignon Curia; and he directed peace aspirations towards the Emperor Charles IV. This is a central aspect of his writings, which admirers of his poetry can easily overlook."

199 In 1996 Ulrich Erckenbrecht published eighty-eight translations of the sonnet into German (see *Shakespeare Sechsundsechzig. Variationen über ein Sonett*: Shakespeare Sixty-Six: Variations on a sonnet, Kassel, 1996). By 2001, however, he was able to include another forty-four versions in his second, enlarged edition.

200 See Harrison, *A Last Elizabethan Journal*, p. 84.

201 See ibid., p. 113.

202 John Dover Wilson, *The Essential Shakespeare. A Biographical Adventure* (Cambridge, 1932), p. 102.

203 See Harrison, *A Last Elizabethan Journal*, pp. 193-94 and p. 351.

204 See Ward/Weed Ward, *Shakespeare's Town and Times*, p. 127.

205 The traditional judgement on Essex, his achievements and his rebellion, is summarized in the entry 'Devereux, Robert (19th [2nd Devereux] Earl of Essex) (1566-1601). Soldier and courtier' by Diarmaid MacCulloch in *The History Today. Who's Who in British History* (London, 2000), p. 242: 'Faced with financial ruin when Elizabeth refused to renew his farm of sweet wines, convinced that his enemies were intent on destroying him and surrounded by young would-be heroes, Essex staged a pathetic attempt at a *coup d'état* in the city of London in Feb. 1601. After trial, in which his former client, Francis Bacon, played an important part in the prosecution, he was executed.' For further reference MacCulloch states Robert Lacey's 1970 monograph: *Robert, Earl of Essex: An Elizabethan Icarus*. This view has generally also been adopted by leading Shakespeare scholars (see, for example, Park Honan, *Shakespeare. A Life*, Oxford, 1998, p. 193). – The attempt at delineating a new image of the Earl of Essex, as presented in this book, draws heavily on Paul Hammer's new research results, published in *The Polarisation of Elizabethan Politics* (Cambridge, 1999). Cf. in particular Chapter 5: 'Matters of intelligence', p. 152–198.

206 Harrison, *A Last Elizabethan Journal*, p. 50–51.

207 Quoted from Kurt Tetzeli von Rosador, 'The Phoenix and the Turtle', in: *Shakespeare-Handbuch. Die Zeit – Der Mensch – Das Werk – Die Nachwelt*. Shakespeare Handbook. The time – The man – The works – The Legacy) Ed. Ina Schabert (Stuttgart, 4th edition 2000), p. 607–608, p. 607.

208 See my lecture 'William Shakespeare: Phönix und Taube. Notate zur Entstehung des Werks und zur Entschlüsselung seiner Figuren als historische Persönlichkeiten' (William Shakespeare: The Phoenix and Turtle. Notes on the composition of the work and the identification of the figures as historical personalities), given on 26 April 2002 at the Annual Conference of the German Shakespeare Society at Weimar, published in *Anglistik* (September 2003), pp. 71-84. In his essay, 'The Phoenix and the Turtle', Tetzeli, in 2000, pointed out that it should be possible to decipher the allegorial language of this (still undeciphered) Shakespearian poem (cf. p. 607).

209 Chester's book was dedicated to the poet Sir John Salusbury (or Salisbury, *c.* 1566–1612), his patron and

the husband of an illegitimate daughter of Henry Stanley, the Catholic fourth Earl of Derby (*c.* 1531–1593). This collection on the allegorical representation of 'the truth of love', made popular by the success of 'The Phoenix and Turtle', also contains other poems on the same theme by anonymous and identified authors, including Jonson and Marston.

210 Wolfgang Weiß, 'Phönix und Taube (The Phoenix and Turtle)', in: William Shakespeare, *Sonette/Epen und die kleineren Dichtungen* (Sonnets, narrative poems and shorter poems). Dual language edition. Epilogue by Wolfgang Weiß (Darmstadt, 1968), pp. 460–465, p. 461.

211 See the internet article by F. D. Hoeniger and I. Lancashire of the Department of English at the University of Toronto from the year 1997: '*Original Text*: Robert Chester, *Loues martyr: or, Rosalins complaint.* Now first translated out of the venerable Italian Torquato Caeliano [pseudonym of], by R. Chester. ([R. Field] for E. B., 1601)', STC 5119.

212 The so-called 'Morris dance' or 'morisco' was the favourite dance of Shakespeare's day, especially in the countryside. It was a mixture of dance and dumb show, executed by dancers in traditional costumes with bells round their knees in the roles of e.g. 'the Moor', 'the hobby-horse', 'Robin Hood', 'Friar Tuck' or 'Maid Marian'. A 'wild morisco' is mentioned in Shakespeare's *Henry VI*, Part II, Act III, sc. 1, 365.

213 Harrison writes about 31 May 1602: 'Sir Anthony Shirley abideth still at Venice, in the utmost extremity, protesting that he is persecuted by those from whom he should have expected comfort. The merchants there are forbidden to speak to him or his [sic], and when he sent to the French King for letters to the French consul at Cairo about his return to Persia, Mr. Wotton told the King that letters had been sent against him by the Queen and the Council. He would have his actions considered apart from the Earl of Essex (by whom he was set out) and to be judged by their merits; [...].' *A Last Elizabethan Journal*, p. 279.

214 'Fair' here means 'free from blemish or disfigurement; clean, clear' or 'free from moral stain, unblemished'. (*SOED*).

215 This reads: 'UNICUS ES PHOENIX CINERES HAEC TUMBA DUORUM / PHOENICUM VERAE RELIGIONIS HABET'. Platter, *Beschreibung der Reisen* (Travel Diaries), II, p. 751.

216 The wording is as follows: 'VNICVS EST PHAENIX CINERES HAEC TV[M]BA DVORV[M] PHAENICVM VERAE RELIGIONIS HABET', and: 'OVOMODO IN VITA SUA DILEXERUNT SE./ITA ET IN MORE NON SUNT SEPARATI'.

217 *The Shakspere Allusion-Book: A Collection of Allusions to Shakspere from 1591 to 1700.* Comps. Ingleby, Toulmin Smith and Furnivall, I, p. 124.

218 *The Shakspere Allusion-Book*, p.123.

219 See my book *The True Face of William Shakespeare*, pp. 89-91 and pp. 143-47.

220 See the introductory section of my book *Die verborgene Existenz des William Shakespeare* (The Secret Life of William Shakespeare)

221 See *Das Geheimnis um Shakespeares 'Dark Lady'*(The Secret of Shakespeare's Dark Lady), p. 74.

222 See Roy Strong, 'My weeping Stagg I Crowne' : The Persian Lady Reconsidered, *The Art of the Emblem: Essays in Honour of Karl Josef Höltgen* (New York, 1993), pp. 103-141, pp. 108-109..

223 See the Chapter 'Das Emblem des Daumenrings der 'Persian Lady" (The Emblem on the thumb ring of the 'Persian Lady') in: *Das Geheimnis um Shakespeares 'Dark Lady'* (The Secret of Shakespeare's Dark Lady), p. 71–79.

224 See ibid., pp. 147–148, footnote 153.

225 Featured with this emblem in ibid., p. 72, fig. 9.

226 See ibid., p. 98f.

227 When, shortly before my book on Shakespeare's 'Dark Lady', went to press, I asked Althorp for an ektachrome of this painting, I was told that the painting was auctioned in 1976, and the new owner was unknown. See *Das Geheimnis um Shakespeares 'Dark Lady'*, fig. 12, p. 76. The new location of the portrait is the Tate Britain Gallery, London, where I finally obtained a transparency. Martin Nickol, however, visited the original in the Tate Britain in summer 2002 to carry out his comparisons.

228 In a reply dated 29 August 2002, Nickol confirmed my observations regarding the bows on the portraits of Sir Henry Lee, Mary Sidney, Lady Wroth, the heir to the throne Prince Henry, and his sister Princess Elizabeth, later Queen of Bohemia.

229 See Alan and Veronica Palmer, *Who's who in Shakespeare's England* (London, 1981, repr. 2000), 'Rutland, Francis Manners'.

230 See *Das Geheimnis um Shakespeares 'Dark Lady'* (The Secret Surrounding Shakespeare's Dark Lady), pp. 71–78.

231 John Horden, 'The Connotation of Symbols', *The Art of the Emblem. Essays in Honor of Karl Josef Höltgen* (New York, 1993), pp. 71–101, pp. 78–79.

232 This was observed by the botanist Martin Nickol when he studied the portrait on 11 July 2002. According to Nickol, the glove decoration and positioning of the earl's fingers also corresponded with the ribbon on the Bible. Nickol's observation regarding the upside-down Bible is supported

by a portrait in the National Portrait Gallery in London of the first Anglican Archbishop, Thomas Cramner (1489–1556), painted by Gerlach Flicke in 1546. In this painting, two books are depicted with the back cover showing, instead of the front cover. As demonstrated by the bookmark ribbon, a third book is held upside down. See Charles Saumarez Smith, *The National Portrait Gallery* (London, 1997), figure on p. 34 and detail on p. 35, Inv.-Nr. NPG 535. Saumarez Smith writes that when the painting was restored, holes in the window shutters in the background became visible – as well as the word 'rot' that Flicke had painted on the archbishop's cushion. The (three) holes in the shutter, the upside-down prayer book and theological works, and the word 'rot' are all negative pictorial or written signs and are obviously meant as hidden criticism of the archbishop himself – from the Catholic point of view. Cranmer was mainly responsible for the religious reform and the introduction of the Book of Common Prayer. He had annulled Henry VIII's marriage to Catherine of Aragon and declared his secret marriage to Anne Boleyn as valid. As shown by the painting 'Allegory of the Reformation' in the National Portrait Gallery (*Fig. 21*), Protestant painters, or those commissioning the painters or their clients, too, did not shy away from heavily criticising Rome, especially the Pope.

233 See *Das Geheimnis um Shakespeares 'Dark Lady'* (The Secret Surrounding Shakespeare's Dark Lady), p. 76.

234 Harrison writes: 'Some also report that she [the queen] showed the skull of the Earl [of Essex] to the Duke [of Biron] and the Frenchmen in her closet, or fastened upon a pole...'. *A Last Elizabethan Journal*, p. 203. Harrison is perhaps too quick to reject this report as 'a ridiculous vain story'.

235 Harrison writes this about the date 9 October 1601. *A Last Elizabethan Journal*, p. 204.

236 In 1608, five years after Queen Elizabeth's death, the famous English playwright George Chapman (*c.* 1560–1634) wrote a play about the political tragedy of Biron and had it staged. He thereby provoked an outcry. The French ambassador to England intervened immediately.

237 Campbell/Quinn, *Shakespeare Encyclopaedia*, 'The Tragedy of HAMLET, Prince of Denmark'.

238 Dover Wilson, *The Essential Shakespeare*, p. 105.

239 Ibid., p. 105.

240 See 'The Image of Man in the Renaissance and Baroque' in my book *The True Face of William Shakespeare*, pp. 13-15.

241 See Caroline Spurgeon, *Shakespeare's Imagery and what it tells us* (Cambridge, 1935, repr. 1971), pp. 316–318.

242 All Lavater quotes taken from Ludwig Lavater, *Of ghostes and spirites walking by nyght* ... (London, 1572), British Library press-mark 718.d.52, pp. 105-106 and pp. 108-109.

243 Walter Bourchier Devereux, *Lives and Letters of the Devereux, Earls of Essex, in the Reign of Elizabeth, James I, and Charles I. 1540-1646*. 2 Vols. (London, 1853), II, pp. 189 ff.

244 See John Dover Wilson, *The Essential Shakespeare. A Biographical Adventure* (London, 1932), p. 106.

245 See John Gee, *New Shreds of the old Snare. Containing The Apparitions of two new female Ghosts*, &c. 1624, p. 17 and p. 20, quoted in *The Shakspere Allusion-Book*, I, p. 327.

246 See Dover Wilson, *The Essential Shakespeare*, p. 111.

247 See Horst Oppel, 'Shakespeare und das elisabethanische Drama' (Shakespeare and Elizabethan Drama), in: *Englische Dichtung des 16. und 17. Jahrhunderts* (English Literature in the Sixteenth and Seventeenth Centuries) (Frankfurt am Main, 1973), pp. 34–81, p. 70.

248 See Schoenbaum, *William Shakespeare. A Documentary Life*, p. 178.

249 See J.C. Cooper, *Dictionary of Symbolism*, (London, 1978), 'Octagon'.

250 The famous sundial of Andronicus of Cyrrhus has an octagonal shape and was built in the first century BC. It is also known as the Tower of Winds and bears depictions of the eight wind gods. The sundial consists of eight plates.

251 The most famous example is the much imitated Church of Our Lady in Aachen. The connections between octagons and the Cult of Mary, which also could have played a role in Shakespeare's plays, were first mentioned to the author by the Professor of English studies in Heidelberg, Dr Kurt Otten.

252 'Wheler Miscellaneous Papers', ii, p.39, quoted in Charlotte C. Stopes, *Shakespeare's Environment*, (London, 1918), p. 120.

253 See R.J. Rohr, *Die Sonnenuhr. Geschichte – Theorie – Funktion* (The Sundial. History, theory and function) (Munich, 1982), p. 82

254 See Robert Bearman, *Shakespeare in the Stratford Records* (Phoenix Mill, 1994), pp.19 ff.

255 William Shakespeare. *A Study of Facts and Problems*, I, p. 75.

256 It can be found in 'State Papers Domestic Eliz. 265/133' and was published in Lawrence Stone's book *An Elizabethan: Sir Horatio Palavicino* (Oxford, 1956), Appendix III: 'Sir Robert Cecil's Intelligence Service in 1598', pp. 325–330.

257 This information is based on Stone, *An Elizabethan: Sir Horatio Palavicino*.

258 William Shakespeare, *King Lear*. Ed. K. Muir (London, 1952, repr. 1973), 'Holinshed', pp. 220–222, p. 222.

259 The first of numerous studies was by Jacob Feis, who published *Shakespeare and Montaigne* in 1884. Another important work is George Coffin Taylor, *Shakespeare's Debt to Montaigne* (1925).

260 Michel de Montaigne, 'An Apologie of Raymond Sebond', in: *Montaigne's Essays*: Renascence Editions, Book II. E-text [www.uoregon.edu rbear/montaigne/ 2xii.htm], provided by Ben R. Schneider, Lawrence University, Wisconsin, 1998, The University of Oregon [101].

261 Montaigne, 'An Apologie of Raymond Sebond' [101]

262 See Ibid. [102]

263 Ibid. [102]

264 Ibid. [102]

265 See 'Samuel Harsnett and King Lear', in: Shakespeare, *King Lear*. Ed. K. Muir, pp. 239–242.

266 See Stone, *An Elizabethan: Sir Horatio Palavicino*, p. 231. He writes: 'It was to grapple with the problems raised by the influx of Jesuits and seminary priests that Walsingham in the 80's built up his system of internal espionage, with the assistance of Thomas Phelippes the cryptographer, Mr. Justice Young, Richard Topcliffe, and Rackmaster Norton.'

267 See Ibid., p. 231. Stone writes: 'The ports were closely watched, the post was screened to catch the papists' letters, stool-pigeons were placed in the jails to extract information from their over-confiding fellow prisoners, and *agent provocateurs* made contact with the most suspect of the recusant gentry.'

268 Quoted from Peter Milward, *Shakespeare's Religious Background* (London, 1973), p. 72.

269 Quoted from ibid., pp. 72-73.

270 See ibid., p. 282, footnote 9.

271 I owe thanks to Professor Alan Bance who made this suggestion.

272 See J. M. Raich, *Shakespeare's Stellung zur katholischen Religion* (Shakespeare's Attitude to the Catholic Religion) (Mainz, 1884), Chapter III: 'Shakespeare's Sterbescenen' (Shakespeare's Death Scenes), pp. 134ff., and Rudolf Böhm, *Wesen und Funktion der Sterberede im elisabethanischen Drama* (Examples and Function of Dying Words in Elizabethan Drama) (Hamburg, 1964).

273 G.B. Harrison, *A Jacobean Journal. Being a record of those things most talked of during the years 1603 to 1606* (London, 1941, rev. And repr., 1946), p. 244.

274 See G.B. Harrison, *A Second Jacobean Journal. Being a record of those things most talked of during the years 1607 to 1610* (London, 1958), pp. 22–23.

275 See *Das Geheimnis um Shakespeares 'Dark Lady'* (The Secret of Shakespeare's Dark Lady), pp. 29ff.

276 See Caroline Spurgeon, *Shakespeare's Imagery and what it tells us* (Cambridge, 1935, repr. 1971), p. 320.

277 See Coleridge, *Table-Talk* (1835).

278 See Swinburne, *A Study of Shakespeare* (1880).

279 See Milward, *Shakespeare's Religious Background*, p. 22.

280 The following events are based on the 20 November 1599 entry in Harrison, *Last Elizabethan Journal*.

281 See Campbell/Quinn, *Shakespeare Encyclopaedia*, 'All's Well That Ends Well'.

282 See Campbell/Quinn, *Shakespeare Encyclopaedia*, 'Spurgeon, Caroline (1869–1942)'.

283 See figure 1994 in: H. Hammerschmidt-Hummel, ed., *Die Shakespeare-Illustration* (The Shakespeare Illustrations), Part 3.

284 See my book *The True Face of William Shakespeare*, pp. 133-134.

285 Harrison, *A Jacobean Journal*, p. 194.

286 See ibid., pp. 206–207.

287 See ibid., p. 210.

288 See ibid., p. 127.

289 See ibid., p. 194.

290 See T. G. Law, ed., 'Documents illustrating Catholic policy in the reign of James VI, 1596–1598', *Miscellany of the Scottish History Society 1* (1893), pp. 3–70; J. D. Mackie, 'The secret diplomacy of King James VI in Italy prior to his accession to the English throne', *Scottish Historical Review 21* (1923–24), pp. 267–282. Also: Hammer, *The Polarisation of Elizabethan Politics*, pp. 171f.

291 See Harrison, *A Jacobean Journal*, p. 244.

292 See ibid., pp. 268–269.

293 See Harrison, *A Jacobean Journal*, p. 270.

294 See ibid., pp. 270–271.

295 'The next was the cause of religion, for which alone he resolved to neglect his estate, his life, his home, his

memory, his posterity and all wordly and earthly felicity whatsoever.' Ibid., p. 271.

296 'His third motive was the promises broken with the Catholics.' Ibid., p. 271.

297 'And lastly that they [the Catholics] generally feared harder laws from this Parliament against recusants.' Ibid., p. 271.

298 See ibid., p. 273.

299 See ibid., pp. 274-276.

300 For a detailed account of the capture of Garnett and Oldcorne and their treatment in the house of Sir Henry Bromley see ibid., pp. 274-275 and pp. 280-282.

301 For a detailed account of Garnett's trial see ibid., pp. 288-295.

302 Ibid., pp. 291-292.

303 See ibid., p. 300.

304 Ibid., p. 301.

305 *A Second Jacobean Journal* (London, 1958), p. 2.

306 Marc Eccles, *Shakespeare in Warwickshire*, (1961), quoted from the *Shakespeare Encyclopaedia*, p. 371.

307 See Bearman, *Shakespeare in the Stratford Records*, pp. 15–16.

308 See Harrison, *A Second Jacobean Journal*, pp. 4–5.

V. SHAKESPEARE'S LATE WORKS:
TALES OF THE SUPERNATURAL AND
FINAL RECONCILIATION

309 See George Sampson, *The Concise Cambridge History of English Literature* (Cambridge University Press, 1941, repr. 1946), p. 144.

310 Quoted from *Shakespeare Encyclopaedia*, 'Burbage, Richard (*c.* 1567–1619)'.

311 Campbell/Quinn, *Shakespeare Encyclopaedia*, 'Taylor, Joseph (1586–1652)'.

312 See *Shakespeare Encyclopaedia*, 'Blackfriars theatre'.

313 Ibid.

314 Ibid.

315 See *Die verborgene Existenz des William Shakespeare* (The Secret Life of William Shakespeare) 'Zur Lage des Blackfriars Theatre' (About the Blackfriars Theatre), pp. 150–153.

316 See ibid., pp.150-153.

317 See Honan, *Shakespeare*, p. 328 f., and Duncan-Jones, *Ungentle Shakespeare*, pp. 205 ff.

318 See *Shakespeare Encyclopaedia*, 'Forman, Simon'

319 See ibid.

320 Peck, ed., *Desiderata Curiosa*, p. 282, quoted from *Akrigg, Shakespeare and the Earl of Southampton*, p. 51.

321 See Stanley Wells, *Shakespeare. The Writer and his Work* (Harlow, 1978), pp. 73–74.

322 See Hammerschmidt-Hummel, *Die Shakespeare-Illustration* (1594-2000) (Illustrations of Shakespeare 1594-2000), Part 3, fig. 18.

323 Horst Oppel, 'Die Gonzalo-Utopie' (Gonzalo's Utopia), in: *Shakespeare. Studien zum Werk und zur Welt des Dichters* (Shakespeare. The Work and World of the Playwright) (Heidelberg, 1963), pp. 220–259, p. 229.

324 Ibid., pp. 230–231.

325 Platter, *Beschreibung der Reisen durch Frankreich, Spanien, England und die Niederlande 1595–1600.* (Description of Travels Through France, Spain, England and the Netherlands 1595-1600), II, p. 837.

326 Ibid., II, p. 837.

327 Rut Keiser, the editor of Platter's *Beschreibung der Reisen* (Description of Travels), II, states this on p. 837, footnote 2.

328 Hecht, referred to by Keiser Platter's *Beschreibung der Reisen* (Description of Travels), II, p. 836, footnote 1.

329 Platter, *Beschreibung der Reisen* (Description of Travels), II, p. 827.

330 See also *Die verborgene Existenz des William Shakespeare* (The Secret Life of William Shakespeare), p. 134 (figure on p. 136).

331 On Fletcher's co-authorship see Horst Oppel, *Shakespeare oder Fletcher? Die Bankett-Szene in 'Henry VIII' als Kriterium der Verfasserschaft.* (Shakespeare or Fletcher? The Banquet Scene in *Henry VIII* as a key to Authorship) Publication by the Academy of Arts and Literature in Mainz (Wiesbaden, 1966).

332 See Ian Wilson, *Shakespeare. The Evidence* (London, 1993), p. 366.

333 Quoted from Wilson, *Shakespeare*, p. 366.

334 H. Hammerschmidt-Hummel, *Die Traumtheorien des 20. Jahrhunderts und die Träume der Figuren Shakespeares* (20th-Century Dream Theories and the Dreams of Shakespeare's Characters) (Heidelberg, 1992), p. 196.

VI. SHAKESPEARE'S LEGACY TO THE CATHOLIC UNDERGROUND AND RETURN TO STRATFORD

335 Quoted in *Shakespeare Encyclopaedia*, 'Mermaid Tavern'.

336 See H. Hammerschmidt, *Die Importgüter der Handelsstadt London als Sprach- und Bildbereich des elisabethanischen Dramas* (The Import Commodities of the City of London and their Impact on the Life-Style, Language and Dramatic Literature of Elizabethan England) (Heidelberg, 1979), pp. 92-101.

337 The author first presented her research results concerning the true meaning of Shakespeare's purchase of the eastern gatehouse of Blackfriars in her book *Die verborgene Existenz des William Shakespeare* (The Secret Life of William Shakespeare) (2001). She owes special thanks to Ian Wilson's research, as published in his book *Shakespeare. The Evidence* (1993).

338 The reply from the German Professor of Law, Dr Hans-Joachim Mertens to H. Hammerschmidt-Hummel, dated 15 December 1998, states: 'Your query whether the Deed of Sale, concerning his property in Blackfriars, which Shakespeare concluded in March 1613, ensured that, even after Shakespeare's death, the *trustees* would be enabled to use the property in Blackfriars according to his wishes, can be answered to the positive. ...' ('Ihre Frage, ob durch den Kaufvertrag, den Shakespeare im März 1613 über das Anwesen Blackfriars Property geschlossen hat, die dort eingesetzten *trustees* in die Lage versetzt werden konnten, das Anwesen Blackfriars Property auch nach dem Tod von Shakespeare seinen Wünschen entsprechend zu nutzen, läßt sich positiv beantworten ... .')

339 John Fortescue to the Earl of Essex, quoted in Chambers, *William Shakespeare. A Study of Facts and Problems*, II, p. 167. On the constant coming and going of priests in the (Eastern) gatehouse of Blackfriars and their quick dissappearance in the nick of time see I. Wilson, *Shakespeare. The Evidence*, p. 374, and J. Morris, *Troubles of our Catholic Forefathers Related by themselves* (1872), I, p. 141.

340 These findings have been published for the first time in my book *Die verborgene Existenz des William Shakespeare* (The Secret Life of William Shakespeare), p. 119.

341 The new calendar was introduced in all Catholic countries in 1582, but was only adopted later by Protestant states. In England, the Gregorian calendar was not introduced until 1752.

342 Printed in: Foley, *Records*, I, pp. 78–86. Although Clarke was a Puritan, his account of the events is sympathetic, and he does not take sides. He attempts to describe the events with great accuracy. Recent research suggests that the author of this report was Thomas Goad.

343 See 'Drury, Robert (1587–1623)', DNB, VI.

344 See 'The Doleful Even-Song', in: Foley, *Records*, I, pp. 78–86, p. 82.

345 See Hammerschmidt-Hummel, *Die verborgene Existenz des William Shakespeare* (The Secret Life of William Shakespeare), pp .127–147.

346 A reproduction of this painting can be found in Roy Strong, *The English Icon. Elizabethan & Jacobean Portraiture* (London/ New York, 1969), p. 240, No. 211.

347 The Globe Theatre could hold between 2,100 and 3,000 spectators (see p. 114).

348 The quotes in this section are from *Shakespeare Encyclopaedia*, 'Globe theatre'.

349 The last Archbishop of Canterbury appointed by the Pope was Cardinal Reginald Pole (1500–1558) under Mary Tudor (see. p. 20).

350 Edmond Howes writes: 'If I shuld here set down the seuerall terrors & damages done this yeere by fire, in very many and sundry places of this kingdome, it would containe many a sheete of paper, as is euident by the incessant collections throughout all churches of this realm for such as haue bin spoyled by fire.' Like other contemporaries, the chronicler also reports that the fire was caused by negligence: 'Also vpon S. Peters day last, the play-house or Theater called the *Globe*, vpon the Banck-side neere London, by negligent discharging of a peale of ordinance, close to the south side thereof, the Thatch tooke fier, & the wind sodainly disperst ye flame round about, & in a very short space ye whole building was quite consumed, & no man hurt: the house being filled with people, to behold the play, viz. of Henry the 8. And the next spring it was new builded in far fairer manner then before.' *The Annales, or Generall Chronicle of England*, begun first by maister Iohn Stow, and after him continued and augmented [...] vnto the end of this present yeere 1614 by Edmond Howes (London, 1615), quoted in *Shakspere Allusion-Book*, I, p. 244.

351 See Vanessa Schormann, *Shakespeares Globe. Repliken, Rekonstruktionen und Bespielbarkeit* (Shakespeare's Globe: Replicas, Reconstructions and Playability) (Heidelberg, 2002).

352 See Chapter 4 ('Shakespeare the Gentleman: Further Purchases in Stratford') in: Robert Bearman, *Shakespeare in the Stratford Records* (Phoenix Mill etc., 1994), pp. 37–43.

353 Platter, *Beschreibung der Reisen durch Frankreich, Spanien, England und die Niederlande* 1595–1600 (Description of the Journeys across France, Spain, England and the Netherlands), II, p. 869.

354 Aubrey writes: 'Now Sr. Wm [Davenant] would sometimes when he was pleasant over a glasse of wine with his most intimate friends e.g. Sam: Butler [author of Hudibras] &c. say, that it seemed to him that he writt with the very spirit that Shakespeare, and was seemed contented

enough to be thought his Son...'. Aubrey's *Brief Lives*. Ed. with the orig. manuscripts and with an introduction by Oliver Lawson Dick [1949] (Harmondsworth, Penguin Books, repr. 1978), 'Davenant'.

355 See H. Hammerschmidt-Hummel, *Das Geheimnis um Shakespeares 'Dark Lady'* (The Secret Surrounding Shakespeare's 'Dark Lady'), p.154, footnote 18.

356 See S. Schoenbaum, *William Shakespeare. A Documentary Life*, p. 249.

357 See my book *The True Face of William Shakespeare*, p. 178, note 69.

358 In *The Works of William Shakespeare. The Text*. 8 Vols. (London, 1844), p.cclii, Collier states: 'We are left in utter uncertainty as to the immediate cause of the death of Shakespeare ....'

359 See Lane, *John Hall and his Patients*, p. xvi.

360 Lane, *John Hall and his Patients*, p. xxii. Lane refers to the in-depth research by J.E.D. Shrewsbury, *A History of Bubonic Plague in the British Isles* (Cambridge, 1970), pp. 276–277, in which the plagues of the years 1558, 1564, 1581, 1604 and 1608–10 are mentioned. She continues: 'By 1616, however, a far more severe affliction, a typhus epidemic, appeared and was noted by Hall as "the new fever" when he attended Lady Beaufou near Warwick in July 1617.'

361 See Dr. John Hall, *Select Observations*, 'Observ. LXXVII', quoted in: Lane, *John Hall and his Patients*, p. 138.

362 The epidemic must already have started in 1616. This is shown by the fact that in this year there was an unusually high number of burials. See Lane's statistic published in *John Hall and his Patients*, p. xxiv.

363 This is because Cooke was acquainted with Hall and his assistants, as well as with his wife Susanna.

364 See *Ungentle Shakespeare* (London, 2001), 'Shakespeare in bad company: George Wilkins', pp. 205–213, and p. 224. The author writes: 'Most likely both men [Shakespeare and Belott] often dined or supped in Turnmill Street, where Shakespeare customarily stopped on his way back from the Globe Theatre, at least on days when he had not been invited to dine more splendidly with aristocratic patrons or with his fellow King's Men. A barge across the Thames from Paris Garden to Queenhithe would carry him to a point from which a walk due north would lead to Turnmill Street, in its 'suburb without the walls'. From here, after dinner or supper, it would be a short stroll south-east to sleep at Silver Street, back within the City walls and under the City's jurisdiction' (p. 208). It is, however, hard to imagine that Shakespeare, on his way back from the Globe Theatre, stopped at Wilkins' inn in Turnmill Street, as this lay too far outside the north-western London city walls. The Mountjoys did not live far from Aldersgate (see *Fig. 60a*). The distance from their house in Silver Street (opposite St Olave's) through Aldersgate, in a north-westerly direction to the corner of Turnmill and Cow Cross was roughly twice as far as the distance from the north bank of the Thames to Silver Street. It is therefore unlikely that, after a long day's work, Shakespeare would leave the Globe Theatre, catch a ferry across the Thames to Queenhithe landing stage, walk along Bread Street to Cheapside and further to Aldersgate, and from there about the same distance again to to Turnmill Street, just to have dinner and company at Wilkins' inn.

365 See *Ungentle Shakespeare*, p. 224

366 Some of the medical conclusions were pre-published in conjunction with my proofs of authenticity for the Chandos Portrait, the Flower Portrait and the Darmstadt Death Mask in *Shakespeare-Jahrbuch* (The Shakespeare Yearbook) (1996), in *Anglistik* (Sept. 1996 and March 1998) and in the annual journal *Symbolism* (New York, 2000). There is a full account of these and other medical findings in my book *The True Face of William Shakespeare*. See pp. 67–80, and fig. 64.

367 See the expert opinion of the ophthalmologist Prof. Walter Lerche, 'Shakespeare Portraits' (11. April 1995).

368 See *The True Face of William Shakespeare*, pp. 72-74.

369 See ibid., p. 70 and figs. 60 and 67.

370 The investigations were commissioned by the President of the Darmstadt Technical University, Prof. Johann-Dietrich Wörner, and were performed by Dr. Rolf Dieter Düppe. The results were first interpreted by Prof. Hertl (see his expert opinion dated 15 August 1997).

371 See 'Gutachterliche Stellungnahme zu der Prominenz der linken Stirnseite an der Darmstädter Shakespeare-Totenmaske und auf dem Flower-Porträt' (Expert opinion of the protrusion on the left side of the forehead on the Darmstadt Shakespeare Death Mask and in the Flower Portrait) by Prof. Hans Helmut Jansen (28 February 1996).

372 See 'Gutachterliche Stellungnahme zu den Shakespeare-Porträts Chandos und Flower und der Totenmaske in der Hessischen Landes- und Hochschulbibliothek Darmstadt' (Expert opinion on the Shakespeare Portraits Chandos and Flower and the Darmstadt Shakespeare Death Mask in the Hesse *Land* and University Library in Darmstadt) by Prof. Jost Metz (23 January 1996).

373 The text was originally in Latin, but a translation appears in *Shakespeare Encyclopaedia*, under 'Shakespeare, Judith (1585–1662)'. See also E. R. C. Brinkworth, *Shakespeare and the Bawdy Court of Stratford*. Illustrated by Wendy Jones (London/

Chichester, 1972), p. 78–80.

374 'Shakespeare's Will', in: Chambers, *William Shakespeare. A Study of Facts and Problems*, II, pp. 169–180, p. 170.

375 'Shakespeare's Will', in: Wilson, *Shakespeare. The Evidence*, pp. 476–479, see also: Chambers, *William Shakespeare. A Study of Facts and Problems*, II, pp. 169–180, p. 173.

376 See *Ungentle Shakespeare* (London, 2001), p. 272.

377 See the entry for 'Schwert' (sword) in: J. C. Cooper, *Illustriertes Lexikon der traditionellen Symbole* (Illustrated lexicon of traditional symbols) (Leipzig, 1986).

378 See *Ungentle Shakespeare*, pp. 262–263.

379 See *Ungentle Shakespeare*, p. 262. The author states that Thomas was the nephew of William Combe. In fact he must have been his brother, because the uncle of the same name had died in 1610. Thomas' brother William was mentioned by Chambers as the 'protagonist of the enclosure controversy'. Chambers, 'The Combe Family', in: *William Shakespeare. A Study of Facts and Problems*, II, pp. 127–141, p. 138.

380 See Chambers, 'The Combe Family', p. 138.

381 Leonard Digges also contributed impressive verses of praise to a volume that contained Shakespeare's poems and appeared in 1640. Digges' homage to Shakespeare was full of allusions to the bard's plays, characters and theatre. The frontispiece of this edition – it was modelled on the famous Droeshout engraving – is also accompanied by stunning lines of praise by an unknown author: 'This Shadowe is renowned Shakespear's. Soule of th'age / The applause' delight. the wonder of the Stage'. They end by wishing that Shakespeare's glory would endure forever, to demonstrate to the world that there will never be another poet to match him in any age to come. The relationship between the Russells, or the Digges, and the Shakespeares must have become much closer after the second marriage of Squire Russell, and it seems that the reverence Leonard Digges' held for Shakespeare and his literary achievement had still increased. Russell lived with his family on his estate at Alderminster, roughly five miles from Stratford. Thus Digges was not just in awe of Shakespeare's works, but also of the man himself, whom he must have met many times when he was still alive and lived a quiet life in Stratford.

382 See *Shakespeare Encyclopaedia*, 'Tyler, Richard'.

383 See *Shakespeare Encyclopaedia*, 'Reynolds, William'.

384 J. C. Cooper, *Illustriertes Lexikon der traditionellen Symbole* (Illustrated lexicon of traditional symbols), 'Ring'.

385 If, in fact, *two* rings, both symbolising the transfer of power, are bequeathed to this relatively small group of people, this may well indicate that one of the bearers was not expected to live for much longer. This could have been Sadler. By giving a ring not just to Sadler, but also to the young Reynolds, Shakespeare could have chosen him to be Sadler's successor on the event of his death. Shakespeare's godson William Walker (just eight years old) is bequeathed 20 shillings in gold. We know that young William (Walker)had been brought up in a Catholic family and was a Catholic. Is he the one Shakespeare had in mind as the future leader of the movement?

386 See *Die verborgene Existenz des William Shakespeare* (The Secret Life of William Shakespeare), p. 123.

387 Lewis, *The Shakespeare Documents*, II, No. 250. See also *Die verborgene Existenz des William Shakespeare* (The Secret Life of William Shakespeare), p. 146.

388 Ibid. , II, No. 250.

389 E.K. Chambers, *William Shakespeare. A Study of Facts and Problems*. 2 Vols. (Oxford, 1930), II, pp. 169-170.

390 For the history of the mask, and other details, see my book, *The True Face of William Shakespeare*, pp. 99-118.

391 See my book, *Die verborgene Existenz des William Shakespeare* (The Secret Life of William Shakespeare), p. 123.

392 Chambers, *William Shakespeare. A Study of Facts and Problems*, II, between pp. 256 and 257, Plate XXIX.

393 See Dover Wilson, *The Essential Shakespeare*, p. 130.

394 Ibid., pp. 130-131.

395 Ibid., p. 131.

396 See Chambers, I, p. 86.

397 Ibid.

398 See the entry 'Fulman, Willliam' in: *Shakespeare Encyclopaedia*, p. 249.

399 See Julian Litten, *The English Way of Death. The Common Funeral Since 1450* (London, 1991, repr. 1992), p. 173.

400 See Litten, *The English Way of Death*. p. 175.

401 The Janssens designed the Earl of Southampton's tomb in St Peter's Church, Titchfield in the 1590s (see my book *The True Face of William Shakespeare*, p. 41). He also created the tomb of the Earl of Rutland.

402 See L. Digges, 'To the Memorie of the deceased Authour Maister W. Shakespeare', in: *Mr. William Shakespeares Comedies, Histories, & Tragedies*. It reads: 'Shakespeare, at length thy pious fellowes giue/The world thy Workes: thy Workes, by which, out-liue/Thy Tombe, thy name must when that stone is rent,/And Time dissolues thy Stratford Moniment,/Here we aliue shall view thee still. This Booke,/When Brasse and Marble fade, shall make thee looke/Fresh to all Ages...'.

403 See Levi Fox, ed., *Correspondence of the Reverend Joseph Greene*, 'IV Shakespearian Matters. (1) The Restoration of Shakespeare's Monument, 1746 and items connected therewith', pp. 164–175.

404 See J. Parker Norris, *The Portraits of Shakespeare* (Philadelphia, 1885), p. 24.

405 See Paul Wislicenus, 'Zur Untersuchung von Shakespeares Totenmaske' (Investigating Shakespeare's Death Mask), *Monatshefte für Kunstwissenschaft* (Art History Monthly) (1915), pp. 279–292, p. 282.

406 See W. Dugdale, *The Antiquities of Warwickshire Illustrated; From Records, Leiger-Books, Manuscripts, Charters, Evidences, Tombes, and Armes...* (London, 1656), p. 523.

407 See my article, 'What did Shakespeare Look Like?', in: Symbolism, pp. 48–50. See also *The True Face of William Shakespeare*, pp. 118-130

408 See my book, *Die verborgene Existenz des William Shakespeare* (The Secret Life of William Shakespeare), p. 165.

409 Ibid.

410 Ibid., p. 271, footnote 27.

ABBREVIATIONS OF SHAKESPEARE'S PLAYS

Eighteen of the following titles are marked with an asterisk (*). These plays, almost half of Shakespeare's dramatic work, did not appear in print before 1623 when John Heminge and John Condell, the poet's close friends and colleagues, published the First Folio edition. They were obviously withheld because of their delicate historical, political and religious references and allusions (see, for instance, JN, pp. 128-135; SHR, pp. 149-150; AYL, pp. 152-158; TN, pp. 158-162; JC, pp. 200-202; MAC, pp. 256-260; MM, pp. 262-265; AWW, pp. 265-268; WT, pp. 287-289, or H8, pp. 294-295). It is significant that, on 8 November 1623, shortly before the publication of the Folio edition, only sixteen of these titles were entered in the Stationers' Register. _The Taming of the Shrew_ and _King John_ were even then not mentioned, although they too were published. It is unlikely that this was an accident.

ADO _Much Ado About Nothing_
ANT _Antony and Cleopatra_*
AWW _All's Well That Ends Well_*
AYL _As You Like It_*
COR _Coriolanus_*
CYM _Cymbeline_*
ERR _The Comedy of Errors_*
HAM _Hamlet_
1H4 _Henry IV, Part 1_
2H4 _Henry IV, Part 2_
H5 _Henry V_
1H6 _Henry VI, Part 1_*
2H6 _Henry VI, Part 2_
3H6 _Henry VI, Part 3_
H8 _Henry VIII_*
JC _Julius Caesar_*
JN _King John_*
LLL _Love's Labour's Lost_
LR _King Lear_
MAC _Macbeth_*
MM _Measure for Measure_*
MND _A Midsummer Night's Dream_
MV _The Merchant of Venice_
OTH _Othello_
PER _Pericles_
R2 _Richard II_
R3 _Richard III_
ROM _Romeo and Juliet_
SHR _The Taming of the Shrew_*
TGV _The Two Gentlemen of Verona_*
TIM _Timon of Athens_*
TIT _Titus Andronicus_
TMP _The Tempest_*
TN _Twelfth Night_*
TRO _Troilus and Cressida_
WIV _The Merry Wives of Windsor_
WT _The Winter's Tale_*

LIST OF ILLUSTRATIONS AND CREDITS

Figures marked with an asterisk (*) are picture and text quotations from books that have been published more than seventy years ago. In a very few cases in which the owners could not be traced, did not reply to the application for reproduction, and did not make any written objections to the photographic reproduction of their artists' works within a fixed period of time, picture quotations had to be taken from works published less than seventy years ago, so that the publication process as well as the publication date of this book would not be jeopardized.

FRONTISPIECE
William Shakespeare – the Chandos Portrait, National Portrait Gallery, London, oil on canvas, c. 1594–1599, authenticated and dated by H. Hammerschmidt-Hummel between 1995 and 2005. See *The True Face of William Shakespeare. The Poet's Death Mask and Likenesses from Three Periods of his Life* (London, 2006), parts III and IV.

1 The Davenant bust of Shakespeare, terracotta, *c.* 1613, Garrick Club, London – authenticated by H. Hammerschmidt-Hummel between 1988 and 2005, see *The True Face of William Shakespeare*, parts III and IV.– p. XII.

2 Town plan of Stratford-upon-Avon, 1759 (© The Folger Shakespeare Library, Photography Department, Washington, DC, Art Vol. d. 94, p. 1). – opposite p.1.

3a William Shakespeare's birthplace in Stratford-upon-Avon (© H. Hammerschmidt-Hummel 2001) – p. 1.

3b Room in which Shakespeare was probably born with furniture from the Elizabethan-Jacobean period (colour postcard J. Salmon Ltd., Sevenoaks, England, *c.*1964) – p. 2.

4 Side view of Holy Trinity Church in Stratford-upon-Avon (© H. Hammerschmidt-Hummel 1996) – p. 4

5a Baptismal font in Holy Trinity Church, from Shakespeare's time (H. Snowden Ward and Catharine Weed Ward, *Shakespeare's Town and Times* [London, ca. 1896], p. 65*) – p. 4.

5 b Restored baptismal font (© H. Hammerschmidt-Hummel 2002) – p. 4.

6 Entry for William Shakespeare in the Stratford parish register ('Baptismal Register, f. 5') (© Records Office, Shakespeare Birthplace Trust, Stratford-upon-Avon – W. Shakespeare's Baptism, 26 April 1564 – Ref. SBT. DR 243/1, baptism. f. 5) – p. 5.

7 Palmer's Farm, Wilmcote near Stratford-upon-Avon, Mary Arden's House (© H. Hammerschmidt 1970). – p. 6.

8a Glebe's Farm, Wilmcote (© H. Hammerschmidt-Hummel 2002) – p. 6.

8b The church in Snitterfield, John Shakespeare's home village, a few miles north of Stratford (© H. Hammerschmidt-Hummel 2002) – p. 7.

8c The church in Aston Cantlow. It was in this church that Shakespeare's parents were married in 1557 (© H. Hammerschmidt-Hummel 2002) – p. 7.

9 Oxford University: Clarendon Building (© H. Hammerschmidt-Hummel 2002) – p. 8.

10 An extract from an Account Book of the Stratford Town Council kept by John Shakespeare, 1566 (© Records Office, Shakespeare Birthplace Trust, Stratford-upon-Avon, Account of John Shakespeare, 1566, BRU 2/1/11) – p. 11.

11 An Elizabethan inn, The White Swan in Stratford-upon-Avon (© H. Hammerschmidt-Hummel 2001) – p. 13.

12a Detail of a coloured fresco in the White Swan in Stratford-upon-Avon © H. Hammerschmidt-Hummel 2001) – p. 13

12b Detail of the coloured fresco in the White Swan: the story of Tobias (© H. Hammerschmidt-Hummel 2001) – p. 14.

13 Maker's mark of the glover John Shakespeare (Sidney Lee, *A Life of William Shakespeare.* Illustrated Library Edition [London, 1899] *) – p. 15.

14 'Mary Shakespeare, née Arden'. (Snowden Ward and Catharine Weed Ward, *Shakespeare's Town and Times* [London, c. 1896] *) – p. 15.

15a Sketch from 1708 – after a portrait of (?) Mary Shakespeare. (Samuel Schoenbaum, *William Shakespeare. A Documentary Life* [Oxford, 1975] *) – p. 16. –

15b Detail of the mouth of the drawing in Fig. 15a – p. 17.

15c Detail of Shakespeare's mouth in the original of the Flower portrait (see *Fig. 106*) – p. 17.

126 Title page of the first edition of Shakespeare's sonnets, 1609 – p. 260.

127 Priest's hole in Clopton House (H. Snowden Ward and Catharine Weed Ward, *Shakespeare's Town and Times* [London, c. 1896]*) – p. 271

128 The Gunpowder Plot conspirators (Johann Theodor and Johann Jsrael de Bry, *Warhafftige und eygentliche Beschreibung der allerschrecklichsten vnd grawsamsten Verrätherey [...] wieder die Königliche Maiestat/derselben Gemahl vnnd junge Prinzen/sampt dem ganzen Parlament zu Londen in Engeland [...]* (True and real account of the most terrible and cruel treachery that has ever been heard of against His Royal Majesty, his Consort and the young Princes as well as the whole Parliament in London, England ...) Printed in Frankfurt, 1606, copy of title page – Private collection. Printed in E. Orlandi, gen. ed., *The Life and Times of Shakespeare* [Feltham, Middlesex, 1968], p. 63*) – p. 273.

129 Portrait of Ben Jonson, c. 1617, after Abraham van Blyenberch or Gerard Honthorst (© National Portrait Gallery, London – Reg. No. 363) p. 279.

130 Modern view of Playhouse Yard in the former monastery of Blackfriars, London (© H. Hammerschmidt-Hummel 2001) – p. 281.

131 Architect's drawing by Udo Schwemmer of the site of the former monastery in Blackfriars, London, based on the research results by H. Hammerschmidt-Hummel (© H. Hammerschmidt-Hummel 1998) – p. 282.

132a Apothecaries' Hall in Blackfriars, London (© H. Hammerschmidt-Hummel 2001) – p. 283.

132b Great Hall in Apothecaries' Hall in Blackfriars (© H. Hammerschmidt-Hummel 2001) – p. 283.

133 Map of London, 1666 (Felix Barker and Peter Jackson, *The History of London in Maps* [London 1990], pp. 34–35*) – p. 284.

134 Tomb of the poet John Gower in Southwark Cathedral, London (© H. Hammerschmidt-Hummel 2002) – p. 285.

135 Portrait of John Fletcher (© National Portrait Gallery, London – Reg. No. 420) – p. 294.

136 'Shakespeare Deed'. British Museum. Eg. 1787 (© The British Library. British Library Reproductions) – pp. 298-299.

137 Remains of a wall in Ireland Yard, Blackfriars (© H. Hammerschmidt-Hummel 2001) – p. 300.

138 Queen Elizabeth on her way to St Paul's Cathedral, London, copper engraving, 1588 (Christopher Hibbert, ed., *Twilight of Princes*, London, 1970, IV, p. 14 – George Weidenfeld and Nicolson Ltd. © 1970 – p. 333.

139 The Shakespeare Hotel in Stratford-upon-Avon (© H. Hammerschmidt-Hummel 2001) – p. 309.

140 Fathers Edmund Campion and Robert Parsons (*Shakespeares England. An Account of the Life & Manners of his Age.* 2 Vols. [Oxford, 1916, repr. 1966], I, p. 50*) – p. 310.

141a Garden of New Place (© H. Hammerschmidt 1996) – p. 311.

141b Fountain in the garden of New Place (© H. Hammerschmidt-Hummel 2002) – p. 311.

142 Modern view of The Crown in Oxford (© H. Hammerschmidt-Hummel 2002) – p. 312.

143 Hall's Croft, residence of Dr John Hall in Stratford-upon-Avon (© H. Hammerschmidt-Hummel 2002) – p. 312.

144 Entry for Hamnet Shakespeare in the register of the deaths of Stratford-upon-Avon, 11 August 1596, Records Office, Shakespeare Birthplace Trust, Stratford-upon-Avon (Sidney Lee, *A Life of William Shakespeare*. Illustrated Library Edition [London, 1899], p. 149*) – p. 313.

145 Page three of Shakespeare's will (© Public Record Office, London – Public Record Office Image Library, Will of William Shakespeare, page 3 of 3 – PROB 1/4 f. 3) – p. 317.

146a-b Dedication by the editors of the First Folio Edition, John Heminge und Henry Condell, to the Earls of Pembroke and Montgomery from 1623. (William Shakespeare, *Mr. William Shakespeares Comedies, Histories, & Tragedies.* Published according to the True Originall Copies [London, 1623], First Folio Edition. Facsimile: Helge Kökeritz, ed., Charles Tyler Prout, introd. [New Haven/London, 1954]) – p. 322.

146c 'To the Great Variety of Readers'. Address from the editors of the First Folio Edition (1623), John Heminge and Henry Condell, to the readers (William Shakespeare, *Mr. William Shakespeares Comedies, Histories, & Tragedies.* Published according to the True Originall Copies [London, 1623], First Folio Edition. Facsimile: Helge Kökeritz, ed., Charles Tyler Prout, introd. [New Haven/London, 1954]) – p. 323.

147 The Darmstadt Shakespeare death mask, 1616. Authenticated by H. Hammerschmidt-Hummel, 1995-2005, Hesse *Land* and University Library, Darmstadt, Germany (Reproduced by kind permission of the Mayor of Darmstadt © Andreas Kahnert 1996) – p. 327.

THE SHAKESPEARE FAMILY TREE

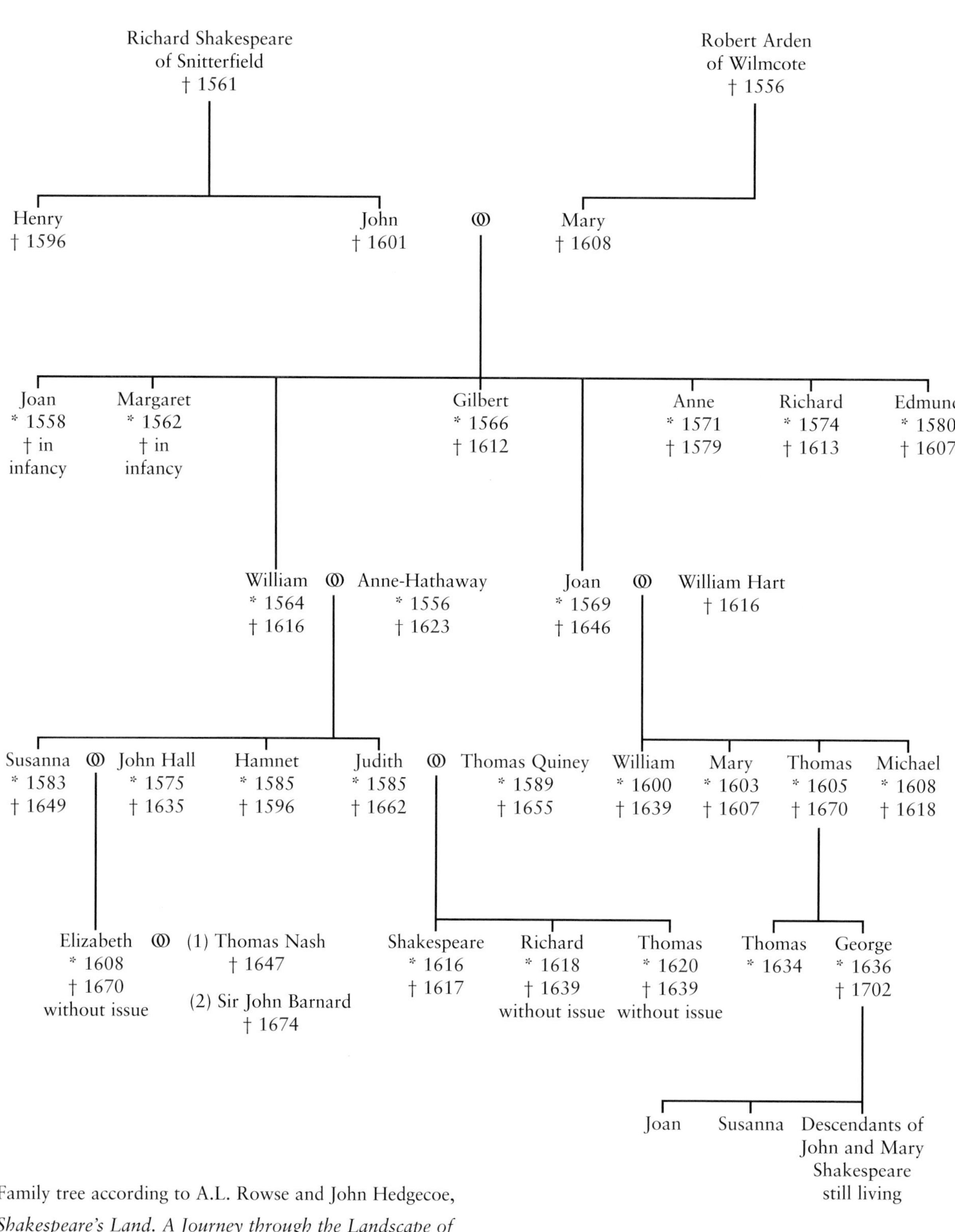

Family tree according to A.L. Rowse and John Hedgecoe, *Shakespeare's Land. A Journey through the Landscape of Elizabethan England.* (Chronicle Books, San Francisco, 1987), p. 14.

CHRONOLOGICAL OUTLINE

1527
Henry VIII (1491–1547), King of England (since 1509) and 'Defender of the Faith' (*Fidei Defensor*), initiates divorce proceedings against Catherine of Aragon (17 May).

1529
Divorce proceedings against Catherine of Aragon held in Blackfriars Monastery (31 May – 23 July).

Cardinal Thomas Wolsey, Lord Chancellor of England, is stripped of his offices of state and forced to hand back the Great Seal. Sir Thomas More succeeds Wolsey as Lord Chancellor.

1530
Wolsey is arrested (4 November) and dies on his way to stand trial (29 November).

1531
The Convocation of Canterbury recognises Henry VIII as head of the Church of England 'so far as the law of Christ doth allow' (24 January); about four months later, the Convocation of York follows suit.

Henry separates from Catherine of Aragon (11 July).

1532
Anti-clerical petition ('Supplication against the Ordinaries') passed by the House of Commons (18 March)

Submission of the clergy (15 May)

Sir Thomas More resigns as Lord Chancellor (16 May).

William Warham, Archbishop of Canterbury, dies (24 August).

1533
Henry VIII marries Anne Boleyn in secret (25 January).

Thomas Cranmer becomes Archbishop of Canterbury (papal appointment of 21 February).

Cranmer pronounces Henry's marriage to Catherine of Aragon null and void (23 May) and his marriage to Anne Boleyn valid (28 May).

Coronation of Anne Boleyn (1 June).

Elizabeth, daughter of Henry VIII and Anne Boleyn, is born in the Palace of Greenwich (7 September).

1534
Act of Succession (March 23) and Oath to the Succession (30 March).

Thomas More and Bishop Fisher arrested for refusing to take the Oath to the Succession.

Act of Supremacy (November). The breach with Rome is complete: Henry is made 'Supreme Head of the Church of England'.

The definition of high treason is extended to cover new offences (November).

1535
Thomas Cromwell appointed as the king's Vicar General

Executions of prominent Carthusian monks (4 May).

Pope Paul III creates Bishop John Fisher a Cardinal (20 May)

Execution of Cardinal Fisher (22 June).

Execution of Sir Thomas More (6 July).

1536
Catherine of Aragon dies (8 January).

Henry VIII dissolves the smaller English monasteries.

Trial of Anne Boleyn (30 April – 15 May).

Execution of Anne Boleyn (19 May).

Henry marries Jane Seymour (20 May or 30 May).

Uprisings in Lincolnshire and Yorkshire, known as 'Pilgrimage of Grace' (October).

1537
The uprisings are suppressed (January – July) and their leaders executed.

Prince Edward born (12 October); the queen (Jane Seymour) dies following the birth (24 October)

1537–1539
The larger English monasteries are surrendered to the Crown and dissolved.

1540
Henry VIII marries Anne of Cleves (6 January). Marriage annulled by Convocation (9 July), decision confirmed by Parliament a few days later.

Thomas Cromwell executed (28 July).

Henry VIII marries Catherine Howard (28 July).

Execution of three Protestants as heretics and three 'Papists' as traitors (30 July).

1542
Catherine Howard executed (13 February).

1543

James V of Scotland dies (14 December).

James's six-day-old daughter Mary becomes Queen of Scots.

Henry VIII marries Catherine Parr (12 July).

Protestant heretics burned at Windsor (12 July).

1546

Anne Askew burned as a heretic in London (16 July) together with other Protestants.

The Duke of Norfolk and his son, the Earl of Surrey, are arrested and charged with high treason (12 December).

1547

Norfolk confesses his guilt in writing (12 January).

Surrey executed (19 January).

Henry VIII dies (28 January).

Edward, Henry's nine-year-old son (b. 1537), ascends the English throne as Edward VI. Lord Protector Seymour (later created Earl of Somerset) rules the country, followed by the Earl of Warwick.

1549

Act of Uniformity passed.

Execution of Thomas Seymour, the Lord Protector's younger brother.

English Catholics revolt.

1552

New Act of Uniformity passed.

Execution of Somerset.

John Shakespeare of Snitterfield, son of the tenant farmer Richard Shakespeare, is recorded as owner or leaseholder of a house in Henley Street, Stratford-upon-Avon (29 April).

1553

Edward VI dies (6 July).

Fourteen days before his death, he grants Stratford-upon-Avon a royal charter. The town becomes a borough, administered by a bailiff (or mayor), fourteen aldermen and a further fourteen leading citizens known as capital burgesses. The seal of Stratford bears the inscription: 'THE SEALE OF THE BOROVGHE TOWNE OF STRETFORD'.

Thanks to Edward VI's charter, the grammar school in Stratford-upon-Avon is refounded. The schoolmaster receives the handsome salary of £20 per annum.

Edward's half-sister Mary (b. 1516), the daughter of Henry VIII and Catherine of Aragon, becomes queen. England becomes Catholic once more.

1554

Mary marries Philip, heir to the Spanish throne, in Winchester Cathedral (July).

1555

Bloody persecutions of Protestants in England (from February 1555 onwards).

Philip leaves England (29 August).

1556

Philip ascends the Spanish throne as Philip II.

The glover John Shakespeare acquires property in Stratford (2 October), consisting of land in Greenhill Street bought from George Turnor, and a house (with garden) known as the 'the Woolshop' in Henley Street bought from Edward West.

John Shakespeare becomes one of Stratford's two bread and ale tasters.

Robert Arden of Wilmcote, a gentleman, dies, leaving his chief property (Asbies, consisting of a house with some fifty acres of land), together with all its produce plus £6.13s.4d, to his youngest daughter, Mary (24 November). Mary must have been able to read and write, as her father had appointed her (together with her sister Alice) executrix of his will.

One of Arden's tenant farmers, Richard Shakespeare of Snitterfield, works the land with his sons Henry and John. John, however, was to become a glover and settle in Stratford (see above, and entry under 1552).

1557

John Shakespeare marries Mary Arden, youngest daughter of his father's landlord, most probably in the church of Aston Cantlow, where the bride lived.

1558

Queen Mary acknowledges her half-sister Elizabeth to be her successor (6 November).

Mary dies (17 November).

Elizabeth becomes queen (17 November).

On the day of Mary's death, the last Catholic Archbishop of Canterbury, Cardinal Reginald Pole, also dies. Out of a total of twenty-seven dioceses, ten are vacant. Of the seventeen bishops who remain in office, one commits apostasy, two die, and two go into exile; the fate of another bishop is unknown. Eleven bishops are sent to prison where they subsequently die, and are revered as martyrs by England's Catholic population.

The Protestant William Cecil (b. 1520), later Lord Burghley, Elizabeth I 's closest adviser, is appointed Secretary of State (20 November).

John and Mary Shakespeare's first child, Joan, is baptised in Holy Trinity Church, Stratford, by the Catholic parish priest Roger Dyos (15 September). She dies in childhood (before April 1569).

1559

Act of Uniformity and Second Act of Supremacy passed. New break with Rome.

The Act of Supremacy declares Elizabeth I to be 'the only supreme governor of this realm ... as well in all spiritual or ecclesiastical things or causes, as temporal'.

Start of the relationship between Queen Elizabeth and Robert Dudley (b. 1532 or 1533).

Roger Dyos, Stratford's Catholic priest, refuses to leave his post. The town council forces him to resign by withholding his stipend. For some years, Stratford has to rely on itinerant preachers.

1560

Francis II of France, husband of Mary, Queen of Scots, dies. Mary returns to Scotland.

1561

John Shakespeare holds office as one of Stratford's two Chamberlains (or treasurers).

John Bretchgirdle, a Protestant, is appointed vicar of Stratford. His Catholic predecessor, Dyos, successfully sues the town and receives generous compensation.

1562

Margaret, second child of John and Mary Shakespeare, is baptised in Holy Trinity Church, Stratford (2 December).

1562–63

A teacher named William Allen is employed illegally for a short time at Stratford Grammar School, where he teaches Latin.

1563

The Thirty-Nine Articles, the historical doctrinal standard of the Church of England, come into force.

Parliament demands that the question of succession to the throne be resolved (January).

Robert Dudley, Elizabeth's favourite, is granted Kenilworth Castle in Warwickshire and large estates in North Wales

John Foxe's *Book of Martyrs*, an account of the persecution of Protestants, is published.

Margaret Shakespeare dies, aged barely four months, and is buried on 30 April.

1563–64

William Allen again illegally employed as temporary Latin master in Stratford.

1564

Christopher Marlowe born in Canterbury, the son of a shoemaker (baptised 26 February).

William Shakespeare, John and Mary Shakespeare's third child, is born at his parents' home in Henley Street, Stratford (23 April) and baptised in Holy Trinity Church (26 April).

Plague breaks out in Stratford (summer), and comes close to the Shakespeares' home. Two hundred townspeople die, but the Shakespeare family is spared.

The town council meets in emergency session in the Guildhall gardens (August). John Shakespeare, one of the fourteen capital burgesses, is present. He makes a generous donation for the relief of poverty in the town.

Elizabeth I elevates her favourite Robert Dudley to the peerage as Earl of Leicester.

1565

Mary, Queen of Scots, marries Henry Stuart, Lord Darnley. She quarrels with him even before the birth of their son James (who was to become James VI of Scotland and James I of England).

John Shakespeare becomes an alderman of Stratford (elected 4 July, takes up office 12 September). He is now officially called 'Master John Shakespeare'. Elizabethan aldermen functioned as an extended arm of government at local level.

John Bretchgirdle, Stratford's Protestant vicar, dies. He leaves his Latin-English dictionary to the Grammar School.

1566

Parliament urges Elizabeth I to marry.

Mary, Queen of Scots' secretary, the Florentine Riccio, is murdered with Darnley's complicity.

Gilbert, fourth child of John and Mary Shakespeare, is baptised in Holy Trinity Church, Stratford (13 October).

1567

Darnley is murdered, probably at the behest of James Hepburn, 4th Earl of Bothwell. A sham trial acquits Bothwell of any involvement. He abducts the queen, (probably) rapes her and succeeds in having his first marriage annulled by the Archbishop of St Andrews.

Mary, Queen of Scots, marries Bothwell in Holyrood Palace.

Lord Darnley's supporters revolt and seize the person of the queen.

Mary abdicates in favour of her son James (b. 19 June 1566). Her half-brother James Stuart, Earl of Moray, becomes regent.

1568

Mary, Queen of Scots, flees to England.

William Allen, former Principal of St Mary Hall, Oxford, emigrates to Flanders with Sir Thomas de Hoghton the Elder of Hoghton Tower, Lancashire. With the support of Philip II of Spain, Allen founds the English College (Collegium Anglicum) at Douai (in Flanders, now in

France). The college offers a basic course of study in the humanities as well as training for the priesthood. It is highly probable that Allen is identical with the former Stratford Latin teacher of the same name (cf. 1562-63 and 1563-64).

John Shakespeare is elected High Bailiff (mayor) of Stratford (4 September), and thereby also becomes a Justice of the Peace.

The coloured wall-painting in King's Hall, Stratford (now the White Swan, close to the Shakespeare family home in Henley Street, Stratford), may date from this year. It depicts the story of Tobias from the Apocrypha. The figures of Tobit and Hannah may represent John and Mary Shakespeare.

Birth of the actor Richard Burbage (baptised 7 July), son of the actor and theatre builder James Burbage. He is destined to become the first and much admired exponent of Shakespeare's leading roles.

1569

Mary, Queen of Scots' presence in England leads to an uprising by the landowning Catholic aristocracy in the North.

Walter Roche, an Oxford graduate, appointed Schoolmaster in Stratford.

Joan, fifth child of John and Mary Shakespeare, is baptised in the church at Stratford (15 April). Her sister of the same name (b. 1558) has already died.

William Shakespeare reaches the age of five and would have entered the preparatory or elementary school attached to Stratford Grammar School, as was customary at the time.

1570

The Catholic 'Rising of the North' is suppressed (February) by Elizabeth I's cousin, Henry Carey, Lord Hunsdon, who was later to become Lord Chamberlain and patron of Shakespeare's theatre company, the Chamberlain's Men.

Elizabeth is excommunicated by Pope Pius V (papal bull 'Regnans in Excelsis', 25 February).

Numerous English Catholics go into exile, mostly to the Catholic Southern Netherlands, then under Spanish domination.

The sons of English Catholics are sent to the English College in Douai in considerable numbers.

1571

Enactment of the first harsh anti-Catholic penal law.

The senior clergy are instructed to acquire copies of Foxe's *Book of Martyrs* so as to make it available to the people.

Edmund Campion, who had been compared to Cicero during his time in Oxford on account of his oratorical talents, abjures Protestantism and goes to Douai to train as a priest.

Simon Hunt, Oxford graduate and secret Catholic, is appointed Schoolmaster in Stratford.

Adrian Quiney, a wealthy silk and textile merchant, is elected Bailiff of Stratford for the third time. John Shakespeare becomes his deputy by being elected Chief Alderman (5 September). Quiney was later to become Judith Shakespeare's father-in-law.

Anne, the Shakespeares' sixth child, is baptised in Holy Trinity, Stratford (28 September).

William Shakespeare, now aged seven, enters the local grammar school. His father is the town's Chief Alderman, former Bailiff, and a Justice of the Peace, and William is therefore following the example of the sons of well-off Elizabethan citizens.

1572

Catherine de Medici, who holds real power in France, even though her second son Charles IX is king, instigates the St Bartholomew's Day Massacre of French Huguenots in Paris (23-24 August), a few days after the wedding of her daughter Marguerite de Valois to King Henry of Navarre, himself a Huguenot. Admiral Coligny, leader of the Huguenots, is killed; Henry of Navarre narrowly escapes with his life.

John Shakespeare and Adrian Quiney ride to London to settle some official business of the borough of Stratford.

According to a Catholic tradition, William Shakespeare receives some of his instruction from a Benedictine monk, Dom Thomas Combe (or Coombes).

1573

Birth of Elizabeth Vernon, daughter of the country squire Sir John Vernon of Hodnet, Shropshire, and cousin of the Earl of Essex (11 January). She later becomes a lady-in-waiting to Elizabeth I, as well as Shakespeare's mistress and Countess of Southampton.

Birth of Henry Wriothesley, 3rd Earl of Southampton, Shakespeare's future patron, friend, and rival in love (6 October).

1574

First licence granted to a theatrical company: a royal patent gives 'Leicester's Men' the right to perform in London and anywhere in the kingdom. It names James Burbage (father of Richard and Cuthbert Burbage), who subsequently built The Theatre in Shoreditch.

Richard, seventh child of John and Mary Shakespeare, is baptised in Stratford (11 March).

1575

Elizabeth I visits Kenilworth Castle, the home of her favourite, the Earl of Leicester.

Stratford's Schoolmaster, Simon Hunt, openly professes his Catholicism. He leaves Stratford for Douai, where he is ordained priest, and subsequently becomes a Jesuit in Rome. Thomas Jenkins, a Protestant, succeeds him.

John Shakespeare buys property in Henley Street, Stratford.

1576

James Burbage builds The Theatre in the parish of St Leonard's, Shoreditch, in the vicinity of the former Augustinian priory of Holywell, just north of the City of London, with the financial backing of his brother-in-law, John Brayne. The cost is 1,000 marks (approx. £666).

The first Blackfriars Theatre is established in a suite of rooms within the precincts of the former Blackfriars monastery, south of Ludgate and Ludgate Street. Under Edward I the Dominican friars received permission to demolish part of the western City wall. Legally, Blackfriars is an enclave or 'liberty', and hence well suited for a theatre.

John Shakespeare applies for a coat of arms (he applies again in 1596).

1577

First execution of a Catholic priest (Cuthbert Mayne).

Alderman John Shakespeare stops attending meetings of Stratford Town Council.

Opening of the Curtain Theatre, Shoreditch.

1578

First (abortive) papal expedition to Ireland.

Edmund Campion ordained deacon, then priest, in Prague.

Robert Parsons appointed English Penitentiary (confessor) at St Peter's in Rome.

The occupation of Douai by the Protestant forces of William of Orange forces the English College to move to Rheims (where it stays until 1593).

The English College, being the only place of higher education for young English Catholics who refuse to take the Oath of Supremacy required by Oxford and Cambridge, is clearly very popular with Catholics back home. Hundreds of students are registered there, mostly under false names.

William Shakespeare is now old enough to leave school; there are several indications that he – like hundreds of young English Catholics – joined the English College in Rheims. The college offers a general course in the humanities based on the educational principles of the Jesuits (with prominence given to rhetoric and the theatre) and a more advanced course leading to the priesthood. Shakespeare's writings show that he is familiar with the names given to the classes in this English college and also with Rheims as a place of study. In his plays, he frequently resorts to the mixed form of tragi-comedy favoured by the Jesuits.

John Shakespeare is in urgent need of ready money, for reasons unknown. He mortgages his wife's inheritance, a house and some fifty acres of land in Wilmcote, to his brother-in-law Edmund Lambert for two years and receives £40 in return (14 November).

The diaries of the English College in Douai (or Rheims) for this year contain an entry for 'Guilielmus', with the surname erased in the nineteenth century, which may refer to Shakespeare.

1579

The Duke of Alençon, heir to the throne of France, arrives in England seeking Elizabeth I's hand in marriage.

John Shakespeare sells one-ninth of the property he inherited from his father in Snitterfield.

Anne, William Shakespeare's seven-and-a-half-year-old sister, dies and is buried in Stratford (4 April).

John Cottom is appointed as Stratford's Schoolmaster (and stays until 1582).

William Allen's third journey to Italy. He helps found the English College in Rome. He and the Jesuit Robert Parsons devise ways of returning England to the Catholic faith.

Ferdinando, Lord Strange, patron of the troupe known as Strange's Men (later Derby's Men), marries Alice Spencer.

1579–1580

Allen, the founder and president of the English College in Douai/Rheims, appeals to the parents of those young English Catholics who wish to study at his college to ensure that their sons come with adequate financial provision.

The English ambassador in Paris urges his government to imprison parents who send their sons to Allen's English College in Rheims.

The so-called 'Rheims Report' of the English College in that city testifies to the success of Jesuit missionaries in England. The Bishop of Worcester, John Whitgift (who was to become Archbishop of Canterbury in 1583), informs Lord Burghley that his diocese and the county of Warwickshire – like Lancashire – are strongholds of clandestine Catholicism and centres of resistance to the new faith.

1580

Rebellion in Ireland, supported by Spain.

Allen returns from Rome to his college at Rheims (April).

John and Mary Shakespeare's eighth child, Edmund, is baptised in Stratford (3 May).

A large-scale Jesuit mission to restore Catholicism in England begins, led by Edmund Campion and Robert Parsons. Fifty-one priests from Rheims and Rome set out for England but are instructed by the Pope only to undertake pastoral work and on no account to engage in political activities. Leaving Rome in the spring, they break their journey in Milan to visit Cardinal Charles Borromeo, who gives them copies of his 'Spiritual Testament' (Catholic articles of faith) to distribute in England.

The Catholic Association is founded in Rome by George Gilbert, the Jesuit mission's chief financial backer (spring). Its members are young Catholics who escort and protect the priests and pave the way for them to enter the homes of the Catholic landed gentry.

In May, Campion, Parsons and their companions visit the English College in Rheims. In June they set out for London, where they are welcomed and looked after by members of the Catholic Association.

Parsons establishes a printing press in East Ham (Essex), which has to be moved repeatedly for reasons of safety.

Publication of Parsons' treatise *A brief discours contayning certayne reasons why Catholiques refuse to goe to church.*

John Shakespeare has been summoned to appear before the Queen's Bench in Westminster so that he can promise to 'keep the peace towards the queen and her subjects' and get a third party to stand surety for him. For ignoring the summons, he is fined £20. He is fined a further £20 on account of a promise of money to John Awdley of Nottingham, which the court deemed illegal.

A total of a 140 citizens are fined by the Queen's Bench, like John Shakespeare, presumably for sending their sons to study in Rheims.

The Jesuit Thomas Cottom is spied upon in France by the English government agent Sledd and betrayed.

Robert Debdale, a priest trained in Douai, acquires Catholic devotional objects – such as crucifixes or rosaries – on the Continent as gifts for his parents and relatives in Shottery, near Stratford. His friend Thomas Cottom, whose brother John is Schoolmaster in Stratford, is asked to bring them over.

Thomas Cottom is arrested on arrival in England. His fellow traveller, a Catholic professor of the University of Douai disguised as a military officer, is chosen as his guard, but immediately releases him. Cottom gives himself up to the authorities because his guard is encountering serious difficulties.

Debdale is arrested on arriving in England but released in 1582 (following the execution of Thomas Cottom). He is arrested again in 1585.

Simon Hunt, who had been Schoolmaster in Stratford when Shakespeare was a pupil at the Grammar School, succeeds Robert Parsons as English Penitentiary at St Peter's in Rome.

The Bishop of Worcester forbids John Frith, the crypto-Catholic parish priest of Temple Grafton, to conduct weddings without his express permission.

The English Catholic Sir Thomas de Hoghton the Elder, who had been head of the de Hoghton family and owner of Hoghton Tower in Lancashire, dies in exile in Liège. He bequeaths £100 to his friend William Allen for the English College in Rheims. Sir Thomas had been living in exile in Flanders since the end of the 1560s. When he left England, his brothers inherited the family wealth.

In the summer, the Jesuit missionary Edmund Campion and his companions stay at Hoghton Tower, Lea Hall and/or Park Hall, where Campion preaches powerful sermons and inspires his listeners with enthusiasm for his cause.

Christopher Marlowe enters Corpus Christi College, Cambridge (10 December).

1580–1581

Parsons and Campion stay for part of the time at the Warwickshire home of Sir William Catesby, father of Robert Catesby (subsequently a leading figure in the Gunpowder Plot) and a relative of Mary Shakespeare, William's mother. When the authorities discover he has been harbouring the two Jesuits, Sir William is arrested (August 1581) and made to forfeit a large part of his fortune in fines.

It is at this time, probably in the house of Sir William Catesby, that John Shakespeare receives his copy of Cardinal Borromeo's Spiritual Testament, which enables him to profess his Catholic faith in writing.

1581

A draconian anti-Catholic law is passed in reaction to the (successful) Jesuit mission. Its provisions include the following:

Catholic missionaries and their converts will be considered traitors. Anyone who incites others to commit treason, shelters traitors, or conceals information about such crimes for more than twenty days, shall forfeit all his property and be sentenced to life imprisonment.

Priests who say mass shall be fined £133, and anyone who attends mass £66. Anyone over the age of sixteen who fails to attend Church of England services shall be fined £20 a month.

Those who employ schoolmasters illegally shall be fined £10 a month and sentenced to one year's imprisonment.

Anyone found teaching without a bishop's licence shall be banned from practising his profession and sentenced to one year's imprisonment, without the right to purchase his freedom.

Alexander de Hoghton's will (3 August) is partly expressed in code ('players' = 'priests'; 'play clothes' = 'vestments'; 'instruments belonging to musics' = 'objects used in the celebration of mass').

William Shakeshafte [= Shakespeare] is illegally employed as a private tutor by the Catholic landowner Alexander de Hoghton (1580 -1582). He is also a member of a secret organisation set up by de Hoghton and his brother to protect Catholic priests hunted by the authorities, and for this he receives £2 a year for life.

Richard Hathaway of Shottery dies, leaving 10 marks (about £7) to his daughter Agnes (Anne), William Shakespeare's future wife, with the proviso that she is not to receive the money until the day of her wedding.

Campion (b. 1540) is betrayed by a government spy, captured, severely tortured, and condemned to death for high treason. He is hanged, drawn and quartered at Tyburn (close to the present Marble Arch). Lord Burghley decides to set an example by having two other priests, Briant and Sherwin, executed. The two priests stood for the English Colleges in Rheims and Rome respectively.

Parsons manages to escape from England with the help of the Spanish ambassador.

1581–1582

Parsons founds an English school at Eu, on the Normandy coast, with the help of the Duc de Guise.

1582

Edmund Campion's martyrdom gives rise to a lament, 'The scowling skies did storm and puff apace', which may well have been written by Shakespeare and inspired by Parsons, who – according to Henry Foley (Records, III, Pt. I, p. 623) – published *Epistle of comfort to the priests* in 1582, giving an account of 'the wonderful stay and standing of the Thames the same day that Campian [sic] and his company were martyred, to the great marvel of the citizens and mariners'. 'The scowling skies' has the line: 'The river Thames awhile astonished stood'.

Parsons publishes An *Epistle of the Persecution of Catholickes* in England.

John Shakespeare, who has not participated in council meetings since 1577, attends one session in order to vote for his friend John Sadler as mayor.

The Jesuit Thomas Cottom is executed (30 May).

His brother John Cottom, Schoolmaster in Stratford, is forced to resign his post and is replaced by Alexander Aspinall, a Puritan.

William Shakespeare returns to his home town of Stratford (summer). In late November he marries Anne Hathaway of Shottery, eight years his senior, who is already pregnant by him.

The Bishop of Worcester issues a licence (27 November) for William Shakespeare to marry Anne Whateley [Hathaway] after a single reading of the banns.

Fulke Sandells and John Richardson, friends of the Hathaways, provide surety of £40 to indemnify the bishop for licensing the marriage (28 November).

The marriage apparently takes place in the church of Temple Grafton, the bride's stated place of residence, where the parish priest is the elderly John Frith, an adherent of the old faith.

Parsons publishes *The first booke of the Christian exercise, appertayning to resolution* in Rouen, a book of devotions which becomes very popular not only with Catholics but also with Protestants.

1583

Susanna, the elder daughter of William Shakespeare and Anne Hathaway, is baptised in Holy Trinity Church, Stratford (26 May).

Archbishop Whitgift takes strong action to remedy abuses in the Church of England.

William Allen, accompanied by his nephew and confidant Thomas Hesketh, travels from Paris to Rheims (February). Apparently Hesketh is one of the younger sons of Sir Thomas Hesketh, Alexander de Hoghton's friend and brother-in-law.

John Somerville plans to assassinate Elizabeth I; his father-in-law, the highly respected Edward Arden of Park Hall, member of a long-established Warwickshire landowning family and a relative of Shakespeare's mother, is drawn into the conspiracy (the Arden-Somerville Plot). Somerville hangs himself in his cell; Arden is hanged in London for high treason.

After a series of successful raids by the authorities in which various Catholic devotional objects are found, ten men from Warwickshire are thrown into the Tower of London, including a Mr Arden (probably a relative of Shakespeare's mother). Arden is horribly tortured.

Dr Richard Barrett, president of the English College at Rheims, informs his predecessor William Allen that the persecution of recusants in Warwickshire is increasing by the day (late December). It is probably at this time that John Shakespeare hides his Borromeo Testament in the rafters of his house in Henley Street. (It is discovered in 1757 during building repairs.)

George Gilbert, founder of the Catholic Association, is sent to Rome with a letter of recommendation from Parsons to Pope Gregory XIII. There the Pope entrusts him with an important mission, but he suddenly contracts a fever and dies the day before his departure.

Lord Burghley publishes his anti-Jesuit pamphlet *The execution of justice in England.*

Due to lack of space, the lower years of the English College in Rheims are transferred to other, newly founded English Catholic schools on the Continent (Pont-à-Mousson, Verdun and Eu).

1583–1584

William Shakespeare is now living in Stratford with his wife and child.

During the season, several companies of actors give performances in the town. Each troupe has its own noble patron: the Earl of Oxford (Oxford's Men), the Earl of Worcester (Worster's Men) and the Earl of Essex (Essex's Men).

1584

The Aldermen of London organise intensive raids in search of forbidden Catholic items such as altars, vestments used in the mass, sacred vessels, images of the Virgin Mary and Catholic writings. They also hope to find out where priests are hiding.

A certain Robert Aden [sic] is recorded as living in the Earl of Southampton's London home (Southampton House). He is probably a relative of Shakespeare's mother, Mary Arden.

In the eastern gatehouse of Blackfriars in London – which Shakespeare was to purchase in 1613 – Alderman Hart confiscates a primer (book of hours), entitled *Officium Beatae Mariae Virginis*, printed with the privilege of the Pope and the King of France. It was found, together with other objects, in the possession of the tenant James Gardyner.

John Donne (the future poet) and his brother Henry matriculate at Oxford. Their uncle, Father Jasper Heywood, a relative of Sir Thomas More, is head of the Jesuit mission to England. The Donne brothers subsequently leave the university without taking a degree, probably because their uncle has been banished from England for being a Jesuit.

The Spanish ambassador, Bernardino de Mendoza, is expelled from England.

1585

Shakespeare's twins, Judith and Hamnet, are baptised in Holy Trinity Church, Stratford (2 February). Their godparents are the Catholic recusants Judith and Hamnet Sadler.

An (unidentified) troupe of actors performs in Stratford.

William Shakespeare flees from his home town of Stratford, apparently for religious reasons. The traditional explanation that he was afraid of being punished for poaching on Sir Thomas Lucy's estate seems to have been an excuse.

Shakespeare travels to Rome, arriving on 16 April. He stays at the pilgrims' hospice attached to the English College, using the pseudonym 'Arthurus Stratfordus Wigorniensis', i.e. Arthur from Stratford in the diocese of Worcester.

The Jesuit Simon Hunt, English Penitentiary at St Peter's in Rome and Shakespeare's former teacher in Stratford, dies unexpectedly in office. Nothing is known about the circumstances.

The Catholic priest Robert Debdale, who had been Hunt's pupil in Stratford and Shakespeare's schoolfellow, is arrested again. He is tried, sentenced to death and executed on 6 October 1586.

Elizabeth I allies herself with the Protestant Netherlands against Spain (August).

Outbreak of war between England and Spain; the conflict is fought out in the Netherlands.

A draconian anti-Catholic law is passed: Jesuits and secular Catholic clergy are to be considered traitors and banished from England; if however they are caught on English soil, they are to be condemned to death; anyone studying at a Jesuit college on the Continent who does not return to England within six months to swear the Oath of Supremacy shall also be considered guilty of high treason.

Parsons goes to Rome to further his plans for the restoration of Catholicism in England. In the course of the year, numerous eminent English Catholics gather around him and William Allen.

On his journey from Rheims to Rome, William Allen is accompanied by Thomas Hesketh. After Allen's death (1594), Hesketh adopts his Christian name as a mark of respect.

Robert Catesby, one of the future leaders of the Gunpowder Plot, studies at Allen's College in Rheims. He and his fellow student Eliot leave the college voluntarily (May), probably to go to Rome.

Lord Henry Howard (the future Earl of Northampton), brother of the 4th Duke of Norfolk (executed in 1572), persuades Lord Burghley to release him from the Tower so that he may go to Warwickshire and take the waters to recover his health; but as soon as he is released, he disappears to Rome.

Henry Percy (1532?-1585), the 8th Earl of Northumberland, imprisoned in the Tower of London for the third time because of his Catholic faith, tries to persuade Elizabeth to free Mary Queen of Scots and show tolerance towards Catholics. He is found shot in his cell. The cause of death is officially given as suicide, but among English Catholics there is talk of murder.

1586

Robert Catesby matriculates at Oxford, but leaves the university after about a year without taking a degree in order to avoid having to take the Oath of Supremacy.

John Gerard (b. 1564), who had studied at the English College in Rheims, goes to Rome where he is ordained as a priest. In 1588 he is accepted into the Society of Jesus.

In Stratford a new alderman is appointed to replace John Shakespeare, who has failed to carry out his duties since 1577.

Anthony Babington, a former page-boy to Mary, Queen of Scots, hatches a plot to release her from captivity and murder Elizabeth I. His plot is uncovered; he is convicted and executed.

Mary, Queen of Scots is condemned to death for having known of, and taken part in, Babington's plot.

1587

Mary, Queen of Scots executed at Fotheringhay Castle, Northamptonshire (8 February).

Queen Elizabeth makes William Davison, Walsingham's colleague as Secretary of State, the scapegoat for Mary's death. Elizabeth had entrusted the death warrant to Davison but without clear instructions for its execution. She has him thrown into the Tower.

On the very day of Mary, Queen of Scots' execution, a magnificent public funeral is held for the English poet, Sir Philip Sidney, who had died of his wounds received at Zutphen in the Netherlands.

Sir William Stanley, the English governor of Deventer in the Netherlands, conspires with the Spanish governor of nearby

Zutphen by ordering the surrender of Deventer and its garrison of 1200 men to the Spanish forces.

William Allen's defence of Stanley's act of desertion is printed in Antwerp as *The copie of a letter written by M. Doctor Allen: concerning the yeelding up, of the citie of Dauentrie, unto his Catholike Maiestie, by Sir William Stanley Knight.*

William Allen is created cardinal by Pope Sixtus V (7 August). If the Spanish Armada succeeds in conquering England, he will become the new Archbishop of Canterbury.

Sir Francis Drake launches a successful attack on the major Spanish port of Cádiz ('the singeing of the King of Spain's beard').

Robert Devereux, 3rd Earl of Essex, Leicester's stepson and Burghley's foster-son, gains the favour of Queen Elizabeth.

The Rose Theatre, built by Philip Henslowe, opens in Southwark.

Probably in this year, the Jesuit and poet Robert Southwell publishes *An Epistle of Comfort to the Reverende Priests, and to the Honorable, Worshipful, and other of the layesort, restrayned in Durāce for the Catholike Fayth*, in which he also refers to 'the wonderful stay and standing of the Thames the same day that Father *Campian* [sic] and his company were martyred ...' (see entry under 1582).

The diaries of the English College in Rheims again contain an entry for 'Guilielmus', with the surname erased in the nineteenth century; the missing name may be that of Shakespeare, or a pseudonym used by him.

The troupes of Essex's Men and Leicester's Men both give stage performances in Stratford.

Christopher Marlowe is sent by the government to Rheims to spy on the students and staff of the English College. In his report, he speaks in positive terms about the English Catholics but has nothing good to say about Protestants.

1588

Defeat of the Spanish Armada.

An engraving shows Queen Elizabeth on her way to a service of thanksgiving in St Paul's Cathedral, with the northern gatehouse of Blackfriars in the background (cf. *Fig. 138*).

Death of Robert Dudley, Earl of Leicester, Elizabeth's long-standing favourite.

Death of Richard Tarleton, the comic actor.

1589

Francis Drake and John Norris lead a military expedition (the 'English Armada') to Spain and Portugal (April), in which Essex takes part, though without the consent of the queen.

Henry III of France assassinated (July).

Parsons founds another English college, in Valladolid (Spain).

1590

The priest Robert Arden, probably a relative of Shakespeare's mother, is appointed English Penitentiary at St Peter's in Rome.

1591

Essex crosses to France in command of an army to support King Henry IV. He and Henry become friends.

The Earl of Southampton and Lord Strange take part together in the festivities held to celebrate the anniversary of the queen's accession (17 November).

Anthony Skinner, William Allen's servant in Rome for many years, and Richard Acliffe, who had been employed by the Bishop of Cassano in the same city, likewise for many years, arrive in Gravesend from the Continent with the intention of continuing their journey to London secretly by rowing boat, but are arrested.

Outbreak of plague in London.

1592

The plague epidemic subsides, allowing Lord Strange's Men to resume their performances at the Rose Theatre (19 February).

Earliest evidence of Shakespeare's presence in London, where this year marks the beginning of his literary career. Like many English Catholics (especially priests), he may well have arrived in the capital secretly by boat.

Shakespeare visits his family in Stratford once a year.

The series of entries in Philip Henslowe's 'Diary' recording the performances of Lord Strange's Men at the Rose Theatre begins. They include 'Harey the vj' (3 March) – almost certainly a play from Shakespeare's *Henry VI* trilogy.

Following the London apprentice riots, the city's theatres are closed for several months (from 23 June).

Robert Greene, well-known writer and dramatist, dies (3 September). His pamphlet *Groatsworth of wit*, in which he refers to Shakespeare as an 'upstart crow', is published on 20 September.

The printer Henry Chettle defends Shakespeare in the pamphlet *Kind-harts dreame* (8 December), in which he declares that people in high places have spoken very positively about Shakespeare's conduct and his gifts as a writer.

The Taming of the Shrew, written and performed *c.*1592, mentions a number of Italian cities, including Rome. The play also alludes to the English College in Rheims and demonstrates Shakespeare's knowledge of French.

Christopher Marlowe is expelled from the Netherlands for attempting to circulate counterfeit gold coins.

Robert Parsons founds an English college in Seville.

The names of John Shakespeare and eight other citizens of Stratford appear on the list of recusants; they are said to have stayed away from Church of England services for fear of being exposed to their creditors.

Plague breaks out again in London, claiming its first victims on 7 September.

Lord Strange's Men perform at court (December).

1592–1593

An anti-Catholic bill is placed before Parliament, under which convicted recusants would have all their property, and that of their wives, confiscated. The bill is considered so severe that Parliament rejects some of its provisions.

1593

London's theatres have to be closed again (late January) due to a fresh outbreak of plague.

Shakespeare's verse epic *Venus and Adonis* is printed in London by Richard Field, who was once his schoolfriend in Stratford (entry in Stationers' Register dated 18 April). The work is dedicated to the Earl of Southampton, a Catholic, and marks the beginning of a close friendship between Shakespeare and Southampton.

This is probably the year in which Shakespeare begins to write his sonnets, which are often autobiographical in nature. They must have been completed *c.*1598.

Love's Labour's Lost is written (and receives its first performance) some time between 1593 and 1595. The play includes a punning reference to the name of Robert Parsons and alludes to his activities. Further passages may refer to Henry of Navarre and the Earls of Essex and Southampton, among others.

Henry IV of France, Essex's friend, converts to Catholicism – to Elizabeth's dismay.

Elizabeth appoints Essex to the Privy Council.

The English College in Rheims returns to Douai, the place of its foundation.

Christopher Marlowe, dramatist and government spy, is himself spied upon by the renegade Catholic priest and government informer Richard Baines – probably on account of his positive comments on the English Catholics at Allen's College in Rheims and his negative remarks about English Protestants.

Marlowe is stabbed to death following a quarrel at the Bull Inn, Deptford, in the presence of Robert Poley, a government spy, and Nicholas Skeres (30 May).

The anti-Catholic bill of 1592-93 becomes law. Anyone over sixteen who has been identified as a recusant must return to his usual place of abode, register with the authorities and not travel outside a five-mile radius without permission. Persons with an annual income of less than £40 must either submit to the established Church or promise on oath to leave the country. If they refuse, or break their oath, they shall be considered guilty of high treason.

Parsons founds an English college at St Omer in France, which later becomes the most important bridgehead for exiled English Catholics and crypto-Catholics on the Continent. It has two libraries, two theatres with a store room for props and costumes, as well as schools of music and rhetoric.

As You Like It may have been written around this time and revised later. The community of exiles living in the Forest of Arden may well be an allusion to the large number of English Catholics (approx. 600-700) living in exile in Flanders. Shakespeare could have met or heard of them during the 'lost years' or when he was (apparently) a student at the English College in Rheims. Though 'Forest of Arden' clearly refers to the English Forest of Arden near Stratford and the maiden name of Shakespeare's mother, it could also be a reference to the Ardennes region of Europe (now divided between Belgium, Luxembourg and France). All the parishes in the present French department of Ardennes belong to the diocese of Rheims.

Henry Donne is arrested for harbouring a Catholic priest. He dies in prison awaiting trial. His brother, the poet John Donne, abjures Catholicism and eventually becomes Dean of St Paul's.

Ferdinando Lord Strange becomes the 5th Earl of Derby (25 September). Through the intermediary of Richard Hesketh, English crypto-Catholics and Catholics-in-exile urge him to lay claim to the throne of England, but he refuses. Derby denounces Hesketh, who is condemned as a traitor and executed.

1594

Shakespeare's tragedy of revenge *Titus Andronicus* receives its first performance at the Rose Theatre (24 January) and is entered in the Stationers' Register (6 February).

Following a performance of the play, Henry Peacham produces a sketch of the opening scene showing Richard Burbage as Tamora, Queen of the Goths, and (?)William Shakespeare as Titus.

Ferdinando Stanley, Earl of Derby, falls ill; his symptoms suggest he has been poisoned. He dies on 16 April, about four and a half months after Hesketh's execution. His theatre company, Strange's or Derby's Men, are forced to find a new patron.

Henslowe's 'diary' records a performance of the *The Taming of the Shrew* (2 May).

Shakespeare's second narrative poem, *The Rape of Lucrece*, is entered in the Stationers' Register (9 May). Like *Venus and Adonis*, it is dedicated to the Earl of Southampton, which shows that a friendship has developed between the poet and his patron.

A new theatre company, the Chamberlain's Men, is formed with Burbage and Shakespeare as its leading lights. Their patron is the Lord Chamberlain Henry Carey, Lord Hunsdon. (After 1603 they were known as the King's Men.)

Southampton's widowed mother marries the Privy Councillor Thomas Heneage. It is possible that *A Midsummer's Night's Dream* was written for their wedding celebrations.

Roderigo Lopez, Elizabeth's personal physician, is put on trial for high treason at the instigation of Essex. Lopez, a Jew, is found guilty and executed (7 June).

Henry Carey obtains a licence from the Lord Mayor of London for his actors, the Chamberlain's Men, to perform at the Cross Keys Inn (8 October).

Shakespeare, Burbage and Kempe perform before the queen at Greenwich Palace (26 and 27 December).

The Comedy of Errors is performed at Gray's Inn (28 December).

Cardinal Allen (b. 1532) dies in Rome and is buried in the English College, in the crypt of the church.

Henry Garnett, Superior (Provincial) of the English Jesuits, who is active in the underground missionary movement, states that he is collecting money for Parsons and emphasises the precarious situation of English Catholics.

1595

William Shakespeare, Richard Burbage and William Kempe receive £20 from the Exchequer for their court performances of 26 and 27 December of the previous year.

Opening of the Swan Theatre in Southwark (*c.* 1595).

Robert Southwell, poet and Jesuit (and evidently a distant cousin of Shakespeare), writes *An humble supplication to Her Maiestie* in which he describes in shocking terms his own predicament and that of his fellow priests, and begs the queen to show clemency.

Southwell is executed.

This is probably the year in which *Richard II* was written and received its performance.

Sir Edward Hoby invites Robert Cecil to his home in order to present 'Richard' to him – almost certainly a reference to Shakespeare's *Richard II*, an historical drama containing clear allusions to Elizabeth I.

The poet Thomas Edwardes, in *L'envoy to Narcissus*, refers to contemporary poets by names from their works: e.g. 'Leander' (from *Hero and Leander*) = Marlowe, 'Adon' (from *Venus and Adonis*) = Shakespeare. Edwardes sees Shakespeare as a genius who stands at the forefront of English poetry, and 'whose power floweth far'.

Having failed to obtain the post of Attorney-General for his protégé Francis Bacon, Essex grants him, by way of compensation, some land in Twickenham which Bacon subsequently sells for £1800.

Beginning of the relationship between the Earl of Southampton and Elizabeth Vernon, a lady-in-waiting to the queen.

Death of Southampton's stepfather, Sir Thomas Heneage.

The Emperor Rudolf II bestows the title of Count of the Holy Roman Empire on Thomas Arundell, Southampton's brother-in-law and a staunch Catholic, at a ceremony in Prague, in recognition of his outstanding service (14 December).

1596

After Thomas Arundell's return to England, the queen has him thrown into the Fleet Prison. She writes to the emperor asking him to refrain from conferring titles on her subjects. Two months later, Arundell is released from jail but banished from court.

Essex sacks Cádiz and is hailed in England as a hero.

Elizabeth appoints Robert Cecil, Lord Burghley's hunchbacked son, Secretary of State (early summer).

The Bishop of Worcester, whose jurisdiction includes Stratford-upon-Avon, informs Lord Burghley that the Catholic recusant threat is particularly great in his diocese.

Henry Carey, patron of the Chamberlain's Men, dies (22 July), and is succeeded as Lord Chamberlain by Lord Cobham. Carey's son George, 2nd Lord Hunsdon, becomes patron of the troupe, known henceforth (until 17 March 1597) as Lord Hunsdon's Men.

Shakespeare, who has been living in the parish of St Helen's, Bishopsgate, moves south across the Thames to Southwark.

Shakespeare writes *The Merchant of Venice*, which contains allusions to the name of Lopez as well as Essex's expedition to Cádiz (news of which reached London in July).

Francis Davison, in a letter to his father William Davison, the former Secretary of State, makes a coded observation to the effect that Robert Cecil wields more power than the kings of Spain and Scotland (late autumn). 'St Gobbo', the nickname by which he refers to Cecil, evidently derives from the character of Launcelot Gobbo in *The Merchant of Venice*. Shakespeare's own choice of the name may have been inspired by the statue of Gobbo on the Rialto in Venice.

Shakespeare's only son, Hamnet, is buried in Stratford (11 August).

James Burbage purchases the former 'great dining chamber', or refectory, of Blackfriars Monastery for £600 (September); here he plans to establish the second Blackfriars Theatre.

John Shakespeare again applies for a coat of arms (20 October). This time he appears to have been successful (see *Fig. 16*).

Composition of *Henry IV, Part 1*, in which the Protestant (Lollard) martyr Sir John Oldcastle (d. 1417) is comically portrayed as a drunken brawler.

Henry IV is performed at court (December).

Lord Cobham and his family, who are related to Oldcastle, take offence at Shakespeare's treatment of their distinguished ancestor; Shakespeare is obliged to change his character's name to Falstaff.

1597

James Burbage dies (January). He bequeaths his valuable property to his sons, Richard and Cuthbert, but their inheritance brings with it serious problems.

The Chamberlain's Men face the prospect of having nowhere to perform, as the lease on their theatre in Shoreditch (The Theatre) has not been renewed.

Lord Cobham dies (17 March). George Carey is appointed Lord Chamberlain and Shakespeare's company is once again known as the Lord Chamberlain's Men.

Early in the year, Shakespeare writes *The Merry Wives of Windsor* at the request of Elizabeth I, who wishes to see Falstaff in love. The first performance is given at Windsor Castle (April or May). Sir Thomas Lucy of Charlecote, near Stratford, a Puritan and ruthless persecutor of Catholics, is caricatured in the rôle of Justice Shallow.

William Shakespeare acquires New Place, one of the two finest houses in Stratford, as his family home (4 May). He carries out alterations to the building, selling the surplus stones to the town. In the garden he erects a free-standing stone monument with an octagonal base. On this octagon there appears to have been a sundial. The poet has the base decorated to illustrate the 'seven ages of man' from *As You Like It*: one side is inscribed with a quotation from the text, the others carved with reliefs each illustrating one of the seven ages (see Part IV, pp. 246–252).

The Jesuit John Gerard and Mr Arden (who has been a prisoner since 1583) make a spectacular escape from the Tower of London by using a rope.

The London theatres are closed following the uproar caused by the *The Isle of Dogs*, a political 'pièce à scandale' by Thomas Nashe and Ben Jonson (performed 28 July). They reopen on 29 August.

Two of Shakespeare's plays are entered in the Stationers' Register: *Richard II* (20 October) and *Romeo and Juliet* (15 November).

Richard II and *Richard III* are both printed in quarto for the first time (15 November).

Shakespeare owes five shillings in tax.

1598

Richard Quiney, a native of Stratford, is asked to contact Shakespeare concerning an investment in the town (24 January).

Southampton quarrels with Ambrose Willoughby, a courtier (late January), because he had started a rumour that Southampton was not the only man in his fiancée's (Elizabeth Vernon's) life. The unnamed man is obviously Shakespeare. Relations between Vernon and Southampton deteriorate and the wedding is postponed (end of January/beginning of February).

Shakespeare is recorded as living at New Place, Stratford, and owning quantities of corn and malt (4 February).

Southampton takes part in an embassy to France led by Robert Cecil. He intends to spend two years travelling on the Continent. Elizabeth Vernon is left behind disconsolate.

Henry IV, Part 1 is entered in the Stationers' Register (25 February).

Love's Labour's Lost appears in print, the first of Shakespeare's plays to bear his name on the title-page (10 March).

The Merchant of Venice is entered in the Stationers' Register (22 July).

Elizabeth Vernon, now pregnant, is banished from court (July). She lives at Essex House, the London residence of her cousin, the Earl of Essex.

William Cecil, Lord Burghley (b. 1520), dies (4 August). His son, Sir Robert Cecil, succeeds him as Elizabeth's chief minister.

Southampton learns that Elizabeth Vernon is pregnant. He comes back secretly to England (end of August) and marries her clandestinely, though not before consulting her cousin, the Earl of Essex, who is his best friend. Southampton then returns to France.

News of the secret wedding reaches the ears of the queen (3 September). She is furious, has Elizabeth Vernon thrown into the Fleet Prison (c. 7 September), notwithstanding her advanced state of pregnancy, and orders Southampton to return home.

In this year, Marcus Gheeraerts the Younger must have painted the emblematic portrait *The Persian Lady*. All the evidence suggests that the subject, dressed as a bride, is Elizabeth Vernon, who had just become the Countess of Southampton. From the signs of her pregnancy, a medical expert has deduced that she is 8-12 weeks away from giving birth. The Countess's daughter Penelope was born on 8 November (see below). Therefore the portrait must have painted at the end of August or beginning of September, soon after the marriage.

The painting *The Persian Lady* contains a poem that has been shown to be by Shakespeare, and is the hitherto missing sonnet that forms the conclusion to his Dark Lady sequence. In it the poet laments that he has been cheated of the fruit of his love, which now belongs to 'others'.

The love triangle that is realistically depicted in Shakespeare's Dark Lady sonnets comes to an end — as the new sonnet reveals — when the poet's mistress is married to his friend. The poet is now excluded from their affections, though the sonnet makes clear that he is the father of the Persian Lady's (i.e. Dark Lady's) unborn child.

Palladis Tamia, or *Wits treasury*, by the writer Francis Meres, a Cambridge graduate, is entered in the Stationers' Register (7 September). The book lists most of the works that Shakespeare had so far written for the stage, as well as a hitherto unidentified play, *Loue labours wonne*. The author compares Shakespeare to the great poets and playwrights of classical antiquity.

Philip II of Spain (b. 1527) dies (13 September).

Ben Jonson is sent to prison. Finding that most of his fellow-prisoners are Catholics (some of whom are priests), he converts to Catholicism (September).

The parish records of St Helen's, Bishopsgate, show that Shakespeare has defaulted on his property tax (1 October). However, they also note that he is no longer resident there.

Richard Quiney from Stratford stays at the Bell Inn on Carter Lane, near Blackfriars. He is evidently in financial difficulties and has been summoned to appear in court. In a letter, he asks Shakespeare to lend him £30, and ends with the words 'The Lord be with yow & with us all amen' (25 October).

Southampton returns to England (early November).

The Countess of Southampton's daughter, Penelope, is born in London's Fleet Prison (8 November). The evidence clearly points to Shakespeare as the father.

Southampton is committed to the Fleet Prison (11 November).

Thanks to Essex's intervention, Southampton is released from prison together with his wife and her baby (late November).

The Chamberlain's Men perform Ben Jonson's social satire, *Every Man in his Humour*, with William Shakespeare and Richard Burbage in the leading rôles.

The authorities raid Blackfriars eastern gatehouse. Two priests manage to escape in time. One day later, the Jesuit Oswald Greenway goes into hiding there.

'The Theatre' in Shoreditch is dismantled and the various parts transported to Southwark on the south bank of the Thames (28 December).

1599

Construction of the Globe Theatre on land belonging to Nicholas Brend, who grants the Burbages a thirty-one-year lease. Their previous landlord Giles Alleyn later sues them (apparently unsuccessfully) for having dismantled The Theatre in Shoreditch.

The building of the Globe is financed by shareholders. Richard and Cuthbert Burbage between them own 50 per cent whilst William Shakespeare, John Heminge, Augustine Phillips, Thomas Pope, and William Kempe own 10 per cent each (contract signed 21 February).

Shakespeare is now living in the Clink Liberty, Southwark, near the Globe.

The historian John Hayward (born c.1564) publishes *The first part of the life and raigne of King Henrie the IV*, which is dedicated to Essex and includes the episode of Richard II's deposition. Elizabeth smells treason and has the author thrown into the Tower.

Essex campaigns against the rebels in Ireland (from April onwards).

Opening of the Globe Theatre (April/May).

The first performance of *Henry V* takes place at the Globe. The play contains clear allusions to Essex, and shows that Shakespeare is one of his fervent supporters.

England's Catholics place their hopes in Essex, who has hinted that should he come to power he will grant religious toleration.

Essex's best friend, the Earl of Southampton, is a Catholic. Priests come and go secretly at his London home, Southampton House.

John Whitgift, Archbishop of Canterbury, and Richard Bancroft, the Bishop of London, order the public burning of banned books ('The Bishops' Bonfire', 4 June). At the same time, Whitgift bans the printing of satires and epigrams, and of plays on the subject of English history.

Shakespeare complies with the ban by composing a tragedy on a Roman theme, *Julius Caesar*, in which the murder of a tyrant is shown on stage.

In Ireland, Essex conducts negotiations with Tyrone, the leader of the rebels, without the queen's authority, resulting in an unauthorised truce.

Publication of the so-called Wright-Molyneux world map, in which 'the Indies', i.e. Asia and the Americas, are drawn according to Mercator's projection. The map appears in a volume of Hakluyt's *Principal Navigations*, but is only present in a few copies. Shakespeare alludes to this new map in *Twelfth Night*.

Following Sir Robert Shirley's expedition to Persia, his ship – the Sophy – returns richly laden. Shakespeare's contemporaries are impressed by Persian luxury.

John Robinson, later to become Shakespeare's tenant in Blackfriars gatehouse, is denounced for harbouring the priest Richard Dudley.

Dr Thomas Worthington, a pupil of Robert Parsons, is appointed president of the English College in Douai (he will remain in post until 1613).

The Swiss doctor, Thomas Platter the Younger, journeys to England via France and the Spanish Netherlands. While in Ghent, seat of a Catholic diocese founded as recently as 1560, he and his fellow travellers visit the double tomb of the first two bishops of Ghent in St Bavo's Cathedral (10 September); the bishops were very close friends during their lifetime and were buried side by side. From the cathedral tower, Platter watches a Jesuit play in the courtyard below.

Platter arrives in England where he visits many places of interest, among them Nonsuch Palace when he saw Elizabeth I in person. He attends a performance of *Julius Caesar* at the Globe (21 September).

Essex returns to England without authority (28 September) and is held prisoner.

It is apparently against this background that Shakespeare composes Sonnet 66, a fierce but coded attack on those who wield power in England. His prime targets include not only Robert Cecil, Essex's chief political rival, but also the queen, who turns sixty-six this year.

The first part of *The Life of Sir John Oldcastle, the Good Lord Cobham*, by Munday, Drayton, Wilson and Hathwaye is premièred at the Rose Theatre (1 November). The authors' aim is to rescue the reputation of Oldcastle, the Protestant martyr, whom Shakespeare had turned into a figure of fun in *Henry IV*. Henslowe, the theatre's owner, rewards them with a ten-shilling bonus.

1600

There are approximately 360 grammar schools in England, roughly one for every 13,000 people.

The Fortune Theatre is built in Golding Lane for Henslowe and his son-in-law Edward Alleyn, as a rival to the Globe.

The comic actor William Kempe leaves the Chamberlain's Men. His place is taken by Robert Armin.

An engraved equestrian portrait of the Earl of Essex is published (2 February), and distributed by his supporters.

William Kempe morris-dances his way from London to Norwich in nine days.

Sir Edward Baynham, and three gentlemen who are friends of Essex, are heard making seditious utterances at the Mermaid Tavern; afterwards they attack the watchmen on the street (25 March).

At court, no one mentions Essex; his existence is ignored.

Essex writes to the queen and complains that he is being treated like a corpse (12 May).

Baynham and his friends are fined and given prison sentences (6 July).

Trial of John Hayward (11 July). He is accused of using his book about Henry IV to comment on contemporary issues.

Four plays owned by the Chamberlain's Men are entered in the Stationers' Register to prevent the printing of pirated editions (4 August). They include three plays by Shakespeare: *Henry V*, *As You Like It* and *Much Ado About Nothing*.

Henry V is entered in the Stationers' Register again (14 August). *Henry IV, Part 2* and *Much Ado About Nothing* are entered in the Register together, described as 'wrytten by master Shakespere' (23 August).

Alarmed by the public circulation of Essex's portrait, the government bans the production and distribution of portrait engravings (August).

Essex is released (26 August), but remains under house arrest in Essex House.

Essex's followers are not satisfied, and seek to have the situation resolved.

Part I of the play *Returne from Pernassus* is performed at Cambridge University. It contains numerous enthusiastic allusions to Shakespeare. The poet is treated as a kind of cult figure, whose portrait students would like to have hanging on the wall of their study.

An unknown artist paints a portrait of the Countess of Southampton in which he subtly inserts the face of William Shakespeare (on the right sleeve, see *Fig. 85b*), thus hinting at an intimate relationship between the Countess (formerly Elizabeth Vernon) and Shakespeare. The poet's face was discovered by the present author during research for her book *Das Geheimnis um Shakespeares* 'Dark Lady' (The secret surrounding Shakespeare's Dark Lady) (1999).

Blackfriars Theatre is leased to the Children of the Chapel, the boy choristers of the Chapel Royal (2 September) who also perform as actors; their manager is Henry Evans.

The comedies *A Midsummer Night's Dream* and *The Merchant of Venice* are entered in the Stationers' Register (8 and 28 October).

William Fulbecke publishes *An historical collection of the continuall factions, tumults and massacres of the Romans* (13 October). He clearly condemns Caesar's murder.

William Hart is born in Stratford to Shakespeare's sister Joan and her husband (also called William).

1601

First performance of *Twelfth Night* (6 January) to mark the visit to England by Virginio Orsini, Duke of Bracciano in Tuscany. In Act IV, Scene 2, Shakespeare uses the words of the clown to disguise references to the name of Robert Parsons and to allude to Edmund Campion ('the old hermit of Prague') and Elizabeth I ('a niece of King Gorboduc').

Southampton is assaulted in the street by Lord Grey of Wilton (9 January), a member of the opposing political camp. Grey receives only a light punishment.

At the request of the the Earl of Essex's supporters, the Chamberlain's Men perform *Richard II* at the Globe, including the forbidden scene of the king's deposition (7 February).

The Essex Rebellion (8 February), led by the Earls of Essex and Southampton. The rebels' chief aim is to march on the seat of government in the Palace of Whitehall and put an end to the power of Essex's enemies.

At the last moment, Essex changes his plan and marches instead into the City of London, where he vainly tries to incite the citizens to join him.

Essex, Southampton and the other conspirators retreat to Essex House, but give themselves up after a brief resistance once their wives and children have been allowed to go free.

Captain Thomas Lee makes an unsuccessful attempt to have Essex freed (13 February). He is tried, found guilty and hanged (14 February).

Essex and Southampton are tried in Westminster Hall by their peers for high treason (19 February).

Essex's enemy Robert Cecil eavesdrops on the proceedings from behind a curtain. Events take a dramatic turn when Essex accuses Cecil of secretly supporting the Spanish Infanta's claim to succeed Elizabeth on the English throne, whereupon Cecil leaps out of hiding, falls on his knees before the peers and manages to convince them of his innocence.

The trial lasts only one day; Francis Bacon's presentation of the case for the prosecution proves decisive, and Essex and Southampton are condemned to death (19 February).

Shakespeare's allegorical elegy, *The Phoenix and the Turtle*, a kind of poetic requiem for Essex and Southampton, must have been composed immediately after the trial. The poem includes cryptic references to other prominent contemporary figures: not only Anthony Shirley, Francis Bacon and Robert Cecil, but also James VI of Scotland and Elizabeth I.

Southampton's death sentence is commuted to a life imprisonment in the Tower.

The Chamberlain's Men are obliged to perform before the queen on the eve of Essex's execution (24 February).

On Ash Wednesday, Essex is beheaded by the sword on Tower Hill (25 February). Afterwards, the executioner barely escapes being lynched by an angry mob in the streets of London.

Other supporters of the Essex Rebellion, including Sir Charles Danvers, a close friend of Southampton's, are executed in March.

Thomas Whittington, Richard Hathaway's shepherd, bequeaths to the poor and needy of Stratford the sum of 40 shillings that Anne Shakespeare owes him.

Shakespeare changes his London address again, apparently to escape the authorities in Southwark. From 1601 or 1602 onwards he lodges with Christopher Mountjoy, a maker of ladies' ornamental headgear, in Silver Street. Here Shakespeare is less likely to attract political suspicion, as Mountjoy is a Huguenot.

Shakespeare seems to be traumatised by the events surrounding the demise of Essex. In his stage plays he now turns towards tragedy. His next play is *Hamlet*, which may be understood as a memorial to his dead hero, Essex. He does not seem to have completed any other new works until 1603.

The poet's father John Shakespeare dies, and is buried in Holy Trinity Church, Stratford (8 September).

Marshal Biron, a friend of Henry IV of France, heads an embassy to England; he is accompanied by twenty French noblemen (7 September). For their audience with the queen, Biron and his companions are conspicuously dressed in black, as a sign of mourning for Essex. None of them is wearing any insignia or decorations. Essex is the chief topic of conversation between Elizabeth and Biron. One tradition relates that she showed her guest Essex's skull.

In the weeks that follow, Elizabeth's exhibits serious abnormalities in her behaviour. She refuses food, stamps her feet, and repeatedly stabs at an arras (tapestry) with her sword.

A government spy informs Cecil that English Jesuits and Catholic priests are operating mainly in three areas – Flanders (especially Douai), Rome and Spain. A group of six or seven hundred English Catholics are living in exile in Flanders, 'the one half priests, scholars, and religious, the other laymen, pensioners, and soldiers'. According to the spy's report – to which a list of names is attached – Parsons is now making an all-out effort 'to overthrow both the laws and State' (11 October).

Death of Nicholas Brend, owner of the land on which the Globe Theatre is built (12 October).

Death of Thomas Nashe (b. 1567), co-author of the subversive play *The Isle of Dogs*.

The queen has a fainting fit at the State Opening of Parliament (27 October).

1602

Sir John Fortescue, a member of the Privy Council, in 'speaking with a dear friend', makes some cryptic, yet telling remarks about 'the weakness of the time', and finds comfort in the fact 'that he was as old and weak as the time itself, being born in the same year as the queen'. He says that 'he would advise his son to take a right course when the hour came'.

It appears that Shakespeare's literary activity is still dormant. He seems to have spent the early part of 1602 in Stratford and possibly also in Warwick, considering the purchase of land.

The Merry Wives of Windsor is entered in the Stationers' Register (18 January).

Performance of *Twelfth Night* in the Middle Temple at Candlemas (2 February).

On 1 May, Shakespeare buys a considerable landholding in Old Stratford from William Combes (127 acres for £320), which guarantees him a substantial income. The transaction is conducted on Shakespeare's behalf by his brother Gilbert.

Shakespeare's friend Richard Quiney dies.

Hamlet is listed in the Stationers' Register (26 July) as having been 'latelie acted by the Lord Chamberleyne his servantes'.

Marshal Biron is condemned to death for alleged high treason and executed in the same manner as Essex (31 July).

Shakespeare buys a cottage and some land in Chapel Lane, Stratford, opposite New Place (28 September).

Troilus and Cressida is written either late in 1602 or early in 1603 (but not printed until 1609). It is a 'problem play' containing echoes of the Dark Lady sonnets and of *Hamlet.*

Robert Cecil adopts the policy of his former rival, Essex, by paving the way for James VI of Scotland to succeed Elizabeth I.

1603

The Chamberlain's Men perform in Richmond Palace (2 February) – their last appearance before the death of the queen.

Troilus and Cressida is entered in the Stationers' Register (7 February).

Security measures in London are tightened (beginning of March).

During the first half of March, 40,000 Catholics have gathered in London to prevent James VI of Scotland from inheriting the English throne. They belong to the 'Spanish party', that branch of the English crypto-Catholics and Catholics-in-exile which supports the candidature of the Spanish Infanta.

The Privy Council decides in favour of the Scottish king as Elizabeth's successor (17 March).

Because of the queen's approaching death, London's theatres are closed (19 March).

Elizabeth I (b. 7 September, 1533) dies at Richmond Palace (24 March). With her the House of Tudor becomes extinct.

Elizabeth is succeeded by James I, the son of Mary, Queen of Scots.

Shakespeare writes nothing to mark the death of Elizabeth. Although many of his fellow poets compose verses in her honour, he pays no tribute to the late queen – not even when he is required to do so (see below).

A considerable number of exiled Jesuits and priests return to England following James's accession, and many recusants openly profess Catholicism and attend mass.

Southampton is released from the Tower on King James's orders (10 April). He and the Countess subsequently play an important role at Court.

Plague breaks out again in London. The theatres are closed (April).

King James arrives in London from Scotland (May 7).

The Chamberlain's Men are renamed the King's Men. Their privileges are confirmed by letters patent in which Shakespeare's name features prominently (May 19).

Lawrence Fletcher joins the King's Men. Fletcher had already performed for the king in Scotland and is James I's favourite actor.

First quarto edition of *Hamlet* published.

The Earls of Southampton and Pembroke are created Knights of the Garter (2 July).

Because of the plague epidemic in London, James I is crowned in a private ceremony (25 July).

Death of George Carey, 2nd Lord Hunsdon (9 September).

The King's Men perform for James I at Wilton House (2 December). The play, for which they receive £30, is thought to have been *As You Like It.*

Shakespeare takes part in a production of Ben Jonson's *Sejanus* (some time between 24 October and 12 December). This is his last appearance as an actor.

Philip Henslowe stops keeping his diary.

Englandes mourning garment, by Henry Chettle, is entered in the Stationers' Register. The author urges his fellow writer William Shakespeare to compose something in honour of the dead queen, but Shakespeare ignores his request.

English Catholics, both priests and lay people, who have been looking forward to an improvement in their lot under the new king, see their hopes dashed.

1604

Shakespeare's name appears in the accounts of Sir George Home, Master of the Great Wardrobe. The King's Men are to take part in the procession that accompanies James I's ceremonial entry into London, and each of them receives four and a half yards of red cloth for his livery.

The theatres reopen following the end of the plague epidemic (April).

Edward de Vere, 17th Earl of Oxford (b. 1550), who had written comedies in his younger years, dies of the plague (24 June).

The Privy Council issues a warrant approving one of Shakespeare's plays, noting in the margin that he is one of the King's Men.

Shakespeare sues the Stratford apothecary Philip Rogers for 35s 10d which he owes for the supply of malt (July).

Peace negotiations between England, the Netherlands and Spain take place in London (Somerset House Conference).

During the conference, twelve members of the King's Men perform in Somerset House on eighteen occasions between 9 and 27 August, for which they are paid £21 12s.

War between England and Spain ends.

Shakespeare writes the problem play *Measure for Measure*, which contains allusions – among other things – to the Anglo-Spanish peace negotiations.

Othello receives its first performance at Whitehall Palace (1 November).

The Merry Wives of Windsor is also performed at court (4 November).

Shakespeare, who is still living in the house of the Mountjoys in Silver Street, London, acts as matchmaker between their daughter Mary and Stephen Belott, who is Mountjoy's journeyman or apprentice. The wedding takes place on 19 November.

Measure for Measure performed at court (26 December).

Second quarto edition of *Hamlet* published.

Henry IV, Part 1 is published in its third quarto edition.

Opening of the Red Bull Theatre, not far from the former Clerkenwell Priory (c.1604).

1605

Shakespeare's comedy *Love's Labour's Lost*, written about ten years previously, is performed at court (some time between 1 and 6 January).

Henry V and *The Merchant of Venice* are performed at court (7 and 10 February).

James I urges the players to perform *The Merchant of Venice* again; the performance takes place on 12 February.

Opening of the Whitefriars Theatre in the Liberty of Whitefriars (between Fleet Street and the north bank of the Thames).

The actor Augustine Phillips dies, leaving Shakespeare a thirty-shilling gold coin in his will (4 May).

Shakespeare pays £440 to purchase tithes on Welcombe property in Stratford (24 July).

Richard III is printed in its fourth quarto edition.

John Robinson, Shakespeare's future tenant in Blackfriars, sends his thirteen-year-old son Edward to be educated at the Catholic English College in St Omer founded by the Jesuit priest Robert Parsons.

David Baker enters the Benedictine Order in Padua and chooses Augustine as his name in religion. He becomes the third (known) member of the restored English Benedictine Congregation. Father Augustine distinguished himself above all in the field of church history.

Ellen Fortescue, wife of John Fortescue, the tenant of the eastern gatehouse of Blackfriars, refuses to shelter the gunpowder plotters Catesby, Percy, Winter and Digby.

Gunpowder Plot (5 November). The sons of Catholic gentry, chiefly from the Midlands (Robert Catesby, Guy Fawkes, Robert and Thomas Winter, Sir Everard Digby and others), disappointed that James I had broken his promise to tolerate Catholicism, had intended to blow up the Houses of Parliament during the State Opening. They would have killed every member of the Lords and Commons together with the king and the royal family. The plot is foiled at literally the last minute.

After the failure of the Gunpowder Plot, the Jesuit John Gerard – disguised, and wearing a wig and false beard – finds refuge in the eastern gatehouse of Blackfriars, from which he is helped to escape to the Continent (St Omer).

John Fortescue, the Catholic tenant of the eastern gatehouse of Blackfriars, moves to St Omer with his family.

Henry Percy (1564–1632), 9th Earl of Northumberland, is suspected of being involved in the Gunpowder Plot and of wanting to be the leader of the English papists. In the following year he is charged with contempt, and sentenced to life imprisonment in the Tower and a fine of £30,000. While in the Tower he is allowed to amass his own library, and to surround himself with learned men. He becomes known as the 'Wizard Earl'.

It is probably towards the end of this year that Shakespeare begins to write *King Lear*. The play refers to 'late eclipses in the sun and moon' which occurred in October and September respectively.

1606

Henry Garnett, Superior of the English Jesuits, is suspected of having been privy to the Gunpowder Plot. He is hunted by the authorities and captured by the Sheriff of Worcestershire, Sir Henry Bromley, together with Father Oldcorne (alias Hall).

Garnett and Oldcorne are taken to the Gatehouse Prison in London (12 February).

Garnett is put on trial for high treason in London's

Guildhall (28 March). The Attorney-General, Sir Edward Coke, presents the case for the prosecution. Garnett is found guilty.

Garnett is hanged in St Paul's Churchyard (3 May).

The list of Stratford recusants dated 5 May contains twenty-two names, among them Shakespeare's elder daughter Susanna, and Judith and Hamnet Sadler, the godparents of his twins. Their offence is their failure to receive communion at Easter (20 April).

Parliament passes a law imposing a fine of £10 for the abuse of the name of God in stage plays (27 May).

Shakespeare writes *Macbeth*, which contains references both to the trial of Garnett and to the low wheat prices of that year which proved ruinous to yeomen and tenant farmers. However, there is no record of *Macbeth* being performed at this time.

The King's Men perform *King Lear* in the Palace of Whitehall for James I (26 December).

1607

New draconian emergency laws against Catholics are passed by Parliament.

Susanna Shakespeare marries Dr John Hall, a physician, in Holy Trinity Church, Stratford (5 June). Hall is a Protestant with Puritan leanings who is nevertheless tolerant of other religious beliefs.

Dom Robert (Sigebert) Buckley, formerly a monk of Westminster and the only surviving member of the old English Benedictine Congregation, professes the novices Sadler and Maihew as monks of the revived English Congregation and appoints them successors to the pre-Reformation community of Westminster Abbey.

The London theatres are closed due to a fresh outbreak of plague (July – November).

Edward, an illegitimate son of Shakespeare's youngest brother Edmund, dies in infancy and is buried in the church of St Giles Cripplegate, London (12 August).

While the *Dragon*, an English ship, is becalmed off the coast of Sierra Leone, the captain has *Hamlet* performed on board (5 September).

King Lear is entered in the Stationers' Register (26 November).

The actor Edmund Shakespeare, John and Mary Shakespeare's youngest son, dies; he is buried in St Saviour's, Southwark (the present-day Southwark Cathedral) on 31 December. It is likely that the cost of the funeral was borne by his wealthier brother William.

1608

Shakespeare's granddaughter Elizabeth, the daughter of Dr John Hall and his wife Susanna, is baptised in Holy Trinity, Stratford (21 February).

It is believed that *Hamlet* was performed again on board the Dragon (31 March).

Antony and Cleopatra and *Pericles* are entered in the Stationers' Register (20 May).

The brothers Richard and Cuthbert Burbage, together with Shakespeare, Thomas Evans, John Heminge, Henry Condell and William Sly, form a seven-man syndicate (9 August) which takes out a twenty-one-year lease on the Blackfriars Theatre. The members of the syndicate are the theatre's 'housekeepers' (or shareholders). Each contributes an equal share of rent to the syndicate. The total raised is then paid to the landlord, Richard Burbage.

The actor William Sly dies and is buried in St Leonard's, Shoreditch (17 August). From now on, the remaining members of the syndicate are each responsible for paying one sixth of the rent on the Blackfriars Theatre.

The playwright's mother Mary Shakespeare, née Arden, dies, and is buried in Stratford (9 September).

The actor Lawrence Fletcher, one of the King's Men, dies. He is buried on 12 September.

Michael Hart, son of Shakespeare's sister Joan, is baptised in Stratford (23 September).

William Walker, Shakespeare's godson, is baptised in Stratford (16 October).

The Venetian ambassador in London attends a performance of *Pericles* (between 5 January and 23 November).

First quarto edition of *King Lear.*

Fourth quarto edition of *Richard II.*

Fourth quarto edition of *Henry IV, Part 1.*

1609

Troilus and Cressida is entered in the Stationers' Register (28 January).

Thousands of young mulberry trees are brought over from France (1 May) and planted in many English counties. The mulberry tree in the garden of New Place, which Shakespeare is supposed to have planted himself, evidently dates from this time.

Shakespeare's Sonnets appear in print for the first time – probably at the author's instigation – and are entered in the Stationers' Register on 20 May. Thus, roughly six months after the death of the poet's mother (September 1608) and a good ten years after the triangular relationship between Shakespeare, Elizabeth Vernon and Southampton came to an end (August 1598), the writer's intimate personal life becomes public knowledge.

George Fortescue, son of the former tenant of the eastern

gatehouse of Blackfriars, John Fortescue, is admitted to the English College in Rome.

Shakespeare has a portrait of the Madonna and Child, which probably belonged to his mother, overpainted with his own image – the so-called Flower portrait.

Thomas Greene, a relative of Shakespeare, is currently his tenant in New Place, Stratford. He occupies the post of town clerk, and assists Shakespeare from time to time with legal advice. In a memorandum, he states that he is living in Shakespeare's property and expects to leave after one year (9 September).

Shakespeare's brother Gilbert is cited by the Court of Requests.

Death of Thomas Combe the Elder of Old Stratford. His son, Thomas Combe the Younger, is Shakespeare's trusted friend and will one day inherit his sword. It is possible that the Combes are related to the Benedictine monk of the same name who is said to have instructed Shakespeare as a child.

Cardinal Borghese discovers that the son of James I's private secretary is being educated by the Jesuits (under the name of his Catholic mother) in the English College at St Omer, one of Parsons' foundations.

Shipwreck off Bermuda: one of the nine ships of the expedition (commanded by Sir Thomas Gates and Sir George Somers) sent to Virginia to relieve the colony of Jamestown becomes separated from the others during a hurricane and is wrecked off Bermuda.

During the Christmas season, the King's Men perform no fewer than thirteen plays at the Palace of Whitehall in the presence of the royal family.

Pericles appears in two quarto editions.

Troilus and Cressida is printed in quarto.

1609–1610

The 'romance' *The Winter's Tale* is written around this time. The plot, in which King Leontes of Sicilia accuses the queen, Hermione, of adultery with his best friend King Polixenes of Bohemia, exhibits certain parallels to the three-way relationship between Shakespeare, Elizabeth Vernon and Southampton. Leontes, believing his daughter to be a bastard, sends her to be exposed shortly after she is born. He also scrutinises his son Mamillius, and satisfies himself that his features resemble his own.

In *The Winter's Tale*, Shakespeare mentions the Italian painter Giulio Romano, a pupil of Raphael, and praises his faithful imitation of nature.

1610

An epitaph appears on Elias James, owner of a brewery in Puddle Dock. Shakespeare is its likely author.

The ship-owner John Jackson (who will become one of Shakespeare's trustees in 1613), marries Elias James's sister-in-law.

Robert Parsons (b. 1546) dies in Rome and is buried in the crypt of the English College church alongside Cardinal Allen.

The Benedictine monk Augustine Baker has been living in hiding for many years (prior to 1610) at the country seat of Sir Nicholas Fortescue in Cookhill, near Stratford. He writes scholarly treatises on church history. As Sir Nicholas is a patient of Shakespeare's son-in-law, Dr John Hall, it is possible that Shakespeare established contact with Baker through Hall. Alternatively, John Fortescue, the former tenant of the Blackfriars eastern gatehouse and a relative of Sir Nicholas, may have been the link.

Some time after 1610 Baker goes to Rheims, where he is subsequently ordained priest (1613).

Shakespeare's title to the land which he purchased in 1602 is confirmed by the Court of Common Pleas.

The so-called 'Bermuda pamphlets' about the famous shipwreck of 1609 are circulating in London. They include William Strachey's letter of 15 July, and two published works – *A Discovery of the Barmudas* by Sylvester Jourdain, and the Virginia Company's official report – both containing detailed accounts of the disaster. Shakespeare is inspired by these narratives to write *The Tempest*.

1611

The Elizabethan astrologer and illegal medical practitioner Simon Forman witnesses a performance of Shakespeare's *Cymbeline* (between 21 and 29 April).

Forman records seeing a performance of *The Winter's Tale* at the Globe Theatre (15 May).

Pericles, *Hamlet* and *Titus Andronicus* are each published in quarto for the third time.

A new edition of *Love's Martyr*, first published in 1601, appears under the title of *The Anuals of Great Brittaine* – exactly ten years after the death of the Earl of Essex. Like the first edition, it includes Shakespeare's elegy *The Phoenix and the Turtle*, a memorial to Essex (and Southampton).

Shakespeare's romance *The Tempest* is performed at court (1 November).

The historian and cartographer John Speed publishes his *History of Great Britaine*, in which he uses the phrase 'this papist and his poet' – apparently a pejorative reference to Parsons and Shakespeare.

1612

Shakespeare's brother Gilbert dies and is buried in Stratford (3 February).

Mountjoy, Shakespeare's erstwhile landlord in Silver Street, is sued by his son-in-law Stephen Belott. Mountjoy makes a statement (3 February), to which Belott responds (5 May). Shakespeare is called as a witness (11 May). His place of abode is given as Stratford.

Stratford town council outlaws theatrical performances (7 February).

The Elector Palatine, Frederick V, arrives in London from Heidelberg (16 October) in preparation for his marriage to James I's daughter Elizabeth in the following year. In 1619 he will become for a brief time King of Bohemia ('the Winter King').

The King's Men perform *The Winter's Tale* (5 November).

Prince Henry, heir to the English throne, dies unexpectedly at the age of 18 (6 November).

Richard III appears in its fifth quarto edition.

Edward Robinson is ordained priest in Rome. His father John Robinson, also a Catholic and Shakespeare's tenant in the eastern Blackfriars gatehouse, is almost certainly the same John Robinson who witnessed Shakespeare's will.

The 5th Earl of Rutland, a friend of the Earl of Southampton, dies.

1613

A bill is laid before Parliament which would force English Catholics to wear red caps or coloured stockings as a mark of identification. However, it fails to become law.

English Catholics are forbidden by law to carry arms.

John Combe, Stratford's wealthiest landowner, dies, leaving Shakespeare £5 in his will (28 January).

Richard, Shakespeare's last surviving brother, dies and is buried in Stratford (4 February).

It is apparently at the beginning of this year that Shakespeare sells his stake in the Globe Theatre and the Blackfriars Theatre, as a result of which he is able to make a significant financial contribution to the survival of English Catholicism. Together with his trustees William Johnson (owner of the Mermaid Tavern), John Jackson (a ship-owner from Hull) and John Heminge (business manager of the King's Men), he purchases the eastern gatehouse of Blackfriars, 'Gatehouse II', for £140 (10 March).

Shakespeare makes a down payment of £80 and takes out a mortgage for the remaining £60.

The gatehouse has 'sundry back-doors and byways, and many secret vaults and corners'. For several decades it has served as a refuge for Catholic priests, offering them both a hiding-place and quick access to the Thames which would enable them to escape to the Continent by boat. Successive tenants have maintained contact with the English College in St Omer (south of Calais) founded by Robert Parsons.

Shakespeare intends the gatehouse to be used to provide board and lodging for Catholic priests and laymen hunted by the authorities, and to facilitate their journeys to and from the continent. The terms of the trust deed ensure that it will continue to fulfil this function even after his death.

Shakespeare and Richard Burbage each receive 44s. for designing an 'impresa' for the Earl of Rutland (31 March).

To celebrate the wedding of the Elector Palatine Frederick V (the future King of Bohemia) to Princess Elizabeth, daughter of James I (20 May), the King's Men perform fourteen plays at court. These include a number of works by Shakespeare, the company's own playwright (*Much Ado About Nothing*, *The Tempest*, *The Winter's Tale*, both parts of *Henry IV*, *Othello* and *Julius Caesar*). The new history play *All is True* (later known as *Henry VIII*), written by Shakespeare in collaboration with John Fletcher, is not chosen on this occasion, but receives its première on St Peter's Day (29 June) at the Globe. The parts of the play written by Shakespeare himself betray his pro-Catholic sympathies – notably in his positive portrayal of Catherine of Aragon.

During the performance of *Henry VIII* or *All is True*, a salvo of cannon is fired to mark the first encounter of Henry VIII and Anne Boleyn. The thatched roof catches fire and the packed theatre is burned to the ground in a very short time. Fortunately there are no casualties. The breeches of one member of the audience catch fire, but another spectator manages to put out the flames with a bottle of beer.

Sir Henry Wotton describes the disaster in a letter to his friend Sir Edmund Bacon (2 July).

After the fire, *A sonnett upon the pittiful burneinge of the Globe playhowse in London* goes the rounds; the anonymous author of the ballad appears to have been a Puritan. Each of the six verses ends with the refrain 'and yett al this is true', an ironic reference to the title of the play. The author can scarcely conceal his 'schadenfreude'. He pokes fun at the leading actors of the King's Men, Richard Burbage, Condell and Heminge, who suffered from smoke inhalation and had a narrow escape. Shakespeare is not mentioned, from which we may conclude that he was not present. There is some suggestion the fire may have been started deliberately, by the Puritans.

Shakespeare's daughter, Susanna Hall, brings an action in the Consistory Court of Worcester diocese against John Lane for defamation of character (15 July)

Shakespeare visits Rome probably for the last time (arriving in October) and stays at the pilgrims' hospice of the English College. He once again employs the pseudonym 'Stratfordus', but this time with the forename 'Ricardus'. Richard is the Christian name both of his paternal grandfather and of his last surviving brother who had been laid to rest in Stratford about eight months earlier in February.

The poet finally retires to Stratford. Modern expert medical evidence suggests this was for health reasons, but growing political pressure on Catholics may also have played a part. From now on he lives in New Place, with his family close at hand.

1613–1614

Following his ordination in Rheims, the Benedictine monk Augustine Baker returns to England. There is no record of where he is living in the years up to 1620.

1614

Many English churches suffer severely from arson attacks – apparently by militant Puritans.

Opening of the Hope Theatre in Southwark.

The reconstructed Globe Theatre opens its doors (June).

Fire sweeps through Stratford (9 July). Fifty-four houses burn down, but Shakespeare's properties are spared.

John and Ellen Fortescue (who are both Catholic), the former tenants of the eastern gatehouse in Blackfriars, who had escaped to St Omer following the Gunpowder Plot, recall their son George from Rome to St Omer.

In Stratford, town clerk Thomas Greene draws up a list of freeholders which shows that Shakespeare owns about 127 acres of land (5 September).

Greene notes in his diary that Shakespeare has ridden to London with his son-in-law Dr John Hall in order to resolve some issues relating to Stratford tithes (17 November).

1615

Shakespeare and other owners of Blackfriars bring proceedings in the Court of Chancery against Matthew Bacon, demanding the release of certain documents relating to the property (26 April).

The court orders Bacon to produce the documents so they can be passed on to the owners (22 May).

Lady Penelope Wriothesley, daughter of the Countess of Southampton and William Shakespeare, marries the Hon. William Spencer (probably in the summer). She lives with her husband at Althorp in Northamptonshire.

The landowners William and Thomas Combe, both of whom are qualified lawyers, seek permission to enclose some of Stratford's common land. The town clerk Thomas Greene, who happens to be a relative of Shakespeare, sides with the borough corporation against the enclosures. Shakespeare appears to distance himself from Greene. Thomas Combe – to whom Shakespeare subsequently bequeaths his sword – insults the aldermen by calling them 'dogs and curs' and 'Puritan knaves'.

Richard II appears in its fifth quarto edition.

1616

Shakespeare draws up his will with the assistance of the Stratford lawyer Francis Collins (ca. 25 January), but later revises it (25 March). The chief beneficiaries are his daughter Susanna and her husband Dr John Hall.

One of the witnesses is John Robinson, who is also mentioned in the will as tenant of the eastern Blackfriars gatehouse owned by Shakespeare.

The will contains a number of coded expressions which point to the clandestine practice of Catholicism in the dramatist's home: 'silver gilt bowl' = ciborium; 'wearing apparel' = vestments; 'bed with the furniture' = secret sleeping quarters.

A list of objects from the room where Shakespeare died was attached to his will, but is no longer extant.

Judith Shakespeare marries the Stratford vintner Thomas Quiney (10 February).

Thomas and Judith Quiney are excommunicated (12 March) because they married during Lent.

Shakespeare's son-in-law Thomas Quiney is summoned by the ecclesiastical court in Stratford to answer charges of immoral behaviour (26 March). He is accused of causing the pregnancy of Margaret Wheeler, who died in childbirth eleven days previously, and is sentenced to do public penance in the parish church. In the event, he is able to buy his way out of the punishment by giving alms to the poor.

Ben Jonson and Michael Drayton visit Shakespeare in Stratford (mid-April).

Shakespeare dies at his home in New Place (23 April).

A Catholic tradition states that during his final illness Shakespeare was under the spiritual care of a Benedictine monk. The monk in question is most likely to have been Father Augustine Baker.

According to a popular tradition, Shakespeare died of a fever contracted during Jonson and Drayton's visit to Stratford.

The most likely cause of Shakespeare's death is a systemic disorder, sarcoidosis, which present-day medical experts have diagnosed on the basis of the four surviving images of Shakespeare (the Chandos and Flower Portraits, the Davenant Bust and the Darmstadt Shakespeare Death Mask, authenticated by the present author in her book – *The True Face of William Shakespeare*, pp. 67-80). The illness is normally fatal, though its development may be very slow. The writer must have been suffering from it for many years, and its successive stages may be traced in the four images.

Shortly after his death, the dramatist's death mask is taken.

The parish register shows that Shakespeare's funeral took place in Holy Trinity Church, Stratford, on 25 April.

As a gentleman, Shakespeare is entitled to a solemn heraldic funeral, supervised by the College of Arms, with the usual badges of honour including helmet and funeral sword.

Shakespeare's son-in-law, Dr Hall, obtains probate of his will in London (22 June).

The eldest son of Thomas Quiney and his wife Judith (née Shakespeare) is baptised with the Christian name Shakespeare (23 November).

A new edition of the poem '*St Peter's Complaint*' by the Jesuit Robert Southwell (executed in 1595) is printed in St Omer, with a dedication to 'to my worthy good cosen Maister W.S. [William Shakespeare]'.

Shakespeare's *Rape of Lucrece* is published in its fifth quarto edition.

Ben Jonson publishes a folio edition of his own collected works.

Tyrone, one-time leader of the Irish rebels, dies in exile.

The actor Nathan Field, also known as Nat or Nid Field, now heads the list of the King's Men, together with Richard Burbage.

The playwright Francis Beaumont dies.

1616-1617

Outbreak of typhus in Stratford.

The sculptor Gheerart Janssen the Younger, from Southwark, works on a bust of Shakespeare, using the death mask (now in Darmstadt) as his model. It forms part of his design for the poet's funerary monument in the Jacobean Renaissance style which is erected against the north wall of the chancel in Holy Trinity, Stratford, above his grave.

Some verses, obviously written by Shakespeare himself, adjuring posterity not to disturb his remains, are inscribed on the stone slab covering his grave. They suggest the poet was afraid his bones might be moved to the charnel house which once adjoined the church.

The native American princess, Pocahontas, is fêted in London.

1617

Williams Leake transfers the copyright of *Venus and Adonis* to William Barrett (16 February).

Dr John Hall and his wife Susanna take up residence in New Place.

Hall begins the second of his casebooks in which he records his successes in treating his patients. His earlier notebook, which may have contained entries about the illnesses of his father-in-law, Shakespeare, including the illness that led to his death, has unfortunately disappeared.

Venus and Adonis appears in its ninth quarto edition.

1618

Shakespeare's trustees John Jackson, William Johnson and John Heminge transfer their responsibility for the eastern gatehouse of Blackfriars to new trustees, John Greene and Matthew Morris, who have now to represent the interests of Susanna Hall as her father's heir (10 February). The retiring trustees imply that Shakespeare's will contained hidden intentions or was subject to special provisions; they allude to the existence of a codicil that has either been lost or removed and may have been identical with the list of objects from the room in which the poet died.

John Robinson, Shakespeare's tenant in Blackfriars, continues to carry out his functions.

1619

The Lord Chamberlain informs the Stationers' Company in writing that the text of plays performed by the King's Men must not be printed without the Company's approval (3 May).

Pericles is performed in the royal apartments for the king's English and French guests (20 May).

Laurence Hayes defends his copyright in *The Merchant of Venice* which has been breached by the printer William Jaggard (8 July).

People living in the vicinity of Blackfriars Theatre complain about the large number of theatregoers, who block the surrounding streets with their carriages.

Anti-Puritan riots break out in Stratford when the Puritan Thomas Wilson is appointed vicar. John Nash and William Reynolds, who had led the opposition to Wilson's appointment, are arraigned before the Court of Star Chamber – together with John Lane and others – for insulting Wilson and disturbing the peace. It is clear from the provisions of Shakespeare's will that both Nash and Reynolds had belonged to his trusted circle of friends (see pp. 320-321).

The Winter's Tale, both parts of *Henry IV*, and *Hamlet* are performed at court during the Christmas period.

1620

There is a record of the presence of Father Augustine Baker, the Benedictine monk, in Devon.

Henry Spencer (the future Earl of Sunderland), son of the Hon. William Spencer (the future 2nd Baron Spencer) and Lady Penelope Spencer (Shakespeare's illegitimate daughter – see pp. 179–182 and *Fig. 88*), is born. Henry Spencer is Shakespeare's natural grandson.

1621

Othello is entered in the Stationers' Register (6 October).

1622

Shakespeare's granddaughter, Elizabeth Hall (1608-1670) marries Thomas Nash, son of the wealthy Stratford landowner Anthony Nash.

First quarto edition of *Othello*.

Henry IV, Part 1 and *Richard III* each appear in quarto for the sixth time.

Stratford corporation pays the King's Men, Shakespeare's former troupe, a sum of money to persuade them not to perform in Stratford.

Anthony Nash, one of the richest men in Stratford, dies. He and his brother John had been close friends of Shakespeare, and both were beneficiaries of his will.

1623

The King's Men perform *Malvolio* (*Twelfth Night*) at court (2 February).

Anne Shakespeare (née Hathaway), the playwright's widow, dies at the age of sixty-seven (6 August). She is buried in Holy Trinity Church next to her husband, but not – as she herself had wished – in the same grave.

During a secret Catholic mass, the floor of an overcrowded third-floor room in the northern gatehouse of Blackfriars collapses (26 October in the Julian calendar but 5 November in the Gregorian calendar).

The event is vividly described in a pamphlet, *The Doleful Even-Song*, which according to Catholic sources was written by the Puritan divine Samuel Clarke. More recent research suggests the author was Thomas Goad.

Ninety-nine people die in the accident, including the celebrated Jesuit missionary Robert Drury, a former rector of the English College in St Omer.

The Bishop of London refuses to allow the victims – with a few notable exceptions – to be buried in consecrated ground. The majority are laid to rest in a mass grave in Blackfriars.

The French ambassador's residence is on the first floor of the gatehouse, but he is away at the time of the disaster. From the first floor, a secret passage led to the clandestine church on the third floor.

Some suspect the event may have been a deliberate anti-Catholic outrage, and investigations were begun – but nothing could ever be proved.

Shortly before all of Shakespeare's plays – with the exception of *Pericles* – are published in the First Folio edition, the London printers Edward Blount and Isaac Jaggard enter the following titles in the Stationers' Register (8 November): 'The Tempest, The two gentlemen of Verona. Measure for Measure. The Comedy of Errors. As you Like it. All's well that ends well. Twelfth night. The winters tale. ... The thirde parte of Henry the sixt. Henry the eight. Coriolanus. Timon of Athens. Julius Caesar. ... Mackbeth. Antonie and Cleopatra. Cymbeline.' These plays have never been published before – obviously because they were politically dangerous. *The Taming of the Shrew* and *King John*, which are also published for the first time in the First Folio, are not mentioned in the Stationers' Register entry of 8 November – apparently because they were even more dangerous in religious and political terms.

Publication of the First Folio. This first complete edition of Shakespeare's plays is printed by William Jaggard and his son Isaac, and financed by Edward Blount, Isaac Jaggard, John Smethwick and William Aspley. The editors are Shakespeare's friends and fellow-actors, John Heminge and Henry Condell. The text of the plays is preceded by a number of eulogies in verse by well-known contemporary authors and an engraved portrait of Shakespeare by Martin Droeshout the Younger (based on the authentic 'Flower portrait' of 1609). In an epigram facing the portrait, Ben Jonson, now the most important living English dramatist, who had been a friend of Shakespeare, praises the engraver for creating a true likeness of the Bard and also expresses the 'work/author identity' (see *Fig. 90a*).

1624

John Gee, Oxford graduate and government informer, draws up a list of Catholic priests and Jesuits who are living in London.

Gee makes ironic and cryptic remarks about Jesuit drama. He says that if the Jesuits clubbed together to form their own theatre company, they could provide such strong competition to the main London theatres (the Fortune, the Red Bull, the Cockpit and the Globe) that the theatres would be forced to close.

1625

Death of King James I (b. 1566).

His son Charles becomes King of England as Charles I. His reign will be marked by constitutional conflict culminating in the Civil War.

1632

Thomas Cotes, who has taken over the press of Isaac Jaggard (the printer of the 1623 First Folio), brings out the Second Folio of Shakespeare's plays. It re-uses the Droeshout engraving from the First Folio. The eulogies preceding the text include an anonymous 'Epitaph on the admirable Dramaticke Poet, W. Shakespeare'. The author of this glowing eulogy is John Milton, a fervent admirer of Shakespeare and his works, who declares that, with his 'unvalued [i.e. priceless] booke' (the folio edition of his dramatic works), Shakespeare has created for himself such a splendid monument that kings would wish to die for it.

1633

The carriages bringing people to the Blackfriars Theatre continue to block the neighbouring streets (see entry under 1619). The Privy Council prohibits the parking of carriages in Ludgate Street and St Paul's Churchyard.

1634

Lieutenant Hammond arrives in Stratford with a company of soldiers from Norwich. Together they visit Shakespeare's tomb in Holy Trinity Church, where Hammond is very impressed by Shakespeare's monument.

1636

The scholar and antiquary Sir William Dugdale visits Stratford and produces drawings of important monuments, including one of Shakespeare's memorial (published in 1656 in his *Antiquities of Warwickshire*). As far as we can tell, the facial features of the bust in Dugdale's drawing, including the length and shape of the nose and also the moustache, match those of the four authenticated images of Shakespeare (the Chandos and Flower portraits, the Davenant bust and the Darmstadt death mask – see *The True Face of William Shakespeare*). However, the bust must have been damaged during the Civil War and was later repaired in a makeshift manner. This explains why the nose and moustache of the bust differ from those of the death mask and the other authentic portraits.

1637

Alderman Baldwin Brooks (a future Bailiff of Stratford), accompanied by several undersheriffs, forces his way into New Place where Shakespeare's widowed daughter Susanna is living. They seize books and other valuable items from Shakespeare's former library – his 'study of books'.

1638

English Catholics bring out a reprint of the Borromeo Testament under the title *The contract and testament of the soule*. The work was originally written by Cardinal Charles Borromeo of Milan, and distributed by the English Jesuit missionaries Edmund Campion and Robert Parsons from 1580 onwards.

1640-1641

Like his brother William, Thomas Combe appears on the list of Stratford recusants. Thomas had belonged to Shakespeare's inner circle of friends, and the dramatist had bequeathed him his sword as a symbolic gesture.

1642

Start of the Civil War. The Puritans order the closure of all theatres.

Parliamentary troops invade Coughton Court, the Warwickshire seat of Sir Robert Throckmorton, a Catholic. They loot and burn Catholic books and destroy Catholic images.

In Stratford-upon-Avon, there are violent skirmishes between Cavaliers and Roundheads.

There is looting and destruction, and the old market hall is destroyed by an explosion.

1643

Henrietta Maria, Charles I's Catholic queen, passes through Stratford on her way from Milford Haven to Oxford, where the court has had to seek refuge. She stays for three days at New Place with Shakespeare's daughter Susanna, who gives her a book which must have come from her father's library.

It is most likely in this year that Captain James Cook(e), an army surgeon, visits Shakespeare's daughter Susanna Hall and receives from her the second casebook kept by her husband, Dr John Hall, which begins in 1617. It seems the first casebook (prior to 1617) was not handed over to Cooke – presumably because it contained entries concerning the diseases of William Shakespeare, including the poet's last illness, which his son-in-law must have treated.

1644

The diarist John Evelyn stays at the English College in Rome, where he sees an Italian comedy performed by the students.

Royalist soldiers force their way into New Place.

Oliver Cromwell's cavalry (the 'Ironsides') win a decisive victory over the Royalists at Marston Moor. Cromwell himself is a strict Puritan, convinced of his divine mission.

The Globe Theatre, rebuilt after the fire of 1613, is the first of the London playhouses to be demolished. A contemporary, John Chamberlain, once described the theatre as 'the fairest that ever was in England'.

1645

Royalist troops attack seats of the landed gentry in the Midlands (spring). They also commit excesses in Stratford, where plague breaks out again.

Parliamentary troops under Cromwell occupy the area around Stratford (May). Following their victory at Naseby, the forces of Cromwell and Sir Thomas Fairfax take up quarters in and around Stratford (June) and cause extensive damage.

Clopton Bridge, Stratford's crossing of the River Avon, is demolished (December) so as to prevent the Royalists from reaching the west of the country.

1646

Some of Stratford's inhabitants report details of the damage they have suffered as a result of the war to the authorities in Coventry.

The members of Shakespeare's family make no such claim, even though New Place, and especially Shakespeare's monument in the parish church, must have suffered substantially.

The troops of Colonel Thomas Morgan engage in looting while they are billeted in and around Stratford.

1648

Cromwell defeats the Scots in the Battle of Preston.

1649

Trial and execution of Charles I (b. 1600).

1653

In his *Miscellania*, the dramatist Richard Flecknoe wistfully recalls the days when Shakespeare's plays were performed in the Blackfriars Theatre, now closed for ever.

Cromwell is made Lord Protector.

Cromwell sells Charles I's valuable collection of paintings. Much of the collection is now in the Louvre.

Under Cromwell, English churches have to endure iconoclastic excesses: many paintings, sculptures, altars and other objects are damaged or destroyed.

In the years which follow, the theatres are demolished. Even the Blackfriars Theatre falls victim to Puritan cultural vandalism.

James Cook(e) publishes some of the notes from Dr Hall's second casebook, having translated them from Latin into English. The title reads: *Select Observations on English Bodies: or, Cures both empericall and historicall, performed upon very eminent Persons in desperate Diseases*. First, written in Latine by Mr. John Hall Physician, living at Stratford upon Avon in Warwick-shire, where he was very famous, and also in the Counties adjacent ... Now put into English for commmon benefit by James Cooke Practitioner in Physick and Chirurgery. London ..., 1657.

1658

Death of Oliver Cromwell (b. 1599). His son Richard succeeds him, but resigns after less than a year.

1660

Charles I's son returns from exile in the Netherlands and ascends the throne as Charles II.

The Restoration era begins.

1663

Publication of the Third Folio of Shakespeare's plays – once again with the engraved portrait by Droeshout. However, the quality of the engraving deteriorates with each new edition.

1664

A reprint of the Third Folio appears in which the original thirty-six plays are supplemented by a further seven. These include *Pericles*, and six plays which are not by Shakespeare: *The London Prodigal, Thomas Lord Cromwell, Sir John Oldcastle, The Puritan, A Yorkshire Tragedy* and *Locrine*.

1666

Immediately following the Great Fire, Charles II commissions Wenceslaus Hollar to produce a detailed map of London. It shows a footpath leading across the old Blackfriars Monastery precincts, starting from the exact spot where Shakespeare's eastern gatehouse once stood, and running in a broad left curve past the site of the Blackfriars Theatre (in which the dramatist had also held a share) to finish at a landing stage on the River Thames. This could be the old escape route used by many Catholic priests.

1667

The biographer and antiquary John Aubrey begins writing his *Brief Lives* (not published until long after his death, which occurred in 1697). In addition to an entry devoted specifically to Shakespeare, the work contains further information about the poet.

Death of Penelope, Lady Spencer, née Wriothesley, Shakespeare's illegitimate daughter by Elizabeth Vernon, Countess of Southampton and formerly lady-in-waiting to Elizabeth I. She had borne seven children, of whom one died in childhood. Lady Spencer's descendants include the 9th Earl Spencer and his three sisters, one of whom, Princess Diana, died in 1997.

1670

Death of Lady Elizabeth Barnard, née Hall, the daughter of Dr John Hall and Susanna Shakespeare. She is the poet's only legitimate granddaughter, and with her the line of his legitimate descendants dies out.

1676

John Ogilby completes his map of London. In 1998 it was used by the present author and the architect Udo Schwemmer, in conjunction with other documentary and pictorial sources of the sixteenth and seventeenth centuries, as the basis for their sketch map 'The site of Blackfriars, the former Dominican friary in London, in the time of Shakespeare, showing the position of the gatehouses and theatre' (see *Fig. 131*).

1688 (approx.)

The Anglican clergyman Richard Davies acquires the notebooks of his late friend and fellow-clergyman William Fulman, which contain a number of interesting details of Shakespeare's life. Davies adds various comments in his own hand, among them the statement: 'He dyed a Papist'.

1756

The Rev. Francis Gastrell, an Anglican clergyman, becomes the owner of New Place.

1757

During repairs to Shakespeare's birthplace in Henley Street, Stratford, his father's Borromeo Testament is discovered among the rafters. The Shakespeare scholar Edmond Malone later examines it, and prints the text in his complete edition of *The plays and poems of William Shakspeare* (1790). However, following Malone's death in 1812, the original document was no longer to be found among his papers. It may have been removed in an unauthorised manner, and subsequently destroyed, by someone who found John Shakespeare's Catholic confession of faith an embarrassment.

1758

Among the papers of the Stratford historian and Shakespeare enthusiast Robert Bell Wheler is a record of fixtures and other objects left in New Place by Henry Talbot, who sold the house to Gastrell. They include 'Shakespeare's head' (probably a painting) in the hall, six 'family pictures' in the other rooms, and, in the 'wildernesse', i.e. the overgrown garden, 'a stone-dyal' (sundial).

Gastrell cuts down the mulberry tree that Shakespeare planted.

1759

Gastrell has New Place demolished on the pretext that he finds the numerous tourists wanting to visit Shakespeare's home a nuisance. A more likely explanation, however, is that he had discovered objects or other features of the house which to him, an Anglican clergyman, were evidence of Shakespeare's secret Catholicism and may have offended his religious and patriotic sensibilities.

INDEX

Bold pagination indicates illustrations or captions.
All plays are listed under the heading of plays.